Conceiving Identities

Conceiving Identities

Maternity in Medieval Muslim Discourse and Practice

Kathryn M. Kueny

SUNY
PRESS

Cover image: The figure of a pregnant woman.
From *The Anatomy of the Human Body* (*Tashrih-i badan-i insan*), written in Persian at the end of the fourteenth century by Mansur ibn Ilyas.
Copy completed 8 December 1488 (4 Muharram 894 H) by Hasan ibn Ahmad, a scribe working in Isfahan.
National Library of Medicine MS P18, fol. 39b

Published by State University of New York Press, Albany

Printed in the United States of America

For information, contact State University of New York Press, Albany, NY
www.sunypress.edu

Production, Ryan Morris
Marketing, Michael Campochiaro

Library of Congress Cataloging-in-Publication Data

Kueny, Kathryn [date]
Conceiving identities : maternity in medieval Muslim discourse and practice / Kathryn M. Kueny.
p. cm.
Includes bibliographical references and index.
ISBN 978-1-4384-4785-8 (hc : alk. paper) 978-1-4384-4786-5 (pbk : alk. paper)
1. Motherhood—Religious aspects—Islam. 2. Women in Islam. I. Title.

BP190.5.M67K84 2013
297.5′77—dc23 2012045678

10 9 8 7 6 5 4 3 2 1

Contents

Acknowledgments

The writing of this book was not unlike the process of giving birth: waves of anticipation and excitement tempered by doubt, discomfort, and brief episodes of pain. Many friends, family members, and colleagues, however, have eased the burden with humor, confidence, and encouragement. I would like to thank them profusely for their unyielding support in my ability to produce this book, and for their vital contributions—in the form of praise, criticism, funding, or time sacrificed—to its creation.

I would like to thank my editor at SUNY Press, Nancy Ellegate, for her confidence in the value of my work. The anonymous reviewers of the manuscript offered insightful commentary throughout that enhanced greatly the quality of the final version. The former director of faculty development at Fordham University, James S. Wilson, was greatly instrumental in helping me to articulate the broader contours of the project, in particular, in its initial stages. With his help, I was awarded a Fordham Faculty Fellowship in the spring of 2011 that allowed me a semester off from teaching to work full time on bringing the manuscript to near completion. My research could not have been conducted without access to Princeton University's Firestone Library. I am grateful for a series of Fordham University FREP grants (facilitated by James Wilson) that covered access privileges to this gem of a facility. I wish to thank, also, the chair of the Department of Theology at Fordham, Terry Tilley, who likewise has been supportive of my research throughout his tenure. Audiences at the SBL/AAR conferences, Patristic, Medieval, and Renaissance conference, and Fordham University who have heard portions of this work also provided helpful commentary. Fordham graduate student assistants also contributed much to the final production of the manuscript: Jen Jamer, who worked tirelessly on the index, and Alex Miller, who helped edit the final proofs.

Colleagues and friends provided me with the guidance, insight, support, and encouragement I needed throughout the extended period of research and writing. I wish to thank Gordon Newby, Jane McAuliffe, Brannon Wheeler, Amir Hussain, Kecia Ali, Elizabeth Johnson, Robert Grimes, SJ, Melissa Naud, Sue Hanks, and Karen Clark in this regard.

An earlier version of part of chapter 1 was originally published as "Reproducing Power: Qur'ānic Anthropogonies in Comparison," in *The Lineaments of Islam: Studies in Honor of Fred McGraw Donner*, ed. Paul M. Cobb (Leiden: Brill, 2012), 235–60.

Part of chapter 5 was originally published as "The Birth of Cain: Reproduction, Maternal Responsibility and Moral Character in Early Islamic Exegesis," *History of Religions* 48, no. 2 (November 2008): 110–29. Copyright 2008, The University of Chicago Press.

When all is said and done, nothing could have been accomplished without the love, support, and sacrifice—often in the form of his own precious time—of my husband, J. Andrew Foster. His keen eye for weaknesses in the argument, his critical assessments of the thesis, and his extended commentary and input on various drafts of the chapters, were invaluable. The gifts of our children, Joe, Iris, Eli, and Leo, have been nothing short of miraculous. Their entry into the world provided me with the initial impulse to explore broader questions concerning the formation of life and the making of mothers that ultimately led to the composition of this work. Watching each one transition from infant to child to young adult in the blink of an eye has only confirmed my thesis that the force of life is much greater than any individual desire to imagine or capture it in single, tangible form. It is to my family, therefore, a source of warmth, stability, and light in the cosmic flux, and to families everywhere, that I dedicate this book.

Introduction

Generating Normative Discourse

God, as conceived by the men who guard Islam's early traditions, fashions only perfected beings in the wombs of women. As noted by Abū ʿUthmān ʿAmr ibn Baḥr al-Jāḥiẓ (d. 869 CE), a famous ninth-century Arab author of prose, literature, and Muʿtazilite theology,[1] each part of the body—hand, leg, eye, ear—is "designed to the highest standard of wise appropriateness,"[2] which is "evidence of Divine wisdom, design, and execution."[3] Given this belief in God's infinite wisdom and perfected design, humans are left to contemplate why many divine creations, brought forth from a mother's womb, fall short of that ideal. For Jāḥiẓ, one without hearing is like "someone absent though present and dead though alive";[4] those who lose their memories "cease to be human beings and become beasts."[5] And, this is from a man who himself suffered from severely deficient eyes.[6]

As Jāḥiẓ's own condition poignantly illustrates, the world humans experience is laden with anything but perfection, especially with regard to birth and reproduction. As every woman knows, pregnancies are fraught with danger. Conception may or may not occur, conception may take place only to be followed by a miscarriage or stillborn child. Both mother and child may die as a result of the traumatic experience of giving birth and/or being born. Mothers may undergo the successful delivery of a child only to find its limbs twisted in ways that do not conform to that divinely perfected, ideal human whom God designed, and men have come to expect. In other words, actual human experience and the ideal world that scholars such as Jāḥiẓ describe are disjointed—often wrenchingly so.

Jāḥiẓ's example, however, illustrates the contradictions that surface when natural, timeless biological functions, such as reproduction and birth, become inextricably bound up with local and specific theological and social systems of language, medicine, law, myth, and ritual to circumscribe what it means to be a mother. Such discussions about the formation of human life during the seventh to fourteenth centuries CE were crucial for the creation of a normative Muslim discourse surrounding women's biological, social, and religious roles as mother. To date, no study exists that considers how Muslim scholars of this period mapped the female reproductive body according to broader, cosmological schemes in order to define a woman's maternal identity. By examining systematically the discourses and practices surrounding maternity and how medieval Muslim theologians appropriated and channeled female reproductive power, this study fills a significant scholarly void concerning the historical construction of Muslim women's identities.

To meet this goal, this book has three aims: First, it brings to light relatively unknown medieval Muslim exegetical works, medical treatises, legal pronouncements, historical narratives, zoological texts, and folklore traditions that frame traditional understandings of motherhood and maternity. Second, it offers a foundational survey of the seminal discourses and practices concerned with women as procreative agents. This survey illustrates how medieval Muslim scholars prescribe visions of the pious "mother" and how their discursive strategies often conflict with the biological realities of the female reproductive body. Third, this study probes how ordinary women struggle to bridge the gap between their ideologically fashioned selves and their actual experience. By close consideration of rituals, gestures, laws, theories of procreation marginal to orthodox discourse, and folk medicine, this study reveals how medieval women embrace, multiply, but often question the maternal identities imagined for them by the tradition and thereby reinvent themselves as mothers and Muslims.

Maternity provides an excellent example for a study of how a mother's identity is formed because of the very liminal nature of conception, gestation, and birth. Maternity exaggerates the porous nature of women, whose boundaries are penetrated by others from within and without, in the form of sperm, child, and even God. As a result of these incursions, a woman's identity is no longer fixed but severed and fluid.[7] The boundaries of her own body shift continuously to accommodate from one to two or even three sentient beings; even more disturbing, there is no clear indication as to when precisely those alterations take place. Upon giving birth, the contours of a mother's physique again erode as they are scrutinized, penetrated, and breached by physicians, midwives, family, society, and the child itself. For example, the blurring of boundaries between mother and child extend well into subsequent activities of suckling, nurturing, and teaching.[8]

The messy, unpredictable, and perplexing experience of reproduction that takes place outside the bodies and control of men presents an ideal occasion for examining how a mother's identity is imagined, constructed, and then reified through the language of medicine, law, myth, and ritual. These discourses create maternal identities that strive to seal up a woman's porosity and to stabilize her mutability, and, as a result, protect society from the perceived instability and dangers associated with the marginality of the female reproductive body, especially when that body is then faulted by men for producing less than desirable outcomes. Through formal discussions of reproduction, pregnancy, birth, and postpartum rituals, elite Muslim scholars generate the boundaries necessary to define and regulate a woman's potent, unrestrained maternal body, and establish her place as subordinate to men in the begetting of the kind of superlative life they determine God desires.[9]

In addition to outlining traditional discourses that circumscribe a mother's identity, this study also seeks to uncover the experiential, maternal activities that lie in the spaces betwixt and between orthodox visions of the reproductive body. Medieval Islamic history is, more often than not, written, defined, and studied by male scholars and theologians.[10] Contemporary or medieval studies about law, war, leadership, politics, theology, and economics may all attempt to reconstruct or record what "really" happened in order to buttress prescriptive views about the Muslim tradition, but they only reveal just part of the story. Unfortunately, the topics of what legitimately comprises "history" (as evinced by the subject list above) are often limited to what men—in the past and present—privilege as significant and worthy of recording.

Since women left no written records, it is impossible to assume that their voices and contributions to Muslim discourse and practice, if any, may be fully uncovered. It is likewise inconceivable and, in fact, detrimental to the feminist project, to believe medieval Muslim women had a rich, alternative tradition or theology of their own, which contemporary scholars need only amplify.[11] Rather than remain complicit in the assumption that women had no meaningful presence in our understanding of medieval Islamic history, or falsely assume a rival female agency that continuously subverted male authority, this study attempts to seek out disruptions in the medical, literary, theological, or legal narratives where alternative modes of maternal subjectivity may have thrived and flourished. Such disruptions destabilize the regulatory discourses and practices that (re)produce the ideal mother whose body readily and easily generates the life God (and men) command. It is in these breaches of instability where maternal experience and voice, in dynamic exchange with a God that may or may not conform to masculine ideals, may be revealed and imagined, even if to a limited extent.[12]

Methodological Concerns

As noted above, this work examines a variety of sacred, medical, exegetical, legal, and literary texts to illustrate the varied and contradictory ways male elite scholars imagine, define, and regulate women's maternal bodies in medieval Islam. By cutting a broad swath through numerous genres of literature and across time and space, this study in no way claims to be exhaustive in its efforts to flesh out a quintessential portrait of the medieval Muslim mother. Rather, its point is to reveal just some of the inherent discursive dynamics at play in the construction of maternal identities.[13] Because reproduction takes place deep within the female womb, in a place concealed far from the naked eye, a close analysis of how it was imagined, moderated, and controlled sheds light on the many ways medieval Muslim scholars wrestled with the complexity of its inner workings, and were often perplexed by unexpected outcomes over which they had no clear understanding or command. The desire to know and govern this mysterious, even inscrutable, process drove male elites to speculate almost obsessively over reproduction.

The sense that women, as sources of life, served as intermediaries between God and men in the bearing of life gave women a more potent—but feared—status. Men viewed women as potent because their reproductive efforts were essential for fashioning a perfected (male) Muslim, and feared because that power was her exclusive privilege. Men could only do so much, as their paternal roles are confirmed externally and only subsequently to the birth of a child. The literary, medical, legal, and ritualistic tendencies to circumscribe, denigrate, but also elevate a mother's status highlight the perceived social and cosmological dangers posed by the female reproductive body, and the male impulse to privilege yet suppress her unique abilities to produce life in conjunction with, but also separate from, both God and man.

To demonstrate how medieval Muslim scholars sought to normalize the liminal nature of the maternal body, each chapter describes in detail what a sampling of medieval Islamic texts, which range primarily from the seventh to twelfth centuries CE (and occasionally beyond) and represent a particular discursive authority on the maternal body, have to say about maternity and maternal identities. In addition to this descriptive analysis, each chapter also explores in depth the language/genre these texts employ to frame such discussions. Special focus is given to the medical descriptions and proscriptions surrounding women's reproductive bodies and practices, the didactic stories of the virtues and moral failings of "good" and "bad" mothers stretching back to the mother of us all, Eve, the legal guidelines regarding intercourse, birthing, inheritance, and nursing, and the ritual prescriptions surrounding new mothers and their newborn infants.

These discourses illustrate how, with striking (and persistent) consistency, maternal identities are constructed, enforced, and reified in the social context through consistent appeals to the greater cosmos. In reference to broader cosmological schemes, the Qur'ān intimates an ephemeral, maternal body that responds in dynamic, intimate, and often ineffable ways to God's calls to procreate. However, in order to assert their own ascendency over such a potent, sovereign female reproductive body, male scholars appeal to this same cosmic authority to overlay their own privileged medical, legal, and theological knowledge onto its inner workings. As a result, male physicians, legalists, theologians, and historians demarcate a subsidiary female physiology that may be capable of giving birth, but not of reproducing the perfected life God demands. In a variety of discursive contexts, men institute their own power to replicate themselves, in the precise form God desires.

In addition to the close analysis of various medieval texts, this study employs anthropological, cultural, and Gender Studies theories to discern how Muslim mothers cultivate, modify, or expand dramatically the identities constructed for them. Judith Butler, Carol Delaney, Lynda Birke and other feminist scholars have demonstrated persuasively there is no such thing as a "natural" body that exists outside the language used to define it.[14] Even the interiority of the body, which houses seemingly neutral, fixed biological processes such as blood flow, digestion, or cell division, can only be known in terms of the social, cultural, and historical images through which it is described.[15] Such descriptions give the appearance of solidifying a person's physical nature in terms of gender, sexuality, or able-ness, while in reality both bodies and their social, cultural contexts remain in a constant state of flux. Judith Butler captures the processes involved in the social, cultural stabilization of core, bodily identities, in particular as they pertain to sex and gender, in her theory of "performativity." Butler shows that physical bodies are not biologically determined but rather socially interpreted through a repetition of stylized acts (performances) in time, which leads to the formation of a core gender identity.[16]

This core gender identity, however, influences but is also constrained by larger "frameworks of intelligibility" that prescribe what types of sex and gender society deems acceptable and therefore "natural." This book draws from Butler's work and others in three ways: one, to reconstruct the cognitive frames of intelligibility through which medieval Muslim scholars organize, encounter, and evaluate the arbitrary content of culture to privilege or suppress particular maternal ideals, habits, displays, and activities; two, to explore the mother's performative responses to such constraints, which are often complicit in the maintenance of patriarchal structures seemingly disparate from their own interests; and three, to identify disruptions within such normative frames of intelligibility where a variety of maternal subjectivities may proliferate because of the failure of discursive, paternal regimes to legislate or confine fully their own ideals.[17]

In its attempts to sift out maternal experience from the creation of maternal identities, this study takes the position that all female action, desire, or striving does not always result in "resistance" to oppositional forces or perspectives. In order to bypass this notion of resistance so persistent in many feminist works, this book incorporates the understanding of "agency" put forth in Saba Mahmood's groundbreaking *The Politics of Piety*. Mahmood has demonstrated how contemporary Muslim women willingly embody (rather than subvert) patriarchal norms through repetitive practices; thus, she locates agency *within* structures of power rather than outside of them.[18] Like Mahmood's monograph, this work demonstrates how believing women, through pre- and postnatal rituals, habits, and practices, often create corresponding, inward dispositions that conform but also contribute to the "ideal mother" within a medieval context.

For example, medieval Muslim women embrace the ceremony of the *taḥnīk,* during which the father chews a few dates, and then places the masticated juices in an infant's mouth to be consumed as the child's first food rather than its mother's milk.[19] Although contrary to what is natural, this tradition symbolizes the father's acceptance of the child as his own, the child's loyalty to the father, and the infant's initiation into the Muslim community through the paternal, rather than maternal, line. By withholding her breast from her baby's mouth, and handing the child over to the father to be nourished, the mother cultivates the perceived virtue of subordination to both husband and God. Her willing suppression of her own maternal instincts secures the infant's place within the community, and so allows her to seal her identity as "ideal mother" in the eyes of believers. In this and other examples, it is important to recognize that agency often operates within—rather than outside—dominant structures of power.

However, this view of compliant or even complicit female agency does not preclude medieval mothers from also transforming traditional, patriarchal norms when their bodies bar them from realizing prescribed theological ideals. Alternative depictions of procreation that undermine the heterosexual dynamic, along with female folk remedies designed to enhance or suppress fertility, disrupt normative ideologies to expand the narrow bandwidth of elite male constructions of mother and God to include the more intricate and complex potentialities of both intimated in the Qurʾān and un/orthodox theologies. This project therefore builds on the work of Mahmood, Butler, and others through a fuller consideration of religious belief in the wider discussion of female agency and embodied practice in the medieval period.

In sum, this study assesses the religious and social contexts in which medieval Muslim maternal identities were articulated, disrupted, embodied, or performed in all of their varied states. In order to enhance their capital within a particular theological field, mothers would have sought to internalize and project outward those theological ideals prescribed for them, or perhaps to expand or modify them through alternate or more desirable forms of piety, through bodily practices. Such bodily practices would include participating (or not participating) in pre- and postnatal ritual performances, conforming to ideal models of piety, adhering to or thwarting particular sex acts, or adopting a variety of reproductive controls (including magic) to enhance or suppress fertility. Through an analysis of both the language used to describe and discuss women's maternal bodies in diverse genres of medieval Islamic literature, along with what can be discerned with regard to female practices accompanying reproduction and birth, this book seeks to reconstruct how believing men and women conceptualize and, to a limited extent, experience maternity in the medieval period, and how these articulations inform (and were informed by) their understandings of God.

Chapter 1: On Wombs, Women, and the Hand of God: The Bearing of Life in the Qurʾān

Chapter 1 examines Islam's foundational, sacred text, the holy Qurʾān, to determine its understanding of God's hand in the reproductive process and to flesh out the plethora of biological and moral roles men and women play (or may not play) in response to God's call to reproduce human life. How God defines mothers explicitly and obliquely within the Qurʾān establishes the contours for all subsequent discussions of maternal identity. Medieval jurists, theologians, doctors, and moralist exegetes all habitually appeal to the Qurʾān's guidance and authority in order to construct, reify, and enforce a normative maternal identity.

Chapter 1 explores the Qurʾān's sophisticated depictions of human creation and reproduction in order to show how the sacred text emulates, encodes, but ultimately critiques both Greek medical wisdom and other Near Eastern creation narratives to project its own image of God. In the many instances that probe how God generates human life, the Islamic deity assumes traits familiar from other Mediterranean contexts such as artisan, farmer, force of nature, loving consort, mother, and midwife. In the composite roles he takes up in the procreative process, God projects masculine and feminine qualities simultaneously to demonstrate both immanent and transcendent aspects of the divine nature and to confirm his supreme and uncontested power over every manifestation of life. The dialectic between these oppositional renderings of his being serves to insulate God's nature from any positive (and therefore restrictive) identity. His projection of a multiplicity of gendered roles in the procreative process, however, necessarily impacts the masculine and feminine subjects with which he interacts to generate life in nontraditional ways.

These complex and diverse descriptions of God's personae and how these personae interact with humans to generate life point to a uniquely Qurʾānic impulse to disrupt pagan, "scientific" theories of fetal development even as they are appropriated, along with other Near Eastern versions of God's generative efforts. Such disruptions inflate the Qurʾān's own theological vision that God alone holds supreme command over and above all of human creation, including sexual reproduction, at the same time that he necessarily engages that creation through a plethora of erotic, immanent exchanges. This vision of God's unrivaled omnipotence that is both transcendent yet immanent, masculine yet feminine, counteracts the traditional pagan and Near Eastern privileging of binary sex roles that assumes a masculine, generative creator and a passive, feminine recipient of the life he alone produces. It also questions the innate, dichotomous, and hierarchical relationship between men and women based on reproduction,[20] and the male's self-proclaimed authority within the context of that relationship to govern and suppress the maternal body so that he alone may proliferate the type of life God commands in an earthly capacity.

Because of his supreme omnipotence over all human life, the Qurʾān boldly asserts that God has full knowledge of what every womb contains, what every womb bears, and what changes take place within a woman's womb.[21] Surprisingly, perhaps, omnipotence and omniscience in this case do not seem to translate into perfected progeny. And so the question arises: given God's inherently apophatic identities, what are the appropriate human responses to his reproductive commands? In other words, how should humans—especially mothers—through their own bodies, moral choices, and pious practices, interact with an ever-changing, ever-shifting divine will to generate (or not generate) life?

Chapter 1 explores further the Qurʾān's plethora of maternal responses to God's rather incongruous procreative desires. Mary, for example, engaged directly, without the help or intervention of any man, in a kind of erotic interchange with the breath and spirit to embody God's command to procreate. Mary's direct, physical response to God's command, however, is countered by more prescriptive efforts to curb such intimacies between God and the female body. For example, Abraham's and Zakarīyā's wives waited passively while their husbands prayed to God to facilitate life in their barren bodies. Likewise, the prophet's wives suppressed their own biological desires for children of their own so that they might serve as moral surrogates for anyone who follows the one, true God. The strict etiquette surrounding divorce, infant care, and sexual mores also serve to counter the unbridled reproductive potency embodied by Mary. Ranging from erotic exchange to the suppression of female desires, Qur'ānic depictions of appropriate female responses to God's procreative demands are as multifaceted as their references to God's apophatic, generative identity.

Chapter 2: Mapping the Maternal Body: The Mechanics of Reproduction

Medieval discourse strives to suppress the Qur'ān's celebration of God's multifaceted identity and tolerance for feminine reproductive potency by subjecting both to patriarchal visions of a male God who interacts solely with the female body through channels approved by men. Thus, it becomes incumbent upon men to articulate an ideal maternal body that will respond to God's call to procreate in an appropriate and productive fashion. The male impulse to assert control over the maternal body suggests a certain level of discomfort with the Qur'ānic ideal that God creates in wombs whatever, and however, he pleases. Such a statement assumes an erotic intimacy between women and God that leaves men completely out of the equation. In order to privilege their own procreative power, men usurp God's omniscience and omnipotence through a variety of authoritative discourses to guarantee the entire reproductive process is directed toward their desired outcome of self-replication.

Through detailed analyses of medieval Islamic medical texts, along with folklore works and *ḥadīth* that focus on reproduction, chapter 2 demonstrates how male physicians and scholars draw upon the Qur'ān, theological beliefs, and Greek medical wisdom regarding procreation to circumscribe female reproductive anatomy. The Islamic medical texts emphasize how the orderly and perfected mechanics of heterosexual reproduction, which they define and deem as normative, alone bear witness to God's will and his creative ideals.

Privileging the many Qur'ānic passages that emphasize the necessity of male and female pairings, the majority of medieval Muslim physicians elaborate Hippocratic, rather than Aristotelian, models of reproduction. Hippocratic reproductive theory dominated medieval Muslim thinking.[22]

In contrast to the Aristotelian model more familiar to Westerners, the Hippocratics (rightly) assigned women an active role in reproduction. Because Muslim scholars believed that women actively contributed to the formation of life, however, the feminine role in the process was scrutinized in great detail and heavily regulated so that women's bodies might bear the appropriate results. For example, because they thought the female body to be naturally weak,[23] early Muslim physicians suggest women's bodies are inimical to childbearing, which sets potential mothers in willful insubordination to God's plans for humanity. Thus, the failure of a pregnancy (which is a failure to replicate believing men) becomes an indictment not only against a woman's anatomy but also her moral character, which, for medieval physicians, were indistinguishable.

Drawing primarily from the works of several prominent medieval physicians who focus in depth on gynecological topics, which include ʿArīb ibn Saʿd (d. 980 CE),[24] ʿAlī ibn Sahl Rabbān al-Ṭabarī (d. 870 CE),[25] and Ibn Qayyim al-Jawzīya (d. 1350 CE),[26] along with other popular medical and folklore treatises,[27] chapter 2 describes in detail how medieval Muslim doctors, scholars and *literati* encode the female body as the weaker sex. As a result of their efforts, the entire course of reproduction, from the first act of sexual intercourse to the suckling of the newborn baby, becomes a precarious endeavor with physical and moral dangers lurking deep within a mother's body, or in her interactions with a hostile, outside environment. In order to ward off potential hazards that might derail God's perfected procreative processes, medieval physicians assert knowledge of, or control over, every stage of the reproductive act by concocting remedies and solutions to ward off any pre- or postnatal problems that could undermine the divine hand. In this way, they assert themselves between women and God, and, in fact, assume the power of God, as the authoritative begetters of life.

Muslim medical treatises offer a wide range of "practical" prescriptions that are predicated upon a weak woman to claim knowledge, power, and control over the reproductive process. For example, texts advise how and when women are most likely to conceive, how they might beget males, what foods, drugs, and drinks pregnant women should eat and avoid, or how they can prevent miscarriages or birth anomalies. The entire medical discourse is framed to curb the damage a woman can do or to overcome the hurdles her physical limitations impose. Because women are believed to be inadequate to bear children, men must lead them carefully along a proper, restricted course of moral thought and physical action toward parturition. In the context of such deliberations over the prescriptions to which women must heed, Muslim physicians inextricably weave social identities with both natural law, which demarcates the female body as naturally weak, and divine law, which ultimately dictates and governs the natural world where all is subordinate to the one true God. Fortunately for women, men possess full knowledge of both.

The treacherous and precarious path, which women—who are already viewed as fragile and frail—must tread toward a successful birth outcome, undermines the Qur'ānic ideal of God's many-sided, procreative identities and feminine reproductive power. Unlike the Qur'ān, which often emphasizes a mother's strength and faith through her direct and solitary choice to embody the divine will, medical and legal discourse relentlessly directs matters to manage and control actively the female reproductive body. On a social level, men become the intermediaries between women and God by defining the ideal, "maternal" role. Women may conceive and give birth, but it is only the men who can guarantee the superlative life God demands.

Chapter 3: Paradigms of the Good Mother

Chapter 3 studies how the theme of the "ideal" mother, who is subordinate to both men and God, is reiterated and embellished in literary and theological depictions of Mary, Khadīja, Āsiya, Fāṭima, and ʿĀ'isha. Each figure, with the exception of ʿĀ'isha, embodies a single, ideal aspect of motherhood as defined by men. Mary, the mother of Jesus, displayed an unflinching willingness to submit to God in her acquiescence to his command to conceive her son out of wedlock, and to bear him alone and in pain. Although not a biological mother, Āsiya demonstrated a readiness to break from her husband's tyranny and abuse to rescue, nurture, and rear a future prophet, despite torture and persecution.

In addition, Khadīja, the prophet's first wife and guarantor of his genealogical line, illustrates the links between belief in God, faith in husband, and a prolific womb, even in old age. Fāṭima, conceived from the fruits of paradise, went on to become the mother of martyrs who sacrificed themselves for the faith. These four women, whom the *ḥadīth* deem to be the "best among women,"[28] reveal how "good mothers" must be steadfast in belief, robust in womb, ready to sacrifice all for their children, husbands, or God, and prolific producers of offspring who will grow to defend and protect the faith.

Each exemplary mother is either explicitly or implicitly compared to ʿĀ'isha, the prophet Muḥammad's youngest wife, whose personal history often challenged masculine ideologies. ʿĀ'isha is nowhere described as the "best among women" but rather as "the superiority of *tharīd* to other meals," *tharīd* being a dish made of bread soaked in broth.[29] Falling short of being the "best," ʿĀ'isha is clearly set apart from the other four women because of her inability to bear the prophet's offspring, a failing that is oftentimes equated with disobedience or impiety.[30] On a narrative level, ʿĀʾisha's personal history offers a diachronic analog to biological realities and theological ideals. She, like the realities of human reproduction, is a mixed bag that disrupts men's concerted efforts to circumscribe the female body. Her deficiencies are accentuated and ideals reasserted by the tradition's taking measure of this woman against these other four martyrs and mothers who are objects of maternal perfection.

Chapter 4: Postpartum: Making the Good Mother through Public Rituals and Embodied Practices

Public rituals and embodied practices reinforce the normative discourses surrounding a mother's willingness to conceive, bear, and nurture children. Childbirth, after all, is a liminal moment that disrupts patriarchal power and control in that the labor, delivery, and birth of an infant takes place among the company of women, not men. Postpartum rituals and practices such as breastfeeding, *taḥnīk,* circumcision, *ʿaqīqa,*[31] and *kunya,* therefore, serve to transfer a mother's authority over the newborn to the father. As such, these rituals and practices repair the social ruptures incurred as a result of childbirth through the reaffirmation and reinforcement of paternal norms that emphasize a woman's identity qua mother, and confer the child's biological relationship to the father. Her willing participation in such postpartum practices bestow upon a woman her pious and privileged status as "mother" among the community of believers through the ritual socialization of her child into that same group. Her ritual gestures allow her to proximate, though not fully emulate, the paradisiacal ideals identified in chapter 3.

Chapter 4 will also examine how these socialized rituals exclude some women (such as ʿĀʾisha) from embracing the familial, religious, and communal norms that serve to anchor a woman's identity more firmly within the larger community of believers when their bodies fail to comply with the ideal maternal form. For example, women who bear no children either because of someone's sterility or a propensity for miscarriages are never granted a *kunya,* a title mothers assume after they have borne children that literally replaces their own given names with that of "mother of the child." Women who have no infant to breastfeed are blocked from establishing an extended network of blood ties with their own children or others from among her family or the community of believers. Childless women are likewise denied the opportunity to suckle a child in paradise, and have no one to intervene for them on the last day. For barren couples, the wealth of the family must be transferred laterally rather than linearly, a secondary provision put forth in the Qur'ān that stifles a husband's ability to secure his own legacy among future generations. Women without offspring are also denied the everyday parties and celebrations surrounding the practices of circumcision, hair cutting, or sacrifice that bring honor and recognition to individual families but also secure for them a definable and privileged place within the community.

In sum, chapter 4 examines how such rituals and embodied practices confirm the images of the ideal mother put forth in the Qur'ān, medical wisdom, exegetical works, and law within everyday life. Such rituals serve well those women whose reproductive bodies reflect the ideal; however, such practices marginalize others whose anatomies are blamed for failing to produce offspring that are the ultimate adhesive to a communal life structured around paternal relations. Out on the edges of social acceptability, however, childless women who bear the burden of their lot without question hold the potential to become universal paragons of piety and subordination, whose pain and suffering generate demonstrations of God's beneficence for all to witness and praise. Through their marginality, these women create new avenues of piety not readily recognized within normative, paternal discourse.

Chapter 5: Mother as Monster

Chapter 5 takes up an examination of "bad mothers," that is, mothers whose bodies either intentionally or unintentionally meddle with God's perfected procreative processes, thereby producing anomalies or monsters who thwart the paradisiacal ideal. Such literary examples taken from far-off civilizations or within the animal world function to discourage women from deviating from the perfected maternal path that reproduces the desired believers both God and men command. Eve, as portrayed in Muslim exegesis, is a prime example of a mother in the center whose moral disposition directly impacts her ability to bear children successfully. Eve undergoes several miscarriages before she finally dedicates what is in her womb to God.[32] However, even after she grants her children to God, the residue of impiety remains embedded in the somewhat shaky futures of several of her offspring.[33] Clearly, no mother should question the authority of God, because terrible things could happen to her body or to her offspring if she does.

Chapter 5 will explore this and other examples of ordinary women found in theological treatises, zoologies, folklore, and entertainment works to demonstrate how the male elite fashions female characters who wittingly or unwittingly violate natural and divine laws through sexual improprieties and, as a result, become infertile, miscarry, or produce reproductive anomalies or monsters. Such examples convey strong warnings to ordinary women. The various examples of reproductive failures and monstrous forms illustrate the different ways in which medieval scholars imagine how impiety corrodes the female body and subverts God's procreative plans. These maternal "monsters" directly defy the ideals put forth in the foundational texts and rituals, and project what might happen if unguarded female anatomies are left to their own devices.

To illustrate this point further, chapter 5 will examine the *ḥayawān* (bestiary) literature, a popular, folklore genre that provides detailed analyses of sexuality, intercourse, reproduction, and birth in the context of unusual animal behavior.[34] By way of analogy, these imaginatively elaborate analyses of animal life fuel analogous debates on human morality, the impact of the environment on the formation of human biology and the soul, and reproductive physiology.[35] The *ḥayawān* literature serves as a safe forum through which male scholars explore the implications of human sexual practices generally considered degenerate within the tradition. What aberrant animals will suffer for their "unnatural" behavior becomes a coded discourse that aims to circumscribe human sexual expression with its dire warnings over the reproductive implications for deviance. Since each and every woman has the potential to thwart God's procreative processes through depraved thoughts and practices via her reproductive power, scholars take great pains to advise women about the hideous and shocking consequences of bad mothering through detailed depictions of monsters and other natural aberrations that occur in the animal world.

In the course of these descriptions that presume a woman's moral efficacy with regard to reproduction, elite male scholars assume that females have a natural propensity for disobeying God. This disobedience manifests itself in bad births. Therefore, men must control women further to ensure positive birth outcomes that do not entail disturbing perversions such as those found in the animal world. If bad outcomes persist, they are due to a woman's intransigence or to her guardian's impotence. Such direct challenges to God's reproductive processes can only be imagined as the result of female deviance, rather than chance, nature, or an ineffable divine will. In probing the source of this deeper question about the range and limits of female power, chapter 5 brings to light how medieval scholars assert that the human life God desires could only be brought forth through the male's necessary interference with or control over the female reproductive body, a position that directly counters Qur'ānic understandings of God's solo role in creating in wombs whatever, and however, he pleases.

Chapter 6: The Cure of Perfection

While chapters 3, 4, and 5 discuss how the medieval scholarly elite imagined and reified the ideal mother through rhetoric and practice, chapter 6 explores how women diffuse the traditional, patriarchal norms imposed on them when their own bodies hinder them from realizing these theological ideals. Driven by their unique experiences, women see that the perfected pregnancies God wills—or perhaps better put, that male scholars have come to expect—are not always attainable nor often, in fact, desirable. In this chapter, alternative theories about God's wondrous reproductive practices, along with heretofore ignored magical and folk remedies, through which medieval women control their own fertility, determine their child's sex, or assure a safe pregnancy and delivery, reveal how women questioned the paradigm of the ideal mother while often forging new visions of God.

Chapter 6 demonstrates how nonorthodox theories of creation embedded in discussions of wind eggs, spontaneous generation, and metamorphosis often, like the Qur'ān, emphasize the feminine role in the generation of life. Marginal to the dominant discourse also are a number theological positions and religious rituals that further envision God's reliance on human participation in the realization of his creative efforts. For example, while most types of bodily mutilations and excessive adornments are condemned by Muslim legal scholars,[36] circumcision—which is a radical human alteration of the body subsequent to its creation—becomes an obligatory act required to purify both males and, to a lesser extent, females. The ritual cutting of the foreskin affirms the necessary intervention of humans in God's efforts to generate perfected human beings.

These theological positions marginal to the dominant discourse disrupt male assertions of power over both the maternal body and its reproductive capacities. Such disruptions, however, open up interpretive spaces where women may take control of their reproductive lives from the hands of men and perhaps even God (as he is defined by men) as they direct and navigate their own fertility, in/ability to conceive, ease in delivery, or the sex/appearance of the child through folk medicine, magic, and direct manipulations of nature. These women, and to some extent nonelite men, strive to do all they can to ensure the reproductive goals they define and determine for themselves while still acknowledging and accepting the Qur'ānic ideal that it is God's plan that will ultimately prevail.

In times where childbirth was often a dangerous enterprise, and infant death common, as evidenced by the *ḥadīth*'s depiction of a special place in paradise for women who have suffered through the deaths of one or more of their children,[37] it is not hard to understand why women would want to participate in God's creative act to let their own hopes, desires, fears, and joys be known. Implicit in women's curative practices is that female reproductive defects that have been catalogued, characterized, and controlled by men can be overcome via direct human intervention, which can be theologically conferred, or at the very least their potentially negative consequences can be negotiated or ameliorated.

Chapter 6 will explore further in depth how folk remedies serve to elaborate feminine visions of God that rival what males vocalize as being God's will. It is through direct participation in their own life cycles that women tap into marginal theologies, such as those of the Muʿtazilite al-Jāḥiẓ and the Qurʾān itself, to challenge normative, elite male constructions of a God who demands perfection from faulty female bodies that never will conform to these ideal expectations. In the lived experiences of everyday life, this chapter demonstrates how women reclaim the Qurʾānic vision that only God, and not men, know the true contents of the womb, and that ultimately only God, and not men, cause a life to be or not to be, in whatever form, or through whatever means, he chooses. Here, chapter 6 explores more fully the role of female agency as ordinary women work within dominate structures of male power to realize those structures in more perfect—and practical—form.

Conclusion: The Making of Medieval Muslim Mothers

Given that this study explores the formation of medieval Muslim maternal identities, it is vital to show how often a particular theological, biological, or social vision of motherhood in the medieval Islamic period was articulated within its broader sectarian context. In other words, the Muslim position on particular aspects of the female reproductive body was fashioned in conformity to, or in contrast with, visions held by neighboring Jews, Christians, and pagans. This chapter will make some broad suggestions as to what might distinguish the "Muslim mother" from others around her, and point to some areas for future study.

As chapters 1 and 2 show, the Qurʾān's views on reproduction were formed in dialog with an already established Greek medical tradition. This dialog with Greek tradition continued on into Muslim medical corpuses, where Hippocratic understandings of the female body were fused with broader theological interpretations about the nature of God and the sanctified relationships between men and women. Here, scholars try to resolve the inherent conflicts between their theological understanding of God as the sole progenitor of life and their biological knowledge of how human reproduction took place.

Similarly, the Qurʾānic proliferation of maternal responses to God's command to procreate stands in direct conflict with Jewish and Christian beliefs that labor pains are punishments for female transgressions. Chapter 3's review of the exegetical literature shows how portrayals of Mary were also honed in light of Jewish and Christian views on maternal morality, responsibility, and the extent to which a mother's thoughts, words, and deeds are impressed upon her offspring.

Chapter 4 refers to shared Abrahamic ritual practices, such as circumcision, to suggest how an infant's socialization into the wider community of believers was cast in a distinctively Islamic way that served to separate Muslim mothers and babies from their Jewish or Christian counterparts. By way of contrast, the fifth chapter argues that when it comes to reproductive anomalies, Jewish, Christian, and Muslim mothers were accused in similar fashion of engaging in immoral practices that led to monstrous births. Such references to Greek, Christian, or Jewish practices will be woven into each chapter and summarized in the Conclusion to demonstrate how the elite scholars' formation of an ideal Muslim mother was dependent in many ways on what Jewish, Christian, or pagan mothers were or were not.

To conclude, this interdisciplinary study will serve Islamicists, scholars of religion, and historians concerned with the creative impulses underlying the formation of a normative, Islamic tradition. The extensive discussions of medieval Muslim exegesis, medical works, legal materials, histories, zoologies, and folklore that frame traditional understandings of motherhood and maternity will provide a useful resource for scholars and students interested in premodern Islam. The subsequent description and analysis of these texts will not only benefit them but also scholars and students with an interest in Gender Studies and/or cultural anthropology, as the book's thesis will provoke discussion, argument, and reflection upon how communities deploy both religious and "scientific" discourses to fashion a gendered subject and rationalize practices that ingrain it within a social group as normative.

These scholars and students will also find value in the wider discussions of female agency and embodied practice in the sections describing how medieval women adopt, revise, and even question these norms imagined for them by the tradition and thereby reinvent themselves as mothers and Muslims. Finally, for generalists in the Humanities and Social Sciences, the liminal moments and dominant/marginal voices surrounding maternity call attention to Islam's multivocal, rather than essentialist, nature. All too often the preserve of political scientists who treat Islam as a global monolith to be reckoned with, this study will challenge such views by demonstrating how the Islamic "tradition" is never fixed but subject to constant negotiation and debate by ordinary men and women struggling to understand their place in the world.

1

On Wombs, Women, and the Hand of God

The Bearing of Life in the Qur'ān

> It is he that fashions you in wombs as he pleases.
>
> —Sūra 3:6

The Qur'ān hardly provides a comprehensive, systematic manual of reproductive theories and practices; rather, it projects a series of brief vignettes that disclose disparate and fragmentary conceptions of procreative processes and agents of creation on both a cosmic and individual level. These vignettes adumbrate the diverse nature of God's generative role and his creative endeavors, which the Qur'ān presents as inscrutably analogous to both human reproduction and maternal identities. Just as God's creative agency and impulses transcend human comprehension, so, too, does human reproduction necessarily remain a mystery to ordinary men and women who struggle to comprehend its elusive intricacies and so better control its often volatile outcomes. Finding maternal paradigms such as Mary, whose piety led to the birth of Jesus, is one such strategy, but attaining Mary's status proves elusive if not illusory. For most men and women, the Qur'ān's many displays of profound creative and reproductive uncertainties that disclose God's incomparable and mystifying omnipotence prevail.

As the examples below will show, God is at once transcendent word, artisan, farmer, midwife, philosopher, and intimate sexual partner.[1] In his donning of these varied roles, the divine encompasses all aspects of human creativity, sexuality, knowledge, and gender, yet transcends them as his identity can never be captured fully in a single image. The polyvalence of God's procreative agency renders both men and women deficient to replicate his ways or assume his generative powers as their own. The exceptionally pious seem exempt to this rule, but only to a limited extent. God and God alone creates in wombs whatever, and however, he pleases.[2]

Divine procreation has among its analogs the mysteries of human reproduction, as it, too, defies rational comprehension and human efforts to determine its outcomes. The Qur'ān presents an array of crucial episodes where women may or may not give birth to show how they are incapable of replicating God's creative efforts to reproduce life, and that God generates in wombs what he pleases. For example, some women remain barren all their lives, even those married to prophets, while others receive a wealth of progeny. Some mothers deliver perfected babies who suffer no infirmities whatsoever, while others bring forth infants who are blind, deaf, or dumb. As one mother's child flourishes well into old age, another's will die while suckling, for no apparent reason. Such profound uncertainty over a mother's ability to dictate reproductive ends likewise serves to underscore God's absolute dominance over all life.

There are a few exceptions to this rule. The extraordinarily pious, such as Mary, who conceived Jesus freely without a human father, do seem capable of determining reproductive ends through their faithful words and actions. However, despite the fact that Mary's exceptional piety gave way to a fertile womb, the Qur'ān still preserves the enigma surrounding Jesus's conception and birth by veiling the actual event behind a panoply of conception narratives that evade any singular interpretation of what actually takes place. Mary's piety may have led to a purified and productive womb, but only God can cause it to conceive the life he desires, in the ways he prefers it to occur.

The majority of ordinary women who struggle to approximate Mary's example, however, can never be assured the same result. Such women may cultivate similar virtues; however, they will not be guaranteed the same reproductive outcomes Mary enjoyed as a result of her perfected actions and purified nature. Therefore, the Qur'ān's array of snapshots projecting the capricious nature of divine creation and human reproduction structure an ambiguous maternal identity that may be pure, pious, and perfected, but also may be deficient, defiant, and flawed in terms of faith and a willingness to sacrifice all to God. The Qur'ān's broad template of diverse and confounding models of creation, reproduction, and maternal identities only grows narrower and more restrictive as subsequent medieval medical scholars and exegetes privilege only those images that support their own patriarchal constructs of God, birth, and motherhood.

The Many Ways God Creates

Near Eastern Foundations of Human Creation: Clay, Mud, and Water

In order to show God's complete mastery and supreme power over all life, the Qur'ān reiterates familiar Near Eastern and Mediterranean stories that stress the generation of life from God's word, or from his hands-on fashioning of inanimate, earthy materials. For example, the Qur'ān emphasizes how God only has to say the word *Be!* and whatever he intends or wills comes into being (*kun fayakūn*).[3] The generation of matter from a single word or command resembles Yahweh's formulaic statements in Genesis 1, where he says "Let there be [light]" and there is [light] (*yəhî* [*ōr*] *vayəhî* [*ōr*]).[4] The Qur'ānic God's calling things into being from afar emphasizes his absolute and utter transcendence over whatever he creates.

Such depictions of God's remote transcendence are mediated through those verses that emphasize his manual fashioning of life from earthy substances, which resemble what is found in Genesis 2:7: "The Lord God formed man of the dust from the earth (*vayyîṣer yəhwâ 'ĕlōhîm 'et-hā'ādām 'āfār min-hā'ădāmâ*)."[5] In contrast to the Hebrew dust (*'āfār*), the Qur'ānic God prefers clay (*ṭīn*) in his molding of humanity: "It is he who created you from clay (*ṭīn*) then decreed a term."[6] However, the Qur'ān does not limit him to *ṭīn* alone. Other verses mention God's use of potter's clay (*ṣalṣāl*);[7] mud (*ḥamā'*);[8] sticky clay (*ṭīn lāzib*);[9] and dust (*ṭurāb*).[10] Water (*mā'*)[11] also serves as a foundational basis for God's formation of life, both human and otherwise, and mirrors, perhaps, ancient Mediterranean or Near Eastern flood narratives, where life emerges after the subsiding of the waters.[12] In all of these examples, God chooses some natural resource he alone shapes into life with his own hand,[13] without help or intervention. He is not limited to a single substance in his creative efforts, but has access to any he chooses.

The Qur'ān is relatively silent as to why God decides to utilize one substance over another, although the text does note that sticky clay (*ṭīn lāzib*) appears to be the stubborn, stinking substance God uses to create those "who see signs but turn them into mockery" (37:14). Many Qur'ānic commentators, however, connect the type of clay God prefers in fashioning a human with her innate, natural disposition. For example, when God created the first human being, Adam, he selected *ṭīn*, the purest form.[14] Humans shaped from *ṭīn* would be born untainted and righteous, though later may be "muddied" by their actions.[15] Some exegetes suggest that extraordinary human beings, such as prophets, were formed from specific types of purified clay.[16] Others propose that human skin color stems from the type of clay originally chosen by God.[17] Such exegetical speculations, however, cannot counter the fact that the Qur'ān bars absolute certainty over God's reasons for selecting particular raw materials to form humans. In theory, he can create humans from any substance he deems worthy, as underscored by the listing of the variety of materials he has at his disposal.

God's supreme, solitary role in the fashioning of life is further underscored through the absence in these examples of any feminized earthly counterpart who must yield her natural substances to God's hand. God's dependency on the earth's role in human creation is implied in Genesis 2:7, as Yahweh Elohim necessarily creates man of the dust *from the earth* (*'āfār min-hā'ădāmâ*).[18] By way of contrast, the Qur'ān eliminates the feminized earth as an intermediary source that God must reckon with to extract his foundational, masculine substances—clay (*ṭīn*) or water (*mā'*)—to generate life. In fact, all of the earthly substances listed above are masculine nouns, which further modulates traditional constructs of binary sexual pairings in the begetting of life.

Several Muslim exegetes continue to privilege this Qur'ānic notion of creation as a solitary act, to the point where God alone even multiplied Adam's progeny without the help of Eve. Tha'labī (d. 1063 CE), for example, relates how God created Adam, and then stroked his (Adam's) back, from which he withdrew offspring who were then destined for the Garden or Fire, a phenomenon also explored at some length by Ibn Kathīr (d. 1373 CE).[19] This homoerotic image of God stroking Adam's back to generate human life without a female counterpart is underscored by the Qur'ānic examples noted above that emphasize God's dominant, creative power as he alone acts upon passive, masculine substances in solitary fashion. In its elimination of any human or nonhuman helpers, female partners, or feminine repositories in the procreative process, the Qur'ān portrays its deity as a more supreme, and powerful version of the biblical Yahweh Elohim.

Pagan Agricultural Models of Human Creation: Earth, Soul, and Sperm

The Qur'ān, however, refuses to limit God's creative nature to that of transcendent utterer of a word or aloof, omnipotent artisan. In order to refine the divine identity projected in many Near Eastern, biblical traditions, many Qur'ānic verses instead highlight God's intimate—almost sexual—interactions with a feminized earth. For example, Sūra 71:17–18 mentions that "God caused you to germinate from the earth (*anbatakum min al-arḍ*), then he will return you into it and bring you out again." Sūra 53:32 also asserts how God "knows you very well since he produced you from the earth (*anshāʾakum min al-arḍ*)." These passages uniquely refer to God not as an artisan but as a farmer who plants crops, watches them grow and die, and then resurrects them each spring.

Here, the earth serves as a willing, animate recipient of God's "seed"[20] rather than a static storehouse of natural resources to be mined and molded by him, as is the case in Genesis 2:7. This intimate partnership between God and earth is mirrored in human life also, as in Sūra 2:223, where women are depicted as "tillage" (*ḥarth*) for men to plough. Such agricultural metaphors that depict the earth in terms of female sexuality appear throughout Greek literature. For example, the Hippocratics liken the female body to a plowed and seeded field.[21] Further, in Pindar's *Pythian IV*, Lemnian women are described as "foreign furrows."[22]

God's intimate relationship with the feminized earth reverberates elsewhere in the Qurʾān. For example, in Sūra 99:5, the earth (*al-arḍ*) serves as one of the few nonhuman, loving beneficiaries of God's revelation (*bi anna rabbaka awḥā lahā*). The bee, whose gender is ambiguous,[23] is another.[24] Later exegetes flesh out this intimate partnership by relaying that when God sent Gabriel to the earth to gather for him some of her clay out of which he would fashion Adam, the earth refused, saying, "I take refuge in God against your taking something away from me and mutilating me,"[25] a statement that may reveal an exegetical critique of the artisan model. While ultimately the earth could only protest against and not reject God's request, her dissenting voice forced the angels to extract bits of clay from different points on her "skin" (*adīm*) so as not to disfigure her.[26]

Such examples of God's partnering with the earth counter his image as the solitary, creative force who self-generates life at will. As a loving consort who pairs with a feminized earth, whose own identity is shaped by her having been chosen by God and her willingness to accept God's procreative plans, the divine in these verses becomes much more immanent, human, and masculine than his more abstract, omnipotent role as artisan. However, as a practitioner of both artisanship and husbandry, and transcendent utterer of word in his production of human beings, God's uniqueness as creator ultimately surpasses any single quality or characteristic ascribed to him by either the Qurʾān or its antecedents.

The intimate relationship between God and the earth is reflected further in the many Qurʾānic passages that feature the integral role of sexual pairing in the procreative act. Such ruminations are similar to what is presented in Genesis 1:27, where "God created humankind

(*ʾeṯ-hāʾāḏām*)," then "male (*zāḵār*) and female (*nəqēḇâ*) he created them." Likewise, in Sūra 4:1, "your Lord created you (pl.) from a single soul (*min nafsin wāḥidatin*)[27] and from it [her] he created its mate (*wakhalaqa minhā zawjahā*)."[28] What distinguishes the Qurʾānic example from its biblical counterpart is that the word for soul, *nafs*, is feminine and the mate (*zawj*) formed from this generic feminine soul is masculine. In contrast, the biblical version presents *ʾeṯ-hāʾāḏām* as a generic or even masculine form that is then split into male and female parts. While binary sexual pairing is a persistent theme throughout the Qurʾān, the fact that it reverses the biblical order of who's initially derived from whom either underscores the significance of the feminine role in the begetting of life or, perhaps, renders both masculine and feminine forces impotent when compared to God's ultimate power.

The Qurʾān provides many other examples that stress the importance of sexual pairing in earthly reproduction, but do not privilege one sex over the other.[29] In Sūra 92:3, "the male and the female (*al-dhakara wa al-unthā*)" together serve as signs of God's creative power. The reasons God has produced both "the male and female (*al-dhakara wa 'l-unthā*)" are revealed further in Sūra 49:13: "to make nations and tribes so that you might come to know one another." What has taken place between God and the earth in primordial times is reflected in the subsequent sexual acts that are mimed throughout human generations. Aside from humans, most animate forms of life also come from pairs. Sūra 42:11 asserts how God "has made pairs (*azwājan*) for you among yourselves, and of the cattle pairs (*azwājan*), multiplying you thereby."[30] Clearly, both sexes play an equally vital role in the engendering of any life form.

While the Qurʾānic God himself does not engage in carnal relations, except, perhaps, in the case of his interactions with Mary and the earth,[31] his creative power underlies the mechanics of sexual fusion so that human reproduction must also be considered a divine feat. In this light, God becomes inextricable from the natural, human laws that govern his generative acts; in fact, he causes them to be. As such, God is simultaneously an analog for and an agent of creation. His creative forces, which engendered the first human being, continue to penetrate every act of human copulation. Masculine and feminine properties contribute to the procreative process, but neither takes precedence, as God dominates all. When it comes to human reproduction, God is "closer to you than your jugular vein."[32]

According to the Qurʾān, sexual pairing serves as more than just a sign of God's power and greatness; it is a fact of nature. The Qurʾān offers many explicit, scientific details, based on Greek medical wisdom, as to how humans are produced through sexual pairing, in particular through sperm: "He has created humankind (*al-insān*) from a sperm drop (*nuṭfa*)."[33] The Qurʾān mentions further how the human being (*al-insān*) was "created from flowing water (*khuliqa min māʾin dāfiqin*) proceeding out from what lies between the loins (*ṣulb*) and the chest-bone (*tarāʾib*)."[34]

The masculine word "water" (*māʾ*) in this case most likely refers to semen, given the Qurʾān's direct reference to the fact that the *māʾ* comes from various parts of the human body.[35] The idea that sperm comes from all parts of the body is Hippocratic;[36] later Muslim physicians, however, also professed this view.[37] Given that the word *insān* refers to humankind more generally, it is worth noting the Qurʾān assumes, like the Hippocratics and Galen, that both males and females produce sperm from different parts of their bodies that then combines in the womb to form life.[38] Other verses underscore this two-seed reproductive theory, including those that refer specifically to mixed or mingled sperm (*nuṭfatin amshājin*).[39] The fact that God creates humans from the sperm he spawns within them—both male and female—and determines the outcome of each individual mixture suggests that he alone dictates the laws of nature governing reproduction.

Therefore, the Qurʾānic sperm is not produced from the loins of God, which would limit his identity to that of a paternal figure and privilege the male role in procreation, but rather serves as a foundational, generic substance (like clay) that God crafts to utilize in the process of human reproduction. Here, God dons the role not of parent but of neutral inseminator as he creates human beings in pairs, male and female, from a sperm drop (*nuṭfa*) lodged in place.[40] Just as the single soul (*nafs*) is a feminine noun from which its masculine mate (*zawj*) is generated, so too is one name for the primary, physical substance so key to all of human reproduction—the *nuṭfa*—feminine. Here, unlike clay and "water" (*māʾ*), God acts upon feminine materials to generate life on both a cosmic and human level. Human beings may serve as the source or vehicle for such sperm, but God alone causes it "to be"[41] and determines what it will become deep within their bodies.

His private workings within the inner confines of the human body—either male or female—to generate "water" (*māʾ*) or sperm (*nuṭfa*) suggests a profound, erotic intimacy with both nature and human life that again casts into relief his image as transcendent pronouncer of "Be!" and the lone, omnipotent artisan who requires no assistance or partnership in the production of life. Such conflated assertions about his identity that fuse together artisan, agriculturalist, and transcendent models of generation resist any human impulse to pinpoint precisely the nature of God or the extent of his powers. Such uncertainties about God's role as creator or precisely how he generates life in theory prevent men or women from modeling themselves off of him in their reproductive capacities, or from structuring their societies to reflect a particular cosmic order based on familial relations.

While God may create the sperm that generates all human life, the Qur'ān undercuts male procreative primacy by asserting boldly that he is in no way to be understood as a husband or father.[42] Many Qur'ānic verses note how both pagan Qurayshī and Christian audiences accused God of fathering daughters or sons during the time of Muḥammad. For example, several of the Qur'ān's polemical statements against the Quraysh serve to counter the pagan praise for Muḥammad's (extra-Qur'ānic) Satan-inspired revelation that the goddesses al-Lāt, al-'Uzzā, and Manawāt, whom the Quraysh venerated as God's daughters, "are the *gharānīq* (exalted females) whose intercession is approved."[43] Clearly, the Qur'ān avows, this statement could not have come from God, for "would God choose daughters for himself and sons for you alone?"[44] Such countercriticisms allow the Qur'ān to distance further its deity from any paternal characteristics derived from his generative role in the creation of life. God is not bound by binary sexual mores.

Christians are also subject to such polemical attacks for reasons having to do with their understandings of Jesus as God's son. The Qur'ān posts dire warnings against "those who say [God] has taken a son,"[45] and repudiates the Christian idea that God could serve as father, since "God begets not, nor was he begotten."[46] Certainly, God could have a child if he chose to do so,[47] but ultimately "it is not fitting for the compassionate (*al-raḥmān*) to have a son."[48] Despite his close associations with sperm, earth, nature, and the human body, and his role as lone artisan in the creation of human life, the Qur'ān makes clear God should not be tied to any overtly paternal qualities or attributes. As such, he transcends human categories that ascribe to him a concrete gendered or familial role in the procreative act, in particular, fatherhood and what has come to be its privileged, social role in the generation of life.

While many Qur'ānic passages flatly deny God's role as a father, some do explore his intimate relationship with wombs, which further repudiates his paternal role by casting him into a maternal light (despite the fact that the word for womb [*raḥim*] is masculine). The arena in which God creates is often the womb,[49] whose secrets are hidden to men and women in "shadows of darkness (*thalmāt*)."[50] The word for womb (*raḥim*) is derived from the same root as mercy (*raḥma*), which forms two of God's ninety-nine names: the merciful (*al-raḥman*) and the compassionate (*al-raḥīm*).[51] God, therefore, is inseparable from a woman's reproductive parts, from which he generates life. In addition to womb, the root *r-ḥ-m* also implies blood ties, kinship, pity, and tenderness.[52] The Qur'ān suggests God's mercy and tenderness are ever-present in the womb, which, like human beings, cannot escape God's complete knowledge of all its inner workings.[53] In theory, this mercy and knowledge will be cast further upon all those whom God creates in their mothers' bellies, "one creation after another."[54] God's close connection with the masculine womb, embedded deep within the female body, is also well attested in many *ḥadīth,* which, for example, note how God appoints an angel to guard over every womb.[55]

In addition to highlighting God's maternal associations with the womb, the Qur'ān also underscores his role as midwife when mothers give birth. Not only does God have complete knowledge of what takes place in the womb, but he himself delivers his followers "out from the bellies (*buṭūn*) of your mothers knowing nothing and gave you hearing, sight and hearts, that by chance you may give thanks."[56] Through such dealings with the womb and what it produces, God's identity becomes intimately entwined with both the mother in whose womb he creates life, and the life form he fashions and carries forth into the world.

Interestingly, this passage notes that the ability to see and hear is something God grants humans subsequent to their birth. In other words, humans are neotenous, or perhaps even nonhuman, as they exit the womb, and therefore require God's continued hands-on molding, nurturing, and rearing to bring them to their current physical and moral state, where they may worship him fully and freely. While God certainly displays all the characteristics of a good mother in these examples, he is never explicitly referred to as one. Whatever maternal characteristics God may display, they are entwined with his identity as transcendent word, solitary artisan, and masculine consort with a feminized earth. By amalgamating disparate identities, and suggesting that God embodies them all, the Qur'ān affirms no clear attribute can possibly capture God's true procreative identity or the precise nature of his generative powers.

Greek Medical Theories and the Qur'ānic God: Seed, Blood, Flesh and Bones

Still other Qur'ānic verses combine the different artisan and agriculturalist models together into a single trope that serves to frame an epigenetic depiction of fetal development that reflects, to varying degrees, Greek medical theories. In its articulation of Hippocratic, Galenic, and, to a lesser degree, Aristotelian models of fetal development, the Qur'ān demonstrates God's mastery of the reproductive techniques described by them, but emphasizes that his creative efforts are not bound by them. While mechanistic processes drawn from Greek philosophy and medical wisdom may play an important role in the production of offspring as they generate heat, friction, or *pneuma* from seminal fluid, the laws of nature become subordinate to the one God who alone possesses the power to engender humans from nonliving matter.

The Qur'ān's epigenetic portrayal of fetal development, which follows the creation of life from clay, to sperm, to blood clot, to lump of flesh, to bones, appears in Sūra 23:12–14: "We have created man from a scion, from clay (*walaqad khalaqnā al-insāna min sulālatin min ṭīnin*); then we placed him as a sperm drop (*thumma ja'alnāhu nuṭfatan*) in a secure place; then we created out of the sperm drop a clot of blood (*thumma khalaqnā al-nuṭfata 'alaqatan*); then we created from the clot a lump of flesh (*fakhalaqnā al-'alaqata muḍghatan*); then made the lump of flesh into bones (*fakhalaqnā al-muḍghata 'iẓāman*); then covered the bones with flesh; then fashioned him into another creation (*khalqan*)."[57]

In this example, God pinches off a small, clay, homuncular mass that he then places "as a sperm" in the womb. The fashioned mass then progresses along the precise path outlined by Greek medical scholars: from seed, to mixed seed, to coagulated blood, to flesh, to bones.[58] According to Hippocrates, for example, it is at this point, when the bones and limbs have been articulated, that the "fetus" comes into being.[59] Likewise, the Qur'ān acknowledges the presence of yet another "creation" after the bones are covered with flesh.

Where the Qur'ānic version differs from the Hippocratic descriptions of fetal development, however, is in its insertion of God's active hand throughout the entire process. This form of divine control is seen most clearly in the Qur'ān's adaptation of Hippocratic models to secure God's primacy as he places clay as "sperm" in the womb just prior to the various stages of fetal development. This added prequel to the Hippocractic process ensures that human reproduction is not an activity separate from divine procreation. God's initial, creative act of generating the first man from clay is still evident in the very conception of each and every human being via sexual intercourse. Thus, human reproduction becomes the analog to all of divine creation in its ever-shifting mysteries and polyvalence.

Including clay in the Hippocratic stages of human reproduction has significant theological consequences. First, it connects biblical antecedents of dust formation with contemporary Greek medical wisdom, and demonstrates how the Qur'ān supersedes them both. Second, it affirms that the divine creation of the first man and subsequent acts of human reproduction are, in essence, indistinguishable. Because human sexuality and reproduction mirror God's initial creative acts, the Qur'ān breaks from the biblical narrative in Genesis by no longer casting human reproduction as a distinct form of divine punishment upon those who disobeyed God.[60] God is no longer absent from earthly, human reproduction, which men and women suffer as a consequence of disobedience or sin, but remains an intimate partner within it as he navigates the entire course of sperm generation, conception, fetal development, birth, and life itself from both inside and outside the womb. And third, God's formation of a clay homunculus as "sperm" ensures that his creation of each human being is flawless and unadulterated, since nothing is left to chance or nature. The Qur'ānic God has no need to "blot out from the earth the human beings [he] has created"[61] for their initial creation is one of divine intent and perfection.

The Qur'ān continues to appropriate and revise Greek medical wisdom through its discussions of another essential ingredient required in the process of human creation: the animating breath. As noted above, Hippocrates divides the embryo into four stages: sperm, coagulated blood, flesh, and bones (and other bodily members). In his model, breath (*pneuma*) enters into the developmental process during one of the earliest stages, after seed from both mother and father mixes in the womb, and is gathered into a single mass that condenses as a result of heat.[62] According to Hippocrates, since the lifeless mass is housed in a warm environment, it "acquires breath."[63] This warm breath, however, must escape, so it hollows out a passage for its release. Once the passage of escape has been formed, it "inspires" from the mother a second quantity of breath, which is cool air. Hot air, in other words, necessarily draws cool air into itself to "feed upon" as it expels warm air in return.[64]

Hippocrates identifies two sources of air for the seed: this internal breath generated by heat, but also the cool, outside air inhaled by the mother.[65] The continuous breathing in and out of the seed allows it to inflate and to develop a membrane around its surface, similar to the way a crust is formed on the surface of bread when it is baked.[66] In other words, Hippocrates likens the female body to a hot "oven" where bread, the staple of life produced through women's labor, is cooked. Because a woman ceases to menstruate when she becomes pregnant, the excess blood descends and surrounds the membrane. The seed contained within the membrane then draws this blood into itself via the essential breath.[67]

The process of tearing the membrane in order to "breathe in" blood from the mother further results in coagulation around the areas of rupture, which causes the mass to grow.[68] Thus the breath (*pneuma*) generates the evolution of what is eventually to become a living being from the first stage of development (seed), to the second (coagulated clot), and then to the third (flesh), when the coagulated clot connects with the umbilicus, and flesh begins to form.[69] At this point in the process, the breath (*pneuma*) serves as the principle organizer of matter, a force that drives nonliving material into living beings. For the Hippocratics, breath is the power that first generates life inside the womb, and then determines, guides, and drives its progression toward a completed human form.[70]

While the four Qur'ānic stages of fetal development resemble the Hippocratic model, they differ radically from it in that they do not evolve one from another, but rather stand as separate and distinct divine acts as noted by the repetition of the verb *khalaqnā* (we created).[71] Rather than breath driving the transformation of the mixed seed into progressive permutations of fetal development, it is God who creates each stage separately. Here, God leaves nothing to natural, mechanistic processes; each movement is not caused by another but rather is rooted in his creative efforts.

There is never a moment in the Qur'ānic scheme—as there is in the Hippocratic model—where any of the various fetal forms would be caught betwixt and between a sperm drop or clot of blood; a clot of blood or lump of flesh. An entity that is neither a sperm drop nor a clot of blood, nor one that is in the nebulous process of transforming from one state to another, could potentially fall outside God's jurisdiction. Likewise, God is not bound by the Hippocratic mechanics of fetal development, as he may disrupt the progression at any point with a new creative act. By deemphasizing the "natural" mechanisms that drive the embryo from one stage to another, the Qur'ān offers a "corrective" to past pagan philosophers who wrongfully left God out of the equation.

When the Qur'ān does take up notions of breath, they tend to reflect more the Aristotelian, as opposed to the Hippocratic, understanding of *pneuma* in terms of the necessary, biological role it plays in the animation of life. The Qur'ān, however, critiques and transforms Aristotelian conceptions of breath according to its own theological principles. Such principles devalue the primacy of the male in the reproductive act, which marks both males and females as equally (in)significant in the generation of life, and elevates God's power over all of creation.

Aristotelian notions of breath are elaborated through the Qur'ān's discussion of two specific cases where God generated life outside the normal course of human reproduction: the creation of Adam from clay, and the conception of Jesus, son of Mary, without a father. In each instance, the Qur'ān draws upon Aristotelian theories of *pneuma* to describe how life comes to be, but amends them according to the theological belief that God alone, as opposed to man or nature, has the power to produce life.

Like Hippocrates, Aristotle also views *pneuma* as heat. However, for Aristotle, this heat is not generated by the friction caused when two seeds mix together, but rather is imparted by the male semen, which is a compound of *pneuma* (hot air) and water.[72] This heat, however, is no ordinary heat; Aristotle likens *pneuma* to the divine element of the stars.[73] Aristotle believes only males contribute semen or seed, and thus *pneuma*, or *ether*, to the generation of life.[74]

Unlike the Hippocratic model so favored by the Qur'ān where both parents generate seed, females supply only the "prime matter" (menstrual blood) upon which the semen, or vital heat, acts.[75] The male, therefore, becomes the sole active partner in the process of reproduction, the transmitter of the *pneuma* that generates the movement,[76] or produces the "effect" inside the passive female body.[77] Rather than two matters colliding and mixing together to produce heat, as in the Hippocratic model, the male semen alone contains the *dynamos* that causes the inactive material in the female to take on a particular shape or character,[78] and imparts to it the same movement with which it is itself bequeathed.[79]

Once inside the womb, the water portion of the semen dissolves and evaporates, and the vital heat (*pneuma*) is left to form, differentiate, and organize the new individual. Aristotle links the activity of the animation and formation of an individual being to the idea of the soul (*psuchē*),[80] which he defines as "the essence (or reality) of a particular body."[81] Here, the soul (*psuchē*) serves as principle of life because it is the source of its movement, its final cause (for the sake of which the body exists), and the "essence" of all living bodies.[82] Although Aristotle, like Hippocrates, confers breath or *pneuma* as the animating or organizing principle for life, he deviates from his predecessor by maintaining that the breath also transmits the soul, the essence that makes something a distinct living being. He also parts company with Hippocrates by locating the source for both breath and soul within the male, who alone produces semen from heated blood.

In the Qur'ānic example of Adam's creation, God tells the angels he is going to produce a man (*bashr*) from clay (*ṭīn*), and "when I have fashioned him and breathed into him from my spirit (*wanafakhtu fīhi min rūḥī*), fall down before him."[83] In many respects, the "breath" imparted by the deity that carries the spirit (*rūḥ*) functions analogously to the male semen that transmits the soul in Aristotle's paradigm. Like the Aristotelian male, God in this passage serves as the active force in the reproductive process, the lone transmitter of the *pneuma* that animates life from passive, inanimate material. However, the Qur'ān continuously casts into relief his male-like dominance over female matter with projections of his maternal concern for human development and his transcendent word that causes life to be without active intervention. This panoply of images assures no singular divine identity is privileged.

Qur'ānic descriptions of Mary's conception of Jesus also mirror Aristotelian paradigms of the role of the animating breath in human reproduction. Here, the divine breath allowed Mary to conceive Jesus without a human partner, just as it allowed for the generation of Adam without a father (or mother, for that matter).[84] The Qur'ān notes in Sūra 21:91 that because Mary guarded her private, sexual parts (*aḥṣanat farjahā*), "We breathed into her from our spirit (*fanafakhnā fīhā min rūḥinā*) and made her and her son a sign to the world."

Sūra 66:12 gives a slightly different version of the story that emphasizes the more overtly sexual nature of the breath's role in reproduction. Here, the breath did not enter *her* but *it,* meaning her vagina (*fanafakhnā fīhi min rūḥinā*). The emphasis on Mary's vagina in Sūra 66:12 elicits more explicitly the Aristotelian model of male semen carrying the essential breath of life that activates the inanimate matter in Mary's womb. Here, Jesus's conception may follow the natural course of reproduction outlined by the Greeks (minus the human father), but the Qur'ān ensures the precise details of the event still remain inaccessible to humans through its multiple and often contradictory depictions of what actually took place.

How medieval exegetes seek to explain who blew what where reveals a desire to resolve the Qur'ān's ambiguity over what took place between God and Mary. Such interpretive efforts likewise strive to diffuse suggestions of an erotic encounter that may have occurred outside the realm of male knowledge and control. To strip Mary of her dangerous, procreative potency and her intimacy with God, some medieval scholars work to revise the literal reading of Sūra 66:12, which proposes the spirit was blown into *it,* meaning her vagina (*farj*). While these scholars assume *farj* to mean vagina,[85] they advise it was actually the angel Gabriel, and not God, who breathed the strong current of air either directly or indirectly into Mary's *farj*. Although the Qur'ān does not mention Gabriel as the one who exhaled the conceiving breath into Mary's private parts—in fact, the Qur'ān utilizes the ubiquitous "we" as the subject imparting the air—the majority of scholars make him the agent of the breath.[86] Gabriel did not take liberties with Mary on his own initiative, however, as a husband might decide to act upon his wife;[87] rather, God dispatched him to her.[88]

In their efforts to sever the intimate liaison between Mary and God so clearly implied by Sūra 66:12, medieval exegetes draw upon the familiar patterns of conception and reproduction offered by Aristotle, where a male figure (Gabriel) necessarily imparts the life-giving force (semen) into the woman's womb.[89] Such interpretations that favor the masculine role in human generation make God's inscrutable creative efforts subject to human reproductive practices, which limits his ability to create whatever, and however, he pleases. They also restrict Mary's own erotic agency in her partnership with God to conceive life.

Despite their insistence on a male figure imparting the animating breath, a number of medieval exegetes were still uncomfortable with the fact that Gabriel, let alone God, would have had access to Mary's vagina. They intimate the spirit was more likely blown into *her* (as suggested by Sūra 21:91), but suggest that could mean anyplace on Mary's person. Therefore, they project Gabriel did not exhale his breath into Mary's vagina, but rather into a hole or opening in her outer garment, and she conceived.[90] Ismāʿīl ibn ʿUmar ibn Kathīr (d. 1373 CE), for example, proposes God commanded Gabriel to breathe the breath into a slit (*jīb*) in Mary's garment, and then the breath descended into her vagina and she conceived Jesus,[91] just as a woman becomes pregnant after sexual intercourse with her husband.[92] He also reports how some scholars assert Gabriel's breath emanated directly into her chest; others that Gabriel exhaled into her mouth.[93] The desire to privilege the male generative role in Jesus's conception, but lessen the erotic intimations of that encounter, seem to fuel these medieval exegetical musings.

In contrast with these interpretive perspectives, the Qurʾān draws from the same biological paradigms to relay the many ways Mary conceived Jesus without a male partner. After all, God creates whatever, and however, in wombs as he chooses. While some Qurʾānic passages are patterned according to Aristotelian views of reproduction, others break that pattern by broadening God's procreative capabilities. For example, in yet another account of Jesus's conception (Sūra 19:17), Mary received not the breath that contained the spirit in her vagina, but directly "our spirit (*rūḥanā*), who appeared to her as a man in every respect (*basharan sawīyyan*)" to tell her the Lord would give her a son. Here, the feminine spirit (*rūḥ*) is cloaked in the guise of a man (in every respect), who, through his very foretelling of what was to be, that is, by his *word,* bequeaths her a child.

In this Qurʾānic verse, the necessary, animating breath of life that must somehow be inserted or generated in Mary's womb—so vital in both Hippocratic and Aristotelian paradigms and in many Qurʾānic verses—is absent. The Qurʾānic God, contrary to those who imply otherwise, can cause life to be in the womb without breath or *pneuma* by simply sending his spirit (*rūḥ*) upon Mary without any necessary contact with her reproductive parts, just as he cast down his spirit (*rūḥ*) on or into the night of destiny.[94] The fact that the spirit, *rūḥ,* is feminine in this example (even though it appears in the guise of a man) further underscores the point that God's creative efforts critique but also transcend the laws of science and nature that elevate the role of men acting upon women in the generation of life.

God's choosing of Mary to bear his "signs"[95] in many ways mirrors his intimate partnership with the earth to create life in the artisan and agricultural motifs noted above.[96] In theory, Mary, like the earth in the eyes of exegetes, could have voiced some resistance to what was about to be done to her. In fact, she did cry out to the spirit (in the guise of a man) who confronted her, asking, "How can I have a son when no man has touched me and I am not unchaste?"[97] He replied, "So it will be (*qāla kathāliki*)," and it was.[98] She, like the earth, could have protested, but instead she accepted what had been decreed.

The fact that Mary acquiesced to God's request and bore and delivered his prophet Jesus successfully, but in great hardship, humiliation, and pain, points to her extraordinary piety, superior physical aptitude, and free acceptance of God's will. Contrary to the Aristotelian depiction of reproduction, where the womb is a passive receptacle for man's generative seed, the Qur'ān portrays those feminized partners (Mary, soul, earth) who received God's breath, spirit, or creative hand through whatever mode he wished to send them, as active, willing, and necessary agents in the generative process. After all, God could have generated life from masculine substances alone, or caused life to "be!" without the help of female agents. His inclusion of them in his procreative efforts, however, became necessarily entwined with the life he drew forth from them.[99] Their active responses to God's desire to create life becomes an essential feature of his procreative efforts and, as such, a revealing measure of an exemplary maternal piety for all to emulate.

What further separates Qur'ānic depictions of life-giving breath in the reproductive process from their Greek counterparts that emphasize the male role in the begetting of life is the presence of the spirit (*rūḥ*), which deviates radically from the Aristotelian *psuchē*. In the creation of both Adam and Jesus, the breath that enlivened them stemmed from the spirit of God. The spirit not only separates the animate from the inanimate, but, in contrast with the *psuchē,* humans from animals. Humans alone share in the divine nature via the spirit. For example, Sūra 32:7–9 speaks of God creating all humanity (*al-insān*) from clay (*ṭīn*), and then making his (its) progeny (*naslahu*) of a "water despised" (*mā'in mahīnin*), or sperm. However, unlike the Mary passages where the spirit, via the breath, was blown directly into her *farj,* God "breathes in him/it[100] of his spirit" (*nafakha fīhi min rūḥihi*), and finally bestows upon "you" (m. plural) the faculties of hearing, sight, and understanding. Clearly, life does not begin until the breath animates the inanimate sperm, as suggested by the shift in pronoun from "him/it" to "you." Human sperm alone does not carry the essential life force that allows someone to access and comprehend God's revelation; that vital element, which separates humans from animals, is rooted in, and can only be transmitted by, the divine.

The idea that God's spirit contains within it the ability to see, hear, and understand his signs—a crucial criterion for defining human existence—is underscored by the fact that it is only human life that may potentially receive his spirit, and not animal life. In the Qur'ān, animal life absorbs only the animating breath. For example, in Sūra 5:110, Jesus was instructed to fashion the likeness of a bird (*kahaya'ti al-ṭayri*) from clay (*ṭīn*), and by God's leave, to breathe into it so that it became a real bird.[101] Jesus's breath served to enliven the clay figure of the bird just as God's breath brought to life the clay figure of Adam. However, Jesus's breath in this case did not transmit the spirit. Jesus's inability to transfer the spirit to the bird may be due to the fact that he was merely a man and not God or that nonhuman beings cannot be the recipients of God's spirit. Clearly, if God had wanted him to, Jesus could have infused the bird with his spirit. Therefore, it seems likely that God does not want his spirit to dwell in animals, which possess no innate capacity to see, hear, and read his signs.[102]

Sūra 32:7–9, where God makes progeny from a "water despised" and bestows upon "you" the faculties of sight and sound, along with the many passages on Mary and Adam, critiques the atomistic, Hippocratic view that life is the byproduct of two nonliving matters colliding randomly in a warm environment. Rather, these passages suggest that while male and female sperm may meet and unite in women's wombs, only God, and not friction, or heat, supplies the necessary breath and spirit to generate human life. In the context of the Qur'ān, strict adherence to the Hippocratic model would give human beings, both male and female, or nature the ability to animate human life, a divine power that would challenge God's supreme authority. In addition, the Qur'ān's emphasis on God's spirit allows the text to distinguish the creation of human life from other, inferior forms (animals) that cannot see and hear his signs.

This same passage (Sūra 32:7–9) also underscores the theological idea that only God, and not the human male, serves as the sole source for and transmitter of the *pneuma* and the spirit. As depicted in the Qur'ān, God in many ways embodies the Aristotelian life force, an image so clearly expressed in the Qur'ānic verses depicting God's breath descending into Mary's *farj* to impregnate her. However, he is not bound to imparting it in the same way males must insert the life-giving breath via their sperm into the bodies of women. Also, while human conception and fetal growth may follow Hippocrates's two-seed theory and four-stage path, as suggested by the Qur'ān's many references to sexual pairing, mixed sperm, and embryonic development, only God can generate that path through his word, breath, or spirit, or his molding and fashioning of clay into sperm that he then plants in the womb, after which he "brings you out as infants, then allows you to come of age, then become old men."[103]

Perhaps, then, one of the reasons why the majority of medieval medical scholars, such as Rabbān al-Ṭabarī, Ibn Qayyim al-Jawzīya, and ʿArīb ibn Saʿd favor the Hippocratic (and Galenic), two-seed model of human conception over the Aristotelian view that males alone impart the *pneuma* to generate life is to distinguish clearly between human and divine reproduction.[104] If human males were allowed to cast out the animating "breath" (let alone the "spirit") through their own semen, what, then, was there to distinguish them from God? As Sūra 5:110 suggests, even Jesus, who was, after all, a man, cannot send forth the spirit as he animates the clay bird via his breath. Only God can impart the "dynamos" that has the effect of granting humans their life, which implies animation, but perhaps more importantly, the unique perception to see, hear, and comprehend that which is divine.

Of course, the Qur'ān also asserts that God can simply bypass any paradigm analogous whatsoever to human sexual reproduction through a singular word. After all, Sūra 3:59 points out that "[t]he similitude of Jesus before God is as that of Adam. He [God] created him [Adam] from dust (*ṭurāb*), then said to him: 'Be!' And he was (*kun fayakūn*)."[105] The feminine spirit that appears as a man also gives this same abstract, nondescript phrase (*kun fayakūn*) to Mary as she inquires how could she have a son when no man has touched her. Clearly, God's creative impulse transcends human comprehension at the same time that it engages it.

In sum, the Qur'ān displays a number of Near Eastern artisan paradigms, pagan agricultural motifs, and contemporary Greek medical theories to demonstrate the varied and contradictory ways God generates life. The Qur'ān's modifications of these models all point toward a radically transcendent, omnipotent creator. God is at once the sole fashioner of human life from (masculine) substances he alone chooses but also intimate male partner with a number of feminine subjects who are active agents alongside him in the procreative process. Likewise, God appears as both omnipotent molder of humans from clay and maternal midwife to the (male) wombs that serve him. He also takes on the role of astute physician as he demonstrates his mastery over contemporary medical wisdom about how life is conceived and how it develops in the womb, and omnipotent lord as he transcends the laws of nature that govern such mechanistic processes in light of his own will, which may be generated by a single word.

Such colorful and diverse models of how life is re/produced and the roles God assumes in his generative efforts reflect the Qur'ān's rhetorical desire to evoke dialog, debate, and general human uncertainty about how (what and why) God creates. In this way, the Qur'ānic God is able to embody yet surpass the limited identities, ideologies, and characteristics assigned to him by past authoritative Near Eastern/Mediterranean traditions, human sexuality, or natural law as articulated through Greek medical wisdom. By vocalizing multiple images of God's creative activities and projecting a variety of models to explain God's procreative efforts (only to undermine them), the Qur'ān provides only fleeting glimpses into God's ineffable power, a power that ultimately defies any humanly derived classificatory schemes, gendered roles, or metaphorical descriptions.

The Volatility of Divine Procreation and its Structuring of Equivocal Maternal Identities

The polyvalence of God's procreative agency makes it difficult for ordinary men and women to assume his generative powers as their own, and thereby determine the reproductive outcomes they (and God) desire. While the exceptionally pious seem exempt from this rule, the majority of ordinary women, who struggle to approximate their superlative example, are never guaranteed similar results. A woman's inability to replicate the ideal procreative goals dictated by God or embodied by his most exemplary servants leads to the Qur'ān's referencing of a variety of maternal identities that conform yet contrast with its pure, pious, and perfected paragons. While the Qur'ān never attempts to resolve such tensions between the real and the ideal—but merely displays, exploits, and explores them—later exegetes take it upon themselves to restrict the revelation's polyvalence to justify male power and control over deficient maternal bodies.

The Fate of Wombs

God's complete mastery over human reproduction is reiterated throughout the Qur'ān, so much so that ordinary women appear to exercise no power over their own reproductive bodies to secure a productive womb. Throughout the Qur'ān, wombs generate life, or not, in a variety of permutations, for no apparent reason, other than the fact that God causes it to be. For example, God alone is fully cognizant of miscarriages, premature deliveries, and stillbirths.[106] Not only is God aware of which women will suffer barrenness, he takes it upon himself to make some sterile (*ʿaqīm*).[107] His dominance over the womb is so complete that he knows what sex a child will be before it is born.[108] He "grants whomever he wishes females and whomever he wishes males."[109]

His absolute power and knowledge over the womb do not cease the moment a child is born. From conception to death, God navigates the child through all the stages of her life: he creates humans from a weak substance,[110] brings them out as infants, and then makes some of them die and some grow old.[111] Women assist God in his efforts, but are never able to exert complete control over what he deems to be.

Despite the apparent randomness of procreation due to God's ultimate authority over all life, there are some contrary suggestions in the Qur'ān that piety produces a proliferation of offspring, impiety a dearth of progeny. For example, Sūra 71:10–12 exclaims, "Ask forgiveness from your Lord . . . he will cause the sky to open upon you in torrents and provide you with wealth and sons." Likewise, Sūra 22:2 reveals how the Day of Judgment will be marked by miscarriages, along with the rejection of a nursing child by its mother.[112] The Qur'ān also states, "He who hates you shall remain childless," which indicates God often punishes a man who curses believers through his wife's womb.[113]

These simple statements that link progeny or the lack thereof with reward and punishment propose that there are times when God's procreative actions are conditional upon human behavior. The Qur'ān may assert God creates in wombs whatever, and however, he pleases, but it just as frequently suggests that righteous wombs are automatically blessed with an abundance of offspring and that the wicked are eradicated by their sterility. God's inscrutable intentions render human assertions of power over the generation of life moot, since their efforts may or may not result in "prudent" offspring.

The Qur'ānic God often rewards or punishes his followers by acting upon their bodies, both inside and outside of the womb. Here, a child's outward form is directly linked to piety and sacrilege. For example, the revelation acknowledges that progeny do not always come into the world with hands, legs, eyes, and ears fitting "the highest standard of wise appropriateness."[114] Although God "originated you and created for you hearing, sight, and hearts,"[115] he may also rescind his gifts if you "forget" his revelations.[116] Those who become blind and deaf bear the physical marks of God's wrath; thus, "the blind (*al-aʿmā*) and the seeing are not equal."[117] More dramatically, God transmutes his creations as a result of their transgressions. Sūra 5:60, for example, reports how he made those whom he has cursed into "monkeys and swine (*al-qirdata wa al-khanāzīr*)."[118] A child may exit the womb in an ideal condition, but God is free to corrupt her as he wills in punishment for her moral decadence. All of these examples move in the direction of God's punishing transgressors through disfigurement. Human piety would seem to guarantee nothing, but impiety will forever be requited.

However, other passages cast such *hubris* in sharp relief. For example, not all Qur'ānic passages associate blindness and deafness with divine punishment, but maintain a certain randomness with regard to whom God chooses to suffer physical deficiencies, which undermines the causal connection between piety and physical perfection. Some suggest "blindness," "deafness," "lameness," and "sickness" are integral parts of God's greater plan to test his servants. This theme of divine testing is underscored further in Sūra 90:4, which states, "We have created man to try him with afflictions." The later Muslim tradition also embraces the theme that bodily imperfections serve as God's way to test his followers. According to tradition, individuals who undergo pain on earth will be rewarded in the afterlife.[119] In contrast with the above examples, good mothers may generate sickly children, and deviant women may be the source of robust offspring. Here, personal piety has little or nothing to do with the incidence of birth defects. God demands faith in all circumstances.

Similarly, other Qur'ānic passages maintain God afflicts certain individuals with physical flaws so that others who gaze upon them may praise him for their own health and well-being.[120] Such afflictions are designed to instill gratitude among his servants and are not necessarily permanent; Jesus, after all, healed the blind, which is considered a miracle.[121] Whatever the case, if a mother is fertile, infertile, or bears a child that is blind, deaf, or one that carries no affliction at all, she may never be fully certain as to whether the outcome is due to piety, impiety, reward, punishment, test, divine sign, or simply divine fate. These disruptions in causal certainty create a volatile maternal identity that must continuously strive for a knowledge and perfection that forever remains elusive. God alone has the power to generate in wombs what he wishes.

And yet, as if to ensure no single understanding of divine intent prevails, the Qur'ān asserts that some pious individuals have indeed achieved such a lofty state of perfection that they are guaranteed ideal maternal outcomes. For example, the Qur'ān tells how the upright and pious Abraham was old and his wife was barren.[122] Yet, he desired a child. Not willing to accept the procreative outcome initially fated for him by God, Abraham asked the Lord to grant him a righteous son.[123] As soon as Abraham made his request, "we announced to him the good news of a prudent boy (*ghulām*)."[124] Here, Abraham demonstrates his piety by believing God will grant him a son, despite the fact that the deity initially chose to make his wife sterile.[125] In a similar tale, the righteous Zakarīyā also cried out to his lord for offspring. As in the case of Abraham, "we listened *to him,* and we granted Yaḥyā *to him,* and we cured his wife's [barrenness] *for him.*"[126]

Clearly, there are instances when God's actions are conditioned by righteous men who display exceptional piety. But what about their wives? While Abraham's wife never seems to have doubted the power of God to grant the couple a son, she did laugh upon hearing the news of what was to transpire.[127] Her impious chortling could easily have warranted divine retribution and not God's merciful dispensation. However, it did not. Did Abraham's faith outweigh Sarah's incredulity? Only God knows. He bestows healthy children upon whomsoever he wills beyond even nature's constraints should he choose.

As all of these examples show, God will create whatever, and however, in wombs as he pleases, and humans must negotiate as best as they can the discrepant signs he conveys through his capricious reproductive efforts. At times exceptional piety does condition the divine hand, but most humans may never hope to achieve the same degree of righteousness as Abraham or Zakarīyā. Certainly, for those who cannot be counted among the truly righteous, the vagaries of human reproduction may or may not be prompted by any one particular cause, or follow any single pattern, which only emphasizes God's complete command over the creation of all life. Men and women may engage in sexual acts in the hopes of bearing children, but only God has the power to engender a living being from those acts, in whatever form he chooses.

Divine Sign and Maternal Exceptionality: Mary and the Mother of Moses

Not only does the Qur'ān assert humans bear little or no control over their own reproductive fates, but it also warns that progeny, like excessive wealth, can become a temptation for men and distract them from God.[128] Not surprisingly, the Qur'ān counters its own dire warnings with numerous statements and examples that laud the bearing and nurturing of children, and thus the mothers who conceive, raise, and rear them.[129] Despite its overwhelmingly positive views of motherhood, the Qur'ān never articulates fully its vision of the "ideal mother" nor precisely how one comes to guarantee the offspring it praises. Instead, it projects a variety of images of mothers whose piety may or may not bring forth healthy and righteous progeny. The Qur'ān instructs ordinary women to emulate these pious maternal models as best they can, even though their actions may never garner the same results.

The Qur'ān does not merely hold up specific maternal exemplars but radiates a variety of maternal images that emphasize a woman's unique procreative power. Unlike the term *father,* the Qur'ān extols the concept of the "mother." Sūra 42:7, for example, refers to Mecca as the "mother of cities" (*umm al-qurā*). Ibn Kathīr elaborates this reference further by stating that Mecca is called the *umm al-qurā* because it is the grandest city and the leader of all towns. He also reports that the earth was made starting from Mecca.[130] In these examples, the term "mother" is reserved to describe a purified, perfected receptacle through which God reveals a multiplicity of signs.

In general, the Qur'ān portrays the "mother" as holding a more intimate relationship with God than men. For example, the Qur'ān refers to itself as the mother of the book (*umm al-kitāb*).[131] Here, the Qur'ān casts the mother of the book as being preexistent, or "with God" (*ʿindahu*), and associated with hidden meanings or his wisdom (*ḥakīm*) in ways similar to the female personification of wisdom (*ḫokhma*) in the book of Proverbs, who was "set up from everlasting, from the beginning, or ever the earth was."[132] Such profound intimacy with wisdom and knowledge blurs the lines between God and his *umm* in ways that destabilize his identity in the eyes of humans. As such, the Qur'ānic *umm* becomes a lofty ideal that finds its concrete expression in Mary, the paradigmatic mother.

The Qur'ān features just one mother who serves as a purified, ideal type much in the same way as the *umm al-kitāb* or the *umm al-qurā*: Mary, the mother of Jesus. Not surprisingly, she bore one of God's prophets—who himself was a bearer of wisdom and deliverer of portions of the heavenly book—and not an ordinary man. Mary faced many hardships in her bearing of God's messenger, but was able to overcome them through her strivings for an exceptional piety that was predetermined by the divine hand. While the Qur'ān shows that Mary willingly gave in to God's desires to generate a life by causing it to "be," it also projects that there was little she could do to derail the course of predestined reproductive events. This tension between divine fate and human agency structures Mary's narrative throughout.

The Qur'ān begins Mary's story with references to her pious ancestry. According to the Qur'ān, God granted Adam, Noah, and the families of Abraham and ʿImrān, the paternal line into which Mary was born, a special privilege.[133] As is the case with the Bible's treatment of some of its righteous figures,[134] the Qur'ān provides Mary with an impeccable genealogy. After Mary was conceived, the Qur'ān relates how her mother, assuming that she was a boy, dedicated "him" to God's service.[135] After Mary came into the world—and it is obvious that "he" was really a she—God still accepted her mother's dedication, even though males, rather than females, traditionally perform service in the temple.[136] Mary, however, was no ordinary woman. Rather, she was so pure that she was "mistaken" for a male, but that identification was acknowledged by God as correct on some level. Here, her mistaken identity presumes that males are considered intrinsically more pious than women. Clearly, the extraordinary piety required to prepare her body for the conception of Jesus pushed Mary to the limits of female gender identity.

Be that as it may, many medieval exegetes underscore the piety of Mary's mother, and perceive that it was her devout prayer that led to Mary's conception and her subsequent divine favor. The famous medieval Qur'ānic commentator, Muḥammad ibn Jarīr al-Ṭabarī (d. 923 CE), for example, describes how the wife of ʿImrān (Ḥanna) prayed to God for a child after seeing a bird feeding its young, and God answered her prayer with Mary.[137] Although Ḥanna's prayers were answered with a girl instead of the boy she longed for (in contrast to male pleas that tend to produce robust sons), her daughter Mary became one of God's chosen servants who went on to bear an extraordinary prophet. While exegetical works propose how Ḥanna's devotion led to a fertile womb and the bearing of an exceptional daughter, the Qur'ān projects that most women must take comfort in the fact that God only "adds to creation as he pleases."[138]

The Qur'ān relays further how ʿImrān's wife named her daughter Mary, and then depicts how God placed her under the care of Zakarīyā, who would oversee her work in the temple. Throughout her temple service, the Qur'ān notes how angels informed her that "God has chosen you and purified you and chosen you above the women of the worlds."[139] In addition, God provided her with a miraculous sustenance so that Mary never had to ask Zakarīyā for food.[140] Obviously, Mary was an exceptional woman. Her uniqueness, however, stems from the fact that God designated her for greatness, and cultivated her perfected nature, even prior to her birth. God's supreme power over Mary refutes any trinitarian assumptions that Mary or her son could be rendered as deities.[141] Whether the Qur'ān's version of the story intends to tamp down any divine pretensions for Jesus, it clearly illustrates that God alone orchestrates the procreation of his most loyal servants. God sanctified Mary so that she might become the pure conduit for a divinely privileged creation.[142]

Mary's maternal superiority is tied to the rather unusual circumstances surrounding the conception of Jesus. Although no other human conceptions and births are mentioned in the Qur'ān, most prophets in the Islamic tradition are viewed as having been conceived through natural, sexual intercourse between husband and wife. For example, Abū Muḥammad ʿAbd al-Mālik ibn Hishām (d. 833 CE), the prophet's biographer who revised Ibn Isḥāq's earlier version of the *Sīrat rasūl Allāh,* relates how the prophet Muḥammad's mother, Āmina, invited her husband ʿAbdallāh to have sex with her; he complied, and she became pregnant.[143] Little is known of Āmina, other than the fact that she was the most excellent of women among the Quraysh in birth and position at the time.[144] Even though the prophet's conception was like any other, a number of extraordinary events did portend his future greatness. Āmina, like the mother of Mary, dedicated her child to God, who instructed her to call him Muḥammad. When she was pregnant with him, she claimed she perceived a light coming forth from her by which she could view the castles of Buṣrā in Syria.[145] However extraordinary, such signs do little to compete with the elaborate miracles and divine intimacy associated with the conception and birth of Jesus.

As noted above, the Qurʾān depicts Mary as withdrawing from her family to a place of seclusion, and then having "our spirit" in the form of a man either sent to her,[146] a more nebulous "spirit" breathed into her[147] or it (her *farj*),[148] or God's word (*kalīma*) cast into her through his utterance of "Be!"[149] These varied depictions of how Mary conceived Jesus ensures humans will never fully comprehend—let alone replicate—God's procreative actions. The fact that God can bypass human sexual intercourse altogether to engender a single child in multiple ways attests to God's superior authority over men to generate life in any way he pleases.

Despite God's complete control over the course of Jesus's birth, the Qurʾān depicts Mary as more than just a passive receptacle for his creative efforts. Repeated again and again throughout these stories is the fact that Mary freely guarded her *farj*, and that her efforts to do so somehow facilitated her son's conception. This brief but significant narrative detail indicates that her superlative moral character somehow evoked this unprecedented reproductive act. As procreative partner with a God who requires no human assistance in causing life to "Be!," Mary's own pious efforts to protect her *farj* and accept God's plans for her are shown to have been that much more extraordinary than any other woman's. Even though God created her "pure," Mary's exemplary status goes above and beyond what was predestined for her because she herself mirrored that same virtue through her own cultivation of an unparalleled piety that surpassed even the efforts of righteous mothers such as Āmina. In this instance, piety may have generated progeny, but only in ways inaccessible and unattainable for most women.

Mary's unique procreative partnership with God is woven throughout other elements of her narrative. After being impregnated by God's spirit, the Qurʾān relates how Mary gave birth to the prophet Jesus under a date-palm tree. There, she cried out how she wished she had died before having to endure the pain of parturition. However, her despair ceased when she heard a voice telling her God would provide her with fresh drink and fruit to alleviate her pain. As displayed in his intimate exchange with the earth to bring forth life, God served as attentive lover or midwife, caring for the woman with whom he was most intimate and for the child his breath and spirit generated.

At this point in the story, Mary was instructed not to talk to anyone and she abided, even when her own people accused her of fornication. Jesus, however, spoke from the cradle on her behalf, protecting the reputation of the mother who bore him.[150] Just as Mary willingly guarded her *farj* to conceive God's word, so, too, did she freely accept the suffering her choices and actions entailed. In all of these examples, Mary's pious efforts evoked an immediate divine response via breath, fruit, or protection. However, for most ordinary women such as the wives of Abraham or Zakarīyā, God remained unswayed by their well-intentioned attempts to elicit his intervention in their reproductive lives.

In sum, these Qur'ānic passages emphasize the extraordinary circumstances surrounding Mary's pregnancy and Jesus's birth: a miraculous conception unique in its display of divine intimacy, and the conception and birth of a healthy child without the help or guidance from scholars, doctors, or midwives.[151] Mary is also furnished with a divine sustenance and an infant prodigy who protected his mother's character from slander. Such profound events were certainly sealed by God when he secured Mary's fate, but here their fruition also depended upon Mary's protection of her *farj* and her willingness to embody God's will. Thus, Mary's reflexive agency became an essential part of a broader reproductive fate established by God prior to her birth. Such apparently contradictory claims underscore God's singular power to generate life as he pleases, even if it implicitly circumscribes his omnipotence by making him reliant on Mary to carry out his will.

Like Mary, the mother of Moses also experienced hardship and pain in her bearing and nurturing of a prophet. Similarly, she bore these sufferings without any assistance from her husband or any other man; only God came to her aid when her infant faced death. She also received a direct revelation from God (*wa awḥaynā ilā ummi Musá*).[152] Unlike Mary, however, the piety of Moses's mother often wavered as she confronted such hardships. Given her weaknesses, the mother of Moses does not quite measure up to the exceptional status of Jesus's mother. Surprisingly, perhaps, the Qur'ān makes no judgment with regard to her inadequacies. Rather, it simply demonstrates how God intervened in her life to correct them so that she would not fail in carrying out his plans.

Having just suckled her child in the hostile environs of Egypt, where the Pharaoh commanded all the sons of a certain group be killed,[153] Moses's mother feared for her son's safety. God sent her a revelation (*wa awḥaynā ilā ummi Mūsá*)[154] that instructed her to place him in the river. If she did, he would be restored to her and made one of God's messengers.[155] After seeing Pharaoh and his minister Hāmān plucking the baby Moses from the water with the intention of slaying him, Moses's mother almost revealed who he was in order to save him. However, God stepped in to give her the strength to conceal Moses's identity so that she might remain a true believer.[156] God also prevented Moses from suckling in the house of Pharaoh, so that his own mother could then be called upon to serve as wet nurse to him.[157] According to the Qur'ān,

God restored Moses to his true mother so that she would rejoice and no longer grieve, and learn that God's promise was true.[158]

As in the case of Mary, Moses's mother was groomed for her role through divine intervention and fate. To protect his infant prophet, God combated the hostile circumstances surrounding Moses's mother so that she could prevent Pharaoh from slaying her son, who was destined to grow up to deliver God's word. Clearly, she required more of God's assistance and intervention than did Mary to carry forth his will, as her inner strength and piety appear to be less cultivated. After all, Moses's mother attempted to put her own love for her child over and against God's plans for him, and therefore required divine correction. Surprisingly, the Qur'ān does not render her less praiseworthy for her weaknesses in this regard. Rather, the example of Moses's mother severs the link between exceptional piety and the automatic production of righteous offspring by suggesting that God engenders what he will in wombs despite a woman's moral deficiencies.

In comparing the examples of Mary and the mother of Moses, it is clear that piety often evokes selection and reward, but selection and reward may just as easily elicit piety. This causal tautology only underscores God's supreme command over the wombs in which he chooses to engender the life he desires. When it comes to reproduction, nothing is certain, and little is guaranteed. While Mary's extraordinary piety may have incited God to generate a righteous prophet in her womb, it is also true that less devoted women, such as Moses's mother or even Āmina, may garner God's favor in raising infants into adulthood. Therefore, the Qur'ān contrasts the extraordinary life of Mary with the mother of Moses to underscore the point that while a purified body and perfected piety may guarantee the production of righteous offspring, God may still reward less than exemplary maternal behavior with a favored son. As the life of Moses's mother demonstrates, ordinary mothers are never expected to replicate Mary's stellar example without the help and intervention of God. Left to their own devices, however, they must still strive to conform to the divine will as best as they can.

Paradigms of the Real: Ordinary Mothers

In its discussions of women who are not prophet-bearers, the Qur'ān emphasizes the importance of a woman's willingness to accept God's procreative desires, whatever they may be. For example, the Qur'ān refers to Muḥammad's wives as exemplary "mothers" of believers (Sūra 33:6).[159] Unlike Mary and the mother of Moses, however, these women remained childless. However, the Qur'ān projects their sterility as a personal sacrifice they had to make in order to ensure Muḥammad's status as "not the father of any of your men,"[160] and to establish a community based on confessional, rather than familial, ties.[161] Here, piety and *infertility* become inextricably linked.

Because God has not perfected them before they were born, Muḥammad's wives had to struggle to achieve a state of purity on their own by adhering to strict codes governing habit and behavior. In order to fulfill divine expectations, for example, the wives were expected to cover themselves, maintain their modesty, remain in their homes, speak justly, and not rebel.[162] Their efforts, however, did not induce progeny, as God had other plans for them. Instead, Muḥammad's wives were instructed to turn their maternal instincts outward to care for all believers as mothers would their own children. The wives' barrenness reminds all women who seek to bear children without divinely perfected and purified bodies, or the help of divine intervention to ensure the livelihood of their offspring, that God may, but does not always, reward piety with robust offspring. In this case, sterility becomes a condition for their piety.

For ordinary women whose bodies do little to display divine signs, healthy progeny are never guaranteed and a barren womb is never praised.[163] Given the uncertainty of their reproductive lives, however, all women are advised to cultivate the same maternal virtues of sacrifice, submission, and purity as Mary and the mother of Moses in the hopes that their efforts will lead to procreative success. Despite the fact that these women may still suffer the volatile consequences of an inscrutable divine will in the form of miscarriages, stillbirths, barrenness, and fetal deficiencies, they can be assured that their efforts will be measured in terms of pious intent rather than fruitful outcome. Like Muḥammad's wives, God has plans for every believer.

Because piety may stimulate the divine hand—although it is not guaranteed—the Qur'ān calls for ordinary women—in imitation of Mary and the prophet's wives—to perfect and purify their bodies as much as possible to prepare them for God's animating breath, or whatever else he might hold in store for them. Good women, therefore, must cover their genitals (*ʿawrāt*), in particular around strangers and young boys.[164] The guarding of one's *ʿawra* is so important that even in menopause, when a woman is theoretically past her childbearing prime, the Qur'ān advises it is still better for women to remain chastely dressed.[165] Believing women are also required to draw their veils over their bosoms so as not display their beauties (*zaynatahunna*).[166] To secure a purified vessel in which God may engender life, only a woman's husband is permitted to impregnate her, and then, only when she is not menstruating.[167] At least in theory, if a woman does not strive to protect her *ʿawra* from illicit contact and impurity, God may withhold offspring from her as punishment for her transgressions. The possibility of a causal link between maternal piety and progeny is enough to engender rightful action.

Like modesty, adhering to licit sexual relations also allows women to cultivate the virtuous maternal behaviors that—at the very least—seem to be prerequisites for God's full range of reproductive plans. The Qur'ān strongly advises both men (and women) to avoid all prohibited marital or sexual relationships, which include marrying their fathers' wives, stepmothers, mothers-in-law, women who have nursed them, maternal or paternal aunts or uncles' wives, sisters, half-sisters, nieces, daughters, stepdaughters, daughters-in-law, or sisters-in-law.[168] Women must take care to guarantee their bodies are free of physical and moral corruption; otherwise, God has the right to refuse to create offspring in their tainted wombs.

Once a child is conceived, the Qur'ān makes clear that mothers must be willing to shoulder the heavy burden of bringing the child to term. Over and over again, the Qur'ān emphasizes the difficulties of childbirth. Like Mary, in "weakness upon weakness" a woman must carry and nourish the fetus;[169] in great difficulty she must give birth.[170] After giving birth, women may continue to sacrifice themselves by breastfeeding for up to two years.[171] In theory, ordinary women, like the earth, could resist or protest against having to endure such hardships. However, the fact that they choose to endure the pain and agony of parturition, the physical demands of breastfeeding, or a lifetime of barrenness, miscarriages, or stillbirths draws them closer to God in an intimate procreative partnership that may approximate—although not fully reflect—that of Mary's.

A mother's sacrifice of her own wants and needs in service of God's reproductive intentions broadly captures the pious maternal virtues ordinary women must work to cultivate. Women who perfect such virtues, however, may or may not garner the same positive reproductive outcomes as Mary, who was selected, purified, and perfected by God even before she was born, or even the mother of Moses, whose child God saves through his manipulation of events. However, without the pious efforts of women in their everyday lives to purify their *'awrāt*, adhere to licit sexual relations, and suffer for the health and well-being of their children, all hope would be lost.

While the Qur'ān projects, in various ways, how a woman's cultivation of pious virtues may affect her reproductive fate either positively or negatively, it also counters such causal links with illustrations of how God ultimately creates in wombs whatever, and however, he chooses. God may decide to test a good woman by inflicting her with one miscarriage after another, or to try others around her by bringing forth children from her womb who cannot see or hear. While Mary's perfected piety calls forth the birth of Jesus, the nameless wife of Abraham, who laughed in the face of God, still conceived and bore a healthy and robust child well into old age upon her husband's request.

The Qur'ān may construct an ideal motherhood around childbearing, but still claims that exemplary "mothers" may be barren but capable of nurturing God's creations. Barrenness, after all, even has a positive effect in that it protects one from the iniquities of excess wealth and distraction from God. Such profound contradictions and ambiguities in the Qur'ān's depictions of mothers continue to accentuate God's supreme but mysterious generative power over all of life, and the plethora of maternal identities formed in relation to God's inscrutable procreative potencies. In whatever ways they can, through whatever means are available to them, good mothers must work to realize and embrace a divine will that may never be fully determined, defined, or fully understood in their own reproductive lives.

Conclusion: The Burden of Life

In all of these snapshots of God's engendering efforts, the Qur'ān underscores God's complete and incontestable control over the divine, natural, sexual, and social processes governing the generation of human existence. God, at once transcendent word, artisan, farmer, midwife, and intimate sexual partner, embodies all aspects of human creativity, sexuality, and gender. Ultimately, he exceeds them all. Within this context, humans, in particular mothers, play a vital role in securing the successful bearing and nurturing of God's procreative plans at the same time they are shown to exert little influence or control over God's generative acts, given his absolute command over all life. The ideal mother, therefore, is one who embodies the role of both subordinate recipient of God's procreative desires but also willing agent who enables his plans, whatever they may be. The paradoxical nature of her role, however, underscores God's complete jurisdiction over all of human reproduction.

In general, the Qur'ān offers a template of diverse conceptions of procreative processes, agents of creation, and maternal identities on both a cosmic and individual level. This broad template of generative possibilities guarantees no singular notion of God comes to dominate any other, and that God's generative potencies are never replicated by mothers or fathers who could then claim divine power for themselves. Given the Qur'ān's rhetorical emphasis on the ineffability of God's nature, the inscrutability of his procreative powers, and the plethora of maternal responses to his engendering endeavors, it is perhaps surprising that medieval discourse narrows so severely the interpretive possibilities to service a patriarchal agenda in their subsequent readings of God's creative identity and the maternal body.

When it comes to replicating themselves, most men bear little resemblance to Abraham or Zakarīyā, who needed only to pray to God for robust sons to appear in their wives' previously barren wombs. In order to secure the life a few pious men so easily attain, medieval scholars, physicians, and exegetes struggle to harness both the capricious nature of God's generative powers as well as the female wombs that operate in "shadows of darkness." Their rhetorical efforts to resolve the Qur'ān's intentional ambiguities result in a more constrictive rendition of God's supreme omnipotence over all life, and a paternal casting of maternal identities that depicts women as weak, subordinate to men, and physically and/or morally deficient.

For example, medieval Muslim physicians suggest women's bodies are frail and therefore inimical to childbearing,[172] a position that sets potential mothers in willful insubordination to God's procreative plans for humanity. Thus, the failure of men to beget life becomes an indictment not only against a woman's anatomy but also her moral character. Male physicians try to offset that inherent female weakness with medicine, diet, and their own critical scrutiny of every aspect of a woman's reproductive body.

By rendering themselves the primary authorities over what a womb produces, male scholars assume divine procreative power for themselves, a paternal posture that contradicts the Qur'ān's open-ended, persistent vision of God's incomparable, transcendent omnipotence to create in wombs whatever, and however, he pleases. From such a broad template of interpretive potentialities, chapter 2 shows how medieval medical scholars selectively isolate and privilege the Qur'ān's more patriarchal presentations of God's procreative agency and maternal deficiency over all other possible readings that preserve the text's vital ambiguities.

2

Mapping the Maternal Body

The Mechanics of Reproduction

> [O]ne (of those instruments) is complete and extends outwards while the other is incomplete and held back on the inside, as if it were an inverted male organ.
>
> —Ibn Sīnā

According to Helen King, the human body is simultaneously a physical and symbolic artifact; as such, it is both naturally and culturally construed.[1] Many feminists take this perspective one step farther to suggest there is no "natural" composition to the body whatsoever. Even "sex," which distinguishes females from males on the basis of their reproductive organs and structures, is always subject to cultural understandings of gender.[2] For example, Judith Butler has argued that there can be no "sex" that is not already gender, or rather, "sex by definition will be shown to have been gender all along."[3] For Butler and other feminists,[4] there is no "natural body" that resides outside the discourse and cultural forms through which it is identified. Even internal, physiological processes, which have long been protected under the guise of perceived biological fact, are equally susceptible to the political, social, and cultural narratives that gender the body.[5] Given the difficulties in separating the vagaries of language from biological "fact," it is hard to deny that the material reality of the body is inextricably entwined with the cultural forms through which it is gleaned intelligible.

This chapter will focus on the medical narratives through which medieval Muslim physicians map one particular bodily, gendered experience: maternity. As Carol Delaney argues, it is a natural fact that babies come out of women's bodies. However, notions of how babies are conceived, how they are formed, and how their identities come to be vary considerably across cultures.[6] In order to appreciate fully the meaning of "maternity" in the medieval Muslim medical context, it is important to examine how both maternity and paternity are constructed in relation to one another within traditional theologies of procreation and the broader social/legal/medical constructs governing the relationships between men and women, husbands and wives, parents and children.[7]

Despite the fact that the Qurʾān and subsequent medical literature assert that men and women contribute equally to the generation of life, and that only God—not men—imparts the life-giving "breath," male physicians tend to favor the seed/soil theory of procreation in their clinical discussions of the maternal body. Although medical scholars confirm a woman's "sperm" must mingle with the man's to generate life, they still cast the mother as the passive partner in whom the privileged male seed is planted. Just as God produces human life from a willing and loving earth in Sūras 71:17–18 and 53:32, so too do men bring forth offspring from a receptive female—albeit passive—body.[8]

In fact, medical depictions of male and female reproductive organs have come to mirror this seed/soil theory. For example, Abū ʿAlī al-Ḥusayn ibn ʿAbdallāh ibn Sīnā (d. 1037 CE), the Persian author of what became the standard medieval medical text, *The Canon of Medicine,* states, "The instrument of reproduction of the woman is the womb and in the origin of its creation it is identical (*mushākila*) to the instrument of reproduction of the man, that is, the penis and what goes with it. However, one (of those instruments) is complete and extends outwards while the other is incomplete and held back on the inside (*muḥtabisa fī al-dākhil*), as if it were an inverted male organ."[9] Maternity thus becomes tied with the female body's natural (albeit inferior) inclination towards receptivity, nurturing, and birth as opposed to active co-creator of the life God commands. As both micro- and macrocosms come to align with one another, women bear the burden of life while men alone guarantee the offspring God prefers.[10]

The power to procreate, imagined as divine power, thus transforms a patrilineal system into a patriarchal one with the father as a more powerful, more perfected naturalized divinity whose duty it is to ensure, define, and protect the progeny both he and God desire.[11] Such paternal, patriarchal views challenge the Qurʾān's theological vision of a multigendered, divine immanence/transcendence that creates in wombs whatever, however, and through whomever he wishes, despite the best (and worst) of human intentions.

The works of ʿArīb ibn Saʿd,[12] ʿAlī ibn Rabbān al-Ṭabarī,[13] and Ibn Qayyim al-Jawzīya,[14] along with other medieval medical, exegetical, and folklore treatises,[15] serve as the basis for this chapter's descriptions of the rhetoric and discourse appropriated by medieval Muslim physicians and scholars to cast the female body as the passive, more dependent sex that must be controlled and dominated by men. Because they construe women's bodies as "naturally" weak, male scholars view the entire course of reproduction, from the first act of sexual intercourse to the suckling of the newborn baby, as a potential threat to God's perfected procreative activities necessarily borne out by men to secure the production of what they identify as ideal offspring.

To keep hazards at bay, medieval physicians assert knowledge of, or control over, every stage of the reproductive act by surveying and circumscribing the female body, and by working to cure any problem within it that might interfere with man's desire to replicate himself. As a result of their efforts, physicians privilege the Qurʾān's more traditional reproductive roles for men and women over and against its more ambiguous and open-ended treatment of sex and gender in the procreative act. Assuming the role of custodian and surveillant of women's bodies, male medical scholars and physicians, like the Qurʾānic God, claim both the knowledge and power to generate life. By gaining access to what the Qurʾān holds to be the exclusive preserve of God, men, rather than women, come to embody the deity's elusive, ineffable efforts to produce life. In this way, male scholars attempt to manage the apparent randomness of reproductive outcomes the Qurʾān preserves and celebrates to highlight God's incomparable power over all of human existence.

The Two-Seed Theory: On Male and Female Sperm Production

As noted above, medieval Muslim medicine adheres primarily to the Hippocratic model of reproduction that assumes both males and females produce sperm that, when mingled together in the womb, begets life.[16] The idea that women generate "sperm" is documented in Greek medical literature, where scholars report that women, like men, emit a kind of "seed" at the end of erotic dreams.[17] This same Greek medical wisdom appears under the guise of many *ḥadīth,* which suggest that since women are the twin-halves of men (*shaqāʾiqu al-rijāli*), they too must bathe if they have expelled some sort of moisture as the result of a sexually arousing dream.[18] These *ḥadīth* statements (and the Greek medical wisdom they contain) are verified further by the Qur'ān, which also maintains that both men and women contribute equally to the reproductive process.[19] However, because mothers do contribute much to what their wombs produce, and nurture new life in "shadows of darkness," their bodies become objects of scrutiny and control for men who assume divine procreative power for themselves.

Resemblance, Heredity, and the Two-Seed Theory

For medieval Muslim medical scholars, the two-seed theory offers a convenient antidote to the perplexing biological question of how a child might come to resemble one parent or another, neither, or both. Theories surrounding resemblance, however, challenge the Qur'ānic ideal that God fashions what he pleases in the womb since the image of the parents determines what form the child will take. More importantly, perhaps, such theories raise fundamental social questions and anxieties regarding paternity.

Following Hippocratic thought, many Muslim sources assert males and females both emit seed that carries traits inherited by offspring. For example, in the *Muwaṭṭa'* of Mālik ibn Anas (d. 795 CE), the earliest extant composition of Islamic law, a tradition reports how Umm Sulaym asked the prophet Muḥammad if a woman should take a bath after an erotic dream. 'Ā'isha said to her, "Silly, does a woman also have an emission?" However, the prophet responded, "May your right hand be dust-laden! From where, then, comes the similarity of features?"[20] In this statement, the seed that dominates, either the male's *or* the female's, carries the traits that shape a child's features.

Despite the fact that children are comprised of sperm stemming from both the mother and father, many medieval Muslim scholars recognize that a child may not resemble either of its parents.[21] To explain this rather common but unsettling occurrence, they assert the semen from any one parent may also contain characteristics from prior descendants that then become manifest in subsequent generations of offspring. Thus, a child may not necessarily resemble the mother or the father, but perhaps some distant relative, such as a grandfather.[22] So, despite their belief that one seed—either the male's or the female's—would eventually dominate another, at least in theory Muslim scholars are open to the possibility that a child may look nothing like its parents. Such dependence on natural, mechanistic explanations for what takes place in the womb, along with human judgment in determining what constitutes "like" characteristics, stand contrary to Qur'ānic declarations that God simply creates whatever he pleases in the womb.[23]

Much more problematic than the fact that such theories of resemblance contradict Qur᾿ānic theology is that they clearly raise much concern and anxiety about paternity, especially when a child looks nothing like its father, or as a fallback, one of his distant male relatives. The Hippocratic, two-seed theory of reproduction, in conjunction with Muslim notions of heredity, assumes males to be essential, but not singularly vital, for generating offspring. As a result, children may often look nothing like their fathers, since male dominance over the forming and fashioning of progeny is tentative at best. In order to assert paternal control over a child's unpredictable features, Muslim scholars had to manufacture social and biological connections with the father to demonstrate that male participation in the procreative process was inherently, if not visually, dominant.[24] Such manufacturings often occurred to the detriment of the woman's equal partnering with men in the begetting of life.

Certainly, many medieval Muslim accounts stress the need for men to accept the vagaries of inherited traits, since the refusal to do so could create an insurmountable social crisis. Muḥammad ibn Mūsá al-Damīrī (d. 1405 CE), composer of one of the two standard medieval zoological lexicons that has inestimable value for Muslim folklore,[25] reports how the prophet Muḥammad explicitly advises fathers not to disown sons who look nothing life them, because children frequently receive hereditary traits (*naj῾a ῾irq*) from distant ancestors, just as red camels oftentimes produce ashy-colored offspring that resemble prior relatives.[26] Clearly, the concern here is for fathers who were too quick to neglect their children because of deep insecurities about their own paternity.

However, the majority of medieval scholars contradict this sound prophetic advice, along with the Qur᾿ānic edict that God fashions in wombs what he pleases, by claiming offspring must always resemble the fathers who sired them. For example, Abū Zayd Ḥunayn ibn Isḥāq al-῾Ibādī (d. 872 CE), the famous Assyrian Nestorian Christian physician who translated Greek medical works into Arabic and Syriac during the Abbasid caliphate, records how what is in the womb must fully reach the shape and form of the father, otherwise it should not be called offspring.[27] Muḥammad ibn Ismā῾īl al-Bukhārī (d. 870 CE), compiler of one of the most authentic collections of Sunnī *ḥadīth,* preserves a tradition that suggests point blank that one can prove adultery without witnesses if the child does not look like the father.[28] Also, in the *Mishkāt al-maṣābīḥ* (ca. 1337 CE), a popular collection of *ḥadīth* drawn from older sources, which were adapted by Walī al-Dīn al-Tabrīzī as an ethical guide for those who wish to live "a life pleasing to God,"[29] the prophet uses resemblance to determine whether or not a woman committed adultery,[30] a position that counters the need for four witnesses mandated by the Qur᾿ān in cases of fornication.[31] Likewise, Muḥammad uses paternal resemblance to accuse a woman of lying when she states that her husband is impotent. He declares, "By God, these boys resemble [their father] as a crow resembles a crow!"[32] In yet another example, the prophet explains how a white man could beget a black and reddish son because his own father was leprous, a fact the man had wished to conceal.[33] In this case, a father's true identity is revealed through his child's features.

Clearly, in each of these anecdotes, paternal uncertainty lies at the heart of scholarly opinion that offspring must always take after their fathers.[34] The idea that the father alone imparts hereditary traits, or that his traits necessarily dominate the mother's, is even rooted in animal husbandry practices. For example, scholars note that if the veins under the tongue of a male ram are white, the ewes will give birth to white lambs; if the veins are black, the females will drop black lambs. If the veins are of two different colors, the progeny will be variegates, and if they are reddish, they (the young) will come forth reddish.[35] Analogously, while both men and women may produce the sperm that mingles together to generate life, it is still the father's that must reign over the mother's to impress itself upon a child's features. Not surprisingly, only the father's sperm can impart the image that socially confirms his privileged procreative status.

In their utilization of arguments from heredity, men place themselves as second to God in terms of producing the kind of life he commands. The life he commands becomes synonymous with children who resemble their fathers, and not their mothers or some third party. In order to appease paternal anxieties, male physicians see the need to deemphasize the reproductive role of the mother, who becomes a passive recipient of prevailing male seed that must engender a child who resembles the father who sired it, rather than an equal contributor of generative sperm. Such views contradict the Qurʾān where God displays total control over the womb and its contents, or invites women to participate along with him in the production of life. In the context of the revelation, children can look like mothers, fathers, grandfathers, or no one at all. In the everyday world, however, a man must work to establish a dominant connection with his child, even if it means suppressing a woman's reproductive capacity, accusing her of adultery, or rejecting his own progeny on the basis of dissimilarity.

Competition and the Necessity of One Seed to Dominate the Other

The desire to shore up the tenuous nature of paternity is also evident in more strictly "biological" explanations of how reproduction takes place. In their descriptions of reproductive theories and practices, medical scholars take great care to secure the primary procreative role of the male, which is far from obvious.[36] For example, in order to explain how children come to resemble parents, most medieval Muslim physicians, like their ancient Greek counterparts,[37] favor a biological model based on the cultural practice of competition, which envisions a stronger, more potent sperm emerging to assert control over a thinner, weaker sperm. They propose that within the confines of the womb, one of the two sperms emitted by either the male or the female eventually comes to dominate (*muḥīl*) the other (*mustaḥīl*), and then transform it according to its own inherent characteristics.[38] In the case of resemblance, which sperm would prevail over the other would depend on its superior quantity and/or quality.[39] If children are to resemble fathers, then it follows that the most optimal, or natural, reproductive scenario would be for the male sperm to rule over the female sperm.

Muslim physicians project a variety of scripts to account for why one seed might be "superior" over another. One suggestion is that the child takes after the first parent to reach orgasm.[40] Here, either the force of the orgasmic experience empowers and strengthens the sperm, allowing it to dominate the weaker,[41] or the first sperm released is simply greater in quantity, and therefore able to overpower what comes second.[42] Again, if children must resemble fathers, then it is more appropriate and natural for men to achieve quicker, more forceful orgasms than women. Likewise, children resembling mothers or no one at all would be products of a failure on the part of male sperm to overcome the female's.

However, scholars acknowledge that there are cases where one sperm will not necessarily be stronger than the other. For example, if the two sperms emitted are balanced and blended equally, the child would resemble both parents. The inability of one sperm to dominate the other is far from optimal, as such a condition holds the potential to produce reproductive anomalies, such as the hermaphrodite.[43] The preference for paternal resemblance, and the desire to avoid producing a hermaphrodite, lead medical scholars to modify and denigrate Hippocratic (and Qur'ānic) theories that value an equal balance of male and female sperm mingling in the womb to produce life. Their interpretive efforts likewise turn women into more passive receptacles for male seed, which carries within it the divine power to generate more optimal forms of life.

The Two-Seed Theory and Sex Determination

At least in theory, if not practice, both mothers and fathers have equal opportunity to contribute to the similitude of their offspring. However, when conversations shift to determining the sex of the child, the medical discourse privileges the male's role in seminal emission, or the quality or quantity of the seed he expels. In the context of discussing what seminal qualities are linked with "maleness" and "femaleness," medical scholars denigrate the woman's reproductive status as secondary to the man's. For example, medieval physicians associate the superior qualities of heat, dryness, strength, and aggression with the production of male offspring and tie the inferior properties of cold, wetness, frailty, and passivity to the production of female offspring. Such superior qualities become manifest in an offspring's very appearance, as the males of any species are deemed more beautiful than its females.[44] A closer look at how these social and cultural values become embedded in reproductive discourse demonstrates how Muslim physicians weave female subordination, weakness, and vulnerability into the very fabric of the natural world, which male scholars determine is divinely construed and socially confirmed. By making the male primarily responsible for sex determination, physicians undermine the Qur'ān's praise of God's unique power to choose what sex a child will be.

Many medical accounts report how the man's seed, when dominant, produces male offspring while the woman's seed, when more powerful, produces female offspring. Damīrī and others note that the seminal fluid of a man is white while the seminal fluid of a woman is yellow. If the semen of the man is above that of the woman when the two come together in the womb, the child will be male. But, if the semen of the woman is above that of the man, the child will be female.[45]

Interestingly, despite his reliance on such natural, mechanistic explanations for sex determination, Damīrī is quick to note that ultimately the sex of the child can only be specified "by order of God."[46] Here, Damīrī suggests that God either mans the natural processes that dictate whether a child will be male or female, or simply knows what the outcome might be.[47] In Damīrī's model, which parallels today's scientific theories that the male alone carries the Y chromosome that leads to the creation of male offspring, women may bear sons but will never generate them.[48] While the Qur'ān certainly lauds the birth of females,[49] it still subordinates the social, political, and cultural position of women to that of men.[50] Within the framework of this paradigm, women are prevented from directly generating and replenishing the optimal and ideal patriarchal structures that sustain the social, political, and religious order.

Other accounts contradict Damīrī's example by proposing that either the man or the woman can produce male or female offspring. However, rather than empowering women by giving them the ability to produce males, such notions further link the more positive qualities having to do with strength with males, and the more negative traits having to do with weakness with females. Rabbān al-Ṭabarī, for example, cites Hippocrates in suggesting that maleness is created from a union between the strongest seeds from both the woman and the man.[51] As a result, males may produce females with one wife, but males with another wife.[52] Rabbān al-Ṭabarī, like Hippocrates, believes that parts of the human body from which seeds are drawn are humors that possess different potencies.[53] When mixed in a ratio that favors strength, males result and when the weak element dominates, females.[54] ʿArīb ibn Saʿd offers another explanation along these lines by suggesting that the sperm itself, when emitted from either the male or female or even when mixed, can become thin and weak, which, of course, results in female offspring.[55] In this scheme, the female sex is always a byproduct of frailty, even when that frailty is actually dominant.

Likewise, in many medical treatises heat, too, becomes associated with the male, coldness with the female. Rabbān al-Ṭabarī, citing Aristotle, notes that if the quality of heat achieves supremacy over the female seed, the child will be a male, and if coldness dominates it, the child will be female.[56] Wetness and dryness are also factors, as it was believed women are born out of moist semen, while men emerge from dry and thick semen. Standard medical opinion also asserts male fetuses become evident in just thirty days, but females in forty-two days. Medical scholars assume that the female seed, being cooler, thinner, moister, and weaker, simply takes longer to set than the male seed, which is hotter, thicker, dryer, and stronger.[57] As a result of their excess moisture, female fetuses are slower to move, or "quicken" than males.[58]

In confirmation of this theory, Ḥunayn ibn Isḥāq records how more women are born in southern areas (than men) because moistness is predominant there and likewise affects seed production.[59] Unlike the above examples, the female seed in this case is neutral, denied of any potential to dominate the male's. Rather, it waits passively for its transformation into one sex or another by hot, cold, wet, or dry qualities in the surrounding environment, or those same elements embedded within the male sperm.

These examples demonstrate that while the majority of Muslim physicians adopt the Hippocratic, two-seed theory of reproduction, they still wrestle with the idea that females could contribute more to the procreative process than simply matter, which is the popular Aristotelian view.[60] In fact, some Muslims jurists reject Hippocrates wholeheartedly to suggest that males alone produce the life form of the child, including Mālik, who, in the *Muwaṭṭaʾ*, relates how ʿAbdallāh ibn ʿUmar disapproved of castration because "the completeness of the created form is in the testicles."[61] However, many physicians and scholars still retain the two-seed theory since the Qurʾān advances it, but propose that while female seed may be analogous to male semen, it functions as little more than matter. Ibn Qayyim, for example, cites the prophet, who said, "The man's sperm is thick and powerful; as for the sperm of the mother, it is delicate.[62] From it is the flesh and blood."[63] Here, the female seed takes on a vital but subsidiary role in the procreative process.

This strong association between heat and masculinity is further underscored by ʿArīb ibn Saʿd, who suggests the quicker and harsher the thrusts of the penis, the more likely a male will be produced. Presumably, this outcome is the result of friction, which is, not surprisingly, tied to male strength and performance. Females, he notes, will result from a gentler and slower penile stroking.[64] Abdallāh ibn Muslim ibn Qutayba (d. 889 CE), a prominent medieval linguist, philologist, and scholar of *ḥadīth,* goes so far as to say that the most fit among women to give birth to virtuous sons is a frigid one. Frigid women are not desirous of men, and therefore exert no influence whatsoever over the quantity or quality of male sperm produced.[65]

The above examples demonstrate how the gendered traits of weakness, coolness, passivity, and frailty come to make up the natural or ideal physiology of the female sex. While the Qurʾān emphasizes the female's direct receptivity to God's procreative desires through the subjection of her will to his, medieval physicians sever that intimacy by inserting men between women and God as those who alone can secure the life he commands. Because of their weak, cold composition, women' s bodies are simply incapable of carrying out the divine's procreative plans, and thus they become dependent on men for reproductive success.

In addition to emphasizing the competition between male and female seed, or the male and female qualities contained within that seed, Muslim medical treatises, following in the footsteps of Hippocrates, Galen, and other Greek scholars, also focus on the influence of the right and left sides of the testicles and/or womb in sex determination.[66] The right and left sides of the human body are not viewed as neutral; the right side was considered hotter,[67] and thus superior, to the left, which was cooler.[68] Thus, the warmer sides of the body produced males, the cooler sides females.

Scholars such as Ibn Qayyim and Rabbān al-Ṭabarī, following the Hippocratics and other Greek scholars, suggest the womb, like the male testicles, has two distinct pouches, or cavities.[69] The right "cavity," therefore, like the right testes, would be hotter than the left. A number of Muslim scholars follow their Greek predecessors by suggesting that the male sex is generated when seed from the right testicle flows into the right cavity of the womb and mixes with the female seed lodged there, and vice versa for the creation of females.[70] In this configuration, males differentiate sex to a limited degree by virtue of their seed; however, the environment of the womb at conception may also contribute to the formation of a child's sex.

The medical literature takes into account that the realities of reproduction do not always follow such nice, neat paths from right to right or left to left when it comes to sex determination.[71] Rabbān al-Ṭabarī, for example, considers what would happen if other combinations were to occur. For Rabbān al-Ṭabarī, if the seed were to flow from the left testicle to the right side of the womb, the child would be a "masculine female," and if it gushes from the right testicle to the left side of the womb, the child would be a "feminine male."[72] In either scenario, the environment of the uterus may affect but not completely dominate or transform the father's semen either by heating or cooling the seed.[73] This limited assertion of feminine power only results in a less than optimal offspring, an anomaly that is neither fully male nor fully female.[74] In this case, a woman's total passivity during the sexual act is preferable to any sort of exertion or dominance that may impede the male sperm's ability to overpower completely her own.

In sum, while the two-seed theory carries the potential to reflect a more egalitarian view of procreation, one of the many models put forth in the Qur'ān, its actual articulation through Muslim medical discourse emphasizes a more patriarchal understanding of the female reproductive role as subordinate to the male's. This subsidiary reproductive role is underscored by the fact that medieval men understand a woman's body to be naturally weak, cool, moist, and passive, and that female, feminine, or "mixed" offspring result when the man's sperm fails to dominate and suppress completely the woman's. In these examples, which privilege Aristotelian paradigms to explain resemblance and reproduction, the male body becomes the only one capable of fully implementing God's procreative plan, provided it is not contested by the female's. Consequentially, suspicion is cast upon the maternal body—in particular the potentially hostile environment of the womb—because of its inclination to thwart, transform, or undermine the sex God (or men) intended. Thus, the medical literature denigrates the Qur'ān's portrayal of the intimate, active, and sacrificial role of women and their wombs in the process of reproduction, as well as its insistence upon God's ability to create in wombs whatever, and however, he pleases, by making men God's primary reproductive agents.

The Capricious Nature of Conception

In much of the medical literature, medieval physicians probe the minute processes of conception, from what types of individuals were most likely to conceive, to what frame of mind one had to be in to produce the most robust offspring. In the course of these discussions, the maternal body is scrutinized in infinite detail for any flaws, weaknesses, or deficiencies that might prevent a woman from fulfilling her role as bearer of life. In addition, the men who conduct such inquiries now become the authoritarian voice, second only to God, for determining and controlling a woman's physical or mental condition so that she would be able to meet divine standards and expectations, which they now defined. Thus, medieval medical scholars privilege the Qur'ān's intimations of the female body's inherent insufficiencies (e.g., the wife of Abraham) over and against its more persistent views of the mother's womb (e.g., Mary) as ideal receptacle for God's generative efforts.

The Glories of Sexual Intercourse and Procreation

As noted in chapter 1, the Islamic tradition lauds both sexual intercourse and procreation.[75] In fact, according to some medieval exegetes, God designed humans for the very purpose of mating. Jāḥiẓ, for example, notes how males grow hair on their chins to separate them from females, "whose fresh faces move men to ensure the continuation of the species."[76] He also observes that since the male needs to expel his fluid into another creature to create offspring, God endowed him with a "projecting instrument" that can expand to allow the sperm reach the far recesses of the uterus.[77] For Jāḥiẓ, God fashioned the penis with a perfect balance of strength and flaccidity to accomplish his goals. After all, if a man's penis were limp all the time, how could it reach the end of the vagina to ejaculate its seed? Contrarily, if it were constantly erect, how could a man turn over in bed or walk about in public "with that thing protruding in front of him?"[78]

The female, on the other hand, who needs to incubate the two fluids together and bear the fetus until it is fully developed, was carved a hollow receptacle for that very purpose. Jāḥiẓ goes on to note how God designed the womb specifically to support the fetus, the blood from the mother to nourish it, and her breasts like small skin flasks, hanging there to satisfy its needs upon birth.[79] In these examples, the woman's body is cast in terms of an ideal receptacle for receiving, nurturing, and bearing what men ultimately engender.

Not only does sexual intercourse fulfill God's command and design to produce offspring, but so too does it provide many physical, spiritual, and psychological benefits for its participants, as long as it is approached with the utmost care.[80] After all, when a man's penis achieves an erection, he loses two-thirds of his mind.[81] However, if intercourse does not exceed the bounds of moderation, and is performed in legal and acceptable contexts, it revives inward energy, and dissipates sad thoughts, melancholy, and depression.[82] Ultimately, men and women who come together in coitus enjoy intimate relationships by blood and marriage, and revel in raising children and being pleased by them.[83]

Pleasure is often enlisted as both an enticing side benefit of procreation for both partners, and an essential part of conception. Abū Jaʿfar Aḥmad ibn Abī Khālid ibn Jazzār al-Qayrawānī (d. 979 CE), the noted Tunisian physician and author of the *Zād al-musāfir,* which was adopted in sixteenth-century Europe as an essential medical textbook (*Viaticum peregrinantis*), suggests God built in an unfailing and never absent sense of great pleasure with any act of intercourse so that the species of animals would survive.[84] Ibn Sīnā also emphasizes the importance of pleasure in ensuring a successful conception. If emissions from the man and the woman occur at once, the contraction of the vagina produces an effective suction that lures the male semen into the womb. Therefore, synchronized orgasms generate a better chance for inception.[85] The famous Persian theologian, philosopher, and mystic, Abū Ḥāmid Muḥammad ibn Muḥammad Ghazālī (d. 1111 CE), too, warns against two close relatives marrying one another, because familiarity does little to incite desire. A lack of desire produces weak children or none at all; ignited passions beget strong ones.[86]

However, there can be many dangers lurking in this joy-ridden exercise. It should only be indulged in when there is a strong desire, and only when this desire is aroused neither by effort nor erotic ideas or sights.[87] Too much of a good thing (or too little) can also have disastrous consequences. Excess amounts of intercourse, for example, can result in tremors and palsies, and it can weaken the faculties and dim the eyesight.[88] On the other hand, extended bouts of abstinence can elicit different types of diseases.[89] For women in particular, desisting from sexual intercourse can result in "hysterical suffocation" (*ikhtināq al-raḥim*).[90] Without intercourse, sperm builds up in the womb and then rots, poisoning the rest of the body. Ibn Jazzār notes this disease mostly afflicts widows, or women who have reached sexual maturity without knowing any man.[91] In these examples, both God and nature confirm sex is an essential benefit for men and women, when approached with reverence, awe, moderation, and piety. Men or women unwilling or unable to have sex are rendered deficient, both physically and spiritually.[92]

Medieval physicians go on to point out that while God both designed and compelled men and women to procreate, they are not always successful in that endeavor. Therefore, to maximize reproductive success, these medical scholars carefully map out the optimal conditions under which couples are most apt to conceive, the proper steps they must follow to guarantee robust sperm production, and any potential problems or difficulties to avoid that might inhibit them from securing a positive outcome.

For example, several scholars emphasize the importance of foreplay before sex, as passion is key to abundant sperm production. The more pleasure a man experiences, the more sperm will empty out of him, which increases his chances of producing offspring and benefits his own health and well-being.[93] Therefore, in order to arouse passions, a man should shower his wife with affectionate words, fondle her hand, lick her body, gaze upon her, and refrain from any grievance he might have against her.[94] Before engaging in coitus, he should trust in God, find peace within his own soul and seek consent, pleasure, and happiness from his partner.[95] He should even pursue peak environmental conditions by making sure there is no southerly wind blowing during his act of coitus, as it produces lazy souls,[96] or it generates delicate, soft, unformed seed that lacks enough maturity to mate.[97]

Men are encouraged to exercise caution in choosing a suitable partner for sexual relations. They are instructed never to have intercourse with a woman who has refrained from sexual relations for a long period of time, nor with a sick woman, as her condition might impact his ability to produce a robust child, or effect his own health and well-being.[98] In each example, men must discipline themselves and their partners to secure the most desirable procreative outcome, which God commands but never guarantees. While Abraham had only to ask God for a prudent boy (*ghulām*) to receive one,[99] most men must control assiduously every aspect of their lives (and those of their potential spouses) in the mere hope of generating heirs. Rather than leaving the outcome in God's hands, as the Qur'ān suggests, men preempt fate to take it upon themselves to ensure reproductive success.

The Hazards of Sperm Production

Even if males enter into an act of coitus under ideal conditions, medieval physicians realize sperm can still be quite finicky, and fail to generate offspring. While the best seed is that which is "flawless, excellent, and numerous,"[100] in reality a number of circumstances produce a less than perfect product. In general, healthy men generate healthy seed; old, sick, lazy,[101] or diseased men put forth deficient or weak seed.[102] Even one's mood can affect the quality and quantity of sperm produced. ʿArīb ibn Saʿd, quoting Hippocrates, professes that men do not ejaculate sperm in one state every time; rather, sperm changes with the conditions of both the soul and the body. A happy soul strengthens the body, and a stronger body gives rise to more robust sperm.[103] Likewise, sad, sick souls only yield weak, thin sperm.[104]

As noted above, medieval scholars assume more powerful sperm creates males, while weaker sperm spawns females; therefore, females would be the product of "sad," old, or diseased sperm.[105] Because they assume one's emotions and health affect directly a child's sex, several scholars recommend exercises males can perform if they want their wives to bear male or female offspring. For example, ʿArīb ibn Saʿd, via Galen, argues that men must strengthen their bodies and ease their minds if they want to fortify their sperm enough to produce males, and weaken themselves ("by the strength of God," presumably because that act would defy their inherent, masculine natures), and thus their sperm, to the point at which it gives rise to females.[106] These examples show how medieval Muslim medical discourse connects healthy physique, peace of mind, "excellent" sperm production, and masculinity with the generation of male offspring that will, in all likelihood, resemble their fathers.[107] In contrast to the Qurʾān, men participate, along with God, in the intimacies of both fetal sex formation and resemblance within the womb.

While they do mention penile disease,[108] or impotence,[109] in general most scholars view a male's inability to produce rich, healthy seed as a temporary condition that requires only slight adjustments in diet, thought, or practice. For example, ʿArīb ibn Saʿd explores a variety of remedies to cure a man's inability to sustain an erection, depending on its causes. For ʿArīb ibn Saʿd, a mere balance in the body's temperature needs to be maintained to produce a suitable erection. So, if erectile dysfunction results from the body sustaining too much cold, men should simply coat their penises with ointment or warm oil, and consume a drink of crushed *ambergris* or musk. If there is too much heat, he should drink cow's milk and cottonseed, eat sour pomegranate and lettuce, or sip barley or whatever else might be moist and cool. If the loss in stiffness stems from an excess in dryness, more moisture should be applied through bathing, rubbing oil, or the consumption of moist foods. Likewise, foods that seem dry will counter excesses in moisture.[110] Some scholars also suggest men who excessively masturbate easily lose their erections when it comes time for intercourse.[111] The key here, of course, is for them to stop pleasuring themselves or at least aim for less frequency.

In these examples, men need only to cut back on their erotic thoughts and behaviors, or adjust their diets or habits, to enjoy positive procreative results. If a man has a prominent erection but produces too little sperm during an act of intercourse, this problem can readily be rectified through minor adjustments in his daily routine. Ibn al-Jazzār, for example, identifies a number of foods men can consume that are known for their abilities to yield larger quantities of sperm: chickpeas, beans mixed with something that adds warmth, moist meat, egg yolks, pine nuts, and peppercorns.[112] The *Ṭibb al-aʾimma* recommends hot, tender endive, for it increases semen, improves the color, and increases the number of males.[113] The Shīʿite *imāms* are also recorded as recommending a meal of parched barley (*sawīq*) for the begetting of strong, healthy children.[114] With a few modifications in their diet, thought, or behavior, men can generate optimal erections, numerous and flawless sperm, and, in some cases, with God's help, the choice sex and like features of their child.

The Infirm Nature of the Womb

When it comes to wombs, scholars point to more serious and complex defects and problems that cannot be rectified through simple changes in habit, diet, or thought. Jāḥiẓ, for example, notes that most children are born in perfected form.[115] Deviations from that perfected form are often caused by ailments in the womb or in the tissues from which the fetus is composed, "just as an imperfection in the wool or in a tool prevents the craftsman from making something correctly, as he intends."[116] Often, medieval physicians believe little can be done to correct the innate weaknesses of the womb, and are satisfied simply to identify and catalog its flaws. By recounting such flaws, men recuse themselves of any responsibility for procreative success or failure. However, when a woman's gynecological problems do seem solvable, these elite scholars often blame women for somehow shirking their responsibilities in maintaining a clean and proper vessel for conception. Medical discourse, therefore, suggests men need only to tweak their physical and mental states to participate alongside God in generating optimal life, while women, because of the very nature of their bodies, can only inhibit their efforts.

In medieval medical treatises, physicians cast the road to conception as a treacherous one; only the most perfected of female specimens will conceive. For example, women most capable of conceiving must be of normal weight and size; heavy women will have a hard time reproducing, as fat cuts off the mouth of the womb, which prevents male seed from entering.[117] Even the healthiest of male seed often falls prey to a woman's inhospitable body. Rabbān al-Ṭabarī, citing Hippocrates, proposes that very cold women do not get pregnant because coldness solidifies the seed, and the very hot also do not get pregnant because heat burns the seed. Likewise very dry and wet women fail to reproduce because their dryness shrivels the seed and their wetness causes it to slide out.[118] Here, no diets or special recipes can counter such detrimental bodily imbalances that freeze, burn, dry, or drown healthy male seed. In each case, male scholars depict the female body as a hostile barrier to persistent, well-intentioned, and optimal male efforts to carry out the divine will.

In order for women to conceive, they must begin with a healthy, regular menstrual cycle. That, too, however, is portrayed as the exception rather than the rule. For example, if women exercise too much or have dark skin (presumably, darkened by living in hot, dry climates), they'll experience little or even no discharge.[119] In ancient Greek medical texts, as in the Islamic works, heavy loss of blood was considered preferable to light loss, since both Greek and Muslim physicians believed menstrual blood nourished the fetus and so more was favorable than less.[120] By way of contrast, women who are moist and fleshy or light in color (presumably, lightened by living in cool, wet climates) will have healthier, more robust flows.[121]

Since scholars believe a single tube connects precariously the woman's uterus to her head, even the smallest of afflictions, such as a nosebleed, could block the discharge of menstrual blood.[122] In addition to worrying about a bloody nose, women also had to face the possibility that some obstruction might fall haphazardly into the mouth of the womb, which would prevent the menstrual blood from exiting. If this happens, the menstrual blood becomes congested, causing the heart to palpitate, the woman to tremble or faint. Scholars liken a woman with a blocked flow to something hideous or monstrous, a social pariah: she refuses to eat and will crave clay and coal as her belly turns black and her bile a bright red.[123]

These examples demonstrate how a woman's menstrual flow, integral to her ability to conceive, falls victim to random afflictions to her body, or, more disturbingly, to the inherently weak nature of her person. In either case, there is no behavioral or dietary regime she can adopt to prepare her body to conceive. The random nature of such female afflictions has an added benefit of recusing men from their inability to procreate as well. While the Qurʾān portrays God as finding many suitable vessels through which to advance his reproductive agenda, the medical works suggest such receptacles are few and far between. Male sperm may flow aplenty, but even the most consummate of sperm will fail when confronting a flawed womb.

For Muslim scholars, the preferred time for conception was right after a woman completes her menstrual cycle, when the vessel of the womb would have cleansed itself of all remaining blood.[124] If any trace of blood stays in the womb, it decays and putrefies,[125] and corrupts both the male and female seeds when mixed.[126] Scholars also feared bits of menstrual blood would severely attack the male sexual organ by causing ulcerations[127] and/or prevent conception altogether.[128] Because of its potential biological and social hazards, men must strictly regulate menstruation, especially when it crosses with ritual. Ghazālī, for example, discusses at length how husbands must teach their wives to abstain from prayer during their monthly flow, but also instruct them when precisely to resume prayer after the bleeding has stopped.[129]

Folk wisdom even goes so far as to suggest that if a woman becomes pregnant with menstrual blood still in her womb she will bear a defective child.[130] Here, the womb's biological purging of the putrefied blood mirrors the Islamic tradition's command for a woman to cleanse herself ritually after menstruation.[131] Or, it may be scholars believe the ritual cleansing serves to affect the internal distillation of the womb. Whatever the case, physicians locate the cause of an "unclean" womb in both a woman's body and with her failure to fulfill her pious obligations. In this light, a woman's inability to cleanse herself fully may stem from a defective womb, but that defective womb becomes indistinguishable from her deficient piety. By linking bodily defects with impiety, scholars hold women responsible for their in/ability to conceive, or the type of child they can produce.

Despite the inherent flaws in her physique, piety, or menstrual cycle, a woman may still be fortunate enough to conceive. In discussions centered around the mechanics of conception, medieval physicians personify the female womb as a kind of lustful harlot, a "greedy" creature[132] that is strongly attracted to seminal fluid,[133] one that sucks or breathes in the male sperm through its hungry "mouth," holding it tightly for itself.[134] Ironically, the type of language employed to describe the womb's reproductive activities suggests that the lucky women who do conceive possess bodies that are somehow wanton or loose.[135] Once conception occurs, however, the woman (and presumably her womb) becomes modestly chaste and no longer desires to have sexual intercourse.[136] At this point, the womb mirrors the more conservative values of chastity by sealing itself up to prevent further seed from entering it.[137] If the womb were to remain promiscuous and open to more male seed, that seed might mingle with the first and produce a child that could potentially have two fathers.[138]

Here, Muslim physicians fashion the biological structure of the womb to mirror their moral desire to prevent a religious crime. As many texts show, the idea that a child can have two fathers is not just physiologically impossible, it is also confirmed legally: the Shāfiʿītes, for example, rule that a child can have only one mother and one father.[139] The closure of the womb also wards off the potential for children to become "mixed up." The sense here is that more seed added during the development of the fetus would result in a strange and corrupted life form, such as, for example, fetal twins becoming mixed and entangled into one monstrous being in the womb.[140] Nature, therefore, does not allow *male* seed to violate normative expectations of what God would ultimately deem as human. Contrarily, nature does permit the woman's defective, weak physique or character to corrupt male seed once she has it trapped inside her womb. The idea that a woman's behavior can impact the physical development of a fetus runs contrary to many Qur'ānic passages, which hold that God has his own reasons for generating particular human forms within the womb. It does, however, reflect some of the Qur'ān's more general prescriptions that circumscribe female sexual behavior.

Constructing the Maternal Body

According to medieval Muslim literature, once a child is conceived and sealed up in the womb, its development follows the neat, epigenetic path of fetal development designated by God and laid out in the Qur'ān.[141] Bukhārī, for example, notes how the first stage of fetal formation ("sperm drop") begins with the collection of material for the body during the first forty days and forty nights. During the second stage ("clot of blood"), the sperm drop becomes a coagulum of thick blood for another forty days. The third stage ("lump of flesh") brings forth a more substantial piece of fleshy material for the same forty-day period. At this point, according to tradition, God sends an angel to the fetus to inscribe four things: her livelihood, her date of death, her deeds, and whether she will be a wretched one or a blessed one in the hereafter. Then the soul is breathed into her.[142] Some traditions note that one of the angelic inscriptions includes the determination of the child's sex,[143] although others suggest sex is differentiated earlier, just after the first forty-day period.[144]

Whatever the case, the Muslim exegetical tradition follows the Qur'ān by asserting infallible divine destiny is imprinted on the child *in utero,* even before the fetus becomes a life through God's breath: Would his limbs be full or imperfect? God makes them full and perfect or otherwise as he desires. What about his livelihood, death and disposition? God decides about his fortune/misfortune.[145] As the renowned traditionalist Muslim ibn al-Ḥajjāj (d. 875 CE) records: "There is none born but is created to his true nature . . . quite as beasts produce their young with their limbs perfect. Do you see anything deficient in them? Then he [the prophet] quoted the Qur'ān: The nature made by God in which he has created men, there is no altering of creation. That is the right religion" (30:33).[146] In theory, only God dictates each precise transformation a fetus undergoes, from his physical development, to his moral disposition, to the path he will eventually take in life. Ideally, nothing is left to chance, random occurrence, or human interference.

The Violable Maternal Body

Medieval Muslim physicians, however, recognize that pregnancies do not progress neatly along such nice, divinely determined paths laid out in the Qur'ān and confirmed by its exegetes. Drawing from Greek medical literature, Muslim physicians lay out the many potential hazards that challenge Qur'ānic and traditionalist accounts of what God has formed and inscribed in the deep recesses of a woman's womb. Physicians, for example, note how the transition from sperm drop to clot is inherently dangerous.[147] To reinforce this point, ʿArīb ibn Saʿd cites astrologists, who claim that since Saturn governs the drop of sperm during the first month (a star ruled by its coldness, dryness, and rottenness), it lies motionless and without sensation, vulnerable to random, natural elements, both internal and external.[148] Once this period of danger passes, he notes, the fetus will prevail over destruction and wasting away by will of God, at least until the eighth month.[149] Interestingly, this view defies the Qur'ānic position that God creates human life in discrete stages. God's power is undermined as forces of nature are shown to seize control of his procreative efforts, if men and women are not careful.

However, whether the time under consideration is before or after the first forty days, physicians acknowledge that the fetus is greatly susceptible to destruction throughout the entire gestational period. In order to comprehend how and why pregnancies fail, and who or what might be responsible for their failures, medieval medical writings devote much space to discussing miscarriages, which were believed to occur frequently and at the slightest provocation.

Physicians place the causes of miscarriage not in the hands of God, but deep within the maternal body. Such medical assertions counter the Qur'ān's position that God causes miscarriages to come about to signal some greater cataclysmic event, such as the onset of the Last Day. In the medical literature, pregnancies end not because God wants them to, but because women's bodies are inherently weak and not well suited for the challenge of bearing children. As a result of their weakness, men must be even more vigilant in ensuring reproductive success.[150]

For medieval physicians, the causes of miscarriage are many. For example, the mixed seed may or may not stick to the womb, especially if its membrane is too thin.[151] If there is too much moisture in the womb, the seed may simply slip out.[152] Miscarriages may also result from tumors in the womb, reductions in the embryo's nourishment, a drying up of the woman's blood, or a pushing on her breast.[153] Women may also abort as a result of their own corpulence, a fall, a strike, an increase in fatigue, an excess in their worrying or anxiety, a general weakness of the womb and its ligaments, an accumulation of sticky gastric juices that open up the uterus,[154] a hemorrhaging of blood, or even diarrhea.[155]

Miscarriages are also instigated by the more innocuous, everyday hazards a woman encounters in her daily life. For example, a woman may miscarry if she experiences a good fright or scare, or because she heard a loud sound or got too close to things that in her condition caused the fetus to be expelled.[156] A woman's cravings for foods that are unavailable for her to consume may also prompt a miscarriage.[157] In this case, her own, carnal desires distract her body from caring properly for the fetus. These examples illustrate how a woman's mental condition is impressed directly upon the fetus, which suggests her body is even in greater need of male expertise, discipline, and control to suppress or curb her emotions and appetites. Clearly, while the fetus is moving along a divinely ordained path, an unstable womb or even a woman's frivolity, hunger, or ignorance can do much to interfere with its orderly progression.

Given their near-obsessive interest in concocting ways to prevent miscarriages, it is evident Muslim physicians believe in most cases that God does not destine the fetus to die but rather that women do not take proper caution for or care of what they are carrying, or that women's bodies are simply not well equipped for the task. Because women often failed to bring a pregnancy to fruition, men needed to be that much more vigilant in protecting the fetus from female ignorance, carelessness, or weakness, or in devising ways to overcome the female body's inherent deficiencies. As a result of their concern, elite scholars rendered women incapable of caring for their own bodies.

For example, medieval physicians advise pregnant women to refrain from excess movement and jumping until they enter the second month. In some cases they prevent women from such mundane practices as walking, for fear the jiggling might loosen the seed from the womb.[158] Physicians also apprise men to refrain from mentioning foods their wives might crave, so that their insatiable desires may not prompt an expulsion of the fetus.[159] For example, men are instructed to substitute harmful forms of clay a woman might crave with the more preferable clay from Nashāstaj, which they mix with lettuce, endive, radish, and oxymel (*sakanjabīn*).[160] They are also advised to temper excess gas with pomegranate drinks fused with peppermint water, quince (*safarjal*) flavored with spices, or a beverage derived from cassia bark (*darṣīnī*)[161] to prevent preterm births. Rabbān al-Ṭabarī even prescribes a particular stone that men might attach to women that contains antidotes for miscarriage, a custom that stems from Jewish practice.[162] In all of these examples, men position themselves between women and God to take control of female frailties or the womb's "shadows of darkness," where, because of a woman's physiological or character insufficiencies, men feel the need to assist him in generating the life he commands.

Even when pregnancies do not result in miscarriages, much could still go wrong. For example, as the embryo develops, men feared a woman's womb might be too tight to accommodate normal growth. Rabbān al-Ṭabarī draws carefully the analogy to what happens when a young, flowering cucumber is placed in a narrow vessel. The cucumber expands in size and shape equal to the inside of the vessel. If the container is small and confined, then the child will also become small, or even weak.[163] Likewise, if a tree is forced to grow between stones, it is not destined to flourish. The stones in this case represent a small, cramped womb, which would choke off vital nourishment for the child and ultimately stunt its growth.[164]

Additionally, if healthy male sperm falls on an uneven or deviated womb, so too will the limbs of the fetus twist or fail to sprout altogether, as when liquid lead is poured into a crooked mold and the resulting product is likewise defectively fashioned.[165] In these examples, the womb, appearing as nothing more than a container, will either produce strong, healthy children or else generate inadequate life forms by literally squeezing or suffocating them to death. Women can do little to expand, hone, or modify their own deficient vessels so that they may properly accommodate a growing child. However, by claiming such intimate knowledge about the inadequacies of the maternal body, men are able to distance themselves from the responsibilities of generating malformed, sickly, or weak offspring. They are also able to shift the theological focus from a respect for God's inscrutable reasons to create whatever he wishes in the womb to a documenting of the causes of why women must be at fault for producing substandard offspring.

The Transparent Maternal Body

As the maternal body grows more and more violable in the eyes of medieval physicians, it also becomes increasingly transparent.[166] The transparency of the maternal body is evident in external signs that gave medieval scholars a window into what was happening internally, since these men were prevented from visually accounting for the hidden workings of the womb, and banned from the experience of pregnancy itself. The male scholar's revealing and reading of such "signs" functions in similar fashion to the modern obstetrician's analysis of the data produced by intrauterine pressure catheters, ultrasonic devices, and subcutaneous electrodes.[167] In the modern context, such reproductive technologies serve to promote "the consolidation and maintenance of scientific authority, as well as paternal privilege, promotion of the institutions of heterosexual marriage and the traditional family structure, the continued accumulation of profit for medical institutions, and the reproduction of men's objectification of women's bodies for cultural and social gain."[168] Likewise, medieval physicians cast the maternal body as a gage through which they could predict, control, or regulate the life they believed God desired.

Because the maternal body bore the auguries of the burgeoning fetus, maternal success or inadequacy would be apparent for all to see. In medieval medical texts, maternal success reveals itself through a number of external signs. For example, if a woman urinates on chickpea or lentil seeds planted in the ground and the plants grow, she is pregnant.[169] Here, the life within her is so bountiful and exuberant it can even generate life outside of her. Other tests include the fumigation of a woman's vagina with incense[170] or some other powerful substance such as garlic.[171] If the scent comes out of her nostrils, she is pregnant, because it is clear to all that the channels from the womb up to the mouth have opened wide so that blood may flow freely to the fetus. Another pregnancy test includes a woman imbibing honey blended with water before she sleeps. If she gets colic upon awaking, she is pregnant. The idea here is that the womb wraps itself around the sperm, which causes cramping, discomfort, and gas.[172] A sign of conception also becomes manifest when the mouth to the womb turns dry right after coitus,[173] for it is prevented from receiving more sperm.

Scholars note that a woman's face will also give away her condition. ʿArīb ibn Saʿd, quoting Hippocrates, states that a woman is pregnant if her eyes are sunken deep and their whites change from their natural color to a discolored form. Signs of conception also include trembling at the time of intercourse, a slight pain below the navel, an increase in breast size, and a dusty-colored face.[174] Through their ability to discern and interpret such external signs, men's knowledge and expertise of the maternal body take precedence over women's experience, and, to some extent, God's omniscience. In contrast to the Qurʾān, medical writings allow men to insert themselves between God and the womb in order to usurp an intimate and mysterious partnership previously inaccessible to them. They also demonstrate their command of the scientific knowledge God has mastered, but ultimately transcended.

The maternal body also exposes the sex of the child to its male audience, whose novel expertise allows them to read the signs. Medieval medical scholars put forth the idea that the excess heat associated with the male fetus permeates the entire maternal body, as did the cold connected with the female fetus. Rabbān al-Ṭabarī, for example, asserts that if the color of a woman is splendid and beautiful, the fetus she is carrying is a male; if her color is ugly and greenish, the fetus is a female.[175] ʿArīb ibn Saʿd elaborates these observations by suggesting a woman who is carrying a male will be agile in movement, and cheerful and intelligent in soul.[176] He also adds that a mother who is carrying a female will experience general unhappiness, a dulling of the senses, a sluggishness in movement, and a corruption and greening of her skin.[177]

Ḥamdallāh Mustawfī Qazwīnī (fl. 1330–1340 CE), who compiled the most famous zoological works of the time period, under the regime of Abū Saʿīd Bahādur Khān, asserts that gender may be determined by a man's squeezing out a bit of a woman's breast milk on the palm of his hand, and then casting a louse into it. If the louse makes its way out, the child will be a girl, if not, a boy, since the milk of a woman who carries a girl is thin and that of one who carries a boy is thick.[178]

Further, if the woman scratches the right side of the breast or womb, she bears a male. Or, if her right breast is larger than her left, especially her nipple, and if all the blood vessels on her right half are harder and fuller than the vessels on the left half (especially the veins under the tongue), the child will be male.[179] A woman raising her right foot upon walking carries a male; her left, a female.[180] When fat accumulates on the right side of the womb, the child will be male, if on the left, female.[181] If a woman finds a heaviness on the right side of the womb, and she prods it, and her eye moves to the right, the child is a male, the opposite a female.[182]

Even if she tries to hide such revealing characteristics, a woman is rendered incapable of concealing what is flourishing within. By marking the mother's external form with signs of its own identity, the fetus transforms the maternal body to expose itself to its true owners—the male observers whose sperm works in partnership with God to generate life—and to place its livelihood, care, and future in their hands. As a result, both mother and child become subject to male propriety, scrutiny, and control.

The transparent maternal body not only reveals its successes, but sadly, too, its failures or inadequacies. For example, Rabbān al-Ṭabarī suggests that if a woman is not bearing children, her urine should be cast upon a head of lettuce. If the lettuce dries up, her seed is corrupt.[183] Here, urine that kills a living plant shows evidence of a body incapable of supporting life.[184] Physicians note also how the female body bears the signs of the death within it; as the child inside her begins to decline, a woman's appearance transforms from one of glowing health to distorted sickliness. Her breasts shrivel,[185] her eyes grow sunken, her face, body, and legs swell, her ears and nose turn white, and her lips become green.[186] A woman cannot even hide what she consumes; what she eats shows up on her child's body, apparent for all to witness. For example, whenever a woman satisfies her cravings by consuming clay (*ṭīn*) or coal (*faḥm*), those materials literally stick to the child's head, causing an abnormal defect.[187]

Nowhere is the maternal body more transparent—and, in fact, inconsequential—than in the case of dream interpretation. In these examples, men transfer female procreative power and experience to themselves through their own abilities to seize particular dreams that indicate desired reproductive outcomes. Dreams are not just passive signs revealing what has already come to pass; rather, they appear to provide the means through which certain men can directly interfere with the inner workings of the pregnant body.

Damīrī suggests that one who is able to seize the image of a rare bird (*anqā'*) in a dream may become the father of a courageous son, if his wife is pregnant.[188] Likewise, if his wife is carrying a child, a man who dreams of taking a lion to his lap will be blessed with a boy.[189] For men with expectant wives, birds of prey,[190] unstrung pearls,[191] and calves[192] also invoke male children; scorpions in the belly indicate hostile offspring.[193] If a man dreams of a fish coming forth from his pudendum, his pregnant wife will give birth to a girl.[194]

Dreams also have the power to affect negatively a pregnancy. If a man dreams a lump of congealed blood comes out of his nose, penis, arms, belly, or mouth, his wife will abort the fetus before it has completely formed.[195] Through the very act of dreaming, the husband is able to take control of his pregnant wife's body and dictate a fetus' sex, prescribe its disposition, or expel it through his own orifices. In these cases of dream interpretation, the flesh concealing the maternal body becomes so translucent as to dissolve, which allows men to assume female procreative power for themselves in order to redirect reproductive outcomes to their own desired ends.

In all of these examples involving the transparent maternal body, medical literature turns what the Qur'ān asserts to be a moral law, "that it is unlawful for [women] to conceal what God creates in their wombs" (Sūra 2:28), into natural law. Because men now deem themselves responsible for bearing the life God commands, they no longer allow women the choice or opportunity to conceal what they hold deep within their wombs.[196] In fact, Muslim ibn al-Ḥajjāj's authoritative collection of *ḥadīth* takes this Qur'ānic prohibition one step further to assert that those whose mothers veiled them in the womb are themselves evil.[197] In order to avoid such hazards, male medical scholars expose the maternal body through natural signs, which allow men to appropriate a mother's reproductive power and experience. Thus, unlike in the Qur'ān, where God works directly with, in, and through women to create and nurture life, men now insert themselves between women and God to usurp his creative powers in order to realize his will.

Premature Births: The Eighth-Month Child

If women are able to maneuver their burdens successfully through the many obstacles that threaten the livelihood of their fetus during the early months of gestation, more danger awaits them toward the end of their pregnancies. According to ʿArīb ibn Saʿd, women are pregnant for approximately nine to nine and one-half lunar months.[198] Fetuses that are born before or after this time period may live but are often subject to disease or even death. For example, physicians assert a fetus cannot live in the womb after 288 days.[199] Some women believe they might be pregnant for ten or eleven months, but medical scholars suggest their ignorance or misunderstanding is due to air coming down from the belly during coitus that bloats the womb or blocks the menses.[200] Here, scholars portray women as being confused or misguided by their own bodies. Men alone hold knowledge superior to a woman's actual experience of her physical self. Unlike Mary, who bore Jesus without the help or advice of any man, ordinary women in these examples seem incapable of navigating their own bodies through pregnancy and birth.

Physicians all agree that babies born during the eighth month had the least chance of survival. The eighth month is a period of great liminality, the moment where the child begins to position itself for delivery. As it begins to move down in the uterus, the fetus becomes subject to a variety of diseases.[201] ʿArīb ibn Saʿd notes how the natural progression of the growing, seventh-month fetus down into the uterus causes the surrounding membrane to tear and turn weak. These tears and weaknesses cause the womb to convulse and the umbilicus to stretch during the eighth month, which induces great pain or fevers for both mother and fetus, and makes them susceptible to weakness, illness, disease, and death.[202]

To avoid such disasters, men urge women to exercise great caution during the eighth month by avoiding fatigue, bad food, baths, and excessive sneezes.[203] Strangely, medical scholars believed that babies born prematurely in the sixth or seventh month had a better chance at life than did children born during the eighth month.[204] While they may be thin, weak, and bear the burdens of physical limitations for some time,[205] these premature babies somehow do not fall prey to the same types of calamities and diseases as do those born during the eighth month.[206]

The peculiar belief that the eighth-month child would be in greater danger than the seventh-month child is rooted in numerology. In the ancient world, the number seven had positive connotations as it was a primary number and therefore more powerful, while the number eight did not.[207] For example, the Hippocratics assert the seventh-month child thrives because of the inherent properties and qualities of the number seven.[208] A healthy, full-term baby will be born at 280 days, which represents a cycle of seven periods of forty days.[209] Likewise, ʿArīb ibn Saʿd notes the seventh month is governed by the moon, which has quick movements, while the eighth month by Saturn, which is cold, dry and rotten. Saturn will silence the fetus and cause it to become ill.[210] In these examples, the inherent qualities of numbers, or the planets, rather than the divine will, dictate whether or not a pregnancy will be successful.

Ironically, the eighth month may be a period of great danger, but those children who are born during this time and survive, and the mothers who deliver them, are often those who hold an elevated status in the medieval Islamic tradition. The most famous eighth-month child is Jesus, son of Mary, whose birth during this dark and treacherous time serves as a sign for all of God's creation. However, scholars are quick to note that he was the last; no child born after the eighth month from that time forward would live.[211] Other traditions also feature infamous eighth-month births. For example, the Christian saint Felicitas delivered a viable child during the eighth month so that she could experience the joys of martyrdom.[212] For most women, however, a premature delivery during the eighth month exposes their inability to carry a child to term.

The Perils of Parturition

Both mother and child face even more perils as the child is ready to be born. Medieval Muslim literature offers many traditional accounts of both mothers and children perishing through the very process of giving birth or being born. Sad and grief-laden images of dead babies, women, and children abound; there is great sympathy in the early Muslim tradition for the pain and agony a family will suffer as a result. Muḥammd ibn Yazīd ibn Māja's (d. 887 CE) authoritative *Sunan*, for example, notes that pregnant women who die in childbirth become martyrs.[213] Women who lose at least three small children automatically are elevated to paradise as well.[214] Newborns and those young ones who are still breastfeeding will ascend straight to the Garden upon death, along with martyrs, prophets, and the infant girls buried alive.[215] Clearly, survival for both mother and child was feared to be the exception to the rule. In the medical literature, death, though sometimes avoidable, is always an ever-present, inherent side effect of childbirth.

Although some scholars deem it legal for male physicians to look upon the forbidden parts of a woman during childbirth,[216] it is more likely that midwives attended women in labor. The fact that men did not witness the actual birth of the child, however, did not stop them from speculating on the difficulties and dangers mothers, their midwives, and the child itself were certain to face during this perilous process. Therefore, they lay out detailed instructions for both mothers and midwives to ensure the successful birth of a healthy child.

For example, physicians predict women may faint from their labor pains, so they command midwives to keep the mother conscious throughout her delivery.[217] They discuss how the baby's legs might appear before its head, or the fetus may come out on its side, or be obstructed altogether.[218] If the legs come out first, the midwife must manually turn the entire body around, which might lead to immediate death of both mother and child from the twisting and pressure, or elicit other illnesses and maladies.[219] If the hand[220] of the fetus comes out together with the head, physicians portend the mother will suffer greatly. In this case, physicians instruct the midwife to push the fetus back inside, straighten or flatten it out, and then gently push out its head. If the head comes out but the rest of the body does not follow, the midwife may have to twist the baby's entire body around again and pull the legs out first.[221]

Medieval physicians do not always possess great confidence in the midwife's expertise. They observe, for example, that some midwives manipulate the heads of fetuses so roughly that their shapes become distorted. They note further that if the midwife fails to conduct even one of her movements properly, the mother may die.[222] One scholar even goes so far as to suggest only God, and not the midwife, can successfully flip a breech baby around in the womb by sending forth a special wind (*rīḥ*) to do the job.[223] Clearly, a midwife's skills can only take her so far under the critical and watchful eyes of male physicians. She must rely in part on the scientific knowledge imparted by men to deliver life successfully, although in reality she would most likely draw upon her own experience and expertise.[224]

Here, too, mothers are portrayed as knowing little about what takes place during labor, or what happens after their children are born. In the medical texts, they are portrayed as being totally reliant on both the midwife and the male physicians who guide her. Fortunately, the laborious maternal body, which has become severed from a woman's own identity, imparts signs that only experts can read. For example, some scholars suggest if labor pains are located in the pubic region and belly, labor will be smooth; if there are pains in her backbone, labor will be difficult.[225]

Difficult labor may also be associated with the delivery of a female as opposed to a male. Scholars note how male and female babies exit the womb in the positions taken by their mothers and fathers during coitus: male children lie face downward while females lie face upward,[226] which makes for a more difficult labor and delivery.[227] Additionally, because females were considered moister and colder than males, and less able to move, their delivery took longer than that of males, as they could do little to help pull themselves out of the birth canal.[228] Again, transparent maternal bodies reveal much about the level of a woman's pain during labor, which is often tied to the sex of the child. Upon seeing such signs (as relayed through the midwife), physicians with their expertise would then offer remedies to assuage their suffering, in a way similar to how God came to Mary's aid during her parturiency.[229]

Medieval Muslim scholars can also read the signs on a woman's postpartum body and predict whether or not she would be a successful breastfeeder. They noted that a woman with large breasts would fail because the excess flesh would prevent the tongue of the infant from sucking. Women with small breasts would likewise fail, as their inadequate size would inhibit an infant from being able to suck.[230] Even a woman's demeanor is read and monitored with great care. Ḥunayn ibn Isḥāq, for example, observes that women become soft-hearted, languid, and gentle after bearing children, because their natures are weak and during delivery they lose a great deal of blood.[231] He observes how a woman's physical ordeal during labor and delivery is essential to transforming her into an ideal mother. As her body embraces all the passive, gentle, submissive qualities of the perfect mother upon giving birth, she becomes more and more dependent upon men to protect her.

Mapping the Maternal Body

These examples demonstrate how medieval Muslim physicians mapped "natural" reproductive processes and the maternal body according to social, cultural, and theological assumptions about the subordinate status of women. Such assumptions about the weakness of women's bodies, their in/ability to care for or nurture the life within, and their natural tendency to fall into moral or physical decay all challenge the more privileged reproductive roles of women in the Qurʾān, and reinforce its more traditional understandings of women as subordinate to men. In these examples, medical scholars emphasize the seed/soil relationship between men and women, and suggest the womb/soil itself must be heavily monitored and controlled so as not to corrupt or subvert God's procreative plans as transferred through male seed.

The medical literature describes in detail how male scholars take it upon themselves to assert knowledge and control over the maternal body to ensure the successful life that God commands. As men take ownership over her body through their unique ability to know, control, and interpret the signs it reveals, a woman is severed from her own identity, experience, and unique relationship with God. What emerges from the medical discourse are more traditional roles for both men and women. Such traditional roles are not only reinforced via "science" and "nature," as this chapter suggests, but through the Muslim exegetical tradition's treatment of ideal, pious mothers who embody the perfected traits all women should emulate, but most likely cannot. How biological visions of the maternal body become manifest in paradigmatic constructions of pious mothers is the subject of chapter 3.

3

Paradigms of the Good Mother

Muslim exegetical writings draw upon the Qur'ān but flesh out further its basic, revelatory proclamations with expansive details from the prophet's biography (*sīra*), medical wisdom, law, and tales from the *isrā'īlīyāt*.[1] In the context of filling in the narratives surrounding Qur'ānic references to human reproduction and motherhood, these authoritative, prescriptive, and folkloric writings hone further the paradigms of the good mother along patriarchal lines. In general, medieval Muslim theologians, legalists, and exegetes identify four women whom they elevate above all others. Through extensive elaborations of their lives, these scholars depict this group of prodigious women—Mary, Āsiya, Khadīja, and Fāṭima—as embodying a variety of flawless maternal physiologies, virtues, and behaviors that conform to patriarchal ideals of subordination to God, and, just as importantly, to the male prophets, fathers, husbands, or children these women are fated to serve in their reproductive capacities. As such, the Qur'ān's many snapshots of God's polyvalent procreative powers and its open-ended visions of the real and ideal mother give way to more hierarchical structures of reproductive power, where women may bear offspring, but only men have the generative power to garner the superlative life God desires.

Narratives depicting the lives of Mary, Āsiya, Khadīja, and Faṭima, whom the *ḥadīth* deem to be the "best among women," reveal how exegetes and other male theologians, philosophers, and legal scholars construct images of "good mothers" who are defenders of the faith, purified in womb, and subordinate to God, the men who guide them, and the male children they attend. In theory, all mothers must seek to embody the same moral and physical "goodness" as these four women because they, too, provide the vessels in which perfected male sperm begets life. Because women's bodies are inherently weak and their piety often suspect, however, it becomes incumbent upon men to make sure their sperm falls upon virtuous ground if they are to realize God's procreative commands.

For example, Ghazālī instructs believers to marry wives of a good lineage so that the children they produce will also be of a stellar quality. If a potential bride is not well-bred, she will be unable to raise her children well. He recalls the prophet as saying, "'Beware of the green dung [*khaḍra al-diman*].' It was asked, 'What is the green dung?' He said, 'The beautiful woman with an evil origin.' The prophet continued, 'Exercise care in choosing wives for your sperm, for a [bad] hereditary quality is wont to return.'"[2] Clearly, bad wombs engender bad children, either morally or physically, no matter how superior the quality of male sperm. In order to produce good children, a mother's womb must be made to conform to the perfected standards embodied by the heavenly queens as much as possible. Texts containing authoritative medieval exegesis, law, and theology, therefore, outline the parameters of perfected and pious wombs that will serve as the best of all possible vessels to house and nurture the flawless male sperm they receive.

In their detailed depictions of the four paradisiacal mothers, medieval scholars map the ideal womb ordinary women must strive to attain so that men may avoid the "green dung" and be blessed with numerous and righteous children. For example, Mary, the mother of the prophet Jesus, displays an unrivaled purity and an unflinching faith as she conceives her son out of wedlock when God commands, and bears him alone in pain and hardship. Although not a biological mother, Āsiya, Pharaoh's wife who lived during the time of the prophet Moses, resists her husband's tyranny, rejection of God, and physical abuse to rescue, nurture, and rear a future prophet. Khadīja, the prophet's first wife and mother of his genealogical line, forges the links between belief in God, service to his prophet, and a prolific womb, even in old age. Fāṭima, according to the Shīʿites, was conceived pure from the fruits of paradise to secure her father Muḥammad's genealogy and to go on to become the mother of martyrs who sacrifice themselves for the faith.

Through the very act of narrating these four women's life stories, medieval male elites transform ordinary female bodies into paragons of absolute perfection by which they measure the deficiencies of all other mothers. By purifying bodies from the dross of menstruation or an appetite for sex, curbing the agonies associated with pregnancy and childbirth, and removing any physical weaknesses or moral failings, medieval exegetes carve out pristine wombs through which men, and God, may acquire desired progeny. Good mothers, therefore, represent perfected and purified vessels that reflect and facilitate male procreative plans that, at least in theory, reflect the divine will. They faithfully offer up their wombs to bear or nurture righteous children, and unselfishly serve the young prophets, husbands, fathers, and scholars whose difficult task it becomes to navigate often flawed, faulty, or insubordinate female morals and physiologies to ensure that the will of God is realized.

Within medieval exegetical discourse, each exemplary mother is either explicitly or implicitly compared to ʿĀʾisha, the prophet Muḥammad's youngest wife, whose personal history reinforces but also challenges masculine ideologies of bodily perfection and subordination. ʿĀʾisha is nowhere described as being the "best among women" but rather as "the superiority of *tharīd* to other meals," *tharīd* being a dish made of bread soaked in broth.[3] Falling short of being the "best," ʿĀʾisha is clearly set apart from the other four women. Why she is often excluded from the list of four may have to do with her sterility, a bodily imperfection that in her case—contrary to the Qurʾān's depiction of the prophet's wives' barren righteousness—is equated with impiety, jealousy, and her own claims to authority, power, and wisdom within the tradition. These "facts" embroidered into her biographical narrative, at least at the outset, do little to contribute to the maternal ideal envisioned by male elites.

Despite ʿĀʾisha's apparent shortcomings, foibles, and general insubordination, however, many medieval exegetes continue to stress the prophet's unyielding support and love for her. In this light, the complaints, reproductive disappointments, and jealousies she is often faulted for reinforce but also undermine the patriarchal paradigms of perfection impressed upon her, and provide another path to God for women whose bodies and minds strive to emulate but never quite conform to those of the paradisiacal queens. In their struggles to come to terms with their often heartwrenching reproductive fates, ordinary mothers such as ʿĀʾisha may still embody God's will by engaging in similar battles for the faith undertaken by the "best among women," contrary to what much of the scholarly discourse implies.

The Perfected Women of Paradise

Medieval Muslim tradition provides lists of the perfected women of paradise that include various combinations of Mary,[4] Āsiya,[5] Khadīja,[6] and Fāṭima.[7] The qualities of these four women are evaluated in a variety of different ways. Muḥammad ibn ʿAbdallāh al-Kisāʾī (d. 1002 CE), the collector of folkloric tales about the prophets transmitted by popular preachers (*quṣṣās*) that had wide public appeal, for example, notes all four appear as being even more consummately beautiful than the dark-eyed houris of paradise.[8] In his own famous literary work, *Stories of the Prophets,* which falls into the same popular genre as Kisāʾī's, Ibn Kathīr moves away from their outward appearance to suggest Mary and Āsiya are praised because they both raised young prophets.[9] He notes Khadīja could also be rendered perfect because she, even more than Muḥammad's own mother, tended to the needs of the prophet for twenty-five years.[10] She sacrificed her own wealth and property for him, and comforted him during times of trial. Fāṭima also falls into this category for she helped her father Muḥammad in his mission and fought against Meccan persecution. Shīʿites, of course, elevate her over all other women (except, perhaps, Mary) for generating the prophet's genealogical line.

Ibn Kathīr argues that ʿĀʾisha, too, might also be considered as perfect as the other four, since she was Muḥammad's most beloved wife. She was the only virgin he married, she was intelligent and knowledgeable in matters of religion, Qurʾānic verses were revealed on her behalf, and she carried forth Muḥammad's message after his death.[11] Given these laudable qualities, it is strange that scholars rarely add ʿĀʾisha to the list of four paradisiacal women, but rather place her in a special category. Though praiseworthy, the superiority of *tharīd* still falls short of the "best."

Lurking beneath their lack of enthusiasm for ʿĀʾisha's candidacy is, perhaps, her barren womb. Outside the depiction of the prophet's wives in the Qurʾān, barrenness often serves as a mark against women unless they show some exceptional measure of piety, submission, or sacrifice to God's will. After all, the Qurʾān often links sterility with divine punishment.[12] Because ʿĀʾisha's womb resisted her own desires to bear the prophet's progeny, scholars speculate that perhaps God's refusal to bestow his mercies upon her had to do with a less than steadfast piety, an unwillingness to subordinate herself completely to both God and men, and a general unfitness for motherhood. Whatever the case, ʿĀʾisha falls short of the patriarchal vision of the maternal ideal so favored by the male elite. However, because most women will never be blessed with the conceiving, bearing, or nurturing of God's prophets, the life of ʿĀʾisha offers an alternative model of maternal piety that bypasses the male ideal to weave the reproductive struggles of ordinary women into the larger context of a lived faith.

Maryam bint ʿImrān, Willing Receptacle for "Our Spirit"

Most medieval scholars agree that Mary serves as quintessential mother.[13] As such, her womb stands as the consummate vessel to receive God's word, spirit, and/or prophet Jesus outside the normal course of human sexual intercourse. Following the Qur'ān, exegetes assert that Mary's own piety and purity play a major role in forming her exceptional status as receiver of God's word and willing bearer of his signs. They conclude that her piety and purity stem from the same factors intimated by the Qur'ān: predestination, a privileged genealogical line, her well-guarded chastity, and her extraordinary obedience to God.[14] Unlike the Qur'ān's emphasis on Mary's reflexive agency in cultivating a piety that mirrors divine fate and expectation, medieval exegetes intimate her overall "fitness" to conceive Jesus in many ways depends upon male assistance in the form of patronage, knowledge, and protection to ensure she fulfills God's intended path.

For example, while the Qur'ān allows for Mary's free acceptance of her fate to carry out God's will, and even dwells on her exclamations of pain and regret as she is called upon to bear life alone,[15] many medieval scholars and theologians assert that her feminine vulnerabilities in no way interfered with the divine plan. In other words, while maintaining that Mary's body was, for the most part, that of an ordinary woman, they strive to control or even eliminate the vagaries and realities of Mary's biological and religious life that might have thwarted, compromised, or contradicted the preordained outcome. As in the case of Muslim physicians, who seek to assert the power of medical wisdom over maternal bodies, traditional scholars and exegetes strive to impress a more perfected ideal of purity, piety, and obedience onto the biological bodies of all women—including Mary's—as they are measured over and against the mother of Jesus's ideally constructed life.

The Qur'ānic Mary

As summarized in chapter 1, Mary the mother of Jesus had to confront the difficulties and responsibilities of conceiving a child outside of wedlock, when no man had touched her. She guarded her womb against any unlawful entry, yet, like the earth itself, opened herself freely to God's spirit. While the labor pains she endured before delivering Jesus were so great that she cried out, "Oh, would death have overcome me before this,"[16] she nevertheless suffered through them alone under the trunk of the palm tree. Mary, in fact, is even granted a kind of divine authority to command the date tree to bend low so that she may resuscitate herself through its fruits.[17] This authority stems from her unique status of willing bearer of God's word.

Mary's response to God's efforts through her willingness to endure the pain and suffering required of her becomes a virtue to which all women can aspire, despite the fact that they will never be called upon to bear one of God's prophets without a husband. In fact, Sūra 32:7–9 suggests ordinary women repeatedly mimic the role of Mary as their wombs, too, receive the "water despised" (*mā'in mahīnin*) into which God's spirit, via the breath, is blown (*nafakha fīhi min rūḥihi*). What separates these women from Mary is obviously the lack of intimate interaction with God, and his choosing of them for an exceptional task. For ordinary women, men now take the place of God as lover through a reenactment of this extraordinary event, although males cannot, of their own volition, generate the animating life force that holds the spirit. The response of women to the divine breath entering their bodies via male sperm, however, must still reflect that of Mary's, as only God, and not men, can generate life.

Even though the Qur'ān holds that Mary's reproductive success was inextricably tied to God's choice and protection, there was still room for agency as she alone protected her *farj* and accepted her lot. However, these Qur'ānic narratives, when framed within the medieval exegetical works that single out Mary as the quintessential mother, have the adverse effect of limiting her own efforts, and creating insurmountable barriers between the mother of Jesus and ordinary women who wish to conceive and bear a righteous child as easily as Mary. The exegetical idealization of chaste, asexual behavior undermines the erotic intimacy and exchange involved in the mutual, procreative act between God and Mary, along with Mary's free compliance to God's will. It also casts into sharp relief the ordinary female body that, unchosen, must engage in carnal practices with men—rather than the divine breath—who now command a woman's reproductive fate.

As confirmed by the medical literature, attempts by ordinary women to reproduce a healthy life were viewed as only marginally successful, and required strict conformity to male authoritative claims, unlike Mary's solitary, fruitful encounter depicted in the Qur'ān. Therefore, the average woman would have to ponder if her own impiety, impurity, or insubordination to male control were preventing her from conceiving or carrying a child to term. After all, in contrast with Mary, whose purity and chastity stem from her chosen status, most women face the daunting prospect of cultivating similar virtues on their own without divine help, intimacy, privilege, or intervention. The fact that traditional commentary often underscores Mary's humanity in the face of such perfection only places a further burden on ordinary women to achieve a maternal ideal that should, in theory, be wholly attainable.

The Exegetical Mary

In conformity with the Qur'ān, medieval exegetes all cast Mary as an ideal mother; in fact, according to many Qur'ānic commentators, her name means "pious."[18] Although every scholar maintains that Mary was extraordinary, they do not suggest she in any way breached the boundaries of her humanity.[19] She is not even considered a prophet.[20] However, many pious men debate the extent to which her body was analogous to that of ordinary women, given her exceptional piety. The results of their speculations are mixed. Some exegetical writings tend to suppress her human nature to emphasize her unique status as mother of Jesus. After all, any human who is chosen by God to carry forth his procreative plans must somehow transcend her own limited, bodily capacities, the assumption being that God's breath would never directly grace an ordinary woman. As a result, Mary can be admired but not fully emulated.

By way of contrast, other traditional voices highlight her humanity to demonstrate her pious actions are readily, but not easily, attainable by all women. Because they accentuate her human nature, these scholars tend to undermine the receptive, participatory role Mary embraces as a result of her physical interactions with God in order to preserve both his transcendence and her modesty. Good women would not expose their wombs to such an erotic exchange, whether divinely sanctioned or not.

In order to preserve further female chastity, piety, and the integrity of divine transcendence, most exegetes insert the angel Gabriel as a buffer between Mary and God. For example, Ṭabarī, like other exegetes, recounts how Gabriel appeared to Mary in the shape of a beardless youth with a shining face and curly hair to announce the birth of a male child. However, rather than having that male form blow the spirit directly into her *farj*, an erotic, sexual encounter between spirit and flesh, he breathed it into the fold of her garment, which she had removed (conveniently) and cast aside. It was only after Gabriel departed that Mary put the garment on and became pregnant.[21]

Likewise, Ibn Kathīr notes how a number of companions report that Gabriel, averting his eyes in modesty, blew directly into her breast or chest, and from there the air passed down into her vagina.[22] As a result, no direct, sexual contact between Mary and God, or Mary and Gabriel, ever occurred. Clearly, the traditional accounts work to preserve a particular, human understanding of God's transcendence and Mary's bodily integrity despite Qurʾānic proclamations suggesting otherwise. A chaste, asexual exchange between a young woman and an angel, or better yet, a cloak, was far preferable to an erotic, intimate encounter with a God who calls into question his own transcendence via his quick breath that penetrates receptive female flesh.[23] The result of such descriptive efforts to preserve Mary's chastity and righteous intentions further idealizes her in relation to her earthly counterparts, who must engage in carnal relations with men to conceive.

On Mary's Selection

Medieval exegetes are unified in their claim that Mary was destined for greatness even before she was born. For example, many scholars tie Mary's exceptional status to her family, which is rooted in the genealogies of Abraham and ʿImrān. This genealogical line is lauded above all others because the families were all pious people of *islām*.[24] Some scholars more inclined to gnostic interpretations argue that these special individuals even received a kind of spiritual breath within the womb that separated them from all other peoples.[25] Presumably this breath would have been different from the one depicted in the Qurʾān that animates all human life.[26] In either case, whether achieved through piety or genetics, the family of ʿImrān, daughters and sons alike, were destined to do wondrous things. By embedding Mary within a divinely privileged genealogical framework, medieval scholars make the extraordinary piety that prompted the conception of Jesus even that much more unattainable for ordinary women. However, hers is still the model by which ordinary mothers are measured as they try to avoid the fate of the "green dung."

The exegetes also treat the exceptional circumstances surrounding the actions of Mary's mother before her daughter was born as contributing to her daughter's privileged condition. Although they make no rhetorical claims that Mary was "immaculately conceived,"[27] medieval scholars still propose the events that led to Mary's birth were far from ordinary. For example, Mary's mother Ḥanna, like Abraham's consort before her and Zakarīyā's wife, had been barren well into old age. However, after viewing signs of fertility in the world around her, her fate was about to change.[28] One day, Ḥanna saw a bird feeding its young. She yearned for offspring, praying that God would grant her a child. Miraculously, as he did for Abraham and Zakarīyā, God answered her prayers, and she conceived Mary. After her husband died, Ḥanna vowed to dedicate the child in her womb to the service of God and the temple, where the young child, presumably a boy, would live in total isolation.[29]

It was Ḥanna's unflinching devotion to God, generated from her own will, that evoked God's engendering response. Ḥanna as depicted in these examples resembles closely the biblical Ḥanna, who also prayed to God for a child; upon conceiving Samuel, she, too, dedicated him to service in the temple.[30] Perhaps this parallel tale explains why Ḥanna the mother of Mary had been expecting a boy. Whatever the case, both examples underscore how God rewards exceptional piety with offspring, even when that piety is demonstrated by a woman.[31] Medieval exegetes thus privilege a particular reading of the Qurʾān that highlights the causal connection between piety and progeny without taking into account those passages that sever the link between the two: God creates in wombs whatever, and however, he pleases.[32] For elite scholars, good women need only to pray, and then they, too, will conceive.

Once Ḥanna saw she had delivered a girl, she was profoundly disappointed. In fact, Maḥmūd ibn ʿUmar al-Zamakhsharī (d. 1144 CE), the prominent Muʿtazilite commentator on the Qurʾān, notes in his discussion of Sūra 3:36 that ʿImrān's wife even feels sorrow for having delivered a female instead of a male, since she assumes God would have no use for her offering once he realizes the sex of the child.[33] Both the Qurʾān and many of its commentators note how it would have been highly unusual—even unnatural—for women to serve the temple. For example, Ṭabarī reports how males are simply more capable of enduring the hardship of temple service than females since they are physically stronger. He adds that females would also be incapable of serving the temple properly because of the impurities associated with menstruation and parturition, which of course, males did not have to endure.[34]

Obviously, Mary's exceptional physical constitution allowed her to fulfill successfully her obligations in the temple. Other commentators underscore this point by asserting Mary's femaleness was not a mistake but actually a gift from God. God knew all along what Ḥanna was carrying and welcomed her daughter's service in the temple.[35] Daughters, of course, are praised throughout the exegetical literature since Muḥammad was the proud and loving father of four.[36] Whatever the case, medieval scholars seal Mary's unique status by linking her privileged position with her mother's exemplary devotion to God.[37] Mary's prodigious nature becomes the unattainable standard by which all women are measured as they struggle to imitate her praiseworthy piety, which stems from fate, an exceptional physical nature, and her mother's extraordinary faith.

In addition to her praiseworthy heritage, Mary's distinctive status is further molded through assertions about her physical perfection, purity, and obedience. Medieval scholars confirm Mary's physical perfection and purity in a number of ways. For example, Ṭabarī, in conformity with the Qurʾān, emphasizes how Mary and her son Jesus were protected from the stab of Satan's finger at birth, a pain endured by all human infants that renders them susceptible to the devil's wiles. Such assertions inoculate both Jesus and his mother from the sins the rest of Adam's children are destined to commit.[38] By protecting Mary from engaging in any potential wrongdoing, male scholars constrict her ability to assert her own agency in ways that might challenge God's procreative intentions, and her own worthiness to realize them.

Medieval scholars also confirm Mary's ideal maternal role through their rhetorical purification of her body to make it a more suitable vessel for God's generative plans. For example, Ashʿarite commentator Fakhr al-Dīn al-Rāzī (d. 1209 CE) reports how, as a baby, Mary never nursed at the breast; rather, she received sustenance directly from paradise.[39] Since medieval scholars believe breast milk was converted menstrual fluid, which is, in fact, unformed semen, Mary's purified nature would have been compromised had she been allowed to ingest such earthly impurities. Again, these exegetes construct a maternal narrative no woman could possibly fulfill on her own without the help of the divine hand.

Miraculous events and other wondrous signs also confirm Mary's extraordinary nature. Mary, like her son Jesus, spoke in infancy.[40] The Mālikite Qur'ān commentator from Córdoba, Abū ʿAbdallāh al-Qurṭubī (d. 1230 CE), further underscores her exceptionality by noting how God made her of consummate stature, so that she grew up in one day as a child would grow in a year.[41] Kisā'ī notes she was also incredibly beautiful.[42] Damīrī suggests that Mary was so idyllic she never ingested impure foods, such as those tainted with blood. He recalls how Mary asked her Lord to feed her with flesh free of blood, so God plied her with locusts.[43] Such embedded details convert her body from that of an ordinary woman who cries out her regrets for having to bear a child out of wedlock into a locus of pristine signs for men to interpret and fashion according to their own perceptions of an ideal mother.

The exegetical demand for Mary's purity and perfection led to some debate among traditional scholars as to whether or not Mary would have been subject to menstruation. Rāzī and others illuminate reports of Mary being free from all impurities associated with menstruation and parturition.[44] For these scholars, her bodily purity necessarily rendered a womb most suitable to conceive the baby Jesus. As noted among medieval physicians, remnants of menstrual blood in the womb may lead to a child who suffers from epilepsy or other physical challenges.[45]

In contrast, however, other scholars such as Zamakhsharī emphasize how Mary both menstruated and endured a full forty days of postpartum bleeding after she delivered Jesus.[46] Here, Mary may have boasted an ordinary, impure womb but somehow her extraordinary piety was able to overcome any deficiencies associated with it to provide the exceptional environment necessary to receive God's breath, spirit, and word. Good mothers must be disposed similarly to a purified womb or equally excellent in pious behavior to conceive and nurture successfully the male sperm required to generate a healthy and righteous child.

Whether or not scholars agree that Qur'ānic references to Mary's purity refer to her physical composition, they all accept the pristine intent of her obedience and submission. For example, according to Ṭabarī, Mary's purification refers not to her body but to the cleansing of her faith from all doubts and impurities that plague the rest of Adam's children.[47] Qurṭubī confirms this interpretation by noting that when the spirit spoke to her, she assented to the words of God and did not have to ask for a sign.[48] This subordinate acquiescence to God's request without pause or question illustrates her unflinching obedience,[49] a virtue all potentially good mothers must strive to achieve.

Zamakhsharī and others assume, however, that Mary's flawless piety did not stem from her own agency, but from divine efforts to create a purified receptacle for the "word" (*kalīma*).[50] Rāzī, too, notes how God made the mother of Jesus completely and exclusively devoted to him, and granted her guidance and protection from error. He favored Mary with hearing the words of the angels, and purified her from the rejection of faith, disobedience, unsavory actions, and bad habits,[51] presumably all qualities and characteristics that plague every other woman. Rāzī also adds how God protected her from the suspicions and accusations the Jews held against her so that she did not have to experience unjust persecution for sexual impropriety.[52] By delimitating the type of female body God deems acceptable to impregnate, these scholars succeed in producing an ideal mother no woman could possibly attain, yet one to which all women are compared.

Because they make God solely responsible for creating a perfected vessel in which to generate Jesus, these scholars—Ashʿarite and Muʿtazilite alike[53]—deemphasize Mary's own agency and experience so valued in the Qurʾān. While the Qurʾān praises Mary's willful protection of her *farj* and her deliberate receptivity to God's procreative advances, scholars such as Zamakhsharī prefer to cast Jesus's conception solely in terms of a sign or miracle that reveals divine power.[54] Ṭabarī underscores this position by suggesting the miracle of Jesus's conception had little to do with Mary's own efforts and experience and more to do with negating what the Christians have said about him being the son of God.[55]

Likewise, Ibn Kathīr reports how Mary would have suffered little in the bearing of Jesus and instead calls upon her to increase her own devotion and worship to show the gratitude she owes to God for the generous favor she received.[56] In imitation of Mary, good mothers must also suppress their own agency and experience in order to be equally grateful for what God has produced—or not produced—in their wombs. While the Qurʾān holds many of these same theological positions expressed by medieval exegetes, it also undermines them with examples of Mary's agency and receptive nature in receiving God's word. The exegetes, therefore, bypass the Qurʾān's polyvalence to emphasize a more patriarchal understanding of Mary's role in conceiving Jesus.

These patriarchal efforts put Mary's body and mind firmly under the control of God's incomparable, transcendent power, which male scholars take upon themselves to define and impart. Medieval commentators are not content to live with the Qur'ān's persistent message that God can cause anything to "Be!" in any way he chooses, even if it means through an erotic, sexual encounter with a woman. Rather, they strip Mary of her own reproductive power and experience, and place her firmly under male/divine interpretive authority and protection. If exceptional piety indeed produces righteous offspring, then Mary becomes the quintessential mother in whose purified and perfected womb God deems worthy to generate one of his most beloved prophets to carry forth his message into the world. After all, the Qur'ān does hold that piety produces a proliferation of offspring, impiety a dearth of progeny.[57] Like Mary, women striving to become good mothers must also work to cultivate similarly virtuous and purified wombs that are suitable for receiving the divine breath in the form of life-generating male seed, and thus avoid accusations of being the "green dung" that may potentially corrupt a man's sperm.

Male exegetes underscore the links between piety, fertility, and a pure and perfected womb by rewarding Mary's righteous deeds and intentions with a fruitfulness so abundant that it breaches the boundaries of her body and extends outward to others as a kind of blessing.[58] For example, Mary's fecundity elicited the sudden fertility of old Zakarīyā and his barren wife. Kisā'ī notes that at precisely the moment Mary conceived Jesus, Zakarīyā's penetration of his wife also generated John.[59] Zamakhsharī observes that when Zakarīyā saw Mary's provisions of summer fruits in winter and winter fruits in summer, he realized that it may be possible for a barren woman to conceive a child.[60] He raised his hands to heaven and asked for a good offspring, and Mary plied him with grapes, figs, and dates, all fruits that have medicinal and magical associations with fertility.[61] Lo and behold, after consuming the succulent fruits, Zakarīyā and his wife conceived John. When Mary experienced birth pains and retired to the trunk of a palm tree, God also sent forth fresh dates and water, again, signs of the life and fertility he deemed acceptable to generate in her perfected womb.[62]

Even her son Jesus, though celibate, exudes fertility. Kisā'ī relays how Jesus himself served as midwife to deliver a child who was stuck halfway in, halfway out of a king's wife's womb.[63] He muses further how Jesus's own ascetic lifestyle will be overcome as he will marry an Arab woman after returning from heaven to battle the Antichrist, and she will give birth to a child who will perform the pilgrimage.[64] Ghazālī likewise speculates that Jesus will indeed marry when he returns to the world just prior to Judgment Day.[65] Every traditional example privileges reproductive power as it flows through the entire line of purified vessels cultivated among the family of 'Imrān/Amran: from forefather (Abraham) to mother (Ḥanna) to daughter (Mary) to son (Jesus). The underlying message that piety is necessary to generate righteous offspring is persistent throughout the entire line.

As the medical literature stresses again and again, for the majority of women, a successful pregnancy without complications appears to be the anomaly and not the norm. It certainly is never a given. Female bodies are portrayed as inherently weak, and therefore require male authority, intervention, and wisdom to overcome their failings in the hopes of generating the life God desires. Exegetes overlay the weak female body with perfected, purified, and therefore abundantly fertile wombs to exaggerate the gap between the real and the ideal that must be bridged via male control. By linking piety with fecundity in the maternal ideal, male elites cast a dark shadow over the virtues of most women, who never receive God's favors and whose wombs present a number of obstacles to reproductive success. These virtues are measured against, but also rectified through, the exegetical example of Mary, who becomes the procreative model all women must emulate—as best they can—in order to bear the healthy and righteous life both men and God require.

Āsiya bint Muzāḥim, A Prophet's Surrogate Mother and Queen of Paradise

Because she, too, is lauded in the Qur'ān, albeit briefly, exegetes often feature Āsiya as the second-in-command among the most praised woman of paradise. In contrast to Mary, Āsiya bore no biological children of her own. Her maternal status is established solely through her surrogate relationship with the baby Moses. While the Qur'ān contains few references to Pharaoh's wife, medieval exegetes extol her complete obedience to God and her unflinching willingness to sacrifice herself to him in order to serve his prophet Moses, even at the cost of her own life. In addition to pure wombs and pious intentions, good mothers must also cultivate the virtues of obedience to the point of self-sacrifice in service of God's creations, as demonstrated by Āsiya.

The Qur'ānic Āsiya

Despite the fact that Āsiya is perhaps the second most important "queen" of paradise, she is barely referred to in the Qur'ān, and is never given a name. In the revelatory context, her story is tied with that of Moses and his mother, and that of her husband, the Egyptian king. The Qur'ān narrates that after Moses's mother cast her baby into the river, the "people"[66] picked him out, presumably to kill him, for "he would be for them an adversary and a cause of sadness, for Pharaoh and Hāmān and their cohorts were sinful."[67] The wife of Pharaoh (*imrātu fir'awna*), however, saved him from his adversaries by saying, "He is a joy of the eye for me and for you [Pharaoh]. Do not slay him; he may be of use to us, or we may take him as a son" (Sūra 28:9). The irony of her statement is evident as Moses eventually rose up to destroy Pharaoh and his household.

In the Qur'ānic context, Pharaoh's wife represents resistance to such fated destruction, as she willfully distanced herself from her husband and all of his iniquities in order to save the baby Moses. Clearly, she had no idea who Moses was or what God had destined him to be, as suggested by her unwitting comment that the young boy might benefit their family. Yet, when she discovered Pharaoh's intentions for Moses, she garnered the inner strength to battle her husband's injustices.

Consequently, in Sūra 66:11, both Āsiya and Mary are held up as righteous servants over and against the wives of Noah and Lot, who deceived their husbands and profited on their behalf. While Mary guards her *farj* and receives the breath that contains "our spirit," the wife of Pharaoh cries out to be delivered from her husband and his wrongdoings: "O my Lord! Build for me a house in the Garden with you, and save me from Pharaoh and his doings, and save me from the people that do wrong." Sūra 66:11 bounds both women together via their willingness to submit to God's will despite the tremendous adversity and dire consequences their decisions evoke.

The Exegetical Āsiya

The exegetical literature gives the Pharaoh's wife a name and continues to stress the many parallels between Āsiya and Mary in order to confirm their mutual piety, obedience, and willingness to sacrifice themselves to God by nurturing and raising his future prophet. Like Mary, the exegetes demonstrate how God also protected, elevated, and guided Āsiya on an arduous and challenging journey to carry out his will. Because she was chosen for such a difficult path, she was no ordinary woman. However, in the process of designating her unique status as God's chosen one, the exegetes often eliminate what the Qur'ān so clearly emphasizes: Āsiya's free agency to critique and thwart her husband's intentions to kill one of God's servants. As is the case with Mary, they root her words and actions in a preordained, divine will in order to generate an ideal that conforms to the pattern of maternal obedience. As such, Āsiya becomes a paragon of righteousness destined to act to save the baby Moses not of her own volition but because God ordained her to sacrifice both her womb and her life to nurture, raise, and save his prophet.[68] Good mothers must follow suit, as they are called upon to devote their lives to what God has engendered.

Āsiya, like Mary, was chosen for greatness from birth. Exegetes supply Āsiya, too, with a privileged genealogy where she is linked with other significant prophetic figures in history. For example, Kisā᾽ī demonstrates how Āsiya was directly related to Moses, as he in fact was the son of her uncle Amran.[69] The linguistic associations between the family of Amram and ʿImrān (Mary's lineage) have long been noted by scholars.[70] Āsiya, like Mary, thus becomes part of the same string of privileged families whom God demarcates to carry out his will on earth. Even without the genealogical connections, exegetes show how Āsiya's birth parallels paradigmatically those of other extraordinary, Qur᾽ānic figures. Ibn Kathīr, for example, records how Muzāḥim, the father of Āsiya, married a woman on the same day that Joseph married Zulaykha, and that he went into her and begat Āsiya on the same night that Zulaykha conceived Manassah.[71] Here, too, as in the case of Mary's son Jesus and Zakarīyā's son, the double birth signifies future greatness.

Exegetical depictions of Āsiya's early years also demonstrate a desire for God to have destined her early on to be separate and unique from ordinary women. Just as Mary spoke in infancy, so too did Āsiya utter words from the cradle.[72] Her marriage and eventual martyrdom at the hands of the evil Pharaoh were not presented as the unfortunate result of the vagaries of human history she had to struggle to overcome, but a divinely planned event that points to God's greatness. For example, Kisā᾽ī notes that when Āsiya reached her twentieth year, a white bird in the form of a dove appeared to her with a white pearl in its mouth. "Āsiya," the bird said, "take this white pearl and when it turns green it will be time for you to marry; when it turns red God will cause you to suffer martyrdom."[73]

Here, her ultimate confrontation with Pharaoh, an infidel to whom God had given her as a husband,[74] is deemed inevitable, along with the sacrifice and suffering she would undergo as a result of this divine plan. Because God ordained it to be, exegetes divorce the Qur᾽ānic Āsiya from her own courageous decision to oppose her powerful husband. In the Qur᾽ān, her faith in God is presented as that much stronger because she demonstrates it without the providential buffer for the consequences. However, the exegetical Āsiya became much less the free agent as God directed the course of her life from start to finish to carry out his plans.

While Mary's womb demonstrated an abundance of fertility and a receptivity to life, Āsiya's uterus remained barren. As in the example of the prophet's wives in the Qur᾽ān, barrenness becomes an expression of piety. Exegetes assure their constituencies that her childlessness did not stem from the fact that Āsiya's womb was flawed or incapable of bearing children, or that God refused to reward her piety with offspring. Rather, medieval exegetes highlight the fact that when Āsiya came to live under Pharaoh's roof, Pharaoh attempted to have sex with her, but was rendered unsuccessful. God barred him from penetrating her and, in case that did not do the trick, made him impotent to boot.[75] Through the detailing of this story, medieval scholars secure Āsiya's womb as being perfectly fit for generating children had God not intervened. In this example, it is Pharaoh who was impotent, and not Āsiya who was barren.

Āsiya's empty womb thus resembles Mary's fertile one in that it submits to the divine will without question and thus becomes the vehicle through which God conveys his mercy and blessings. Barrenness in this instance serves as a mark of God's greater plan to which good women must abide. Given his ungodly disposition, Pharaoh must be deprived of fathering his own offspring through God's punishment of his reproductive organs. The king's sinful actions not only led to the death of his own genealogical line, but eventually his own life. Pharaoh's impiety is displayed again and again throughout the exegetical literature in reports about how he slaughtered twelve thousand women and seventy thousand babies just to avoid his ultimate destruction at the hand of a child.[76] God would never reward such depraved actions against mothers and children with abundant fertility and righteous offspring.

While God stripped Āsiya of her ability to bear progeny, he still rewarded her piety with a favored child. Thus, Āsiya's extraordinary maternal status becomes inextricably tied to her surrogate mothering of God's prophet, Moses. The fact that she, rather than Moses's own mother (whom the Qurʾān also glorifies) is elevated to the status of paradisiacal queen exemplifies the exegetical concern for the extraordinary piety and sacrifice women must display to secure the livelihood of one of God's young prophets. Āsiya became one of the ideal queens perhaps because she underwent many more trials than Moses's mother to protect Moses from Pharaoh's wrath. Like Āsiya, good mothers must also embody a complete and self-effacing commitment to the life God fosters, even if it means sacrificing their own lives in the process.

Stories about the birth and early years of Moses are riddled with marvelous signs that are often conveyed through the women around him. For example, medieval texts describe how Moses was conceived miraculously and spared from Pharaoh's wrath. Because Pharaoh was out to kill all Israelite babies, God concealed the signs of pregnancy for Moses's mother.[77] His mother delivered him safe within the cover of night with no one to help her but her daughter. Upon birth, Moses shone with a bright light. Moses's mother nursed him in constant fear of discovery by Pharaoh, lest he be killed. Tales also tell how whenever she went out of the house she would conceal him in the oven. One day when she was out (after tucking Moses safely inside the oven), her daughter lit the stove; miraculously, Moses was spared.[78] Clearly God's plans could only be fulfilled through his necessary interventions in the body and actions of Moses's mother and not solely because of her own noble efforts. Left solely in the hands of Moses's mother, the child would have burned up in the oven.

Despite Moses's mother's piety and courageous devotion to her son, it is Āsiya who is praised most for saving Moses and caring for him after his mother placed him in the Nile to protect him from Pharaoh's intent to kill any potential threat to his reign. While her husband wished to slay him, it was Āsiya who begs for his life. Pharaoh was not keen on sparing him, but Āsiya persuaded him that if he did indeed turn out to be the enemy, Pharaoh still had the opportunity to slaughter him at will.[79] Exegetes also laud Āsiya for reuniting Moses with his birth mother so that he could nurse from her breast and maintain genealogical purity. Prior to this reunion between true mother and son, potential wet nurses were brought from all over the kingdom. However, in conformation to Sūra 28:12, God caused Moses not to latch onto the breasts of the nurses provided, so as not to suckle from anyone but his true mother.[80]

Āsiya also supported Moses financially as he was growing up. For example, she paid all the expenses for the boy so he could live with his own mother while she nursed him for three years.[81] By supporting him and his mother for three years, she surpassed what the Qur'ān stipulates is required for husbands and fathers; they only need to provide for suckling children for up to two years.[82] While Āsiya was not in a position to offer her own breast, she was responsible for protecting Moses's physical constitution so that it was not tainted with the milk/blood of another genealogical line that could then claim Moses as its own. In each of these exegetical scenarios, Āsiya was able to carry out God's will as protector and nurturer of Moses solely because of her own pious efforts that were, of course, divinely cultivated.[83] Perfected wombs, therefore, are those that embody fully God's plans, and good mothers are those who strive to protect and nurture the life God creates, even if it costs them their own lives.

Given their emphasis on divine fate and intervention in the lives of these women, medieval scholars seem reluctant to place the livelihood of God's prophets entirely in the hands of female servants. For example, traditional sources relate how Āsiya endured many cruelties at the hand of Pharaoh because of her Israelite faith.[84] In her final moments, they relate how he cast her down upon a rock. God, however, heard her prayer and took her soul to himself, so that only her body fell on the stone. It is also reported that Pharaoh scourged her to death, but as a result of Moses's praying to God, she experienced no pain.

Another tale reports how Pharaoh ordered iron stakes to be driven into Āsiya's breast until she collapsed. At this point Gabriel descended upon her, informed her that she would dwell in paradise, and that God would join her there with Muḥammad. He handed her a cup of paradisiacal nectar to drink, and took her soul so that she felt no pain from Pharaoh's torture.[85] If left to endure the tortuous pain alone, Āsiya may have relinquished her faith, and Pharaoh would have triumphed over Moses. As they flesh out Āsiya's narrative, traditional sources attempt to guarantee she will stay the course often by inserting men or male angels to intervene at key moments in the story. After all, it is Moses who prays to God to remove her pain, and Gabriel who buffers her agony as she undergoes Pharaoh's torment.

As is the case with Mary, male scholars assert their own knowledge of divine intent over female agency to guarantee Āsiya's role in raising, nurturing, and protecting the baby Moses. The scholarly concern for controlling the behavior of God's female servants is, perhaps, rooted in the example of Moses's mother, who almost blurted out Moses' identity as he was pulled from the water, had not God strengthened her heart,[86] or hid him in the oven not knowing her daughter would light it inadvertently. While good mothers must be willing to sacrifice their own wombs and lives to nurture and protect God's creations, they must also recognize that their good intentions may not counter sufficiently their limitations and weaknesses, which may interfere with God's procreative plans. Āsiya, after all, could only exercise her own agency to a point; after that, she forfeited it into the hands of God's (male) servants who ultimately shielded her from anything that might jeopardize her faith and God's plans for Moses: her pain, choices, and even her own progeny. Therefore, to approximate the maternal ideal as mapped by medieval exegetes, ordinary women must also be willing to submit their agency and their bodies to those male authorities who can guarantee their wombs do not corrupt good male seed.

Khadīja bint Khuwalid, Bearer of the Faithful

Muḥammad's first wife, Khadīja, is neither mentioned nor given reference in the Qurʾān. Only the wives Muḥammad married after the *hijra* are addressed as a group in just a handful of passages.[87] As she is not mentioned in the Qurʾān, she is not subject to the same standards of perfection and purity as Mary or Pharaoh's wife. Rather, medieval scholars highlight information regarding Khadīja's faithful support and loyalty to Muḥammad, along with the prolific nature of her womb, in their references to the prophet's first wife, whom he married prior to the *hijra*. The lack of excessive detail surrounding her life perhaps suggests that her virtues were so well known, and her lofty status in relation to the prophet so clearly apparent, that medieval scholars did not require extensive persuasion or proof in support of her favored position in paradise.

According to traditional accounts, Khadīja's first encounter with Muḥammad began with her hearing a pagan prophesy that a prophet called Aḥmad would be sent down to bear God's message, and that this prophet required someone to volunteer to become his wife.[88] Khadīja, without hesitation, stepped forward. Other traditions also point to Khadīja's keen ability to see signs of Muḥammad's future greatness, which prompted her to marry him.[89] Khadīja's love for and loyalty to the prophet Muḥammad and his message stemmed from her own volition, and not from divine selection, which makes her more easily emulated by ordinary women. Unlike Mary and Āsiya, she was never divinely chosen for greatness, nor purified in body; rather, her dedication to the prophet came out of her own understanding and recognition of who he was and what his message represented.

In contrast with the other two paradisiacal queens, there is nothing extraordinary in Khadīja's genealogy or background that might signal her vital role as first convert and financial backer of Muḥammad's mission. In order to contrast Khadīja's rather ordinary nature with her extraordinary role, traditional sources relate a number of details about her prior marriages, career, and the children she bore with either past husbands or Muḥammad. For example, reports show she was married twice before Muḥammad, to ʿAtiq ibn ʿĀʾidh ibn ʿAbdallāh ibn ʿUmar of the Makhzūm, and then to Abū Hāla ibn Zurāra al-Nabbāshī of the ʿAmr ibn Tamīm.[90] To the latter she bore two sons with the usually feminine names of Hind and Hāla, and to ʿAtiq a daughter Hind. Sources report that she was probably divorced from Abū Hāla, but it is most likely that ʿAtiq died.[91] Before she married Muḥammad she owned a great amount of property, which she secured either through her husbands' estates or her father's, and engaged in her own trade.[92]

The gritty details of her life—her divorces, deaths of her children, her efforts in business—make her a much more accessible figure to ordinary women than either Mary or Āsiya, whom exegetes portray as being formed, purified, and guided by God throughout their lives. Like Khadīja, most women might imagine that they, too, would be as supportive of the prophet as she was, given the opportunity. Whether or not they would have been capable of bearing his children, however, is something over which they could exert little control.

The medieval sources relay how the prophet himself confirms the extraordinary role Khadīja played in his life because she—alone among all of his wives—bore his children.[93] As in the case of Mary, exegetes link a fertile womb with piety, which Khadīja demonstrated in abundance.

Khadīja bore Muḥammad four girls (Zaynab, Umm Kulthūm, Fāṭima, and Ruqayya) and one, two, or three boys (al-Qāsim and ʿAbdallāh,[94] or al-Qāsim, al-Ṭāhir, and al-Tayyib[95]). Khadīja's sons, al-Qāsim and ʿAbdallāh died in paganism while Khadīja was still alive; however, daughters Zaynab, Ruqayya, Umm Kulthūm, and Fāṭima embraced Islam and migrated with Muḥammad to Medina after their mother's death. Fāṭima lived on to bear the prophet's grandchildren; the rest of Khadīja's daughters died relatively young without supplying the prophet any descendants.[96] As noted above, Muḥammad took great pride in his daughters, and many traditions record his praising the begetting of girls. For example, the prophet said if a man has two daughters and treats them well, as long as they remain with him they will cause him to enter paradise.[97]

In general, a womb as prolific as Khadīja's is a wifely virtue supported by many *ḥadīth* passages and is considered one of the greatest advantages of marriage by Ghazālī.[98] Khadīja, therefore, fulfilled her divinely prescribed role by having children. Ghazālī even goes so far as to suggest God created the womb solely to serve as a repository for sperm,[99] and that anyone who refrains from "tilling" (either male or female) violates both nature as well as divine ordination.[100] The prophet himself stated how "the best of your women are the affectionate child bearers."[101] He also describes women "as child bearers, mothers, and nursers who are compassionate toward their children; those who pray will enter paradise, provided they do not commit wrongs against their husbands."[102] The Shīʿite traditionalist Muḥammad ibn Yaʿkūb al-Kulaynī (d. 941 CE) also records sayings from the *imāms* that praise the benefits of childbearing, especially for men, when he reports how a righteous child makes for a happy man.[103] Such traditions emphasize that giving birth to more children leads to a larger, more robust community (of Shīʿites, of course).[104] Good mothers, therefore, produce children for the sake of their husbands, to maintain the health of the community as a whole, and to fulfill the destiny of their divinely constructed physiologies.

The message revealed in the exemplary paradisiacal models of Khadīja, Mary, and even the barren Āsiya is that God saves both men and women through their children. Mary's son defended her in infancy by proclaiming her innocence, Moses prayed for the alleviation of Āsiya's pain as she underwent torture by her husband's hand, and Khadīja will rest forever in the Garden because, as the *ḥadīth* note, if a woman has lost three, two, or even one of her children, she will go straight to paradise.[105] As a mother who struggled through the pains of both childbirth and the death of two young sons, Khadīja becomes a much more accessible role model for ordinary women who might also experience joy and tragedy as children are born, flourish, and then die. Her example, however, and that of Mary and even Āsiya, would have provided little relief for barren women, or those who suffer miscarriages or stillbirths, who would not have the opportunity to be saved by God through their children. Such women would be left to ponder the causal connections between piety and fertility as applied to their own tragic experiences.

Medieval literature confirms the fact that men, too, have much to gain from their wives bearing them righteous children,[106] which places an even heavier burden on women to fulfill this role. Early sources reveal how the prophet began to practice *taḥannuth* after the birth of his daughters. *Taḥannuth* refers to the Qurayshī practice of sojourning to Mt. Ḥīrā᾿, feeding the poor, and circumambulating the Kaᶜba. It was during such a sojourn that Muḥammad received his revelation from God.[107] Here, the generation of offspring—the creation of a family—led to revelation and prophecy. In another example that celebrates familial bonds, Ghazālī reports how a young child who precedes her father in death will serve as intercessor for him.[108] Children, in fact, can drag their parents into heaven,[109] and offer their parched fathers goblets of water to drink as they are standing in line on Judgment Day.[110] Ghazālī also records how the prophet claimed, "A man has intimate relations with his wife, and is thus decreed for him the reward of a male offspring who fights for the cause of God and is martyred."[111] In this case, male offspring support God's community through their defense of the faith and can also, through their martyrdom, bring pious gains to the ones who fathered them.

Contrary to the Qur᾿ān's take on reproduction, the father in medieval exegetical literature serves as the direct cause of his son's existence by merely ejaculating his sperm into the mother's uterus, even though God is still revered as the ultimate source of all life.[112] Thus, a father is lauded for the causation and subsequent accomplishments of his son. A wife who generates no progeny deprives her husband from securing such potential rewards gained through a child that dies in martyrdom or otherwise, or from contributing his share to the maintenance and protection of the community of believers. Khadīja, through a prolific womb most likely attained through her unyielding support for her husband and his message throughout their married life, was the only one of his wives who spared the prophet from such a fate.

Khadīja's exceptionality is not only confirmed through her fruitful womb, but also through her role as surrogate mother to Muḥammad, a theme evident in the medieval texts and even more obviously emphasized in modern exegetical works.[113] According to most traditional sources, Khadīja was forty at the time of her marriage; Muḥammad just twenty-five. Some early sources, however, suggest that she may have been closer to twenty-eight, which makes more sense given that she bore five children with Muḥammad.[114]

The fact that the majority of commentators preserve a significant number of traditions that underscore her "elderly" status reveals their desire to place her in a more maternal role in relation to the prophet Muḥammad, even more so than to her own children.[115] After all, the prophet's own mother died when he was six; his marriage to an older woman serves to underscore Khadīja's caring and nurturing role to the budding prophet. Clearly this element of motherhood, manifested through her prolific womb but also through her surrogate, "maternal" role in relation to the prophet, has boosted her status to being one of the "best" of all women, either in her own time or for all time.[116] A good mother is one with a strong, pious, and fertile womb who is also willing to sacrifice all to the husband who generates life within her. Without such life, neither husband nor wife would achieve happiness, a chance at paradise, or a fulfillment of divine destiny.

Traditional accounts emphasize again and again the maternal care and support Khadīja was able to provide Muḥammad throughout his mission, a support that is inextricably linked with her devotion and unyielding piety. After all, she was the first to believe in God and his messenger, and in the truth of his message. Given her inherited wealth, she, like Āsiya for Moses, backed financially his prophetic mission. God comforted him by her when he went home; she strengthened him, lightened his burden, proclaimed his truth, and belittled men's opposition to him.[117] Defense and protection of a young prophet in the face of adversity is an ideal maternal trait shared by all three women of paradise. For example, when the prophet received his first revelation, it was Khadīja who confirmed that he saw an angel and not a devil.[118]

In this way, Khadīja's loving and caring maternal associations with a prophet—borne out of her own choice and not predestination—establish significant parallels with the pious maternal achievements of both Mary and Āsiya. Mothers who are kind, loving, helpful, and protective of God's (male) prophets, whether out of their own volition or by the hand of God, are either given receptive wombs to bear his creations or rewarded with (and through) surrogate sons. Women who have no children or no surrogates to nurture are left to speculate on the reasons why God did not honor their pious efforts to carry out his will. These images of an ideal mother who bears righteous children with ease or nurtures God's prophets into and through adulthood cast into sharp relief the often unfortunate and difficult circumstances of ordinary mothers whose wombs are fraught with barrenness, miscarriages, stillbirths, or impious offspring. Such images invite scholars to speculate further on the causes for such discrepancies between the ideal and the real, which they often root in the weaknesses of a woman's body or the frailties of her piety.

Fāṭima bint Muḥammad, Conceived from the Fruits of Paradise and Mother of Martyrs

Like Khadīja, Fāṭima is nowhere mentioned in the Qur'ān. The ideal, maternal role of the prophet Muḥammad's daughter Fāṭima varies greatly depending on whether sources come from Sunnī or Shīʿite traditions. The Sunnī traditions emphasize her ordinary nature: the difficulties in her marriage with her husband ʿAlī, her jealous encounters with the wives of the Prophet, in particular ʿĀ'isha, and her dependency on the prophet Muḥammad. Yet, despite these deficiencies, traditional Sunnī sources also accentuate her willingness to step in as surrogate mother to Muḥammad after Khadīja died, and to commend her patience in marital relations with ʿAlī, her weak physical constitution, and the death of her beloved father. Shīʿite traditions, on the other hand, are concerned primarily with Fāṭima's extraordinary role as bearer of the prophet's descendants, who were to become the future *imāms* and martyrs for the faith. These sources, through a variety of means, transform her body into a purified vessel, even more so than Mary's,[119] that is protected from the vagaries of a flawed human nature.

In both Sunnī and Shīʿite examples, Fāṭima is lauded for her willingness to suffer grief and pain, and to sacrifice her own body to bear and support the prophet's grandchildren. The differences between the two sources have to do primarily with positions on genealogical succession. Shīʿites favor the prophet's biological successors who carried forth the essential inspiration (*ilhām*) to lead the community forward into its triumphal future, while Sunnīs privilege individual faith and piety as essential elements of leadership and authority. Both, however, still praise a woman's ability to procreate healthy and righteous offspring who will contribute to their religious and political goals.

Fāṭima in Sunnī Exegesis

According to Sunnī sources, Fāṭima was born in Mecca, and emigrated as a Muslim convert to Medina with her father after her mother's death.[120] While these sources make no claims that Fāṭima was destined for greatness from birth, like Mary or Āsiya, they do admit the presence of God's hand in shaping some of the events in her life. For example, the prophet Muḥammad believed a divine command would determine for him who would be wedded to Fāṭima. ʿAlī was the one designated through divine sign, and sources suggest she was married to him when she was nine, fifteen, or eighteen.

Like her mother, Fāṭima was also blessed with a prolific womb. Out of all her siblings, Fāṭima is the only one who bore successfully children who lived to go on to reproduce. For example, her sister Ruqayya, who had married ʿUthmān ibn ʿAffan, suffered a miscarriage during the first emigration, and then lost a second child, ʿAbdallāh, at the age of two when a cock pecked his face and he died. She bore no children after that.[121] Another sister, Umm Kulthūm, died without bearing children whatsoever.

Fāṭima, on the other hand, was blessed with four children, including two boys, who carried forth the prophet's lineage. Sunnī sources relate how her sons Ḥasan and Ḥusayn were born in quick succession shortly after her marriage, one year after the other. Despite such fecundity, tradition holds that Fāṭima was of a weak, bodily constitution. She did not feel strong enough even to nurse her own children. To denigrate her affiliation with her own sons, some traditions even hold that one of the wives of ʿAbbās served as a wet nurse, making the two boys foster children (blood relations) of those who went on to establish the ʿAbbāsid empire. In addition to her two sons, Fāṭima also bore two daughters, Zaynab and Umm Kulthūm, the latter in the last year of her relatively short life.

While Sunnī sources cast a somewhat ambiguous light upon ʿAlī,[122] their treatment of Fāṭima is much more generous (though still equivocal), especially when it comes to the warm and loving relationship she had with her father. In general, the Sunnī traditions speak of a close bond between Muḥammad and his daughter. Sources reveal that despite her own tremendous grief when Khadīja died, Fāṭima, in all of her frailties, stepped into the demanding role as Muḥammad's surrogate mother. In fact, her *kunya* became *Umm Abīhā* ("mother of her father"), rather than Umm Ḥasan, the more natural title she should have assumed, given that mothers were traditionally given names that linked them with their first-born sons.[123] As such, Sunnī sources emphasize what they deem to be her more important role as *"Umm Abīhā"* over and against her biological role as mother to her own children. Both her ability to produce offspring, more so, perhaps, for her father (to whom she became "mother") than for ʿAlī, and her maternal nurturing of the prophet Muḥammad after Khadīja's death, led to her extraordinary status as a paradisiacal queen.

The prophet was equally as loyal to her as she was to him. Sunnī sources are filled with short vignettes that highlight the close, domestic relationship they shared. For example, when the prophet woke up every morning, he went and announced the hour of prayer first at Fāṭima's door. When Muḥammad became owner of northern Ḥijāz, he gave his daughter eighty-five loads of wheat, just as he had done for his wives. Fāṭima is also praised for her willingness to nurse her father back to health after he suffered injuries during his many battles. For example, after the Battle of Uḥud, sources reveal how she tenderly treated her father's wounds as a mother would her son's, or even, perhaps, as a wife would her husband's. And, on Muḥammad's deathbed, Fāṭima was told she'd be the first to join him in the afterlife, a prediction that came true, according to sources. Muḥammad also confided in her that she would become the chief of the women in paradise, with the exception of Mary.[124] Fāṭima, ʿAlī, Ḥasan, Ḥusayn, and Muḥammad are all described in intimate, familial terms as the privileged ones of the cloak (*aṣḥāb al-kisāʾ*). At one point in time Muḥammad is said to have covered them all with his cloak, saying, "These are the members of my family."[125]

Yet, despite the positive treatments noted above, many Sunnī sources also dwell on her many flaws. For example, they note how Muḥammad did not favor Fāṭima among his daughters. Some put forth that Muḥammad had declared Zaynab to be the most preferable and capable of the three. Others declare he considered Ruqayya the most attractive. Fāṭima, by way of contrast, is described as being physically weak, thin, and subject to frequent illnesses.

A number of Sunnī traditions also emphasize her pitiful nature. For example, sources note that given the prophet's deemphasis of wealth, Fāṭima could bring no dowry to her marriage with ʿAlī. ʿAlī himself, at times, is described as being poor and not very intelligent; he is often depicted as quarreling with his new wife.[126] He even contemplated taking on a second wife, much to Fāṭima's dismay. Clearly Fāṭima endured many humiliations and difficulties during her marriage to ʿAlī, a union that was, ironically, ordained by her own father.

Her relationship with the prophet's wives was equally strained. Sources reveal she did not have good relations with ʿĀʾisha, and many examples show how often she tried to intervene—without success—in the intrigues that divided the mothers of the believers, who often scorned her advice. Despite her deficiencies, however, Fāṭima is never portrayed as the "green dung" as Sunnī sources describe the children she bore as "chiefs of the youth of paradise"[127] who were loved[128] and protected[129] by the prophet Muḥammad, who claimed them as his own flesh.[130] Her combined role as a surrogate mother to her father, who was willing to sacrifice all to secure his well-being, and also bearer of his offspring (once removed), elevates her to the paradisiacal status of Mary, Āsiya, and Khadīja.

Fāṭima in Shīʿite Exegesis

In contrast to Sunnī perspectives, Shīʿite sources extol Fāṭima as mother of the prophet's grandchildren, who were destined to become the future *imāms*. Her strong associations with motherhood are rooted in her very own name. Muḥammad Bāqir ibn Muḥammad al-Taqī al-Majlisī (d. 1699 CE), one of the most influential Shīʿite clerics of all time, for example, identifies the root *f-ṭ-m* as meaning "to wean."[131] In order to purify Fāṭima's body enough to bear the future *imāms*, like her paradisiacal predecessor Mary, Shīʿite traditions assert her own miraculous birth, and also that of her sons, Ḥasan and Ḥusayn. As a perfected and purified vessel, Fāṭima's body surpasses even that of the exegetical Mary in terms of its sanctity. Mary, after all, was conceived through normal sexual relations between husband and wife. Majlisī, however, intimates that Fāṭima was conceived through even loftier means:

> Muḥammad is reported to say: On the night of the *miʿrāj* when I reached the sixth heaven Gabriel took my hand and brought me into paradise. There I saw a tree of light before which stood two angels. On the tree I beheld some fresh and fragrant dates. I ate one of the dates[132] and it became sperm in my loins. When I returned to earth I had intercourse with Khadīja and she became pregnant with Fāṭima. Thus Fāṭima is a human *ḥūri* because she has the appearance of a human female form and the characteristics and moral attributes of a *ḥūri*. Now whenever I am near Fāṭima I smell from her the odor of paradise.[133]

In this example, the prophet's sperm contains the heavenly spark that would generate a daughter free from earthly contamination who would be worthy to bear his future progeny.

Majlisī continues to demonstrate how Fāṭima was like no ordinary woman by asserting that Khadīja's labor with Fāṭima was assisted by four paradisiacal women: Sarah, wife of Abraham, Āsiya, Mary, and Kulthūm, sister of Moses.[134] Like Mary and Āsiya, as a sign of God's favor and her own greatness, Fāṭima spoke from her mother's womb, where she consoled her mother Khadīja for the ill treatment she suffered from the Qurayshī women of Mecca, who had refused to help deliver her righteous daughter.[135]

These examples illustrate how Shīʿite exegesis purifies Fāṭima's body in order that it may bear the future Imāms in a way similar to how Christians cleansed Mary to prepare her for the conception and birth of Jesus.[136] Like the Islamic Mary, Fāṭima in Shīʿite sources was both virginal (*batūl*) and free of menstruation.[137] As is the case with both Jesus and his mother Mary, the births of Ḥasan and Ḥusayn were predestined to be even before they were conceived. In fact, their births were foretold to the prophet in dream. Umm Faḍl had a vision in which a piece of the prophet's flesh, or one of his members, was cut off and thrown in her lap. She told her dream to the prophet, who interpreted it as Fāṭima having a child.[138] Here, the role of ʿAlī is bypassed as the prophet himself symbolically impregnated his daughter through his own flesh. Surprisingly, perhaps, as in the case of the Sunnī examples, Fāṭima's marriage to ʿĀlī is often ignored as she is linked more directly to the prophet. In contrast to the Sunnī examples, however, Shīʿite sources portray Fāṭima less as the *Umm Abīhā* and more as his wifely consort lauded because she bore his own flesh and blood.

Unlike the Qurʾānic Mary who cried out in pain as she was delivering Jesus alone under the date tree, Shīʿite exegetes report how Fāṭima bore none of the suffering, pain, or anxiety associated with pregnancy or childbirth. While pregnant, at no time did Fāṭima crave food or drink; rather, she was constantly satiated with milk and honey.[139] Like Mary, when it was time to deliver her son, Fāṭima retreated from all human contact, and was provided with a heavenly sustenance.[140] However, this divine sustenance did not appear as relief to a thirsty, suffering woman about to give birth because Fāṭima experienced none of the usual labor pains. Rather than enduring any hardship whatsoever during childbirth,[141] sources reveal how Fāṭima's body was so extraordinarily honed that it quickly recovered after giving birth to her first son, Ḥasan, to the extent she was able to conceive Ḥusayn on the same day.[142] Such a unique feat also suggests she experienced none of the impurities of postpartum bleeding or even physical or mental fatigue, and therefore would not have inconvenienced her husband, as would most new mothers, by withholding sex from him.

Fāṭima's extraordinary maternal physique is also reflected in the robust and idyllic nature of her children. Ḥusayn, the martyr whose wrongful death will be vindicated at some future date, was in the womb for only six months,[143] which points to his superior nature. Shīʿite sources reveal God sent down Luʿayya, the most beautiful of all *ḥūris*, to deliver the boy.[144] She washed the child with the waters of paradise and rubbed his gums with her spittle, as did also the angel Gabriel.[145] The rubbing of the gums suggests divine ownership of the child; rather than Ḥusayn belonging to ʿAlī, or even Fāṭima, these gestures sealed him instead to the heavenly sphere. Ḥasan and Ḥusayn's purity and unique natures are also emphasized by the fact that they, by many accounts, were born circumcised.[146] While Mary's suffering, pain, and dependence on God are highlighted as pious virtues in the Qurʾān, the Shīʿites problematize these same qualities through their complete sanitization, purification, and idealization of Fāṭima's body, along with those of her sons. Clearly, no other woman could possibly emulate this paradisiacal creation.

Remarkably, as mentioned above, many Shīʿite sources emphasize the role of the prophet as a kind of doting husband to his expectant "wife" (daughter). Thus, we are told how Ṣafīya, the daughter of ʿAbd al-Muṭṭalib, was Fāṭima's midwife who delivered the child while the prophet waited outside the birthing room like an impatient husband. As soon as the child was born, the prophet called out, "O Aunt, give me my son." She, however, protested, saying, "O messenger of God, we have not yet cleaned him." He retorted (sarcastically), "You clean him! Nay, God himself has cleansed and purified him."[147] Some scholars have gone so far as to say that the prophet himself acted as midwife at the birth of Ḥusayn, and that his hands were thoroughly stained with the blood of childbirth in the process.[148] The staining of his hands in this example establishes the paternal, genealogical connection between Muḥammad and his "children."

In these Shīʿite examples, Fāṭima serves as the necessary link between the prophet and his heirs that bypasses that of their own father. Thus, Muḥammad's own daughter—even more than his wives—becomes the purified vessel through which succession is guaranteed. Fāṭima's role as child bearer, therefore, facilitates Muḥammad's status as paternal generator of martyrs, a lofty position praised in the eyes of God. Here, fathers become second to God in generating the superlative martyrs God commands, and mothers the supporting vessels that must be acted upon for this purpose. Despite her extraordinary purity, Fāṭima assumes a subordinate position in ensuring the praiseworthy status of Muḥammad as father of sons who grow up to fight for the cause of God. Even though they will never attain the same level as Fāṭima in terms of their perfection, good mothers must also strive to become the purified vessels through which men can generate the future pillars of the faith and achieve glory for themselves.

Fāṭima's laudable, maternal sympathies for her own sons reappear in the grief she demonstrates over their deaths. According to Shīʿite traditions, Fāṭima weeps eternally over her two sons in death, and her tears in paradise kindle God's wrath.[149] Her suffering and grief over the death of both her beloved father and her two sons become praiseworthy qualities and characteristics that seal her status over and above ordinary women. However, her most prestigious roles in Shīʿite traditions lie in the fact that she was chosen and purified by God to serve as surrogate wife to the prophet, and to bear him the future political and spiritual leaders of the Shīʿite community.

In sum, in both Sunnī and Shīʿite visions, Fāṭima's selfless, maternal subordination to male prophetic figures places her squarely beside Mary, Āsiya, and Khadīja. A good mother must seek to continue the paternal line (however it may be defined, as illustrated by both Sunnī and Shīʿite traditions) by cultivating a pure womb and idyllic virtues as best as she can; however, unlike the Shīʿite Fāṭima, she must often strive to do so without the help of divine intervention.

The Ideal Mothers of Paradise Reflected in the Good Mothers on Earth

The medieval exegetical works assert again and again how all four paradisiacal women—Mary, Āsiya, Khadīja, and Fāṭima—embody the ideal characteristics of motherhood. The fact that the noble mothers of paradise donated their own bodies, identities, and internal volition in support and sustenance of God's prophets is a consistent theme throughout all of these exegetical narratives. Fortunately or unfortunately, most women will not be called upon to bear God's prophets. However, in their everyday lives, as foci for God's reproductive activities, they, too, must strive to embody these same qualities, as best they can, to foster the righteous life both men and God desire. Otherwise, their bodies may never become the suitable vehicles necessary to transform healthy and robust male sperm into pious progeny who may worship God, protect the faith, and bring glory, honor, and a place in paradise for the men who generate them.

The volatile nature of the female body, so clearly mapped in medieval medical texts, often prevents women from embodying the ideal. Weak, frail, and impure female physiologies only underscore the stark gap between average mothers and the maternal paragons they must come to model in order to acquire the stellar progeny both men and God desire. Exegetical projections of the ideal mother onto the bodies of ordinary, less than perfect women, however, serve to fashion and form good mothers who must struggle continuously to cultivate a purified womb, perfected piety, and an ethics of relentless self-sacrifice directed toward husbands, fathers, and children.

In painting their portraits of the maternal ideal, medieval male exegetes succeed in creating a standard by which to compare, and often denigrate, all other mothers. If a woman fails to bear her husband children, and shows no other signs of extraordinary piety, then her behavior becomes suspect, and subject to male scrutiny and repair. Of course, such standards of perfection and profound fecundity contrast sharply with the Qurʾān's polyvalent, often contradictory snapshots of how God creates or does not create offspring and in whom. After all, Abraham's doubting wife still conceived a child well into old age, and the wombs of the prophets' wives were closed in pious response to Muḥammad's fatherless status. As these examples show, only God, and not men, can determine what lies deep within the "shadows of darkness." Such sound Qur'ānic advice, however, is often ignored by elite scholars who construct ideal maternal models by which they measure the ordinary women who often struggle—and fail—to replicate the righteous worshipers of God men desire to produce.

The "Mother" of Believers Who Bears No Fruit: The Liminal Status of ʿĀʾisha bint Abī Ṭālib

Nowhere is the patriarchal privileging of the link between piety and a fertile womb more apparent than it is in the life of ʿĀʾisha. As noted above, Ibn Kathīr suggests that ʿĀʾisha, too, might also be considered among the paradisiacal queens. However, most traditions imply she is not among the best, but rather must be considered as "the superiority of *tharīd* to other meals," *tharīd* being a dish made of bread soaked in broth.[150] The ambiguity of ʿĀʾisha's status raises questions as to why she is not considered among the "best." After all, the prophet Muḥammad considered her to be his favorite wife. She was the only virgin he married[151] in a context where virginity was highly praised. Throughout his life and into his death, ʿĀʾisha nurtured and supported him as much as Khadīja and Fāṭima, and she was the transmitter of traditions that went on to stand as the basis for Islamic law and practice.

However, the one shadow cast over ʿĀʾisha is the fact that she was never able to bear the prophet's children, and, unlike the fearless and obedient Āsiya, she resented her inability to do so. Despite the fact that all the other wives the prophet married after the death of Khadīja never bore children, ʿĀʾisha seems to carry the brunt of this burden. In contrast with Khadīja, her maternal impulses to nurture the prophet stubbornly did not translate into a prolific womb.

For example, ʿĀʾisha's virginity should have made her a prime candidate for a fecund womb. According to tradition, the prophet instructed his followers to "[m]arry virgins, for they have the sweetest mouths, the most prolific wombs, and are satisfied with little."[152] A man will also be most attached to the woman with whom he has had his first intimate relations; likewise, he will be somewhat repelled by a woman who has been touched by another husband.[153] As medieval scholars have shown, desire is an essential component of male virility and fertility. Without it, little sperm will be produced, and no children will be sired. Virgins, then, would be the sole object of their husbands' sexual lust, which, in theory, should result in an abundance of male seed and thus the proliferation of offspring.

Despite her virginity, ʿĀʾisha never conceived. Certainly, the prophet was not at fault, given the number of children he fathered with Khadīja, who was by no means a virgin when he married her, and the fact that he was able to impregnate his concubine, Māriya the Copt, while he was married to ʿĀʾisha. And certainly, in practice, it seems the prophet did not take his own words about virginity to heart, given his great love and respect for his first wife, Khadīja, and the fact that the rest of his (seven to ten) wives were widows or divorcées. Thus, the reason for ʿĀʾisha's barrenness becomes an analog by which medieval exegetes measure her piety over and against the theological ideals embodied by the women described above, and the biological realities of the female body that these exceptional women were somehow able to thwart through God's helping hand, a hand that somehow refused to grace ʿĀʾisha in the same way it did with other faithful female servants.

The debate over the piety of barren wives pivots around the life of ʿĀʾisha who became, according to some, a mother to all believers, even though she herself was childless. As noted in chapter 1, the reference to the "mother of the believers" is Qurʾānic and applies to all the prophet's wives, despite the fact that none of them bore his children.[154] The fact that the prophet is "father to none of your men"[155] obviously depends on his wives' infertility. In this light, the Qurʾānic category of "mother" is equally as problematic as "father" when it comes to addressing the prophet and his wives.

Even though the Qurʾān disallows for God and/or the prophet to establish paternal relations with their followers, Muḥammad's many biographers recall how ʿĀʾisha greatly lamented the fact that she was barren. Rather than accepting her fate in blind support of the prophet's necessarily nonpaternal role among his followers, ʿĀʾisha questioned God's sacrifice of her womb in support of this cause. Barrenness brought with it a stigma that somehow called into question a woman's ability to be a good wife to her husband, as exemplified by Khadīja and Fāṭima. Ghazālī, for example, instructs men to avoid marrying women who are barren.[156] He records many *ḥadīth* that reveal the prophet's disparagement of women unable to produce children. For example, Muḥammad notes how "a straw mat in the corner of the house is preferable to a barren woman."[157] The prophet also suggests "a black child bearer is better than a beauty that cannot give birth."[158] It is clear to see why ʿĀʾisha would have been distraught over her predicament.

Given these prophetic criticisms, childlessness was obviously the cause of great anxiety and speculation among male scholars. The legal determination of the barren party, for example, translates into a variety of negative social repercussions. In Islamic law, a man may divorce his wife if she is unable to produce heirs.[159] Likewise, Jāḥiẓ suggests people unable to procreate are banned from securing relationships generated through blood and marriage, or from simply enjoying the raising of children and being pleased by them.[160] Inheritance, too, casts a pallor on barrenness as fathers are unable to pass their wealth directly to their children.[161]

Obviously ʿĀʾisha's sterility bore no resemblance to Āsiya's, as that would have indicted the prophet's inability to procreate. Likewise, the prophet could not be faulted for choosing a less than perfect wife. Sources instead prefer to blame an impious character flaw that resurfaces again and again in ʿĀʾisha's biography: her jealousy. According to traditional sources, God considers certain types of jealousy to be laudable; other types detestable. The jealously God favors is what results from just suspicion, and the type he loathes comes from unfounded suspicion (i.e., pride in falsehood).[162] ʿĀʾisha's envy apparently stemmed from the latter.

The *ḥadīth* record her as being incredibly jealous of Muḥammad's first wife Khadīja, whose prolific womb, borne out of a perfected piety, produced many children, including the two sons who died tragically at such young ages. As a result of her jealousy, ʿĀʾisha referred to Khadīja as that "toothless old woman whom God had replaced with a better." On this occasion, the prophet Muḥammad rebuked her, retorting, "She believed in me when I was rejected; when they called me a liar, she proclaimed me truthful; when I was poor, she shared with me her wealth, and God granted me her children while withholding those of other women!"[163]

By withholding children from some women and granting them to others, medieval exegetes show God to have rewarded some wombs over others for reasons having to do with piety. In this passage, the verdict is clear: ʿĀʾisha did not garner God's favor in the same way as did Khadīja, and she had the gall to question him on his judgment in withholding children from her. In contrast to ʿĀʾisha, true paradisiacal queens only support, nurture, and care for their prophets; never do they question them, and certainly they are not rebuked by them. Exegetes record this example to demonstrate that ʿĀʾisha's jealousy was not just but unfounded, and to root her barrenness firmly in her impiety, which is inextricably tied to the disobedience to her husband. These scholars' chastisement of ʿĀʾisha's behavior elevates their own status to that of God's as they, too, deem which wombs are worthy of offspring, and which are not.

ʿĀʾisha is faulted further for her response to God's will in making her barren. Medieval scholars note how ʿĀʾisha once stated, "God has given you better than her (meaning Khadīja) in exchange."[164] This phrase mimics a divine revelation sent to Muḥammad that promised more obedient and pious wives would be given to him in replacement for ones divorced (presumably because they did not fulfill their ideal roles).[165] Clearly, ʿĀʾisha was not subordinating her own will to God's or the prophet's and was, in fact, challenging his (their) rule over her womb. As Jāḥiẓ notes, bad things happen to good people to stop them from taking for granted the security that encourages the wicked to trust in sinful things and slackens the efforts of the righteous to do good.[166] Because ʿĀʾisha was unwilling to accept her lot, many medieval Muslim scholars underscore the causal link between ʿĀʾisha's barrenness and her moral behavior. The paradisiacal mothers noted above display no insubordination whatsoever to God or to his prophets. According to male exegetes, their prolific wombs, with the exception of Āsiya's, whose womb was still obedient and submissive despite its barrenness, are signs of his approval of their unflinching obedience to what best serves men and God: the bearing and nurturing of the children he creates.

Her jealousy, however, was not aimed solely at Khadīja. ʿĀʾisha displayed similar rages against other women, who she perceived might lure the prophet away from her. For example, the prophet's biography relates how ʿĀʾisha intensely disliked a woman named Juwayrīya, who was one of the captive girls of the Banū al-Muṣṭaliq. Apparently, she was a most beautiful woman, and captivated every man who saw her. ʿĀʾisha, worried that she might also enamor her husband, went to Muḥammad with a plan for him to marry off Juwayrīya. The prophet eventually followed her advice and discharged the woman in question to ʿĀʾisha's cousin, who proposed marriage to her, and she accepted.

Here, ʿĀʾisha's jealousy appears as excessive and ungrounded in actual fact. The prophet never approached Juwayrīya in any way, nor did he express any amorous words about her. He himself rebuked men for displaying fierce jealousy over their wives for whom there was no warranted justification or suspicion.[167] ʿĀʾisha's baseless mistrust in the prophet invited equal censure. Her words and actions questioned her support and loyalty to her husband, which contrasted sharply with Khadīja's maternal sacrifice and devotion to her husband, or Fāṭima's wifely care for her father. ʿĀʾisha's vacillating obedience allows exegetes to assign moral causes to her barren womb.

Notably, the prophet never divorced ʿĀʾisha or any of his other wives because they were barren; this, however, did little to squelch the speculation reflected in many *ḥadīth* and other traditional sources that

ʿĀʾisha's impiety somehow caused her infertility. Linking infertility with impiety suggests many medieval Muslim scholars believe the activities that go on inside a womb are far from random. Clearly, the implication is that God does not create righteous offspring in morally tainted wombs. ʿĀʾisha's childbearing difficulties stand as dire warnings of how moral inadequacies, in addition to the numerous bodily imperfections outlined in the medical literature, lead to barrenness. Good mothers strive to overcome such deficiencies, and with the help of scholars, husbands, fathers, and male children, they may surmount them.

Despite their stern reproof of ʿĀʾisha's behavior, many exegetes counter their condemnations of her barrenness, jealousies, and quick temper with depictions of the prophet's extraordinary love for his youngest wife. For example, several *ḥadīth* report how the prophet used to lay his head in ʿĀʾisha's lap during her menstrual period and recite the Qurʾān.[168] The prophet's complete disregard for her impure womb as he tenderly stroked her hair intimates that many scholars viewed ʿĀʾisha as less an "unfit mother" and more a mediating figure between the paradisiacal four and ordinary women.

While not quite the perfected ideal, ʿĀʾisha still embodies many of the good maternal qualities ordinary women should invoke in the context of their own families at the same time her all-too-human foibles reflect the jealousies and pains they, too, experience on a daily level. Her fierce devotion to her husband buffers any unwarranted bursts of jealousy; her loving memory of his every word and action combats her often questionable obedience to his will. In their projection of such contradictory emotions, desires, and intentions, many scholars model ʿĀʾisha after the plethora of women whose barrenness incites anger, pain, and jealousy rather than passive acceptance of divine fate. As the "superiority of *tharīd*" to all other meals, ʿĀʾisha becomes a maternal model not wholly unattainable; rather, she reflects for ordinary women what are all too often real responses to life experiences. While she may never achieve the consummate status of the four paradisiacal queens, as her barren womb and sharp tongue suggest, through her strivings to serve her husband, overcome her jealousies, and bear him the children he desires, she guides ordinary women toward the paradisiacal ideals that so often evade them, and helps them avoid the many pitfalls along the way.

A Piety Within Reach? Good Muslim Mothers

The exegetical constructions of the paradisiacal mother reveal how male scholars strive to press upon the ordinary female body perfection, purity, or piety. Through targeted rhetorical strategies employed to narrate these four mothers' maternal lives, medieval male elites seek to fashion women with weak bodies and morals into paragons of piety. By distilling bodies, obviating suffering, controlling female agency, or turning wives into mothers or daughters into wives, scholars demonstrate the difficult path ordinary mothers must tread to become the purified, fertile vehicles necessary for the transmission of God's word or the propagation of his faith. Such views contrast with the Qur'ān's many passages that emphasize a more symbiotic relationship between God and his female servants to generate life, its celebration of rare moments breached by God through his intimate associations with women and wombs, and its assertions that God often creates in wombs what he pleases.

Male scholars encode this paradigmatic ideal of the "good mother" further through the public rituals and embodied practices that reinforce the normative discourses that affirm a woman's willingness to conceive, bear, and nurture children under the guidance of men. As the medical literature has shown, for ordinary women wrestling with their own violable bodies and the vagaries of reproduction, the path to paradise—forged through the bearing of children—was often elusive. It could only be realized through the transference of women's own reproductive power to men, and maybe not even then. Women sanctioned male generative authority primarily through their performance of prescriptive postpartum rituals and practices, such as the *taḥnīk,* circumcision, *ʿaqīqa,*[169] *kunya,* and breastfeeding. With her full participation in these practices, a woman seals her status as "good mother," and grants men the sole right to guarantee for her child a meaningful life.

4

Postpartum

Making the Good Mother through Public Rituals and Embodied Practices

Public rituals and embodied practices serve to bridge the gap between the perfected queens of paradise and the real women whose lives and bodies often thwarted their efforts to achieve the ideal states of motherhood personified by Mary, Āsiya, Khadīja, and Fāṭima. As noted in chapter 3, for real women, the path to paradise was certainly forged through the bearing of children, but more so perhaps through their willingness to relinquish those children—and their reproductive power—to men. By surrendering their reproductive potency and the life it generates to the care, protection, and authority of men, woman are able to offset their inherent physical and moral weaknesses, and mime more fully the good mother. Such conceding of their procreative agency takes place through postpartum rituals and practices, all of which counter the woman's vital and singular role in the process of giving birth, which, by nature, norm, and necessity, evades male command.[1]

Through male-initiated practices such as *taḥnīk* (rubbing an infant's palate with dates), *khitān* (circumcision), *ʿaqīqa* (sacrifice of a goat upon the birth of the child), *tasmiya* (the naming of the child) and the *kunya* (a mother's taking the name of her male child), *ḥalaqa* (shaving of the head), and *adhān* (recitation of the call to prayer sequence in a newborn's ear), men reassert control over both their wives and their children postpartum as heads of the family and second only to God in begetting life. Such God-given control is already stipulated in the marriage contract, through which men are awarded unilateral control over the continuation or termination of the relationship. In fact, in early Sunnī jurisprudence, the *milk al-nikāḥ* (ownership in marriage) becomes analogous to the relationship between a master and slave concubinage.[2] However, the dominance of the husband over his wife must be reestablished practically through postpartum rituals.

Men even regulate breastfeeding practices to such an extent that the intimate bond forged between mother and child through nursing is severed to accommodate paternal power and control. In each one of these postpartum activities, including breastfeeding, a mother embodies a subordinate position to men as she actively transfers her own ability to generate life to her husband, and her exclusive, intimate authority over her child to its father. Her acquiescence to the status quo through habituated action and self-sacrifice, however, allows her to overcome her physical and moral weaknesses to mimic more closely the perfected ideals articulated through the lives of the pious queens of paradise, and to reinforce her identity as "good mother" in response to those ideals.

A Mother's Willing Subordination: Some Theoretical Considerations

Feminist scholars have long argued that a woman's subordination to patriarchal power results in her inherent suppression, silence, or passivity.[3] In order to counter such images of the repressed female, especially in historical studies, feminist scholars have looked to carve out women's "space," or have tried to demonstrate how women have struggled to resist dominant structures through alternative practices.[4] However, as recent studies have shown, it is not always fair or productive to confine women's voices to expressions of resistance, a concept that has become synonymous with a liberal, Western feminist agenda.[5]

While it is impossible to reconstruct fully individual, female experiences from elite, male-generated texts, this chapter argues it is still useful to describe how, within the context of ritual practice, medieval Muslim mothers may have exercised agency in ways that confirmed, rather than defied, the dominant structures of power.[6] Agency, in this light, can be understood as "a capacity for action that historically specific relations of subordination enable and create"[7] rather than a "capacity to realize one's own interests against the weight of custom, tradition, transcendental will or other obstacles (whether individual or collective)."[8] Agency in the former—but not the latter—sense can be detected throughout the numerous and varied postpartum rituals and practices described below, where women who bear children willingly acquiesce their reproductive authority to patriarchal forms of control through gesture, and thus become identified with and lauded as good mothers.

Expressions of female agency that reinforce the conditions of patriarchal subordination are best understood in light of intricate processes of self-formation.[9] Selves do not appear in a vacuum. An autonomous individual realizing its "own interests" implies an *a priori* self with constituted interests prepared to battle already identified forces that oppress it.[10] Rather, in light of current feminist studies, the "self" must be viewed as a much more fluid and unstable entity, created and recast through repeated performances of prior established conventions and ideologies that comprise the social world surrounding it.[11]

Applied to this study, a "good Muslim mother" who overcomes her physical and moral limitations to mirror the female paragons extolled within traditional contexts would be created and confirmed through actions, efforts, and desires that are themselves the products of theologically constituted power structures that privilege the bearing of children as a divinely mandated goal.[12] Thus, a woman performs certain bodily actions and disciplines to cultivate the self, in this case, to strive to conceive and give birth successfully, nurture an infant, and publicly socialize a child as its father's progeny. Through her efforts, she aims to realize states of "happiness, wisdom, purity, perfection or immortality in accordance with a particular discursive tradition."[13] Here, the particular discursive tradition articulated through medieval Muslim texts that create (and circumscribe) the conditions of maternal agency and enactment consists of Qur'ānic and prophetic affirmations of procreation, didactic stories about the virtuous, self-sacrificing examples of Mary, Āsiya, Khadīja, and Fāṭima, and the medical prescriptions wherein knowing men determine the contours and define the care of a "normative" female body.

This chapter examines how medieval women exercised agency within the context of patriarchal subordination through the lens of *habitus*. *Habitus*, in its classical, Aristotelian sense,[14] refers to "a specific pedagogical process by which moral virtues are acquired through a coordination of outward behavior (e.g., bodily acts, social demeanor) with inward dispositions (e.g., emotional states, thoughts, intentions)."[15] In the medieval Muslim context, a similar notion of habituated learning through practical knowledge is coined by the term *malaka*, which has been translated as "habit."[16] Conceptually, *malaka*, like *habitus*, can be similarly construed as "an inner quality developed through outer practice until that quality comes to regulate and govern one's behavior without conscious deliberation."[17] A woman's willing participation in the predominately male rituals and practices pertaining to the care and socialization of her child postpartum, such as *taḥnīk, khitān, ʿaqīqa, adhān, tasmiya,* and the *kunya,* as well as her acquiescence to male regulations regarding breastfeeding, creates a particular, maternal disposition that interacts with the very dominant discourses through which her identity and status as pious mother are formed, reinforced, and evaluated.

As the examples elaborated below show, it is clear that such practices and rituals function to bond the child more closely with his father than his mother, and thereby reinforce the dominant patriarchal structures through which men position themselves as second only to God as procreative determinants.[18] In reality, however, the issue is far more complex. A woman is not silenced through her consent but rather is afforded agency insofar as she is willing to subordinate her own prominent, reproductive role to paternal authority.[19] Even though the woman is excluded from participating directly in many of the postpartum practices listed above, her embodying of the natural (divine) order of the world through willful subordination, repeated again and again as the mother allows the father to take over her role incrementally through a series of infantile rituals, becomes a prized virtue that contributes to the creation of her pious, maternal self. It is through such directed efforts to maintain what God has willed that she exercises her agency,[20] and comes to embody the "good" mother.

As noted in the example of ʿĀʾisha, however, childless women often threatened the dominant patriarchal understanding of the good mother. After all, paternal identity depends on a man's wife giving birth to a child. A man's social status, therefore, hinges upon his appropriation of the child his wife bears through the rituals and embodied practices that create his role as father, head of the household, and generative partner with God. Without a child, no such role can be activated or sustained. Ironically, the paternal structures so vital to social stability are contingent on the childless women against whom the norm is necessarily defined, privileged, and praised.[21]

Examples of childless women on the margins show how these females did little to resist the paradigms of the good mother articulated in traditional sources and reinforced through postpartum rituals, but rather appropriated such practices in new ways that allowed them to embody, as closely as possible, the paternal ideal. Such efforts articulate a more nuanced theological understanding of "motherhood" that further accommodates women who cannot fulfill their role as natural child bearers. A woman's noble efforts to suffer her fate turn her into a model of piety and subordination for all women to emulate, and God's grace upon her becomes a sign of the mercy and benevolence only he can give.

In sum, rituals and embodied practices both regenerate but also are constrained by the images of the ideal mother put forth in the Qurʾān, medical wisdom, exegetical works, and law within everyday life. Such rituals and practices serve to distinguish the "maternal" from the "paternal," and to endow the latter with a primary, creative, and engendering role that becomes embedded within nature and the very fabric of the cosmos itself. Women whose reproductive bodies conform to the ideal hold a sacrosanct place in this cosmic theater. However, those whose anatomies are often blamed for failing to produce offspring become marginalized, since they are unable to participate in essential practices that articulate acceptable social identities and sustain the father's primary procreative role.

Such marginalization, however, invokes theological, social, ritual, and communal accommodation that equates a childless woman's suffering and pain with the more general acts of self-sacrifice demonstrated by the paradisiacal queens. A woman's willing acceptance of her reproductive lot—whatever that may be—thus, too, becomes a vital act men depend on to position themselves as second only to God in engendering the superlative life he desires.

Childbirth as Liminal Moment: An All-Female Affair

As noted in chapter 2, the maternal body, whether trying to conceive or already pregnant, falls under the jurisdiction of elite male scholars who strive to control anomalous conditions, often attributed to women, that might subvert a healthy life from being born. Given men's desire to monitor every facet of gestation, it is rather surprising that the actual act of giving birth likely took place within an all-female space. As an all-female affair, childbirth becomes a liminal moment, a breach that interrupts constant male surveillance and vigilance over the female body. This breach would have been reinforced further through purity laws enacted through postpartum bleeding, where a mother must abstain from intimate relations with her husband, and refrain from public rituals, such as the *tawaf,* until the cessation of blood.[22]

Such a breach is ultimately overcome through a reassertion of male dominance over the mother postpartum, who relinquishes her procreative power so glorified in the Qur'ān to that of men through her participation in a series of actions and infantile rituals that facilitate the shift from (natural) body to (cultural) symbol or, in Lacan's terms, from sheer anatomy to universal semantics.[23] Such actions and rituals seal the child's religious, familial, and gendered identity but also her bearer's status as "mother." Additionally, they work to seat the "father" as head of the family and society, and the prime begetter of life on earth, second only to God. In other words, after a woman delivers her child among the company of women, patriarchy reconstructs itself through rituals and embodied practices, which attempt to bundle the womb and its contents with patrilineal kinship and place the entire package under the sole jurisdiction of men.

Midwives as Navigators of Liminality

The liminal event of childbirth would have been navigated by the midwife and other female attendants, who work with the mother to bring forth her child into the world. In medieval Muslim society, midwives were both idealized and demonized, most likely because of their vital role as deliverers of life, and because their efforts took place in an all-female space inaccessible to men. As noted in chapter 3, the idyllic Luʿayya, the most beautiful of all houris, served as Fāṭima's midwife.[24] She lovingly cleansed the child Ḥusayn with paradisiacal waters and rubbed his gums with her own spittle.[25] Certain Shīʿī traditions even laud the prophet Muḥammad for acting as midwife and delivering Ḥusayn with his own hands,[26] although this is the only example of a male serving in that capacity (other than Jesus). Midwives were often valued so highly they were given special legal exemptions. Medieval Sunnī jurists, for example, accepted the testimony of midwives verbatim regarding certain issues, such as the infant's first cry upon birth, the age of a miscarried fetus, the establishment of paternity through the fixation of the child's birth date, or the verification of a woman's identity as mother of her child.[27]

Perhaps because their domain rests outside of male control, many scholars were somewhat skeptical of midwives, and sought to exert control over their activities, along with the maternal body, as suggested in chapter 2.[28] They describe midwives as being "rough" with the mother and child and often ignorant about what needs to be done in times of crisis.[29] Such ignorance, of course, requires immediate male intervention. By idealizing or demonizing the role of the midwife, male physicians and scholars reveal their own inadequacies in not being able to dominate a process so vital to the generation of life, a process that maintains the divinely ordained cosmic whole.

Despite such ambivalent views about female birth attendants, midwifery manuals and other forms of *ṭibb* literature agree that women, and not men, generally attended the birth and delivery of a child. Burhān al-Dīn al Marghīnānī, who authored the great Ḥanafī juridical work, *al-Hidāya*, states how, ideally, women should be trained as doctors so they could minister to their own sex.[30] Whether or not there were actual women doctors in the medieval period, the midwifery manuals' extended compilations of therapeutic recipes suggest folk remedies may have been transmitted to physicians via an already established female tradition, as opposed to the other way around.[31] For example, the manuals' direct commands to midwives (*qawābil*), or to the physicians who would be instructing midwives, all underscore the fact that birthing practices, including those that require complex medical wisdom and technical knowledge, would have been performed by women and not men.[32] Certainly, propriety and tradition would also have dictated the exclusive presence of women, and not men, during both labor and delivery.[33] Given the midwife's prominent role in delivering babies, men were left to speculate on what took place within those closed female circles, and often had to rely on secondhand information, prior medical tradition, or their own imaginations to fill in the gaps of their knowledge.

In general, the *ṭibb* literature paints a portrait of women giving birth in the warm and nurturing company of women, with the midwife (*qābila*) at the helm. Medical texts present her as the central figure around which all aspects of labor, delivery, and after-birth care revolve. In fact, the historian Abū Zayd ʿAbd al-Raḥmān ibn Muḥammad ibn Khaldūn al-Ḥaḍramī (d. 1406 CE), in his famous *Prolegomenon* (*Muqaddima*), notes the term *qābila* (midwife) implies both "giving and receiving."[34] The woman in labor gives up her embryo to the midwife and the midwife receives it from her in a kind of intimate, mutual exchange reminiscent of the Qurʾān's many depictions of God's loving, caring intimacy with female agents to generate life. *Ṭibb* texts capture this intimacy in their narrations of how midwives created a conducive environment for delivery by lighting fires and placing curtains on the doors to prevent the mother from catching cold; likewise, it is noted that they protected the expectant mother from excessive summertime heat by preparing a quiet place shaded from the sun, in a room that opened to the north.[35]

Male medical scholars acknowledge the fact that unlike Mary and Fāṭima, ordinary women experience great difficulties during labor. They describe in detail how midwives try to ease the woman's pain in any way possible. For example, according to these male elites, dedicated midwives prepare fatted chicken broth (*maraqa*), or supply bread, water, and drinks fused with water to counter labor pains.[36] They recite Qurʾānic verses that mention Mary's labor pains (Sūra 19:23–25) or God's supreme authority over all life (Sūra 16:78) to remind women in labor that they are not alone.[37] If a woman is going through a particularly severe bout of discomfort, the midwife might daub her face with spices of radish (*fujl*) and watercress (*jirjīr*) that are mixed with milk and crushed cinnamon.[38] Other accounts describe the attending midwife's preparation of warm milk fused with dates and almond oil,[39] or drinks made of musk and fruit juice to ease the anxieties of women as they face the often uncertain outcomes of their pregnancies.[40] Likewise, to release pain, a midwife lays her hands on the parturient female to massage her back, buttocks, and lower extremities adjacent to the uterus.[41]

The midwife, however, is not the only female in attendance; she relies on other women—presumably friends and family members of the pregnant woman—for help. A number of other women in attendance provide moral support as they assist the mother to work through each cycle of contractions (*makhāḍ*) by coaxing her to walk around or ascend the stairs, and then sit on her bed and take a rest.[42] When the midwife sees signs that the mouth of the womb has extended, she seats the pregnant woman in the birthing chair, and places a towel under the mother's feet in order to keep her from injuring herself.

At this point, two other women position themselves on the right and left side of the mother to assist her as needed. A third woman sits with her back braced against the birthing woman's back in order to provide support and leverage as the midwife works with the mother to push the child forth into the world.[43] To what extent these texts' descriptions mirror reality is unclear; whatever the case, they provide at least some glimpse into an otherwise closed environment where a woman about to give birth would have been surrounded by the intimate company of female family members, friends, and medical experts to support her and guide her through this arduous time.

In addition to facilitating the actual delivery, the midwife also plays a vital role in the moments subsequent to the baby's birth, even more so than the mother. For example, she first removes the placenta from the womb, often by making the woman sneeze if it proves too difficult to extract.[44] Next she cuts the umbilicus with a piece of glass (*zujāja*) or a thread or a reed resembling a knife.[45] The midwife is the first person to inspect the child; she ensures the head is shaped well and the child is healthy.[46] After she inspects the child, she washes him in a saline solution to remove the dirt. Scholars note women from Egypt often bathed infants with cold water from the Nile to cleanse them, rather than salt water.[47] Some midwives drip warm water to clear the baby's eyes, others boil myrtle water infused with *ʿafs* (gallnuts)[48] or ashes (*ramād*) for this same purpose. After she attends to the child's needs, the midwife carefully treats the mother's torn vagina.[49] In all these examples, the midwife is the authoritative, ever-present expert who ensures the safety, health, and care of both mother and child.

Reports show that the first food to enter the child is honey, which the midwife administers. She dips her fingers into the honey and the newborn sucks the liquid from them.[50] Physicians believed that honey would purify his stomach and clear his passages.[51] In addition to its cleansing properties, however, honey is also connected with the divine healing of the human soul. For example, the Qurʾān describes it as a "healing for the people" (*shifā'un lil-nāsi*); a "sign for those who give thought" (*l'āyatan liqawmin yatafakkarūna*).[52] Likewise, a *ḥadīth* states, "You must use two sources of divine healing: honey and the Qur'ān."[53]

Given the infant's emergence into the world in a state of purity (*fiṭra*), honey, which is placed on par with the Qur'ān in terms of promoting the well-being of the entire human person, both body and soul, seems the appropriate first drink. The striking image here, however, is the primary role of the surrogate mother (embodied by the midwife) in the transference of one of God's signs that is directly associated with his healing word into the body of the purified infant. In this light, divine word becomes food, transferred initially from woman to child.

After this intimate moment between child and midwife, however, the circle of women surrounding the child begins to expand outward into the social world. Sources note how a wet nurse is called upon to suckle the child for the first four days,[54] the purpose here being that a mother's colostrum, which is often thinner, yellower, and produced at less volume than breast milk, is somehow detrimental to the child.[55] Presumably, the mother would take the child to her own breast after that; however, it is unclear how readily her milk would have flowed after a four-day hiatus without excessive intervention.[56] The prominent roles of both midwives and wet nurses[57] suggest that perhaps during medieval times, the bond between mother and child was less sacrosanct than society assumes it to be today.[58] The extended network of women involved in the birth and care of an infant indicates his social identity may have been more important than his exclusive relationship with his mother. Of course, the elite, scholarly texts under consideration may simply wish to emphasize this point.

Much of the discussion about midwives, however, goes above and beyond the idyllic scenarios of the warm and comforting birth room described above where children are eased out of the womb and embraced by the mother's friends and family members. In other words, midwives were not just birth attendants but sophisticated physicians in their own right. This fact is evident in the medical literature that is primarily concerned with cases where midwives would be called upon to perform extraordinary procedures to save the life of the mother and/or that of the child. To ensure their readiness, male scholars took great care to arm the midwife with both the knowledge and tools necessary to deal with any anomalous or abnormal situation in the birth room that may have confronted her.[59]

While the rhetoric suggests male physicians would instruct midwives on various medical techniques, it may be they are simply describing what midwives already did when confronted with anomalous conditions, or what they believed would be the right thing for them to do in those same situations. In other words, the medical knowledge would lie with the midwife. For example, if delivery is difficult, it is noted that a midwife should make an incision in the fetal membrane with her fingernail to allow the water out, and put pressure on the woman's abdomen until the infant emerges.[60] If the fetus remains stuck, she is to apply an enema made from the mucilage of fenugreek and sesame oil.[61] Much is relayed about how midwives must work quickly both inside and outside the womb to reposition fetuses that present their feet, hands, or backs first rather than their heads.[62] Interestingly, male physicians seize this moment in the discussion of potential crises to tout some extraordinary cases the midwife might someday encounter, such as wombs that can carry two, three, seven, ten, or fifteen fetuses, all fully formed.[63] The fact that these men rely on such formulaic, Classical, tropes involving monstrosities reveals the limits of their own, firsthand experience.[64]

In the medical literature, physicians also familiarize midwives with the tools necessary to extract dead fetuses, whose continued presence in the womb would compromise the mother's life. In each of these cases, physicians command midwives to use any means available to save the life of the mother, no matter how extreme. The well-known Andalusian surgeon Abū al-Qāsim Khalaf ibn al-ʿAbbās al-Zahrāwī (d. 1013 CE), for example, instructs the midwife to stick hooks (*ṣinnārāt*) in the eye sockets or any other soft spot, and then "extract it [the fetus] evenly, as one pulls out a tooth."[65] If the head proves to be too large, a spike-shaped scalpel (*shūkīya*) may be employed to split it open to let the water drain out, which would make for easier extraction.[66] The head may also be smashed with a cephalotribe (*mishdākh*).[67] If circumstances dictate such a move, the midwife may need to cut the fetus up and extract the parts piecemeal.[68]

Even though male physicians appear knowledgeable about what instruments should be used in these life or death scenarios, and the general proficiencies involved, the nitty-gritty, anomalous details of such extreme procedures remain obscure, which suggests they may have been lost within the midwife's—and not the medical doctor's—memory. For example, how does one know when a fetus is dead? Is it more important to deliver the child alive at any cost, or would midwives have to weigh the mother's life against the child's, and opt for extraction before the child actually died? The midwife would have wielded much power and expertise in these split-second decisions. However, the criteria she would have used in her determinations remain tantalizingly undocumented. Unfortunately, there are no firsthand accounts of these heart-wrenching scenes, but one can assume what was covered in the manuals did not begin to address the trials, tribulations, joys, and tragedies these women confronted in their daily lives.

When Life Begins: Newborns and Social Identities

The expertise of the midwife, and the all-female space that envelops the new mother and child, disrupt the dominant structures of power that defined women as secondary to men. Men begin to counter this disruption by taking measures to facilitate the child's rebirth into its social life through ritual and practice where men—not women or God—demarcate the parameters of human existence. According to the Qur'ān, the life God bestows upon his creations is sparked by his breath and ensoulment.[69] Only he is aware of what wombs bear, and when life begins and ends.[70] Midwives and mothers, however, would certainly have been the next to know if a fetus were alive or dead in the womb.

In terms of a newborn's socialized human identity, however, men alone determine when new life begins or ends. According to the *ḥadīth,* "life" begins with the public affirmation of a child's first cry.[71] Prior to that moment, what a mother carries and brings forth from her womb bears no publicly recognized social existence. For example, despite the fact that the midwife testifies that a newborn did indeed cry upon exiting the womb, a male judge must confirm her testimony.[72] She may attest to life but that attestation carries no weight until it is rendered legitimate by the judge who represents the public at large.

The judge's stamp of approval on the midwife's testimony allows the infant to hold a lawful place in society. Infants whose cry has been confirmed may inherit property;[73] infants silent upon exiting the womb are not only denied an inheritance, they are also deprived of prayer recited over them upon their death.[74] As these cases illustrate, a child is born twice: first from the womb of the mother, and second into a social world where men define the parameters of a meaningful life. With the legal confirmation of the cry, patriarchy triumphs over and against the liminal moment of childbirth, where first God, and then women, attest to the presence or absence of life.

Rules of inheritance likewise underscore the significance of the cry as demarcating the child's social birth. A majority of jurists agree that fetuses that die in the womb should only be considered partially but not fully "alive." Thus, if one injures a woman's womb and causes her to abort, the blood money for an unborn (dead) fetus becomes a male or female slave, that is, its potential life is valued at less than a free person's.[75] However, "if a fetus comes out of the womb alive, the full blood money is due it. It is alive if it cries."[76] Additionally, funeral prayers may be uttered over infants born alive, but not those who die in the womb or during the process of being born.[77] While a mother may attest to her child's life in the womb or in the few tender moments postpartum, that life bears no concrete reality in the "public" sphere. If the infant dies before public (male) recognition, it simply has had no existence.

Contrarily, several scholars mark the origins of human life prior to the cry, which reveals the paternal desire to delimit life socially and legally not just after birth, with the cry, but also inside the woman's body and even prior to conception. For example, Ghazālī calls for miscarried fetuses being given names, and thus identities as persons, postmortem.[78] Likewise, abortion rulings harken back to Qurʾānic notions that human life actually commences with ensoulment, which occurs at one hundred and twenty days.[79] Prior to that time, most jurists would allow a woman to have an abortion, since they believe some form of life begins at conception, just not *human* life.[80] After one hundred and twenty days, abortion is prohibited.

Minority positions, which follow the dictates of Aristotelian views on reproduction, debate further the issue by locating human life within the male sperm. For example, the Mālikites argued that since the destiny of semen is ensoulment, once the semen settles in the womb husbands or wives cannot induce abortions.[81] This paternal understanding of the potentiality of male semen to contain publicly recognized life is further reflected in Mālikite rulings on the distribution of blood money: A man's penis incurs full blood money as do his testes.[82] Therefore, if a doctor performs a circumcision and cuts off the glans, he must pay the requisite blood money.[83] There seems to be no such compensation if a womb (not bearing a child) is harmed.[84] Again, in these examples, life may begin before the child utters his first sound, but its very existence depends on male recognition and, in some cases, the male semen's bearing of the life force.

Other scholars also argue for the integrity of life prior to parturition. Ibn ʿArabī, for example, states the unborn child in the womb has the potential to develop all the perfections of human existence by comprehending the divine names.[85] This idealized image of the fetus's primordial omniscience or wisdom appears also in medieval Talmudic exegesis, which claims the purified fetus "looks and sees from one end of the world to the other," and is "also taught the Torah from beginning to end."[86] Each of these examples shows how male elites, through their social, legal, or, in the case of Ibn ʿArabī, theological criteria that determine when life begins, exert control over a process that—practically speaking—involves the bodies and intimate knowledge of God and women. The effects of their efforts to confirm life both licitly and publicly serves to subsume the intimate associations between God, mother, and child under the counsel of men.

Kinship: The Womb as Social Property

In the company of women who witness parturition, there is no question as to whom the child belongs; however, paternal ties have yet to be asserted and confirmed by the community at large. Such paternal ties are established via the rhetorical linkage between kinship and the mother's womb. Blood ties, maintained through kinship, become the basis upon which to establish the intricate web of relationships that identify and order human beings in the world. The womb serves as the primary source for the creation of all kinship relations for the newborn; the Qur'ān, in fact, presents the womb as the source for all human relationships. Wombs negotiate mutuality and reciprocity, the source through which "you demand one of another" in kinship.[87]

However, the paternal ties that dictate such relationships become more heavily emphasized with the child's rebirth into the world of men. As the child's existence is conferred socially and legally, its paternal associations become the predominant, organizing feature in establishing his identity, even though maternal bonds and motherly love are still lauded as "natural" and thus necessary for the child's care and well-being.[88] Such paternal control over the womb, and thus the kinship ties created there, are often asserted retroactively through legal decisions regarding adultery, paternity, inheritance, and the offspring of freed slaves, to locate the male presence in the womb both subsequent and prior to birth. Such an emphasis on fatherhood and paternal relations in these cases counters Qur'ānic images of both God and Muḥammad as *antipater,* and the womb as intimate partner with God.

Rulings on adultery, for example, solidify and privilege the paternal connections between father and child. However, these paternal connections are almost always described in social, rather than biological, terms. For example, if a woman commits adultery and becomes pregnant, "the child belongs to the bed and the adulterer gets nothing."[89] Likewise, if the mother is an unmarried slave girl, the legal father is also not the adulterer but rather the man who was her master at the time she gave birth to the child.[90] Only when the mother is a free unmarried woman does the child become detached from any paternal ties, and is thus labeled a "child of fornication (*walad al-zinā*)."[91] In these examples, adulterous men can lay no claim to the children they father; rather, offspring belong to the husband (or master) of the wife, if relevant.

Such a view that the husband "owns" his wife's womb is confirmed in Zamakhsharī's commentary on Sūra 2:233, which suggests wombs may be places of safekeeping, but only at the discretion of the husband.[92] The husband's ownership of his wife's womb, and therefore what it contains, is further underscored in legal proclamations concerning the fate of an adulterous woman who becomes pregnant, and gives birth. According to the *Mishkāt,* the prophet ordered a woman who confessed to fornication to give birth to the child, and then suckle it for two years and wean it. After that, she must be stoned.[93] Here, the woman's womb and breasts serve as the vehicles through which the husband's property must be sustained and delivered, since he is the owner of the "bed."

Legal opinions regarding the status of pregnant female slaves also sever further a woman from the contents of her womb. Mālik, for example, records traditions that argue if a slave woman who is married to another slave is set free while pregnant, "the *walā*ʾ of what is in her womb goes to the person who set the mother free because slavery touched the child before the mother was set free."[94] In this example, the mother's change in status cannot override the fact that the slave owner was officially the possessor of her womb and its contents. A second example relays how the slave girl, and what she carries in her womb, belongs to the one who has bought her (whether or not the buyer stipulates that).[95] Further indications of the master's complete ownership over the bodies of his female servants occur in legal discussions about the *umm walad,* a term that refers to the female slave who bears the child of her master. Here, if a master claims a child to be his own, or at least does not deny that he had intercourse with the enslaved mother, both woman and child will be freed upon the master's death.[96] Here, the status of the father literally transforms that of mother and child to reflect his own. Again, in all of these examples the mother is not in full possession of her child; neither is the biological father. Rather, her womb becomes a public entity that can be bought, sold, freed, or enslaved by its male owner, whether he is actually related to the child or not.[97]

All of these examples reinforce the importance of paternal dominance over, and responsibility for, a child. Because men own the womb that bears their offspring, a mother should never assign her child's paternal heritage wrongfully, nor should fathers deny their genetic connection to their offspring. For example, Ibn Māja relates that the prophet said: "Any woman who attributes her child to people to whom he does not belong, she has no relation to the right religion [*dīn*] of God. She will never enter paradise. As for any man who rejects his child he knows to be his own, God himself will hide from him on the day of resurrection and disgrace him before the witnesses."[98]

Such proclamations counter pagan, *jāhilīya* practices, where a child's maternal ties were often privileged over and above his paternal ones. For Muslim scholars, such practices led to chaos and disorder that undermined the *dīn* of God. A list of *jāhilīya* marriage practices describes how prostitutes used to fix flags on their tents, and would have sex with any number of men who came to visit them. If one became pregnant and gave birth, all the men who ever came to visit her would be gathered for scrutiny by a *qā'if* (person skilled in recognizing the likeness of a child to his father). The *qā'if* ruled the child belonged to the man he most resembled.[99] In another *jāhilīya* example, the mother herself named one of the men she had sex with as the father.[100] These examples demonstrate how a patriarchal system based on blood relationships replaced a matriarchal one founded on female power and preference, which descended into, at least for Muslim scholars, complete pandemonium.[101]

The shift from a maternal to paternal system was gradual and never quite complete in the early decades of Islam. Evidence shows how the early caliphs were given the difficult task of sorting out the agnatic lineages of those born prior to the advent of Islam (or at least the figures of the caliphs were utilized to establish normative practice). In these situations, the caliphs often had to step in and establish paternity, which suggests that constructing male lineage was so vital an issue as to be taken up by rulers, and to be asserted even in cases that defied absolute clarification.

For example, Mālik reports a situation where two men each claimed to have fathered a woman's child. The second *rashidūn* caliph, ʿUmar ibn al-Khaṭṭāb (d. 644 CE), summoned a *qā'if,* who determined both men were indeed the fathers. ʿUmar ibn al-Khaṭṭāb beat him.[102] He then consulted with the mother, who noted she thought the first man was the father until she menstruated. After that, she hooked up with a second gentleman. Given the timing of both the encounters and her menses, she did not know who the father was. Because of the complexity of this situation, ʿUmar empowered the child to choose one of the men to be his father.[103]

In another instance, a woman gave birth to a fully developed child four and a half months after her husband died. Since she had waited the prerequisite period before remarrying, it was unclear to whom the child belonged. ʿUmar ibn al-Khattāb consulted with some wise old *jāhilīya* women, who informed him the woman continued to menstruate after her first husband's death, which dried the child out in her womb. When she remarried, the new husband's semen watered the child, causing it to grow again in the womb. As a result of this information based on traditional, female gynecological wisdom, ʿUmar delegated the child to the first husband.[104] The fourth caliph, ʿAlī ibn Abī Ṭālib (d. 661 CE), on the other hand, is reported to have simply assigned a child by lot to one of three men who had intercourse with the mother.[105] Each of these early Islamic rulers found creative ways to incorporate ambiguous heritages into the new, patrilineal system that required clear lines to be drawn from father to son (or daughter), and son (or daughter) to father. Such lines asserted paternal authority and power over maternal bonds, and confirmed the primacy of social birth over what took place solely among the company of women.

Breastfeeding: Forging Patrilineal Links between Mothers and Children, Brothers and Sisters, Neighbors and Friends

Breastfeeding for up to two years is a practice lauded in the Qurʾān and in traditional sources. Upon parturition, the breast assumes the role of the umbilical cord and external placenta.[106] As such, breastfeeding becomes a prolongation of gestation in which the mother, having given her life to the child *in utero,* now donates her milk to guarantee her infant a healthy life.[107] The circularity of giving and receiving milk in order to produce milk again creates an intimate bond between mother and child,[108] which, as in the case of pregnancy and childbirth, occurs outside the experience of men.[109] As an extension of pregnancy and an act that begins postpartum among the company of women, breastfeeding has the potential to waylay the child's social rebirth into a meaningful life. To secure a quick transference of the infant from its natural state, defined solely by its association with women, into a culturally significant position among the world of men, male elites sought to control every aspect of the milk flowing from a mother's breasts into her child's mouth.

Despite the fact that the father cannot physically nurse his child, he still defines and oversees the terms of the suckling relationship between mother and infant. Through his financial support of the breastfeeding mother, employment of a wet nurse, observance of the kinship connections solidified through blood, breast milk, and his own semen, the father reroutes the intimate ties between mother and child so that he becomes the primary source of nourishment for his own progeny.

While men struggle to repair the disruption of the social order brought on by the liminal moment of childbirth through reassertions of paternal authority and privilege, women also face the prospect of reintegration into a postpartum world, where "mothers" must be defined over and against "fathers." To this end, the woman exercises agency by becoming the willing and necessary vehicle through which the father bestows a meaningful life upon his child. Her acquiescence to the divinely affirmed social order, where men stand as the primary begetters of life, is expressed through her acceptance of the child to her breast, but more importantly, through her adherence to the paternally driven rules and regulations surrounding the feeding of her child.

On the Goodness of Breastfeeding

Medieval scholars and theologians view a breastfeeding mother as the optimal mother who provides her child with the best love, nourishment, and opportunity for a healthy life. In conformity with this view, Fakhr al-Dīn al-Rāzī encourages mothers to feed their own infants. Suckling is not imposed, he notes, but "it is more proper for the child to be fostered with his mother's milk than with the milk of other women."[110] The only time suckling is mandated, rather than encouraged, is in the case of adultery, where a woman essentially relinquishes her authority over the child. As noted above, an adulteress must suckle her child for two years and then wean him before she is stoned.[111]

In addition to viewing the mother's milk as the best milk for her child, medieval scholars also praise the self-sacrificial nature of breastfeeding. For example, traditional scholars note how, with each suck from her breast, a mother receives the reward of one good deed.[112] Scholars recognized that breastfeeding took such a toll on the body that they deemed nursing mothers exempt from the fast.[113] Other texts praise exemplary mothers who struggle to breastfeed at any cost. The banished mother Hagar bore no concern for herself but for her child as she frantically ran the hills of Ṣafā and Marwa in search of water to drink to make her milk flow sufficiently to suckle the baby Ishmael. In response to her profound expressions of faith, dedication, and self-sacrifice, God miraculously provided the necessary water for their sustenance.[114] Such tender images inform the "natural" bonds established between mother and child through breastfeeding.

Despite such idealized views of the devoted, self-sacrificing nursing mother, medieval sources do not condemn mothers who hand their children over to nursemaids. Certainly, it is within a woman's rights to not nurse her child.[115] After all, the Qur'ān allows for a certain flexibility in this regard; no burden should be imposed on a mother and/or father they cannot bear.[116] The revelation also proposes both the mother and father can determine the time of weaning, and the employment of a wet nurse, if necessary. In fact, a whole business evolved around the profession of wet nursing in medieval times; clearly it was a common, and necessary, practice prior to the advent of infant formula.[117] However, the professional wet nurse was rarely praised, and was often deemed mercenary in her desire to offer her breasts in exchange for money.[118]

However, astonishing stories still surround those rare wet nurses willing to take on the responsibilities of another woman's child without payment, which suggests again a privileging of women willing to sacrifice their bodies for another with little or no compensation. For example, hagiographical sources idealize the prophet Muḥammad's wet nurse, the bedouin Ḥalīma bint Abī Dhuʿayb, who was the only woman willing to suckle the orphan Muḥammad, because his father was dead and therefore could not pay her for her services. Even though she was poor, she took on this responsibility and was rewarded for her efforts. When she nursed him, her own breasts became excessively engorged, and she and all her family's livestock produced milk abundantly during a time of great famine.[119] In this example, the causal connection between piety and fecundity is clear.

Likewise, paradise is filled with unnamed, dedicated wet nurses who selflessly suckle infants upon their arrival in the Garden after an untimely death. Stories abound about how Ibrāhīm, the prophet's son who tragically died at age two, received a wet nurse to nurture him in paradise.[120] Clearly, traditional sources praise the intimate bond between mother and child created through breastfeeding, and the many self-sacrifices they, or their nursemaids, were willing to endure while carrying out this difficult but honorable task. By selflessly suckling their newborns, both mothers and wet nurses model themselves after the ideal women of paradise who continuously sacrifice themselves for the sake of their children.

On the Right to Breastfeed

The mother's inherent right to breastfeed her child is advocated in every source. In Sūra 2:233, the Qurʾān commands mothers to suckle their offspring for two years, if "one desires to complete the period of suckling" (*liman ʿarāda ʿan yutimma al-raḍāʿata*). Here, the "one" desiring the mother to nurse her child appears to be the father, according to traditional accounts.[121] The Qurʾān, however, stipulates that for every child a man desires to have breastfed, he is obliged to pay the mother her expenses, whether he is married to her or divorced.[122] While fathers may command their wives (or ex-wives) to breastfeed if they can support them, they do not have the right to preclude a mother from breastfeeding. If she wants to nurse her child, he must provide for her for the two-year period.[123]

Traditional sources view breastfeeding as highly beneficial to the child, and encourage it despite difficult circumstances, such as divorce.

However, they warn against divorced parents using children as weapons to harm one another. Accounts admonish a divorced mother who seeks revenge on her husband by refusing to suckle his child, especially if the husband provides for her with what God has enjoined him, "for her milk is best for it [the child] and she is usually kinder and more gentler to it [the child] than any other woman."[124] Here, refusing to suckle the child is equivalent to rejecting the benefits God has bestowed upon his creation.

In addition, fathers should not try to bully their ex-wives by taking the child to another woman to be nursed.[125] By suckling the child even when divorced, a mother cultivates the maternal virtues of both kindness and gentleness. In addition, by suppressing her own anger toward her ex-husband, her body becomes the sole source through which the father is able to solidify his relationship with the child. Despite the fact that the parents will part ways once the child is weaned, and the mother will most likely have custody of her child (if she does not remarry),[126] the father maintains the authority he established over both mother and child by providing for their maintenance and well-being during the two years of suckling.

Interestingly, medieval Muslim views on breastfeeding obligations mirror medieval Jewish perspectives, which suggests motherhood was constructed along similar lines in both monotheistic traditions. Jewish women are encouraged to suckle, if they are able, but no man can coerce his wife to suckle his friend's child as well.[127] Jewish sources, similar to Islamic texts, declare a woman's wishes to breastfeed her child will always take precedence over the father's desire to prevent her from doing so, although there is some practical evidence to the contrary.[128] According to the *Tosefta Niddah*, if the husband of a nursing woman dies, she is not allowed to marry for twenty-four or eighteen months, for fear that the stepfather might cut off the baby from his suckling.[129] Here, the desire to assert proper paternal authority is, perhaps, even more pervasive than it is in the Islamic examples.

Jewish husbands were likewise obligated to support their ex-wives financially for nursing a child; however, the women could choose not to nurse, and therefore severed themselves from any obligation toward children or ex-husbands.[130] In both the Islamic and Jewish examples, women are encouraged to breastfeed but not necessarily forced to do so, and in general their desires are privileged over and above their husbands' if they choose to suckle their children. Husbands, however, always bear the financial burden for supporting a nursing mother. Therefore, his wealth becomes the ultimate source for the milk, and thus the primary determiner of the child's health, nourishment, and identity.

Milk and Paternal Blood Relationships

The father's desire for the mother to suckle his child, even after divorce, makes little sense unless contextualized in broader discussions of how breast milk reinforces a father's paternal relationship to the child. Most Muslim physicians, like their Greek predecessors,[131] assume breast milk is generated from the leftover blood of the menses, which has been stored in the womb to nourish the growing fetus.[132] The blood that nourishes the child in the womb now rises up to the breasts, where it converts to milk for the child to suck.[133] Scholars prove that menses becomes breast milk by the fact that nursing women no longer experience their monthly periods.[134] As the examples above show, physicians glorify the woman's body for its ability to generate the most perfected of all foods to nourish the newborn.[135] They also laud those women who freely submit their bodies to the needs of their dependent infants. However, some scholars propose that while the mother's milk does play an essential role in her child's livelihood—her body best suited for such a role—it is still the father's semen that serves as the ultimate source for the creation of milk.

For example, Abū Walīd Muḥammad ibn Aḥmad ibn Rushd (d. 1198 CE), the prominent Andalusian scientist, theologian, and philosopher known in European literature as Averroes, argues that male semen stimulates pregnancy, which leads to delivery and the subsequent conversion of blood to milk.[136] Bukhārī also records that if one suckles from a wet nurse's breast, her husband will become a foster father to him.[137] Such views reflect structurally Aristotelian claims that menses, milk, and semen stem from a single substance: blood.[138] In this scheme, male semen stands as the most complete concoction over the other two, with menses being the crudest form, with milk in the middle.[139] Aristotle, in fact, identifies cases where men have actually produced milk, which suggests they, like women, have the capability to nurse children had they not evolved to a superior physical form beyond that.[140] Likewise, in Ibn Rushd's example, the father becomes the patron source for his wife's breast milk, for without his semen directing her inferior substances to a desired end, milk would never be produced. The circle between blood, menses, and semen is completed via the child's ingestion of breast milk, which is, in fact, connected with the father's semen, and thus to his own, growing virility.[141]

Nowhere is the male absorption of the maternal role as ultimate provider of nourishment for her child more explicitly acknowledged than in Shīʿite tales depicting the prophet Muḥammad's nursing of his grandson Ḥusayn. In his *Manāqib Āl Abī Ṭālib*, Imāmī exegete and *faqīh* Abū Jaʿfar Muḥammad ibn ʿAlī ibn Shahrāshūb (d. 1192 CE) relates how the prophet forbade Fāṭima to nurse her son, and instead inserted his own tongue or thumb into the child's mouth to suckle him for forty days.[142] This transference of nutrients from the prophet's own body to his grandson's bonded the blood and flesh of Muḥammad with the blood and flesh of Ḥusayn, which subordinated the mother's biological connection with her child.[143] Through this maternal act of nursing, Muḥammad transfers the imāmate through the progeny of Ḥusayn.[144] However, by offering her own maternal role to her father, Fāṭima's decision to withhold her breast from her hungry son becomes a willful act of piety to be emulated by all women who symbolically sacrifice the intimate bond they have with their children for the good of the divinely prescribed social order and the maintenance of the community. Without such a sacrifice, neither they nor their children would have a clear or valued identity in the postpartum world.

Milk and Maternal Blood Relationships

Despite the fact that men assert themselves to be the primary source of their child's food, as those who don the physical tools to breastfeed women are not without power. Given that physicians believe breast milk was generated from converted blood, they argue that kinship relations could be established through suckling. By breastfeeding another woman's child, to whom she was unrelated, a woman could mimic the process of reproduction as blood, the source of milk, transmitted kinship.[145] Suckling relationships, which were governed by the same laws as kin relationships,[146] had the benefit of allowing for further exogamy. Not only were close relatives prohibited from marrying one another, but so, too, were children nursed by the same woman. Thus, men and women who suckled from the same breast would have to seek alternative marriage partners. For example, a woman told ʿUqba b. al-Ḥārith, a prominent transmitter of *ḥadīth,* that she had suckled both him and his wife. The prophet said he must divorce his wife.[147] To a limited extent, women possessed the power to establish kinship relations through their own deficient form of semen, namely, breast milk.

Such power, however, was curbed through a number of proscriptions limiting the time frame during which a woman could mimic such reproductive relations. Breast milk may be potent but it is, after all, only a lesser, incomplete form of semen. These proscriptions appear to have been formulated in response to several episodes where men felt the need to exert control over women's power to transform the social order through suckling. For example, Mālik reports how a wife used suckling to prevent her husband from having sex with a slave girl. In order make the slave girl off-limits to the husband, the wife nursed her at her breast. This act prevented the husband from having further intercourse with her, as she was now his milk sister. As punishment, the caliph ʿUmar told the man he should beat his wife, since "kinship by suckling is only by suckling the young."[148] Mālik establishes what constitutes the "young" at age two; after that, blood relations can no longer be claimed through the breast.[149]

Clearly, such proscriptions constrain a woman's ability to restructure the patrilineal social order according to her own desires. To avoid repeated episodes of jealous women taking matters into their own hands when it comes to manipulating a man's right to engage in sex with concubines, many *ḥadīth* reports declare a child (under the age of two) must suckle at a woman's breast at least five times before a marriage (or here, sexual relations) could be decreed unlawful.[150] Also, during the five discrete periods of suckling, the milk must fill the child's entire stomach and serve as the sole form of its food.[151] A quick nip at the tit is an insufficient justification to restructure the social fabric along maternal lines.

Such restrictions may curtail a mother's ability to mimic the reproductive power of a father, but they are often used by men to assert control over women. For example, Sahla bint Suhayl ʿAmr al-Qurayshī said to the prophet Muḥammad that her adopted son Sālim used to see her dressed scantily. The prophet replied that she should nurse him, thereby establishing kinship ties with him.[152] Here, the prophet recommends a suckling relationship be set up between a mother and her grown adopted son so that no impropriety is committed as a result of the two interacting with one another. Of course, the logistics of initiating such a feat could be considered impious and improper in and of themselves; however, in this case, the end would necessarily justify the means. This example reveals a situation where what is forbidden to women to perform somehow becomes acceptable for men to command.

Male Control over Breastfeeding Practices

The closed circle of women surrounding the birth of a child was further disrupted through the rules and regulations surrounding breastfeeding, which often involve a husband reestablishing normative sexual relations with his nursing wife. Clearly, a mother was off-limits to her husband for a forty-day period after childbirth, as the *lochia* would render her impure.[153] However, after the forty days, when a mother would be breastfeeding her child, there seems to be two schools of thought as to when husbands and wives could once again engage in sexual intercourse.

Ibn Qayyim, for example, recommends nursing women refrain from sexual relations throughout the entire lactation period.[154] The concern here has to do with the possibility of a nursing mother becoming pregnant while she is nourishing the first child. For Hippocrates, milk flowing from the breast of a pregnant woman always means the fetus she is carrying will be weak.[155] A *ḥadīth* found in the collection of Ibn Māja makes the same exact point.[156] ʿAbd Allāh ibn Muslim ibn Qutayba (d. 889 CE), a medieval philologist and lexicographer of Persian or Turkish descent, discusses how the ancient Arabs disliked the suckling of one child while pregnant with another.[157] Likewise, the *Mishkāt al-maṣābīḥ* professes that a child whose mother suckled him while pregnant will suffer later in life.[158] The Sunnī Muslim biographer from Baghdad, Muḥammad ibn Saʿd (d. 845 CE), who narrates the lives of prominent Muslim figures in the early history of Islam, notes that the prophet was dismayed when he was unable to touch his wife Umm Salama because she was breastfeeding. However, once he found her a wet nurse, he was able to resume sexual relations with her.[159] In these examples, breastfeeding puts a wedge between husbands and wives; paternal authority could not be fully reestablished until sexual relations were reinstated.

In order to restore normative relations, scholars noted some exceptions to the rule. For example, the idea that pregnancy would compromise the health of a suckling child is negated by appeal to other cultural practices. Ibn Māja, for example, records a *ḥadīth* that describes how the prophet had wanted to prohibit *ghīla* (a man having intercourse with his wife while she is breastfeeding), but then saw the Persians and Greeks doing it and that it did not kill their children.[160] This passage may point to a reversal of prior practice, or may suggest a growing acceptance of a new mother's use of contraceptives. According to Elisheva Baumgarten, medieval Jewish law permits nursing mothers to use a *mokh* (cervical sponge) for the mandated twenty-four month period of suckling in order to prevent the conception of a child who would then compromise its sibling's milk supply.[161] It is possible the Persians and Greeks also allowed for such contraceptive use. Whatever the case, allowing husbands to engage in sexual relations with their nursing wives serves to repair the social breach brought on by childbirth and early infant care, and to reestablish patriarchal order through the reconstitution of the household hierarchy.

Even more restrictions are placed on the daily activities of professional wet nurses, since they don the role of surrogate mother.[162] Through such restrictions, men continue to assert control over the feeding process, as they believe the child to be weak and vulnerable without their full participation in the activity.[163] Given that the father of the child would be purchasing the services of the wet nurse, it was up to him to control her diet, behaviors, and habits, as these could be easily transferred to the child. Such rules and regulations regarding her diet and behavior would have been intimately tied with medical wisdom at the time.

Medieval physicians assume an intimate connection exists between the uterus and the breast, which is not surprising given the anatomical map of the female reproductive system they had in mind, with a single tube linking the two together.[164] However, they believe the link between the uterus and the breast also extends to the body and mind of the nursing woman herself. Thus any of the wet nurse's unpleasant or problematic traits or defects would be imprinted on the child through her breast milk.[165] For example, Jāḥiẓ muses that if a nursing woman drinks wine, she will make her baby drunk as it feeds; if she takes a laxative, the infant, too, will have diarrhea. He advises wise men to choose wet nurses free from any physical or mental illness.[166] Muslim physicians counsel fathers to instruct wet nurses to avoid any foods that might compromise the health of the child's brain, including salty, fatty, pungent, spicy, acidic, or unwholesome foods.[167] For example, leeks and garlic can cause ulcers in the child.[168] Wet nurses should avoid having sexual intercourse, as it spoils the milk.[169] If her milk becomes exceptionally thin, she should increase her consumption of foods such as rice, meat and white egg yolks, and lengthen the amount of sleep she gets.[170]

If men are to employ a wet nurse, they should seek out women who are young, preferably between twenty and thirty years of age, pink in color, not ill or irritable (so as not to transfer to the child those same qualities). She should have good, plump breasts; not too small and not too large. Most importantly, perhaps, the wet nurse should not be pregnant, for then the milk is spoiled and returns to water.[171] ʿArīb ibn Saʿd mentions that women who have had two to three babies provide the best milk; if the child of the wet nurse is female that is more preferable.[172] Contrarily, Ibn Sīnā suggests the sex of her last born child should be male.[173]

Not only does the father of the child that requires a wet nurse display complete control over the female body, but so too does the husband of the wet nurse. Medieval jurists discuss the fact that wet nurses who offer up their breasts for hire must receive permission from their husbands. For example, Mālikī jurist Khalīl ibn Isḥāq (d. 1374 CE) states that the husband of the wet nurse is entitled to cancel his wife's contract if he did not authorize it in the first place. In general, husbands have a stake in their wives' professional lives given that they are the ones who initially impregnate their spouses and put them into the position of being able to produce milk. Also, husbands of wet nurses must agree to refrain from intercourse with their lactating wives during the stipulated time period so as to prevent them from becoming pregnant, and thus breaching their contracts.[174] In sum, the wet nurse is subservient to the men who require the services her body provides.

Such rules and restrictions regulate the wet nurse's potential power over the child, and elevate that of the father who sired him, and that of the man she is married to. Men exert control over wet nurses similar to what they wield over their wives to protect their child from harm. As such, they move the child away from the circle of women who surrounded him from the moment of birth into a social world where it becomes the man's responsibility to generate and nourish the life God commands. The mother's role is also shaped in the process as her breasts become the property of the child's father, and serve to solidify his position as head of the household and second only to God in procreative power. Her means of support are illustrated through her willingness to breastfeed the child, and emphasized further through the consent she gives for her own husband—or her male client and the child she is servicing—to participate in postpartum ritual practices.

Paternal Rites and Maternal Agency in Postpartum Ritual Practices

Patriarchy continuously reasserts itself through a series of postpartum rituals, which have the effect of further repairing the breach brought about through childbirth, solidifying the womb's connection with kinship, and placing the womb and its contents more firmly under the jurisdiction of men. While postpartum rituals reestablish male authority to create Muslim fathers, they also generate women's identities as good mothers. Such identities become more clearly articulated as women consent to paternal authority through repeated performances during which mothers transfer their sanction over the child to men. Such ritual performances often involve bodily iterations of significant events in sacred history, the internalization of legal prescriptions grounded in divine authority, or the embodiment of the paradigmatic examples of selfless mothers.

The Taḥnīk: The Sealing of Blood Relations through Paternal Food

Evidence for the transference of female authority to men appears in a number of postpartum rituals such as the *taḥnīk*. Like paternal control over breastfeeding practices, the *taḥnīk* ceremony, which the prophet Muḥammad initiated but which then became a recommended duty for men,[175] symbolizes even further the father's replacement of the mother as nurturer of the child. During the *taḥnīk*, the prophet Muḥammad (quintessential father) chews a few dates, and then places the masticated juices in an infant's mouth to be consumed as the child's first food rather than its mother's milk.[176] It is important to note the *taḥnīk* was only performed on males, and not females, which suggests structural parallels to Jewish practices of circumcision that underscore patriarchal inclusion into a religious group.[177]

The replacement of the mother with the father as the prime nurturer of the child serves to establish lineage between fathers and sons, the son's loyalty to the father, and the communal recognition of the infant's identity as his father's son. However, by refusing to suckle her child, and instead handing the infant over to the father to be fed, the mother cultivates the perceived virtue of subordination to both husband and God. It is ultimately her willing suppression of her own maternal instincts and biological functions that secures the infant's place within the community, rather than simply the father's ritual actions. Through such consent to the status quo, a woman is able to seal her identity as "good mother" in the eyes of believers and, most importantly, in the eyes of God.

According to tradition, the *taḥnīk* ceremony is deeply rooted in the actions of the prophet Muḥammad. Bukhārī records how after Asmāʾ conceived and bore ʿAbdallāh b. al-Zubayr, the prophet asked for a date, which he chewed. He then put some of its juice in the child's mouth so that the first thing to enter the child's stomach was the prophet's own saliva.[178] Here, the date serves as the vehicle through which the prophet's spittle enters the child's stomach as his "first food." Other traditional accounts of the same event describe how Muslims rejoiced at the birth of ʿAbdallāh ibn al-Zubayr, considered to be the first child born in the Islamic era, for they believed the Jews had bewitched them (*ʿinna al-yahūd qad saḥaratkum*) so they would not be able to produce any offspring.[179] The prophet's gesture of placing his own saliva—via the date—into the child's mouth protects ʿAbdallāh and all other children born after the advent of Islam from harm.

In addition to its defense against evil, the *taḥnīk* ceremony also provided a context in which the male child was given a name and a blessing, and thus a social identity.[180] The protective quality of the prophet's saliva, along with the name and blessing, were all a part of the child's social rebirth as his father's son, and as a publicly recognized member of the Muslim community. However, mothers also played a significant role in this process of rebirthing the child under paternal terms by handing the child over to the father, and through their efforts, secured for him and themselves an integral place in society.

To illustrate this point, in the following tale, Umm Sulaym, one of the earliest converts to Islam in Medina, guarantees her son's livelihood by relinquishing her own care of him and by handing him over to authoritative men who would then provide him with the essentials for his survival:

> On the authority of Anas. b. Mālik: Abū Talḥa had a son who was sick. Once, while Abū Talḥa was out, the child died.

> When Abū Talḥa returned home, he asked, "How is my son?" Umm Sulaym replied, "He is quieter than he has ever been." Then she brought supper for him and he took his supper and slept with her. When he had finished, she said to him, "Bury the child." The next morning Abū Talḥa came to the messenger of God and told him the story. The prophet said to him, "Did you sleep with your wife last night?" Abū Talḥa said, "Yes," The prophet said, "O God, bestow your blessing upon them with regard to that night of theirs." Umm Sulaym gave birth to a boy. Abū Talḥa told me [Anas b. Mālik] to take care of the child until it was taken to the prophet. Then Abū Talḥa took the child to the prophet and Umm Sulaym sent some dates along with the child. The prophet took the child and asked if he had something with him. The people replied, "Yes, a few dates." The prophet took a date, chewed it, took some of it out of his mouth, put it into the child's mouth and did *taḥnīk* for him, and named him ʿAbdallāh.[181]

This vignette makes a number of didactic points. It cautions against newborn infants being left in the sole care of their mothers. Here, while the father is away, an infant dies unexpectedly, for no specified reason. This unfortunate situation is rectified only when the prophet, via the father, is informed and then calls upon God to allow the couple to conceive another son.

After the second child was born, the men donned a maternal role as Umm Sulaym's son, Anas ibn Mālik, watched over his newborn brother until the prophet could perform the *taḥnīk* ceremony with dates mixed in saliva. Here, the prophet and father become the generative source of both biological and social life. They become the rightful guardians over the newest member of the Muslim community through their nourishment and protection of the child. The lesson is clear: danger preys upon newborns because mothers cannot sustain and secure their livelihood. Just as Moses's mother would have burned her son in the oven had God not intervened, so, too would Umm Sulaym's second son have perished if Abū Talḥa had not stepped in to shield the child from harm.

Just as fathers must come to emulate the prophet as performers of the *taḥnīk,* so, too, must mothers mimic the gestures and intentions of Umm Sulaym, who was known for her courage, bravery, and steadfast faith.[182] Like Umm Sulaym, the mother must play a vital, albeit secondary, purpose in confirming both the prophet's and the father's role in bestowing life. After all, she is the one who will hand her child over to be cared for and watched over by men. She is the one who will provide the dates, which become a substitute for her own breast milk, along with her sexuality and reproductive power, to the prophet via the father.

For medical scholars, dates have a long established association with sexual potency and fertility. Jalāl al-Dīn al-Suyūṭī (d. 1505 CE), the well-revered Egyptian author who wrote on a wide range of topics, for example, notes that a woman who eats dates, or inserts date palm blossoms into her vagina, will produce children with ease. Given that dates are hot and dry, they also increase sexual power (especially when combined with pine kernels).[183] As noted in chapter 3, Mary plied Zakarīyā with dates, which allowed him to impregnate his wife after a long period of barrenness.[184] In the example of Umm Sulaym, however, dates and their various potencies necessarily fall under the jurisdiction of men. The woman plays an important role as the provider of dates for her child's first food, but the food must now be administered by men. The act of handing over both dates and child typifies the sacrifice of a mother's procreative authority to the father's control. By inserting dates mixed with saliva into the child's mouth, the father, via the prophet, passes along his own reproductive power to his child.

Despite the father's central role in this ceremony, the mother's biddable gestures are also key in facilitating the child's rebirth into the world of men, as well as advancing her own nascence as self-sacrificing "mother." Without her willingness to conform to such normative paradigms of female piety, the community would not survive. The community's flourishing, therefore, depends on a woman's own cultivation of those maternal virtues that lead to her securing the child's identity and position (and her own, as well) under the guardianship of men.

Circumcising Men

Circumcision, which is nowhere mentioned in the Qur'ān[185] but is considered *sunna* (recommended) or even *wājib*[186] (duty) for men but *makrūma* (a noble deed) for women,[187] stands as another postpartum ritual that facilitates the infant's rebirth into a social world marked by paternal authority. In the more prominent and mandatory practice of male circumcision, the cutting of the foreskin serves to separate further the child from his mother through the solidification of his ties with God, his father, and the patriarchal line of prophets whose penises all resemble the child's own. Through the creation of such paternal ties that bind, circumcision establishes for the child a strong affiliation and identity with a particular religious community. Through the marks on his genitals, the child is well positioned to go forth with others like him to defend the boundaries of the community and to reproduce and sustain life and proper faith (which are, in many ways, indistinguishable) within it.

There is much debate in medieval sources as to when male circumcision (*khitān*) should be performed. Medieval scholar Muḥammad ibn Abī Bakr ibn Qayyim al-Jawzīya (d. 1350 CE) notes that Abraham was eighty years old (or one hundred and twenty, in some traditions), Ishmael thirteen years, and Isaac seven days.[188] While eighty years of age seems a bit extreme to undergo the procedure (though not unheard of),[189] the debate is centered around whether a child should be seven days old or approaching the time of puberty.

There is much support for both opinions. For example, some medieval texts record how many prominent figures were circumcised at seven days after the day of birth (the eighth day of life), including Muḥammad, who was purportedly circumcised by his grandfather, ʿAbd al-Muṭṭalib,[190] and Ḥasan and Ḥusayn, who were either cut by their mother Fāṭima or her father Muḥammad.[191] Other scholars debate the seventh day as normative, since it mimics what the Jews practice.[192] These scholars point out that while Isaac may have been circumcised on the seventh day, that practice is only *sunna* for his particular tribe. Muslims, on the other hand, should adhere to the example of Ishmael, who was thirteen years old.[193] Whatever the case, it is clear that circumcision serves as a rite of passage into an established faith community.

The preference for the "*sunna* Ishmael" is often supported by the argument that circumcision is necessary for the initiation of boys into acts of worship. Before the time of puberty (*al-bulūgh*), boys are not responsible for the performance of mandated religious rituals, and therefore do not need to be circumcised.[194] Sources claim anyone who is not circumcised, however, cannot serve as an *imām,* his prayer is rejected by God, his witness is not accepted in court, he is not allowed to perform pilgrimage to Mecca, and the eating of his sacrifice is forbidden. In short, uncircumcised males are barred from participating in communal life.[195] Even the witness (*shahāda*) of an uncircumcised male is prohibited, which makes the cutting of the foreskin a prerequisite for entry into a perfected faith.[196] On a more mundane level, *khitān* has many physical benefits, such as protecting against the obstruction of urine (*iḥtibās al-būl*) by the foreskin, which could also potentially defile one's ritual purity and prayer.[197] By ensuring that their sons undergo the procedure, fathers carve out a secure, legitimate, and valued space for their progeny among the community of believers. Without such a space, their offspring would have no social or religious identity, protection, or value.

The thirteenth year may also be privileged over the seven-day mark because of its association with the preparation of young men (and women) for marriage, which appears to be the reason why pre-Islamic Arabs promoted the practice. For example, Philo of Alexandria (d. 50 CE), the well-revered Hellenistic Jewish philosopher, records that "the Egyptians, in accordance with the national customs of their country, in the fourteenth year of their age, when the male begins to have the power of propagating his species, and when the female arrives at the edge of puberty, circumcise both bride and bridegroom."[198] Here, circumcision eases the transition of a boy from childhood to adulthood.

Anthropologists have long noted that circumcision rituals enable a child with an ambiguous gender to become a socially recognized, sexual male capable of reproducing. For example, the German Coptologist Otto Meinardus argues how, in some African traditions, circumcision eliminates the extraneous skin that feminizes the male organ; once removed, males take on the social, psychological, and physical characteristics of their adult gender.[199] In similar fashion, Carol Delaney has proposed in the context of contemporary Muslim societies that the cutting of the foreskin transforms boys into socially gendered beings through a public display of what had previously been covered.[200] By literally "pruning" the penis, the male organ, like a plant or tree, becomes fruitful and productive,[201] which serves to transform boys into men whose identities are defined by their ability to generate life in godlike fashion.

Along these theoretical lines, circumcision has also been linked with symbolic castration.[202] Here, the father ritually cuts the penis so the son cannot rival the father in his relations with the mother. In other words, the snipping of the foreskin solidifies the familial hierarchy and maintains the father as the prime generator of life with the mother in a secondary role. Such theoretical paradigms are often reflected in concrete examples that can be found in medieval depictions of the animal world, as put forth in many *adab* works. The Arabic term *adab* refers to an expression of a particular attitude or habit toward life, which became the focus of a new genre of literature in the ninth century The new genre was concerned with all sorts of issues connected with the relationship of human beings with the world around them.[203] For example, Abū Ḥayyān al-Tawḥīdī (d. 1023 CE), a Persian literary scholar and philosopher, notes that in the animal world, if the female of the wild ass (*ḥimār al-waḥsh*) has given birth to male young, the father ass pulls out their testicles and chews them with his teeth, lest the young become his rivals and make him share the she-ass with them.[204] In this example, animal behavior serves as a unique context in which to reveal, entertain and resolve certain social anxieties.

Whether a circumcision is performed at seven days, thirteen years, or somewhere in between,[205] this practice, like the *taḥnīk,* constructs a sacred time marked by male exclusiveness during which a father removes his infant or child from his mother's care and socializes him as a potential procreative agent, and also as a productive member of society.[206] The child's entrance into society is further underscored by those traditions that advocate circumcision for a child of seven or ten years of age, around the time when he begins his religious education under the tutelage of his father.[207] While women may bring forth children into a state of nature, circumcision may be understood as a child's true birth into his true cultural state,[208] where men, like God, have the power to create life.[209] Through a single cut, men become symbolically aligned with God the Creator, while women become relegated to what was created, namely, both nature and the earth.[210]

Women's associations with nature and the earth are already established in the Qur'ān: "Your women are as a tilth [*ḥarth*] to you, so approach your tilth however you will."[211] Because of their strong emphasis on the male generative organ, circumcision rituals leave the woman who bore the child in a somewhat culturally deficient and ambivalent social position.[212] Unable to transcend her own nature, she must derive her agency, and thus her cultural identity as mother, from her support of the father's ability, through ritual, to establish a rightful place for her son in the world. Thus, good mothers ensure the circumcisions of their sons, which in some sense allows them, like their husbands, to play a vital role in the regeneration of the patriarchal order, upon which their identity depends.

In addition to arguments that circumcision creates procreative agents capable of harnessing divine power,[213] or that the uncircumcised would be banned from taking part in key communal practices, medieval Muslim scholars also recommend the ritual through the sheer fact that many significant figures in monotheistic history performed it for pious reasons. True Muslims, therefore, must emulate their forefathers' exemplary behavior. Many traditions explore *khitān's* strong associations with Abraham. Bukhārī, for example, records God's messenger as saying, "Abraham performed his circumcision with a pick-axe when he was eighty years old."[214]

For Ibn Qayyim, Abraham's self-circumcision with such a crude instrument indicates a great inner strength and conviction.[215] Ṭabarī supports these virtues by linking circumcision with a series of tests Abraham faced to demonstrate his unflinching faith. These six tests were the star, the moon, the sun, the fire, emigration, and circumcision.[216] In other accounts, tests of fire, emigration, circumcision, and the attempted sacrifice of his son are used to demonstrate how Abraham remained steadfast in his faith.[217] By circumcising one's sons, Muslim fathers firmly root their offspring in communal practice and the pious discipline and disposition of their founding father, Abraham.[218]

Traditional sources, in particular, the Qur'ān and *ḥadīth,* also fuse circumcision with notions of *fiṭra,* covenant, and purity, all three of which are grounded in Abrahamic practice. The concept of *fiṭra* appears in the Qur'ān as a kind of true or original religion God created ([*al*]-*dīni ḥanīfan fiṭrata allāhi*) that demands a response from all humans according to their "God-given nature."[219] In other words, *fiṭra* denotes an innate understanding of the oneness of God, and submission to that oneness. As such, *fiṭra* is also linked with the idea of God's preexistent covenant (*'ahd*) to humanity. This primordial covenant has nothing to do with the biblical contract involving land, kings, or progeny,[220] but rather humanity's initial response to God's revelation at the dawn of creation.[221] This inherent impulse of all humans to heed the divine message is coexistent within an infant at birth. For example, Mālik reports how "every child is born on the *fiṭra* and it is his parents who make him a Jew or a Christian. Just as a camel is born whole—do you see any difference?"[222] In Muslim belief, infants do not enter life into a state of "original sin," but come into the world in a state of pure and perfected humanity, without physical or moral taint.[223]

In addition to its associations with creation, submission, and the pure religion of the one true God, the root *f-ṭ-r* also denotes splitting, or cleaving. The Qur'ān employs *f-ṭ-r* as splitting or cleaving in passages that deal with the final hour. As Sūra 73:18 claims, that devastating time will come "when heaven shall be split [*munfaṭir*], and its promise shall be performed." In this example, cleaving generates the requisite opening through which the divine promise may be revealed.

Such notions of splitting or cleaving are made manifest in a number of purity practices that embody the *fiṭra,* or the true, original religion of God. Here, those elements that stain, compromise, or obscure the pure condition into which one is born must be removed. For example, Bukhārī records: "The messenger of God said, 'Five practices are characteristic of the *fiṭra*: circumcision, shaving the pubic region, plucking the armpit hair, clipping the nails, and cutting the mustache short.' "[224] Each of these practices involves some sort of trimming or pruning of excess material from the body; a paring down of extraneous matter to reflect, as closely as possible, the physical form in its original, perfected condition. Both Ṭabarī and Ibn Qayyim link these five duties with the faith and covenant of Abraham (*milla Ibrāhīm*).[225] Abraham, having circumcised himself, embodies this primordial, unadulterated form of natural submission to the deity that all humans innately possess.[226] Through cuts in his foreskin, he opens himself up to the pure state of submission sparked in response to God's revelation at the dawn of creation.

The insistence that humans must take part in perfecting God's creation by removing foreskins and excess hair or nails furthers man's role as co-creator with the divine. Man, at least according to these purity prescriptions, has an obligation to alter temporarily, or even permanently, in the case of circumcision, the body's physical articulation so that it reflects more closely the divine ideal of human perfection. Here, a child does not exit from his mother's womb in perfected form, but rather must be made so through ritual acts committed by his father, or, in some instances, on behalf of the father via the mother.

In general, Islam frowns upon permanent modifications of the created body, such as tattooing or creating a space between the teeth.[227] Circumcision, however, seems to be the exception to the rule in that it parallels medieval rabbinic perspectives that cutting the foreskin was designed to repair nature, since "man is not born intact and still requires fixing of body and soul."[228] As stated in *Genesis Rabbah,* "Whatever was created in the first six days requires preparation, e.g., mustard needs sweetening, vetches need sweetening, wheat needs grinding, and man, too, needs to be finished off."[229] In the Islamic context, too, the commands of the *fiṭra* require human tinkering with or even direct intervention in God's creative process by the cutting of the foreskin, although it is unclear as to why, if humans were born perfect and pure, such an alteration of that particular physical trait would be necessary.

Yet, it does appear that some medieval Muslim scholars view the uncircumcised body as inferior to the circumcised one. After all, if a child is born into a state of *fiṭra,* he must be free of excess hair, nails, and foreskin. Many traditions point out the fact that laudable, exemplary servants, to whom God revealed his word, were born circumcised, including Ādam, Shīth, Idrīs, Nūḥ, Sām, Ibrāhīm, Dā'ūd, Sulaymān, Lūṭ, Ismā'īl, Mūsá, 'Isā and Muḥammad.[230] These parallel the *Midrash Tanḥuma*'s list of seven: Adam, Seth, Noah, Jacob, Joseph, Moses, and Job.[231] In fact, the prophet Muḥammad speaks openly of his own bodily perfection. For example, Anas ibn Mālik records the prophet as stating, "For the sake of my honorable position at God's presence I was born circumcised and nobody saw my pudendum."[232] Here, the circumcised penis is a precondition for standing in the presence of God and may even, perhaps, facilitate that presence.

Both Elliot Wolfson and Daniel Boyarin have discussed the intimate connections between circumcision and divine encounter in the context of medieval, rabbinic Judaism.[233] Both quote *Genesis Rabbah,* which reveals how Abraham circumcised himself in order to make God appear:

> "This, after my skin will have been peeled off, but from my flesh, I will see God" (Job 19:26). Abraham said, after

> I circumcised myself many converts came to cleave to this sign. "But from my flesh, I will see God," for had I not done this [circumcised myself], on what account would the Holy Blessed One, have appeared to me? "And the Lord appeared to him."[234]

Boyarin argues that Abraham's self-mutilation creates an essential opening in the body that allows him to receive divine speech and a vision of God.[235] For Boyarin, the act of circumcision feminizes the body through the creation of a manmade porta, which can then be penetrated by God.[236] Contrary to the depictions of circumcision's associations with paternity and patriarchy noted above, these examples, both Jewish and Muslim, link the cutting of foreskin with an oppositional impulse: the necessary reversal of one's gender to encounter God.[237] In this light, Muslim fathers would not circumcise their sons to make them more male, but rather to make them more open, receptive, and vulnerable to the revelation, in other words, more feminine.

The necessity of feminizing the male body in order to make it more capable of receiving the divine word echoes throughout Muslim depictions of circumcision as characteristic of the *fiṭra.* In the fivefold lists of *fiṭra* practices, the markers of male sexuality—in particular, postpubescent hair and the penis itself—are plucked, trimmed, or cut to create a pared-down (and thus feminized or perhaps nongendered) human form more capable of reflecting its true "God-given nature," a nature fully receptive to God's revelation.

The depilated and clipped male body shares much in common with Qurʾānic portrayals of those privileged feminine (or feminized) recipients who, perhaps by their very natures, as culturally constructed, offer unique opportunities for divine penetration. Examples from chapter 1 recall how the spirit and bearer of God's word entered Mary through her *farj* (or a slit in her garment) and God's revelations to the earth will occur only during those devastating hours preceding judgment, when the sky will split open (*inshaqqat*) and the earth cast forth what is within it.[238] In this light, fathers who ritually circumcise their sons seek to feminize the male body in order to prepare it for penetration by God's primordial revelation, or covenant. The fact that pubescent boys will undergo the practice at the same time they become responsible for fulfilling ritual obligations and studying the Qurʾān, which fulfill that covenant, further underscores this point. Such feminizations of the body, however, also allow men to usurp for themselves the open, receptive reproductive power of Mary as God blew his breath into her *farj,* and she conceived.

Medieval scholars, of course, provide more mundane, practical justifications for the practice of male circumcision than the loftier discussions noted above. For example, a circumcised penis serves to distinguish Muslims (*ʿibād al-raḥmān*) from Christians (*ʿibād al-ṣalabān*)[239] and unbelievers (*kāfirs*).[240] Ibn Qayyim, for example, notes that Christians wrongfully rejected circumcision and replaced it with baptism.[241] According to Ibn Qayyim, Christians failed to understand that circumcision is the practice of the *ḥunafāʾ* commanded by the covenant (*ʿahd*) of Abraham and the covenant of the seal (*khātim*) of the prophets.[242] The link between circumcision and the seal of the prophets also appears in the *Midrash Tanḥuma,* which may shed light on what Ibn Qayyim may be suggesting here. According to the *Tanḥuma,* God places the seal and the name (*hashem wahaḥotem*) upon the circumcised who enter into the Garden of Eden. *Ḥotem* (seal) in this context suggests a signing or sealing of a document; circumcision, therefore, stands as the literal mark or seal of God's protection, beneficence, and privilege established through the covenant.[243] Similarly, Muslim fathers who mark their sons' foreskins place them firmly in line with the chain of (male) prophets who bear the same "seal" (*khātim*), and provide those who don the brand with the same truth and guidance of the covenant.

While the cutting of the foreskin grounds male infants and children in culturally and theologically privileged roles as procreators, ritual performers, followers of a particular prophetic line, and the ones most receptive to divine covenant and revelation, the equivalent female practice (*khafḍ,* which means "lowering" or lessening)[244] serves no similar purpose. Female circumcision involves a cutting of the clitoris, to greater or lesser degrees.[245] The piece that is cut resembles "the comb of a rooster under the *farj*"; its function is to conceal the [clitoral] glans in the *farj*.[246] Like its male counterpart, the precedence for female excision can be located in sacred history; however, it does not represent a pious practice to be emulated. Ibn Qayyim, for example, traces the practice of female circumcision back to the time of Abraham, but locates it in a conflict between Sarah and Hagar. Sarah was jealous of Hagar because she had conceived Ishmael, and she swore to cut off her rival's limbs. Abraham, fearing Sarah would cut off her nose and ear, ordered her instead to pierce her ears and to circumcise her.[247] In this example, Hagar does not demonstrate her faith by circumcising herself; rather, it is forced upon her by a woman in a state of jealous rage.

Likewise, female excision does not lead to an established cultural identity or a prominent place for girls among the community of believers. While male circumcision prompted ritual and communal celebration,[248] no such ceremonies accompanied the female version. In contrast to the male procedure, medieval sources do not identify female circumcision as a necessary prerequisite for ritual practice,[249] and only rarely suggest it may be a requirement for converts.[250] Rather, the clipping of clitoral skin has more to do with curbing women's sexual desires than anything else,[251] a side effect of the practice not mentioned with regard to male circumcision.

The lack of an association between male circumcision and the suppression of sexual appetite is surprising, especially given the fact that prominent scholars such as Ghazālī note that sex may distract one from God if not performed with the proper intentions,[252] and that medieval Jewish scholars suggest one of the primary benefits of circumcision is its curbing of desire so men can focus more exclusively on the Torah.[253] In theory, Muslim men could assert mind over matter without physical modification. However, in the case of girls, female excision allowed fathers—and mothers, too—to assert their control over their daughters' lust, which might potentially damage the paternal authority necessary to manage the household's status and reputation.

Like the ritual of the *taḥnīk,* male circumcision severs the child from his mother and binds him more closely with the community of men. Such a severance is symbolized by the cutting of the foreskin; the exposure of the glans parallels the rebirth of the male into his religious and cultural role as producer of progeny and performer of mandatory ritual practice. Ironically, revealing the glans also serves to reverse his socially constructed, gendered identity by opening him up to the revelation of God. His ability to embody both male and female procreative roles—an ability facilitated by both his mother and father, who insist the ritual be performed—allows him to mimic the divine's ability to transcend gender when it comes to procreative power, a trait that reinforces his status as the mirror image of God on earth.

Namings, Shavings, and Sacrifices: Newborn Recognition

Both Muḥammad ibn ʿĪsá al-Tirmidhī (d. 892 CE) and Aḥmad ibn Shuʿayb al-Nisāʾī (d. 915 CE), prominent collectors of *ḥadīth,* record traditions that show how, on the seventh day after his birth, the child receives its name (*tasmiya*), his hair is shaven, and the *ʿaqīqa* is slaughtered on his behalf.[254] All three practices, like circumcision, create a new identity for the child by binding him more closely with his father through the severance of his maternal bonds. As such, these practices facilitate the child's rebirth from his natural state into his cultural role, which is defined by his relationship with his father and his ability to engage in ritual practices that define the faith.

The naming of the infant, which is the sole prerogative of the father,[255] seals the child's identity with his patriarchal lineage; the haircut serves to articulate his gender and secure his future fecundity, and the *ʿaqīqa* symbolizes the father's protection of and responsibility to his child through his expiation of the child's wrongdoings (presumably, until he's old enough to take on that responsibility himself). In (perhaps conscientious) contrast to Jewish practices, Muslim sources tend to identify the practices of the naming, first haircut, and *ʿaqīqa* on the seventh day of life as essential infantile rites aimed to accomplish the same symbolic ends as the *taḥnīk* and circumcision. All four contribute to the child's rebirth into the world as his father's child and a social being, capable of performing the faith, appropriating the word (revelation), and regenerating God's creation.

Appropriate Naming

The right of naming the child, in particular, the son, belongs solely to the father, and not the mother.[256] Through the *tasmiya*, the father in many ways stands in for Adam, whom God teaches the names of all things.[257] By giving his son an identity, the father bestows upon both mother and child concrete realities that become connected with him. This association between fathers and sons is formalized through the father's taking on the title of his son (*kunya*), whom he in fact names.[258] Thus, for example, the prophet Muḥammad became Abū Qāsim after the birth of his son Qāsim with his first wife, Khadīja, and later Abū Ibrāhīm through his son Ibrāhīm, whom he begot with his Egyptian concubine, Māriya. The *kunya* facilitates the son and the father taking on new identities relationally tied with one another and, in many ways, solidifies patriarchal power.[259]

Ibn Qayyim notes that although the child may take after the mother in terms of freedom and slavery, he comes to resemble the father in terms of kinship (*al-nasab*).[260] The name of the child, which the father alone bestows but is then reflected back onto him, embodies these kinship ties that bind. In fact, the *kunya* so closely invokes familial lineage that the prophet Muḥammad prohibited any of his followers from using his own; no other father could call himself Abū Qāsim or Abū Ibrāhīm.[261] While mothers also take on the names of their sons (*kunya*) as *umm* (mother) so-and-so, it is still through the father's initiative that the mothers are brought into the broader kinship circle. Mothers, after all, do not have the power to name, but only to be named.

Medieval sources also point out that it is the father's duty to choose an appropriate name for his child, one that reflects fully the values of his religion. Such decisions are freighted with great responsibility, for picking the wrong name could ostracize the child among his fellow believers.[262] Names associated with servitude to God, such as ʿAbdallāh or ʿAbd al-Raḥmān are preferable, along with the names of the prophets,[263] except for ʿĪsá (Jesus). If a child is called ʿIsá then his father's *kunya* would be Abū ʿĪsā, which would make the heretical claim that Jesus had a father.[264]

Other titles must be avoided as well. True believers must shun names that denote service to anyone other than God. Kings or sultans should never serve as namesakes; *Shāhnashāh* (king of kings) is reserved for God alone.[265] Ibn Qayyim also refers to sources that forbid a father to give his child one of the names of "Satan," such as *Khinjab,* and *al-Walahān,* and *al-ʿAwar,* and *al-Ajdaʿ*. Children are not to be called by the names of angels, either; Jibrīl, Mīkāʾīl, and Isrāfīl are off-limits.[266] The father's careful choosing of an appropriate title for his child has the effect of carving out a privileged and respected place for himself and his progeny—along with the mother who bore them—among the community of believers. The prophet, after all, often changed men's *jāhilīya* names to reflect the tenets of the new faith.[267] In order to emulate the prophet's *sunna,* the father must also select a similarly suitable Muslim name for his child. Likewise, mothers must trust that their husbands will choose wisely, as their own named status within the community, as well as their children's, depends on this decision.

Slaughtering Sheep and Cutting Hair

Both the cutting of hair (*ḥalaqa*) and the slaughtering of sheep (*ʿaqīqa*) accompany the naming of the newborn (and, for some, the cutting of the foreskin) that takes place on the seventh day. As such, all four practices facilitate the father's begetting of the child's new social, cultural identity. Medieval accounts present differing and often conflicting views about the necessity, performance, and purpose of both the *ḥalaqa* and *ʿaqīqa,* which were either performed together, or as discrete indications of piety.

As for their necessity, some scholars argue the *ʿaqīqa* is recommended practice (*sunna*);[268] others suggest the prophet disliked it,[269] perhaps because it was rooted in *jāhilīya* custom.[270] For example, Ibn Qayyim reports Barīda al-Aslamī as saying: "When we were living during the *jāhilīya,* and a boy were born to one of us, we slaughtered a sheep, and splashed his head with its blood. Now that God has brought Islam to us, we sacrifice a sheep, and shave the child's head, and stain it with *zaʿfarān* (saffron)."[271] According to this statement, the haircut and smearing of saffron are substituted for the wiping of sacrificial blood on the infant's head, which marks the *jāhilīya.*[272]

The aversion to smearing blood on the head is reflected also in prophetic example. When Ḥusayn was born, the prophet took him in his arms, shaved his hair, and performed the *ʿaqīqa.*[273] However, other traditions record the prophet performing the *ʿaqīqa* for his grandsons without mention of the haircut, which signals no substitution for blood was necessary.[274] Clearly, no single view dictated the necessity of carrying out one or both of these practices. Whatever custom prevailed, performance of the *ʿaqīqa,* and to a lesser extent the *ḥalaqa,* demonstrates the father's symbolic acceptance of his responsibility to socialize his child in the ways of Islam, and to protect him from pagan influence.

There is also much debate over how (and for whom) the *ʿaqīqa* should be executed, as well as its overall purpose. Bukhārī, for example, reports that a father should offer the *ʿaqīqa* for a newborn boy to relieve him from his suffering, or harm.[275] Other scholars dispute this point, and argue the *ʿaqīqa* should be offered not just for baby boys, but for girls, too.[276] However, most learned men advise just a single sheep for girls, and two for boys,[277] with a minority, namely, the Mālikites, arguing for equality between the sexes, with one or two sheep apiece.[278]

The argument for equal treatment for boys and girls reflects Qur'ānic, and also prophetic, reverence for daughters.[279] Whether it's one sheep or two, the father's impulse to slaughter mimics symbolically the mother's own spillage of blood during the violent act of childbirth. Just as the mother brings forth her child into a state of nature through pain and gore, so, too, does the father deliver his son or daughter into a more meaningful life through a similar gesture of sacrifice and bloodshed. In this way, the *ʿaqīqa* mimes the act of childbirth—this time under male tutelage and control—as the infant is reborn into a world where fathers take over the primary role for generating the type of meaningful life God desires: true worshipers who adhere to the tenets of faith.

As noted above, the haircut often accompanies the sacrifice of sheep. Scholars point out the word *ʿaqīqa* may either refer to the hair on the head or the sheep that is slaughtered; in some cases, the haircut may serve as a replacement for the slaughter.[280] Ibn Qayyim, for example, describes how the prophet instructed his daughter Fāṭima to shave her son Ḥasan's head rather than perform the *ʿaqīqa.*[281] In accordance with her father's wishes, Fāṭima cut off Hasan's hair and gave its equivalent weight in silver to charity (*sadaqa*),[282] an act that parallels precisely the distribution of the meat from the *ʿaqīqa* to the poor.[283] Through such acts of severance and distribution, the child's rebirth into its social existence is marked by a commitment to ensuring the health and well-being of the community. The mother or father[284] act on behalf of the helpless infant, but the assumption is that the child will eventually shoulder the obligation of caring for the poor as he grows older.

In the absence of any sacrifice, it appears the haircut may be undertaken by women. Through the very act of cutting off the hair that accompanied the newborn at birth, a woman transfers her own maternal bonds with her child to the father. In general, hair, as a part of the body "capable of painless amputation, infinite manipulation, and endless regeneration,"[285] stands as a convenient symbolic device for facilitating shifts in life passages and transformations in identity.[286]

Like foreskin, hair, too, serves to articulate the dialectic between nature and the norms and constraints of culture.[287] For example, bodily hair must removed to ensure a state of *fiṭra,* yet hair must not be cut while in a state of ritual purity, as commanded by the rules of the *ḥajj*. As a gesture that eases such transformations in status, the first haircut at seven days of age quickly seals off the liminal period of childbirth, where newborns thrive in a natural state among the company of women without paternal connection, oversight, or socialization.[288] This natural state is not positive or even neutral; male scholars characterize it by weakness, or even harm.[289] Ibn Qayyim, for example, notes that shaving the head removes weak hair and replaces it with stronger hair; it opens the skin, strengthens the eyes, and improves the sense of smell and hearing.[290] In other words, the act of managing and controlling one's hair makes one more fully human. It is fitting, then, that in some cases the mother would perform the first haircut; through an act of ritual severance, she freely submits to the patriarchal order that lends meaning to her child's birth and subordinates her own life-bearing status to that of the father. Her cultivation of such ideals and virtues generates and seals her own identity as a "good" mother.

Whispering the Adhān and Iqāma: Protecting Families from Evil

The *adhān* refers to the recitation of the formula used for calling to prayer, and the *iqāma* pertains to the words chanted in the mosque during the opening of a prayer. The child's father whispers both in the ears of a newborn in order to acquaint him with the basic principles of Islam, protect him from the wiles of Satan, and encourage him to accept the faith.[291] Ibn Qayyim, for example, testifies to the importance of the *adhān* as the words to the call to prayer contain the bare essentials of Muslim belief: the splendor of God and his greatness. He identifies the words themselves as having the sacred potential to brand the child with the mark of Islam from the very moment he enters into the world.[292] He adds that the sound of the *adhān* also provokes the flight of Satan, who lies in wait for the newborn at birth. The fact that a child's first supplication will be to God and the religion of Islam, and not to Satan, gives him a healthy advantage in his fated, life-long struggle against the devil.[293]

The *adhān,* whispered into the ear at birth, and the *tawḥīd,* recited in the ear at death, appear as bookends in human life to cordon off firm believers in the one true God from undesirable influences. By receiving such testimonies of faith uttered in their ear by their fathers, believers exit this life in the same, pure state they enter it in, and vice versa.[294] By performing the *adhān,* fathers impart a meaningful life into the bodies of their infants by equipping them with the tools necessary to adhere to the rightful path of God. Therefore, the *adhān,* like the practices of *taḥnīk,* circumcision, naming, haircutting, and sacrificing, facilitates the father's separation of the child from his mother as he literally breathes into him a meaningful social existence defined by faith. This symbolic breath of life, marked by the divine word, underscores the father's procreative power as essential in begetting the proper life God commands.

Those on the Outside: The Ritual and Practical Marginalization of Childless Women

As these examples show, the paternal role, along with its maternal counterpart, depends on the very act of a woman's giving birth. The man's familial and social appropriation of his child from the one who bore him through postpartum rituals and embodied practices solidifies a man's identity as father and head of the household, and, most importantly, his position as procreative partner with God. The father's words and actions, buffered by the mother's unflinching support, thus regenerate the cosmos through the creation and replication of the very life God desires.

Given the patrilineal nature of this constructed cosmic order, barren women undermine the very foundations that sustain a meaningful life at the same time they serve as essential foils against whom the norm is defined and justified.[295] Because of their ambiguous status as potential but unrealized mothers, or as the necessary "other" by which the blessings of fertility may be measured, traditional sources do not condemn such women, but rather attempt to articulate a more nuanced theological definition of "motherhood" to try and accommodate those females whose weak or flawed bodies both threaten and sustain the status quo. In the eyes of medieval scholars, barren women, like their fertile counterparts, must work to cultivate the same maternal virtues of piety, obedience, and subordination despite the fact that they might never receive God's blessings, and thus become more fully integrated into communal life. However, by striving to become "good mothers," no matter what the outcome, barren women may be shown to reinforce male procreative privilege as they work to generate a vessel perfected and purified enough to be graced with a child, like Mary's mother Ḥanna.

Infertile women threaten paternal privilege as they are unable to transfer willingly their reproductive power to men through gesture and ritual, and thus cannot contribute to the familial or communal order medieval men assert God has sanctioned. On a very basic, physiological level, as noted in chapter 2, the barren female body counters divine wisdom, design, and execution, all of which tailor particular body parts for the purposes of reproduction.[296] After all, as Jāḥiẓ notes, wombs are patterned to support fetuses, and breasts shaped like small skin flasks aptly positioned for the child to suckle.[297] Without a child to conceive or nourish, such female body parts serve no intended purpose; their gratuitous presence mocks both the cosmic and social orders as reminders of what should be, but obviously is not.[298]

Barren women, therefore, reside in a permanent state of liminality, since their own bodies and identities cannot be defined in relation to men's. For example, the lack of a *kunya* withholds women from securing a privileged, familial, and social identity for themselves or their husbands. As noted above, the common name husbands and wives derive from their children serves the purpose of grounding women in a widened paternal context that is confirmed socially. Likewise, women who have no infant to breastfeed cannot create an expanded network of blood ties with their own children or others among their family or the community of believers. Without the ability to establish such an expansive network of familial relations, few will inherit from them. In the absence of offspring, the wealth of the family must be transferred laterally rather than linearly, a secondary provision put forth in the Qur'ān that stifles a husband's God-given right to sow his own legacy among future generations. Unmoored, barren women are left adrift in a world organized around kinship ties.

Childless women are also unable to impart a privileged status upon men as begetters, sustainers, and regenerators of righteous progeny that will grow to serve God and protect the faith as they are excluded from engaging in the ritual practices of *taḥnīk,* male circumcision, hair cutting, or sacrifice. Barred from these rituals, they bring no honor or recognition to their families, and prevent their husbands—and thus themselves—from securing a definable place within the community. Without children to intervene for them on the last day, barren women also put their own fates, and those of their husbands, in jeopardy. Clearly, as the example of ʿĀ'isha has shown, women who produce no progeny are depleted of all agency to confer male procreative authority, and thus to secure a privileged status for their husbands both within the community of believers and beyond.

To eliminate any threat these women on the margins may present to the dominant discourse that privileges kinship relations, paternal authority, and progeny, scholars construct a more universal understanding of "motherhood" that includes expressions of piety in the form of obedience, suffering, and self-sacrifice to ensure barren women continue to strive to become good mothers despite the uncertainties of their reproductive futures. This universal understanding of motherhood is rooted in the examples of the prophet's wives. Although some of his wives were fertile with other men they had married, once they were wedded to the prophet they bore none of Muḥammad's offspring.[299] Bereft of the prophet's children in order to service his role as "not the father of any of your men,"[300] Muḥammad's wives become models of piety to be emulated by all barren women.[301]

As noted in chapter 1, each of these wives receives a generic, communal *kunya* as "mother of believers" (*umm al-mu'minīn*).[302] This title confers an exalted and honored status upon the women whose role it was to nurture and care for the community of believers, rather than their own children.[303] A "mother" in this context is thus defined through the obedience and devotion she demonstrates in order to nurture the whole of the Muslim community.[304] For barren women, such a role carves out a meaningful identity and place within the community they are unable to secure through their own bearing of children.

Even though it is conferred by the Qur'ān, exegetes continue to depict the role of universal nurturer as secondary to that of biological mother. In fact, medieval scholars employ such an image to discipline obstinate female bodies so God might (eventually) deem them suitable to become a "good mother," that is, one who conceives. For example, despite her prestigious title of *umm al-mu'minīn*,[305] medieval scholars emphasize how ʿĀ'isha begged Muḥammad for a "real" *kunya*, that is, one based on kinship relations, since all his other wives had such a title (based on the children they bore with prior husbands). To appease her, Muḥammad gave her the name "*Umm* ʿAbdallāh." ʿAbdallāh was her young nephew, the son of her sister Asmā' and her husband Zubayr ibn al ʿAwwām. ʿAbdallāh was believed to have been the first Muslim child born in Medina.[306] However, "*Umm* ʿAbdallāh" may simply refer to "mother of *any* servant of Allāh" (given the generic name of ʿAbdallāh), which solidifies ʿĀ'isha's role as nurturer of all the faithful, no matter what their kinship affiliation.

This example illustrates ʿĀ'isha's rejection of her Qur'ānic title in favor of a more established and approved maternal identity to ground her in a broader concrete social and familial context. Her longings for both a child and the accompanying shift in her own status and identity underscore the exegetical privileging of those mothers who provide men with the progeny necessary to structure and give meaning to their lives. Certainly, barren women must strive to become the nurturers and caretakers of all of God's creations, but for exegetes childbearing still remains the optimal goal as it reinforces male procreative power and the social structures that support it.

While barren women occupy an ambiguous position among traditional scholars, more sympathy abounds for women who are childless as a result of miscarriages, stillbirths, or the death of a young daughter or son. They have, after all, demonstrated a willingness and fitness to conceive a child, even if tragedy has struck. In addition, their sufferings on behalf of their fate appear greater than those endured by barren women. For example, the prophet often expresses an intense sadness for the miscarried fetus: "A miscarried fetus sent before me is dearer to me than a horseman whom I leave behind."[307] Muḥammad also empathizes with the pain of mothers whose young children die while nursing. Khadīja, for example, laments the fact that even though her milk is flowing, her son Qāsim will never drink from it. She cries, "Would that God have let him live until he had finished breastfeeding!" The prophet lovingly consoles her by saying, "He will complete his breastfeeding in paradise."[308]

Likewise, the prophet assures mothers that children who die while suckling will continue to feed from the breasts of wet nurses in paradise.[309] For mothers who lose three (or two or one) of her children, the prophet comforts them by claiming their maternal pain will screen them from the fire.[310] All of these heartbreaking vignettes demonstrate the fact that a mother's suffering over her loss of a young one is equated with the pious actions of martyrs. By bearing fully their pain, mothers who miscarry or fail to raise children into adulthood are carved a special place among the faithful, despite the fact that they are unable to forge meaningful identities or ties within the community. Theological accommodation thus assures more abstract, universal rewards for these grieving women's pious efforts, and presumably, brings honor to their husbands as well. Unable to generate the future believers and protectors of the faith that God commands, these suffering women are promised a paradisiacal payoff for their displacement on earth. To a greater extent than barren women, these bereft servants come to mirror more closely the best of all women who are willing to sacrifice all to care and nurture the bearers of God's word.

Conclusions: Muslim Mothers as Communal Anchors

In sum, a mother's willing consent to her child's participation in postpartum rituals and embodied practices repairs the cosmic and social damage caused by the very act of giving birth. Parturition, which occurs solely among the company of women, threatens the patriarchal boundaries that demarcate a child's (and its parents') very existence. The lines that define his existence, however, depend on the discourses and practices that distinguish the "maternal" from the "paternal," and endow the latter with a superior, generative role that mirrors both divine creation (as narrowly construed) and female reproduction. Through her participation in postpartum gestures and rituals, a woman willingly transfers her own ability to generate life to the husband, and her exclusive, intimate authority over her child to its father. Her acquiescence to the status quo, achieved through habituated action and self-sacrifice, allows her to embody more closely the perfected bodies and ideals articulated through the lives of the pious queens of paradise. However, rather than subordinating themselves directly before God, as did these righteous women, good mothers submit to God via the men who represent him.

Theological assurances provide barren women, and women who have lost children through miscarriages, stillbirths, and infant death, with alternative paths to many of these same goals. Given that these women are excluded from the very rituals and practices that allow men to beget and regenerate life, some medieval scholars find ways to accommodate them by formulating new types of familial bonds, emphasizing maternal virtues that must be expressed for all of God's creations, or by easing their unspeakable pain and suffering with paradisiacal reward, which also brings glory to their husbands.

In addition to the postpartum rituals and embodied practices outlined above, such alternative theological assurances also have the advantage of supporting the position of men as begetters of meaningful life. These perspectives also serve to enforce, rather than challenge, many of the same maternal virtues demonstrated by the pious queens of paradise, including self-sacrifice, suffering, and an utter devotion to a God whose procreative desires are circumscribed by men. These maternal virtues broaden the medieval understanding of the "good mother" to discipline and accommodate those marginal women whose bodies bear no meaningful life.

Such theological accommodations, however, do little to squelch many of the suspicions or uncertainties raised by those who benefit from the usurpation of female procreative power. The mother whose body or child does not conform to the "ideal" thus becomes the subject of much scholarly speculation and scrutiny. Chapter 5 examines medieval portrayals of the "bad mother," who, in contrast with the "good," is the mother whose body meddles with God's (and man's) procreative prowess, thereby producing "monsters."

In various depictions of the bad mother, such corruptions of the human form are far from accidental; rather, they are borne out of the mother's witting or unwitting violation of natural and divine laws through her own sexual improprieties, perversions of faith and practice, or bodily deviations. As a result of her impious beliefs or actions, the bad mother becomes infertile, miscarries, or reproduces anomalies or monsters. The various examples of reproductive deviations flesh out the different ways in which elite scholars imagine how impiety and immorality corrode the female body and subvert God's (or man's) procreative plans. They also serve to warn women about the heinous consequences of bad mothering, and their negative impact on the cosmic order, so that they may stay the righteous path.

5

Mother as Monster

> My mother says that I am his. But I don't know. Does anyone really know his father?
>
> —*The Odyssey*

Unlike the stellar Mary, Āsiya, Khadīja or Fāṭima, "bad" mothers defy both God's and man's reproductive command through sexual deviance and corrupt faith, ritual, and practice. Bad mothers don't confirm social births; rather, they undo both the ritual and theological structures that give their children (and themselves) a legitimate, meaningful life. As a result of their transgressions, they produce not the righteous prophets God demands but rather anomalies or "monsters" that disrupt the social and cosmic orders.

In their elaborate depictions of the grotesque phenomena borne out of sexual aberrance in nature, medieval Muslim scholars project how human iniquity and perversion—both male and female—likewise corrode the reproductive body to the point at which it generates similarly corrupt offspring or other birth anomalies that thwart God's procreative plans. The mere presence of these deviant beings in literary texts warns both good and bad mothers of what will happen if they do not submit fully their reproductive lives to the care of elite men who alone possess the proper knowledge and authority to fashion an appropriate female womb through which they can beget healthy and righteous believers who will worship God. The threat of monsters also holds men accountable for their own sexual behaviors and iniquities, since they are the guarantors of the superlative life wombs must produce under their protectorate.

Eve (*Ḥawwa*), as portrayed in Muslim exegetical texts, provides an instructive example of a mother whose questionable morals impact directly her ability to bear and nurture perfected progeny. After all, Eve's miscarried fetuses, slain babies, and incestuous, murderous son bear little resemblance to the ideal offspring produced by the paradisiacal queens. The unfortunate circumstances surrounding her rather wayward reproductive life bear witness to the causal connections between maternal piety and fetal development, where unbridled female power, moral turpitude, and weak bodies and minds prove to generate less than optimal offspring, or even monsters.

In order to show how medieval scholars link female impiety with flawed wombs, this chapter reads the narratives of Eve's reproductive life through broader discursive discussions about monstrosities in both the natural and human worlds. Through a variety of discursive contexts found in travelogues, bestiaries, sacred histories, medical wisdom, entertainment literature, and laws governing sexual practices, medieval Muslim *literati* explored how impious intent in the form of sexual deviation and perversion, either in the natural world, or in human life, engenders monstrous forms. In the case of Eve and all mothers who follow her example, the monstrous forms on the margins come to press upon the children in the center when they bear no physical or moral resemblance to their fathers. Nonresemblance between parents and children in the center creates a fundamental, primordial disorder by revealing the superficial authority of all paternities.[1] By producing "monsters," ordinary mothers undo the familial, communal, and ritual/practical structures that imbue their own lives, and those of their children, with meaning.

In these literary contexts, the "monstrous" ranges from a wildly fantastic "other" roaming the margins of civilization to a slightly deviant "self" barely distinguishable from those in the center. The corrupt behaviors that produce one form of monstrosity or another, however, are to be measured by degree rather than kind. For example, the hairy, grunting creatures produced when men copulate with animals may seem more strikingly aberrant than a child who lusts after his twin sister and murders his brother. However, for medieval scholars, both often share much in common as the visual embodiments of maternal indiscretions to be avoided so one does not disrupt paternal reproductive authority. Both Cain and the human/bear combination (for example) were generated as the result of the same violent incursions into the base, normative rituals, practices, laws, and beliefs that make one a believer who resembles his father, and thus a fully human being.

Some Introductory Remarks on the "Monstrous"

Medieval authors of zoological works or other forms of *adab* often preface their works with introductory remarks that imply the half-beasts or mixed-up animals they catalogue serve as potent vehicles through which God's magnificence and ultimate transcendence are displayed.[2] Out on the frontiers of both civilization and human life, the grotesque and monstrous bear little resemblance to any known reality. As embodiments of nonbeing, their forms disrupt the essential relationship between the sign and the signified.[3] The disturbance of this essential relationship between the sign and the signified in turn negates positive, rational, human constructs that order and make sense of the world, in particular those having to do with God's identity or nature, since he alone is given ultimate responsibility for producing such creatures. In the absence of these constructs, humans—by contemplating the monstrous—are presented with a rare opportunity to grasp and affirm the paradoxical nature of God's unique transcendence,[4] "a reality which *is-not*."[5] In sum, the "monster" on the margins, in all of its contorted and deviant resplendency, provides a rare opportunity through which believers may experience the ineffable glory of God that transcends the rational limitations imposed on his nature.[6]

Upon closer consideration, however, it is clear that monsters on the periphery or even in the center do not always glorify God but personify the human chaos and corruption that continuously threatens to dismantle the current religious and social order, where men struggle to replicate themselves in like form.[7] In the context of travelogues and other types of entertainment literature, aberrant anatomies outside the boundaries of the civilized world that appear part-human, part-beast, mirror not divine glory but an idolatrous, heathen perimeter that casts into relief an ideal, faithful center where children look like parents. These creatures on the margins are shown to come into being through unnatural or unspeakable acts among beasts, humans and beasts, or humans who simply deviate from the norm. If men indeed serve as God's reproductive stewards on earth, then they must take care to make sure such grotesque life forms stay on the margins of civilization or remain outside of a pious human life, and are not concocted deep within the "shadows of darkness," or the believing woman's womb.

Not only do such aberrations appear out on the geographical periphery of civilization, but so too do they lurk among the world's fauna. The deviant reproductive practices that occur among animals provide ripe opportunities for medieval scholars to measure the threat of sexual deviance over and against normative reproductive processes.

Certainly, on the surface, the variety in numbers and kinds of species that exist gives humans a small but inadequate glimpse into what God is capable of creating.[8] However, a closer look at much of the *ḥayawān* (bestiary) literature[9]—anthologies that deal with animals yet touch upon questions of theology, metaphysics, politics, and sociology[10]—reveals deeper anxieties about the unusual sexual practices and orientations typical of many living creatures that are all too readily mimicked by humans when they deviate from the divine laws designed to suppress such iniquities. Such anxieties expressed through the fantastical explorations of the natural world only serve to reinforce the normative reproductive practices underscored by the legal, exegetical, and theological materials discussed above.

For example, transsexual hares, crossbred horses, and promiscuous animals such as the parents of the giraffe all engender mixed-up offspring with no socially recognized identity or status. Crossbreeds are sterile, and at least three different fathers may call the giraffe their son. Depictions of such aberrant animal behavior define the parameters of deviance but also reinforce normative human laws that regulate sexual intercourse between one male and one female, and promote the necessary copulation between like-types. They also facilitate an infant's rebirth into his publicly recognized social identity as his father's child, and govern the essential barriers between humans and animals. Clearly, parents' prenatal activities, like those displayed by the hare or parents of the giraffe, hold the potential to impact profoundly their children's features as well as their fates.

As scholars move from the disordered periphery and into the ordered center, the points of contrast between the deviant and the splendid, or the deviant and the norm, become more difficult to discern. On the comfortably distant margins, "monstrosities" remain, for the most part, the absolute other. As displays of human degeneracy or God's splendor, they offer no tangible, physical threat to the "not me."[11] In the center, however, the "monster" stands in all too intimate proximity to what is normative, close enough to blur the lines between self and "other." It may be easy to account for the strange creatures that inhabit far-off lands, or populate the animal kingdom in terms of splendor or deviance, but how does one accommodate the anomalous births (resembling Cain's, the hare's, or the giraffe's) among friends, neighbors, family members, or in one's own womb?

In the center, whether the monster mirrors the splendors of God or deviant maternal behavior ultimately depends on the community's discretionary judgment. When scholars suspect maternal impiety or sexual transgression, the creature with anomalous features may be deemed grotesque; when its mother is beyond reproach, his aberrant anatomy may signal God's magnificent power. For example, nowhere do exegetes render Cain's impulse to kill, or a child's resemblance to several fathers, as wondrous displays of divine magnificence. Such offspring are simply products of bad parenting, or more precisely, bad mothering.

On the other hand, in cases that have no connection whatsoever with sexual impropriety or moral turpitude, unusual anatomies may be praised as exhibits of God's rich design and unique intent, his eternal wisdom and mercy.[12] Damīrī illustrates this point in a tale about how the prophet fell prostrate when he saw a dwarf (*al-nughaysh*).[13] Similarly, Jāḥiẓ describes how God disciplines men through physical deformities they must endure to develop patience and piety.[14] Clearly, the community's basis for evaluating aberrant anatomies is heavily dependent upon its assessment of a mother's moral character. In the center, such communal, paternal judgment becomes even more transparent and urgent than it is out on the margins. To avoid the fate of being deemed a bad mother, ordinary women must adhere more closely to the sexual proscriptions articulated and enforced by men so that their bodies only produce well-formed, righteous progeny and not the grunting, grotesque, or murderous offspring that undermine male procreative authority.

Taxonomic Transgressions: Monsters on the Margins

According to Jeffrey Jerome Cohen, monsters "police borders" between "self" and "other" as their very form indicates what happens when individuals step outside communally prescribed boundaries; thus their presence on the margins prevents transgression and preserves the homogeneous center.[15] Cohen suggests that the assertion of borders, and the monsters that guard them, in particular serve to reflect and control the behavior of women, or to establish the essential homosocial bonds that privilege patriarchal authority. For example, monsters skulking the edges of civilization don the tangible stigmata of unnatural copulations that took place far beyond acceptable cultural or taxonomic bounds. Therefore, a good mother must guard her *farj*, seek legitimate partners, and not engage in any sexual improprieties in order to avoid giving birth to similarly heinous beings.

The grotesque forms that patrol the margins also become convenient scapegoats that display the flaws, faults, defects, or idolatries of other ethnicities or rival religious groups.[16] Such scapegoats likewise serve to warn women not to stray too far across communal lines in choosing appropriate fathers for their children. As the following examples show, the monster as he appears in medieval Muslim texts reveals the underlying communal values, norms, judgments, and power structures that separate the reproductive lives of good mothers from those who are "bad," that is, those who disrupt the paternal structures that provide women and their children with a meaningful life.

Anatomical Wonders in Far-Off Places: Human/Animal Mixtures

A common monstrous trope that permeates both medieval travelogues and bestiaries is the human/animal mixture. Such an anomaly, produced through deviant human sexual intercourse with beasts, crosses the fundamental boundary between species so clearly drawn in the Qur'ān. The Qur'ān, after all, states only humans—and not animals—receive God's spirit (*rūḥ*), which allows them to see, hear, and interpret his word.[17] The heinous examples of hideous creatures roaming freely in far-off lands certainly display God's power, but they also warn women never to transgress the divinely mandated divide that separates God's "viceregents"[18] from all other life forms. The lurid depictions of monsters on the borders, therefore, serve to dissuade both women and men from violating the tradition's strict prohibition against humans having sex with animals. As the prophet said, "If anyone has sexual intercourse with an animal, kill him and kill it [the animal] along with him."[19]

A relatively extended list of monstrosities appears in the zoological portion of Qazwīnī's *Nuzhatu-l-qulūb*. In the fifth section of this work, Qazwīnī mentions a number of curious animals (*ḥayawānāt*) in far-off (non-Muslim) lands that resemble men to lesser and greater degrees. In their disturbing appearance these animals that bear human-like (*ādamī*) characteristics[20] underscore permissible forms of sexual intercourse: the necessity of like "pairs" (species) coupling in order to generate offspring in their own image that will come to worship the one God.

For instance, Qazwīnī describes a type of animal (*ḥayawān*) called the *asbsār* (a horse-like creature) that inhabits islands in the China Sea (*baḥru shīni*).[21] It is tall in stature with a head like a horse and body like a man, and it has two wings.[22] The *sulaḥfātī,* out on the isles of the Indian sea (*jazā'īri hindi*), bears a body like that of a tortoise, but has a countenance like that of a man.[23] The *sadsār,* dwelling on the isles of the Indian and Ethiopian seas (*baḥru hindi wa zindi*), is an animal with a dog-like head and a body like a man's.[24] It also has two faces: one like a dog's and one like a man's. This creature feeds on animals, and some animals feed on it.[25] The human features of these fantastical creatures hint they may have been generated through some sort of sexual deviance that occurred between man and animal.

Qazwīnī describes further the *dū paykar,*[26] a beast with one body, two heads, and a voice "like that of birds, but it has meaning, though it cannot be well understood because of the rapidity of [its] speech."[27]

Likewise the *ṭayir,* an animal shaped like a man with two wings, has the capability of speech, though no one can understand its language.[28] From India (*hind*), however, comes the *zāghsār,* an animal with a head like a man's and a body like a crow's. The *zāghsār,* a gift to the caliph from India, delivers deeply cryptic messages to humans. It utters things like "I am the crow, the prodigy," or "I am the lion with the lioness."[29]

In these examples of bizarre anatomies, the taxonomic violations are even more prominent as the creatures under scrutiny share many human-like qualities: the ability to see, hear, and perhaps comprehend the divine revelation. However, upon closer scrutiny it appears these wondrous creatures can only express such human-like characteristics in a highly corrupted form. The degradation of God's perfected creations thus condemns more forcefully the sexual deviance that produced such beasts in the first place, and reinforces more strongly the appropriate and permissible reproductive behavior necessary to generate more desirable offspring.

Such sexual perversion is explicitly mentioned in the *Nuzhatu-l-qulūb*'s description of the *khirṣsār,* an animal born of a bear and man that matches the human being in form and speech, but is hairy like a bear. In medieval contexts, an excess of body hair on men, women, or animals often implies violence, a lack of civilization,[30] or an unbridled, unrestrained sexuality.[31] After all, the Dajjāl (false Christ) is thought to have abundant hair, along with a protuberant eye.[32] Even though it can speak, the *khirṣsār* lacks the essential qualities that make one fully human: it possesses no understanding or judgment, and its speech cannot be comprehended by others.[33] In other words, this creature possesses no ability to form communal relations, an essential quality that makes one human but also serves as a fundamental characteristic of faith.[34]

Like the *khirṣsār,* the *mālūf,* a hairless, tailless, ape-like creature,[35] dons the shape of a human being but lacks its civility. She has a beautiful face but cannot speak or comprehend speech. Men have sex with her and beget sons who resemble their mother in that they cannot utter a word.[36] Born out of prohibited sexual relations between human and beast, these offspring reflect and promote a degenerate creation. They are plagued with compromised anatomies, and lack the optimal "human" tools necessary to hear, speak, comprehend, or communicate God's revelation. Certainly, offspring produced through acts of bestiality do not evoke the same glories of God to create in wombs as he pleases, as, for example Mary's conception of Jesus without a husband.

Other aberrant anatomies likewise point to deviant sexual behavior, and encourage women to adhere more closely to prescribed sexual relationships and behaviors in order to generate perfected and righteous children. In his *Ḥiyāt al-ḥayawān*, Damīrī describes a creature that manifests the taboo of humans crossing faith boundaries during an act of coitus. He tells the woeful tale of how a Jew fornicated with a Christian woman, and she gave birth to an offspring with a human body and the face of an ox.[37] The zoological treatises often equate Jews with animals, and warn God's "perfected of perfections"[38] to avoid intercourse with them since the offspring produced from such a liaison would barely resemble a human being.

The equating of Jews with animals is underscored throughout the *ḥayawān* literature. Both Damīrī and Qazwīnī, for example, describe a creature called the *shaykh al-yahūdī*, commonly called the "Jew." This creature has a countenance like a man with a white beard, but a body in the form of a frog. On Friday night, the *shaykh al-yahūdī* hops out of the water and stays on land until Saturday night. This beast suffers whatever violence is done to it, and never breaks for the water during that time. At sunrise on Sunday the "Jew" hops back into the sea.[39] The message embedded in these tales is clear: good Muslim mothers do not copulate with Jews or members of other faiths, since such liaisons reveal their indiscretions by producing grotesque anatomies. Perfected and righteous offspring are only generated in good and pious wombs, which only allow penetration by like members of the faith.

The depictions of monstrous offspring aim to evoke fear and revulsion in ordinary women who may even be contemplating an abominable act. Mothers cannot hide from their sexual transgressions since they become visually imprinted upon the offspring they produce. Such embodied manifestations of individual sin and iniquity emphasize a woman's dire need for the medieval tradition's strict prohibitions against bestiality and other types of sexual perversions and cultic transgressions.[40] The grotesque manifestations of misguided lusts and desires that patrol the borders of humanity for all to see, however, serve to police proper behavior of aberrant mothers more effectively than any abstract prohibition.

Aberrant Behavior in the Animal World

Zoological treatises also serve to regulate the sexual behaviors of mothers in their extensive descriptions of unusual practices of coitus among animals. Their cataloguings of crossbreeds, hermaphrodites, transsexuals, hypersexed animals, and creatures that bear the unhappy likeness of rival ethnic and religious groups warn those who trespass the norms of their own species (or religious and ethnic identities) that their actions may generate similarly corrupt offspring. Like the animals under consideration, mothers, too, if they are not careful, may breed "monstrous" progeny with no clear social identity, communal standing, or ability to comprehend God's word. The distorted offspring unable to forge any meaningful paternal connections do little to confirm the procreative authority of men, and thus the social, communal structures that likewise privilege the status and identity of "good mothers."

Crossbreeds: Sterile Wombs and Bad Dispositions

Medieval scholars argue that crossbreeds that occur in nature may only result from the coition of two different animals that have relatively similar characteristics.[41] They view the "mixed" stock begotten from such couplings, however, as corrupt and degenerate versions of their parents, who embody the perfected characteristics of their created form. Damīrī, for example, argues any mixed breed will be more miserable, unstable, misshapen, and evil than the parents that generated it, since the worst elements of the mother and father combine in the body of the offspring.[42] Because they are sterile, crossbreeds are also deemed despicable in that they are incapable of fulfilling their divinely ordained role of procreation, which further solidifies their marginal, debased status.[43]

Zoological treatises dwell on a number of crossbreeds that are barren, have strange appearances, or display bad dispositions. For example, the mule (*baghal*), a mix between the horse and the ass, cannot reproduce, although apparently it once conceived a black stone and a white mule in its womb.[44] The rhinoceros (*karkadann*) is the product of coitus between a mare and an elephant. It, too, is barren, and has a violent temper.[45] The panther (*fahd*), known for seeking out human excrement for medicinal purposes,[46] occasionally copulates with the bear, and generates a wild beast (undeserving of a name) with a strange appearance.[47] In Greece, bulls with four horns may deviate from their natural coupling with cows in order to mount mares; from this crossing, peculiar-looking horses appear.[48] Lions mating with leopards beget cheetahs. Cheetahs are naturally bad-tempered, fierce, and fond of wine,[49] a prohibited substance that often leads to moral and pious indiscretions.[50]

As these examples show, the creation of hybrids through crossbreeding is never a neutral event in the animal kingdom but rather an activity ripe with stern lessons for humanity, where "mixed breeds" also occur.[51] In the human context, taxonomic purity becomes equated with maternal morality and piety,[52] and not just good behavior or temperament. In terms of appropriate sexual behavior among mothers, the message is clear: the best and most perfected offspring are generated when like produces like, each according to his God-given kind. Therefore, good mothers should not stray too far beyond their own likeness in their copulative desires and practices, or else deficient offspring may result.

The literary community often draws explicit parallels between degenerate crossbreeds among the world's fauna, and human "hybrids." Both Ibn Qutayba and Jāḥiẓ, for example, state that the child of a masculine female and effeminate male has a worse nature than that of the mule.[53] Jāḥiẓ also reports that when a man from Khurāsān mates with an Indian woman, the offspring may *still* have a good nature if well raised. In this example, it appears that such "crossbreeding" between members of two separate ethnic groups would most likely generate a child with a bad disposition that can only be offset by good training.[54] These vignettes demonstrate how good mothers may be identified as those who copulate within their own taxonomic groups. Straying too far outside the lines may produce less than optimal offspring that are as sterile as the mule, as bad-tempered as the cheetah, or as violent as the rhinoceros.

The one possible exception to the rule of "like copulating with like" occurs in cases of women engaging in sexual intercourse with beings on par with or above their own humanity, which would include jinn or angels. In the case of jinn, scholars appear to be divided as to whether or not such liaisons are desirable, legal, or fruitful. Some scholars support the permissibility of jinn for sex by referring to Bilqīs (Sheba) whose father was the king of Yemen, and whose mother was a jinn (ʿUmāra).[55] They back their position with the Qurʾānic verse, ". . . and share with them [jinn] your wealth and children."[56]

As for angels, scholars also acknowledge some of their more successful sexual liaisons with humans. For example, Jāḥiẓ states that whenever an angel rebelled against God, he was sent down to earth in the guise of a man, as was done in the case of Hārūt and Mārūt. In this manner some of the angels had intercourse with some of the daughters of Adam, who then gave birth to Jurhum.[57] The Jurhum, however, were a righteous group in that they are noted for giving protection to Ishmael and Hagar.[58]

While many scholars endorse human/jinn copulations,[59] uncertainty about the resultant progeny still plagues debates on the topic. Some elites dispute the idea that humans and jinn could mate at all based on their biological difference. The Ḥanbalīs, for example, argue that it would be impossible for the humors of jinn to mingle with those of the human, given that the bodies of jinn are supple and ethereal, while human bodies are weighted with impurities.[60] The Qurʾān underscores the necessity of like mating with like by stating "God has made for you *among yourselves* wives" (emphasis mine).[61]

Even if such matings were fruitful, scholars deliberate the quality of the resultant offspring. While most scholars agree Bilqīs was an extraordinary woman, they also emphasize she had feet like an ass and hairy legs, telltale marks of the jinn.[62] In order to become a Muslim, marry the king, and produce a child, Bilqīs had to submit to Solomon's removal of those animal-like features (the hair on her legs) that distanced her from her humanity.[63] The need to purify Bilqīs of her jinn heritage before her coupling with Solomon may be tied to the suspicion that jinn oppose human beings by having souls like those of the devils,[64] or that jinn are actually Iblis's progeny.[65] Such demon-like qualities most certainly would compromise the offspring produced from these taxonomic transgressions. Clearly, even in the case of jinn, crossbreeding results in the begetting of less than perfected Muslim beings, and should be avoided by good mothers whose duty it is to confirm the male's superior ability to beget righteous offspring in their own image.

Transsexuals and Hermaphrodites: Ambiguous Producers of Life

In addition to crossbreeds, much is made in the *ḥayawān* literature about animals that have the ability to change their sex from one year to the next, or can take on the role of both male and female because they possess a penis and a vulva. As noted in chapter 2, medieval scholars believe ambiguous genitalia is produced naturally during the act of sexual intercourse, when male and female sperm come together in equal strength or heat in the womb.[66] While jurists such as the Ḥanafite al-Sarakhsī (d. 1091 CE) have argued that the *sharī'a* readily accommodates hermaphrodites by assuming them to be inherently male or female[67] despite the presence of ambiguous sex organs, no such premise exists in the animal world, where crocodiles, hyenas, or kites can embody both sexes simultaneously, or on a rotating basis.

The general anxiety created when certain animals do not fit into one taxonomic, legal category or another becomes manifest in the descriptions of these unusual animals' unruly dispositions. Although hermaphrodite and transsexual animals are able to replicate themselves, scholars attribute their unusual anatomies—and those of their offspring—to their inherently immoral behaviors and/or characters. In order to avoid generating similarly deviant offspring, good mothers must adhere to the sexual mores prescribed for them by those men who wish to replicate only the distinct male and female "pairs" God initially created.

For example, Qazwīnī notes how the crocodile (*timsāḥ*) has both a male organ (*dhikr*) and female parts (*farj*).[68] He suggests further that the crocodile is likewise hideous in appearance, and its flesh is unlawful to consume. It has a violent temper, and it can kill a number of large animals, including humans.[69] Like the crocodile, the hyena (f. *ḍabuʿ*, m. *ḍibʿān*) dons male and female organs "in the manner of a hermaphrodite [*khunthá*], and every year the organs of one sex [over the other] are excited."[70] Depending on which organ is stimulated, the hyena can impregnate females like a male or conceive like a female.[71] Perhaps because of the transformative nature of its gender, writers on the natural world depict the hyena as exuding an unbridled sexuality. For example, the female ravishes the corpses of men, engages in necrophilia with them, and drinks their blood afterward, lustful, unnatural, ungodly acts that then prompt them to menstruate and thus conceive and replicate their own monstrous natures.[72]

Despite evidence to the contrary,[73] hermaphrodite life forms—whether animal or human—are hardly neutral. In the *ḥayawānāt* they are shown to have strong associations with the devil. Damīrī, for example, notes how God created Iblis as a hermaphrodite. Like the hyena, Iblis dons both male and female genitalia. On his right thigh God created a penis and on his left thigh a vagina. The two thighs then rub together in order to copulate. In a single act of "intercourse" Iblis's thighs produced ten eggs, out of which seventy male and female devils are born.[74] In contrast with Mary's miraculous conception of Jesus without a husband or God's solitary formation of Adam, this depiction of how life may be generated without the benefit of sexual coupling does not glorify God's omnipotence but rather underscores the perversion of Iblis, who stands opposed to all that is good and divine.

In the hermaphroditic anatomies of the crocodile, hyena, and devil, violence, blood, fecundity, and impurity are all wrapped up in an insatiable appetite for sex and erotic stimulation that destabilizes the normative boundaries between male and female pairs reinforced by the Qurʾān and *sharīʿa*.[75] In some cases this fundamental challenge to normative boundaries is encoded within the very presence of the dual sex organs that are likewise stamped upon the offspring's body, which resembles its "mother" in terms of its ambiguities and deviance. The moral lesson is clear: offspring with dual sex organs are the products of overzealous sexual cravings and violence that all good mothers must seek to avoid.

Transsexual animals are also fairly abundant in the animal kingdom, and many medieval *adab* writers and naturalists depict them as having similarly disruptive natures as the hermaphrodite. For example, the male spider (*ʿankabūt*) spins its thread and becomes the female who lies in wait to kill its prey.[76] The kite (*ḥidāt*) is one year a male and one year a female.[77] The meat of the kite is forbidden to consume, and it is referred to as a scoundrel and the basest of all birds.[78] The hare (*arnab*), also one year a female and one year a male, menstruates in the manner of women.[79] While the Shāfiʿīs allow for hare meat to be consumed, some of the law schools question its inherent impurities.[80]

As in the case of animals that embody both sexes, transsexual *ḥayawānāt* transgress taxonomic boundaries that define normative views of sexuality; as a result, they are viewed as impure, hypersexual, or as having unsavory dispositions. The female form in particular becomes associated with blood, death, and violence. The didactic point to be drawn from such examples is that mothers who willingly defy the fundamental norms of their prescribed sexual roles will likewise produce offspring similarly corrupted in form and temperament.

Despite the fact that Islamic law can accommodate individuals with ambiguous sex characteristics,[81] medieval *literati* often suggest such persons bring chaos into the world. Damīrī, for example, discusses the strange (*gharīb*) case of a neighbor who remained a girl for nearly fifteen years until she developed a male organ and grew a beard.[82] Al-Rāzī also describes a Kurdish woman who became a public curiosity because of her full, luxurious beard. He reports further how a woman who gave birth to children afterward grew a male organ on her body.[83] Such anomalous figures turn normative expectations upside down, but not necessarily in a way that glorifies God.

For example, even though *sharīʿa* carves out public spaces for hermaphrodites to pray, observe rules of modesty, or marry,[84] the medical scholar ʿArīb ibn Saʿd undermines their normative treatment with reports on how those with ambiguous sexual organs often bear children from their rear ends, sources of profound impurity that corrupt both mother and child.[85] In addition, the philosopher Ibn Sīnā notes how "extra organs" should be relegated to the status of *ʿayb* (defect), at which point they could be surgically removed.[86] Because of such assaults on the natural order of God's ideal world as men define it, perhaps, the prophet cursed men who resemble women and women who resemble men.[87] These examples suggest that when good mothers deviate from expected reproductive norms, through which men secure the generation of righteous offspring, they destroy the very structures that lend meaning to their lives and the lives of their children.

Hypersexed Animals

In addition to crossbreeds, hermaphrodites, and transsexuals, medieval zoological texts also catalog those bizarre animals that result when different species mount a female and produce a single offspring that resembles its multiple fathers, or multiple offspring in a single pregnancy that take after their individual fathers. In either case, the large amount of sperm that accumulates in the womb—a product of excessive sexual excitement and/or promiscuous intercourse—engenders taxonomic anomalies. In the animal kingdom, such anomalies may simply point to the "creatures and shapes you never imagined God had created."[88] However, when humans give birth to offspring with evidence of multiple paternities, the emphasis shifts from their being displays of God's glory to public shows of maternal sexual deviance and promiscuity, qualities good mothers would do well to avoid.

In the animal world, the giraffe is the most visible manifestation of an offspring with more than one father. Many theories exist as to the origin of this animal, whose name (*zarafa*) means collection. According to Damīrī, the giraffe (*zarafa*) is produced when the hyena mounts a she-camel, and produces a male crossbreed that then mounts the cow.[89] Clearly, the hyena is a suspect animal from the start; whatever it generates will likewise be similarly tainted. Other scholars suggest the giraffe may be the result of indiscriminate sexual intercourse, which appears to be rampant and unbridled in the animal world. For example, Abū Ḥayyān holds that storks are "naturally" inclined toward fornication and adultery.[90] Qazwīnī notes how four-legged female animals are instinctively driven to coupling with numerous males.[91] Ibn Qutayba describes female dogs that produce litters with black, white, and reddish pups, each of which reveals precisely the various fathers who leaped their mother.[92]

As for the giraffe, stories abound about wild animals assembling together at the watering hole to engage in wanton sex, which causes the seminal fluids of each male to mix freely together in a single womb. As a result of such orgiastic revelries, the female gives birth to kaleidoscopic offspring, such as the giraffe, that vary in appearance, color, and form.[93] Of course, some scholars such as Jāḥiẓ, for example, refute this theory on the basis that few animals can fertilize another species. Moving away from the evaluative diagnosis of sexual promiscuity, but still unable to explain precisely how the giraffe achieved its rather unusual form, Jāḥiẓ asserts that the giraffe is simply one of God's amazing creations.[94] Here, Jāḥiẓ shows himself to be one of the few scholars who tries to offset patriarchal notions of reproductive causality with more open-ended, Qurʾānic visions of God's ability to generate in wombs whatever, and however, he pleases.

In many traditional sources, however, improper sexual practices are what lead women to conceive something like a giraffe, and therefore are strictly prohibited. Mālik, for example, reports how it is forbidden for a man to have sex with a female slave who is carrying another man's child,[95] in theory, so the two sperms cannot mix together and corrupt the fetal form. Likewise, the *Mishkāt* confirms it is unlawful for a man who believes in God and the last day to "water what another has sown with his water."[96] Again, underlying such prohibitions is the scientific belief that one man's sperm may contribute to what has already been generated by another man's seed. Thus, the child produced could end up with two fathers. Good mothers must observe such proscriptions and never engage in sex with multiple partners. If they do, the appearance of the child will expose their iniquities through its uncanny resemblance to its two (or more) fathers.

Ibn Qutayba reports on this strange phenomenon in a story about the caliph ʿUmar, who found himself in the unfortunate position of having to determine paternity in a case where a child's heritage was similarly "mixed-up."[97] The idea that a child could have two fathers is not a rarity; in fact, it is explored at some length in Jewish texts. The *Yerushalmi Yebamoth,* for example, suggests that since conception occurs within three or forty days of cohabitation, a woman who copulates with another man during this period allows for the mixing of the two sperms together, which results in a child with two fathers.[98] Clearly, a human child with such polyvalent features like the giraffe would not be received with the same enthusiasm as the comparable wonders of nature in the animal world. As a result of promiscuous female behavior, a Muslim child with "mixed-up" features would be instantly marginalized without the infantile rituals of *taḥnīk,* circumcision, naming, the haircut or sacrifice, or laws of inheritance that socialize him in a world where a single paternal identity prevails.

In distant lands or the wilds of the animal kingdom, monstrous forms prompt communal affirmation of normative practices, which become inextricably tied to what it means to be a good mother. Mothers whose offspring conform to normative shapes, sizes, and appearances obviously embrace right belief and practice. On the other hand, those who shun what is proper may give birth to the physical signs of their sexual or cultic defilements. When women adhere to normative practices, monstrous or mixed forms may be considered a wondrous sign of God's omnipotence, a source of reflection and contemplation for rational men. However, when mothers are suspected as deviating from the norm of acceptable sexual behavior, the monstrous or mixed creature produced becomes the visual embodiment of God's wrath or punishment, a warning for those who venture too closely to the edges of their humanity.

Eve, Bad Mothering, and the Monster Next Door

The communal judgment that sets the criteria to distinguish the truly heinous from glorious divine sign becomes even more crucial in the civilized center. In the center, taxonomic breaches are less apparent and more evasive than out on the margins. Men are not flagrantly copulating with animals; women are not engaging in wild orgies at the watering hole; humans do not flip their sex from one year to the next. The aberrant anatomies or moral characters produced among friends, neighbors, and relatives generally do not appear to diverge all that greatly from the norm. To explain the subtle deflections in the appearance or disposition of the community's children, medieval Muslim scholars draw upon many of the same tropes they employ to evaluate the contorted heathens on the margins or the promiscuous, sexually ambiguous creatures in the animal world that threaten to disrupt the human realm. They look to fundamental categories that have been violated, cultic or sexual norms that have been trespassed, or, at last resort, when no clear cause can be assigned, the elusive divine intentions randomly at play in human life.

When contemplating the variance that occurs among "us" as opposed to the "other," scholars often blame female piety for impacting negatively the development of the fetus. A close analysis of the life of Eve reveals how lessons from the margins—both geographical and animal—are brought to bear on maternal intent, belief, and behavior in the center to explain physical or moral aberrations in human offspring. These lessons serve to steer pious women away from emulating the habits of bad mothers. After all, the righteous queens of paradise only generate the "perfected of perfections" in their wombs.

The Reproductive Life of Eve

The reproductive life of Eve is overshadowed by the incestuous, murderous actions of her son, Cain. Although the Qur'ān is silent on the issue of what brother killed whom, the majority of Muslim exegetes agree it was Cain who killed his brother Abel.[99] As often is the case today,[100] medieval exegetes and other *literati* expand their circle of blame outward from the perpetrator to include the mother who bore and raised him. For Muslim exegetes in particular, the question of whether Cain was innately flawed, or later corrupted through his own actions, is firmly rooted in broader discussions and debates about the role Eve played as mother, and the conception, birthing, and nurturing of her notorious son. Added to these conversations are careful analyses of Cain's own sexual, reproductive role as exegetes debate the extent to which a flawed maternal character is imprinted upon the offspring of future generations. All of these deliberations draw heavily from contemporaneous medical wisdom about how reproduction takes place, and reflect structurally the findings in zoological texts and folklore that explore monstrous births among both humans and animals.

Before the birth of her murderous son Cain, Eve's procreative history was already checkered with barrenness, miscarriage, violence, and an unnatural fecundity. According to medieval exegetes, who diverge radically from the Qur'ān's silence on the issue,[101] Eve's maternal difficulties stretch back to her questionable actions in paradise. According to Ṭabarī, God said, "Eve, you are the one who beguiled my slave (Adam). You shall not have a single pregnancy that will not be difficult. When you desire to give birth to what is in your womb, you will quite often be on the verge of death."[102] Such foreboding came to fruition in Eve's initial attempts to conceive.

When Eve first had sex with Adam, she became pregnant with twins, a male and a female, but in the eighth month aborted them.[103] As noted in chapter 2, scholars of medicine, such as Rabbān al-Ṭabarī, often wrote about the dangers surrounding the eighth month of pregnancy, since eight is not an optimal number like nine or seven,[104] and that it is during the eighth month that the fetus confronts a variety of diseases that generally prove fatal.[105] Either Eve's twins fell prey to the perils of the month ruled by the cruel Saturn,[106] or God's own words were simply being fulfilled through the death of her children.

According to Kisā'ī, Eve conceived another set of twins after aborting this first set, but miscarried for a second time during the eighth month of pregnancy. She conceived a singleton the third time, and here Iblis, or Satan, came to her and asked if she wanted the contents of her womb to live. Eve said yes, and he told her to name her perfect little boy ʿAbd al-Ḥārith, which means "slave of the earth cultivator," or "slave of Iblis."[107] She agreed, and the child lived.[108] Soon after the birth, an angel came to her, asking why on earth she would name the child ʿAbd al-Ḥārith, and not something more appropriate such as ʿAbd al-Raḥmān, which means "servant of God." In a reversal of communal practice where the father, and not the mother, provides the child with a suitable Muslim name and thus ensures its paternal status within the community and the eyes of God, Eve accidentally dedicated her child to something other than God through her ignorance of traditional norms. Her misguided actions thus link her with both Moses's mother, who inadvertently placed her child in the oven, and Umm Sulaym, whose child died under her watch.[109] Frightened as to the consequences of their actions, Adam and Eve abandoned their child, and God caused it to die.

Eve conceived again, and this time successfully gave birth to twins, whom she fittingly called ʿAbdallāh and Amatallāh, which mean, "(male) servant of God," and "(female) servant of God," respectively. This set of twins was followed by twenty-one more pairs like it, all of whom were dedicated to God. As Kisā'ī narrates the story, at the midway point in her childbearing career, Eve bore the prophet Abel and his sister, and then Cain and his sister. Eve continued to give birth after these two infamous brothers until she totaled 120 pregnancies.[110] Ṭabarī offers a different version of this story, having Satan slay a number of the infants even after they were committed to God as punishment for Eve's and Adam's refusal to submit to his cunning ways.[111] In his telling of the story, their initial mistake in dedicating their children to him is indelibly impressed upon the lives of subsequent offspring through sudden infant death.

Each of these examples casts the deaths of Eve's infants as direct punishment for her choosing Satan to be her first master. Eve's miscarriages and the slayings of her babies were all caused by her ignorance of God, which was further emphasized through her sorry attempts to socialize her child without the help and guidance of men. Throughout medieval Muslim literature, miscarriages and infant death often serve as portents of impending punishment. The Qur'ān, in fact, discloses that the simultaneous miscarriages of all pregnant women will serve as signs of the last judgment, when those who have turned away from God will be severely and eternally burned in the fires of hell.[112]

Such a view that God uses women's reproductive bodies to carry out his wrath is not confined to the Islamic context. In similar fashion, Talmudic sources also link miscarriage with punishment. Here, under less extreme circumstances than the final judgment, a woman miscarries as punishment for her groundless hatred.[113] Muslim texts likewise infer that impiety leads to miscarriage. It is only when Eve acknowledged the existence of God and placed him above all else that her womb began to respond properly and profitably.

The *ḥadīth* mention many other examples supporting the link between a lack of divine reverence and negative reproductive consequences. Bukhārī, for example, relates a story about Solomon, son of David, who declared:

> "Tonight I will go round one hundred women, every woman will bear boys who will kill in the cause of God." An angel said to him, "Say: If God wills." But Solomon did not say it; he forgot. So he had sexual relations with them, but none of them delivered except one woman, who delivered a half-person (*niṣfa insān*).[114] The prophet said, "If Solomon had said, 'If God wills,' God would have fulfilled this desire and that saying would have made him more hopeful."[115]

In this example, men become impotent, wombs dry up, and the "*niṣfa insān*" is left to bear the brunt of his parents' impiety for not acknowledging God as the sole source for life. Barrenness and the delivery of a child with an aberrant physical form stand as punishments aimed directly at wayward parents, who "forget" God's central role in the reproductive process.

Other sources also stress the dire consequences a child may endure if his parents are not properly focused on God during sexual intercourse.[116] For example, many *ḥadīth* emphasize the need for humans to utter the following phrase during any carnal act, so that Satan will not interfere with conception and pregnancy: *bismillāh Allāhumma jannibnī al-shaytān wa jannib al-shaytānu ma razaqtanā* (in the name of God, God, protect me from Satan and protect what you bestow on us from Satan).[117] Ghazālī also instructs couples to call upon God to avert the devil so that if a child results from an act of coitus, the devil shall not harm him. A man should also ask God to "cause [the child] to be good progeny if you cause him to issue forth from my loins."[118]

Likewise, Ibn ʿArabī speculates on how parents who have consumed unlawful foods may produce children with souls that are dark, filthy, and evil. Their souls are corrupt because the sperm that generates the child is formed out of unlawful nourishment and nurtured by a tainted soul; therefore, the child must be in accord with the defiled soul.[119] To ward off Satan, Ghazālī, insists a man must chant the *adhān* in the right ear of a newborn and the second call in the left; this practice has the added benefit of repelling epilepsy.[120] Ibn Qutayba suggests something as minor as jealously can prevent a woman from ever giving birth to virtuous sons,[121] so that particular iniquity must be avoided. The causal connection between jealousy and fertility was, after all, what stymied ʿĀʾisha's attempts to conceive a child.

Medieval Muslim texts also restrict deviant or unlawful sexual practices that may interfere with a woman's conception of a prudent child or a fetus's proper development by showing them to cause birth defects.[122] Suyūṭī mentions men must take care to purify themselves before engaging in sex. He notes that whoever has a wet dream and does not wash before having sexual intercourse will produce an idiot or an epileptic.[123] Penile contact with menstrual blood can lead to impotency in males,[124] and sex with kindred wives gives rise to weak children.[125]

Scholars are particularly concerned with sex during menstruation, as that practice is strictly forbidden in the Qurʾān.[126] Ghazālī boldly asserts that sex with a menstruating woman will engender leprosy in offspring, and sodomy causes permanent harm.[127] ʿArīb ibn Saʿd states that if a trace of menstrual blood remains in a woman's womb after her period, it will corrupt the mixing of sperm together inside the womb.[128] To emphasize the dangers of monthly blood, he adds that if a woman becomes pregnant while menstruating she will bear an absentminded child, and if she becomes pregnant during her menstruation her child will be loathed.[129] While men, too, are responsible for adhering to lawful sexual practices, it is the woman's body that creates the hostile environment that impacts the child's growth and development. Although she may not generate something as monstrous as the *khirsṣār,* the epileptic, weak, or despised progeny still bears the marks of sinful trespass.

Interestingly, Muslim scholars distance themselves from their Jewish counterparts by allowing for a broader repertoire of sexual positions that will leave no visible marks on the child generated. While both groups prohibit sex with a menstruating woman, Muslim scholars permit men to have vaginal sex with their wives from the back, which the Jews claim would create a squint-eyed child. So that Muslims would not follow the ways of the Jews, the Qur'ānic verse came down, "Your wives are a tilth to you, so come to your tilth however you will."[130] This statement allows for any sexual position to be undertaken except anal sex[131] and having sex with one's wife while she is menstruating.[132]

By way of contrast, the Shī'ites more narrowly define deviance and more tightly regulate sexual practice than do their Sunnī counterparts to prevent anatomical flaws in the offspring generated from despicable, unlawful, or even suspicious acts of coitus. The sixth Shī'ite Imām Abū 'Abdallāh is reported as saying, "Do not have intercourse with your wife while you have your hair dyed, for if you are blessed with a child, it will be a hermaphrodite (*mukhannath*)."[133] The fifth Shī'ite *imām,* Imām Muḥammad al-Bāqir (Abū Ja'far al-Bāqir) (d. 733 CE), also warns against a man having intercourse with his wife when a child can see the action (apparently from inside the womb). Such a child will be known for being dissolute (*al-fisq*) and immoral (*al-fujūr*).[134]

The Imāmī Shī'ite treatment of the *walad al-zinā* (the offspring resulting from illicit sexual intercourse) illustrates most effectively the idea that maternal deviance can be impressed upon the child's features or affect negatively its disposition. The prolific Shī'ite scholar Abū al-Qāsim 'Alī ibn Ḥusayn al-Sharīf al-Murtaḍá (d. 1044 CE), for example, argues those created from adulterous sperm will never choose a good and virtuous road.[135] 'Abdallāh ibn Ja'far al-Ḥimyarī (ca. ninth century CE), compiler of the *Qurb al-isnād* and author of a book on the occultation, likewise suggests it is impossible for the *walad al-zinā* to serve as a wet nurse, for the suckling infant may imbibe corrupt characteristics from the milk.[136] Marriage with a *walad al-zinā* is not recommended, but if it does occur no children should be produced. The implication here is that the *walad al-zinā,* a product of a prohibited adulterous affair, has despicable traits that are passed on to progeny.[137] In these examples, children, like monsters and animals on the margins, bear the indelible marks of a mother's sexual trespass.

According to the Shīʿite *imāms*, periods of liminality also pose a great danger for sexually active couples. For example, Imām Muḥammad al-Bāqir reports that the prophet disapproved of coitus on the night in which a person intended to travel, for if he were blessed with a child, it would be squint-eyed (*aḥwal*).[138] Imām Muḥammad al-Bāqir goes on to discuss the prophet's concern for children conceived between dawn and sunrise, between sunset and nightfall, during an eclipse of the sun, or on the day of an earthquake. The prophet claims these children, when born, will possess detestable qualities.[139] Sex should also be avoided in the middle of the month, when the crescent moon shifts from one stage to another and begins to wane. Children generated during this time of flux will be poor, and subject to trials.[140] Likewise, children conceived on the night of a new moon (*hilāl*) will be born insane (*makhbūt*).[141]

Sunnīs are not immune to the fear that any kind of liminality may affect adversely a pregnancy. Ibn Sa'd, for example, reports how Ruqayya, the prophet's daughter, suffered a miscarriage during the first emigration.[142] Ghazālī warns how coitus is undesirable during three nights of the month: the first, last, and middle. He claims the devil is present if a woman is ovulating on one of these nights; additionally, evil beings copulate on these nights, so it is best for men to avoid emulating such figures.[143]

With all of these examples, both Sunnī and Shīʿite scholars suggest that by ignoring God, attempting to usurp his creative powers, or deviating somehow from his straight path (either intentionally or even inadvertently), women (and men, too) can impact negatively those divinely controlled bodily processes that ensure the birth of a healthy, moral child. The violation of normative practice exposes the entire human reproductive system to the wiles of Satan, or to unknown forces in nature that somehow embody what is not God. Good mothers would do best to avoid such questionable practices, and, like the paradisiacal queens, strive to adhere to the strict codes of purity, piety, and right behavior enforced by men to ensure their wives give birth to the perfected and righteous offspring both they, and God, desire.

Given the many causal connections between impiety, barrenness, and the birth (or destruction) of flawed children, it may be that Eve's ignorance of God, sexual impropriety, or even malignant natural forces invoked her son Cain's murderous intent. The problem with this scholarly explanation is that it contradicts the many Qurʾānic statements that assert "no soul shall bear the burdens of another,"[144] and "it is he who shapes your bodies in your mothers' wombs as he pleases."[145] These revelatory passages disassociate Eve from Cain's fate since her impious actions would have had no effect whatsoever on her son's moral disposition; in theory, only her own womb would have suffered the consequences of her lack of faith. The causes of Cain's moral downfall would thus be attributed to his own actions, or to God's eternal wisdom that simply cannot be replicated by man.

Many medieval scholars also concur that once a mother has given birth, the child stands alone as an individual before God. Ibn Qutayba, after all, notes that if a man rapes a woman, and she becomes pregnant as a result of his violence against her, the son she bears will not be evil like the father, but in fact virtuous.[146] And, in all of the exegetical works describing the first family, it is never God who punishes the offspring for Eve's transgressions; rather, it is Satan who kills them to punish Adam and Eve for choosing the divine over him, or Adam and Eve who insist God destroy the infants dedicated as servants of Satan.[147] Although in each instance the infants were, indeed, put to death, God never marked the children for death in retribution for Eve's initial or subsequent crimes. Early Islamic exegetes for the most part agree individuals are judged for their own faith, actions, and intentions independently before God. Neither a mother's piety nor impiety guarantees her child's success or demise in this world. This theological position on individual human accountability would suggest Cain had every opportunity to be counted among the righteous, even if he had emerged from a tainted, flawed, weak, or impious womb.

So why did he fail? Despite theological evidence to the contrary, a number of scholars reject the idea that a mother's piety or impiety have absolutely no impact on the moral or physical composition of her child. While Cain in no way resembles the subhuman *khirṣsār,* the man-eating crocodile, or the corpse-eating hyena, structural parallels persist between the moral and physiological forces involved in his birth and conception and those at play in the reproduction of monstrous beasts on the margins of humanity or in the animal kingdom. Such structural parallels revolve around maternal taxonomic transgressions involving moral equivocations and a variety of bodily, reproductive violations. In the case of Cain, scholars project that such infractions in maternal piety, sexual propriety, or the normal course of conception somehow contributed to the formation of his despicable nature despite adverse theological arguments in defense of his moral independence.

Gestational Anomalies: Cain as Twin Brother

Exegetes who adhere to the causal argument explore the possibility that Cain was driven to murder because something may have gone wrong during the period of gestation. As noted in chapter 2, scholars often view the cycle of conception, gestation, and birth as a treacherous path that often leads to less than desirable birth outcomes. Following the conclusions of Hippocrates, Rabbān al-Ṭabarī discusses how problems in embryonic development occur when a woman's belly constricts and the child is left with little room to grow, or when a woman's womb is weak and the embryo is deprived of vital nourishment.[148] Ṭabarī also notes that good seed can, in fact, fall on rocky ground or a deformed womb, which may lead to the twisting or contorting of a child's limbs.[149] ʿArīb ibn Saʿd suggests, too, that procreation can only take place in wombs free of decay (*al-fad*).[150] Perhaps the fetal Cain encountered a similarly hostile and volatile environment.

The sources reveal little about what went on in Eve's womb after she began to conceive successfully. If anything at all is notable about Eve's womb, other than the fact that it was quite fertile after a slow start, is that it brought forth many sets of twins. Could Cain's contemptible nature in some way have stemmed from the fact that he was a twin? In many mythological contexts, twins represent a category fraught with extraordinary power and danger. Whether identical or fraternal, twins present a unique challenge to any religious, legal, literary, or practical discourse that must navigate alterity; how are two individuals who share the same womb and the same moment of birth identical, yet otherwise; like, yet unlike? Are they halves to a whole, or a whole never realized?

The underlying resemblances of twins suggest an eerie fragmentation of a once-unified self, a fissure so deep it generates great social or psychological confusion that requires immediate repair. Their dichotomous identities, which often embody the polarity of good and evil, signify fundamental moral or ethical contradictions that undermine the social fabric and threaten the cosmic whole. As extraordinary phenomena, twins and the unique events surrounding their births result in real or imagined disruptions of the established individual, familial, social, and cosmic order. From the standpoint of religious discourse and praxis, these ruptures must be repaired through a variety of exegetical and ritual controls. The exceptionality of twins may either be interpreted negatively, that is, they are a danger, or positively, that is, they bring good luck.

If anything extraordinary can be said about twins in the Sunnī Muslim context, it would have to be that their presence is imbued with little to no physiological or mythological significance. As noted above, as Eve's womb became more fruitful, she began to bear twins, including Cain and his sister, and Abel and his sister. Sunnī traditions relate that as Eve's children grew older, Adam began to marry off one of the boys to a sister who was not his twin, since God informed Adam that marrying one's "womb-mate" was strictly forbidden.[151]

These sources acknowledge the problems inherent in incestuous unions, but insist that cross-twin marriage, an exceptional practice granted through God's grace and blessing for the time,[152] to be better than copulation with one's own twin or even worse, one's mother (the only viable alternative). Notably, Shīʿite scholars found even this relatively distant and anomalous form of sibling incest abhorrent; rather than allowing each brother to mate with his sister, the Shīʿites claim God created a female *jinnīya* for Cain to marry, and a *ḥūrīya* for Abel.[153] In Shīʿite traditions, since neither one of these nonhuman beings could bear offspring, God carved out wombs in them so they could conceive.[154]

The exegetical privileging of twins in this case fulfills the practical purpose of explaining how the world became populated without resorting to more problematic forms of incestuous relationships that would have desecrated the very fabric of the cosmic order. What these Shīʿite examples show, as do the Sunnī narratives, is that the divine prohibition against incest is woven so deeply into the fabric of the universe that all reproductive activities, including the social rules governing it, and the biological mechanics driving it, are inherently subject to that law.[155] The exegetes not only construe any sexual union that violates the prohibition without any sort of divine stay, such as son mating with mother, or father with daughter, as a social and moral infringement; more strikingly, they depict it as a natural aberration, since nature too is subsumed under divine law.

Therefore, they assert God must have granted an exemption to Eve's sons, whose only choices were to mate with distant sisters, jinn, and houris, practices that would, in any other context, be considered unnatural and therefore ungodly. In this place and time, however, their sexual behavior must be socially, culturally, naturally, and divinely affirmed in order to shield the perfection of God's cosmos against any threat of corruption caused by even more detestable forms of incest. As a result, Eve's offspring are guarded from any social, moral, or physical consequences that would ordinarily arise out of divine punishment for such an incestuous union that transgresses fundamental sexual boundaries. In theory, such extraordinary divine protection should have prompted the generation of righteous—not murderous—offspring.

Given the somewhat exceptional circumstances surrounding their births, Islamic sources stress the ordinariness of Eve's children. Traditional accounts do not portray Eve's daughters, along with their twin brothers, in any way as two opposite ends of a pole with one twin representing the good, the other evil. Nor do they suggest incomplete remnants of a severed self whose whole is somehow more than the sum of its two dysfunctional parts. Their appearance brought neither exceptional danger nor extraordinary good luck to the first human community.

The only concrete information given about Eve's daughters is that their wombs came to be extremely fruitful (like their mother's), and that some were more beautiful than others.[156] Twinning, in this example, appears to address a practical problem only.

This practical—if not positive—view of twinning is reflected further in other Islamic contexts as well. The Qur'ān mentions twinning in a variety of verses that emphasize natural harmony and balance, for example, that night and day were created as twin marvels, or signs (*ayatayn*),[157] and that men and women are created as equal pairs (*zawjayn*).[158] The *ḥadīth* material suggests women are the twin-halves of men (*shaqā'iqu al-rijāli*).[159] In Islamic legal materials, twins present no great dilemma in terms of inheritance, since all male sons would share equally in their father's property.[160] In theory, Eve's twins should have benefited from the fact that they, too, shared in the natural balance or harmony of the cosmos so lauded in the Qur'ān and Muslim traditions.

This indifference toward who comes out of the womb first, whether twin or otherwise, varies radically from the Jewish context, for example, where birth order reigns supreme in cases having to do with inheritance and covenantal promise.[161] This fascination with birth order appears in many descriptions of Jewish midwives whose attestation of which twin came first is considered valid in court.[162] In Islam, "first-born" is simply not a category that is privileged. Cain may have been born before Abel, but he had a sister with whom he shared his mother's womb, and many siblings who preceded him. Thus, Cain's status as first-born or as twin seemingly had no bearing on his subsequent actions, since prenatal sibling competition was removed from the equation.[163]

Several Muslim physicians likewise confirm the nonexceptionality of twins. They agree pairs of infants are conceived through normal, and not extraordinary, acts of intercourse. For example, Ibn Qayyim, ʿArīb ibn Saʿd, and Rabbān al-Ṭabarī explain the phenomenon of twinning by suggesting the womb has two horns, or cavities, and two children are conceived when an excess of seed is forced into both horns, rather than just one.[164] Other scholars modify this view slightly by claiming humans have but one cavity, and the sperm, which must be expelled in abundance to generate two or more fetuses, simply sloshes to one side and then the other.[165] They note an inordinate amount of semen expelled in the womb may lead to extraordinary cases where women could bear upward of twenty children during the course of four pregnancies,[166] or even seventy fetuses in a single pregnancy.[167] However, even in these rather unusual instances, scholars consider an excess of sperm, often the result of an abundance of sexual excitement, to be completely normal when generated in the context of permissible sexual behavior and sanctioned relationships.

Scholars note if all the sperm exits forcefully from the male and female in its entirety, the multiples will be male, but if it is slightly lighter and wetter, the fetuses will be female.[168] There seems to be no mechanism in place, however, to explain the creation of both males and females in a single pregnancy. Here, the birth of Cain and his twin sister would be considered as somewhat "unusual" since the sperm would need to be dense and light, wet and dry, and hot and cold simultaneously to produce fraternal twins of different sexes in a single womb.[169] Despite this anomaly, scholars still maintain male/female twins would also be generated from a single act of excessively pleasurable intercourse between one man and one woman.

Even though such "natural" explanations for twinning abound, and dual siblings are given no special treatment legally or mythologically, twins are not the neutral category they appear to be at first glance. Read through the lens of monstrosities depicted on the margins of humanity or within the animal world, Eve's generation of multiples becomes a much more suspect phenomenon that may have led to her production of a deviant offspring. As such, Cain's murderous intent may not have been rooted in his own choices, but rather linked to his mother's physical and moral aberrations.

Ḥunayn ibn Isḥāq, for example, refers to twinning as "accidental and unnatural."[170] While not considered deviant, ominous or auspicious, twinning or the production of multiples does indeed become associated with certain types of impure or hypersexed animals, such as the pig, dog, or hare.[171] The pig (*khinzār*), for example, is an animal without any sense of shame. It copulates with its own mother, and in the presence of other pigs several males will satisfy their desire on the same female. The female has the capacity to bear twenty piglets at a time[172] who would, in theory, resemble the various fathers who sired them. Like the pig, female dogs freely welcome the sexual advances of numerous males.[173] Their hypersexuality and promiscuity are manifested in their physical composition: bitches menstruate every seven days.[174] And, as noted above, hares change their sex year in and year out, and either impregnate others or conceive themselves, depending.[175] Hares are also noted for superfetation, where a female becomes pregnant with one set of offspring, and then may become pregnant again before delivering the first set.[176] Superfetation among animals occurs as a result of sex with multiple partners.

Not surprisingly, the pig and the dog are rendered impure.[177] The prohibition against eating pork is well documented in the Qur'ān; dog meat is likewise condemned by the tradition as canines are known to lap blood (*mayta*) with their tongues.[178] The hare, too, is deemed somewhat suspect. Although the Qur'ān in theory would allow for the consumption of the hare (as long as its throat has been cut ritually), and jurists agree it is a product of hunting and is herbivorous rather than carnivorous, some *ḥadīth* do suggest the prophet Muḥammad abstained from consuming the hare,[179] perhaps in part[180] for reasons having to do with its transsexuality. Clearly, mothers of multiples—such as Eve—may also share much in common with these three animals that are known for their promiscuity, impurity, and inordinate appetite for sex.

Thus, a mother who bears undue amounts of twins, like Eve, skirts the fundamental boundaries that separate human from animal in terms of the qualities she shares with dogs, pigs, and hares: an insatiable desire for sex and a misshapen womb. Eve's excessive fecundity, therefore, raises deeper questions about the suitability of her anatomy, purity, and piety for bearing God's righteous servants. Ibn Qutayba says as much as he praises sheep over goats in that sheep bring forth a singleton once a year and no twins, as opposed to the goat that bears three kids or more at one time. Despite the goat's excessive fruitfulness, he notes, it is still the sheep that thrives, is blessed by God, and is never found in decreasing numbers.[181]

Likewise, the prophet once said God has created no animal more honored by him than the ewe (*naʿja*). The ewe is honored because the divine concealed its pudenda while not covering those of other animals.[182] Perhaps Eve, like the goat, was never blessed by God, or her exposed pudenda is suspected of attracting unwelcome, excessive sexual attention. Eve, like the *mālūf,* may be more animal/heathen than human/believer. As a result of her inordinate fertility, Eve bears little resemblance to the queens of paradise who produce optimal numbers of perfected and righteous offspring.

Mothers with hyperactive wombs, like those of pigs, dogs, and hares, contrast sharply with women who have extended gestational periods, and therefore only produce a few children over the course of many years. Scholars view such women as being even more pious and fully human than mothers who give birth in nine months, and their children more exceptional than those that are products of "normal" (and certainly multiple) births. Children who are born after a long period of gestation, for example, are nowhere described as monstrosities, but rather as signs of God's glory. For example, ʿArīb ibn Saʿd describes a baby who remained in the womb sixteen months. When he was born, he already had teeth. He also refers to a woman from the Ḥijāz who was pregnant for thirty months, and another, Fāṭima bint al-Walid b. ʿUtba b. Rābiʿa, who was pregnant with a child for four years.

According to ʿArīb ibn Saʿd, these extraordinary reproductive feats demonstrate that God's signs are greater than what can be calculated and contained.[183] The suffering these mothers must have endured while carrying and expelling these hefty burdens is likewise met with great reward.[184] In addition, those progeny who remain in the womb up to thirty months often grow up to become distinguished members of the Muslim community, as they are born with a "head start" in the pursuit of wisdom and knowledge.[185] As all of these examples show, multiple births in quick succession structurally link both the mother and her offspring with the animal world (goats) and subhuman behavior (Cain), while extended pregnancies over the course of many years generate more civilized, humane outcomes (sheep). Scholars place multiple cavities, an excitable libido, and an innate desire to copulate even in public[186] in opposition with a single womb where exceptional women cover their genitals and refrain from sex for lengthy periods of time to nurture and sacrifice all for the single child within.

Muslim *literati* also link multiple births with the generation of monstrous forms. Creatures such as the *dū paykar,* which may occur as a result of monozygotic twinning or other sorts of gestational malfunctions,[187] suggest the physical (and perhaps moral) constitution of multiples may not be as robust as that of singletons. Physician ʿArīb ibn Saʿd provides some extreme cases where twins are conjoined at the bellies so that their faces face one another, or appear in a single body that dons two heads.[188] Such unusual anatomies obviously disrupt a social fabric founded on paternal rule in which a child's singular identity is necessary to construct that authority.

Since these conjoined twins share an uncanny resemblance to those unusual creatures on the margins born to beasts or heathens, ʿArīb ibn Saʿd expresses concerns about a man engaging in sexual intercourse with their mothers for fear of what such taxonomic transgressions might produce.[189] Given their marginal status, the conjoined twins in this case are not socialized as children but rather labeled as "curiosities" and then offered as gifts to distant rulers[190] or put on display for public viewing.[191] The bearing of such unusual multiples automatically raises questions about the piety, morality, or general fitness of the mother, who cannot generate a child that resembles its father and can be easily assimilated as his progeny among the community of believers.

Contrarily, while many medieval writers and traditionalists suggest such diverse forms of human life may suffer on earth because of their marginalization, they still assert that in no way does God shun their unusual anatomies, unless, of course, these beings bring iniquity upon themselves through their own choices. For example, many *ḥadīth* clarify that people will be resurrected in the state in which they were created.[192] This theological position suggests a mother may bear children who expose her transgressions, but God still accepts them as his own creations.[193] As such, he does not require postmortem modification. However, many minority voices, such as Damīrī, oppose this view, and claim humans may only be gathered on the day of resurrection in perfected form. Perfected form means they will be free from any of the diseases and defects they suffer in the present, such as leprosy, lameness, blindness, or blindness in one eye. At least for Damīrī, humans must have healthy, perfected bodies to last for an eternity in paradise or hell.[194] God alone corrects the physical imperfections wayward mothers impress upon their children.

Medieval Christians share Damīrī's view. Augustine, for example, claims that even monsters will be resurrected, but with an amended body. What prompted his decision was the "double-membered man recently born in the east, about whom most trustworthy brethren who saw him have reported." Augustine found the resurrection of the "double-man" to be distasteful and preferred instead to imagine the rising of two separate, wholly integral individuals.[195] This broad range of interpretations—both Muslim and Christian—suggests that aberrant anatomies may be included into the kingdom of God but may require modification so as not to deflect from what many male scholars define as being truly human.

For Muslim elites, multiple births, aberrant or otherwise, still reflect badly on their mothers. In addition to revealing their mothers' noncivilized, animalistic natures, twin births inevitably raise the possibility that the children generated may have been conceived through a mother's engagement in sexual intercourse with multiple men. As noted above, scholars assert one act of intercourse produces twins or multiple children.[196] In fact, Ibn Qayyim notes that immediately following a single act of intercourse, the womb draws together and embraces the sperm;[197] therefore, it cannot permit the reception of a second fluid, which might mingle with the first and theoretically produce a child who has two fathers.[198] The biological insistence that a child may only be conceived through one act of intercourse, and have only one mother and one father, is also confirmed legally; the Shāfiʿīs, for example, rule that a child can have only one mother and one father.[199]

Despite legal admonitions and scientific arguments against the idea of a child with two fathers, many scholars still entertain the possibility that the integrity of a fetus in the womb may be violated by another man's sperm, as in the case of the giraffe. Ḥunayn ibn Isḥāq, for example, held the position that fetuses are permeable: a father's sperm may continue to shape the form of the child even after conception has occurred. For Ḥunayn ibn Isḥāq, the reason why animals produced in a single litter will often vary in shape, size, and appearance from one another is the result of the male and female (or several males and one female) engaging in numerous acts of sexual intercourse after conception, so that other seed continues to mix with the forms generated from the first conception.[200] Ibn Qayyim supports this theory by suggesting if a pregnant woman has lots of sex then the child will come out very fat; if she abandons sexual intercourse, the child will be emaciated and weak.[201] Here again, male semen entering the womb after conception continues to contribute to the established form, this time, by adding to its size.

Other scholars take a slightly different approach to the open womb theory by suggesting superfetation may occur in humans. According to Aristotle, if the uterus has two horns, then the first horn can become pregnant during one act of intercourse and the other horn can conceive at a later time.[202] As noted above, hares are the quintessential models for superfetation. In the case of the hare, the fetus itself does not receive additional seed; rather, the womb remains open to multiple conceptions. Rabbān al-Ṭabarī, for example, in direct reference to Aristotle, said that he knew of a woman who gave birth in seven months and then put out another child after two months. In this instance, a woman conceives a second time (after the first conception) *by another man* (emphasis mine).[203] Here, scholars draw analogies from the animal world to explain human reproductive anomalies. As in the case of rabbits, superfetation in humans is a direct result of promiscuous, adulterous behavior.

These examples show how a predilection for multiple children places women in the category of those libidinous, hyperfertile creatures that are leaped by multiple animals at the watering hole. The works of Aristotle, for example, which serve as the basis for many reproductive theories put forth by Muslim scholars, suggest that when a woman conceives a second son after she commits adultery, the first will certainly resemble the husband, the other the adulterer.[204] Ibn Qutayba relates a similar story where the caliph ʿUmar struggles to determine the paternity of child whose mother had sex with two men; she was unclear about which man had fathered him. ʿUmar calls upon two *qāʾif*s to ask their opinion, and they reply that both men shared in begetting him. ʿUmar does not believe this to be possible at first, but then exclaims on the basis of resemblance, "It never occurred to me that such a thing could happen, although I knew that if several dogs leg one bitch she brings forth young resembling the different males."[205] Twins and other multiples, therefore, provide an occasion by which the male elite imaginatively project unsavory animal behaviors onto the mothers who bore them.

Such biological theories tinged with moral lessons (or vice versa) are further borne out in mythology. In many religious myths, the presence of twins signals some sort of unusual conception that takes place outside a single act of intercourse between a husband and wife. Twins emerge as products of shady liaisons between a woman and two separate males, one of whom is likely to be something other than human. As a result, one twin often embodies good and the other evil.[206] In the Jewish context, for example, many rabbinic sources that elaborate the details of Cain's conception posit Cain and Abel as twin brothers having the same mother, but different fathers. Some Jewish rabbinic documents, such as the *Targum Pseudo-Jonathan* and the *Pirke de Rabbi Eliezer*, record how Eve was frolicking in the Garden when she was visited by Sammael, the chief of the devils and the angel of death. Sammael rode past her on a serpent, and she conceived. After having sex with Sammael, Adam came to her and she conceived again. As a result of these dual conceptions that led to superfetation, Abel was begotten in the likeness of Adam while Cain was spawned from demonic seed.[207]

Muslim tradition contains no such explicit accusations of Eve copulating with Iblis or an angel of death dressed in serpent's garb; however, there are implicit suggestions that something untoward may have transpired between Eve and Iblis/snake. Qazwīnī, for example, describes how Satan concealed himself in a serpent's head, entered paradise, and tempted Adam.[208] According to one of the prophet's earliest biographers, Muḥammd ibn Isḥāq ibn Yasār ibn Khiyār (d. 767 CE), after Iblis was expelled from the Garden he married the serpent whose mouth he had entered.[209] Eve, too, most certainly would have encountered this devil/snake as she, like Adam, fell prey to Satan's deception.

Such references hint that something heinously sexual between Eve and the serpent/Iblis might have transpired in the Garden. Muslim scholars believe snakes have deep associations with uncontrollable or excessive female lust, violence, sexual perversion, and maternity.[210] In the animal realm, when the male viper (*ufʿuwān*) couples with the female (*afʿā*) she turns on him, and eats his head out of intense love for him.[211] Damīrī observes how some vipers copulate through the mouth,[212] which is depicted as the result of the female engaging in oral sex.[213] This image lends an interesting twist to the story of Iblis marrying the snake whose mouth he entered. Dreams, too, about offspring often involve the presence of snakes. For example, whoever dreams of killing a serpent on his bed, his wife will die; he who dreams of his wife being pregnant and giving birth to a serpent will have an undutiful son born to him.[214]

Snakes may also reveal a woman's inner deviance with respect to sex and reproduction. Jāḥiẓ relates a story about a woman who awoke on the pilgrimage journey to find a snake coiled about her, his head and tail meeting between her breasts. Once they got to Mecca, the snake disappeared. After she completed pilgrimage rites and left Mecca, the snake reappeared and wrapped itself around her body. It hissed, and snakes came out from all over the valley. They bit the woman until marrow oozed from her bones. A slave girl reported that this unfortunate woman had sinned three times: each time she gave birth to a child, as soon as it was born she heated it up and put it in the oven.[215] Such tales of female indiscretion and deviance, buttressed by suggestions of superfetation and its links to adultery, hint that Eve's encounter with Iblis in serpent's guise in the Garden may have generated something more than just disobedience against God.

A Liminal Birth

In addition to speculation that Eve's womb and/or her piety somehow impacted Cain's deviant moral disposition, Muslim scholars project rather unusual circumstances surrounding his birth. While most Sunnī scholars report Cain's birth was as normal as any other for the time, a minority claim that unlike the rest of his siblings, Cain was born under remarkable conditions. These minority traditions describe how Eve became pregnant with Cain and his twin sister (*Iqlima*)[216] in the Garden *before* their descent to earth.[217] In the perfected Garden, before her transgression, Eve, like Fāṭima, bore none of the burdens of an earthly pregnancy; she had no fatigue, no labor pains, and no blood during or after the birth.[218] The recorder of prophets' lives, Abū Isḥāq Aḥmad ibn Muḥammad ibn Ibrāhīm al-Thaʿlabī (d. 1036 CE), quotes the following *ḥadīth* in support of this interpretation: "Were it not for the lapse committed by Eve, women would not menstruate, yet would still be sexually mature. They would bear in secrecy and give birth in secrecy."[219] As a result of Eve's disobedience, however, women's bodies became impure, and necessarily subject to male control and scrutiny.

Thaʿlabī suggests that within the pristine environment of the Garden, Eve nursed Cain with "pure milk" (*min ṭaharat labanihi*).[220] As noted in chapter 4, medical scholars of the time, such as ʿAlī ibn al-ʿAbbās al-Majūsī (d. 994 CE), argue breast milk is formed out of material otherwise evacuated during menstruation.[221] This excess material is then passed up through the body and converted into milk. According to Ibn Qutayba, this link between milk and menstrual blood serves as the basis for the belief that an infant emerges from the womb with a serene glow that quickly dissipates once he sucks from his mother's milk, which makes him resemble her, or the wet nurse.[222]

As discussed in chapter 4, the idea that milk is inseparable from blood is also emphasized in a number of *ḥadīth* that forbid men and women who suckle from the same wet nurse from marrying one another,[223] and in those medical works that prohibit wet nurses from having intercourse with their husbands while they are nursing someone else's child.[224] In the latter case, it is believed a husband's semen serves as a source for milk production in his wife; therefore wet nurses were warned against being sexually active because the suckling would be ingesting her (the nurse maid's) husband's blood that generated the semen.[225] The pure milk Cain suckled from his mother's breast, then, would have been something quite different from what is normally formed out of the womb's remaining bloody (seminal) contaminants.

Ṭabarī and Thaʿlabī go on to report how Abel and his twin (*Labuda*) were then conceived on earth, with Eve bearing all of the earthly symptoms of pregnancy,[226] and presumably, nursing him with milk no longer pure. In this scheme, Cain was, after all, a marvelous birth—beyond human perfection—and should have led a long, happy, and righteous life. If anyone were to bear the stains of evil and corruption, one might assume it to be Abel, and not Cain, for Abel was born into a flawed world that stands in sharp contrast with the ideal Garden.

Not so. Exceptional births (such as Mary's, for example) only bear fruit if they affirm, at least in some way, normative practices. The fact that Cain was the murderer even though he was born in the Garden without impurity, and not Abel, only underscores the idea that if any type of exceptionality, even one that seems quite positive at first glance, evades what is legally, socially, and morally construed, it forebodes ill. In this scheme, Abel, in all his gritty humanness, becomes the more perfected, righteous believer than one who may have been born pure, but to whom no legal, moral, social, or natural prescription applies. According to these traditions, the lack of such necessary and essential boundaries that ultimately separate believers from nonbelievers, which seem to determine who is fully human over and against who is not, indelibly corrupts Cain's nature. In other words, women who "bear in secrecy and give birth in secrecy," even if they are in paradise, generate children whose humanity will never be publicly confirmed, socially circumscribed, or divinely rewarded. In this light, the liminality surrounding his birth, which would have taken place solely in the company of women and not men, affected irreversibly Cain's status before God.

Incestuous Desire

Further attempts to explain the causes of Cain's deviance lie in the inherent problems associated with the stringent taboo against incest. In many exegetical elaborations of the Cain and Abel story, in order to avoid more the abhorrent forms of incest necessary to populate the earth, scholars record how God commanded Adam to give Abel's twin to Cain, and Cain's to Abel.[227] These traditions maintain that Cain's sister was more beautiful than Abel's, and Cain did not want to share what he believed to be rightfully his. According to these narratives, Cain was unrighteous because he declared his twin sister to be his future wife, which underscores how he knowingly and willfully defied God's prohibition against a certain type of incest.[228] Such defiance not only goes against God's will, it ultimately disrupts the very fabric of the cosmos and, of course, the physical and moral composition of future generations. Ibn Qutayba, for example, notes how kindred wives give birth to weak offspring.[229] In theory, sex with one's twin will only generate the most deplorable, grotesque forms of human life. Cain's desire for his twin sister, therefore, places him outside all divine, natural, and social laws that determine his identity as a believer, and therefore call into question his status as a fully formed human.

As the story goes, because Cain was not a believer (for no believer would commit such an act nor is one who commits such an act considered a believer), God could only acknowledge the sacrifice of Abel, who offered a succulent lamb, fresh milk, and rich butter,[230] and reject the rotted crops laid down by Cain.[231] When God granted Abel Cain's twin sister, according to the exegetes, Cain became filled with rage, and killed Abel by smashing his head against a rock.[232] The story ends with Cain and Qalima (his twin) defying God (and natural law) by descending hand in hand from Mount Ḥirā' and fleeing to ʿAdan in Yemen.[233] Not only did he kill his brother, but he also flagrantly denied God's reproductive roadmap for his creations.

But all was not well in ʿAdan. While Cain and his offspring are depicted as being abundantly fruitful throughout the first few generations, a shadow of impiety continued to hang over them, which eventually corrupted and then dried up their seed. For example, one of Cain's descendants, Tūbīsh, is described as the first to play stringed instruments and cymbals.[234] Other children and grandchildren are depicted as godless tyrants who engaged freely in acts of sexual promiscuity and wine drinking,[235] like, for example, the hyena. Eventually, the weak and corrupt offspring of Cain began to mingle with the pure offspring of Seth, and multiply on the face of the earth, so much so that the entire population had to be drowned in the flood.[236]

As in the cases of the *khirṣsār* or *mālūf,* such blatant disregard for taxonomic boundaries compromises the integrity of what it means to be human. While in this case men were not coupling with animals, Eve's marked reproductive life, and later, that of her sons, became inextricably entwined with the production of monsters that patrol the margins. Both types of deviant offspring created under ambiguous and unspeakable conditions mirror egregious and immoral infractions of prescribed borders that separate human from animal, believer from heathen, and good mother from bad. Good mothers never transgress such fundamental boundaries, and, as their reward, they produce the perfected offspring desired by both men and God. As for Cain, it is not solely the quality of his offering, or the fact that God prefers sheepherders to farmers, or even that God was testing Cain's countenance that made him unrighteous. Rather, scholars explore the broader possibility that Eve impressed deviance upon her own child—and subsequent generations—through a womb that bore and revealed the burdens of divine judgment and punishment.

As emphasized in the examples of good mothers, righteous wombs beget nothing but righteous offspring. Unrighteous wombs may produce good children, but more often than not they breed moral or physical deviants who, like the *khirṣsār,* lack the ability to profess or comprehend God's word. And deviants breed deviants, as exemplified by Cain's engagement in an ungodly act of sexual intercourse with his own twin sister. The wine-drinking, sexually perverted despots engendered by Cain's illegitimate wife only serve to underscore this point. Through their recording, expanding, and retelling of Qur'ānic narratives, medieval scholars affirm Eve's reproductive history must have had something to do with Cain's choice to kill his brother. More than Cain's own choices, it was Eve's misshapen, animalistic, and morally compromised womb that corrupted the straight path upon which God can fashion and instruct his "perfected of perfections."

The vitiated reproductive life of Eve illustrates the persistence of a perpetual conflict between the tradition's ideal vision of a radical individualism before God and the practical realities of the intimate moral, biological, and social connections between parents—especially mothers—and children. How the exegetes articulate this conflict and try to resolve the tensions between the real and ideal demonstrates an array of multiple and conflicting interpretive strategies created to navigate the inherently contradictory problem that even though individuals must be free to make their own moral choices before God, those choices are often constrained by maternal behavior, which can affect divinely controlled reproductive processes and familial relationships for generations to come. The exegetical desire to blame mothers for physically or morally flawed offspring even outweighs the Qur'ānic concern to preserve the broader theological and ontological position that individuals be allowed to choose good over evil.

While the extent of the impact Eve's reproductive life has on her offspring remains unclear, the vast majority of debates reveal an inherent bias that only righteous and perfectly fashioned mothers are fully guaranteed of producing healthy and morally sound children. The determination of who precisely is "healthy and morally sound" is communally dependent, and often rests upon male scrutiny and men's relative evaluation of the mother's body and her piety. All other mothers may hope for the best, but can only look to their own words, actions, bodies, and ancestry, all of which have a direct impact on their (socially defined) superior or inferior physical and moral constitution, when God's orderly and perfected paths of reproduction go astray. The assertion of a causal connection between female impiety and monstrous offspring that can be defined, manipulated, and controlled, however, allows male elites to exert their own procreative authority over God's to create in wombs whatever, and however, they please.

Mothers as Monsters to Be Cured

The curiosities that patrol the margins of humanity, along with the lives deemed deficient among ourselves, all reveal how medieval Muslim scholars imagine impiety corrodes the female body and subverts God's procreative plans. Bad mothers and the children who resemble them directly defy the reproductive ideals put forth in the foundational texts, the fertile bodies of perfected paradisiacal queens, and the normative rituals that confirm social birth and normative identity. The *ḥayawān* literature provides a sanctioned forum through which elite male scholars may probe the consequences of human sexual practices generally considered deviant within the tradition. What degenerate animals will suffer for their "unnatural" behavior becomes a barely disguised, coded discourse that aims to circumscribe human sexual activity with its dire warnings over the reproductive implications for deviance. Since every woman has the potential to thwart God's procreative processes through depraved thoughts and practices via her reproductive power, physicians, traditional scholars, and other medieval *literati* often expound the heinous consequences of bad mothering through detailed depictions of monsters and other natural aberrations that occur in the animal world, the margins of humanity, or in the dark recesses of her own womb. Certainly, potential mothers who heard these stories would have taken heed.

The need to curtail women's wayward sexual behaviors becomes even more urgent among the community of believers. Away from the margins, female disobedience more often than not manifests itself in defective wombs and bad births that threaten to blur the lines between self and other/believer and heathen, as in the example of Eve. Unlike in the animal world, anomalous human births rarely evoke God's miraculous power over nature, but rather expose a woman's reproductive aberrancy, as measured by men. Therefore, men must take pains to control female reproductive behavior to determine positive birth outcomes that do not entail disturbing variations such as those found along the margins of civilization, or among the world's fauna. If bad outcomes persist, they are due to a woman's intransigence or to her guardian's impotence, both of which serve to undo the very structures that give fathers, mothers, and children a legitimate, meaningful life.

In probing the source of this deeper question about the range and limits of female power, medieval scholars maintain that the human life God desires could only be brought forth through the male's necessary interference with or control over the fertile female body, a position that directly counters Qur'ānic understandings of God's singular role in the creation of life, or an individual's right to choose his own fate. Ironically, it is men, rather than women, who undermine God's omnipotent and unparalleled procreative power so celebrated in the Qur'ān by trying to protect him from his own polyvalent nature.

The patriarchal norms imposed upon women's bodies, along with limited male visions of God's creative power and transcendence, were directly challenged by maternal experience. Women see that the perfected pregnancies God wills—or that male scholars have come to expect—are not always attainable nor often, in fact, desirable. These medieval male fantasies that fashion an ideal maternal body are undermined by more marginal, imaginative visions of God's omnipotent creative potencies, and practical discussions about magic and folk remedies, through which women control their own fertility, determine their child's sex, define their own agency, or ensure a safe pregnancy and delivery. By asserting reproductive control over their own bodies, women broaden the male construct of the ideal mother while often forging new visions of God, many of which resonate more closely with the Qur'ān's rich and complex expressions of divine omnipotence and immanent transcendence.

Chapter 6 examines how folk remedies bypass what males articulate as being God's will. It is through direct participation in their own life cycles that women tap into marginal theologies, such as that of the Mu'tazilite al-Jāḥiẓ and the Qur'ān itself, to envision a female agency constructed through experience, practice, or habit, and to dispute normative, elite male visions of a God who demands perfection from female bodies that never can conform to ideal expectations. In the lived experiences of everyday life, women reclaim the Qur'ānic position that only God, and not men, know the true contents of the womb, and that ultimately only God, and not men, cause a life to be or not to be, in whatever form, or through whatever means, he chooses.

6

The Cure of Perfection

The monstrous forms on the margins or in the center that result when fundamental boundaries have been transgressed prompt the reestablishment of primary prohibitions necessary to preserve the divinely mandated social order encoded within its established maternal ideals. Such prohibitions both structure and patrol the strictly binary and hierarchical relationships between men and women and establish the father (not the mother) as the principal begetter of the superlative life male scholars have determined God commands, and the mother's womb as the passive but perfected vehicle through which men may realize their goals. These paternal visions of normative human relations that embody what the divine has prescribed as "natural"[1] rest on a particular vision of transcendence where God may initiate the creation of all life, but men are responsible for facilitating his plans as planters of seed, plotters of the female reproductive body, crafters of the ideal mother, Spartan attendants of a child's rebirth into the social world, and determinants of a code of acceptable female behavior that ultimately seals their own authority.

By assuming this responsibility for generating and regulating life on earth, man becomes synonymous with God. This apparent reflection of God, however, flatly contradicts the Qur'ān's portrayal of the divine as polyvalent procreator: transcendent yet immanent; erotic yet ineffable; masculine yet feminine. Such prosaic paternal imaginings of divine power also constrain a woman's own strivings to participate—like the Qur'ānic Mary—directly with God in the begetting of life and restrict her ability to control her own *farj*/reproductive body.

This chapter examines marginal reproductive theories and folk therapies found in medical works, *ḥayawān* literature, and a variety of other medieval treatises to identify those rarefied moments where boundary interruptions between humans and God in the generation of life evoke something other than flurried assertions of patriarchal, social correctives. For example, narratives about "wind eggs" counteract the divinely mandated hierarchical relationships among men, women, and God that male scholars so carefully impose through medical, theological, or proscriptive discourses. Likewise, proposals about spontaneous generation allow for more fluid understandings of "creator" and "created" to emerge for God, men, and women.

A variety of traditionally sanctioned bodily manipulations also emphasize the necessity for human exchange and interchange with God to enact the physical perfections of his creations. For example, the cutting of the foreskin to perfect the human form suggests that God depends on humans to complete what he has engendered. In similar fashion, a woman's decision to employ contraceptives necessitates more direct participation with God, nature, and her own reproductive system to determine the contours of life before or after it comes into being. In each instance, such disruptions to dominant, patriarchal discourses provide unique exegetical or experiential opportunities through which normative, social models of procreation may be recast in ways in which the father's status as second to God's in the begetting of life is never a given, since the feminine is also bestowed with an essential procreative agency, and God is free to create in wombs whatever, and however, he wishes.

These reproductive theories and folk remedies that border the dominant discourses do not move beyond the prevailing patriarchal structures of procreative power, but rather proliferate their possible forms. The recognition that a full range of possibilities exists within the medieval tradition to define how and why reproduction takes place ultimately exposes the failure of heterosexual regimes to legislate or confine fully their own ideals.[2] Within the liminal occasions of this failure, women may construct new alliances with men, nature, and God as they trace their maternal bodies along alternative theological lines. Drawing upon their own experiences in light of theories about God's generative power intimated by Aḥmad ibn ʿAbd al-Ḥalīm ibn Taymīya (d. 1328 CE), Jāḥiẓ, the *ḥadīth,* and the Qurʾān itself, as well as more marginal authorities within the tradition, ordinary women and men reclaim the revelatory vision that only God, and not the male elite, know the true contents of the womb, and that ultimately only God, and not men, causes a life to be or not to be, in whatever form, or through whatever means, he chooses.

God's Curious Means of Procreation: Divine Challenges to Privileged Heterosexual Pairings

As evinced in chapter 1, the Qur'ānic God's creative impulses can never be forced into a single mold. The deity is at once intimate fashioner of man out of (masculine) clay[3] or (feminine) soul,[4] male lover projecting his seed into the warm folds of a receptive earth,[5] nurturing womb that cultivates life, as well as the midwife who brings it forth into the world,[6] force of nature that generates pairs,[7] and transcendent power that merely has to utter "Be!" and it is.[8] These often contradictory snapshots of God's engendering nature capture the multifaceted character of his being that evades men's ability to guarantee fully the conception and delivery of perfected, righteous believers, as the prevailing presence of monstrous forms has demonstrated.

Within the context of his own polyvalent creative techniques, God establishes what may be called the "heterosexual dynamic,"[9] born out of a necessity for earthly reproduction. The Qur'ān asserts that while God creates human life initially, his own generative efforts operate through male and female pairings that continue to reproduce the life he engenders. However, even though sexual pairing is the chosen vehicle through which God brings forth earthly life, the Qur'ān makes clear that the deity's procreative power, unlike that of the human beings he creates, may transcend his usual pattern of generating life through male/female pairings.[10]

As shown in chapter 1, the Qur'ān projects that God may interrupt the human reproductive process at any point through a single word, breath, or action, or through a gender dynamic that is often fluid and dynamic. These interruptions introduce alternative modes of interactions between creator and created that counter the traditional, hierarchical relationships between God and humans, men and women, and humans and animals meticulously defined, controlled, and patrolled by elite male scholars. Their strict governance over sexual roles and the female reproductive body mask the fact that even though men may beget life, their ability to realize the superlative life God desires is at best limited. Despite assertions to the contrary, men, too, are subject to the vagaries of divine power and/or feminine potency as they struggle to reproduce the healthy, perfected worshipers God prefers.

Medieval bestiary authors, travel writers, and even orthodox scholars preserve what may be described as "fringe" displays of God's marvelous procreative abilities in order to highlight God's ultimate transcendence and power over all life. As in the case of monstrous forms, much of the discussion about God's procreative perturbations takes place in the safe haven of the animal kingdom. However, elite scholars draw enough analogies between anomalous animal births and those of human beings to suggest conversations about some of the more awe-provoking births of the world's fauna may well apply to men and women, too.

Their wondrous depictions of wind eggs, spontaneous generation, and metamorphosis that puncture both animal and human realms serve to violate the patriarchal, hierarchical patterns of heterosexual procreation traditional, orthodox scholars strive so hard to maintain. As a result of such infractions, an interpretative space opens up for women to explore more freely their generative potency in relation to God's. This space allows for the broadening of extant views about divine omnipotence, female agency, and maternal well-being intimated in the Qur'ān and other un/orthodox writings.

Wind eggs: Female Impregnation sans Coitus

According to the Qur'ān, the creator of the heavens and earth, when he decrees a thing, only has to utter "Be!" and it comes into being.[11] According to medieval bestiaries, God's ability to call anything to life allows for a variety of nonheterosexual, procreative operations to take place under his watch. For example, bestiary authors such as Abū Ḥayyān note several cases where female animals or birds become pregnant not by sexually coupling, but through a mere blowing of the wind. Abū Ḥayyān describes how female partridges, for example, may be filled with eggs when the wind blows from the (leeward) side of a male in her direction.[12]

In similar fashion, Ibn Qutayba discusses how female palm trees likewise are impregnated by a current or wind when planted next to male palm trees. He weaves a direct analogy between the sexually receptive palm trees and the female partridge, which, he notes, also conceives via the breeze when a male partridge is standing upwind.[13] However, lest God's creative powers be confined to natural processes, it is believed not all wind eggs necessarily require the presence of a male to stand upwind of the female.[14] Ibn Qutayba, for example, notes a mere blowing dust, too, may cause the female partridge to conceive.[15]

Beliefs about begetting offspring via the wind harken back to Greek and Roman times. Aristotle, for example, notes how mares conceive by the wind if not directly impregnated by a stallion. The mares that conceive through encounters with the wind cast off certain objects called "*hippomanes*,"[16] which women collect to concoct fertility drugs and aphrodisiacs.[17] Roman author Lucius Junius Moderatus Columella (d. 70 CE) declares it is the mares' excessive desire for coition, combined with a hypersexed imagination,[18] that facilitates their ability to conceive by the wind.[19] Here, as in the case of multiples, an anomalous conception is caused by female promiscuity. The Roman philosopher, writer, and naturalist Pliny (d. 79 CE), too, describes how mares, in order to capture the elusive breeze, need only to turn their tails up to receive the "genital air" rather than a stallion's "natural seed." The resulting foals of this unusual form of asexual conception, however, have defective constitutions: they live only up to three years.[20]

In addition to mares, Greek and Roman scholars also identify vultures as being particularly susceptible to wind impregnation.[21] Horapollo Nilous (ca. fifth c. CE) even argues that since female vultures conceive by merely opening their wombs to the north wind, they have no need whatsoever for males; therefore, male vultures do not exist.[22] Clearly, when it comes to birds and animals, ancient and medieval scholars feel no need to impress a clear, consistent pattern of heterosexual coupling upon the reproduction of living creatures.[23]

The idea that females can conceive without the presence of males—a phenomenon so lauded in the case of Mary—also appears in Muslim legends about human reproduction on the margins of civilization, which further buttresses the theological stance that God creates in wombs whatever he pleases. Ibrāhīm ibn Wāṣif Shāh (d. 1199 CE), an authority much quoted by Arab historians, for example, in his *Mukhtaṣar ʿajāʾib al-dunyā,* describes an island situated at the edge of the China Sea where women are fertilized by the wind. Like the vulture, they bear only females. Ibn Wāṣif Shāh also observes these women may be fertilized by a tree whose fruit they eat.[24] In addition to air and trees, water (*māʾ*) also provides an analogous function to male seed.[25] Andalusian traveler and collector of marvels (*ʿajāʾib*) Abū Ḥāmid Muḥammad al-Māzinī al-Gharnāṭī (d. 1169 CE), in his *Tuḥfat al-albāb,* identifies a tribe of women who enter the water in order to become pregnant.[26] He mentions that each female bears a daughter but never a son through this erotic, aquatic encounter. Unable to explain fully such a phenomenon, Abū Ḥāmid al-Gharnāṭī emphasizes the fact that such unusual conceptions must be attributed directly to God, who is most wise when it comes to these matters.[27]

Each case demonstrates how women, like mares, partridges, and female palm trees on wondrous occasions conceive through alternative pairings with masculine *or* feminine substances such as the wind (*rūḥ*), trees (*shajarāt*), or water, without coitus with any man. Such curious patterns of reproduction among women on the margins of civilization boost core theological beliefs in God's ineffable, unparalleled generative power. After all, God chose Mary, the quintessential mother, to conceive Jesus in a similarly unique fashion via a spirit, breath, or word blown into her womb.[28]

In this and other examples of nonheterosexual conception, medieval scholars take great pains to assert that divine action never conforms to random patterns in nature but rather disrupts them: God chooses to create in wombs whatever and however he pleases. The *Sīra* articulates this theological position, for example, by asserting Mary's conception of Jesus without a man results from God calling to "be" what he wills, how he wills it, and how he wishes it to be.[29] The natural mechanisms that underlie both the generation of wind eggs and Mary's ability to conceive by the breath may be parallel, but entirely coincidental. Each instance of wind fertilization or water impregnation among birds or women is a discrete, creative act designed to disturb normative, paternal expectations of and control over heterosexual coition in order to demonstrate divine glory.[30]

By way of contrast, medieval Christians frequently use the "wind egg" argument to defend the virgin birth against pagan criticism. To do so, they project the likeness between the partridge and Jesus's mother as homologous rather than analogous. For example, the early Christian author Lucius Caecilius Firmianus Lactantius (d. 320 CE) asks, "But if it is known to all that certain animals are accustomed to conceive by the wind and the breeze, why should anyone think it wonderful when we say that a virgin was made fruitful by the Spirit of God, to whom whatever he may wish is easy?"[31] For Lactantius, the virgin birth is far from exceptional: If nature does it, why can't God? Muslim scholars, on the other hand, do not use arguments from nature to justify God's actions when it comes to Mary's conception of Jesus. God performs such wondrous acts in nature, and among humans, for calculated reasons unbeknownst to man. There are no underlying natural processes that would govern both God's generation of winds eggs and Mary's conception of Jesus without a father.

Whatever the case, in the medieval Muslim context wind eggs challenge the conventionality of heterosexual reproduction and men's privileged role in it borne out in medical, exegetical, and legal discourse. The fact that God can bypass men to generate life by "pairing" with women through wind, trees, breath, water, or his own word, suggests an unparalleled intimacy between the two parties that excludes both husbands and fathers. Women do not passively receive God's life-generating "seed" via his breath or wind, but actively engage the divine imperative to produce life through a variety of different conceptual means.

Unlike men, whose reproductive significance depends upon external recognition for its validation, women pair with God in these examples through their own desire to draw in the feminine, life-animating breath or the masculine, fecund water, and through their unique ability to sustain and nurture that life deep within their wombs, or in far-off places, inaccessible to men. This procreative model that bypasses normative male authority highlights the feminine, generative aspects of the divine, along with his erotic, often passive, immanence, as critical agents in the reproduction of human beings. It also opens up space for women to participate in their own life cycles to facilitate or inhibit their intimate, multifarious partnering with God, to generate what they will outside the dictates of men.

Spontaneous Generation: Life out of Muck

In addition to their acknowledgment of wind eggs, medieval Muslim scholars contemplate the idea that life may be generated outside of heterosexual bounds through the process of spontaneous generation (*tawallud,* or *takhalluq al-ḥayawān min ghayr al-ḥayawān*).[32] Spontaneous generation refers to life coming into being through inanimate matter. Rooted in the classical world, theories of spontaneous generation account for the existence of a variety of both simple and complex life forms. Aristotle, for example, holds some insects are self-generated out of dew falling on leaves,[33] others grow in putrid mud or excrement, and certain types emerge from wood, animal flesh,[34] or hair.[35] Likewise, he asserts a handful of fish are known to spring from mud, sand, or scum.[36] Church Fathers also attribute the appearance of certain life forms to spontaneous generation. Clement of Alexandria (d. 215 CE), for example, refers to moles that spring from the earth, vipers that issue forth from ashes, wasps generated from horse flesh, bees from ox flesh, and beetles from cow dung. He also concludes that some creatures may be engendered from plants, such as the scorpion from basil.[37]

Relying on these same classical sources, medieval Muslim authors of bestiaries and other *adab* writings, like their Christian brethren, espouse similar traditions of inanimate matter begetting life. For example, frogs may be generated spontaneously in stagnant water, or after a copious rain,[38] snakes out of scum,[39] dung beetles from fermenting earth;[40] gnats, worms, and mosquitoes within the bodies of other animals,[41] or from putrid scum.[42] The female bee produces young solely through her absorption of the male's odor.[43] Ants are not engendered by copulation; rather, something falls out of their bodies to the ground that then transforms into eggs. After a fashion, the eggs produce the ant form that is recognized by all.[44] Likewise, Muslim authors observe that at the time of death, the male and female phoenix (*qaqnus*) collect a large quantity of firewood, link their beaks together, and flap their wings. The clash of their wings causes the wood to catch fire, and the two phoenixes are consumed by it. Rain falls on their ashes and a worm appears that eats the ashes and becomes another phoenix.[45]

Spontaneous generation cannot be confined solely to the production of lower life forms, and therefore readily dismissed as marginal. Some Muslim scholars assert if matter is in its most harmonious, well-balanced state, the most perfected of all creatures, namely, the human being, may also be generated.[46] The Andalusian philosopher, naturalist, and writer Abū Bakr Muḥammad ibn ʿAbd al-Mālik ibn Muḥammd ibn Ṭufayl al-Qaysī (d. 1185 AD), for example, in order to ascertain how the human mind progresses without social contact, attributes the birth of his protagonist Ḥayy[47] to spontaneous generation in his mystical work, *Ḥayy ibn Yaqẓān*. According to Ibn Ṭufayl, Ḥayy's birth can be imputed to a mass of fermented clay blended in a perfect balance of hot and cold, damp and dry.[48] The clay "labored and churned," and in the very middle formed a tiny bubble divided in half by a membrane filled by a gaseous body.[49] It joined the spirit of God in an indissoluble bond, and became Ḥayy.[50] Here, what takes place in the earth mimics what Greek scholars suggest happens in a mother's womb as heat acts upon matter to form life.[51]

The birth of Ḥayy suggests how the inherent qualities of matter determine the type of life that may be self-engendered. If the matter reaches a perfected state, a human life may be formed. If not, some lower being may result, or no life at all. To confirm the environmental impact on the development of life forms, historian Ibn Khaldūn professes that if the world were destroyed, along with all of its species, life as it is would reemerge intact through "a kind of fermentation, with the help of appropriate heat, of a kind of clay that corresponds to the temper of (the being to be created)."[52] In this example, the conditions of the earth circumscribe the kinds of living beings produced, since the type of clay affected by heat matches a particular human temperament.[53]

The prominent role of matter in the formation of life is well attested among animals. After all, putrid soil brings forth dung beetles; the noble phoenix rises from the fiery ash. In similar fashion, medieval Muslim scholars assert the maternal womb plays an analogous role to that of the active, determinant character of soil. Ibn Qutayba, for example, paraphrases the sages as saying the *zanj* (peoples that populate the east coast of Africa) are the most inferior of creatures with the worst constitutions. Why? Because their country is hot, and their mothers' wombs burn them. The same principle applies to people living in cold regions: maternal wombs do not cook them sufficiently. As for the people of Babylon, their absolute perfection is due to a temperate climate.[54]

Given the primary and highly influential role of matter or environment in determining the type of life that will result, theories of spontaneous generation are not to be confused with creation *ex nihilo*.[55] In every instance of insects emerging from flesh, or frogs from rain, phoenixes from ash, or humans from perfected soil, there is a principle of life (divine breath, soul, or *pneuma*) that is set into motion by heat (sun or animal bodies) that acts upon matter, which in turn affects life.[56] Matter in these depictions is far from inanimate or passive as it must engage the principle of life as a willing and active partner in the production of life.

To capture the influential and even determinant qualities of matter, many medieval Muslim scholars personify it as a feminine recipient of masculine heat. Andalusian mystic Ibn ʿArabī, for example, notes how "[e]verything that exercises an effect [*muʾaththir*] is a father, and everything that receives an effect [*muʾaththar fīh*] is a mother."[57] This standard blueprint for life production, which necessitates an active agent (heat, breath, soul, *pneuma*) impressing itself upon an animate recipient (matter), underlies everything from God's creation of the world through his utterance of a single word, "Be!," to human reproduction, to conception via the wind, and, in these examples, to the very mechanics of spontaneous generation. As Ibn ʿArabī suggests in a reflection similar to Ibn Khaldūn's, "[H]eaven [husband] cast something of the command that God revealed to it unto the earth [wife], just as the man casts water into the woman through intercourse. When the casting takes place, the earth brings out all the strata of the engendered things that God concealed within it."[58] Thus, the *telos* of all life forms is already embedded within the material world; once it receives the principle of life for its activation, it articulates what was originally "cast" into it from heaven.

While Ibn ʿArabī asserts the "caster" is naturally associated with the male, and the "receiver" with the female,[59] his overall model does not necessarily privilege the dominance and power of the "father" over and against the passivity and submissiveness of the "mother." For example, he argues that "the locus [mother] must be receptive to giving birth . . . and . . . the seed [generated by the father] must accept the opening up of the form within it."[60] Here, Ibn ʿArabī underscores the agential aspect of receptivity, along with the required subordination of the male-generated seed. As the seed must subordinate itself to the *telos* of the form within it, the mother, too, must open herself to the heat and breath that act upon her. In other words, the unique ability to transform energy into discrete living forms cannot take place without her own desire and efforts to receive and realize the effect. In these examples, the womb does not affect the life process negatively, as medical scholars and other traditional writers are so quick to assert, but rather positively, as life could not come into being without the feminine's consent.

In these examples, "mother" and "father" represent two oppositional forces that must act in conjunction with one another rather than personify fixed gender roles. This paradigmatic deconstruction of socially defined gender roles already takes place in the Qur᾽ān's depiction of Mary's conception of Jesus, where the feminine *rūḥ*—the principle of life—acted upon Mary's masculine *farj,* which accepted the gradual unfolding of the form that had been cast within it. Examples of spontaneous generation, therefore, reveal more subtle, relational dynamics between matter and the principle of life and the more fluid notions of gender that serve to disrupt the paternal, hierarchical depictions of human reproduction where men serve as the primary begetters and guarantors of the future generations of worshipers who resemble themselves.

Such disruptions destabilize normative understandings of who functions as the active "giver" and passive "receiver" of life to allow for the construction of illimitable images of interaction and exchange between masculine and feminine, or dominant and passive principles that more closely reflect the Qur᾽ān's varied and multifaceted models of human creation. Such boundless generative models continuously shift and expand (rather than eliminate)[61] the power dynamic through their fluid concepts of animate, receptive "matter" and active but also submissive "heat."

Such ambiguities in the fixed, gendered roles of creator and created leave room for both men and women to manipulate and recast their own reproductive identities and futures in ways that expose and re-encode socially mandated, ineluctable ends. Such dissident reproductive paradigms present unique occasions for women to act upon or interact with God, men, nature, their own bodies, or forces that cannot explicitly be defined or named, to generate or inhibit life. Along with wind eggs, such occasions of spontaneous generation bypass men's authoritative claims over the female body, which is often depicted as a weak, passive, and often defective vehicle they must temper in order to replicate righteous offspring.

Metamorphosis and the Shifting of One Species to Another

The primacy of the heterosexual dynamic is further defused through rare instances of metamorphosis. As chapter 2 has shown, in the course of human reproduction semen is gathered from the bodies of both the mother and father to generate the material form God eventually ensouls.[62] Therefore, offspring will undoubtedly resemble their biological parents upon birth, at least in terms of their humanity. However, the Qur᾽ān offers exceptions to this rule by showing that even when a particular life form is begotten, God still has the power to transform that life into anything he chooses. Repeated instances of metamorphosis where the divine changes adult human beings into apes, monkeys, or swine, often as punishment, demonstrate God's unrivaled ability to manipulate successive stages of human development at any point he desires to deconstruct man's creative efforts to replicate himself in his own image. Men may exercise rhetorical and practical measures to demonstrate they have the entire reproductive enterprise under control, but God proves otherwise.

The Qur'ān contains a number of references to God's turning men into apes, monkeys, swine, and devil worshipers. Such acts of "metamorphosis"[63] serve as divine punishments for some type of transgression. Metamorphosis in these examples implies God's abrupt replacement of forms rather than his progressive transmutation of one species into another. For example, Sūra 2:65 declares, "And you surely know those of you who violated the Sabbath: We said to them, 'Be dejected apes!' "[64] The use of the command "Be!," as in the case of the Qur'ān's depiction of fetal development,[65] marks another of God's discrete, generative acts. Here, he erases the identities of those who violated the Sabbath entirely and replaces them with new, albeit degenerate, creations. Thus, in Sūra 2:65 there are no more Sabbath breakers to occupy a particular identity or space, only apes. Just as the Qur'ān refutes the continuous development of human life from sperm drop to clot of blood, it also denies a liminal stage—an ambiguous midway point—between human and ape. Through a single word, God can destroy, replace, or create whatever, and however, he wills at any moment. Men may try to avert the outcome, but their authority pales in comparison with God's.

While the Qur'ān treats these particular apes as distinct and separate creations from the humans who once profaned the Sabbath, medieval exegetes are willing to entertain a much more fluid understanding of the transmutation of life forms, and to locate the cause for such alterations in human, rather than divine, agency. This tolerance for the blurring of taxonomic categories between animal and human, or human and God, is illustrated in the traditionalist Muslim ibn al-Ḥajjāj's account of the prophet discussing a group of Banū Isrā'īl that was lost and then transformed (by some unknown agent for some unknown reason) into the shape of rats. Here, the Banū Isrā'īl are not rats per se but strange mutations of human beings that merely appear as rats. One can distinguish between the true rat and the false by placing two bowls of milk—one of goat's, and one of camel's—in front of them. The false rats will drink the goat's milk, but not the camel's, since Jewish law prohibits the consumption of the latter.[66]

Strangely missing from this discussion is the instigator of the transformation. There is no mention whatsoever that God is the one who changed the Banū Isrā'īl into rats, which suggests their own transgressions, or some unnamed third party, somehow prompted the mutation of their forms to make them *appear* as rats. Here, humans, not unlike

God, are able to interrupt the normal course of human development to instigate radical alterations in the divinely created form, either of themselves or others.

The ability of humans to interrupt or intervene in God's created form, either as a result of their own efforts, wrongdoings, or some sort of spell cast by others, is displayed frequently in entertainment works and travelogues to explain why people often become entrapped in the bodies of beasts, or vice versa. The *Arabian Nights*, for example, refers to a *jinnīya* who turns the ungrateful brothers of a *shaykh* into dogs; and a sorceress who turns her jealous husband into a half-stone, half-human figure and groups of Muslims, Magians, Jews and Christians into multicolored fishes.[67] In addition, the Berber explorer Abū ʿAbdallāh Muḥammad Ibn Baṭṭūṭa (d. 1369 CE), in his exhaustive *Rihla*, reports on hearing about *yogis* that assume the shape of tigers through their ascetic discipline.[68] These fantastical tales of metamorphosis involve human, rather than divine, manipulations of the natural order. The popular proliferation of beliefs that humans can undo what God has already done most likely prompted Muslim scholars, such as Ibn Sīnā, to declare that humans (in particular, alchemists) are incapable of transmuting the actual "species of things."[69] Such elite proclamations appear to have little effect on common, popular beliefs that God's created beings are continuously open and vulnerable to human manipulation.

As in the case of monsters, cross-species transformations become a convenient way for scholars to turn the proximate other into a subhuman that publicly bears his transgressions in hairier or furrier form. A number of medieval Muslim authors appropriate this effective polemical strategy not only to isolate themselves from other ethnic, religious groups, but also to brand aberrant transgressors as nonbelievers in their own tradition. Damīrī, for example, suggests both serpents and monkeys are transformed out of the Banū Isrāʾīl.[70] The *Sīra* underscores the Qurʾānic point that the Jews are turned into apes for profaning the Sabbath.[71] It is important to note Muslim scholars did not originate this damning association between Jews and apes. The comparison between the two is rooted in rabbinic literature to condemn those who thwart God's covenant, which suggests that both the Qurʾān and its commentators may be employing for polemical purposes an established Jewish tradition rather than creating something new.

For example, some rabbinic sources assert that while Adam, Seth, and Enosh initially resembled God, ensuing generations came to bear the characteristics of apes as a result of their idolatrous practices.[72] Other rabbis claim that half-man, half-animal mutations, mating with ape-like creatures, were among the offspring of Adam and the decadent generations of Enosh.[73] Additionally, medieval Jewish scholars assert God transformed some of the builders of the tower of Babel into apes as punishment.[74] On the Muslim side, not all scholars associate Jews alone with apes. Ibn Māja declares any of the people of the *fiṭra* who drink wine but call it by another name, or who become entranced by music and singing girls, will be transformed into apes and pigs.[75]

Beliefs in metamorphosis for polemical purposes or otherwise challenge fundamental ideas that offspring must resemble parents, animals are what they appear to be, life must progress in predictable ways from conception to death, and that humans are incapable of interfering with God's created forms. As such, the exegetical acceptance of morphed forms and the potential for humans to generate them opens up liminal moments or nebulous spaces for interpretive possibilities betwixt and between taxonomic certainty. The disruption of the boundaries that set apart two discrete species—human/rat—provides a unique opportunity for humans to manipulate or even determine the physical, moral, or even paradisiacal destiny of what something, or who someone, will be.

For example, Jāḥiẓ mentions men from the *maghrib* who refuse to emigrate from lands tainted with bad soil and unwholesome water out of ignorance. Living in such a bad environment makes their skin darker, their tails longer, and their faces more like monkeys.[76] Presumably, had they all been a little smarter (or the soil a little richer), the *maghribi*s could have fended off such a fate. In similar fashion, Imāmī Shīʿite theologian, philosopher and mystic Ibn Abī Jumhūr al-Aḥsāʾī (ca. 1473 CE) suggests the elephant was a former tyrannical pederast; the bear an effeminate man; the pig a Christian; the monkey one who transgressed the Sabbath; the eel a cuckold; the lizard a thief; the bat a stealer of fruit; the scorpion a stingy man; the worm a backbiter; and the rabbit an impure woman who refused to cleanse herself of menstrual blood.[77] Likewise, were these men and women a little better behaved, they could have averted such mutations of their original, created forms.

Unlike the Qurʾānic examples where God simply replaces one species (human) with another (ape) by calling the latter to "Be!," human behavior in these cases works in conjunction with nature, for better or worse, to invoke bodily transformations. Jāḥiẓ, for example, mentions how humans may only achieve a unique state of grace by enduring the harm caused by the poisonous or vicious animals God creates.[78] Without interacting with such nasty creatures, and instead living a passive, easy life within the goodness of creation, humans—like the exegetical Cain—will never be able transform themselves into paragons of virtue.[79] Contrarily, the examples of Jews caught up in rat-shaped bodies, or *maghribis* twisted into monkey-like creatures by bad water and a dim wit, reveal how transgressions, negative choices, and the surrounding environment can all undo what God has originally intended to "Be!"

The fact that nature and/or human striving or passivity have the power to transform God's creations into something more or less desirable challenges paternal privilege to control fully female bodies and dictate reproductive ends. After all, such bodies may simply resist or even change what men—or even God—intend to be reproduced within them. Therefore, a human's ability to mutate her own form or those of others deconstructs what male scholars assert to be God's normative taxonomic categories that determine the integrity of life and provides unique occasions for both women and men to redirect their reproductive fates toward their own desired ends along minority theological lines.

Human Realizations of God's Creations: Clipping, Licking, and Grafting

As these examples of wind eggs, spontaneous generation, and metamorphosis show, God often reproduces life through less than conventional means. The nonnormative paths God chooses to tread to reproduce offspring disrupt the status quo and undermine the primary role men define for themselves in controlling the generation of life. They also challenge the limits of transcendence men place upon God as mothers (and fathers, too) work to increase established beliefs and practices to engage in more intimate, active exchanges with the divine to engender life. Like matter drawing in and impressing upon seed, women in particular, through their bodily responses to God's life force in conjunction with God's submissive acceptance of the opening up of that life within them, have the ability to affect and circumscribe birth outcomes even more than men. Given the unstable nature of gender and power relations that such disruptive models of creation invoke, men, too, at least in theory, would also be freed from their socially prescribed, dominant roles in the procreative process.

The fact that God demands both human passivity and active desire on the part of men *and* women in his creative efforts constitutes a complex gender and power dynamic that plays off his own transcendence and imminence to defy strictly hierarchical or binary relationships between male and female, divine and human. This complex dynamic that disrupts the status quo is further evinced through those instances where God calls upon both men and women to complete the life form he commenced, either by trimming off excess skin, licking or kneading infants into shape, or grafting one life form onto another. Through these intrusive human practices upon which God depends to form and complete his creations, both mother and father become essential agents in God's realization of perfected beings. His need or desire for human participation in the creation also breaks down normative, hierarchical understandings of transcendence that ultimately restrict his identity and power.

Clipping the Foreskin to Perfect Human Forms

As noted in chapter 4, the practice of circumcision is linked with purity practices and a concept known as *fiṭra*. *Fiṭra* can be defined as the pure nature in which God creates humanity.[80] For example, Muslim ibn al-Ḥajjāj states, "There is none born but is created to his true nature. It is his parents that make him a Jew, Christian, or Magian. Just as beasts produce their young with their limbs perfect; do you see anything deficient in them?" He goes on to quote Sūra 30:33, which states, "The nature (*fiṭra*) made by God in which he has created man, there is no altering of creation. That is the right religion."[81]

Here, children emerge from wombs in a pure state, but are subsequently corrupted by parents. The idea of *fiṭra* as a morally pure condition also extends to an ideal bodily composition. Bodies must come to reflect their moral perfection as originally construed and do so through circumcision, shaving the pubic region, plucking the armpit hair, clipping the nails, and trimming the mustache.[82] The intriguing point in these grooming practices is that humans must manipulate their bodies, often permanently, in order to realize God's original plan to create perfected forms (*fiṭra*).

Outside the context of these *fiṭra*-related practices, however, the medieval Muslim tradition condemns permanent alterations of the body. For example, women are prohibited from donning tattoos, plucking their eyebrows, fastening hair extensions, wearing high heels, or filing teeth for purposes of beautification; in sum, they cannot change what God has created.[83] As an integral part of God's design, everything on the body (except for those *fiṭra*-related items listed above) has a dedicated function or purpose, and therefore should not be modified. Jāḥiẓ, for example, states lips are like doors to the mouth that can be opened and closed at will, and give the mouth a pleasing appearance. He states, "Have you noticed how ugly a person becomes if his lips have been cut off?"[84] Such assertions clearly undermine those examples of metamorphosis noted above where humans take an active role in modifying what God has already caused to "Be!"

Clearly, circumcision, along with various forms of hair and nail removal, are exceptions to the rule, perhaps because they, unlike lips that are needed to form words and recite God's message, may potentially cause a person harm.[85] ʿArīb ibn Saʿd, for example, speaks of the need to prune date trees when too many branches take nourishment away from what the trunk can sustain.[86] Likewise, believers must also clip excess armpit hair or foreskin,[87] which may cause wickedness, aggression, idleness, or defection from the true faith.[88] In these examples, humans work alongside God to ensure his creations are perfected as much as possible by protecting them from harm. Since most human beings will never be born into a completely perfected, circumcised state like the Shīʿite *imāms*[89] or Muḥammad[90] (despite the fact that *fiṭra* ensures that they will), God works through them to realize his ideal as much as possible. His reliance on humans to remove what is harmful to perfect his creative efforts as much as possible pairs both males and females more intimately with himself in bringing forth the life he commands. In addition, human assent to his will makes them more active agents—like the Qurʾānic Mary—in the reproduction of life.

Prodding and Licking Offspring into Recognizable Forms

In addition to trimming away harmful parts from the body, humans must also work alongside God to complete the life forms he commands by physically manipulating the twisted limbs of an infant upon birth. According to medieval physicians, infants bear little resemblance to other human beings, let alone their parents, because they are born into a contorted state. For example, Ibn Khaldūn notes that when infants squeeze out of the narrow, vaginal opening, their "humid," soft bones become bent and curved; their limbs and joints radically change shape to where they no longer look like their parents. Therefore, the midwife must massage and correct the newborn child until every limb has resumed the natural pattern and position destined for it, "and (the child) has again its normal form."[91] Theoretically, without such manipulations by the midwife, the child would never realize its natural, pre-birth perfection. Bearing no similarities to its parents, the uncorrected child would become an outcast, something less than human, acknowledged neither by the father nor society at large.

The interventionist approach adopted by the midwife to ensure parental resemblance is also mimicked among animals (or vice versa), where certain species require the mother to reshape offspring that appear dissimilar to their parents. Abū Ḥayyān, for example, mentions how the mother bear (*dubb*) brings forth her cubs (*daysam*) as shapeless chunks of flesh (*fidrat laḥm*) that necessitate her to mold them into their proper form by licking them.[92] In these examples, as in the case of the *fiṭra,* God relies heavily on the female principle to realize what he has ultimately destined for the child. Through their hands and tongues, mothers and midwives play an essential role in enacting the life God commands. Their efforts in carrying out God's reproductive plans disrupt the paternal chain of command established and invoked by men, where elite scholars and fathers guarantee the reproduction of life. They also break down male-imposed notions of divine transcendence, where God's procreative efforts require no receptive counterpart to actualize his intent.

Pollinating New Life Forms

The idea that the life God has created can be improved upon by both men and women, and, in fact, demands their consensual participation, occurs further in practices of pollination and animal husbandry. For example, the father of Mūsá b. Ṭalḥa b. ʿUbaydallāh and the prophet came upon some people pollinating palm trees. The prophet asked, "What are these people doing?" He was informed that they were taking something from the male part and putting it into the female part. The prophet said, "I do not think that this will do any good." When news of the prophet's proclamation reached the people, they stopped their manual pollinations, and their output declined. The prophet heard about their falling yields, and said, "That was only my thought. If it will do any good, then do it. I am only a human being like you, and what I think may be right or wrong. But when I tell you 'God says,' I will never tell lies about God."[93]

In a similar vein, a woman asked the prophet how to preserve the health of her flocks of goats and sheep. The prophet asked her, "What are their colors"? She informed him they were black. He replied, "Cross them with white ones." After her flock presumably became more robust, the prophet sent out a broadcast message to all shepherds: "He who has black goats and sheep shall mix them with white ones, for the blood of a white female is thriftier than that of two black ones."[94] As in the examples of circumcision and kneading contorted infants into shape, here humans manipulate the reproductive life cycle of the date palm tree and black goats in order to avert harm and do good, with the prophet's approval. Humans thus become essential agents in the realization of God's procreative plans, many of which require tinkering, manipulation, or redirection to conform to what they—both men and women—determine to be the divine "good."[95]

Directing Reproductive Outcomes: Women in Intimate Partnership with God

Disruptions to the heterosexual dynamic, either through demonstrations of God's generative anomalies or his need for human partnership, provide practical occasions for women to intervene in their own life cycles through fertility treatments, birth control, abortifacients, and labor therapies to actualize their vision of the type of life both they and God, in partnership, desire. Justifications for such reproductive practices tap into marginal theologies that highlight a woman's intimate and active exchanges with God, nature, and her own body to beget, modify, or even determine life before or after it comes into being. Such marginal theologies, along with their practical applications, challenge elite scholars' fixed rather than fluid notions of gender and power, and their assertions that God's abstract transcendence prevails over his erotic, creative imminence.

Stimulating Sterile Wombs

As noted in the Qur'ān and its exegesis, women with barren wombs, such as Abraham's wife, Mary's mother Ḥanna, and Zakarīyā's wife, tried to overcome their predicament through piety. Their prayers, or, more often than not, the prayers of their husbands, served to stimulate their sterile wombs, but only by the will of God. The ability to invoke divine response through piety alone, however, appears to be the exception. In the medical and *ḥayawān* literature, examples suggest women often take reproductive matters into their own hands in order to influence, modify, or anticipate God's will. Rather than pray to God and passively await a decision often mediated through men, women adopt active measures of their own to stimulate sterile wombs to invoke the life God commands and they desire. Some of these measures utilize the knowledge of physicians or female wisdom; others draw upon direct manipulations of the natural world and the female body to bring forth particular results. As the examples below will show, through fertility treatments women contribute their own efforts to generate life alongside male piety and authority. Such endeavors disrupt the heterosexual dynamic where men alone govern the female body to direct the course of reproductive events along the pristine lives of the paradisiacal queens.

Generally speaking, drugs employed by women to enhance their fertility are geared toward pregnancy retention, that is, the prevention of miscarriages. For example, ʿArīb ibn Saʿd prescribes the boiling of seedless colocynth (*ḥanẓal*) with oil of lily of the valley (*sausan*) to thwart miscarriage or early delivery.[96] The Persian polymath Abū al-Rayḥān Muḥammad ibn Aḥmad al-Bīrūnī (d. 1050 CE) also notes how colocynth cures uterine inflammation,[97] which can inhibit pregnancy. In support of this remedy, Bīrūnī mentions that when she-pigeons consume colocynth, they begin to lay their eggs.[98] *Zurumbād* is also mentioned as a good cure for miscarriages,[99] and Persian physician Najīb al-Dīn Muḥammad ibn ʿAlī al-Samarqandī (d. 1222 CE) references generic aromatics, perfumes, and gums for the same purpose.[100] Strangely, some of the same ingredients employed to enhance fertility are used in contraceptive or abortifacient recipes. Colocynth, for example, appears frequently in discussions about fertility drugs, birth control, and abortifacients.[101]

In addition to the concoctions listed above, women invoke folk therapies or magic to stimulate a sterile womb. In general, folk remedies and magic designed to activate barren wombs work to redirect forces from the natural world into the female body in order to make it more fruitful. For example, since hares are hypersexual and exceptionally productive, a woman who eats a hare's brain or carries it about her, and then has intercourse, will become pregnant.[102] In medical treatises, the brain is often portrayed as having a primary role in directing the functions of the mind and body.[103] To consume a hare's brain is to consume its vital, active force, which results in a more fertile womb. Rather than the brain, Jewish traditions instruct sterile women to consume the hare's stomach in order to cure barrenness.[104]

Women who have recently miscarried are also advised take a frog from the river, spit in its mouth, and then throw it back in the water. When her husband has intercourse with her, she will become pregnant, with God's permission.[105] Since frogs are thought to be the product of spontaneous generation, their inner vitality to replicate themselves may be the natural force that can be harnessed to stimulate conception.[106] Likewise, it is attested that if a woman roasts and eats the testicles of a cock, it will cure her infertility.[107] Here, the hypersexuality of the cock, as contained in its generative organ, may be the vibrant quality that excites a barren womb. In all of these examples, the transference of natural life forces from a fecund plant or animal into the woman's womb remains operative.[108]

Outside these examples of the hare, frog, or cock, what must be consumed and why is often difficult to discern in many folk recipes that attempt to produce life in a barren womb. Oftentimes a remedy will be mentioned in the context of a conditional statement, but no justification for its use is provided. In other words, no clear connection is established between the various qualities or characteristics of the particular animal, bird, or object cited, and the kind of effect some of its body parts or inherent qualities might produce. Perhaps the associations were rooted in common knowledge derived from a complex web of ancient mythology and popular folk wisdom with regard to fertility.

For example, a woman carrying wolf (*dhi'b*) bile upon her body will most likely become pregnant.[109] Wolves are often associated with maternity in ancient myths that refer to their suckling and raising human infants when those infants have been abandoned by their parents, as in the case of Romulus and Remus,[110] as well as Cyrus the Great.[111]

The heart of a wall gecko, hung around a woman's neck, averts miscarriage.[112] Lizards in general are regarded as symbols of fertility, in particular, in parts of South and West Asia, perhaps because they seemingly renew themselves every time they shed their skins.[113] For those who could afford it, shavings of elephant ivory, drunk over the course of several days, will cause women to conceive, by the order of God.[114] Likewise, a woman can insert a piece of hoof into her vagina after menstruation to increase her chances of becoming pregnant.[115] If the shavings of burnt hoopoe (*hudhud*) claws are scraped into a beverage, and a woman drinks it, she will conceive.[116] The drinking of hawk excrement mixed with water will also help her to become pregnant, even if she is naturally sterile.[117]

Some inanimate objects were believed to contain magical properties, including a special magnetic stone worn to prevent miscarriage or invoke conception.[118] Like their Muslim sisters, medieval Jewish women also sought protection against miscarriage by wearing an *eben tekuma*, a preserving stone.[119] In all of these examples of folk therapies, women become agents of their own reproductive destiny by aligning the life forces of nature with those of their own bodies to partner intimately with God to generate the life they believe both he—and they—desire. Such assertions of female agency conform more closely with Qurʾānic narratives of how Mary guarded her *farj*, consented to divine insemination, and bore her child alone and in pain, more so than exegetical images of a divinely purified and perfected vehicle God acts upon to generate life.

Certainly, it is difficult to discern whether medieval Muslim women pursue such fertile outcomes for themselves, or whether men demanded their wives' participation in these cures to realize their own goals of siring offspring. For example, Ibn Qutayba mentions if you (referring to a single male) want your wife to conceive, make her walk around the courtyard ten times so her womb lowers into a more favorable position for conception to occur.[120] This example implies the husband's command over his wife's reproductive body to ensure it generates what he desires.

However, despite such suggestions that husbands may cajole their wives to heal their barren wombs through folk remedies, it is just as easy to imagine women freely hanging geckos around their necks or spitting in a frog's throat during that period of mourning just following a miscarriage without direct coercion from their husbands. A mother's longing for children to nurture and love, in particular after a devastating loss, may prompt her to pursue any means necessary to become pregnant, in spite of, or in accordance with, her husband's help and encouragement. A fecund body fulfills personal expectations and needs that are likewise affirmed and justified through dominant discursive beliefs and practices.

A woman can only increase her joy, status, and piety by satisfying all the demands of her maternal role.

In striving to secure their own fertility in these cases, women become the givers, as well as the receivers, of life. Rather than God bestowing life upon passive female servants through men who work to guarantee self-serving outcomes, women bypass men to impart life upon God as they manipulate forces in the natural world to realize their common reproductive goals. Such jarring assumptions about God's shared power and potency justify bold interactions between nature and the female body that recall the disruptive occurrences of the wind egg, spontaneous generation, and metamorphosis, as well as God's polyvalent modes of creation in the Qur'ān.

A woman's active participation in her own reproductive life finds theological support in, for example, Jāḥiẓ's belief that poisonous creatures play a vital role in God's perfected plan because they evoke pious human action. As medieval Muslim women confront the tragedy of their own barrenness, they strive to do all they can to make sure their bodies are in optimal form to cultivate a womb as prolific as Khadīja's[121] in order to realize the prophet's claim that "the best of your women are the affectionate child bearers."[122] Anything less than their best efforts to stimulate sterile wombs would verge on impiety.

Enhancing Male Potency to Boost Fertility

The medical and *ḥayawān* literatures devote an inordinate amount of discussion to advising men on how to increase their semen, sexual power, and penile erections. Such anxiety over male potency and performance suggests men not part of the scholarly elite place little faith in their ability to secure the type of life God desires. In order to overcome their physical deficiencies and vulnerabilities so clearly apparent when measured against the scholarly ideal, non-elite men, like women, recognize their own limitations and try to manipulate nature in order to procure the desired results.

As noted in chapter 2, male sexual dysfunction was rarely attributed to an inherent deficiency but rather to an imbalance in overall health. Therefore, men only had to adjust their diets and habits to achieve more semen, increased sexual potency, and robust erections. Changes in a man's diet are aimed primarily at balancing the humors, which are assumed to be out of kilter if a man is unable to acquire an erection or father offspring. The humoral system is based on the correlation between the four elements (water, air, fire, and earth), the two qualities that each of these elements possess (coldness, moisture, heat, and dryness), and the temperaments associated with each one. A healthy human body indicates a maintenance of humors in equilibrium; illness points to an imbalance.[123]

An excess of one quality or another that leads to impotence or deficient sperm production can be offset through the consumption of food items that compensate for what the man lacks. For example, a number of moist foods may heighten seminal production if the man bears an excess of dry heat. Foodstuffs that contain a surfeit of moisture include *bahman* (an herb like a carrot),[124] carrots,[125] chickpeas,[126] moist meat, egg yolks,[127] brains, figs, pine nuts, peppercorns,[128] turnips,[129] milk,[130] and fir tree seeds.[131] Texts mention that the consumption of certain types of animals also increases semen, in particular, the black partridge (*durrāj*),[132] the sparrow,[133] and the lizard.[134] In these cases, it is not clear whether the creatures themselves provide the surplus moisture needed to restore the man's ability to produce a sufficient amount of semen, or whether their fecund natures transfer magically their sexual vitality to the man's genitalia. Female partridges, after all, are described as being so desirous for sex that the mere blowing of the wind from the leeward side of the male can impregnate them,[135] and male partridges are depicted as lustful in their need to have sex with one another.[136]

Contrarily, hot and dry plants, birds, or animals play a critical role in increasing sexual power and potency. The absence of such potency and power can be attributed to an excess of moisture and coldness in the male body. Hot and dry foods that serve to counterbalance such qualities include dates, especially when combined with pine kernels,[137] cress,[138] saffron,[139] ginger,[140] peas, onions, grapes, asparagus,[141] parsley,[142] mastic,[143] a concoction of hemp leaves, honey, poppy seeds and milk,[144] and olives.[145] Certain birds, animals, and fish are also said to intensify sexual performance when men consume or internalize their vital potencies. For example, cranes,[146] the *karwān* (a duck-like creature),[147] sparrows,[148] swallows (when the heart is dried and eaten with wine),[149] doves,[150] partridges,[151] peacocks,[152] and a bat's heart tied to a man[153] all increase sexual power. Eating the flesh of the viper (*afʿā*)[154] is especially helpful, given the strong associations between snakes and sexuality.[155] Likewise, the skink (*saqanaūr*),[156] and chickens well boiled with onion and rapeseed[157] endow men with an added sexual virility to sire offspring successfully.

Different types of fish, including the *ḥarīth,*[158] *dubyan,*[159] and *tarīkh,*[160] are known to stimulate penile potency. Adhering to basic practices of the *fiṭra,* such as shaving the pubic hair, may also excite desire for sexual intercourse.[161] A more direct way to usurp generative power is by consuming the reproductive organs of a creature. A straight shot of ground penis and testicles of the ibex (*ayyil*),[162] the penis of a hyena,[163] or testicles of a porcupine (*duldul*), mixed with honey,[164] are all guaranteed to produce the desired results.

Inadequate erections are often attended to through direct manipulations of the penis with certain potions. For example, sustained erections may be achieved when the blood of the sand grouse (*qaṭāt*)[165] or salamander (*samandar*)[166] is rubbed on the penis; likewise, the penis and testicle of the calf, when smoothed onto a man's generative organ, will cause it to grow stiff and powerful.[167] If the blood of the promiscuous *dīk* (cock) is first passed over the fire with honey, and then applied to the end of the penis, it will increase sexual power and the pleasure of intercourse.[168] The earthworm (*kharaṭīn*) first kneaded with Spanish chamomile,[169] *gum euphorbium,*[170] and olive oil and then smeared on the penis likewise strengthens and elevates the male organ.[171]

These examples demonstrate how husbands whose sexual performances often fail to measure up to normative expectations strive to rectify their less than perfect condition through direct manipulations of nature. Their dependence on nature to provide the life forces they require for self-replication interrupts the hierarchical arrangement of God, men, women, animals, and nature upon which the paternal rendition of the heterosexual dynamic so heavily depends. The disruption in the patriarchal chain of command, the usurpation of the vital forces in nature, and the sharing in what plants and animals possess all reveal a more intimate but less certain partnership with God as humans at once become the givers and receivers of life. By acting upon the environment God has ultimately created, but also allowing that environment to work upon and within them, men, women, and God become simultaneously the submissive agents and active recipients in a more complex, ineffable dynamic of exchange and interchange in the production of life.

Disrupting the Fertile Womb: Controlling Conception

An exhaustive study of medieval Muslim views and practices of birth control has been conducted by Basim Musallam in *Sex and Society in Islam*. No attempt will be made here to replicate that study, but rather to draw from it and other materials to demonstrate how women (and non-elite men) tap into marginal theologies and practices to challenge scholarly constructions of a God who demands perfection and compliance from faulty bodies that inevitably thwart ideal, paternal expectations. By disrupting their own life cycles via suppositories, drugs, foodstuffs, and the magical transference of cogent forces in nature in order to manipulate birth outcomes, medieval women reclaim the Qur'ānic vision that it is ultimately God, and not elite men, who can reproduce life, in whatever form, or through whatever means, he chooses.

A woman's appropriation of her own fertility signals her acknowledgment that God may opt to generate life in conjunction with, or contrary to, human desires. While women (and men) may interrupt normative articulations of heterosexual generation in order to activate or disrupt the life that is/not produced, they do so in humility and intimate partnership with God in that they recognize his ultimate governance over all life. Therefore, birth control practices do not dispute God's unrivaled authority over life but rather the paternal images of a predominately masculine God who must act, traditionally through men, upon a more passive or submissive female body to beget the life he—and they—desire at any cost.

Given the discursive emphasis on the male governance of life, and the traditional privileging of fertility, it is surprising, perhaps, that most discussions about reproductive intervention have more to do with pregnancy prevention than pregnancy enhancement. Why would humans wish to thwart God's desire for them to reproduce life? After all, Ghazālī and other theologians emphasize the fact that the primary purpose of coitus is to produce offspring.[172] There are, however, many theological, familial, and communal justifications for averting conception and pregnancy, despite their overall importance in the medieval tradition. For example, while the Qur'ān celebrates the bearing of life, it also warns that children, who are often paired with wealth, can steer one away from God.[173]

Likewise, given the difficulties of childbirth at the time,[174] it was quite possible a mother would die while giving birth, which would compromise the health and well-being of her husband and her other children. Also, if a mother were nursing one child, that child's livelihood would be jeopardized if she were to become pregnant with another. In sum, the overwhelming number of potions, techniques, and remedies for preventing conception point to a desire to protect the overall health and sustainability of the existing family, as well as the community at large. This emphasis on the welfare of the whole takes on a greater value than any single, individual life, in particular if that life has yet to become enlivened or ensouled. Medieval Muslim men and women, therefore, often intervene in their own life cycles to preserve what life God has provided in a way that does not overburden the community or endanger the personal livelihood of any one individual, like the mother, who already sacrifices herself on a daily basis for the well-being of the family, or an existing child whose life depends upon her mother's milk that would be compromised through an additional pregnancy.

Scholars have long argued for the existence of different forms of contraception, including abortion, since the birth of civilization. Throughout time, no uniform opinion about the desire to control fertility or pregnancy prevails; views range from acceptance to tolerance; limited practice to rejection. The ancient Egyptian *Kahun Medical Papyrus,* for example, calls for suppositories consisting of crocodile dung mixed with fermented dough or honey blended with saltpeter for the prevention of pregnancy. The *Ramesseum Papyrus* also advises the use of crocodile dung as a suppository, and includes a description of a pessary made from acacia berries and colocynth mixed with honey.[175] Here, it may be that the efficacies of the Egyptian crocodile god Sobek[176] are what invoke the desired results. Or, since crocodiles are also regarded as symbols of fertility and strength,[177] their dung would serve to counter their fecund effect.

Ancient Greeks also discuss the use of contraceptives and abortifacients. In the *Theaetetus,* Plato has Socrates saying that midwives can cause abortions at an early stage if they believe them to be desirable.[178] Hippocrates notes that women (in particular, prostitutes) should jump up and down to expel the seed in order to keep themselves from becoming pregnant.[179] Aristotle suggests that abortion may be induced before sense and life have begun in the embryo, that is, before "quickening" occurs.[180]

Church fathers ban both contraception and abortion, although obviously they must have possessed much knowledge of local practices and medical wisdom inherited from the Greeks in order to condemn them.[181] John Chrysostom (d. 407 CE) likened contraceptive practices to sowing a field in order to destroy the fruit;[182] Gregory of Nyssa (d. 394 CE) held the unformed embryo is a human being that should never be destroyed.[183] Medieval Jewish rabbis argue it may be the nature of man to subdue, but it is not the nature of woman to subdue. Therefore, they excuse women from this command, and permit them to use freely potions to make themselves sterile (*samā d-ʿaqartā*).[184] Men, of course, were forbidden from using all types of contraceptives, even withdrawal.[185]

In general, Muslim scholars permit the use of contraception and abortifacients, but limit their employment. Their permission rests partly on the theological principle that semen is nothing definite; therefore, a woman faces no consequences if she blocks or gets rid of seminal fluid before it settles in the womb and mixes with her sperm to generate life.[186] This majority view is countered by minority positions, including Ibn Sīnā's argument based on Aristotle that semen is the bearer of the human soul.[187] Despite the fact that the majority of medieval scholars believe semen has no vitality in and of itself, they still place a number of restrictions on the deployment of different types of birth control. For example, women could not gain access to contraception or abortion independent of men.[188] On the flip side, a free woman could refuse to engage in contraceptive practices just to satisfy her husband's request; her own consent was required.[189] Since different forms of contraceptives, especially those applied directly to the penis, were often crude and invasive (see below), they could potentially compromise a woman's sexual pleasure or her desire for children. Given that she has a right to erotic enjoyment and procreation, she could refuse to use or engage in anything that might inhibit the fulfillment of her rights.[190]

Some Muslim physicians, such as Ibn Sīnā, do not advocate the unrestricted use of birth control practices but rather prescribe contraceptives and abortifacients in limited cases where the health of the mother is at risk. These include a fear of childbirth on the part of a young woman, and a desire to protect the well-being of a woman who has a defect in her womb or a weakness in her bladder.[191] In the latter case, it was believed the weight of the fetus, especially in the pregnancy of an early adolescent, may produce a rupture in the bladder (fistula), which causes the woman to suffer incontinence for the rest of her life, constant infections, ostracism, and/or death.[192]

Other physicians, such as Abū Ḥasan al-Ṭabīb (d. 1101 CE), add that abortive drugs may, in fact, be recommended for women who become pregnant before the age of fifteen, most likely because her pelvis would be too small to deliver the child or because of her risks in developing a fistula, or for women who are weak and sickly.[193] Majūsī declares that even in these extreme cases, such remedies should only be prescribed to women who could be "trusted," which indicates a certain fear with regard to female procreative power.[194] Other than preserving a mother's health, contraception could also be employed to protect the life of a nursing child, and to avoid the enslavement of children.[195] In all of these cases, a mother's health and her family's well-being become the major criteria used to judge the permissibility of contraception. The family's survival (and the mother's pivotal role in guaranteeing it) thus takes on a greater value than any potential individual soul that may undermine or threaten what already exists.

In order to preserve further the integrity of the family, Ghazālī permits women to engage in contraceptive measures to preserve their beauty, or to assuage their concerns for having too many children to support.[196] The idea that pregnancy distorts beauty is also prevalent in rabbinic sources, which report that among the generation of the flood, each man took two wives, one to bear children, and the other for sexual gratification. The former was neglected like a widow her whole life, and the latter was given a potion made from roots to make her sterile. She then sat before her husband made up like a harlot.[197]

Ghazālī, however, did not approve of contraception if employed by men or women out of a fear for female children, labor pains, nursing, childbirth, or the uncleanliness childbirth entails.[198] For some scholars, birth control is also shown to have value in the context of prostitution. Jāḥiẓ, for example, records how prostitutes in India use a suppository of elephant dung mixed with honey so as not to lose their customers.[199] Clearly medieval Muslim discussions on birth control, as in any religious tradition, reveal a wide variety of concerns and debates about when life begins, and the value of fetal versus maternal/familial life.

The Theology of Coitus Interruptus

Much of the theological debate over birth control, however, takes place in juridical, rather than medical, contexts of discussions about *coitus interruptus* (*al-ʿazl*), or withdrawal.[200] While the practice has its detractors who argue it interferes with divine fate,[201] most medieval scholars are in agreement over its basic permissibility. Ibn Māja, for example, states withdrawal is permitted, "for there is no soul God has decreed to come into existence, except for what he creates."[202] This statement challenges human assertions of divine fate through an appeal to God's omnipotence. To think that God himself is limited to the confines of his own fate is to restrict his very nature. If he can create via the wind, spirit, ash, or mucky soil, he can certainly override penile slippage to generate life, or, contrarily, to allow his will to coincide with human intention and action to prevent life from occurring. A God who only has to utter "Be!" and it is will never be threatened by human efforts to thwart his plans. After all, God creates in wombs as he pleases.

The *Mishkāt al-maṣābīḥ* concurs with this theological premise, but adds that a child does not necessarily have to come from an ejaculation of all the (seminal) liquid.[203] The *Mishkāt,* therefore, leaves room for a medical or natural justification as to why withdrawal may only be partially effective. God may have decreed a life to be, but only because a bit of semen escaped into the woman's womb. Ghazālī, in fact, cites a *ḥadīth* recorded by Muslim where a man practices *coitus interruptus* with a female slave, but she conceives anyway despite all of his best efforts to prevent her from doing so.[204]

Such claims by the *Mishkāt* and Muslim, of course, subject God's infinite power to the mechanical, physical act of sexual intercourse. In fact, his power to generate life is shown to depend upon human willingness to engage in sex. If God's magnificence is ultimately unquantifiable, illimitable, or ineffable, then he may not only allow for but actually demand human partnership or assistance in the procreative process (just as much as he may bypass and transcend it, as in the case of Mary, wind eggs, or spontaneous generation). Ḥanbalī scholar Taqī al-Dīn Abū al-ʿAbbās Aḥmad al-Ḥalīm ibn Taymīya (d. 1327 CE) intimates as much when he claims only a fool abstains from intercourse with the hope that if God wills him a child somehow he will be given one.[205] Therefore, through sexual intercourse, God invites both men and women to engage in his procreative plans and, in fact, depends on their acquiescence to his invitation to facilitate them.

Suppositories, Spermicides, and Barriers

Medieval arguments about contraceptive devices and methods outside of *coitus interruptus* are also governed by the same theological premise that God's creative power is illimitable, and therefore invites, but does not necessarily require, human partnership. Humans may thus act with God to prevent conception and pregnancy for many of the familial or communal reasons outlined above: the protection of the mother's health, the preservation of a dependent child, the avoidance of economic hardship, and the maintenance of the wife's beauty, which leads to a happier married life and a faithful husband.[206] A woman's consent, and her husband's knowledge, of course, are necessary for engagement in any contraceptive practice. As in the case of *coitus interruptus*, whether they opt for suppositories, drugs, barriers, or the tapping into cogent natural forces, both women and men manipulate nature and their own bodies to provoke a divine response that addresses their own needs and desires that conform to their understanding of the divine will.

Often, however, it appears that elite male scholars and women disagree over what that divine will might entail, to wit, to what extent maternal or familial health (over which the mother surveys) should be valued over potential life (over which the father strives to guarantee in his own image). After all, why should men such as Ibn Sīnā and Ghazālī decide when and if a woman is physically and mentally capable of risking her life and health to bear a child? To override scholarly scrutiny over the suitability of their bodies to bear children, along with their husbands' permission, medieval women take advantage of contraceptive practices to preserve the integrity of the family, bodily health, and the economic well-being of dependent children.

Many of the vaginal suppositories scholars prescribe to be utilized under limited conditions could be concocted easily by women and inserted into their vaginas without knowledge or permission from scholars or husbands. Since a number of these suppositories are to be introduced into the vagina after—rather than before—coitus, the husband would most likely be unaware of his wife's efforts to block his semen from entering her womb. For example, Ibn Jazzār recommends pepper as a suppository to be placed in the vagina after intercourse, a regular—but rather coarse—household item to which women would have had easy access.[207]

Rāzī includes other types of foodstuffs on his list of ingredients best suited for blocking, killing, or countering postcoital sperm, whether male or female: birthwort *(aristolochia)*, spurge (*euphoria*), cyclamen, cardamom, aloe, juice of onion, juice of squirting cucumber; colocynth, iris with honey, cinnamon with myrrh, tar, and juice of pennyroyal leaves.[208] The Syriac physician Abū Zakarīyā Yūḥannā ibn Māsawayh (d. 857 CE), who attended four caliphs, also describes a number of postcoital suppositories made from cabbage seeds, elephant dung,[209] saltwort, black cumin, and myrrh, watercress with tar, and colocynth pulp.[210] Such household ingredients applied after an act of sexual intercourse would surely conceal the mother's desires to preserve bodily health and familial life. However, such instructions might have also been given to the caliphs or their concubines in order to prevent the conception of slaves.

Of course some texts instruct a woman to use certain suppositories before *and* after, during, or just before coitus. Obviously, many of these suppository mixtures would require her husband's assistance, consent, or at the very least his knowledge of her intentions to avoid pregnancy. For example, Majūsī discusses inserting rock salt (a less than stealth ingredient) into the vagina during coitus, or the seed of cabbage and juice of rue during or just after coitus.[211] Ibn Sīnā describes suppositories of tar, applied before and after coitus, pulp of pomegranates with alum before and after coitus,[212] and the flowers and seed of cabbage after menses or before and after coitus. Ibn Jazzār recommends mint as a suppository before sex,[213] and Rāzī prescribes dill[214] in the mouth of uterus, before or during coitus.[215]

It is difficult to believe any of these ingredients would have gone unnoticed by the husband during sex, and therefore their use would indicate mutual consent to control fertility, protect the mother's life, and sustain dependent children. As noted in Ghazālī's advocacy of birth control to promote a vibrant marriage and/or to sustain household economic stability, the overall health of the family as a whole—which leads to communal stability and well-being—becomes the dominant theological value embraced by both husband and wife over and against the life of any single individual. In these examples, husbands and wives in partnership labor along with God by intervening in the natural course of events to realize an outcome that is beneficial to the familial—or even communal—whole. After all, if God depends on humans engaging in sexual intercourse to reproduce life, why would he not count on them to take matters into their own hands to inhibit that life when it proves detrimental to other human beings he has created?

There is also much evidence to suggest that men, too, sought control over their own fertility, with or without the consent of women. Musallam, for example, notes that the erotica literature in particular places a heavy emphasis on male contraception, especially the practice of smearing tar on the penis before intercourse.[216] Majūsī also refers to the practice of men anointing their penises with salt or tar to prevent pregnancy, as does Ibn Jazzār, who adds balm oil and white lead to the list of barrier methods for the man.[217] Other types of ingredients smeared on the penis seem to function more as spermicides rather than barriers. Rāzī notes how onion juice, when daubed on the penis, helps prevent pregnancy.[218] Other physicians suggest colocynth or mint juice act as spermicides to inhibit conception.[219]

Of course, couples can also try to avoid simultaneous orgasms (during which the force of sperm released by both men and women optimizes their chances of conceiving), and women can jump backward, sneeze, or fumigate themselves with elephant dung.[220] Here, it is clear that pleasure without fear of reproduction factors into a man's decision to employ contraception. However, it is most likely that men, too, wish to avoid putting the health of their wives, the mothers of their children, and the integrity of their families at risk by taking action not to incite new life, whether legitimate or not.

The Transposing of Natural Forces

In the context of folk remedies, both men and women engage elite scholarly judgments about when the integrity of family life is in legitimate danger in order to make such intimate, personal decisions for themselves. Outside medical, academic circles, nature becomes a vital, responsive, and easily accessible resource from which women or men could draw certain powers to inhibit conception. It is believed a particular animal characteristic or quality could be transferred directly from nature to the human body to affect the desired result. For example, the mule, a crossbreed between the horse and the donkey, is known for its sterility. Therefore, a woman who wishes never to conceive could consume or manipulate certain parts of its body or what its body exudes in order to achieve her goal. If she employs its ear wax or sweat as a pessary, ties its skin on her,[221] consumes its dung with honey and ginger, drinks its urine,[222] or devours its heart,[223] she will remain barren.

In other examples, if a woman carries sheep's wool about her she will avoid pregnancy.[224] Sheep, after all, bear only one offspring per year, so it may be this lengthy gestational cycle that is transferred to the woman. Lengthy gestational periods also may explain why elephant urine, when drunk, or elephant dung, when hung on her person, prevent a woman from conceiving.[225] While consuming the hare's brain, the central source of its vitality, may incite fertility, ingesting what ultimately leads to its death or what its body expunges induces sterility. For example, if a woman drinks hare blood she will never conceive; if hare dung is hung on her body, she will remain sterile for as long as it remains there.[226] Women who drink the rennet of a hare after having completed their menstrual cycles are also spared from ever becoming pregnant.[227] In these examples, the fundamental barriers between humans and animals become permeable to the point where they allow for a transference of magical powers across species to enhance or thwart fertility. The breakdown in taxonomies further disrupts the tradition's maintenance of the strict hierarchical relationships between humans and animals, men and women, or men and God that necessarily govern human reproduction.

It is often difficult to discern why particular life forces extracted from certain animals work to suppress conception in many examples. For instance, if a woman uses hawk excrement as a pessary she will never conceive and if she is pregnant she will abort.[228] Since hawks are birds of prey, it may be that their life-stifling qualities are thought to curb reproduction; they are also known to be cruel to their young.[229] Perhaps their nonmaternal characteristics serve to counter what is thought to be innately female. The hawk was also considered a deity by ancient Egyptians; the efficacious powers of this bird/god, who had strong ties to the sun, may have been garnered to achieve the appropriate reproductive results.[230]

However, the connections between other animals and their abilities to suppress life are less than transparent. For example, the flesh of swallows protects a woman from becoming pregnant for entire year.[231] Women can spit into the mouth of a water-frog three times (*al-ḍifdiʿ*), return it to the water, and become sterile.[232] Lynx urine, when drunk, also promotes barrenness.[233] Women who carry around a weasel's ankle bone will not become pregnant.[234] A rat's testicle hung on a woman's body will keep her from becoming pregnant as long as she wears it.[235] Tiger bile also works as a contraceptive, and if a woman is already pregnant it will cause her to miscarry.[236] Wolf blood, too, when consumed, will cause barrenness.[237] The smoke from a wild cat's (*daywan*) brain effectively expels sperm from the womb.[238] Some animals possess the power to disrupt menstruation, which impedes conception. The spleen of a black cat (*sinnaur*), tied around a woman, will check menstrual flow; until it is taken off the menses will not reappear.[239] Goat dung serves in this same capacity.[240] The fact that the goat's flesh is perceived to be warm and dry may explain why it is suitable to counter an excess amount of cool, moist menses.[241] Many of these animals have served as past and distant gods; primarily in ancient Egypt,[242] but also in India.[243] Perhaps it was believed their once worshipped efficacy could be captured and directed toward the desired goal.

Miscellaneous contraceptive practices, for which little justification is provided, include a woman painting her body with the afterbirth of her first child,[244] having sex during the days when the sap flows into the wood,[245] tying the leaves of a plant resembling hyacinth to her body,[246] and donning something referred to as "the bead of barrenness."[247] Even removing a woman's desire for sex may serve as a form of contraception. If a woman carries goat liver about her, she will cease to desire a man.[248]

Whatever their origins, all of these "natural" birth control practices reveal the inner hopes and outward efforts of men and women to ward off conception, which marks the need to preserve familial health and maternal well-being. By causing life not to be, humans—particularly women—work alongside God to complete or perfect the healthy familial, maternal, or communal life he commences. Their interference in both the body and creation represents a wholesome responsibility to address the needs of the body and to ward off harm.[249] Such interference is not innovative, but rather rooted in the Qur'ān and marginal theologies where women and God act in intimate exchange and interchange to shape their reproductive fates.

Birth Control That is Done unto Others

It is worth mentioning that some of these folk remedies may have been used for magical purposes to manipulate the life cycles of others. Here, a desire to do good and to ward off harm may still be operative, but the criteria used to weight the outcome would, of course, be relative, and therefore subject to abuse. For example, women and/or men attempt to "cure" certain women of their general lack of desire for men. Through their very gestures, a structural relationship is created between a particular creature and the resolution of a particular problem. In this case, a lack of desire or sexual willingness on the part of a potential childbearer becomes the obstacle that must be removed. By casting a spell, one thus seeks to redirect this structural relationship to resolve ambiguous situations in the real world that are the source for much anxiety.[250]

Medieval Muslim texts suggest this "problem" of a lack of sexual desire (that may, in fact, be linked with sexual orientation) could be rectified if the couple is given a hoopoe heart cooked with sugar to eat. After they consume it, they will demonstrate an unrestrained affection for one another.[251] In a similar vein, if earthworms are tied up in a frigid woman's hair without her knowledge, she will long for sexual intercourse.[252] If the water frog is split into two halves from its head to its end and a woman looks at the two pieces, she will be overcome by sexual desire and her inclination for men will greatly increase.[253] Men can also incite a woman's sexual passions by making themselves overwhelmingly attractive. For example, women simply cannot resist the man who consumes roasted wolf testicles.[254] Likewise, women will lust after the man who carries around the penis and testicles of a hyena. Conversely, when the hyena's private parts are tied onto a woman, men will desire her.[255] Hyenas, of course, are well-known for their hypersexuality. In all of these examples, men seek to transform women's emotions to resemble those of animals in heat, who succumb to an unbridled, desperate passion.[256]

Men and women would have used magical recipes and techniques to cast reproductive harm onto others as well. For example, when the hyena's penis is dried, pounded, and put into a woman's food without her knowledge, she will no longer crave the company of men.[257] Its gallbladder will have the same effect by causing her to despise sexual intercourse.[258] When swallow blood is placed in a woman's food, her sexual desire disappears. If a man comes in to her she is greatly distressed.[259] In addition, if a pregnant woman is made to gaze upon a particular striped snake that slithers in front of her, she will miscarry.[260]

Men's sexual potency is also the target of magical manipulation. Male sexual power is greatly diminished when a lizard (*ḍabb*) runs between a man's feet. He will lose his ability to generate an erection for that entire day.[261] The skin of a dragon, tied on a lover, will cool his passions.[262] If a man consumes frog flesh, his semen will be ruined forever.[263] Bīrūnī even suggests that a man's eating of frogs will cause his semen to spill out of him until it is drained entirely from his body.[264] The leaves of the *banjangusht* plant desiccate seminal fluid and prevent men from having erections.[265] Suyūṭī refers to the fact that the consumption of spleen meat or water lily (both cold and wet substances) removes all desire for sexual intercourse.[266] Magic may even be extended into the womb to affect the offspring produced. *Shawkrān,* a plant similar to aniseed, diminishes male sperm, stops the flow of breast milk, and shrinks the testes of children.[267] Damīrī notes if a pregnant woman is given a little of the brain of a mule to drink, her child will become mad (*majnūn*).[268]

It is unclear in these malicious examples as who may be manipulating whom, and for what purposes. Perhaps a man's mother tries to help her son by making his wife more desirous of sex. It could be a jealous wife seeks revenge on her husband and his mistress by stifling their fertility and sexual desire. A woman's perceived promiscuity may also be the target of some of these seemingly malevolent recipes. After all, a woman who has no interest in sex is in no danger of committing adultery.

In general, the medieval Muslim tradition prohibits such magical spells, and renders those who employ them despicable.[269] Bukhārī, however, states magic can be used to counter magic if it is directed toward a good purpose: what serves to benefit human beings is not forbidden.[270] This theological principle justifies the human ethical initiative to redirect nature toward desired, "good," and pragmatic ends, even if those ends may seem harmful to certain individuals. Of course, God can always override these human goals as he sees fit, but to not strive to achieve what is good is to wallow in a less than perfected state of passivity and complacency that is condemned by scholars like Jāḥiẓ and Ibn Taymīya.

Abortifacients

Recipes for abortifacients also populate the medical and *ḥayawān* literature. In general, the Qur'ān and Muslim tradition condemn any form of infanticide,[271] and among the law schools abortion is only permitted before a fetus has been ensouled, which may occur at forty or up to 120 days.[272] Before ensoulment takes place, however, legal scholars treat abortifacients in the same way as they do contraceptives; since no life yet exists, it is permissible to cause an abortion before human existence commences. However, medical scholars warn against these substances' inherent danger in that pregnant women may "inadvertently" cause an abortion at some later stage of fetal development if they consume such drugs without knowledge of their potential effects. Ibn Jazzār, for example, gives a list of drugs that taint the sperm in the uterus, or kill the fetus and expel it from the womb. He decides to provide such a list so women "would be aware of using them, since they corrupt fetuses."[273]

It appears medieval women willingly employ such prohibitive knowledge to terminate early pregnancies (fewer than forty or 120 days) for the same reasons they would have used postcoital suppositories. In fact, it is often difficult to separate what is technically "contraceptive" from what is "abortive," since most pessaries were inserted into the vagina *after* the act of sexual intercourse. No clear instructions are provided as to how long after coitus such contraceptives might still be effective in curtailing pregnancies. In addition to serving as forms of birth control, evidence indicates abortifacients were frequently used to facilitate the expulsion of fetuses, alive or dead, from a woman's womb immediately before, during, or after a difficult labor. In these instances, an ensconced or deceased fetus would endanger the mother's life.

In general, however, the texts simply reveal too little information to reconstruct the precise circumstances or conditions under which women would have chosen to employ abortifacients to terminate an advanced pregnancy or expel a fetus, dead or alive. It may be fair to say, however, that as in the case of contraceptives, women would have relied on abortifacients for pragmatic purposes: to preserve their own life, health, dependent children, or the integrity of their families. The mother, after all, is key to the survival of the family and its future generations.

Abortifacients were delivered into the female body through fumigants, pessaries, or the manipulation of natural forces. Textual materials provide few hints as to who would have conducted the procedure; the midwife, physician, female family members, or perhaps the pregnant woman herself are all likely candidates. As in the case of contraceptives, the techniques involved were not that difficult to employ, the materials not all that rare, expensive, or unusual to secure. For example, physicians note that fetuses could be expelled when the uterus was fumigated with red peach (*khūkh*),[274] cardamom,[275] or a type of grass (*shaylam*) mixed with barley broth, myrrh, saffron, and storax.[276] Tar suppositories could also be inserted into wombs of pregnant women to instigate abortions,[277] and a kind of tampon soaked in mineral water (*shabb*) acts as both a contraceptive and abortifacient.[278] The juice of squirting cucumber, which is also known to prevent conception, likewise corrupts fetuses in the womb.[279] Some scholars suggest that if a pregnant woman is struck thrice with the root of *ambarbārīs*, a branched tree with thorns in three layers, abortion results. Poultices made from this same tree may also cause an abortion.[280]

Again, it is impossible to retrace precisely the concerns, fears, and pain that would have weighed heavily on the maternal, medical, or familial decisions to terminate a pregnancy, whether viable or not. Despite elite scholarly guidance, warnings, and restrictions, the wide variety of available abortifacient methods and materials suggests women believed themselves to be in the best position to negotiate the perils and dangers of pregnancies to their own bodies and families.

In addition to drugs and tampons, women also had the option to tap into various forces of nature to terminate a pregnancy. However, most of these examples seem to involve expelling the fetus when it has either died in the womb, or when natural labor fails to eject it in a timely fashion. Either way, a woman's life would be in immediate danger if the pregnancy were to continue. Drinking the weight of a dirham of hare blood quickly forces the fetus to fall in the womb, which facilitates delivery.[281] In this example, what ultimately causes the death of the prolific and fertile hare (the release of its blood) can be channeled into an easing out of fetal life. Waste material functions in a similar way. If a pregnant woman carries pigeon dung about her she will immediately give birth.[282] Fumigations with cow dung also invoke parturition and expel the fetus dead or alive, along with the afterbirth.[283]

Here, abortifacients, when used at the appropriate time or under the right conditions, operate in a way similar to the modern-day oxytocin.[284] They serve to resolve difficult deliveries and remove any dead material that could become gangrenous and kill the mother.[285] In rare cases, they may also expel a live fetus before it is viable for reasons medical texts do not fully elaborate. It is possible to speculate, however, that if a mother perishes, her dependent children would become a heavy social burden for others to bear, which compromises the well-being of the community. The above examples of fertility treatments, contraceptives, and abortifacients all reveal how women manage directly their own reproductive successes or failures under the auspices of broader theological truths. Such truths determine when life begins, declare only God can cause a life to be or not to be despite human intentions, deem women as essential partners in the production of life, and weight a mother's life more heavily than the potential one she carries inside her womb.

Easing Labor

While Mary may have willingly suffered the excruciating pains of childbirth alone, without any help or intervention on the part of women or men, most women take it upon themselves to bypass such intense agony to ease their labor or that of others. Male elites may praise the virtues of a mother like Mary who is willing to sacrifice all for her child, but most women accept her exceptionality and realize they can never fully emulate the mother of Jesus, whose praises are sung throughout the Qur'ān and its exegesis. As mothers are called upon to reproduce non-prophetic life, medieval Muslim women, and the men who love them, seek to ease their labor pains as much as possible through any means necessary. God, after all, does not call upon humanity to witness passively the deterioration, corruption, or stagnation of their own fate or existence, as suggested by Ibn Taymīya, Jāḥiẓ, and the Qur'ān itself.[286] Their rightful response to the often dire circumstances of creation is, in and of itself, a pious act.

Prior to Islam, traditional folk wisdom claims if a woman gives birth to a child without resentment or greed, she will experience no labor pains.[287] Likewise, as noted in chapter 3, exegetes such as Ṭabarī view labor pain as a necessary burden all women must endure because of the iniquities of Eve.[288] Therefore, good mothers, like Fāṭima or Mary, would be exempt from the agonies of labor. Muslim physicians also recognize the often intolerable nature of giving birth, and suggest such suffering is something every mother must endure regardless of her righteous intentions. To ease the burdens of pregnancy and parturition as much as possible, these physicians cite a number of recipes designed to ward off cravings, stymie vomiting or gas, and provide relief for labor pains.

In an imperfect world where real women fall short of the ideal, accommodations may be made to secure a mother's comfort.

ʿArīb ibn Saʿd, for example, states that if a pregnant woman craves clay, she should consume clay of *nashāstaj* mixed with lettuce, endive, and radish. Salty fish will counter cravings, also.[289] In order to strengthen the womb during the course of pregnancy, ʿArīb ibn Saʿd also recommends cardamom seed (*qāqulla*), saltwort, cinnamon bark (*qirfa*), mastic bark, and tender date branch sugar, soaked in quince water (*safarjal*).[290] He prescribes pomegranate, honey, and peppermint bark (*naʿnaʿ*) for bouts of indigestion, heartburn, or heart palpitations. Gas, cramps, and vomiting may be resolved through sipping *sakanjabīn* (oxymel), a drink that contains sugar, water, vinegar, and honey, or quince (*safarjal*) and cassia bark (*dār ṣīnī*).[291] Suyūṭī calls for a more generic remedy to cure all gestational unpleasantries by suggesting if a woman inserts the blossom of the date palm into her vagina before intercourse, her entire pregnancy will go more easily.[292]

Both the medical and *ḥayawān* literature contain a plethora of information on how to ease labor pains and facilitate a quick delivery. This information would most likely be utilized by the midwife or the attending women, since rarely were men allowed to witness childbirth. The Fāṭimid physician Aḥmad ibn Muḥammad al-Baladī (d. 990 CE), for example, advises one to wrap an onyx in the hair of the woman in labor, and she will produce the child immediately. A snakeskin wound around the hips of the pregnant woman accelerates birth, as will the root fibers of coriander hung over her thigh.[293] Bīrūnī, citing Galen, states one or two dirhams of saffron (*zaʿfarān*) promote parturition, but three dirhams will kill both the pregnant woman and the child in her womb.[294] ʿArīb ibn Saʿd recommends tying garlic, coriander, and colocynth (*ḥanẓal*), a contraceptive and abortifacient, to the thighs of the woman in labor to ease delivery.[295] In each of these examples, midwives recognize most women's burdens will not progress as smoothly as Mary's or Fāṭima's, and therefore work alongside God to bring forth the life he desires as painlessly as possible.

As in the case of contraception and abortifacients, folk remedies take up much of the discussion about easing labor pains. Again, women tap into natural forces in order to facilitate God's procreative plans, and to help the mother as much as possible in ways that challenge the ideal model of the suffering servant. Qazwīnī, for example, recommends a peacock claw be tied on a woman to ward off the trauma of parturition.[296] Pig dung wrapped in wool serves a similar function,[297] as does goose brain[298] boiled in fennel, cattle bone,[299] and earthworms (*shaḥmat al-arḍ*) dried and given to a suffering woman to drink.[300] Damīrī instructs women to take burnt human hair mixed with rosewater and place it by the pregnant woman's head to ease labor pains during delivery.[301] He also cites Hermes, who says the earwax of a mule dropped into a silver goblet and hung from a pregnant woman will prevent premature contractions,[302] which could cause miscarriage.

A parturient woman may also invoke Qur'ānic verses and various supplications to allay severe labor pains. Sūras 62, 63, and 64, which praise the glories of God, can be written out and given to the woman in labor to drink. Here, the direct ingestion of God's word permeates the female body and reveals itself as "medicine" to ease the agony of childbirth.[303] By affirming God's greatness, a mother can surrender her own pain to God through her recognition of her insignificance in comparison to him.

The following supplications may also be written down to relieve the difficulties of labor: "O creator of life from life, O extractor of life from life, deliver it." According to Damīrī, these words were spoken by Jesus when he passed by a cow whose fetus was presenting itself crosswise, making delivery difficult.[304] Certainly, women agonizing through breach births or something similarly atrocious might receive comparable relief through the prophet Jesus's words. In all of these examples, women work with one another and with God to bring forth the offspring both he, and they, desire, in ways that seek to alleviate the inevitable burden of his female servants as much as possible. Their efforts to both endure pain and relieve it turn everyday mothers and the women who attend them into alternative models of piety, concern, and self-sacrifice who coexist alongside the exegetical paragons of the ideal mother who delivers perfected offspring easily and without pain. These everyday mothers can come to resemble more closely the Qur'ānic Mary, upon whose agency and suffering God must depend to generate his procreative plans.

Directing the Course of Nature: Manipulations of Temperament, Appearance, and Sex

The ability of women to intervene in their own life cycles extends to their limited attempts at fashioning the temperament, appearance, and sex of the child. As noted in chapter 2, men—and not women—assume divine authority to fashion their children according to certain privileged criteria. Many recipes, techniques, and instructions, for example, direct men to intervene in a woman's reproductive cycle to produce healthy, male, and/or pious children.[305] Evidence suggests women often took these matters into their own hands to shape the child as they see fit.

Ibn Qutayba, for example, notes that women can make their children resemble the more noble of the two grandfathers,[306] though he never explains how they were able to accomplish such a feat. ʿArīb ibn Saʿd proposes that good-looking children may be generated if women take the ashes from a donkey or horse hoof, add a coating, then make a *ṣūfa* and place it in the mouth of her womb.[307] Bīrūnī, quoting Pedanius Dioscorides (d. 90 CE), states that if a woman happens to eat the smaller version of *khusa al-kalb* (an aphrodisiac herb), the child in her womb will become female. If the plant is eaten again, the child will return to being a male.[308] Damīrī projects a woman who drinks the rennet of a male hare will beget male children; contrarily, female rennet produces female children.[309] If a pregnant woman carries around the dung of a bird of good omen (*rakhamat*), such as that of a vulture, she will know whether she is carrying a boy or a girl,[310] and, in theory, could change the sex if she so desires. All of these examples, which allow for the metamorphosis of the fetus in the womb, illustrate a woman's ability to participate actively in or alter divine procreative processes.

Conclusion: The Cure of Perfection

Evidence of God's creation of life through wind eggs, spontaneous generation, and metamorphosis, and his dependence on human beings to complete the life he commences, serves to disrupt the paternally structured modes of heterosexual reproduction upon which medical, exegetical, theological, and proscriptive discourses so deeply depend. As such, they call into question "natural" suppositions about maternal passivity, the father's status as second to God's in the begetting of life, and male beliefs that God's creative impulses must always conform to patriarchal, heterosexual patterns. Within these liminal moments that reveal unusual creations and startling demonstrations of a God who often depends on human action to carry out his procreative plans, women encode their own maternal bodies according to a more complex, erotic dynamic where the lines between giver and receiver, male and female, imminent and transcendent, and creator and created remain necessarily indeterminate.

Nontraditional theories of procreation and God's reliance on humans to actualize the life he generates are expressed practically through feminine exercises in fertility treatments, contraception, abortive techniques, and various other manipulations of pregnancy outcomes. These reproductive therapies allow women to bridge the gap between their ideologically constructed selves as prolific mothers, and their actual experience, where failed attempts to conceive invoke barrenness, or pregnancy itself leads to poverty, sickness, pain, hardship for existing family members, or even death. Justifications for such bold maternal assumptions and actions for women to take control of their own reproductive lives are rooted in both nontraditional theories of procreation and normative theologies intimated by Jāḥiẓ, Ibn Taymīya, Ghazālī, *ḥadīth* scholars and the Qur᾽ān itself that privilege the feminine role in the generation of life, castigate human passivity in the face of divine fate, and stress how God alone (not men) creates in wombs what he wills.

It is not difficult to understand why women would want to participate in God's creative efforts to affect their own hopes, desires, fears, and joys. Implicit in women's curative practices is that the reproductive body, which medieval elites scrutinize, control, and often devalue, provides a unique window through which women may come to experience God in an intimate way. In the lived experiences of everyday life, mothers take control of birth outcomes from male scholars as they direct and navigate their own fertility, in/ability to conceive, sex of the fetus, length of gestation, ease in delivery, and the appearance or disposition of the child to determine desired ends. Through whatever means available to them, women actively respond to God's call to further what is good (as they—not men—understand it) while trusting it is only God's plan that will ultimately prevail. Women's practical, bodily engagements with God's multifaceted creative efforts cultivate pious virtues that create a variety of theologies that reveal the failures of paternal structures to regulate fully their own ideals and underlying rationale. Such theologies oppose dominant, patriarchal views about men's primary reproductive role by emphasizing maternal care and well-being, familial welfare, and a more erotic dialog between women and God that preludes the generation of all life.

Conclusion

The Making of Medieval Muslim Mothers

As the examples above have shown, not every child born into the medieval Muslim world appears to have been "designed to the highest standard of wise appropriateness,"[1] which is "evidence of divine wisdom, design, and execution."[2] Barrenness, miscarriages, stillborn infants, and maternal mortality often reveal an experiential reality that disrupts the ideal flow of divine generation, where "he creates you in the wombs of your mothers, creation after creation."[3] Even when pregnancies yield fruit, there is no guarantee that the offspring produced will bear any physical or moral likeness to the ideal form of life scholars such as Jāḥiẓ and other male elites imagine to be the norm. More often than not, the mother is blamed for the discrepancies in her child's physical features and moral disposition. Physicians, exegetes, theologians, and literary writers take great pains to ensure the maternal body and the mother's moral disposition conform to the ideal modes of perfection they construct along paternal lines.

In the context of medieval discourses about reproduction and maternity, contorted limbs and compromised physiologies do little to display God's glory or reflect his ideal, but only serve to undermine the perfected creation, where God "constructed [the sky] and beautified it," producing "no flaws therein"[4] and the beautiful growth in pairs (*zawjin bahījin*) evokes every servant to turn toward him.[5] While medieval scholars assert that the divine realm may be perfect and stable, that perfection is obviously threatened by the impious acts or flawed bodies of women who inhabit a world that is far from ideal. In trying to bridge the gap between the real and the ideal, medieval Muslim scholars, through a variety of literary genres, generate the rhetorical boundaries necessary to map, define, and regulate a woman's potent maternal body and often misguided morals.

Assertions of such control through medical knowledge of the female reproductive system, images of an ideal mother predestined for purity and perfection, and dire warnings about the monsters produced when women engage in sexual impropriety secure a man's power to reproduce superlative believers with consummate physiques and pious intentions that best reflect what men define to be the will of the one true God. In sum, scholars assume that only righteous women are guaranteed of producing healthy and morally sound children. Those whose reproductive lives may be called into question can only look to their own words, actions, bodies, and familial inheritance—all of which have a direct impact on their superior or inferior physical and moral constitution—when God's orderly paths of generation go astray.

The traditional, paternal discourses that circumscribe the "good mother" are not just reinforced through male elite discourse. As depictions of the *taḥnīk,* circumcision, or the first haircut have shown, medieval mothers, through their performative responses to such rhetorical constraints, are also complicit in the creation and maintenance of the very patriarchal structures that seemingly oppose their own interests. Through a variety of infant initiation rituals and other maternal gestures, a mother symbolically transfers her own procreative power to that of men. Her efforts to suppress her own procreative power prove necessary in securing her child's place within the community, as well as in sealing her own identity as a "good mother." Without her active and willing participation in the preservation of her own subordinate but pious reproductive role, a mother would have no authority whatsoever to carve out a place for herself or her children within the broader community that values the role of men as the warrantors of the righteous believers God desires to generate in wombs.

Notably, these views of male procreative power and biddable female agency are also countered by medieval mothers who articulate patriarchal norms in new ways when their bodies and/or moral choices preclude them from attaining the prescribed theological ideals embodied by such prodigious figures as Mary, Āsiya, Khadīja, or Fāṭima, or the perfected biological standards upheld by medical scholars. Female contraceptive practices and fertility enhancements, read through alternative depictions of God's procreative efforts, serve to disrupt normative ideologies in order to bring forth a greater number of elite scholarly depictions of the dynamics that structure the identities of, and relations among, God, mother, and child. These proliferations of normative discourse highlight the polyvalent, reproductive potentialities of all three players intimated in the Qur'ān and un/orthodox theologies that often stand in sharp contrast with more dominant medical, exegetical, and theological projections of a woman's bodily weaknesses and often fickle piety. By garnering forces of nature, weighting the value of potential life, and intervening in their own reproductive cycles to cause or prevent conception based on their assessment of that value, women tap into the erotic partnership God shared with Mary, the earth, and the night to embody the feminine procreative power so readily displayed in the Qur'ān and other marginal discourses.

As argued above, the Qur'ān reveals a multitude of perspectives that depict God's creative nature, and lays out a variety of scenarios through which both real and ideal women must respond appropriately—albeit in different ways—to God's reproductive plans, whatever they may be. Medieval medical discourse as well as traditional exegesis, law, and theology select from this broad palette of possible interpretations more narrow, patriarchal readings that suppress both God's polyvalent identity and female reproductive agency. Such readings find further support and validation through the many prescriptions regarding the pregnant body, projections of the ideal mother, and required postpartum practices that permeate traditional discourses.

As a result of their ability to control the vagaries of female reproductive physiology, men become second in command to God in their power to secure the life he demands. Such paternal constructs of reproduction are countered by alternative, minority theologies that play upon the Qur'ān's many assertions that despite the limited knowledge and power humans may have over the begetting of life, only God creates whatever, and however, he pleases. Among an infinite number of avenues through which he can bring forth life, God often chooses to interact intimately with his female servants as they assist him in his engendering efforts just as easily as he decides to call life to "Be!" from a far-off location inaccessible to human comprehension.

The presence of such opposing views about how God generates life lends insight into Islam's multivocal, rather than essentialist, nature. In general, more patriarchal views about the flawed and weak nature of women inherited from the Greek and Roman medical tradition, or the links among sin, childbirth and punishment so prevalent in the Jewish- and Christian-influenced *isrā'īlīyāt* tend to structure dominant discourses about the maternal body. However, minority voices take these discourses to task by deconstructing the fundamental binaries between creator and created, male and female, immanent and transcendent. Ordinary men and women struggling to make sense of the apparent randomness in their own reproductive lives reveal the nonessential nature of such binaries by intervening in their own fertility, reveling in the awe-provoking instances of wind eggs and spontaneous generation, or perfecting and modifying what God initially creates. Such diverse opinions over how and why life comes to "Be!" shed light on the complexity of medieval Muslim views about God's procreative impulses, a father's tenuous connection with his child, and the all too inscrutable inner workings of the maternal body in its generation of life.

Sectarian Implications

This study will conclude with a few thoughts on how the "Muslim mother" was formed in relation to the pagan, Jewish, Christian childbearers around her. These reflections are far from exhaustive; however, they seek to show how the theological, biological, and social visions of motherhood in the medieval Muslim period did not take place in a vacuum, but were articulated, honed, and enforced within a broader sectarian context. As suggested above, there are as many points of intersection among these various groups as there are divergences. The cursory examples discussed below are intended to point the way for future conversations in the area of comparative medieval sexualities, maternities, and motherhood rather than provide a complete summary of sectarian debate about mothers and children in the medieval period.

In many ways, constructs of a medieval Muslim motherhood stand in sharp contrast with pre-Islamic, *jāhilī* perceptions of maternity, perhaps intentionally so.[6] As noted above, the *rashidūn* caliphs were often given the formidable task of having to determine or even reconstruct the paternity of children born during the *jāhilīya*. Often they had to rely on resemblance,[7] the mother's recollection of her sexual past,[8] the child's choice in the matter,[9] or even random lot to determine who belonged to whom[10] prior to the establishment of more formalized, patriarchal laws governing marriage, intercourse, and adultery. Clearly, with the advent of Islam, a woman's maternal power and authority—underscored by the utter lack of concern for the child's father in these *jāhilīya* cases—were diminished as a "good mother" was now understood as one who ensured her child a proper paternal lineage and identity. Thus, the gradual Islamicization[11] of motherhood was built around men becoming the primary, procreative authorities whose role it was to guarantee the paternity of a woman's children. Men secured paternity by naming the child's father, seeking resemblance in a child's features, proscribing a woman's sexual behavior, or linking fathers with sons through ritual. A well-defined paternal identity provided both women and children with a meaningful familial and social existence, along with a revered status among the community of believers and an honored position in paradise.

As chapters 1 and 2 show, the making of Muslim mothers also took place through dialog with an already established Greek medical tradition. This engagement with Greek medicine continued well into medieval Muslim corpuses, where Hippocratic and Aristotelian understandings of the female body were obviously fused with broader theological interpretations about the omnipotent nature of God and the sanctified relationships between men and women. Despite such theological convictions that highlight the equal contributions of both men and women to the procreative process, and the sovereign power of God to create whatever, and however, he pleases, Muslim medical treatises still tend to map women's bodies along the same patriarchal lines as their Greek predecessors. For example, physicians in both Muslim and pagan circles implicate the same organs and functions in the reproductive process, identify similar situations that mandate male medical intervention,[12] and weight the male role in procreation more heavily than that of the female.

As noted in chapter 2, Muslim physicians, like their Greek antecedents, hold that seeds generated from both males and females mix together in the womb to produce life. While the Qur'ān suggests this mingling process is a neutral one, medieval Muslim scholars, drawing from Greek medical treatises, insist one seed must dominate the other to engender boys or girls. The ability of one seed to dominate the other stems from three causes: the seed's place of origin, its temperature, and its consistency.

Both Muslim and Greek physicians associate the "right" generative organs—both male and female—with the begetting of boys, and the "left" with the engendering of girls. Likewise, they assert boys come from the hot and dry elements embedded within the seed; girls from those that are cold and wet. "Right," hot, and dry qualities translate into stronger seed, which makes a boy; "left," cold, and wet qualities weaken the seed and produce a girl. In both Muslim and Greek traditions, these gendered traits become inextricably linked with a person's essential nature: girls are inherently weak, boys strong. The idea that seeds engage in some sort of Darwinian competition inside the womb, with the stronger seed always coming to dominate the weaker, suggests it is a girl's nature to be submissive to and dominated by men. Here, the natural order of the world justifies the standing social order, and vice versa. Therefore, good Muslim mothers, like their pagan, Greek predecessors, must accept a more subordinate role and allow men to counter their natural, physical deficiencies through medical and practical expertise.

Not only do Greek and Muslim medical treatises portray women as the weaker sex, but so, too, do they show their wombs to be susceptible to corruption in similar fashion. Because of their potential for degeneracy—either moral or physical—female wombs are shown to distort robust "male" seed and divert it from its intended course of strength and domination. As examples in chapter 2 have illustrated, if the female seed is stronger than it "normally" should be, and the male seed is unable to assert full control over it, a hermaphrodite results. Likewise, if good seed falls on "rocky ground," limbs that have been divinely "designed to the highest standard of wise appropriateness"[13] may suddenly become twisted and distorted. A good Muslim mother, at least according to medieval medical literature, must strive to cultivate a passive sexual role so as to avoid the production of such "monstrosities," and work to overcome any of her physical or moral deficiencies that might produce an environment hostile to perfected male seed.[14]

While both Greek and Muslim mothers must contend with a weak physiology and an overall ignorance about its inner workings,[15] Muslim mothers have to wrestle further with the threat of immoral action and impious intent upon their bodies and those of their offspring. As medieval exegetes have demonstrated through their detailed depictions of Eve's checkered reproductive life, a morally degenerate womb often imprints its sedition upon the child. In addition to subjecting themselves to the care and wisdom of men in order to overcome their physical deficiencies, good Muslim mothers—unlike their Greek predecessors—must also strive for moral perfection, as impiety, too, may corrode the ability of healthy male seed to reach its *telos*.

When it comes to ensuring women do not engage in sexual acts that might lead to reproductive anomalies, Jewish, Christian, and Muslim scholars employ similar lessons from the animal kingdom to illustrate the consequences of heinous and immoral practices. All three traditions feature the hare, weasel, and hyena as animals particularly "good to think"[16] about issues of purity, morality, identity, and sexuality. While ancient Jewish texts tend to focus on the im/purity of these animals to assert dietary proscriptions that separate the Israelite from outsiders, Christian and Muslim materials tend to draw more abstract moral lessons from their deviant sexual behaviors to distinguish the pious from the impious.

With its focus on impurities, the Book of Leviticus claims Israel must refrain from the consumption of hares and weasels, as both are rendered unclean. Leviticus 11:6 mentions it is forbidden to eat the hare because it chews the cud, but does not have split hooves; Leviticus 11:29 notes the weasel is among the unclean animals that move about on the ground, and therefore cannot be consumed. The Hebrew Bible does not mention hyenas in the context of dietary laws or otherwise, however, Jeremiah 12:7–9 refers to a streaked creature (*tzavua'*) that may indeed be the Arabic *ḍabuʿ*, or female hyena, even though it is often translated as a "speckled bird of prey." Here, Jeremiah depicts the *tzavuaʾ* as a predator that is about to be devoured by more vicious, carnivorous beasts. In general, the Hebrew Bible condemns the consumption of any predator that might prey on the blood of other animals and present a danger to flocks. Predators would include the bear, lion, wolf, fox, jackal, hyena, weasel, badger, and the mongoose.[17] Any carnivore that rends the flesh of birds or animals is considered impure; to consume one is to compromise one's identity as an Israelite.

The Talmud also refers to the hare, weasel, and hyena in terms of their unfitness for consumption, although it occasionally makes mention of how one's moral comportment is more important than God's dietary restrictions. For example, the Babylonian king Nebuchadnezzar is caught eating a live hare in private, and he is chastised for his actions; however, those who divulge his secret are more strongly reprimanded than the king is for revealing his sins to the public in his absence.[18] In addition to its focus on dietary concerns and moral behavior, medieval Jewish literature also describes both the hare and the hyena in terms of their inherently unstable natures. The *Nishmath Chaim* (ca. 1636 CE) refers to those Kabbalists who say the soul of an unclean person will transmigrate into an unclean animal. Thus, an unclean soul may transmute into an ass, a woman of Ashdod (harlot), a bat, a rabbit, or a hare.[19] The Talmud also notes the hyena's unusual ability to morph its physical self: in seven years, for example, it will turn into a bat.[20] In these examples, the consumption of unclean foods is shown to erase the boundaries fundamental to one's humanity. Although Jewish scholars never link these three animals directly with sexual impropriety, the more abstract lesson to be gleaned from further reflection on these beasts is that good men and women adhere to God's laws. Straying beyond them by consuming unlawful foods or losing one's moral compass results in the loss and degeneration of self, body, and soul.

By way of contrast, medieval Muslim and Christian traditions use the hare, hyena, and weasel to warn believers against mimicking these beasts' unnatural inclinations toward anal intercourse, transvestism, hermaphrodism, and/or lustful promiscuity.[21] The Christian Epistle of Barnabas (ca. first c. CE), for example, suggests that the intent of the Mosaic laws prohibiting the ingesting of the hare, weasel, and hyena is to protect people from taking on the perverse sexual appetites these creatures possess. For example, the Epistle of Barnabas notes that by eating a hare one will morph into a debaucher of young boys, "because the hare grows a fresh orifice in its backside every year, and has as many of these holes as the years of its life."[22] Hyenas cannot be eaten because "that creature changes its sex annually and is a male at one time and a female at another."[23] Those who eat the weasel would likewise become like "abandoned women" who engage in oral sex, and then conceive and give birth through their mouths.[24] In each case, the sexual deviations these animals commit become imprinted on the culprit, the offspring such acts produce, or the peculiar (and rather revealing) way in which a mother gives birth. These Christian examples turn sexual deviation into the dominant criterion that dictates a person's humanity and thus his status in the faith rather than what maintains his purity and ethnic identity through an adherence to specific dietary restrictions.

Muslim scholars draw upon the same trio of hare, hyena, and weasel as the Epistle of Barnabas to warn women (and men, too) not to stray too far from their divinely created sexual paths. As noted in chapter 5, Qazwīnī and Ibn Qutayba refer to the hare (*arnab*) as a transvestite: it is one year a female, the next, a male.[25] Hares, of course, are also cited for their excessive sexuality and fertility as they produce offspring with every menstrual cycle, which may occur on a weekly basis.[26] In contrast, good Muslim mothers conceive and give birth to just one offspring at a time, at acceptable intervals,[27] in order to avoid suspicions of promiscuity and adultery.[28]

In addition to the hare, Muslim zoological texts likewise dwell on the unusual generative organs of the hyena (f. *ḍabuʿ*, m. *ḍibʿān*), which dons male and female genitalia "in the manner of a hermaphrodite (*khunthá*), and every year the organs of one sex [over the other] are excited."[29] Because of its sexual uncertainty, scholars suggest the female hyena falls outside normative boundaries that prescribe a pious, righteous society. Unlike "good animals" that reflect positive aspects of human behavior or the social whole,[30] the hyena engages in unspeakable activities that threaten underlying moral and ethical structures: sex with male human corpses, and the consumption of their blood after coitus. Such perverted, unnatural acts break down the fundamental lines between human/animal, living body/corpse that make one a human, and a righteous servant of God. Good mothers, therefore, must avoid such sexual depravities at all costs.

Lastly, just as Barnabas links weasels with oral sex, so too does Abū Ḥayyān, who projects weasels conceive through their mouths and give birth through their ears.[31] While oral sex is not explicitly prohibited in Islam, there is some question and concern about the release and spread of pollutants that result from that activity.[32] Thus, the weasel that ingests what is impure is shown to give birth to the visual evidence of her transgression. A good mother must avoid similar practices to ensure her children come into the world in a normative, acceptable fashion, and do not bear the observable stains of her sexual wrongdoings.

Unlike Barnabas, Muslim scholars are not implying humans engage in such depraved activities because they have devoured a hare, hyena, or weasel. In fact, in contrast with the Jewish treatment of these animals, some Muslim law schools consider the meat of these animals to be permissible (*ḥalāl*). Shāfiʿī, as noted in chapter 5, permits the consumption of hares, as well as hyenas. Despite the fact that both hyenas and hares have fangs, which would generally render them prohibited (*ḥarām*), Shāfiʿī dismisses the idea that either one is an actual predator.[33] Rather than focus on the inherently impure nature of these animals that somehow transforms human morality when ingested, Muslim scholars emphasize the uniquely human ability to discern right from wrong when it comes to sexual behavior. The deviant sexual practices of these animals that are on display for all to witness assist humans in their choices as part of God's repertoire of "signs" to warn believers to avoid falling away from his path.

Interestingly, in the Muslim context God's signs as displayed through these animals' deviant sexual desires do not seem to include dire warnings against same-sex relationships, as hares are strictly associated with transvestism, lust, promiscuity, and fertility, rather than anal sex. However, given that the *ḥayawān* literature often refers to hare blood as a contraceptive suggests that its Christian associations with same-sex couplings or anal intercourse—both of which do not result in offspring—may still be at play.[34] Such views, however, appear to be marginalized since most warnings against sexual aberrations still assume the fundamental necessity for male/female pairings. After all, female hyenas only copulate with *male* corpses, and while hyenas may possess both male and female genitalia, just one "sex" appears to be active at a time. Good Muslim mothers, therefore, must steer clear of degenerate heterosexual practices, which are defined primarily in terms of oral sex, bestiality, necrophilia, and excess lust, if they wish to generate righteous, healthy believers rather than the twisted forms embodied by the hare, hyena, or weasel. In general, the engagement in sexual activities outside a desire to procreate does not appear to be as great concern to Muslim scholars as it does to the Christian elite.[35]

A final example compares Jewish, Muslim, and Christian perspectives on contraception, in particular, the extent to which all three groups weight the life of the mother over and against the unborn—or the not yet conceived—child. For example, medieval Jews and Muslims hold opposing views on contraception, in particular, *coitus interruptus*. While medieval Muslim elites allow for *coitus interruptus* to be practiced, since God may cause a life to be or not to be despite the best of human intentions, medieval Jewish scholars, such as Maimonides, forbid it.[36] Seed spilling is thought to be unnatural and unproductive, the reasons for it often suspect, as the biblical example of Tamar and Onan so aptly illustrates.[37] Rabbis consider the destruction of male seed for any reason a serious moral offense against God's command to procreate.

Despite such strong opposition against *coitus interruptus,* however, rabbis believed the commandment not to waste seed was binding only for men, and not women.[38] Therefore, while medieval Jewish men would have been prohibited from rubbing tar on their penises to prevent pregnancy,[39] or spilling seed on rocks, women could still utilize the contraceptive sponge (*mokh*)[40] as long as it did not destroy the man's sperm.[41] In this way, medieval Jewish women, like their Muslim counterparts, would have exercised some control over their own fertility.

In general, female contraceptive practices were permissible if done in order to save a mother's life, or to spare her excess suffering during the course of pregnancy and childbirth. Unlike Ghazālī, Talmudic sages were not inclined to permit contraceptive potions or devices to preserve a woman's beauty,[42] or for reasons having to do with poverty.[43] However, like Ghazālī, the Jewish sages were very receptive to contraceptive devices for girls under the age of twelve, for nursing mothers who might compromise the life of the suckling child if she were to become pregnant, and for the prevention of superfetation if she were already pregnant (a criterion not mentioned in Muslim sources).[44]

Abortifacients were also approved under these same circumstances, because medieval Jewish sages believed a mother's life has priority over that of the unborn child. For example, the *Mishnah Oholot* 7:6 (ca. 200 CE) states, "If a woman is in hard travail [and her life cannot otherwise be saved], one cuts up the child within her womb and extracts it member by member, because her life comes before that of [the child]."[45] However, if the greater part of the head has emerged from the vagina, the child is considered a living being, and "one may not set aside one person's life for the sake of another."[46] Clearly, the fetus in the womb was not considered a fully autonomous being until it (or at least its head) emerges from the womb. Abortifacients were also recommended for women with deformed genitalia, a serious health condition, or for whom delivery of an infant would be fatal.[47] As in the case of medieval Muslim mothers, Jewish mothers likewise would have weighted their own lives and livelihood over and against that of an unborn child. Whatever their decision, the issue of whether to have a child or not for both Muslim and Jewish mothers would have been an intimate, family matter that was never to be taken lightly.

While Jewish and Muslim male elites allowed for the use of contraception to limited degrees, medieval Christian scholars did not. Their prohibition against all forms of contraceptive use, however, does not suggest Christian mothers were themselves averse to employing the various potions, sponges, or a variety of other methods to control and regulate their reproductive lives.[48] However, given the Church fathers' stern condemnation of all forms of birth control, including *coitus interruptus*, medieval Christian women would have had a more difficult task securing the theological justification for their use of various forms of contraception. Many women, of course, embraced celibacy as a way to become closer to God, and to avoid altogether the demands that sex and motherhood placed upon them by both husbands and a patriarchal church.[49]

The church's prohibitions against any contraceptive practice or abortifacient (including exposure) were severe. For example, *The Didache* (ca. 100 CE) states in no uncertain terms that "[y]ou shall not use magic. You shall not procure abortion. You shall not destroy a newborn child."[50] Clement of Alexandria makes a strong case against *coitus interruptus* by emphasizing the divinely sanctioned, privileged position of the male sperm in generating new life. He writes, "Because of its divine institution for the propagation of man, the seed is not to be vainly ejaculated, nor is it to be damaged, nor is it to be wasted."[51] *Coitus interruptus*, masturbation, or the use of spermicidal potions, therefore, do "injury to nature."[52]

The absolute stance against contraception stems from the Aristotelian belief that the potential for life is contained within the male sperm, that life begins close to the time of conception, and that the sole purpose of sex is procreation. In contrast with the *Mishnah*'s view that human autonomy begins after the infant emerges from the womb, John Chrysostom argues that even sterilization (castration) must be condemned, as that "prevents their [infants'] beginning to live."[53] Although he condemns all forms of contraceptive devices and practices,[54] Augustine takes a position much like that of Muslim jurists in his statement that killing a fetus that had not yet formed cannot be equated with homicide, "for it could not be said that there was a living soul in that body."[55] However, for Augustine the act is still a crime.[56]

In general, medieval Church fathers consider contraception and the prevention of a child from being born as sins because they interfere with God's purpose to generate life through any and every act of intercourse.[57] Good Muslim mothers, over and against these Christian counterparts, would never assume humans to have that much power and control over God, who alone determines the terms and conditions of life. In addition, rather than valuing the potential life of the unborn over and against her own health, a nursing child, or the livelihood of her family,[58] a good Muslim mother would, in an expression of piety, interfere in her own reproductive cycle to ensure the well-being of the communal whole, if God so desired.

All of these examples show to what extent "good Muslim mothers," as defined by male elite scholars, would have been formed in relation to what pagan, Jewish, and Christian mothers were or were not. Across the board, points of similarity appear in the paternal constructs of "good mothers" that are formed around the shared values of procreation and childbirth, as both are believed to reflect divine desire or command, and/or natural law. In all of these traditional permutations, to greater and lesser extents, the female reproductive body is presented as detrimental to these endeavors, and therefore in need of male knowledge, protection, expertise, and control in order to generate the perfected life God and/or man desires.

Points of departure reveal differing views about the value Muslim scholars place on prenatal life in comparison with that of the mother's, the procreative purpose of sexuality versus its sensual role, and, in contrast to the elite Church fathers, the range and scope of God's omnipotence. Even for Muslim scholars, who seek to usurp divine procreative power for themselves, God's desire to create or not create life can never be eclipsed—but only enhanced—through pious and well-intentioned human efforts.

The maternal body, with its fluid and permeable boundaries, is, like Lévi-Strauss's animals, "good to think." Despite its porous nature, the female reproductive system remains impenetrable to men, who are often left to compensate for their lack of experiential expertise of giving birth through elaborate imaginings of how it functions, how it may be manipulated to produce the desired results, and how they (men) may assume its procreative properties through knowledge and ritual. While medieval male scholars, through a wide range of authoritative discourses, try to contain and control the maternal body's diffusive boundaries along paternal lines, their discursive efforts are often rendered futile by women's own experiences, marginal theologies, and the Qur'ān itself, all of which serve to remind human procreative agents that God alone "shapes you in wombs as he pleases."[59]

Notes

Introduction

1. The works of al-Jāḥiẓ are significant for this study because of his obsessive interest in developing an overarching system to explain both natural and social phenomena. For Jāḥiẓ, instructions from and insight into God and human behavior come from critical contemplation of the natural world. As a Mu'tazilite, Jāḥiẓ believed that wisdom is present in all of God's creation through moral reason. Explanations for human action and, more generally, why the world is as it is become apparent through his many writings. For an extended analysis on the life of Jāḥiẓ and the significance of his work, see Tarif Khalidi's *Arab Historical Thought in the Classical Period* (Cambridge: Cambridge University Press, 1994), 104–107.

2. Abū 'Uthmān 'Amr ibn Baḥr al-Jāḥiẓ (d. 869 CE), *"Chance or Creation"? God's Design in the Universe,* trans. M. A. S. Abdel Haleem (Reading, Berks.: Garnet Publishing, 1995), 76. Not all scholars view this work as a legitimate work of Jāḥiẓ; however, whoever the actual author, the text represents a particular position or opinion that characterizes the thinking about these very human issues during the medieval period.

3. Ibid., 72.

4. Ibid., 80.

5. Ibid., 81.

6. The name "Jāḥiẓ" itself means "pop-eyed," which suggests he suffered from a severe form of eye disease. Muḥammad ibn Mūsā al-Damīrī (d. 1405 CE) notes that Jāḥiẓ was attacked with hemiplegia towards the end of his life, which left one half of his body numb (*Ḥayāt al-ḥayawān al-kubrá,* vol. 2 [Qum: Manshūrāt al-raḍī, 1985], 248).

7. In *Maternal Encounters: The Ethics of Interruption* (New York: Routledge, 2009), Lisa Baraitser describes the maternal body as both "singular and multiple"; it disturbs notions of both unity and the bounded self (22).

8. See, for example, Nancy Chodorow, *Feminism and Psychoanalytic Theory* (New Haven: Yale University Press, 1991), 6.

9. Carol Delaney, *The Seed and the Soil* (Berkeley: University of California Press, 1992), 27.

10. According to a national survey conducted in 2003, male academics outrank females 62 percent to 38 percent ("Faculty Diversity in Higher

Education," Rutgers: Institute for Women's Leadership). In 2001, 33.9 percent of MESA full members were women (A. H. Betteridge, "A Case Study in Higher Education International and Foreign Area Needs: Middle Eastern Studies Association Membership from 1990–2002," Global Challenges and US Higher Education Conference, Duke University, January 2003).

11. Saba Mahmood, "Feminist Theory, Embodiment, and the Docile Agent: Some Reflections on the Egyptian Islamic revival," *Cultural Anthropology* 16, no. 2: 205.

12. For a discussion about "instabilities" in the Book of Genesis, and the potential readings they produce, see Ken Stone, "The Garden of Eden and the Heterosexual Contract," in *Bodily Citations: Religion and Judith Butler,* ed. Ellen T. Armour and Susan M. St. Ville (New York: Columbia University Press, 2006), 50.

13. Or, as Nancy Chodorow articulates it, this study seeks to analyze "an open web of social, psychological relations, dynamics, practices, identities, beliefs" to comprehend "relations of gender and sexuality not immediately comprehended in terms of hierarchy, domination, or inequality or by concepts like patriarchy, male dominance, or the law of the father" (5).

14. See, for example, Delaney, *The Seed and the Soil,* 16, and Elisheva Baumgarten, *Mothers and Children: Jewish Family Life in Medieval Europe* (Princeton: Princeton University Press, 2004), 4.

15. Lynda Birke, "Bodies and Biology," in *Feminist Theory and the Body: A Reader,* ed. Janet Price and Margrit Shildrick (Oxford: Oxford University Press, 1999), 44–45.

16. *Gender Trouble: Feminism and the Subversion of Identity* (New York: Routledge, 2006), 25.

17. Stone describes this phenomenon in the biblical context (54). See also Judith Butler, *Bodies that Matter: On the Discursive Limits of "Sex"* (New York: Routledge, 1993), 237.

18. Saba Mahmood, *The Politics of Piety: The Islamic Revival and the Feminist Subject* (Princeton: Princeton University Press, 2005), 135ff.

19. Muslim ibn al-Ḥajjāj al-Qushayrī (d. 875 CE), *Jāmiʿ al-ṣaḥīḥ,* vol. 6 (Beirut: Dār al-iḥyāʾ al-turāth, 1956–1972), 176. See also Aḥmad ibn Muḥammad ibn Ḥanbal (d. 855 CE), *Musnad,* vol. 3 (Cairo: Al-Maṭbaʿa al-maymanīya, 1895), 106.

20. This innate relationship has been referred to as the "heterosexual presumption," a term coined by Teresa de Lauretis, "The Female Body and Heterosexual Presumption," *Semiotica* 67, no. 3–4 (1987): 259–79. Ken Stone refers to the same concept as the "heterosexual contract" (54). For further elaboration of how pervasive such presumptions regarding the sexual binary are, and how that particular paradigm is justified through appeals to "nature," see Monique Wittig, *The Straight Mind and other Essays* (Boston: Beacon Press, 1992).

21. See Sūras 13:8; 31:34; 35:11; 19:6; 41:47.

22. Basim Musallam, *Sex and Society in Islam* (Cambridge: Cambridge University Press, 1983), 49.

23. ʿAlī ibn Rabbān al-Ṭabarī (d. 870 CE) notes that the maleness of an embryo becomes evident in thirty days, while the femaleness of an embryo only becomes evident after forty-two days. This is due to the fact that the seed that makes the male is stronger and hotter from that which creates the female (*Firdaws al-ḥikma fī ʿl ṭibb* [Beirut: s.n., 1970], 30).

24. *Kitāb khalq al-janīn wa-tadbīr al-ḥabālā wa ʿl-mawlūdīn* (al-Jazāʾir: Maktabat Farrāis, 1956). ʿArīb ibn Saʿd's work is considered one of two important works written on gynecological topics in the Middle Ages (Ron Barkaï, *A History of Jewish Gynaecological Texts in the Middle Ages* [Leiden: Brill, 1998], 43). The other is Abū al-ʿAbbās Aḥmad ibn Muḥammad ibn Yaḥyā al-Baladī's *Kitāb tadbīr al-ḥabālā wa al-aṭfāl,* which was composed at the end of the tenth century.

25. *Firdaws al-ḥikma.* Rabbān al-Ṭabarī was the son of a Syrian Christian father living in Persia on the Caspian Sea, and a convert to Islam. He was the personal physician of caliph al-Mutawakkil (847–861 CE). The *Firdaws al-ḥikma* is recognized as the first and most comprehensive medical encyclopedia of its kind in Islam. Topics in the encyclopedia range from cosmogony, to the nature of man, to embryology, to anatomy, to *materia medica,* to psychotherapy, to pathology and surgery (Sami K. Hamarneh, "Al-Ṭabarī," in *Encyclopaedia of the History of Science, Technology, and Medicine in Non-Western Cultures* [Dordrecht: Kluwer, 1997]).

26. *Tibyān fī al-aqsām al-Qurʾān* (Beirut: Muʾassasat al-risāla, 1994). Ibn Qayyim al-Jawzīya, a fourteenth-century theologian, jurist, and philosopher, advocated an alternative genre to Greek medical wisdom called *al-ṭibb al-nabawī* ("medicine of the prophet"). Religious scholars writing from this perspective featured the medical practices of the prophet Muḥammad's time and the Qurʾān in preference to the medical knowledge assimilated from a Hellenistic context. Such medical wisdom based on the prophet's words and actions as well as divine revelation was deemed more acceptable by many orthodox scholars.

27. For example, ʿAbdallāh ibn Muslim ibn Qutayba (d. 885 CE), *ʿUyūn al-akhbār,* 4 vols. (Cairo: al-Muʿassasa al-miṣrīya al-ʿāmma li al-taʾlīf wa al-tarjama wa al-nashr, 1964); Muḥammad ibn Mūsá al-Damīrī (d. 1405 CE), *Ḥiyāt al-ḥayawān al-kubrā,* 3 vols.; ʿAlī ibn al-ʿAbbās al-Majūsī (d. 994 CE), *Kitāb Kāmil al-ṣināʿa al-ṭibbīya al-maʿrūf bi-al-Malakī* (Miṣr: al-Maṭbaʻa al-Kubrá al-ʻĀmira: 1877); Abū ʿAlī al-Ḥuṣayn ibn ʿAbdallāh ibn Sīná (d. 1037 CE), *al-Qānūn fī ʿl ṭibb,* 3 vols. (Beirut: Dar Sader Publishers, 1970); Abū Ḥāmid al-Ghazālī (d. 1111 CE), *Iḥyāʾ ʿulūm al-dīn,* Part 12, trans. Madelain Farah, *Marriage and Sexuality in Islam* (Salt Lake City: University of Utah Press, 1984);ʿAbdallāh ibn Busṭām Nīsābūrī, *Islamic Medical Wisdom: The ṭibb al-aʾimma,* trans. Batool Ispahamy (London: The Muhammadi Trust, 1991).

28. Abū ʿAbdallāh Muḥammad ibn Ismāʿīl ibn Ibrāhīm al-Bukhārī (d. 870 CE), *Jāmiʿ al-ṣaḥīḥ* (Al-Riyāḍ: Bayt al-afkār al-dawlīa li al-nashr, 1998), "Kitāb al-anbiyāʾ," no. 642, and Muslim, *Ṣaḥīḥ,*"Kitāb faḍāʾil al-ṣaḥāba," no. 5965, for example, mentions Mary the daughter of ʿImrān, and Khadīja. Bukhārī, "Kitāb al-anbiyāʾ," no. 643, and Muslim, "Kitāb faḍāʾil al-ṣaḥāba," no. 5966, adds Āsiya, wife of the Pharaoh, to the list.

29. Bukhārī, *Ṣaḥīḥ,* "Kitāb faḍāʾil al-ṣaḥāba," no. 115. *Tharīd* is a dish made from pieces of bread soaked in meat or vegetable broth.

30. According to tradition, ʿĀʾisha referred often to her own jealousy of Muḥammad's first wife Khadīja, with whom he produced many children, including two sons, who died tragically at young ages. She would often ask why, since she was so much younger and more attractive than Khadīja, and the prophet more intimately involved with her than with any of his other wives, God did not allow her to conceive. However, because ʿĀʾisha once stated arrogantly,

"God has given you better than her [meaning Khadīja] in exchange" (Bukhārī, *Ṣāḥīḥ*, "Kitāb manāqib al-anṣār," nos. 164, 165, 168), many medieval Muslim scholars suggest a strong link between a woman's barrenness and her moral behavior.

31. The *ʿaqīqa* ceremony involves the sacrificial slaughtering of animals, the shaving of the head (and its weight in silver given as charity), and/or the bestowing of the name on a child's seventh day of life.

32. Muḥammad ibn ʿAbdallāh al-Kisāʾī (ca. 1000–1100 CE), *Qiṣaṣ Anbiyāʾ al-Kisāʾī*, trans. W. M. Thackston Jr (Boston: Twayne Publishers, 1979), 72–73.

33. For example, in Ṭabarī (Abū Jaʿfar Muḥammad ibn Jarīr), *Tārīkh al-rasūl wa ʾl-mulūk*, trans. Franz Rosenthal, vol. 1, *General Introduction and From the Creation to the Flood* (Albany: State University of New York Press, 1989), 338–39, Cain's descendants are depicted as godless tyrants who engage freely in acts of promiscuity and wine drinking.

34. Examples include Damīrī's *Ḥiyāt al-ḥayawān al-kubrá*, and Abū ʿUthmān ʿAmr Baḥr al-Jāḥiẓ's *al-Ḥayawān* (Miṣr: Muṣṭafā al-Bābī al-Ḥalabī, 1966).

35. For a more detailed discussion of the significance of bestiaries in medieval Islam, see the entry on "ḥayawān" in the *Encyclopedia of Islam*, 2nd ed. (Leiden: Brill, 1960–2005).

36. Muḥammad ibn Yazīd Māja (d. 887 CE), *Kitāb al-sunan*, vol. 3, no. 1989, states how women cannot have tattoos, pluck eyebrows, or file teeth for purposes of beautification. In other words, they cannot actively manipulate God's creation.

37. Bukhārī, *Ṣaḥīḥ*, "Kitāb al-ʿilm," no. 101; "Kitāb al-janāʾiz," nos. 340, 341, 342, 463.

Chapter 1. On Wombs, Women, and the Hand of God

1. For an incomplete sampling of God's many and varied creative efforts, see Sūras 4:1; 6:2; 7:198; 15:26; 16:4; 22:5; 23:12; 23:12–14; 24:45; 25:54; 31:28; 32:7; 35:11; 38:71; 39:6; 40:67; 42:11; 53:45–46; 55:14; 76:2; 86:6–7.

2. Sūra 3:6.

3. See, for example, Sūras 2:117; 6:73; 16:40; 36:82; and 40:68.

4. Genesis 1:3.

5. For Mesopotamian examples similar to Genesis 2:7, where humans are generated in autochthonous fashion from dirt or clay, see *Atrahasis*, where Nintu creates humans by mixing clay with the blood of a slain God (Stephanie Dalley, trans., *Myths from Mesopotamia* [Oxford: Oxford University Press, 1989], 15). For Greek examples see Hesiod's *Works and Days*, trans. M. L. West (Oxford: Oxford University Press, 1999), lines 47–105, and *Theogony*, trans. Norman O. Brown (Upper Saddle River, NJ: Prentice-Hall, 1953), lines 507–616, in which Hephaestos fashions Pandora from clay. For Roman examples, see Ovid's *Metamorphoses* I.85, where the "son of Iapetus fashioned that earth, mingled with the waters of rain, into the image of the gods that guide the world" (trans. Z. Phillip Ambrose [Newburyport, MA: Focus Publishing, 2004], 4); and *Pseudo-Hyginus, Fabulae* 142, where he used just clay to create Pandora (*The Myths of Hyginus*, trans. and ed.

Mary Grant [University of Kansas Publications in Humanistic Studies, no. 34. Lawrence: University of Kansas Press, 1960]).

6. Sūra 6:2: See also Sūras 23:12; 32:7; and 38:71. *Ṭīn,* which refers to a pure form of clay that remains after the subsiding of water, has a reputation for preventing plague or pestilence, and has the power to purify corrupt water (Edward Lane, *Arabic English Lexicon* [London: Williams and Norgate, 1863], s.v. *ṭīn*).

7. Sūras 15:26; 55:14. Ṭabarī, *Tārīkh,* notes that *ṣalṣāl* is dry clay, which has in it *ṣalṣāla,* or that which makes sounds (*Tārīkh al-rasūl wa al-mulūk,* 26). This same statement is repeated in Abū Jaʿfar Muḥammad ibn Jarīr al-Ṭabarī's *Jāmiʿ al-bayān ʿan taʾwīl āy al-qurʾān,* vol. 4 [Bayrūt: Muʾassasat al-Risāla, 1994] (*Tafsīr al-Ṭabarī*), 477). See also Muḥammad ibn Muḥammad Riḍā al-Qummī (d. ca. 1713 CE), *Tafsīr kanz al-daqāʾiq wa baḥr al-gharāʾib,* vol. 7 (Qum: Dār al-Ghadīr, 2003, 104). Ṭabāri reports further that Adam produced such a sound when Iblīs would pass by him and kick him (*Tārīkh,* 262).

8. Sūra 15:26.

9. Sūra 37:11. Ṭabarī notes the term *lāzib* refers to that which is viscous and sweet smelling, something that sticks or adheres to something else, or that which emerges from *masnūn* or *muntin* slime, meaning "stinking" slime (*Tārīkh,* 258–59). ʿAlī ibn Ibrāhīm al-Qummī (c. 900 CE) notes that *ṭīn lāzib* is that which sticks to the hand (*Tafsīr al-Qummī* [Qum: Dhawā al-Qurbā, 2007], 525).

10. Sūras 3:47; 22:5; 35:11; 40:67.

11. The word for "water" (*māʾ*) can also mean "sperm" or "semen," at least in later Islamic medical texts. See, for example, Ibn Qayyim al-Jawzīya, *Tibyān,* 293. In the following two Qurʾānic examples where water is mentioned, however, it is not clear that human sperm is indicated. In Sūra 24:45, God creates every beast from water (*māʾ*), and in Sūra 25:54, "it is he who created from water [*māʾ*] a human being." In these examples, it appears as though water is just another natural resource God utilizes to generate human life. For a Roman account of water as an essential ingredient in man's creation, see Ovid, *Metamorphoses,* where Prometheus used water from "living streams" to create humans (I:100–10).

12. Genesis 9:1. For a similar version of the flood, see *Gilgamesh* (trans. Dalley, 113–14).

13. The role of God's loving hands in the generation of life is reflected upon by Ibn ʿArabī, who states that "from the first existent thing down to the last of the children—the animals—God did not combine both his hands in anything He created except the human being, that is, in the human being's earthly and bodily configurations. He created everything else either by divine command or with one hand" (*Futūḥāt* I 122.11, quoted and translated in Sachiko Murata, *The Tao of Islam* [Albany: State University of New York Press, 1992], 88). Clearly, Ibn ʿArabī believed the creation of humans was a unique process that separated them from animals. See discussions of Sūra 32:7–9, which also maintains this position, below.

14. Ṭabarī, *Tārīkh,* 258. See also al-Qummī, *Tafsīr kanz,* vol. 11, 98. Al-Qummī also records traditions that assert believers are formed from paradisiacal clay, while the unbelievers are fashioned from clay from hell (ibid.).

15. Ṭabarī actually aligns all the Qur'ānic substances together to suggest the clay from which Adam was originally formed was moistened until it became sticky, and then what was left became stinking slime, and then dry clay (*ṣalṣāl*) (*Tārīkh,* 260–61). There is also the suggestion that God caused Adam's clay to ferment, since he left it lying around as a body for forty years (ibid., 261). These exegetical examples emphasize man's innate, corrupt disposition, a position that contradicts many Qur'ānic passages that stress his purity at birth.

16. The Shī'ite exegete al-Qummī notes how believers are composed from the same type of clay (*ṭīn*) as the prophets (*al-anbiyā'*); however, prophets themselves are formed from the purest kind. The uppermost believers, however, are made from *ṭīn lāzib;* therefore, God will not separate them those who separate from them (*Tafsīr kanz,* vol. 11, 98). In this light, "stickiness" is not equated with stubbornness or insubordination; rather, it suggests a steadfastness in character.

17. Ṭabarī, *Tārīkh,* 258–60.

18. While the Qur'ān does not link "clay" with "earth" in these passages, later exegetes, such as Ṭabarī, do. According to Ṭabarī, Adam was created from the skin (*adīm*) of the earth (*Tārīkh,* 258–59). Skin, however, is also a masculine noun. Here, the skin serves to protect the feminized earth.

19. Ismā'īl ibn 'Umar ibn Kathīr (d. 1373 CE), *Qiṣaṣ al-anbiyā'* (Dimashsq: Dār Ibn Kathīr, 1992), 32. Abū Isḥāq Aḥmad ibn Muḥammad ibn Ibrāhīm al-Tha'labī (d. 1035 CE), *'Arā'is al-majālis fī qiṣaṣ al-anbiyā', Stories of the Prophets,* trans. William Brinner (Leiden: Brill, 2002), 70.

20. See also Sūra 20:53, where the barren, dry earth receives God's water (*mā'*), stirs to life, and then produces rich vegetation in pairs (*azwāj*). The parallels between human reproduction and God's generating life through his "water" (*mā'*) raining down upon the earth is underscored by the fact that these verses on vegetation directly follow the Qur'ān's discussion of how God creates human life in stages (22:5). For further discussions of the link between water (*mā'*) and male semen, see note below.

21. See Ann Hanson, "The Medical Writers' Women," in *Before Sexuality: The Construction of Erotic Experience in the Ancient Greek World,* ed. Froma I. Zeitlin, John J. Winkler, and David Halperin (Princeton: Princeton University Press, 1990), 317, who cites Hp., *Mul.* 1.1, 8.10.1–14.7 L (*Hippokratische Gynäkologie: Die gynäkologischen Texte des Autors C nach den pseudohippokratischen Schriften De Muliebribus I, II unde De Sterilibus,* ed. H. Grensemann [Wiesbaden: Steiner, 1982]).

22. Bruce Karl Braswell, *A Commentary on the Fourth Pythian Ode of Pindar* (Berlin, New York: Walter de Gruyter, 1988), 50. In note 255 (b) in the commentary, Braswell provides an exhaustive list of Greek sources where human reproductive processes are compared to the planting and plowing of a field; for examples, cf. *Thgn.* 581–82, A. *Th.* 753–56 (lyr.), S. *Tr.* 31–33, *Ant.* 569, *OT* 1211 (lyr.), 1256–57, 1484–85, 1497–98, E. *Med.* 1281 (lyr.), *Or.* 553, etc.

23. Edward Lane, *Arabic English Lexicon* (London: Williams and Norgate, 1863), s.v. "n-ḥ-l."

24. Sūra 16:68. See also J. Andrew Foster and Kathryn Kueny, "From the Bodies of Bees: Classical and Christian echoes in Surat al-nahl," *Comparative Islamic Studies* 3, no. 2 (2007): 145–68.

25. Ṭabarī, *Tārīkh,* 258–60.

26. Ibid., 258–59. For *midrashic* parallels of the earth's refusal to allow the angel (either Michael or Gabriel) to extract dust from her surface, see Howard Schwartz and Caren Loebel-Fried, *Tree of Souls: The Mythology of Judaism* (Oxford: Oxford University Press, 2004), 132. Here, the authors cite *4 Ezra* 3:4; *Genesis Rabbah* 14:8; *Midrash Komen* in *Bayt ah-Midrash* 2:27; *Pirkei de-Rabbi Eliezer* 11, 12, 20; *Midrash Tehillim* 92:6; *Y. Nazir* 7.2, 56b; *Seder Eliyahu Zula* 2; *Sefer Zikhronot* 15.

27. Here, *nafs* may be related to the Aristotelian (and Hellenistic) notion of *psuchē,* meaning a quality that is related to the essence of life. Lucretius, for example, states "the psuchē is contained by the whole body, and is itself the body's guardian and cause of its survival; for they cling together with common roots, and manifestly they cannot be torn asunder without destruction" (III.323–26) (*The Cambridge History of Hellenistic Philosophy,* ed. Keimpe Algra, Jonathan Barnes, Jaap Mansfeld, and Malcolm Schofield [Cambridge: Cambridge University Press, 2000], 546).

28. See also Sūras 31:28; 39:6.

29. Fazlur Rahman observes how sexual pairing functions as a universal law operative in all life, in *Health and Medicine in the Islamic Tradition* (New York: Crossroad, 1987), 101. For Qur'ānic examples of universal pairing, see Sūra 13:3: "of each kind of fruit he creates in two sets of pairs [*zawjayni athnayni*]"; Sūra 20:53: "We bring forth diverse pairs of plants [*azwājan min nabātin*]"; and Sūra 51:49: "All things we have made in pairs [*khalaqnā zawjayn*]."

30. For further mention of cattle, see also Sūra 39:6.

31. See below.

32. Sūra 50:16. See also Sūras 2:186; 34:50; 56:85; and 57:4 for examples of God's close proximity to humans, or rather, his almost indistinguishability from them.

33. Sūra 16:4.

34. Sūra 86:6–7. See also Sūra 32:8.

35. Note above: the word *mā'* is often used for semen, in both the Qur'ān and in later sources.

36. Lesley Dean-Jones, *Women's Bodies in Classical Greek Science* (Oxford: Oxford University Press, 1996), 168, notes that Hippocrates believed parts of the body from which seeds are drawn are humors that possess different potencies. See also Hanson, where she discusses how the Hippocratics believe in pangenesis of the seed, i.e., the production of seed by all parts of the body (314).

37. Abū ʿAbdallāh Muḥammad ibn Aḥmad ibn ʿUthmān al-Dhahabī, *Ṭibb al-nabawī* (Mecca; al-Riyāḍ: Maktabat Nizār Muṣṭafā al-Bāz, 1976) discusses how semen flows from all parts of the body (183). ʿArīb ibn Saʿd, in reference to Hippocrates, observes, too, that sperm comes from all parts of the body. He adds, however, that God gives it [sperm] the goodness of his creation (*Kitāb khalq,* 9).

38. See below. The affirmation of combined or "mixed seed," that is, seed emitted from both males and females, appears in Hippocrates, "The Nature of the Child," trans. J. Chadwick, in *Hippocratic Writings,* ed. G. E. R. Lloyd (London, New York: Penguin, 1978), 324. According to Hippocrates, the mixing occurs because the woman will not remain still. Galen, too, asserted that both

males and females produce seed. Galen proposed females possess "testicles" (ovaries) that discharge semen into the uterus (*Galen: On Semen*, ed., trans. and commentary by Phillip de Lacy [Berlin: Akademie Verlag, 1992], II.2–6 [145]).

39. Sūra 76:2. In other Qur'ānic verses, this mixed, seminal fluid is referred to as a "clot(s) of blood (*ʿalaq*)." Lane suggests *ʿalaq* refers to the seminal fluid, after its appearance, when it becomes thick, clotted blood, before it passes to another stage, becoming flesh (s.v. *ʿalaq*).

40. Sūra 53:45–46: *Wa annahu khalaqa al-zawjayni al-dhakara wa al-unthā min nuṭfatin idhā tumnā.*

41. The Qur'ānic God often creates by claiming "Be!" and it is. See, for example, Sūras 2:117; 3:47; 19:35.

42. See Sūra 112:3: "God begets not, nor was he begotten." See also 72:3: "And that he, may our Lord's majesty be exalted, has not taken a consort or a son," and 6:101: "How can he have a son when he has no consort?" It is not surprising that the Qur'ānic God would be viewed as a paternal figure, especially given his relationship with the earth and his role in generating life. The refutation of that role, perhaps, is more unusual, since human reproduction is often mirrored in cosmology. See, for example, Aristotle, who notes that "in cosmology too they speak of the nature of the Earth as something female and call it 'mother,' while they give to the heaven and the sun and anything else of that kind the title of 'generator,' and 'father'" (Aristotle, *GA* 1.2.716a14–18, quoted in Yii-Jan Singh, "Semen, Philosophy, and Paul," *Journal of Philosophy and Scripture* 4, no. 2 [Spring 2007]: 38). Similarly, Ibn ʿArabī also notes how a "father" is anything that exercises an effect and a "mother" is anything that receives an effect (as noted in *The Tao of Islam*, 154). In these examples, the severance of God from a sexual role in human reproduction counters those Qur'ānic passages that link him with a generative function. However, the Qur'ānic disassociation of God with a paternal role counters other traditions, such as Christianity, that refuse to imbue the maternal body with symbolic significance equal to that of the father in the generation of human life (Tina Beattie, *God's Mother, Eve's Advocate: A Marian Narrative of Women's Salvation* [New York: Continuum, 2002], 92).

43. *The Life of Muḥammad: A Translation of Ibn Isḥāq's Sirat Rasūl Allāh*, intro. and notes by Alfred Guillaume (Karachi: Oxford University Press, 1995), 165–67.

44. Sūra 43:16. See also 37:151–53: "It is out of their perversion that they will say: God has begotten, but they are liars. Has he preferred daughters over sons?"

45. Sūra 18:4. See also 19:88. "Those who utter such blasphemies about God's paternal nature will stand by as the heavens crack, the earth splits, and the mountains crumble to dust."

46. Sūra 112:3.

47. Sūra 39:4.

48. Sūra 19:92. See also 19:35. As noted below, the root for the word *raḥmān* comes from the same root as womb. It is ironic that the *raḥmān* could have a son but chose not to.

49. Sūra 2:228.

50. Sūra 39:6.

51. Bukhārī links these terms together in *Ṣaḥīḥ,* "Kitāb al-adab," nos. 16, 17, 18.

52. Murata, 215.

53. Sūra 31:34. See also 3:36, where God knows the wife of ʿImrān is bearing a female and not a male.

54. Sūra 39:6.

55. Murata, 215–17. Bukhārī, *Ṣaḥīḥ,* "Kitāb al-ḥayḍ," no. 315; "Kitāb al-anbiyāʾ," no. 550.

56. Sūra 16:78.

57. See also Sūra 22:5: "We have created you from dust, then from a sperm, then from a clot, then from a sperm, then from a little lump of flesh partly formed and partly unformed in order to show you our power."

58. Hippocrates, 324–29.

59. Ibid, 329.

60. Genesis 3:14–21.

61. Genesis 6:7.

62. Hippocrates, 324.

63. Ibid.

64. Ibid.

65. Ibid., 325.

66. Ibid.

67. Ibid., 326. For the same account reiterated in medieval Muslim medical texts, see also Zakarīyā ibn Muḥammad al-Qazwīnī (d. 1283 CE), *ʿAjāʾib al-makhlūqāt wa gharāʾib al-mawjūdāt* (1973), 349.

68. Hippocrates, 326. See also Hanson, 314. This same narrative concerning the role of "breath" in the reproductive process is repeated in ʿArīb ibn Saʿd, *Kitāb khalq,* 29; and Jalāl al-Dīn al-Suyūṭī, *Ṭibb al-nabawī,* translated as *as-Suyuti's Medicine of the Prophet* (London: Ta-Ha, 1994), who states how the "womb is a greedy creature. When a man's semen meets a woman's fluid the two fluids intermingle. This results in bubbles forming, caused by the heat of the interaction in the same way that bubbles are produced when a thick fluid is heated over a fire. These bubbles then coalesce, making one single bubble, which forms a relatively large sphere. It is inside the sphere that the vital force will enter, by the permission of Allah" (193). Here, only God allows such natural forces to take place.

69. Hippocrates, 326.

70. This understanding of breath as the power that drives fetal development is illustrated further in Hippocrates's description of how breath forms flesh into bones and distinct members of the body (the fourth stage): the flesh fills with air, and then begins to divide and separate. Once the parts of the body materialize, and the bones grow hard "as a result of the coagulating heat," Hippocrates determines the embryo to be a living being (Hippocrates, 328).

71. Rahman, 107.

72. Aristotle, *Generation of Animals,* trans. A. L. Peck (Cambridge: Harvard University Press, 1943), II.ii.736a (163).

73. Ibid., II.iii.736b (171).

74. Ibid., I.xx.729a (111).

75. Ibid. For Aristotle, menstrual blood is really unheated semen. Women do not generate enough heat to convert blood into semen, as do men. Aristotle goes so far as to say the male is separate from the female, "since it is something *better* and more divine in that it is the principle of movement for generated things, while the female serves as their matter" (II.i.732a [133]).

76. Ibid.

77. Ibid., I.xxi.729b (115).

78. Ibid. I.xxi.730a (117).

79. Ibid., II.iii.737a (173).

80. Ibid., II.iii.737a (173). Although Aristotle suggests menstrual discharge is unformed semen (since the female body cannot heat its blood enough to convert it into semen), he asserts this cold substance does not contain the principle of the Soul, or the ability to generate movement, as does the male semen.

81. Ibid., II.iv.738b (185).

82. Ibid., II.iv.738b, footnote "a" (184).

83. Sūra 38:71–72. See also 32:9.

84. Later exegetes also make the connection between Adam and Jesus son of Mary, as neither one had a father. For example, Kisāʾī relates that when Joseph learned of Mary's pregnancy, he asked Mary if anything could grow without seed. She said no, and then he asked her if there can be a child without a father. To this she replied yes: Adam had no father or mother. She tells Joseph the child she is carrying is like Adam, whom God shaped from dust and to whom God said "Be!" and he was (*Qiṣaṣ*, 328–29).

85. Muḥammad ibn al-Ḥasan al-Ṭūsī (d. 1067 CE), *Tibyān fī tafsīr al-Qurʾān*, vol. 10 (al-Najaf: al-Maṭbaʿa al-ʿilmīya, 1957–1963), 54–55. See also Ibn Kathīr, *Tafsīr al-Qurʾān al-ʿaẓīm*, vol. 9 (Jīza: Muʾassasat Qurṭuba: Maktabat awlād al-shaykh lil-turāth, 2000), 67. See also Ibn Kathīr, *Qiṣaṣ*, 585.

86. Ṭūsī notes how Gabriel breathed the messiah directly into Mary's *farj* (54–55). Ṭabarī also reports that Gabriel is the one who blew into Mary's *farj* (*Tafsīr*, vol. 7, 333; 279), as does Muḥammad ibn Aḥmad al-Qurṭubī (d. 1273 CE) (*Jāmiʿ li-aḥkām al-Qurʾān*, [al-Qāhira: Dār wa-maṭābiʿ al-ahaʿb, 1961], 573), Ibn Kathīr, *Tafsīr*, vol. 14, 67, and Maḥmūd ibn ʿUmar al-Zamakhsharī (d. 1144 CE), vol. 4 (*Khashshāf ʿan ḥaqāʾiq al-tanzīl wa-ʿuyūn al-aqāwīl fī wujūh al-taʾwīl* [Cairo: Miṣr al-bābī al-ḥalabī, 1966], 132). Muḥyī al-Dīn ibn al-ʿArabī, by way of contrast, suggests the holy spirit (*rūḥ al-quds*) imparted his breath into Mary, and she bore Jesus (*Tafsīr al-Qurʾān al-karīm*, vol. 2 [Beirut: Dār al-thaqāfa al-ʿarabīya, 1968], 89).

87. See, for example, Qurṭubī, 573, and Zamakhsharī, vol. 4, 132, who both suggest Gabriel's appearance both resembled, but did not resemble, that of a husband.

88. Ibn Kathīr, *Tafsīr*, vol. 9, 67. The intervening role of Gabriel protects the qurʾānic idea that humans and God must remain separate. Otherwise, the divine breath blown into individual humans might have the potential to elevate them above and beyond their humanity.

89. Ṭūsī, vol. 7, 276 suggests Gabriel's life-giving breath impacted Jesus's biology. While the Qurʾān asserts Jesus's unusual conception did not have any impact on his natural, biological composition, Ṭūsī claims Jesus was "superior in

nature, not like the children created from [human] sperm (*nuṭfa*)." Unlike other messengers who received their status later in life as a result of their piety, Jesus, via the breath, was created as a prophet. Here, the breath, occupying the same function as male semen in the Aristotelian context, bequeathed something vital of its nature to the offspring it engendered. Thus, the child (Jesus) resembles his father (Gabriel).

90. Ṭabarī in particular defends this position, and even goes so far as to suggest that the interpretation of the word *farj* actually means fissure, gap, or tear. As he notes, "every fissure [*ṣadʿ*] or gap [*shaqq*] in a wall, or roof, is *farj*." Therefore, Gabriel blew not into Mary's vagina, but rather "in the hole [*jīb*] of her outer garment, and that is her *farj*" (*Tafsīr,* vol. 7, 333).

91. Ibn Kathīr, *Tafsīr,* vol. 9, 67. See also Ibn Kathīr, *Qiṣaṣ,* 585.

92. Ibn Kathīr, *Qiṣaṣ,* 585.

93. Ibid.

94. Sūra 97:1–5. Michael Sells argues that the descent of the spirit upon or into Mary at the conception of Jesus structurally parallels the descent of the spirit on or into the night of destiny (*Approaching the Qurʾan* [Ashland: White Cloud Press, 1999], 183–207, summarized also in the *Encyclopedia of the Qurʾān,* ed. Jane Dammen McAuliffe [Leiden: Brill, 2001–06], s.v. "spirit"). These examples also parallel Sūra 99:5, where the earth is a recipient of God's revelation.

95. Sūra 19:21. Mary, Jesus's birth, and Jesus himself all serve as bearers of God's signs. Elsewhere in the Qurʾān, God's water (*māʾ*) enlivening a barren earth (just as the breath and spirit enliven Mary's womb to produce life) also serves as a "sign" for humankind. For God's *māʾ* raining down upon a barren earth, see Sūras 10:24; 7:57–58; 18:45; 22:63; 25:48; 31: 50:9; 78:16; 23:10–21 and 39:20–21.

96. Reference above. The intimate partnership between God and the earth (*al-arḍ*) is already noted in the Qurʾān. Sūra 99:5 notes how the Lord gave "her" a revelation (*bi anna rabbaka awḥá lahā*).

97. Sūra 19:20. See also 3:47, where she cries out to her lord the same thing.

98. Sūra 19:21. Interestingly, in this example, the spirit can only "say" it will be so but does not seem to be able to utter the generative "be" himself.

99. Here, it seems as though the Qurʾān conforms to Aristotelian notions of conception where women provide the necessary material to be formed by the male semen.

100. Here it is ambiguous whether the "him" or "it" refers to the *al-insān,* the *naslahu,* or to the *māʾ*.

101. See also Sūra 3:49.

102. According to the Qurʾān, some animals do possess certain human qualities, such as the capacity to speak. Solomon speaks of the human ability to comprehend the speech of the birds; likewise, ants are able to converse with their fellow ants (Richard C. Foltz quoting Sūra 27:16–18, in *Animals in Islamic Tradition and Muslim Cultures* [Oxford: Oneworld, 2006], 12). As noted above, also, the bee was the recipient of divine revelation. In general, however, it does not appear that animals have the choice of accepting or rejecting God's revelation in the same way that humans—who possess the spirit—do. They can serve as signs, or even bear them, but cannot witness to them.

103. Sūra 40:67.

104. Obviously, one of the major issues the two-seed theory resolves is that of family resemblance, and that of sex determination. For support of the two-seed theory for those reasons in medical treatises, see ʿArīb ibn Saʿd, *Kitāb khalq,* 9; Rabbān al-Ṭabarī, *Firdaws al-ḥikma,* 34; Suyūṭī, 185. In addition to medical scholars, the *ḥadīth* also support the two-seed theory. For example, Mālik b. Anas records a tradition that has ʿĀʾisha reprimanding the prophet for laughing at the idea that a woman might have some sort of nocturnal emission. ʿĀʾisha claims women must have such emissions, for where else might family resemblance come ("Kitāb al-ṣalāt," in *Muwaṭṭaʾ* [Bayrūt: Dār al-Gharb al-Islāmī, 1994], 2:21.86). See also Abū Dāʾūd Sulaymān ibn al-Ashʿath al-Sijistānī, *Sunan Abī Dāʾūd* (Beirut: Dār al-kutub al-ʿilmiyya, 1996), "Kitāb al-ṭahāra," no. 236. See also Bukhārī, *Ṣaḥīḥ,* "Kitāb al-adab," no. 113; "Kitāb al-ḥudūd," no. 830; "Kitāb al-ʿilm," no. 132.

105. Sūra 3:47.

106. Sūras 13:8; 35:11; 41:47. Similarly, 60:11 demonstrates God's complete omnipotence over all things, as "no disaster befalls but by God's leave."

107. Sūra 42:50.

108. Sūras 3:36; 31:34; 53:32.

109. See Sūras 22:5; 67:14, and 42:49.

110. Sūras 30:54; 40:67.

111. Sūra 22:5.

112. See also Bukhārī, *Ṣaḥīḥ* "Kitāb al-anbiyāʾ," no. 67.

113. Sūra 108:3. It may be that the male organ is also the target, but certainly both parents will suffer as a result of a man's transgressions against believers.

114. Jāḥiẓ, *"Chance or Creation,"* 76.

115. Sūra 67:23.

116. See Sūra 20:124–26: "But he who shuns my reminder will have a life of hardships and we shall raise him up a blind man, on the Day of Resurrection. He will say: Lord, why did you raise me up a blind man, while I was originally capable of seeing? God will say: That is how our revelations came to you, but you forgot them; and that is how, today, you shall be forgotten."

117. Sūra 40:58.

118. Sūra 5:60. See also 7:166. See also Ilse Lichtenstaedter, "And Become Ye Accursed Apes," *Jerusalem Studies in Arabic and Islam* 14 (1991): 153–75; Uri Rubin, "Apes, Pigs, and the Islamic Identity," *Israel Oriental Studies* 17 (1997): 89–105; Michael Cook, "Ibn Qutayba and the Monkeys," *Studia Islamica* 89 (1999): 43–74.

119. Abū ʿĪsā Muḥammad ibn ʿĪsā al-Tirmidhī, *Ṣaḥīḥ al-Tirmidhī* (Cairo: Al-Maṭbaʿ al-miṣrīya, 1931–34), "Daʿawat," 119.

120. Sūra 24:61: "The blind (*al-aʿmā*) are not at fault, the lame are not at fault, the sick are not at fault, nor are you if you eat in your houses." See also Sūra 48:17.

121. Sūras 3:49; 5:113.

122. Sūra 51:41–42. The same sequence of events is repeated in the story of Zakarīyā. Like Abraham, Zakarīyā asks God for a son even though his wife

is barren (*ʿāqir*) and he is old (19:1–10). According to the Qurʾān, barrenness is not simply the inability to bear a child, it also contains an element of external social, familial, or physical destructiveness, as a barren wind (*al-rīḥ al-ʿaqīm*) that "left nothing it came upon, but reduced it to rubble."

123. Sūra 37:101. The practice of men praying for sons is not uncommon in Jewish lore. Baumgarten notes how Beit Shamai believed Jewish law required the father's generation of two sons (29). Fathers, therefore, explicitly prayed for the birth of male offspring. From the moment of conception, special prayers were recited to help women bear sons.

124. Sūra 37:100. Jesus is also referred to as a "*ghulām*" in Sūra 19:19.

125. This choice, perhaps, was reinforced by the fact that Sarah initially laughs at the suggestion she might conceive a child at her ripe old age. Her laughter signals a deeper impiety that perhaps only her husband's profound faith may counter (Sūra 9:71–72). See also 51:29.

126. Sūra 21:90: *astajabnā lahu wa wahabnā lahu Yaḥyā wa aṣlaḥnā lahu zawjahu.*

127. Sūra 11:71. Suzanne Pinckney Stetkevych argues that the Arabic verb *ḍaḥikat,* which occurs in Sūra 11:71, may actually mean "to menstruate" in addition to "to laugh." Most Qurʾānic commentaries go with the meaning of laughter; however, she notes many poetic references link the root *ḍ-ḥ-k* with menstruation ("Sarah and the Hyena: Laughter, Menstruation, and the Genesis of a Double Entendre," *History of Religions* 36, no. 1 [Aug. 1996]: 13).

128. See, for example, Sūra 60:15. Note also 3:14, 18:46, 34:37, 57:20, 58:17, and 71:21, which warn against the accumulation of wealth and children as a substitute for worship of God.

129. Sūra 60:12.

130. Ibn Kathīr, in his *Tafsīr,* commentary on Sūra 3:97, notes Mecca's names include *umm al-raḥm* (mother of mercy), and *umm al-qurā* (mother of the towns). For an exhaustive account of the relationship between Mecca and Eden, see Brannon Wheeler's *Mecca and Eden: Ritual, Relics, and Territory in Islam* (Chicago: University of Chicago Press, 2006).

131. Sūras 13:39, 3:7, 43:4.

132. Proverbs 8:23.

133. Sūra 3:33, as referenced in "Mary," by Barbara Freyer Stowasser, in *Encyclopedia of the Qurʾān,* vol. 3, ed. Jane Dammen McAuliffe (Leiden: Brill, 2001–06).

134. For example, in the Christian gospels Luke seeks to rectify Matthew's genealogy of Jesus as Matthew includes Joseph's royal but wicked ancestor Jechoniah, as well as some less than reputable women such as Tamar, Rahab, Ruth, and Bathsheba, who were often associated with prostitution and/or adultery. Luke, on the other hand, provides Mary's genealogy (or, perhaps, another version of Joseph's) to show how her/his descendants can be linked with David but bypass Jechoniah and, in theory, these four women. In other words, whether he is supplying Joseph's or Mary's genealogy, Luke purifies Jesus's ancestry to show his righteousness and rightful claim to the throne of David. For further explanations of this phenomenon, see, for example, L. Michael White, *Scripting Jesus: The Gospels in Rewrite* (New York: HarperOne, 2010), 477. It

is important to note, however, that the Qur'ān, too, casts many "biblical" figures in a much more righteous light than its biblical counterparts. In other words, the Qur'ān sterilizes biblical histories and persons in such a way as to make these figures paragons of virtue. For example, while the Hebrew Bible mentions Noah's drunkenness, the Qur'ān makes no mention of this detail (Kathryn Kueny, *The Rhetoric of Sobriety: Wine in Early Islam* [Albany: State University of New York Press: 2001], 17–21).

135. Sūra 3:35–36.

136. Ibid.

137. See Ṭabarī's commentary on Sūra 3:35 (*Tafsīr*, vol. 6, 329–30).

138. Sūra 35:1.

139. Sūra 3:42.

140. Ibid., Sūra 3:37. See also Ibn Kathīr, *Qiṣaṣ*, 600, which states how Mary was no partner in divinity.

141. *The Encyclopedia of Islam*, 2d. ed. (*EI*[2]), s.v. "Maryam." See also Sūra 5:116: "And when Allāh said, 'O ʿĪsā b. Maryam, have you said to the people, take me and my mother as two gods besides Allāh?' He answered, 'Far be it that I should say to what I am not entitled.'" Clearly anti-trinitarian sentiments are projected here.

142. A number of medieval scholars—in particular, those from Andalusia—debated whether or not Mary would have been considered a prophet, given that she received a "word." These would include Ibn ʿArabī, Ibn Ḥazm, and Qurṭubī (Murata, 345, n. 28).

143. Muḥammad ibn Isḥāq, *Sīrat rasūl Allāh*, in the rescension of ʿAbd al-Mālik ibn Hishām's *al-Sīra al-nabawīya*, 3 vols. Dār al-kutub al-miṣrīya, n.d. Translated by Alfred Guillaume as *The Life of Muḥammad: A Translation of Ibn Isḥāq's Sīrat rasūl Allāh* (Oxford: Oxford University Press, 1995), 68–69.

144. Ibn Hishām, trans. Guillaume, 68.

145. Ibid, 69.

146. Sūra 19:17–21.

147. Sūra 21:91. See chapter 1, 31.

148. Sūras 66:12; 3:45. See chapter 1, 32.

149. Sūra 4:171.

150. Sūra 19:22–33.

151. The idea that Jesus is generated without a father is seen as one of God's wondrous signs. According to Ibn Kathīr (*Qiṣaṣ*, 575), angels came to Mary and told her a baby would be born to her without a father, who would speak in infancy, calling people to the way of God.

152. Sūra 28:7.

153. Sūra 28:4.

154. The fact that the mother of Moses received a revelation from God makes her a prophet in the eyes of Andalusian scholar Ibn Ḥazm (A. R. Agwan, N. K Singh, *Encyclopedia of the Holy Qur'ān*, vol. 1 [New Delhi: Global Vision Publishing House, 2000], 766).

155. Sūra 28:7.

156. Sūra 28:10.

157. Sūra 28:12.

158. Sūra 28:13.

159. As the prophet's wives are like no other women (Sūra 33:32), ordinary believers are not expected to follow in their path but rather maintain other aspects of a faithful life, such as fasting, guarding their chastity, praising God, and being patient, humble, and generous in charity (Sūra 33:35).

160. Sūra 33:40. Although the Qur'ān does refer to the fact that Muḥammad adopted a son, Zayd, it repudiates his paternal role in relationship to this son, along with the fact that adopted sons are equivalent to one's own offspring (Sūra 33:37). See also David S. Powers, *Muḥammad Is Not the Father of Any of Your Men* (Philadelphia: University of Pennsylvania Press, 2009), 35–71. Even though Muḥammad fathered children with Khadīja, and later his Coptic concubine Māriya, the Qur'ān does not celebrate or even acknowledge this fact.

161. Sūra 33:6. The Qur'ān still acknowledges blood ties are the most important ties one can have with someone. This fact, however, seems to be true for ordinary people, and not the prophet and his wives. This communal vision centered around faith rather than blood is similar to the one in Luke 14:26, where Jesus states, "If anyone comes to me and does not hate his father and mother, wife and children, his brothers and sisters—yes, even his own life—he cannot be my disciple."

162. Sūras 33:32–34; 39:4; 39:65.

163. The barrenness used to describe an old women past her childbearing years (*ʿaqīm*) is also used to refer to the winds sent by God to destroy the people of ʿAd who refused God's signs (*al-rīḥa al-ʿaqīma*). Certainly, it is difficult to render such "punishment" in positive terms.

164. Sūra 24:58. In 7:26, the verbal form is used to instruct the children of Adam to cover themselves. There is, of course, much debate as to what exactly must be covered.

165. Sūra 24:60.

166. Sūra 24:31.

167. See Sūra 2:222 for the prohibition against men having sex with women who are menstruating. For prohibitions against adultery, see Sūras 7:33; 17:32; and 24:26.

168. Sūra 4:22–23.

169. Sūra 31:14.

170. See Sūra 31:14, which mentions how mothers bear children in weakness upon weakness. Examine also 45:15, which states how men should be kind to their parents, as their mothers have borne them and delivered them in great pain. 7:189 speaks of women bearing at first a light burden, which then becomes heavy.

171. Sūra 2:233. See also 45:15, which puts the period of gestation and weaning up to thirty months.

172. Rabbān al-Ṭabarī notes that the maleness of an embryo becomes evident in thirty days, while the femaleness of an embryo only becomes evident after forty-two days. This discrepancy is due to the fact that the seed that makes the male is stronger and hotter from that which creates the female (*Firdaws al-ḥikma,* 30).

Chapter 2. Mapping the Maternal Body

1. Helen King, *Hippocrates' Women: Reading the Female Body in Ancient Greece* (New York: Routledge, 1998), 5.

2. Here, gender can be defined as the behavioral, cultural, or psychological traits typically associated with one sex or another.

3. Sara Salih and Judith Butler, eds., *The Judith Butler Reader* (Hoboken: Wiley-Blackwell, 2004), 91.

4. King, 6. Thus, the human body should not be understood as historically constant, a natural given.

5. Lynda Birke, *Feminism and the Biological Body* (Edinburgh: Edinburgh University Press, 1999), 3.

6. Carol Delaney, "Cutting the Ties That Bind: The Sacrifice of Abraham and Patriarchal Kinship," in *Relative Values: Reconfiguring Kinship Studies*, ed. Sarah Franklin and Susan McKinnon (Durham: Duke University Press, 2001), 452–53.

7. Delaney notes that "[p]aternity has not meant merely the idea of a physiological relationship between a specific man and specific child, as so many people assume, nor the social role built on that recognition. Paternity has meant the *primary, creative, engendering* role ("Cutting," 453).

8. Ibid., 457. Delaney is working within the context of the Hebrew Bible, which takes the Aristotelian view that only men produce seed. Thus, mothers are never the generators of seed, but the mere recipients of it. The Islamic tradition wrestles with the discrepancies between inherited Aristotelian tradition and the Qur'ān's emphasis on Hippocratic views of reproduction.

9. *Qānūn*, (Kitāb 3, Fann 21, Maāla 1, Faṣl 1), noted in Suad Joseph and Afsaneh Najmabadi, eds., *Encyclopedia of Women and Islamic Cultures: Family, Body, Sexuality, and Health* (Leiden: Brill, 2005), 401.

10. Delaney, "Cutting," 457.

11. Ibid.

12. *Kitāb khalq al-janīn.*

13. *Firdaws al-ḥikma.*

14. *Tibyān fī'l-aqsām.*

15. For example, Ibn Qutayba's *ʿUyūn al-akhbār*, Damīrī's *Ḥiyāt al-ḥayawān*, Majūsī's *Kitāb Kāmil*, Ibn Sīnā's *al-Qānūn fī ʿl ṭibb*, Ghazālī's *Iḥyā' ʿulūm al-dīn*, and passages from the *Ṭibb al-a'imma*.

16. ʿArīb ibn Saʿd notes that women have sperm like men (*Kitāb khalq*, 9).

17. Helen King, 136. King observes that the Anonymous writer of the tenth book of the *History of Animals* notes several times that women emit what he calls seed at the end of erotic dreams (*HA* 634b29–31; 635a34–36).

18. Abū Dā'ūd, *Sunan*, "Kitāb al-ṭahāra," no. 236. See also Bukhārī, *Ṣaḥīḥ*, "Kitāb al-adab," no. 113, "Kitāb al-ḥudūd," no. 830; "Kitāb al-ʿilm," no. 132.

19. See chapter 1, 24, for more information about how God creates all life forms in pairs.

20. *Muwaṭṭa'*, "Kitāb al-ṭahara," 2.21.86.

21. The acceptance of this proposition is quite radical, given the fact that Aristotle, for example, states that "anyone who does not take after his parents

is really in a way a monstrosity, since in these cases Nature has...strayed from the generic type (Margrit Schildrick, *Embodying the Monster: Encounters with the Vulnerable Self* [London/Thousand Oaks: SAGE, 2002], 31, quoting Aristotle, *GA* 4.3.767b).

22. Damīrī, 50, tells a tale where a wife gives birth to a black and white son. He is white from the head to the navel, and black in the rest of the body. A Turk cries out that his own grandfather was like that.

23. Sūra 22:5.

24. Wendy Doniger and Greg Spinner, "Misconceptions: Female Imaginations and Male Fantasies in Parental Imprinting," *Daedalus* 127, no. 1c, Science in Culture (Winter 1998): 99. See also Delaney, "Cutting," 452.

25. Joseph de Somogyi, "Ad-Damiri's Ḥayāt al-ḥayawān: An Arabic Zoological Lexicon," *Osiris* 9 (1950): 33.

26. Damīrī, *Ḥayawān,* 24–28. See also ʿArīb ibn Saʿd, *Kitāb khalq,* 10; Bukhārī, *Ṣaḥīḥ,* "Kitāb al-ṣalāq," no. 225.

27. *The Problemata Physica Attributed to Aristotle, the Arabic Version of Ḥunayn ibn Isḥāq and the Hebrew Version of Moses ibn Tibbon, Aristoteles Semitico-latinus* (ed. L. S. Filius, vol. 11, 1999), 275.

28. Bukhārī, *Ṣaḥīḥ,* "Kitāb tafsīr al-Qurʾān," nos. 269, 271; "Kitāb al-dīyāt," no. 407. See also Bukhārī, *Ṣaḥīḥ,* "Kitāb al-farāʾiḍ," no. 762, where resemblance is determined by an examination of the feet; and "Kitāb al-ḥudūd," nos. 837 and 839: here, resemblance is used to prove illicit sexual intercourse. In an example from Mālik's *Muwaṭṭaʾ,* a "professional" scrutinizer of resemblance could not determine the child's father. ʿUmar let the child decide which of the two possible candidates he wanted to serve as his father (36.21.22). Presumably, that gentleman would have to comply.

29. Ignaz Goldziher, *Muslim Studies,* trans. from the German *Muhammedanische Studien,* by S. Stern (Albany: State University of New York Press, 1973), 271.

30. 703–704. See also Ibn Māja, *Sunan,* no. 2004. Nowhere is the significance of resemblance in determining paternity more clear than in the following *midrashic* example. For example, *Numbers Rabbah* states that one must not suppose the features of the infant will necessarily resemble those of an adulterer; however, if a woman conceives from her husband but has had sex with an adulterer, God will still transform the features of the child into those of the adulterer in order to reveal her transgression (9:1).

31. Sūras 24:4; 24:13. See also Bukhārī, *Ṣaḥīḥ,* "Kitāb al-maghāzī," no. 462.

32. Bukhārī, *Ṣaḥīḥ,* "Kitāb al-ṭibb," no. 715.

33. Damīrī mentions that a man by the name of Zurāra b. ʿAmr al-Nakhāʿī went to the prophet and said to him, "Oh prophet, I had a dream on the road that terrified me." The prophet said, what was it about?" The man replied, "I saw that a she-ass—that I had left with my people—gave birth to a kid of black color tinged with red. I saw them coming out of the earth, which shifted about between myself and my son (whose name is ʿAmr), and they kept on saying, 'Burn, burn, the seeing and blind.'" The prophet asked him, "Have you left among your people a female slave secretly pregnant?" And the man replied, "Yes." The prophet said, "Then she has given birth to a boy who is your son." The man said, "But what about the black color tinged with red?" The prophet

replied, "Come near me." And the man approached him. The prophet said, "Your father was leprous, which you conceal" (*Ḥayawān,* 28–29). Here, one's genetic past can never be hidden.

34. Shildrick, 31. Shildrick notes how Aristotle assumes anyone who does not take after his parents is really a monstrosity, since in these cases nature has strayed from the generic type (*GA* 4.3.767b 1953, 401). She argues that for Aristotle, even the birth of a female is considered a monstrosity, the most common type of deformity (*GA* 728a18737a, 27).

35. Abū Ḥayyān al-Tawḥīdī (d. 1023 CE), *Kitāb al-imtāʿ wa al-muʾānsa,* translated by L. Kopf as *The Zoological Chapter of the Kitāb al-imtāʿ wa al-muʾānsa al-Tawḥīdī (10th century), Osiris* 12 (1956): 408–409.

36. Thomas Laqueur, *Making Sex: Body and Gender from the Greeks to Freud* (Cambridge: Harvard University Press, 1990), 58.

37. Aristotle favored a model of competition between opposing influences, a view that is still, though greatly modified, predominant today (A. H. Sturtevant, *A History of Genetics* [Cold Spring Harbor, NY: Cold Spring Harbor Laboratory Press, 2001], 80). See also Dean-Jones, who notes how Aristotle assumed the two "seeds" from the man and woman would mix together in various combinations to produce either males or females. For example, two strong seeds would generate a male, and two weak seeds would generate a female (167).

38. Franz Rosenthal, "Al-Rāzī on the Hidden Illness," *Science and Medicine in Islam* (Aldershot, Hamps.: Variorum, Great Britain, 1990), 52.

39. Muslim, *Ṣaḥīḥ,* "Kitāb al-ṭahāra," no. 608, where "Umm Sulaym asks about a woman who sees in a dream what a man sees. The prophet says to her, 'In case a woman sees that, she must take a bath.' Umm Sulaym said, 'I was bashful on account of that, and said, 'does it happen?' Upon this the prophet said, 'Yes, otherwise how can a child resemble her? Man's sperm is thick and white and the woman's is thin and yellow, so resemblance comes from the one's whose sperm dominates.'" Suyūṭī (d. 1505 CE) also notes the differences in sperm color and consistency: "Ibn ʿAbbās related the *ḥadīth* that the fluid of a man is white and thick, and that the fluid of a woman is thin and yellow. The family resemblance of a child depends on whichever of these two fluids is more subtle or more fine" (*Ṭibb,* 185).

40. ʿArīb ibn Saʿd, *Kitāb khalq,* 9. See also Ibn Qayyim, *Tibyān*: "If it is the man who overcomes the woman, his water will come before hers and the resemblance will be to him. If she is dominant, the resemblance will be to her" (294). Here, sperm follows the same cultural practices of human sexual intercourse, that is, one party must be dominant, and the other more passive and subordinate, or, the receiver. Bukhārī records the same observation in *Ṣaḥīḥ,* "Kitāb al-anbiyāʾ," no. 546; and "Kitāb al-anṣār," no. 275, which states, "As for the resemblance of the child to its parents, if a man has sexual intercourse with his wife and discharges first, the child will resemble the father, and if the woman discharges first, the child will resemble her."

41. Suyūṭī, *Ṭibb,* 185, states that a man's fluid is hot and strong, thick and white, and a woman's fluid is thinner, weaker, and yellow. Whether the child resembles one parent rather than the other depends on how much fluid is emitted,

which fluid exceeds the other fluid, and whose sexual appetite is stronger. Here, Suyūṭī links sexual desire with the production of greater quantities of sperm.

42. Ibid.

43. See below.

44. Ibn Qutayba, *ʿUyūn al-akhbār,* 75.

45. *Ḥayawān,* 157. See also Bukhārī, *Ṣaḥīḥ,* "Kitāb al-anbiyāʾ," no. 546. Ibn Qayyim notes also that "the man's water (*māʾ*) is white and the woman's water is yellow. If they have sexual intercourse and the man's sperm dominates the woman's, [the offspring] will be a boy. And if the woman's dominates the man's, [the offspring] will be a girl" (*Tibyān,* 293). Ibn Qayyim, like Damīrī, also points out that ultimately God is in charge of forming the sex of the child, despite such deterministic explanations. This view of God's role in the process reflects several Qurʾānic statements that indicate God alone knows the sex of the child (Sūras 13:8; 31:34). Like Damīrī and Ibn Qayyim, Fakhr al-Dīn al-Rāzī also suggests that if the sperm of the man is the one that transforms, the newborn child will be male, and if the sperm of the woman is the one that is prevalent, the newborn child will be female (*Al-Tafsīr al-kabīr* [Cairo: Al-Maṭbaʿa al-bahīya, n.d.], 53). In the ancient Greek tradition, Democritus of Abdera (d. 370 BCE) noted that sex depended on the parent whose semen it was that predominated (*GA,* 764A 6–24, as noted by Eugene Stock McCartney, "Spontaneous Generation and Kindred Notions in Antiquity," *Transactions and Proceedings of American Philological Association* 51 [1920]: 64).

46. Damīrī, *Ḥayawān,* 157.

47. Bukhārī, *Ṣaḥīḥ,* "Kitāb al-qadar," no. 594, states the sex of the child is determined in the womb. See also Bukhārī, *Ṣaḥīḥ,* "Kitāb al-anbiyāʾ," no. 550, and "Kitāb al-ḥayḍ," no. 15, which also assert gender is inscribed upon the child in the womb.

48. Guy Garcia, *The Decline of Men* (New York: Harper Perennial, 2009), 2; Edwin H. McConkey, *How the Human Genome Works* (Sudbury, MA: Jones and Bartlett, 2004), 39.

49. The Qurʾān, for example, condemns female infanticide in Sūras 16:57–58; 81:8–9, which was a "*jāhilīya*" practice embraced by pagans who turn away from God. Interestingly, it was also a pagan Greek practice (Sarah Pomeroy, *Families in Classical and Hellenistic Greece: Representations and Realities* [Oxford: Clarendon Press, 1997], 217).

50. See Sūra 2:228, where it is mentioned that men are a degree above women. This statement does not make a value judgment about the superiority of man's nature, but rather suggests men have a financial responsibility to support the family. See also 4:34, which is interpreted in similar fashion by Amina Wadud, *Quran and Woman* (Kuala Lumpur: Penerbit Fajar Bakti Sdn. Bhd., 1992), 70.

51. Rabbān al-Ṭabarī, *Firdaws,* 34. See also Hippocrates, 320, for exact same reference. Dean-Jones suggests Hippocrates supports his conclusions in this regard by referring to couples who have produced a child of one sex together who then are capable of producing children of the other sex with other partners (167).

52. *Firdaws,* 34; Hippocrates, 321. Both sources assert this is true because the same man may emit strong or weak sperm.

53 Hippocrates describes seed as containing both a fiery and moist element. When the fiery element predominates the seed is male; when the moist is dominant, a female (Dean-Jones, 168). ʿArīb ibn Saʿd, in reference to Hippocrates, notes, too, that sperm comes from all parts of the body. He adds, however, that God gives it [sperm] the goodness of his creation (*Kitāb khalq,* 9).

54. For a list of Greek references that make this point, see Dean-Jones 16.

55. ʿArīb ibn Saʿd, *Kitāb khalq,* 24.

56. *Firdaws,* 34.

57. ʿArīb ibn Saʿd, *Kitāb khalq,* 30. ʿArīb ibn Saʿd explains the discrepancies between male and female fetal development by citing Galen, who noted in his interpretation of the words of Hippocrates that females have in them a great moisture and their movements are weak, but the male is hotter and stronger so likewise quickens and clarifies its organs more quickly than the female. See also Rabbān al-Ṭabarī, *Firdaws,* 33, who notes it is customary for the woman to expel the lochial blood when carrying a male child before thirty days, of the female after forty days. In his reflections on Aristotle, he also suggests that because the male is generated from optimal heat, males become the quickest in movement and most audible in word (34). Compare his statements with Leviticus 12:5–8, which proposes a woman will be unclean for two weeks after giving birth to a daughter, but only one week after giving birth to a son. The doubling of the period of uncleanness for a female child is repeated in the *Mishnah Niddah* 3:7, which asserts a male fetus is fully formed after forty-one days, a female after eighty-one. Hippocrates's "Nature of the Child" states movement (equated with life) occurs after three months for a boy, but only after four for a girl, because males are stronger than females (King, 134). Aristotle, on the other hand, adopts the position that it takes males forty days to be fully articulated; girls may only be articulated after ninety (Dean-Jones, 210).

58. ʿArīb ibn Saʿd, 31, describes how Hippocrates, in the book of *Epidemics,* asserts quickening is associated with fetal movement, which was thought to occur after the ensoulment of the fetus. Muslim scholars no where suggest females are slower to be ensouled; however that would have to be the logical conclusion one would draw if movement was synonymous with ensoulment. For women, an excess of moisture isn't all bad. ʿArīb ibn Saʿd notes on this same page that a woman's "sluggishness" gives way to a greater ability to bear more children over the years. Men have less endurance; because of their "heat" they burn out more quickly.

59. Ḥunayn ibn Isḥāq, 629.

60. Nancy Tuana, "Aristotle and the Politics of Reproduction," in *Engendering Origins: Critical Feminist Readings of Plato and Aristotle,* ed. Bat-Ami Bar On (Albany: State University of New York Press, 1994), 202.

61. *Muwaṭṭaʾ,* 51.1.4.

62. Hippon (ca. 450 BCE) also said that the compact and strong sperm produced one sex and the more fluid and weaker the other (Censorinus, *De Die Natali,* 6.6.4), as referred to in Eugene S. McCartney, "Sex Determination," 64, n. 11.

63. *Tibyān,* 295. See also Suyūṭī, who cites Muslim, who records "that the main organs have come from the man's fluid and that the flesh comes from the woman's fluid" (*Ṭibb,* 185). The idea that males contribute the form and females matter is also reiterated in Jewish tradition. For example, the *Midrash Tanḥuma* notes how the creation of the embryo is the product of the cooperation between God, man, and woman, and is assisted by an angel called Night. God says to Night that he must know that tonight this man is sowing the creation of man. Man sows white and woman sows red and they mix and a fetus is created according to the will of God. White gives bones (which structure the form), tendons, nails, and the whites of eyes. Red provides skin, flesh, blood, and blacks in eyes. The spirit and soul, along with image and wisdom, are given by God (Baumgarten, *Mothers and Children,* 41).

64. *Kitāb khalq,* 24.

65. *ʿUyūn al-akhbār,* 67.39.34. See also 65.37.23, where Ibn Qutayba quotes ʿUbayd Allāh ibn Ḥasan: "If you desire your wife to give birth to male offspring, make her angry, and then sleep with her." This statement seems to apply the same principle that male offspring may be more easily generated if the woman simply does not exert her own sexual desire during an act of intercourse. Such passivity allows the male sperm to dominate completely the female sperm, and transform it according to its own kind.

66. Eugene S. McCartney ("Sex Determination,") cites several Greek (and Roman) scholars who adhere to the view that different sides of the body determine the sex of the child: Aristotle, *GA* 765A 4–18; Plut., *Mor.* 905E; Censorinus, *De Die Natali,* 6.6.6; Galen 4.174–75; 19.453, and Galen 4.633 (63, n. 4). See also Hippocrates, *Aphorisms,* no. 48, which states a male fetus inclines to the right, a female to the left. Moses Maimonides suggests that if a male's right testicle is larger than his left testicle he will give rise to male offspring; if it is the left, he will give rise to females. The same applies to the breast of a girl at the time of puberty (reference from *Comment. Epidemianum* VI, 4, from *The Medical Aphorisms of Moses Maimonides,* trans. Fred Rosner [Haifa: Maimonides Research Institute, 1989], 386, no. 1).

67. Citing Hippocrates, Galen believed the right side was warmer than the left because of the anatomical reason having to do with the blood vessels that fed them; the left uterus and the left testicle receive less purified blood and are therefore cooler than their counterparts on the right (Joan Cadden, *Meanings of Sex Difference in the Middle Ages* [Cambridge: Cambridge University Press, 1993], 35).

68. For example, the Hippocratic corpus asserts the superiority of right over left (Helen King, 9). The Pythagoreans also linked the male to the right and the good, and the female to the left and bad (Aristotle, *Metaph* 986a23-b5, as cited by Dean-Jones, 44).

69. Aristotle argues that the womb has two chambers, which serve as analogs to the two testicles (King, 34). By way of contrast, Galen argues the womb has one neck but two chambers (King, 35). For a similar map of the womb, see Ibn Qayyim, *Tibyān,* 305; Suyūṭī, *Ṭibb,* 193.

70. Dean-Jones, 167. She notes how Parmenides also associated the female fetus with the left side of the womb (44). McCartney argues that Empedocles

made the same associations, as noted in *GA* p64764A 1–6 ("Sex Determination," 64). McCartney references Empedocles further, who, he argues, suggests that boys are begotten in the warmer part of the womb, and that this is why men are darker, more stalwart and shaggier than women ("Sex Determination," 64, n. 8). He also refers to Galen, 19.453, who says that the warmer semen begets males, the colder, females. See also Censorinus 6.6.7 (64, n. 8). Moses Maimonides (*Medical Aphorisms*, 266, no. 25) notes that male fetuses, in most instances, are conceived by the woman on the right side of the uterus, whereas the female fetus is conceived on the left side. The reverse of this situation happens only exceptionally (*De Locis Affectis*, VI). See also Pliny, *Natural History*, Book 7, no. 37 (*The Elder Pliny on the Human Animal*, trans. Mary Beagon [Oxford: Oxford University Press, 2005]).

71. Rabbān al-Ṭabarī notes how, ideally, "if the seed from the right [testicle] of the man [flows] to the right side of the woman's womb, the child will be a male. If the seed flows from the left [testicle] of the man to the left of the womb, the child will be a female" (*Firdaws*, 35).

72. Ibid. See also Qazwīnī, *ʿAjāʾib al-makhlūqāt*, for the exact same commentary (351). ʿArīb ibn Saʿd modifies this proposal by suggesting if the seed flows from the left side of the man to the right side of the womb, the child would simply be female, for what comes from the male testicles is strong enough to resist the womb's efforts to transform it. However, if the seed expelled from the right testicle falls into the left side of the womb, ʿArīb ibn Saʿd maintains the child produced will still be a soft, docile, feminine male (*Kitāb khalq*, 24). Abū Bakr Muḥammad ibn Zakarīyā al-Rāzī (d. 925 CE) describes "masculine women" as those who may have little menses or none at all, or may occasionally grow beards (*Kitāb al-ḥāwī fī al-ṭibb* [Haydarabad: Osmania Oriental Publications Bureau, 1960], 54).

73. Cadden, 35.

74. Qazwīnī, *ʿAjāʾib al-makhlūqāt*, 350. See also Rāzī, *Kitāb al-ḥāwī*, 54. Dean-Jones notes that in Greek traditions, when a mother produces male seed, and a father produces female seed, a hermaphrodite results (169). Although Islamic law assumes hermaphrodites innately belong to one sexual category or the other, their legal status remains necessarily ambiguous, which places them on the margins of society. In addition, their default status is always that of a female, which positions them as social subordinates to men (Paula Sanders, "Hermaphrodites in Medieval Muslim Law," in *Women and Middle Eastern History*, ed. Nikki Keddie and Beth Baron [New Haven: Yale University Press, 1993], 74–95).

75. For example, in his *Alchemy of Happiness* (trans. Claud Feld [Armonk, NY: M. E. Sharpe, 1991]), Ghazālī lays forth the benefits of marriage and reproduction. Children, for example, may intercede for their parents on Judgment Day (62). Spouses also provide unyielding support and comfort to their partners (63). Wives also take care of the house for their husbands (64).

76. Jāḥiẓ, *"Chance or Creation,"* 72.

77. Ibid., 76. See also Abū Jaʿfar Aḥmad ibn Ibrāhīm ibn Abī Khālid ibn al-Jazzār, *On Sexual Diseases and Their Treatment: A Critical Addition of Zād al-musāfir wa-qūt al-ḥāḍir* [*Provisions for the Traveller and Nourishment for the Sedentary*], Book 6, trans. Gerrit Bos (London and New York: Kegan Paul International,

1997), who states: "The moment someone desires sexual intercourse or conjures it up in one's imagination a flatulence is stirred up and descends from the heart to the penis through connecting veins. Then it enters the hollow nerve of the penis, which consequently is blown up and stands erect. This completes the natural activity for which it was created" (240–41). Notice how the initial "power" for procreation begins with the male and not the female.

78. Jāḥiẓ, *"Chance or Creation,"* 88.

79. Ibid., 72.

80. ʿArīb ibn Saʿd, *Kitāb khalq,* 17. Sexual intercourse in general is considered to be highly beneficial for both the mind and body. Suyūṭī emphasizes this point also (*Ṭibb,* 18).

81. Ghazālī, *Abstinence in Islam,* trans. Caesar D. Farah (Minneapolis: Bibliotheca Islamica, 1992), 95.

82. Suyūṭī, *Ṭibb,* 18.

83. *"Chance or Creation,"* 120.

84. Ibn Jazzār, 239.

85. Ibn Sīnā's *Qānūn,* Book 3, *fann* 20, and *fann* 21, *maqāla* 1, as cited in *Encyclopedia of Women and Islamic Cultures: Family, Body, Sexuality, and Health.*

86. *Etiquette,* 91.

87. Suyūṭī, 18.

88. Ibid.

89. Ibid.

90. Ibn al-Jazzār, 274. See also ʿArīb ibn Saʿd, *Kitāb khalq,* 21. Ann Hanson notes such suffocation is attributed to an inadequate amount of sex, when the womb is empty and light (576).

91. Suyūṭī, *Ṭibb,* 19.

92. There is much debate about this issue in terms of the prophet John, who was rendered a "chaste man" (*ḥaṣūr*). Ṭabarī and others claim his inability to engage in sexual intercourse was due to the fact that "his generative organ was no bigger than this straw" (*Tafsīr* VI, 377–80 [commentary on Sūra 3:39]). Having such a small organ was considered to be a positive benefit come Judgment Day, as it would not lead one astray. Ibn Kathīr, however, disputes this position, as this condition would be a "defect and a blemish unworthy of prophets." John was capable of having sexual relations, but God protected him from committing them. John's condition stands in contrast with that of impotent men (*Tafsīr,* vol. II, 35–36).

93. ʿArīb ibn Saʿd, *Kitāb khalq,* 10.

94. Ibn al-Jazzār, 249.

95. ʿArīb ibn Saʿd, *Kitāb khalq,* 26.

96. Ibid.

97. Ibid., 25. ʿArīb ibn Saʿd also adds that a north wind prevents the heat from spreading and allows for the completion of the maturity of the sperm. Herdsmen employ this knowledge as they stimulate their own flocks to bear sheep.

98. Suyūṭī, *Ṭibb,* 19.

99. Sūra 37:100. There are a few examples outside of the Qur'ān of men praying directly to God to bring forth children. For example, the Shīʿite *Ṭibb*

al-a'imma says for those who lack of children, they should recite 71:1–12 (to ask forgiveness of their Lord), have sex with their wives on the third night, and hopefully they will have a boy (171). The Shī'ite *imāms* also prescribe a number of actions that should accompany one's invocations to God. Imām Ja'far al-Ṣādiq notes that "when she enters her month write for her the *sūrat al-qadr* and protect what is in her belly with this invocation written with musk and saffron. Wash it [the paper on which the invocation had been written) out and make her drink its water and sprinkle her genitals with it. Such actions keep both wife and child from trial, mental disorder [*al-khabl*] and madness" (122). The necessity of reciting "and appointed for you (16:7–9) hearing sight, and hearts..." will lead to the child being born healthy (127).

100. 'Arīb ibn Sa'd, *Kitāb khalq,* 9.

101. Ibid., 11.

102. Ibid., 10, 19. See also Suyūṭī, *Ṭibb,* 186.

103. 'Arīb ibn Sa'd claims that youths tend to bear more males, because of their strength, happiness of soul, and gladness (*Kitāb khalq,* 25).

104. Ibid.

105. 'Arīb ibn Sa'd notes how the elderly tend to produce females (*Kitāb khalq,* 25).

106. Ibid., 24. 'Arīb ibn Sa'd suggests there may be some instances where men may want girls, in particular if they have too many boys already. He also notes that good health before coitus leads to male offspring (ibid., 26).

107. Ibid., 26.

108. See, for example, Ibn al-Jazzār, where he discusses various diseases that harm males: involuntary erections (250); constant excretion of sperm (251); nocturnal emissions (252); ulcers of the penis (254); and tumors of the testicles (255).

109. The discussion of impotence comes up in Muslim commentary on the celibacy of John (b. Zakarīyā). Certainly in prophets impotency may serve as a sign of God's greatness; however, for ordinary men, it is a burden, or even a defect (see above).

110. 'Arīb ibn Sa'd, *Kitāb khalq,* 14–15.

111. Ibid., 15.

112. 243.

113. 177.

114. This tradition is attributed to Imām Ja'far al-Sādiq, 111.

115. *"Chance or Creation,"* 113. Jāḥiẓ also advises, "Consider how a child's body grows in all its members while remaining constant in essence, form, and shape. Even more amazing is the way it develops in the womb, where no eye can see and no hand can reach, yet the baby comes out well shaped and complete with all the components it needs for its welfare: stomach, limbs and body fluids in addition to its truly wisely designed and very finely structured bones, flesh, marrow, muscles, veins and cartilage" (*"Chance or Creation,"* 78).

116. Ibid.

117. 'Arīb ibn Sa'd, noting Hippocrates (*Kitāb khalq,* 19). See also Hippocrates, *Aphorisms,* 5.46. For ancient Greek medical depictions of what type of woman is more likely to conceive, see King, 141, who quotes Hippocrates's

Prorrhetic: "This is how you can tell which women are more likely, and which are less likely to conceive. First their appearance. Small women are more likely to conceive than large, thin more likely than fat, white than red, black than livid, those with prominent veins. You should enquire about her menstrual periods, if they appear every month and if they are sufficiently heavy, a good color and same amount on some days every month. Wombs should be healthy, dry and soft."

118. *Firdaws,* 36. See also ʿArīb ibn Saʿd, *Kitāb khalq,* 20; Hippocrates, *Aphorisms,* 5.62.

119. ʿArīb ibn Saʿd, *Kitāb khalq,* 20. Second-century CE medical writer Soranus of Ephesus suggests women can stop menstruating altogether if they exercise too much (*Gynecology,* translated by Owsei Temkin [Baltimore: Johns Hopkins University Press, 1956], 133).

120. King, 31. Ibn Qutayba notes, "Some of the physicians say: The embryo is nourished by menstrual blood flowing up through the navel cord along with its other food. In their opinion it is for this reason that pregnant women do not menstruate" (*ʿUyūn al-akhbār,* 64).

121. ʿArīb ibn Saʿd, *Kitāb khalq,* 20.

122. Ibid. According to Greek physicians, any kind of affliction having to do with the head, like a nosebleed, can block discharge of menstrual blood. This idea stems from the view that in women's bodies, there is one tube (*hodos*) that connects nostrils and mouth with the vagina. In this light, both ends of the tube have a mouth (*stoma*), so the two become analogous (Catherine Blackledge, *The Story of V: A Natural History of Female Sexuality* [New Brunswick: Rutgers University Press, 2003], 214).

123. ʿArīb ibn Saʿd, *Kitāb khalq,* 20.

124. The Qurʾān forbids intercourse with women who are menstruating (2:222). For the opposite view, see Pliny, *Natural History,* Book 7, no. 67, who states that the easiest conceptions are said to take place when menstruation is starting or finishing.

125. ʿArīb ibn Saʿd, *Kitāb khalq,* 10. The word he uses for putrefaction is *al-fād* (wickedness, depravity), which ascribes a moral element to a defective womb.

126. Ibid., 28. This time was also recommended by the Hippocratics. In the "Nature of the Child," Hippocrates states the most favorable time for conception is just after menstruation, when the womb was empty of blood but remains open to receive semen (Helen King, 135).

127. Suyūṭī, *Ṭibb,* 18. This view of menstrual blood's toxicity is fairly tame when compared with, for example, Pliny's, who suggests that menstrual blood has the power to turn new wine sour, kill crops and bees, cloud mirrors by its very reflection, blunt knife blades, dull the gleam of ivory, and corrode bronze and iron. He notes also how dogs go mad after they have tasted it and their bite is imbued with a deadly poison (*Natural History,* Book 7, no. 64).

128. ʿArīb ibn Saʿd, *Kitāb khalq,* 20.

129. Ghazālī adds that if the husband is diligent in teaching her, she will not have to go out and ask the *ulema* about it (menstruation), which shows further how the regulation of the body is paternal and social (*Etiquette,* 103).

130. Prominent scholars warned against men of having of sexual intercourse with women until they have cleansed and purified themselves (ʿArīb ibn Saʿd, *Kitāb khalq*, 28).

131. Sūra 2:222.

132. Suyūṭī, *Ṭibb*, 193. Suyūṭī suggests there is an angel in the womb who cries out for the male semen: "O Lord, grant just one drop of semen!"

133. Ibid.

134. See Helen King, 28, who notes that the work of pseudo-Aristotle (third century BCE) states the womb breathes in the male semen in much the same way as the mouth and nostrils inhale substance, and the route from the vulva to the inside of the womb is like the path from nostrils to larynx. ʿArīb ibn Saʿd also suggests the womb has a neck analogous to the throat. The womb has a strong, muscular flesh, and it has a mouth that discards menstrual blood from it and receives the sperm and the fetus in it (*Kitāb khalq*, 18).

135. Since women are viewed as being perpetually moist and cold—and thus imperfect—they must try to perfect themselves by becoming more dry and hot. Thus, women perpetually crave heat, which can be procured through sex. Women, therefore, are thought to be in a condition of relentless desire for sex with men (Sara Poor, *Mechthild of Magdeburg and Her Book: Gender and the Making of Textual Authority* [Philadelphia: University of Pennsylvania Press, 2004], 63).

136. Suyūṭī, *Ṭibb*, 193. Clearly, this view is not based on Aristotelian tradition, but on Hippocratic tradition (see below). Aristotle, for example, holds the position that no female among males is receptive to coitus after impregnation except the woman and the mare (*HA* VII, iv. 585a8–23).

137. ʿArīb ibn Saʿd, *Kitāb khalq*, 18. See also Hippocrates, *Aphorisms*, 5.51, which states that during pregnancy the mouth of the womb is closed. See also Ibn Qayyim, *Tibyān*, 304.

138. One of the reasons why Islamic law abhors adultery is to prevent a child whose descent is (literally) "mixed up." The Jerusalem Talmud, by way of contrast, suggests a woman may indeed become impregnated by two men. If a woman has intercourse with a second man within three days of having sex with the first man, the sperm could mix together and produce a child with two fathers (*Yerushalmi Yebamoth* 4; 5c). Rabbān al-Ṭabarī references Aristotle, who said that he knew of a woman who gave birth in seven months and then put out another child after two months. According to Aristotle (as paraphrased by Rabbān al-Ṭabarī), the woman became pregnant again (after the first conception) by another man (35). The issue of whether or not a child could have multiple fathers and therefore be of a "mixed" nature is explored further in the animal world. Damīrī records a number of authoritative statements about the *zarafa*. Some authorities, he notes, explain how beasts and wild animals collect together at the watering hole in the summertime, and that they all have promiscuous sexual intercourse with one another. As a result, some animals conceive, others do not, and sometimes, after several males mount the same female, the seminal fluids become mixed up, and, as a result, females give birth to animals varying in appearance, color, and form. Damīrī goes on to suggest Jāḥiẓ does not accept this explanation for the appearance of the *zarafa*, and argues instead that God creates whatever he pleases. The *zarafa* is a creature onto itself, according to Jāḥiẓ,

because it is able to bring forth one like itself, a fact which has been visually affirmed (Damīrī, *Ḥayawān,* vol. 1, 534). Ibn Qayyim asserts only one man can father a child, and only one mother (based on Shāfiʿī law), as the womb closes itself so as not to add a second water. The womb draws together and embraces the water (*māʾ*); it does not permit the reception of the second water (*Tibyān,* 304).

139. Rabbān al-Ṭabarī, *Firdaws,* 305.

140. Ḥunayn ibn Isḥāq, 517.

141. See chapter 1. Fazlur Rahman notes how "the Qurʾān looks upon the process of the creation of a fetus as a series of genuine transformations or creations, the last being the ensoulment." Resurrection is the same kind of transformation (111).

142. *Ṣaḥīḥ,* "Kitāb al-tawḥīd," no. 546.

143. For example, Bukhārī states, "The Prophet said, 'At every womb God appoints an angel who says, O Lord, a drop of semen, O Lord, a clot, O Lord! a little lump of flesh. Then, if God wishes its creation, the angel asks, will it be a male or a female? A wretched or a blessed? And how much will his provision be? And what will his age be? So it is written in the belly of his mother' " (*Ṣaḥīḥ,* "Kitāb al-ḥayḍ," no. 315). See also Suyūṭī, who suggests destiny cannot be established until the soul is breathed into the form created in the womb (*Ṭibb,* 194).

144. Suyūṭī, *Ṭibb,* 185, 193.

145. Muslim, *Ṣaḥīḥ,* "Kitāb al-qadr," no. 6395. See also no. 6393.

146. Ibid., no. 6423.

147. ʿArīb ibn Saʿd, *Kitāb khalq,* 40.

148. Ibid., 37.

149. Ibid., 40.

150. Of course, the alternative explanation would have to be that God utilizes maternal bodies to carry out his plans to destroy life. However, if this were the case, why would male physicians work so hard to prevent failure from taking place? Perhaps men tried to challenge God, or assert their power over him, by securing the life he destined to fail.

151. Rabbān al-Ṭabarī, *Firdaws,* 39; ʿArīb ibn Saʿd, *Kitāb khalq,* 44.

152. Rabbān al-Ṭabarī, *Firdaws,* 39.

153. Ibid.

154. ʿArīb ibn Saʿd, *Kitāb khalq,* 44. See also Ibn Jazzār, 40.

155. ʿArīb ibn Saʿd, *Kitāb khalq,* 44. See also Hippocrates, *Aphorisms,* 5.34, where it is stated that frequent diarrhea in a pregnant woman renders her liable to a miscarriage.

156. Rabbān al-Ṭabarī, *Firdaws,* 39. In Jewish texts, it is mentioned that a woman miscarried as the result of a barking dog (Elijah Judah Schochet, *Animal Life in Jewish Tradition: Attitudes and Relationships* [Jersey City: Ktav Publishing, 1984], 120). In Pliny, *Natural History,* Book 7, no. 42, we hear how sneezing after intercourse causes a miscarriage, and that the very smell of lamps being put out can also cause an abortion (ibid., no. 43).

157. Ibn al-Jazzār, 286.

158. ʿArīb ibn Saʿd, *Kitāb khalq,* 42. ʿArīb ibn Saʿd remarks how Galen analogized the connection between the fetus and the uterus as that between the fruit and the tree. For in the beginning of its generation the fruit is connected

by means of weak suspensions. It therefore falls off quickly, when a strong wind blows, which moves it violently. But when it grows, the fruit's connection with the tree becomes stronger, and it becomes more unlikely that it will be torn off. When it is fully grown, the fruit falls off without anything disturbing it from the outside. Adhering to this model is, as Galen says, the case of the fetus. For in the beginning, when the seed has fallen into the uterus, its connection with it is weak. When the woman jumps or slips and falls, or she takes a laxative or receives venesection or suffers an excessive evacuation from her bowels, or the blood bursts forth from the neck of the uterus, or the uterus is otherwise moved rather heavily by movements of the body or affectations of the soul, the connection between the fetus and the uterus is quickly severed. See also Ibn al-Jazzār, 285, for similar observations.

159. ʿArīb ibn Saʿd, *Kitāb khalq*, 41.

160. Ibid.

161. Ibid, 40.

162. Rabbān al-Ṭabarī, *Firdaws*, 39. In the medieval Jewish tradition, as a protection against miscarriage, a pregnant woman wore an *eben tekuma*, a preserving stone. Women who already miscarried, those who are pregnant or those who wish to become pregnant also wore them ([*Shabbath* 66b], as referenced by Julius Preuss, *Biblical and Talmudic Medicine*, trans. Fred Rosner (Northvale, NJ: J. Aronson, 1993), 385.

163. Rabbān al-Ṭabarī, *Firdaws*, 36. See also Hippocrates, 322–23; Ḥunayn ibn Isḥāq, 435; Helen King, 35, who cites Aristotle (*GA* 9.67.482).

164. ʿArīb ibn Saʿd, *Kitāb khalq*, 31–32.

165. Ibid., 37.

166. For a discussion on how the transparency of the maternal body serves as a means through which women's reproductive powers are appropriated and reinscribed, see Deborah S. Wilson, "Technologies of Misogyny: The Transparent Maternal Body and Alternate Reproductions in *Frankenstein, Dracula,* and Some Selected Media Discourses," in *Bodily Discursions: Genders, Representations, Technologies*, ed. Deborah S. Wilson and Christine Moneera Laennec (Albany: State University of New York Press, 1997), 106.

167. Anne Marie Balsamo, *Technologies of the Gendered Body: Reading Cyborg Women* (Durham: Duke University Press, 1995), 89.

168. Ibid., 94.

169. Rabbān al-Ṭabarī, *Firdaws*, 36.

170. ʿArīb ibn Saʿd, *Kitāb khalq*, 19.

171. Rabbān al-Ṭabarī, *Firdaws*, 36, states if a woman sleeps on garlic and wakes in the morning to the smell of garlic, she is also pregnant. This tradition is also repeated in Damīrī, *Ḥayawān*, 61. ʿArīb ibn Saʿd also describes how, if a woman sleeps on garlic, and there is found in the morning a smell of garlic in her nose, she is pregnant. This smell would be the results of all the tubes being open during pregnancy (*Kitāb khalq*, 28). Hippocrates takes a similar approach. He notes if a woman has not conceived, and one wishes to determine whether conception is possible, he should wrap her in a cloak and burn incense underneath her. If the odor seems to pass through the body to the nose and mouth, then she is not sterile (*Aphorisms*, 5.59; Helen King, 31).

172. ʿArīb ibn Saʿd, *Kitāb khalq,* 28; King, *Hippocrates' Women,* 33. According to the *Aphorisms,* pregnancy could be ascertained by investigating whether the womb was open or closed—since it was believed to be closed upon conception—by administering hydromel, a mixture of honey and water. If colic followed, the woman was pregnant (5.41).

173. ʿArīb ibn Saʿd, *Kitāb khalq,* 28.

174. Ibid.

175. *Firdaws,* 35. See also Suyūṭī, *Ṭibb,* 195; Rebecca Flemming notes that Hippocrates had observed if a woman is pregnant with a male child, she will have a good complexion; if with a female, a poor complexion ("The Pathology of Pregnancy in Galen's Commentaries on the *Epidemics,*" in *The Unknown Galen,* ed. Vivian Nutton [London: Institute of Classical Studies, 2002], 109). See also Hippocrates, *Aphorisms,* 5.42.

176. *Kitāb khalq,* 24.

177. Ibid. See also Pliny, *Natural History,* Book 7, no. 41.

178. *Nuzhatu al-qulūb,* trans. Lieut-Colonel J. Stephenson as *The Zoological Section of the Nuzhatu-l-qulub* (London: Royal Asiatic Society, 1928), 45.

179. *Kitāb khalq,* 25. See also Suyūṭī, *Ṭibb,* 195.

180. Rabbān al-Ṭabarī, *Firdaws,* 36. See also Suyūṭī, *Ṭibb,* 195.

181. ʿArīb ibn Saʿd, *Kitāb khalq,* 25. He adds that despite all of these external signs, only God can determine the sex of the child.

182. Ibid., 24–25.

183. *Firdaws,* 36. Rabbān al-Ṭabarī notes one can use the same technique to determine if the male seed is corrupt.

184. ʿArīb ibn Saʿd, *Kitāb khalq,* 19.

185. Rabbān al-Ṭabarī, *Firdaws,* 35; ʿArīb ibn Saʿd, *Kitāb khalq,* 44. This phenomenon was also noted by Moses Maimonides (*Medical Aphorisms,* 267, no. 26) who also suggests if a woman is carrying twins and only one of her breasts withers, then just one of her fetuses will be aborted (*De Locis Affectis* VI). Perhaps all three authors are drawing their discussions from Hippocrates, *Aphorisms,* 5.37. In *Aphorisms,* 5.38, it is also determined that if a woman's right breast contracts, the male child will be lost; if the left side contracts, the female will be aborted.

186. ʿArīb ibn Saʿd, *Kitāb khalq,* 44.

187. ʿArīb ibn Saʿd, *Kitāb khalq,* 40, who notes Galen on this issue. See also the Hippocratic *De superfoetatione,* where it is suggested that if a pregnant woman has the desire to eat coal and earth, the child will carry a black mark on its head (cited by Jan Bondeson, *A Cabinet of Medical Curiosities* [Ithaca: Cornell University Press, 1997], 146).

188. Damīrī, *Ḥayawān,* vol. II, 90.

189. Ibid., vol. I, 22.

190. Ibid., 624.

191. Ibid., 609.

192. Ibid., vol. II, 22.

193. Ibid., vol.II, 46–47. He also notes how sows indicate large offspring (vol. I, 435–36).

194. Ibid., vol. I, 572.

195. Ibid., vol. II, 75.

196. The womb's innate transparency coincides neatly with traditional, theological understandings that wombs are inherently connected with kinship. The *ḥadīth,* for example, suggest wombs do not belong to women but are owned by families and the community at large, all of which have a stake in what they produce (Ibn Māja, *Sunan,* vol. 3, no. 892).

197. Muslim, *Ṣaḥīḥ,* "Kitāb al-qadr," no. 6393.

198. *Kitāb khalq,* 32. See also Rabbān al-Ṭabarī, who identifies much greater variability. If the image is completed in thirty-five days, the fetus moves in seventy days, and would be born in two hundred and ten days. If the image is completed in forty-five days and it moves in ninety days, it is born in 270 days. If the image is completed in fifty days, movement will take place in one hundred days and birth will take place in three hundred days (*Firdaws,* 33). See also Preuss, *Biblical and Talmudic Medicine,* where the *Niddah* lists the normal duration of pregnancy as 271–273 days (38a, as cited on page 383).

199. ʿArīb ibn Saʿd, *Kitāb khalq,* 37. Some extreme examples in folk literature defy these assertions. See chapter 5, 189, for examples of superhuman offspring who are noted for spending inordinate lengths of time in the womb.

200. Ibid., 33.

201. For a discussion of this phenomenon in the Greek context, see Dean-Jones, 210. ʿArīb ibn Saʿd notes that Saturn once again governs the eighth-month child. Saturn is cold and dry and rotten, and it will silence the fetus and cause it to become ill and if it is born in this month it will not live (*Kitāb khalq,* 37). Note the connection between the first month and eighth month in terms of danger.

202. ʿArīb ibn Saʿd, 36. Hippocrates identifies the dangerous first and sixth forty-day periods during pregnancy as dangerous (*Women's Life in Greece and Rome: A Source Book in Translation,* ed. Mary R. Leftkowitz and Maureen B. Fant [Baltimore: Johns Hopkins University Press, 2005], 241–42).

203. ʿArīb ibn Saʿd, *Kitāb khalq,* 37, 42. See also Pliny on sneezes that result in miscarriages (*Natural History,* 7.6.42).

204. Rabbān al-Ṭabarī, *Firdaws,* 33–34. Pliny notes children born before the seventh month are never viable (*Natural History,* 7.6.38).

205. ʿArīb ibn Saʿd, *Kitāb khalq,* 36, 37.

206. The idea that a child will not survive if born during the eighth month can be found as late as the nineteenth century in Jewish texts. For example, according to the *Mishna berura,* the child born in the eighth month will most likely not survive. The text instructs it is forbidden to handle such a child upon birth, so as not to desecrate the Sabbath (*Mishnah berurah: The Classic Commentary to Shulchan aruch Orach,* trans. and commentary by Israel Meir [ha-Kohen], Aharon Feldman, and Aviel Orenstein, vol. 3 [Nanuet, NY: Feldheim, 1986], 143).

207. Pliny, *Natural History,* 186. In support of this point, translator and editor Mary Beagon cites Virgil, *Ecl.* 8.75 and Servvius comm. ad loc.; Pliny, *HN* 28.23.

208. Beagon cites the Hippocratic treatise, *On Fleshes* 8 613L (186). Rabbān al-Ṭabarī also confirms the inherent qualities of the number seven (*Firdaws,* 33–34).

209. Here, Beagon cites Hippocrates, *On the Eighth Month Child* (7, 7.446; 10 7.452; 13, 7.458 L), 186.

210. ʿArīb ibn Saʿd, *Kitāb khalq*, 37.

211. Ibn Qutayba, *ʿUyūn al-akhbār*, 66: It is related in a *ḥadīth* that Jesus the son of Mary was born by his mother after eight months of pregnancy, and therefore, no child that is born after eight months will survive. ʿArīb ibn Saʿd confirms this view, suggesting Jesus was born after the eighth month in order for God to grant a sign for his creation. No one after him would be born at this point in a woman's pregnancy and live.

212. L. Stephanie Cobb, *Dying to Be Men: Gender and Language in Early Christian Martyr Texts* (New York: Columbia University Press, 2008), 112–13. Both Felicitas and her child serve as signs of God's protection and favor.

213. Ibn Māja records how being killed in the cause of God is martyrdom, when a pregnant woman dies in childbirth, that too is martyrdom, and dying by drowning or burning or pleurisy is also considered to be martyrdom (*Sunan*, vol. 3, no. 2803).

214. See, for example, Bukhārī, *Ṣaḥīḥ*, "Kitāb al-janāʾiz," nos. 340, 463; Muslim, *Ṣaḥīḥ*, "Kitāb al-birr wa al-ṣila wa al-adāb," no. 6367.

215. Jane Idleman Smith and Yvonne Haddad, *The Islamic Understanding of Death and Resurrection* (Albany: State University of New York Press, 1981), 173. According to Aḥmad ibn Ḥanbal, Muḥammad listed four types of people who would dwell in paradise: the prophet, the martyr, the newborn child, and the newborn girl buried alive (*Musnad*, vol. V, 58). Smith and Haddad (173) note that in paradise there is a tree named blessed (*ṭubba*) which is full of nurture. Every boy who dies while still at the breastfeeding stage will be able to feed from that tree (Suyūṭī, *Bushrá al-kaʾīb bi liqāʾ al-ḥabīb* [al-Zarqā', al-Urdun: Maktabat al-Manār, 1988], 75–76).

216. Gerrit Bos observes that the majority of Muslim scholars would have prohibited a male physician from looking upon a woman's private parts, which, for him, explains why Arab physicians did not perform well in the field of women's diseases. However, he does provide some notable exceptions to the rule, including al-Zahrāwī, who designed a number of vaginal specula. He also declares the Ḥanbalis permitted physicians access to women's bodies (Introduction to *Ibn al-Jazzār on Sexual Diseases and Their Treatment*, 51).

217. ʿArīb ibn Saʿd, *Kitāb khalq*, 47.

218. Ibid., 48.

219. Ibid., *Kitāb khalq*, 50.

220. Ibid., 50. ʿArīb ibn Saʿd notes that the Arabs say that if the hand of the fetus comes out from the womb before the body itself emerges, the child will be a notable figure. However, if something like the legs come out before its belly, the child will be an orphan. Clearly, this statement suggests a mother will most likely die if the child is breech or has difficulty exiting the womb.

221. Ibid., 48.

222. Ibid., 47–48.

223. ʿArīb ibn Saʿd, *Kitāb khalq*, 46.

224. See chapter 4.

225. ʿArīb ibn Saʿd, *Kitāb khalq,* 46.

226. Rabbān al-Ṭabarī, *Firdaws,* 33. See also Preuss, *Biblical and Talmudic Medicine,* 396, which describes the medieval Jewish belief that if the child lies face downward coming out it is a boy, face upward, a girl. See also ʿArīb ibn Saʿd, *Kitāb khalq,* 29, which asserts the face of the male will lie next to the back of the woman and the face of the female lies toward the diaphragm.

227. In general, when babies enter the pelvis before birth, they should be face down for an easy delivery. The back of the head, which has the smallest diameter, should lead the way. If a larger diameter of the head may not be well accommodated by the pelvis, this would make for a more difficult birth (Roger W. Harms, *Mayo Clinic Guide to a Healthy Pregnancy* [New York: Harper Paperbacks, 2004], 189).

228. See Flemming, "Pathology," 107, for a discussion of this phenomenon in the Greek context.

229. In Sūra 19:24–26, God comforts Mary with water, fresh dates, and the shade of a palm tree.

230. ʿArīb ibn Saʿd, *Kitāb khalq,* 55.

231. 465.

Chapter 3. Paradigms of the Good Mother

1. The *isrāʾīlīyāt* refer to biblical lore, both Jewish and Christian. This genre of literature includes rabbinic material, Jewish traditions, and canonical and noncanonical gospel references.

2. Ghazālī, *Etiquette,* 90–91.

3. See, for example, Ibn Kathīr, *Qiṣaṣ,* 579; Qurṭubī, *Jāmiʿ li aḥkām,* vol. IV, 82–84.

4. Aḥmad ibn Ḥanbal mentions Mary alone as being "best among women" in *Musnad,* vol. 3, 135. See also Sulaymān ibn Dāwūd al-Ṭayālisī, *Musnad* (Ḥaydarābād, 1903), no. 504; Qurṭubī, *Jāmiʿ li aḥkām,* IV, 82–84. Aḥmad ibn Ḥanbal also refers to Mary as being the head of the women of paradise (vol. 3, 64; 80). Ibn Kathīr suggests Mary was the best of all pious women of all times. To support his position, he quotes a *ḥadīth* from al-Tirmidhī that the best women of the world are four: Mary, Āsiya, the wife of Pharaoh, Khadīja bint Khūwaylid, and Fāṭima bint Muḥammad (*Qiṣaṣ,* 576).

5. Bukhārī notes that only Mary and Āsiya, wife of Pharaoh, attained perfection (*Ṣaḥīḥ,* "Kitāb al-ghusl," nos. 113; 166).

6. Ibn Ḥanbal notes how Khadīja is among the best of all women (*Musnad,* vol. 1, 84; 116; 132; 143). Ibn Kathīr mentions Khadīja along with Mary and Āsiya (*Qiṣaṣ,* 579). Ṭabarī identifies both Mary and Khadīja, and then, in another tradition, Mary, Āsiya, Khadīja, and Fāṭima (*Tafsīr,* vol. VI, 393–98).

7. Bukhārī suggests Fāṭima to be the mistress of all the women of paradise ("Kitāb faḍāʾil al-ṣaḥāba," no. 819).

8. Kisāʾī, *Qiṣaṣ,* 213.

9. *Qiṣaṣ,* 579–81. After all, Mary brought up Jesus and Āsiya looked after Moses.

10. The fact that she was a good fifteen years older than the prophet reinforces her maternal role toward him.

11. Kisāʾī, *Qiṣaṣ,* 579–81.

12. Sūra 108:3.

13. Although many traditional scholars suggest Mary is the best among women of her own time, both Rāzī and Qurṭubī surmise Mary is the best of all women in an absolute sense. (A. J. Wensinck and Penelope Johnstone, "Mary," in *The Encyclopedia of Islam,* 2d ed., ed. H. A. R. Gibb et al., 12 vols. [Leiden: Brill, 1986–2004]).

14. For Qurʾānic examples of Mary's purity, see Sūras 3:33, 19:21, 21:91.

15. For a depiction of Mary's pain in bearing Jesus, see Sūra 19:23.

16. Sūra 19:23.

17. Sūra 19:24–25. Michael Sells suggests Mary was instructed, in prophet-like fashion, to command the date tree to bend over, so that she may reach its fruits (129). Such an image stands in direct dialog with the *Pseudo-Matthew* (chapter 20) where Mary, while resting under a palm tree, desired some fruit to satisfy her hunger. Joseph could not reach it, but the child Jesus commanded the tree to bend over so that Mary could pluck some dates (James E. Bowley, *Living Traditions of the Bible: Scripture in Jewish, Christian, and Muslim practice* [Chalice Press, 1999], 91). The Qurʾān's insistence on Mary's ability to command the tree attests to her elevated status, and also, perhaps, supports the view that Jesus is not God.

18. *Encyclopedia of Islam,* 2d, s. v. "Mary."

19. Ibn Kathīr, *Qiṣaṣ,* 600. Scholars for the most part believed Mary's physical nature was that of an ordinary woman (Ṭabarī, *Tafsīr,* vol. VI, 400).

20. Jane Dammen McAuliffe, "Mary and Fāṭima in Qurʾānic Exegesis," in *Islamochristiana* 7 (1981): 21. McAuliffe references Rāzī, where he connects Mary's divine selection to her mother's prenatal dedication of her to God's service (*Tafsīr al-kabīr* [Cairo, n.d., al-Maṭbaʿa al-bahīya al-misrīya], vol. 8, 45). He insists that Mary's being the recipient of the angels' announcement in no way implies that she is a prophet (which is only reserved for men). Thus, the divine favor of sending Gabriel must be attributed to Jesus or Zakarīyā and only secondarily to Mary.

21. Ṭabarī, *Tafsīr,* vol. VI, 22.

22. Ibn Kathīr, *Qiṣaṣ,* 585.

23. Ibn Kathīr reports that many people accused Zakarīyā of having sex with Mary, and they set forth to kill him. Others accused her of having sexual intercourse with Joseph (*Qiṣaṣ,* 590). Jesus clears his mother of all such accusations (ibid., 591).

24. Ṭabarī, *Tafsīr,* vol. VI, 326–27, as cited by Ayoub, *The Qurʾān and Its Interpreters,* 86.

25. Ibn ʿArabī, *Tafsir al-Qurʾān,* vol. I, 180. In these examples, there is no evidence of God blowing the spirit directly into the *farūj* of any of the other women of ʿImrān.

26. Sūra 32:7.

27. The Qurʾān seems to affirm Mary's virginity and virtue, but repudiates the doctrine of the "immaculate conception" as it is understood in Catholic

terms, which frames the issue in light of Mary's preservation from "original sin" at the moment of her animation (Cleo McNelly Kearns, *The Virgin Mary, Monotheism, and Sacrifice* [Cambridge: Cambridge University Press, 2008], 254).

28. Kisāʾī, *Qiṣaṣ,* 327. Amran and Anna (or Ḥanna?) are her parents. Kisāʾī reports that one day, while Amram's wife was sitting in the house, she saw a dove brooding over her young. Anna wept and said to her husband to pray to God to bless them with a child. Rise up, he said, perform ablutions and pray, we will ask our lord. When they prayed they fell asleep. Amran dreamed of someone saying to him, O Amran, God has answered your prayer. Rise up and lie with your wife, and she will conceive. He did and she did.

29. Ṭabarī, *Tafsīr,* vol. VI, 329–30. Kisāʾī, *Qiṣaṣ,* 327. Ibn Kathīr summarizes the following tale: Ḥanna says to her husband, if we are blessed with a male child, I shall consecrate him to the temple. Her husband replies that what she is carrying in her womb is female. Ḥanna states that since she has dedicated what is in her womb to the Lord's service, he must accept the offering from her, even if the child is female (Sūra 3.35). When her time came, indeed, she gave birth to a girl and named her Mary (Ibn Kathīr, *Qiṣaṣ,* 571).

30. 1 Samuel 2:1–10.

31. Ḥanna is the only woman to utter prayers directly to God in the Hebrew Bible. Notable, also, is the fact that Ḥanna is one of several women in the Hebrew Bible who have the authority to name their children. In each case, the child receiving the name thereby comes under the influence of the one who does the naming (Lilian R. Klein, "Hannah: Marginalized Victim and Social Redeemer," in *A Feminist Companion to Samuel and Kings, Volume 5,* ed. Athalya Brenner [London: Sheffield Academic Press, 1994], 98). Interestingly, Zamakhsharī notes that ʿImrān's wife (like the biblical Ḥanna) is the one who names her daughter Mary (*Kashshāf,* vol. 1, 355–57).

32. For example, see Sūra 3:6.

33. *Khashshāf,* vol. 1, 355–57.

34. Ṭabarī, *Tafsīr,* vol. VI, 334.

35. Rāzī, *Al-Tafsīr al-kabīr,* vol. VIII, 26–29, as cited by Ayoub, *The House of ʿImrān,* 96.

36. Carl Ernst, *Following Muḥammad: Rethinking Islam in the Contemporary World* (Chapel Hill: University of North Carolina Press, 2004), 91.

37. See, for example, Ṭabarī, *Tafsīr,* vol. VI, 336–41, who links God's protection of Mary from Satan with her mother's plea for God to protect her daughter and her offspring from the devil.

38. Ibid. See also Ibn Kathīr, *Tafsīr al-Qurʾān,* vol. II, 30–31; Qurṭubī, *Jāmiʿ li-aḥkām,* vol. IV, 65–67. The exceptionality of Mary is underscored by Bukhārī, who records Muḥammad as saying that Satan touches all the offspring of Adam. The pain of Satan's touch explains why a child cries loudly at the time of birth (*Ṣaḥīḥ,* "Kitāb al-anbiyāʾ," no. 641).

39. Rāzī explains how paradisiacal angels gave Mary the essential sustenance she required. As a result of their nurturing, she did not nurse at her mother's breast even for a day, and she, too, like Jesus, spoke in infancy (*Tafsīr al-kabīr,* 102, as cited by McAuliffe, 25).

40. Rāzī, *Tafsīr al-kabīr,* 102, as cited by McAuliffe, 25. Damīrī lists the names of four extraordinary individuals who spoke from their cradles: The

friend of Jarīj, who talked of his innocence of the charge of adulterer; the witness of Joseph, who talked of his innocence to Zulaykha; the son of the woman attending Pharaoh's daughter, who warned against infidelity; and Jesus son of Mary, who talked of his mother's innocence (*Ḥayawān*, vol. 1, 79). In each case, it appears the need to speak from the cradle stems from a desire to remove all accusations of adultery from a given victim.

41. Qurṭubī, *Jāmiʿ li-aḥkām*, vol. IV, 69–71; Zamakhsharī, *Kashshāf*, 357–58; Ayoub, *The House of ʿImrān*, 100–102.

42. Ibn Kathīr notes how God causes Mary to flower into a beautiful girl; God always provided for her by giving her winter produce in summer and summer produce in winter (*Qiṣaṣ*, 574; 584).

43. Damīrī, *Ḥayawān*, vol. 1, 268. He adds that upon consuming the insects, she cries, "Oh God, make them live without having to suck milk, and make them follow one another without the aid of a voice."

44. Qurṭubī quotes traditions that reveal how Mary was exempt from the menstrual impurities endured by all women (*Jāmiʿ li-aḥkām*, vol. IV, 69–71). Some interpreters have recorded traditions that state Mary's purity would also have included chastity as well as freedom from bleeding (Rāzī, *Tafsīr al-kabīr*, vol. VIII, 46; ʿAbdallāh ibn Umar al-Bayḍawī [d. 1286 CE], *Anwār al-tanzīl wa asrār al-taʾwīl* [Istanbul: s.n., 1911], vol. I, 155; McAuliffe, 22). Mary's choosing and purification, according to Rāzī, reflect both a spiritual purification and the purification from menstruation or from being with men (*Tafsīr al-kabīr*, vol. VII, 46).

45. Ghazālī, *Etiquette*, 107. This tradition appears to be quite common in antiquity and in medieval times. For example, Pliny the Elder noted that children conceived during menstruation would be born stillborn or flawed (*Natural History*, 7.15, 87). Also, according to the Pseudo-Albert, in his *De Secretis Mulierum*, children conceived by a menstruating woman were likely to have epilepsy or leprosy (Karen Cherewatuk, *Marriage, Adultery, and Inheritance in Malory's Morte Darthur* [Suffolk and Rochester, NY: Boydell and Brewer, 2006], 38).

46. Traditions on the forty days of isolation that Mary is said to have observed after the delivery of her child until she was healed of childbirth further indicate to many interpreters that Jesus's birth was, at least in its physical manifestation, an ordinary event (Zamakhsharī, *Kashshāf*, vol. III, 21; Ibn Kathīr, *Qiṣaṣ*, vol. II, 393). Kisāʾī notes that when Mary begins to menstruate, she says, "I have seen a horrible thing." Right after she is done menstruating, she returns to the temple and there is visited upon by Gabriel (*Qiṣaṣ*, 328). Note that she is visited by the angel at a time that would have been the optimal moment for conception.

47. Ṭabarī, *Tafsīr*, vol. VI, 393–98; Ayoub, *The House of ʿImrān*, 122–23; McAuliffe, "Mary and Fāṭima in Qurʾānic exegesis," 20. Ṭabarī suggests it is not Mary's body that is purified but her religion that is cleansed of the doubts and defects of normal female religious behavior. On the point of God's choosing Mary over the women of mankind, Ṭabarī opts for a chronological distinction. The choice is not, in his view, over the women of all time but only over the women of Mary's own time (*Ṭafsīr*, vol. III, 262).

48. Even Zakarīyā asked for a sign when he received glad tidings (Sūra 19:7–10).

49. Qurṭubī, *Jāmiʿ li-aḥkām*, vol. IV, 82–84.

50. McAuliffe cites Zamakhsharī as saying, in his *Kashshāf,* that "truly God chose you" means God chose you "at the time when he received you from your mother and nourished you and selected you for an exalted mark of esteem" (21). She notes also, on that same page, how commentators remark on the verbs *iṣṭafā* (chosen) and *ṭahara* to mean that Maryam was miraculously preserved from all bodily impurity and from spiritual failings.

51. Even though the Qur'ān mentions that God elected and purified Mary, it still commands her to be obedient, which suggests she had the option to do otherwise. See for example Sūra 3:37–38: "The angels said, O Mary, verily God has elected you and purified you and elected you above the woman of all created beings. O Mary, be obedient to your Lord and prostrate yourself and bow down with those who bow down." McAuliffe notes the Shī'ite Abū al-Futūḥ Rāzī (d. 1131) as saying Mary is chosen because of her consecration to God's service; she is physically purified from the blood of menstruation and parturition and from all male contact, and her preference over the women of mankind refers just to her time period (*Tafsīr Rawḍ al-Jinān wa rūḥ al-Janān* [Tehran: Kitābfurūshī-ye-Islāmīya, AH 1382, vol. 3, 36], as cited in "Mary and Fāṭima," 23).

52. McAuliffe, "Mary and Fāṭima," 23.

53. One might think that the Mu'taziles like Zamakhsharī would emphasize Mary's own willingness to accept the challenges placed upon her.

54. Zamakhsharī, III, 362. Ṭabarī suggests again the importance of Jesus being born without a father, and states that the fact Jesus is the son of his mother Mary negates what Christians have said about him being the son of God (Ṭabarī, *Tafsīr,* vol. VI, 412–13; Ayoub, *The House of 'Imrān,* 131–32). Rāzī adds that God granted her Jesus without a father (*Tafsīr al-kabīr,* vol. VIII, 45–46). Most commentators agree the fact that Mary conceived Jesus without a father was a kind of divine favor, or miracle. See, for example, Qurṭubī, *Jāmi' li aḥkām al-Qur'ān,* vol. IV, 63–64; Qummī, *Tafsīr kanz,* vol. I, 102; Zamakhsharī, *Kashshāf,* vol. I, 361–62. Jāḥiẓ states that God created a child out of a woman, without the intervention of any man, but he has never created a child out of a man without a woman. Thus, it is especially to woman and not to man that he vouchsafed this wonderful sign, this signal token, when he created the messiah in Mary's bosom, without a man (Charles Pellat, *The Life and Works of al-Jāḥiẓ: Translations of Selected Texts* [London: Routledge and Kegan Paul, 1969], 257). Kisā'ī records that when Joseph learns of her pregnancy, he asks, Mary, does anything grow without seed? She says no. He says, can there be a child without a father? And she says yes, that Adam was without father or mother. She goes on to tell him the child she is carrying is a gift from God. He is just like Adam, whom God shaped from dust and to whom God said "Be!" and he was. God caused Jesus to speak from his mother's womb and say, O Joseph, what are these words that you speak? (*Qiṣaṣ,* 328–29). Ibn Isḥāq relays how, if they say, Jesus was created without a male, tell them [God] created Adam from earth by that same power without a male or a female. And [Adam] was as Jesus was: flesh and blood and hair and skin. The creation of Jesus without a male is no more wonderful than this (*Sīrat rasūl Allāh,* 226–27). It is interesting that the flesh, blood, hair, and skin are normally formed by the substance that is in the mother's womb.

55. Ṭabarī, *Tafsīr,* vol. VI, 412–13.

56. Ibn Kathīr, *Qiṣaṣ,* 575.

57. See chapter 1.

58. In Jerusalem, in Ḥammām Sittī Maryam near St. Stephen's gate, where it was believed Mary once bathed, the place would be visited by women seeking a cure for barrenness (R. Kriss and H. Kriss-Heinrich, *Volksglaube im Bereich des Islam,* vol. I [Wiesbaden: O. Harrassowitz, 1960], 169; T. Canaan "Mohammedan Saints and Sanctuaries in Palestine," *Journal of the Palestine Oriental Society* iv, no. 1–2 [1924]: 1–84).

59. Kisā'ī, *Qiṣaṣ,* 328, following Sūra 19:16ff.

60. *Kashshāf,* vol. I, 359.

61. Kisā'ī declares that when Zakarīyā finds out these fruits were given to Mary by God, he raised his hands to heaven and said, "Lord, give me a good offspring from you" (3:38). Mary then offered him a stalk of grapes and some dates and some figs (which are well-known fertility drugs), which he ate" (*Qiṣaṣ,* 328). Gabriel descends upon him and said, after Zakarīyā presumably consumed the fruits, that God has answered his prayer.

62. Barbara Freyer Stowasser, *Women in the Qur'an, Traditions, and Interpretation* (London, New York: Oxford University Press, 1996), 161, note 71.

63. According to Kisā'ī, Jesus's attendance at a difficult birth was one of his many miracles. Jesus heard that the wife of the king was having great difficulty in giving birth, as half of the child had emerged and half remained, so he told the people to inform the king that he would place his hand on her womb, and she would expel the child in haste. The people went to the king, and the king wanted to see Jesus. Jesus told him his wife's womb was carrying a beautiful boy. One of his ears was longer than the other, and his chest bore a black mole. On his stomach was a white birthmark. Jesus placed his right hand on the woman's abdomen and said, Come forth! And she gave birth to a boy of the exact description Jesus had provided (*Qiṣaṣ,* 331).

64. Kisā'ī, *Qiṣaṣ,* 334.

65. Ghazālī, *Etiquette,* 48.

66. The Qur'ān never explicitly references Egypt, or any other biblical location, for that matter. Historical and geographical details, especially those associated with the biblical covenant, are absent.

67. Sūra 28:8.

68. Like Mary, Āsiya, too, is perhaps referred to as a prophet by Andalusian scholar Ibn 'Arabī (Murata, 345 no. 28).

69. Kisā'ī, *Qiṣaṣ,* 217.

70. Ibid., 214.

71. Ibid., 213–14.

72. Qurṭubī references several exceptional individuals who spoke in the cradle: the man who witnessed the innocence of Joseph son of Jacob; the infant of the chambermaid of Pharaoh's wife; John the Baptist, the companion of Jurayj, and the companion of the tyrant. The tradition of the chambermaid finds this young woman refusing to refute the fact the God is God, so the Pharaoh ordered a cauldron be heated, and she be cast into it. She asked him if he would gather her bones and those of her children in one place. He agreed, then had her and

her children thrown into the fire. As a very young child—a nursing infant—was about to be thrown into the fire, he called out to his mother, saying, "Cast yourself mother, and do not hesitate, for we are in the right!" (*Jāmiʿ li-aḥkām,* vol. IV, 91–92).

73. *Qiṣaṣ,* 214.

74. Ibid.

75. Ibn Kathīr, *Qiṣaṣ,* 309. God's ability to cause impotence to protect women close to prophets is also demonstrated in the case of ʿĀʾisha. The young man with whom ʿĀʾisha was wrongfully accused of having an affair with was also found to be impotent in the "affair of the necklace" (*Sīrāt rasūl Allāh,* 499). In similar fashion, the Egyptian Maʾbūr, who used to go visit upon Māriya, the prophet's consort, was claimed to be a eunuch (Ibn Kathīr, *al-Sīra al-nabawīya,* 370).

76. Ibn Kathīr, *Qiṣaṣ,* 309.

77. Ibid., 311; Kisāʾī, *Qiṣaṣ,* 215–16.

78. Ibid.

79. Kisāʾī, *Qiṣaṣ,* 217.

80. Ibid. For similar accounts of Moses refusing to nurse from any other woman aside from his own mother, see Flavius Josephus, *Jewish Antiquities,* trans. Louis H. Heldman, *Loeb Classical Library* (Cambridge: Harvard University Press, 1998), 5.224–28.

81. Ibn Kathīr, *Qiṣaṣ,* 313.

82. Sūra 2:233.

83. Ibn Kathīr, *Qiṣaṣ,* 312.

84. Stowasser notes how both Ibn Kathīr and Kisāʾī link Āsiya with significant Jewish and Christian figures of the past. Kisāʾī connects her with the Christian martyr St. Catherine of Alexandria and also Esther, adversary of Hammān (151, note 15).

85. Kisāʾī, *Qiṣaṣ,* 233.

86. Sūra 28:10.

87. In general, the prophet's wives are mentioned in the context of conduct. For example, the prophet's wives must not display lewdness (Sūra 33:30); and they, unlike other women, must not leave their houses (33:32–33). If men would like to speak to the prophet's wives, they must do so behind a curtain (33:53); in general, they must conduct themselves in a respectful fashion (33:28–29).

88. Muḥammad ibn Saʿd, *Ṭabaqāt al-kabīr, juzʾ 8,* translated as *The Women of Madina* by Aisha Bewley (London: Ta-Ha, 1995), 9.

89. Ibn Isḥāq, *Sirāt rasūl Allāh,* 82–83.

90. M. J. Kister, "The Sons of Khadīja," in *The Life of Muḥammad,* ed. Uri Rubin (Sydney: Ashgate Variorum, 1998), 62.

91. Fatima Mermissi, for example, mentions how Khadīja inherited a great amount of wealth from her late husband (*The Veil and the Male Elite: A Feminist Interpretation of Women's Rights in Islam* [New York: Basic Books, 1992] 27).

92. *Encyclopedia of Islam,* 2d, s.v. "Khadīja," by W. Montgomery Watt.

93. Bukhārī, *Ṣaḥīḥ,* "Kitāb al-anṣār," no. 166, notes how the prophet responds to ʿĀʾisha's jealousies that it was only from Khadīja that he was able to have children.

94. It may be that ʿAbdallāh was another name for al-Qāsim.
95. M. J. Kister, "The Sons of Khadīja," 70.
96. *Encyclopedia of Islam* (2d), s.v. "Khadīja."
97. Ghazālī, *Etiquette,* 114.
98. Muḥammad ibn ʿAbdallāh al-Khaṭīb al-Tabrīzī (ca. 1337 CE), *Mishkāt al-Maṣābīḥ,* trans. James Robson (Lahore: Sh. Muhammad Ashraf, 1981), 659, who records, on the authority of Abū Dāʾūd, Nisāʾī, and Tirmidhī, "marry women who are loving and very prolific; for I shall outnumber this people by you." See also Ghazālī, *Etiquette,* 53.
99. Ghazālī, *Etiquette,* 54.
100. Ibid. Ghazālī asserts that God has preordained a certain number of individuals to populate the world, and it is up to humans to achieve the divine goal.
101. Ibid., 57.
102. Ibid., 121.
103. Abū Jaʿfar Muḥammad ibn Yaʿqūb ibn Isḥāq al-Kulaynī (d. 941 CE), *Furūʾ min al-kāfī* (Qum: Dār al-ḥadīth, 2008), "Kitāb al-ʿaqīqa," no. 10416.
104. Ibid., no. 10413.
105. Ghazālī, *Etiquette,* 58. See also Bukhārī, *Ṣaḥīḥ,* "Kitāb al-ʿilm," no. 101; "Kitāb al-janāʾiz," nos. 340, 643; Muslim, *Ṣaḥīḥ,* "Kitāb al-birr wa al-ṣila wa al-adāb," nos. 6311, 6367; Tirmidhī, *Ṣaḥīḥ,* 8:36, 64; Ṭayālisī, *Musnad,* nos. 508, 562, 2304.
106. Ghazālī, *Etiquette,* 57.
107. M. J. Kister, "*Al-Taḥannath*: An Inquiry into the Meaning of a Term," *Bulletin of the School of Oriental and African Studies* 31, no. 2 (1968): 223.
108. Ibid., 54, 58.
109. Ibid., 58. According to Ibn Māja, even the miscarried fetus (*al-saqṭ*) will drag his mother and father by his umbilical cord to paradise (*Sunan,* nos. 1608, 1609).
110. Ghazālī, *Etiquette,* 59.
111. Ibid, 109.
112. Ghazālī, 109.
113. Stowasser, 122–26.
114. This tradition is recorded by both Ibn ʿAbbās and Ibn ʿAsākir (Ibn Kathīr, *Al-sīra al-nabawīya,* trans. Trevor Le Gassick [Reading, UK: Garnet Pulbishing, 1999], 417). See also Kister, "The Sons of Khadīja," 69.
115. This also connects her to the figures of Abraham's and Zakarīyā's wives, who were well into old age when they bore their sons.
116. Stowasser, 80.
117. Ibn Isḥāq, *Sīrat rasūl Allāh,* 111.
118. Ibid., 107.
119. Fāṭima is also referred to as is "the mistress of all the women of paradise" (D. A. Spellberg, *Politics, Gender, and the Islamic Past: The legacy of ʿĀʾisha bint Abī Bakr* [New York: Columbia University Press, 1996], 159).
120. The following summary of the Sunnī view of Fāṭima comes from *The Encyclopedia of Islam,* s.v., "Fāṭima" by H. Lammens, unless noted otherwise.
121. Ibn Saʿd, 24–25.

122. Sunnīs walk a thin line in terms of their disparagement of ʿAlī. After all, the prophet said, "whoever gives his daughter in marriage to a licentious man has betrayed her womb" (Ghazālī, *Etiquette*, 91). The father of Fāṭima would never be accused of such treachery. In addition, many Sunnī supported the primacy of Fāṭima and ʿAlī over ʿĀʾisha and Abū Bakr (D. A. Spellberg, *Politics, Gender, and the Islamic Past: The Legacy of ʿĀʾisha Bint Abī Bakr* [New York: Columbia University Press, 1994], 34).

123. Gerhard Endress, *An Introduction to Islam* (New York: Columbia University Press, 1988), 151; Annemarie Schimmel, *Islamic Names* (Edinburgh: Edinburgh University Press, 1990), 3.

124. McAuliffe, "Mary and Fāṭima," 20.

125. *The Encyclopedia of Islam*, s.v. "Fāṭima." Ghazālī notes how the prophet emphasized the familial connections between the two: "The prophet asked his daughter Fāṭima, 'What is best for a woman?' She replied, 'That she should see no man, and that no man should see her.' So he hugged her and said they were descendants of one another (Q. 3.33). Thus he was pleased with her answer" (*Etiquette*, 100.) Here, chastity and modesty appear to be prerequisites that bind such familial ties with the prophet.

126. Susan Sered, "Rachel, Mary, and Fatima," *Cultural Anthropology* 6, no. 2 (May 1991): 134. ʿAlī is said to have acted so harshly toward Fāṭima that she complained often to her father about his treatment.

127. Tirmidhī, *Ṣaḥīḥ*, vol. 5, 660; Ibn Ḥanbal, *Musnad*, vol. 1, 62, 82; vol. 3, 3, 64; vol. 5, 391.

128. Aḥmad ibn Muḥammad ibn Ḥajar al-Haythamī, *Ṣawāʿiq al-muḥriqa fī al-radd ʿalá ahl al-bidaʿ wa al-zandaqa* (Riyad: Dār al-waṭan; Beirut: Muʾassasat al-Risāla, 1997), ch. 11, sect. 3, 292.

129. Tirmidhī, *Ṣaḥīḥ*, vol. 5, 699; Ibn Māja, *Sunan*, vol. 1, 52; Ibn Ḥanbal, *Fadāʾil ahl al-bayt min kitāb fadāʾil al-ṣaḥāba* (Tehran: al-Majmaʿ al-ʿĀlamī li al-Taqrīb bayna al-Madhāhib al-Islāmīya, 2004), no. 1350.

130. Ibn Ḥanbal, *Musnad*, vol. 4, 172; "*Fadāʾil al-ṣaḥāba*," no. 1361; Ibn Ḥajar al-Haythamī, *Ṣawāʿiq al-muḥriqa*, ch. 11, sect. 3, 291.

131. Mary F. Thurkill, *Chosen Among Women: Mary and Fatima in Medieval Christianity and Shiʿite Islam* (South Bend: University of Notre Dame Press, 2007), 6, quoting Majlisī, *Biḥār al-anwār* (Tehran: Dār al-kutub al-Islāmīya, 1957–), vol. 43.2, 18.

132. Here, another example of dates serving as fertility drugs.

133. McAuliffe, 26, quotes Safavid theologian Muḥammad Bāqir Majlisī, *Jalāʾ al-ʿuyūn* (Tehran: Kitāb furūshī-ye-Islāmīya, 1348), ch. 3, 126–27.

134. Ibid., 26.

135. Ibid.

136. See Thomas Izbicki, "Doctrine of the Immaculate Conception," in *Women and Gender in Medieval Europe: An Encyclopedia*, ed. Margaret Schaus (New York: Routledge, 2006), who describes the extolling of her purity and excellence in the medieval period, and the claims that she was created in her mother's womb by the Holy Spirit and thus free of original sin.

137. McAuliffe, 23.

138. Mahmoud Ayoub, *Redemptive Suffering in Islām: A Study of the Devotional Aspects of ʿĀshūraʾ in Twelver Shīʿism* (The Hague: Mouton, 1978), 74.

139. Ibid., 71.

140. Ibid., 72.

141. Sered, 138.

142. Ayoub, *Redemptive Suffering,* 71, from Kulaynī, *Kāfī,* vol. 1, 363.

143. Ayoub, *Redemptive Suffering,* 71.

144. Midwives sent from heaven are not an uncommon occurrence. Preuss, *Biblical and Talmudic Medicine,* 404, notes how legend relates that under Egyptian bondage, when the time to deliver the baby was at hand, a woman would go out into the field and deliver that child under an apple tree. God would then send someone, an angel from heaven above, who would cleanse and manipulate the child, in the manner of the midwife (*Sotah* 11b) and who would cut his navel, bathe him, and anoint him (*Ex Rabbah* 23.8), or the mother herself would cut the navel with a sharp stone. In Byzantine art, midwives are often placed among the angels and shepherds who surround and attend Jesus just following his birth (John Beckwith, *Early Christian and Byzantine Art* [New Haven: Yale University Press, 1986], 316; Ormonde Maddock Dalton, *Byzantine Art and Archeology* [Ithaca: Cornell University Library, 2009], 654; Sirarpie Der Nersessian, *Études byzantines et arméniennes: Byzantine and Armenian Studies* [Paris: Impr. orientaliste, 1973], 519.

145. Ayoub, *Redemptive Suffering,* 75.

146. Muḥammad ibn ʿAlī ibn Bābawayh al-Qummī (d. 939 CE), *ʿUyunu akhbarī al-riḍā,* vol. 1 (Najaf: Haydariyyah Press, 1970), 169.

147. Ayoub, *Redemptive Suffering,* 75.

148. Ibid.

149. McAuliffe, "Mary and Fāṭima," 23, who cites the Shīʿite Abū al-Futūḥ Rāzī, *Tafsīr Rawḍ al-Jinān wa rūḥ al-Janān* (Tehran: Kitābfurūshī-ye-Islāmīya, AH 1382), vol. 3, 36.

150. See, for example, Ibn Kathīr, *Qiṣaṣ,* 579; Qurṭubī, *Jāmiʿ li-aḥkam,* vol. IV, 82–84; Ibn Māja, *Sunan,* nos. 3280, 3281, which report the prophet as saying, "Many men have attained perfection but no women have attained perfection except Maryam bint ʿImrān and Āsiya, wife of Pharaoh. And the superiority of ʿĀʾisha is like the superiority of *tharīd* over other foods."

151. Bukhārī, *Ṣaḥīḥ,* "Kitāb al-nikāḥ," no. 14, where ʿĀʾisha mentions she is the only virgin (*bikr*) the prophet married.

152. *Mishkāt al-Maṣābīḥ,* 659; Ibn Māja, *Sunan,* no. 1861.

153. This implies, of course, that the first husband will still be attached to his first wife. Ghazālī, *Etiquette,* 90.

154. Sūra 33:6.

155. For an exhaustive study of this term, see David Powers, *Muḥammad Is Not the Father of Any of Your Men.*

156. Ghazālī, *Etiquette,* 90, 57.

157. Ibid., 57.

158. Ibid.

159. Sharon N. Covington and Linda Hammer Burns, *Infertility Counseling: A Comprehensive Handbook for Clinicians* (Cambridge: Cambridge University

Press, 2006), 412; Marcia C. Inhorn, "'The Worms are Weak': Male Infertility and Patriarchal Paradoxes in Egypt," in *Islamic Masculinities*, ed. Lahoucine Ouzgane (London: Zed Books, 2006), 232.

160. Jāḥiẓ, *"Chance or Creation,"* 120.

161. According to Islamic law, those heirs mentioned in the Qur'ān (*aṣḥāb al-furūḍ*) are guaranteed an assured share of the inheritance. These would include the husband, wife, father, mother, sons, daughters, paternal grandfather, maternal grandmother, son's daughter, full sister, consanguine sister, and uterine brother and uterine sister. Offspring rank the highest among the relatives listed (Stephen P. Heyneman, *Islam and Social Policy* [Nashville: Vanderbilt University Press, 2004], 64).

162. Ghazālī, *Etiquette*, 100.

163. Nabia Abbott, *Aishah, the Beloved of Muḥammad* (Chicago: University of Chicago Press, 1942), 48; Ibn Ḥanbal, *Musnad*, vol. VI, 117f and 154.

164. Bukhārī, *Ṣaḥīḥ*, "Kitāb al-anṣār," nos. 164, 165, 168.

165. Sūra 66:5 states, "It may be, if he divorced you two, that God will give him in exchange consorts better than you, who submit (their wills), who believe, who are devout, who turn to God in repentance, who worship, who travel and fast, previously married or virgins."

166. *"Chance or Creation,"* 118.

167. Ghazālī, *Etiquette*, 99.

168. Bukhārī, *Ṣaḥīḥ*, "Kitāb al-ḥayḍ," no. 296; "Kitāb al-tawḥīd," no. 639.

169. In general, the *ʿaqīqa* ceremony involves the sacrificial slaughtering of animals, the shaving of the head, and the bestowing of the name on a child on the seventh day of life.

Chapter 4. Postpartum

1. Baumgarten, 112, argues that the postpartum process is, for women, a reversal of the social order. It is a time enveloped by female friends during which women celebrate their identities. See also Natalie Zemon Davis, *Society and Culture in Early Modern France* (Stanford: Stanford University Press, 1975), 124–51; Adrian Wilson, "Ceremony of Childbirth and Its Interpretation," in *Women as Mothers in Pre-Industrial England, Essays in Memory of Dorothy McLaren*, ed. Valerie Fildes (London and New York: Routledge, 1990), 88–93.

2. For an in-depth discussion of the concept of *milk* ownership and the analogous relationship between husbands and wives, as well as masters and slaves, see Kecia Ali, *Marriage and Slavery in Early Islam* (Cambridge: Harvard University Press, 2010), 181.

3. See, for example, Caroline Squire, *The Social Context of Birth* (Oxford: Radcliffe Publishing, 2009), 10–11, who notes how feminist theory is more often than not used to trace the origins of women's subordination; Heidi Tinsman, *Partners in Conflict: The Politics of Gender, Sexuality, and Labor in the Chilean Agrarian Reform, 1950–1973* (Durham: Duke University Press, 2002), 12; Saba Mahmood, "Feminist Theory," 205.

4. Mahmood, "Feminist Theory," 205–206.

5. Ibid., 206; *The Politics of Piety,* 6; Lisa I. Knight, *Contradictory Lives: Baul Women in India and Bangladesh* (Oxford: Oxford University Press, 2011), 182. See also Tinsman, who explains that patriarchy can no longer be understood as a "master grid," but as "a multiplicity of arrangements derived from broad principles legitimating men's authority over women" (12–13). Patriarchy must be understood as a more fluid and dynamic concept, and relations between men and women undergo continuous negotiation and change.

6. See Chodorow, 5–7.

7. Mahmood, "Feminist theory," 203.

8. Ibid., 206.

9. Ibid., 210.

10. Here, liberalism can be understood as a constituted desire for freedom that is supposedly embedded within all human subjects.

11. Judith Butler, "Performative Acts and Gender Constitution: An Essay in Phenomenology and Feminist Theory," in *Performing Feminisms: Feminist Critical Theory and Theatre,* ed. Sue-Ellen Case (Baltimore: Johns Hopkins University Press, 1990), 272.

12. For a slightly different perspective on self formation than that presented by Mahmood, see Lisa Baraitser, *Maternal Encounters: The Ethics of Interruption* (London; New York: Routledge, 2009), 19, who describes "maternal subjectivity" as a useful concept to refer to the ways "fantasy, meaning, biography, and relational dynamics inform how each woman takes up a position in relation to a variety of discourses about mothering."

13. Michel Foucault, *Ethics, Subjectivity, and Truth,* vol. 1. *Essential Works of Foucault, 1954–1984,* ed. Paul Rabinow (New York: The New Press, 1997), 24, as cited by Saba Mahmood, "Feminist Theory," 210.

14. Mahmood distinguishes between Bourdieu's notion of *habitus* and that held by Aristotle. She suggests Bourdieu employs *habitus* as a "theoretical concept to explain how the structural and class positions of individual subjects come to be embodied as dispositions" (Mahmood, *The Politics of Piety,* 136). Bourdieu suggests *habitus* operates on an unconscious level, while Aristotle suggests the act of "coordination" is, in fact, conscious (ibid.). In other words, Bourdieu's model leaves out the essential quality of self-determination (ibid., 138).

15. Mahmood, "Feminist Theory," 215.

16. Ibid. See also her *Politics of Piety,* 136.

17. Ira Lapidus, "Knowledge, Virtue, and Action: The Classical Muslim Conception of Adab and the Nature of Religious Fulfillment in Islam," in *Moral Conduct and Authority,* ed. Barbara Metcalf (Berkeley: University of California Press, 1984), 38–61, cited by Mahmood, "Feminist Theory," 215.

18. Yoram Bilu argues that male initiation ceremonies are corrective mechanisms designed to establish firmly the secondary male identity where the attainment of this identity has been at risk because of the prevalent presence of women in a male child's early life ("From *Milah* [Circumcision] to *Milah* [Word]: Male Identity and Rituals of Childhood in the Jewish Orthodox Community," *Ethos* 31, no. 2 [2003]: 177). Quoting David D. Gilmore (*Manhood in the Making* [New Haven: Yale University Press, 1990], 27), Bilu suggests that boys "must overcome the previous sense of unity with the mother in order to achieve an

independent identity defined by his culture as masculine" (177). Therefore, men, like women, are made, not just born. He bases these observations on the works of Nancy Chodorow (*The Reproduction of Mothering: Psychoanalysis and the Sociology of Gender* [Berkeley: University of California Press, 1978]), Margaret Mahler, Fred Pine, and Anni Bergman (*The Psychological Birth of the Human Infant* [New York: Basic Books, 1975]), and Robert Stoller (*Presentations of Gender* [New Haven: Yale University Press, 1985]).

19. Suad Joseph, in her introduction to the edited volume *Intimate Selving in Arab Families: Gender, Self, and Identity* (Syracuse: Syracuse University Press, 1999), observes how individuals are active participants, "both caused and causative of the relations of inequality in patriarchal systems" (14).

20. Mahmood suggests *habitus* here is acquired through "human industry, assiduous practice and discipline such that it becomes a permanent feature of a person's character (*Politics of Piety*, 136). She argues further that the significance of such humanly generated practice and discipline coincides with the Muslim tradition's emphasis on human action and deliberation (rather than divine grace or will) as essential in the formation of moral conduct (*Politics of Piety*, 138).

21. *Bodily Citations*, 7. Here, the editors discuss Butler's views on how social norms define the realm of viable subjectivity. However, just as such norms demarcate what is intelligible and acceptable, they also determine what lies outside those borders. According to the editors, these outlying areas are called the "abject" by Butler. Those who reside there are given no status in society; however, they are necessary for the legitimation of viable subjectivities.

22. Durrīya al-ʿAyṭah, *Fiqh ʿibādāt ʿalá al-madhhab al-Shāfiʿī* (Damascus: Maktaba Dār Bayān, 1975).

23. Bilu, "Milah," 193.

24. See chapter 3, note 144.

25. Ayoub notes that Safīya, the daughter of ʿAbd al-Muṭṭalib, also served in this capacity (*Redemptive Suffering*, 75).

26. Ibid. See also ʿAlī ibn Ḥasan ibn ʿAsākir, *Tārīkh al-kabīr* (Damascus: Maṭbaʿat Rawḍat al-Shām), 314.

27. For legal opinions on this issue, see Judith Tucker, *Women, Family, and Gender in Islamic Law* (Cambridge: Cambridge University Press, 2008), 142, who cites the Ḥanafī scholar al-Marghinanī's *Al-Hidāya*. For further Ḥanafite support for the testimony of midwives, note Muḥammad ibn Aḥmad Sarakhsī's *Kitāb al-Mabsūṭ*, vol. 30 (Miṣr: Maṭbaʿat al-Saʿadah, 1906–1913), 70. The prominent *ḥadīth* scholar ʿAbd al-Razzāq ibn Hammām al-Ṣanʿānī (d. 827 CE) also reports traditions in support of such findings. See his *al-Muṣannaf*, vol. 8 (Al-Majlis al-ʿilmī, and Beirut: Al-Maktab al-islāmī, 1970), 333, as cited by Avner Giʿladi, "Liminal Craft, Exceptional Law: Some Notes on Midwives in Medieval Islamic Writings," *International Journal of Middle East Studies* 42 (2010): 194.

28. See chapter 2, 78–79.

29. See chapter 2, 77.

30. Noted in Tucker, 183.

31. See Nancy Demand, *Birth, Death, and Motherhood in Classical Greece* (Baltimore: Johns Hopkins University Press, 1994), 65, who cites John Riddle's *Contraception and Abortion from the Ancient World to the Renaissance* (Cambridge:

Harvard University Press, 1992), 81, 91. Riddle suggests evidence for a female medical tradition resides in the fact that the Greek materials are often poorly presented (which is the case in Muslim medical compilations); in addition, midwifery manuals provide compilations of extended lists without commentary, both of which suggest a certain unfamiliarity with the processes. Likewise, Abū Zayd ʿAbd al-Raḥmān ibn Muḥammad ibn Khaldūn (d. 1406 CE), *The Muqaddima: An Introduction to History,* vol. 2, ed. N. J. Dawood; trans. Franz Rosenthal (Princeton: Princeton University Press, 1989), 370, argues that "[m]idwives [are] best acquainted with these sorts of treatment skills. We likewise find them better acquainted than a skillful physician with the means of treating the ills affecting the bodies of little children from the time they are sucklings until they are weaned. This is simply because the human body, at this stage, is only potentially a human body. After [the child] is weaned, [its body] becomes actually a human one. Then, its need for a physician is greater [than its need for a midwife]." Ibn Qutayba, suggests the presence of a tradition of "women's wisdom," even in *jāhilīya* times. He records Muḥammad ibn al-Jahm (ca. ninth c. CE) as saying, "Do not look with contempt on many a cure you see practiced by old women; for a great deal of their knowledge has come down to them from the ancient physicians, such as flies dipped in antimony with which one rubs the eyes, increase the visual power and the sharpness of sight and tighten the pores in which the hair on the edge of the eyelids is fixed" (*ʿUyūn al-akhbār,* 104.79.32).

32. Abū al-Qāsim Khalaf ibn ʿAbbās Zahrāwī (d. 1013 CE), *Kitāb al-taṣrif li man ʿajiza ʿan al-taʾlīf,* translated as *Albucasis on Surgery and Instruments: A Definitive Edition of the Arabic Text with English Translation and Commentary* by M. S. Spink and G. L. Lewis (London: The Wellcome Institute of the History of Medicine, 1972), ch. 75, "On the Training of Midwives." At times throughout the chapter the midwives are addressed directly; at other instances a ubiquitous "you" (in the masculine singular form) is given instruction as to what must be relayed to the midwives.

33. Ibn Khaldūn suggests midwifery as a rule is restricted to women since they, as women, may see the pudenda of other women (*Muqaddima,* vol. 2, 368).

34. Ibn Khaldūn, *Muqqadima,* vol. 2, 368.

35. ʿArīb ibn Saʿd, *Kitāb khalq,* 48.

36. Ibid., 47.

37. *Ṭibb al-aʾimma,* 83.

38. ʿArīb ibn Saʿd, *Kitāb khalq,* 53.

39. Ibid., 48. Further reflecting on the benefit of dates, milk, and almond oil, Muḥammad ibn Abī Bakr ibn Qayyim al-Jawzīya asserts the prophet himself ate dates on a regular basis, and in general they are considered a fruit, a medicine, and drink and a sweetmeat. They also may be used to protect one from harm, poison, or witchcraft (*Medicine of the Prophet,* trans. Penelope Johnstone [Cambridge, UK: The Islamic Texts Society, 1998], 211). See also Bukhārī, *Ṣaḥīḥ,* "Kitāb al-Aṭʿima," 49.

40. ʿArīb ibn Saʿd, *Kitāb khalq,* 49.

41. Ibn Khaldūn *Muqaddima,* vol. 2, 368.

42. ʿArīb ibn Saʿd, *Kitāb khalq,* 46.

43. Ibid.

44. Ibid., 52. See also Ibn Khaldūn, *Muqaddima,* vol. 2, 369.

45. ʿArīb ibn Saʿd, *Kitāb khalq,* 50. He notes that the midwife will not cut the umbilicus if the child requires a lot of pulling and twisting to come out; only if it cries or sneezes or urinates (which means it is actually alive).

46. Ibid., 47.

47. Ibid., 51. The medicinal qualities of the Nile are well known. In his article on *al-Nīl* (*Encyclopedia of Islam*), J. H. Krammers notes a tradition practiced by Christians and Muslims that involved bathing in the Nile on the eve of the Epiphany, in memory of the baptism of Christ (B. T. A. Evetts, *Churches and Monasteries of Egypt and Some Neighboring Countries Attributed to Abu Salih the Armenian* (*Anecdota Oxoniensa,* Semitic Series), 7 [Oxford: The Clarendon Press, 1895], 129); ʿAlī ibn al-Ḥusayn al-Masʿūdī describes this same festival, which he calls *Laylat al-ghifās* (*Murūj al-dhahab wa maʿādin al-jawhar* [al-Qāhira: al-Maṭabʿa al-Azharīya, 1885–87], ii. 364). The water is also known for having medicinal qualities, and *baraka* (blessings).

48. Gall nuts are known to be rich in tannins, which serve to treat ulcerated or inflamed tissues (Samuel Philip Sadtler and Henry Trimble, *A Text Book of Chemistry: Intended for the Use of Pharmaceutical and Medical Students* [Philadelphia: J. B. Lippincott, 1895], 727).

49. Ibn Khaldūn, *Muqaddima,* vol. 2, 369.

50. ʿArīb ibn Saʿd, *Kitāb khalq,* 50. On the practice of putting honey in the newborn infant's mouth, see also Ibn Sīnā, *Qanūn,* vol. 1, 153.

51. ʿArīb ibn Saʿd, *Kitāb khalq,* 50. Ibn Qayyim also notes that honey removes impurities from the veins and the intestines (*Ṭibb,* 23).

52. Sūra 16:69.

53. Ibn Qayyim, *Ṭibb,* 7.

54. ʿArīb ibn Saʿḍ, *Kitāb khalq,* 50.

55. Ibn Qayyim suggests the common view of Muslim physicians is that a wet nurse should be hired for the first two or three days of an infant's life as the milk is thought to be spoiled (*Tuḥfat,* ch. 16). Soranus, *Gynecology,* makes this same point, but suggests breast milk is actually spoiled for the first twenty days (as referred to by Dean-Jones, 222). In medieval Spain, women were instructed not to breastfeed their children during the first eight days, a belief that became detrimental to infants who did not receive the necessary colostrum during their first few days of life (Baumgarten, 120, referencing R. Menaḥem ibn Zeraḥ, *Ẓeida laDerekh* [Warsaw: Bi-defus Ḥ. Ḳelṭer, 1880], Part 1, Rule 3, ch. 14).

56. It is clear that "relactation" is possible in infants under six weeks of age; however, it often requires a concerted effort on the part of the mother to produce a substantial milk supply (Judith Lauwers and Anna Swisher, *Counseling the Nursing Mother* [Sudbury, MA: Jones and Bartlett, 2010], 539).

57. Maya Shatzmiller argues for the wide use of the wet nurse in later medieval times. She identifies it as a legitimate profession for women, along with hairdressing ("Aspects of Women's Participation in the Economic Life of Later Medieval Islam: Occupations and Mentalities," *Arabica* T. 35, Fasc. 1 [March 1998]: 42).

58. Even the scientific community is on board with the sacrosanct nature of maternal bonding. Not only is maternal bonding essential for forming mean-

ingful familial and social relationships, it is said to serve as the foundation for all cognitive, neurobehavioral, and social-emotional relationships. For example, scientists have suggested maternal bonding allows for longer periods of brain development, a precondition for higher intelligence. Science has assigned a biological (specifically, neuroendocrinological) cause for maternal bonding: oxytocin, which is linked with uterine contractions, milk production, and general maternal behavior (Ruth Feldman, Aron Weller, Orna Zagoory-Sharon, and Ari Levine, "Evidence for a Neuroendocrinological Foundation for Human Affiliation: Plasma Oxytocin Levels Across Pregnancy and the PostPartum Period Predict Mother-Infant Bonding," *Psychological Science* 18 no. 11 [November 2007]: 965–66). It is interesting that in modern times, the mother can still be blamed for child deficiencies.

59. Al-Zahrāwī, 468.

60. Ibid., 470.

61. Ibid.

62. Ibid., 472.

63. Ibid., 474.

64. For example, Rabbān al-Ṭabarī mentioned, citing Aristotle, a woman who bore twenty children in the course of four pregnancies; another bore sixty children during the course of thirty-five pregnancies (*Firdaws*, 25).

65. Al-Zahrāwī, 476.

66. Ibid., 478.

67. Ibid.

68. Ibid., 480.

69. See Sūras 3:49 and 32:7–9.

70. Sūra 13:8.

71. Ibn Māja, *Sunan*, nos. 2750 and 2752.

72. Gilʿadi, "Minimal Craft, Exceptional Law," 194.

73. Ibn Māja, *Sunan*, nos. 2750 and 2751. Ibn Māja adds that a child born dead cannot be considered an heir. See also ʿArīb ibn Saʿd, *Kitāb khalq*, 51, who notes: "[T]he Arabs say that the crying of the male child is a sign of his well-being. If he does that he will be a chief. He raises his voice crying and the *ʿahl al-fiqh* say a child is not born an inheritor or has the ability to inherit until he cries."

74. *Mishkāt*, vol. 2, 354; Ibn Māja, *Sunan*, no. 1508.

75. Mālik, *Muwaṭṭaʾ*, 20.76.243. See also Bukhārī, *Ṣaḥīḥ*, "Kitāb al-ṭibb," nos. 654 and 655; Ibn Māja, *Sunan*, no. 2639.

76. Mālik, *Muwaṭṭaʾ*, 43:7.5.

77. Bukhārī, *Ṣaḥiḥ*, "Kitāb al-janāʾiz," no. 440.

78. Ghazālī, *Iḥyāʾ ulūm al-dīn*, vol. 2 (Ḥalab: Dār al-waʿy, 1998), 68–69.

79. Musallam, 57. The 120 days coincide with quickening, that is, when the mother feels the child inside her begin to move. Prior to the onset of ultrasound, if a mother did not feel her child move, it is not surprising she (or those observing her) may have believed the being inside her was not yet a human life.

80. Ibid., 58.

81. Ibid., 57.

82. Mālik, *Muwaṭṭaʾ*, 43.7.6.

83. Ibid., 43.5.

84. At least as far as I have been able to discern; there is no mention of this phenomenon in the material under review.

85. Murata, 44.

86. *Babylonian Talmud, Niddah* 30b; Bilu, "Circumcision," 42–43. This idealized state of existence is short-lived. According to Jewish sources, at the moment of parturition, an angel strikes each newborn male on its upper lip, and the newborn forgets all his prior wisdom. Ibn ʿArabī also suggests infants are no more intelligent than animals upon birth. He adds it is not until they reach puberty that they gain reason, a quality that clearly distinguishes them from animals (Murata, quoting from the *Ikhwān al-ṣafā*ʾ, 44).

87. Sūra 4:1. Summary presented in Abdulaziz Sachedina's *Islamic Biomedical Ethics: Principles and Application* (Oxford: Oxford University Press, 2010), 116. See also Ibn Māja, *Sunan*, no. 1892, where wombs are associated with kinship.

88. Mothers, however, are supposed to care for children, and to love them more than anything: Ibn Māja notes on the authority of Naṣr ibn ʿAlī al-Jahḍamī, ʿAbd al-ʿAlāʾ, Saʿīd, Qatada, and Anas ibn Mālik: "The Prophet said, 'I start prayer and I want to make it long but then I hear an infant crying so I make my prayer short, because I know the distress caused to the mother by his crying' " (*Sunan*, no. 989; see also nos. 990, 991). Interestingly, it is the prophet who empathizes with the distress the mother would feel as she hears her child crying. The prophet in this case, perhaps, takes on a maternal role. Perhaps this maternal role compromises or undermines the strictly paternal authority commanded by the medieval tradition, or, perhaps, it symbolizes the total usurpation of the uniquely maternal role by the male. Another proponent of the natural bond between mother and child is Rāzī. Rāzī, in his commentary on Sūra 2:233, notes that an "infant's need for its mother's attention is stronger than the need for its father. For no mediator whatsoever comes between the infant and its mother's care, whereas the care of its father reaches him through mediation" (as quoted by Avner Giʿladi, *Infants, Parents, and Wetnurses: Medieval Islamic Views on Breastfeeding and Their Social Implications* [Leiden: Brill, 1999], 19).

89. Bukhārī, *Ṣaḥīḥ*, "Kitāb al-buyūʿ," no. 421, "Kitāb istitāba al-murtaddīn wa al-muʿānidīn wa qitālihim," no. 807; "Kitāb al-farāʾiḍ," no. 741, "Kitāb al-aḥkām," no. 293; Muslim, *Ṣāḥīḥ*, "Kitāb al-nikāḥ," nos. 3435, 3436, 3437; Abu Dāʾūd, *Sunan*, "Kitāb al-nikāḥ," nos. 2267, 2268; Aḥmad ibn Ḥanbal, *Musnad*, vol. I, 25, 59, 65; Ṭayālisī, *Musnad*, nos. 86, 1127, 1444. Patricia Crone, in *Roman, Provincial and Islamic Law: The Origins of the Islamic Patronate*, discusses how the Arab maxim *al-walad li al-firāsh* is the Islamic version of the Roman principle *pater est quem (iustae) nupiae demonstrant* (Cambridge: Cambridge University Press, 2002), 10. She notes also there is a parallel Jewish version of the same statement (11).

90. Ella Landau Tesseron, "Adoption, Acknowledgement of Paternity, and False Genealogical Claims in Arabian and Islamic Societies," *Bulletin of the School of Oriental and African Studies* 66, no. 2 (2003): 176. See also M. S. Sujimon, "Istilḥāq and its role in Islamic Law," *Arab Law Quarterly* 18, no. 2 (2003): 119.

91. Tesseron, 176.

92. Giʿladi, *Breastfeeding*, 19, note 21.

93. *Mishkāt,* 759–60, which discusses a woman who became pregnant as a result of fornication and then confessed. The prophet instructs that the child in the womb be born, and then suckled and weaned. Then the woman should be stoned. See also Ibn Māja, *Sunan,* no. 2694. Mālik, *Muwaṭṭa'*, 41.1.5, asserts that pregnant women should not be killed or stoned until they give birth, when the baby can be entrusted to someone else. Here, embedded in this statement, is the idea that the womb and the child it produces do not really belong to the woman, but to the public at large.

94. *Muwaṭṭa'*, 38:11.

95. Ibid., 40:1.

96. For a complete discussion of the status of the *umm walad* in Mālikī circles, see Jonathan E. Brockopp's *Early Mālikī Law: Ibn ʿAbd al-Ḥakam and His Major Compendium of Jurisprudence* (Leiden: Brill, 2000), 164–200.

97. The prophet Muḥammad, for example, set Māriya the Copt free as she bore Ibrāhīm, his own child (Ibn Saʿd, *Nisā'*, 154–55).

98. *Sunan,* no. 2743. See also Aḥmad ibn Ḥanbal, *Musnad,* vol. II, 26. Tesseron underscores this link between claims of false paternity with infidelity in her discussion of how medieval Muslim law forbids the denial of a genuine child, along with forged pedigrees. She states that the prophet has been reported to have said, "Whoever knowingly claims descent from someone other than his father is an infidel." She states further how Ibn Baṭṭāl argues that a person who pretends to be the offspring of someone other than his biological father lies about God. It is as if he were saying, "God created me from the sperm of so and so, whereas he was created by the sperm (in reality) of someone else." No one can claim to possess the knowledge of God (178).

99. Bukhārī, *Ṣaḥīḥ,* "Kitāb al-nikāḥ, nos. 58, 59. Of course, as noted in chapter 2, legal scholars still employed resemblance to ascertain cases of adultery. See Bukhārī, *Ṣaḥīḥ,* "Kitāb al-ṭalāq," nos. 230, 236.

100. Ibid., "Kitāb al-nikāḥ," no. 58, vol 7. Or, instead of the mother determining paternity, the public may call in the *qā'if.*

101. Of course, the idea that *jāhilīya* women were once in charge may serve as a "foil" that rationalized current patriarchal practices within the burgeoning Muslim community. John Wansbrough asserts this function of the *jāhilīya* "against which the articulation of the community can be measured" in the context of kinship (*The Sectarian Milieu: Content and Composition of Islamic Salvation History* [Oxford: Oxford University Press, 1978], 33).

102. As noted in chapter 2, a child with two fathers is often rendered to be a physical impossibility (Ibn Qayyim, *Tuḥfat,* 304). See also al-Suyūṭī, who notes that after a drop of semen reaches the womb, a woman no longer desires to have sexual intercourse (*Tibb,* 193). Chapter 5 relays notable exceptions to this rule, which suggest a lingering suspicion of children with duel paternities.

103. Mālik, *Muwaṭṭa'*, 36.21.22.

104. Ibid., 36.21.20. It seems, in these examples, that the semen, which is produced from blood, would have contributed to the "fattening" of the child.

105. Abū Dā'ūd, *Sunan,* "Kitāb al-ṭalāq," no. 31; Nasā'ī, *Sunan,* "Kitāb al-ṭibb," 50; Ṭayālisī, *Musnad,* no. 187.

106. Mara Mabilia, *Breast Feeding and Sexuality: Behavior, Beliefs, and Taboo among the Gogo Mothers in Tanzania* (New York: Berghahn Books, 2005), 101.

107. Ibid., 103.

108. Ibid., 102–103. Mabilia notes this circularity is rooted in biology: The baby's stimulation of the nipple allows for the secretion of milk (let-down reflex), which then allows the process to continue.

109. Ibid., 103–105. Mabilia argues the bond between mother and infant is not natural but social in that it becomes fraught with already established sets of values, affections, emotions, and feelings that tie the mother more closely with her child, and, as a result, extend outward to include other subjects in the circle.

110. Giʿladi: *Infants, Parents and Wet Nurses,* 18. See also Rāzī's commentary on Sūra 2:233.

111. For an example of an adulteress ordered to suckle, see the *Mishkāt,* 759–60. See also Ibn Māja, *Sunan,* no. 2694; Mālik, *Muwaṭṭaʾ,* 41.1.5.

112. Alieh Schleifer, *Motherhood in Islam* (Cambridge: Cambridge University Press, 1986), 52–53. Medieval sources also note that if a mother is kept awake by her child at night, she receives the reward of one who frees seventy slaves for the sake of God.

113. Ibn Māja, *Sunan,* no. 1668. The same holds true for medieval Jewish women (*Babylonian Talmud, Taʾanit,* 27a; *Mishna Nidda,* 4).

114. Bukhārī, *Ṣaḥīḥ,* "Kitāb al-wuḍū," no. 567.

115. See below. Maya Shatzmiller notes how a case came up where jurists had a great deal of difficulty in retaliating against a mother who refused to nurse her baby, which caused death ("Women and Wage Labour in the Medieval Islamic West: Legal Issues in an Economic Context," *Journal of the Economic and Social History of the Orient* 40, no. 2 [1997]: 186).

116. Sūra 2:233.

117. Infant formula did not make its appearance until the twentieth century (Lauwers, 4). For a full discussion of wet nursing as a profession, see Shatzmiller, "Women and Wage Labour in the Medieval Islamic West."

118. Giʿladi, *Breastfeeding,* 106.

119. Ibn Isḥāq, *Sīrat rasūl Allāh,* 70–71.

120. Bukhārī, *Ṣaḥīḥ,* "Kitāb al-adab," no. 215.

121. Wael Hallaq, *The Origins and Evolution of Islamic Law* (Cambridge: Cambridge University Press, 2005), 23.

122. Giʿladi, *Breastfeeding,* 96.

123. Mothers, however, have prior claim to breastfeeding (Giʿladi, *Breastfeeding,* 19, n. 22, references Ṭabarī's commentary on Sūra 2:233).

124. Bukhārī, *Ṣaḥīḥ,* "Kitāb al-ṭalāq," no. 273.

125. Ibid.

126. *Al-Hidāya,* vol. I, trans. Charles Hamilton (Karachi: Daruʾl-Ishaat, 1989), 1760.

127. Preuss, *Biblical and Talmudic Medicine,* 406 (*Kethuboth* 5:5).

128. Ibid., 407, (*Kethuboth* 61a). Some practical evidence exists to the contrary, however. Shatzmiller identifies a statement recorded in the *Geniza* that permits a husband to prevent his wife from nursing someone else's child, and

permits him to force his wife to nurse her own child if she refused to do so ("Women and Wage Labour in the Medieval Islamic West," 185).

129. *Tosefta Nidda* 2:7; *Mishna Sitah* 4:3.

130. *Kethuboth* 59b.

131. Flemming notes Hippocrates and Galen both assert milk uses up the material otherwise evacuated during menstruation ("The Pathology of Pregnancy," 106). According to these scholars, breast milk is simply menstrual blood diverted and refined (Helen King, 34).

132. Ibn Sīnā, *Qānūn,* vol. 1, 151. When an infant is born, nature moves the blood to the breasts, which changes it to milk. See also ʿArīb ibn Saʿd, *Kitāb khalq,* 54; Jāḥiẓ, *"Chance or Creation,"* 72; Ḥunayn ibn Isḥāq notes the substance out of which milk is produced is blood. He also adds that nature has made milk veins wide in animals that have few offspring, and who produce them with difficulty, and whose offspring are weak (421).

133. ʿArīb ibn Saʿd, *Kitāb khalq,* 30, who is paraphrasing Galen. See also Aristotle, *HA,* 7:3:21.For Jewish examples promoting the same theory, see *Babylonian Talmud,* "Niddah," 9a.

134. ʿArīb ibn Saʿd: *Kitāb khalq,* 54. For examples from the Aristotelian context, see Thomas Walter Laqueur, *Making Sex: Body and Gender from the Greeks to Freud* (Cambridge: Harvard University Press, 1990), 36. Since all the blood rises to the breasts, there is no longer any excess blood that can be expelled.

135. ʿArīb ibn Saʿd, *Kitāb khalq,* 54.

136. Vol. 5, 270, quoted in Giʿladi, *Breastfeeding,* 80. Giʿladi also provides a detailed discussion on "sire's milk." He elaborates how Sarakhsī adopts the view that a wet nurse's husband should be regarded as the "milk father" of his wife's nurslings. Just as semen is the cause of her pregnancy and childbirth, intercourse with her husband is the source of the nurse's milk (Muḥammad ibn Aḥmad Sarakhsī. *Kitāb al-Mabsūṭ,* vol. 30 [Cairo: Maṭbaʿat al-Saʿada, 1906–1913], 293–94). On milk fathers, see also Bukhārī, *Sahīh,* "Kitāb al-nikāḥ," no. 40, who reports, "If one drinks a woman's breast milk, then her husband will be as a foster father to him."

137. Bukhārī, *Ṣaḥīḥ,* "Kitāb al-nikāḥ," no. 40.

138. *PA* 650a8ff, as cited by King, *Hippocrates' Women,* 35.

139. Teresa M. Shaw, *The Burden of Flesh: Fasting and Sexuality in Early Christianity* (Philadelphia; Fortress Press, 1998), 69.

140. Lacqueur, 36; Aristotle, *HA* 3.20.522a19–20.

141. Bilu makes this observation in the context of discussion on the Sambia in the Eastern Highlands of Papua New Guinea. Initiation ceremonies of the Sambia seek to undo the intimate mother-son bonding—*sans* father—that occurs postpartum ("Milah," 176).

142. Ibn Shahrāshūb, *Manāqib Āl Abī Tālib,* vol. III (Najaf: Haydariyyah Press, 1956), 207; Ayoub, *Redemptive Suffering,* 75.

143. Ayoub, 75.

144. Ibid. Interestingly, the prophet had commanded Fāṭima not to nurse Ḥusayn's older brother Ḥasan. However, the prophet went on a trip and Fāṭima could not stand to see her child cry of hunger, so she fed him. Although she

was the daughter of the prophet, her blood could not transfer the *imāmate;* only her father's could serve in that capacity (Ibn Shahrāshūb, vol. 3, 209). Men nursing infants is not an uncommon trope in medieval literature. For example, in the ritual of Leipzig Maḥzor, the male teacher acts out the response to Moses's rhetorical question in Numbers 11:12. He carries the child as a nurse carries a babe to his bosom/lap. He then proceeds to feed the child, not from the physical breast but with symbolically equivalent baby foods, especially milk and honey (Ivan G. Marcus, *Rituals of Childhood: Jewish Acculturation in Medieval Europe* [New Haven: Yale University Press, 1996], 91). The image of Christ feeding believers with his breasts is common in medieval Christian theology. Bernard of Clairvaux speaks of Christ being "your mother." Julian of Norwich also refers to Jesus as a mother who feeds his followers with his breasts (Sarah Salih and Denise N. Baker, *Julian of Norwich's Legacy: Medieval Mysticism and Post-Medieval Reception* [New York: Palgrave Macmillan, 2009], 108).

145. Giʿladi, *Breastfeeding,* 21. Giʿladi notes how W. Montgomery Watt had suggested this was a nod to matrilineal groups (*Muḥammad at Medina* [Oxford: Clarendon Press, 1956], 81). On breast milk transferring kinship, see Bukhārī, *Ṣaḥīḥ,* "Kitāb al-nikāḥ," nos. 39, 166.

146. Bukhārī, *Ṣaḥīḥ,* "Kitāb al-ṣawm," nos. 812, 813, 827, 828; "Kitāb al-nikāḥ," nos. 43, 46; Ibn Māja, *Sunan,* no. 1937; Ibn Saʿd, *Nisāʾ*, 64.

147. Bukhārī, *Ṣaḥīḥ,* "Kitāb al-nikāḥ," 41.

148. Mālik, *Muwaṭṭaʾ*, 30.1.13.

149. Ibid., 30.1.6. Or, he reports, when the child is in the cradle (30.1.11). See also Ibn Māja, *Sunan,* no. 1945.

150. See, for example, Ibn Māja, *Sunan,* no. 1942.

151. Ibid., no. 1946.

152. Abū Dāʾūd, *Sunan,* no. 1764. See also Ibn Saʿd, *Nisāʾ*, 190.

153. Postpartum bleeding can occur anywhere from thirty-six days to six weeks (Mavis Kirkham, *Exploring the Dirty Side of Women's Health* [New York: Routledge, 2006], 41).

154. *Tuḥfat,* 141–42.

155. Hippocrates, *Aphorisms,* 52.

156. *Sunan,* vol. 3, no. 2012.

157. *ʿUyūn al-akhbār,* 66.

158. Vol. 2, 688.

159. *Nisāʾ*, 64. See also Tirmidhī, *Sunan,* vol. 3, 459.

160. Ibn Māja, *Sunan,* 2011. See also ʿArīb ibn Saʿd, *Kitāb khalq,* 55.

161. Baumgarten, 124; *Tosefta Niddah* 2:6; *Babylonian Talmud, Yevamot* 34b; Musallam, *Sex and Society,* 25.

162. The Qurʾān, for example, refers to wet nurses as, literally, "your mothers who suckle you" (*ummahātukum allātī arḍaʿnakum*) in Sūra 4:23.

163. ʿArīb ibn Saʿd, *Kitāb khalq,* 56.

164. Ibid., 20. See also chapter 2, note 122.

165. Ibn Sīnā, *Qānūn,* 152.

166. Jāḥiẓ, trans. Pellat, 1969, 168.

167. ʿArīb ibn Saʿd, *Kitāb khalq,* 55–56.

168. Ibid., 56.

169. Ibid.

170. Ibid.

171. Ibid., 55. In the Jewish context, the same warning can be found in the *Tosefta Niddah,* 2:4.

172. ʿArīb ibn Saʿd, *Kitāb khalq,* 55.

173. *Qānūn,* vol. 1, 151–53.

174. See Shatzmiller, "Women and Wage Labour in the Medieval Islamic West," 185–89.

175. Avner Giʿladi, "Some Notes on Taḥnīk in Medieval Islam," *Journal of Near Eastern Studies* 47, no. 3 (July 1988): 177. Giʿladi notes occasional references to mothers performing the ceremony, in particular Aḥmad ibn Ḥanbal's wife, Umm ʿAlī (n. 13, 177). See also Ibn Qayyim, *Tuḥfat,* 66. However, it is important to note that a woman served in this capacity upon the request of her husband, who commanded her to perform the ceremony. In *jāhilīya* times, it appears mothers used to perform the ceremony unaided by husbands, which may account for the shift in favor of men. Again, however, the portrayal of female authority in this instance could be the result of an intentional "foil" against which more patriarchal forms of society are measured. See above.

176. Ibn Ḥanbal, *Musnad,* vol. 3, 106. Some traditions emphasize the rubbing of the date on the child's palate. For examples of this practice, see Giʿladi, "Taḥnīk," 176.

177. See below for examples of connections between the *taḥnīk* and ritual transferences of female reproductive power.

178. Bukhārī, *Ṣaḥīḥ,* volume 5: nos. 245 and 248. As reported by Muslim, the first thing in the child's stomach is the saliva of the prophet (*Ṣaḥīḥ,* "Kitāb al-adab," no. 5344). In other *ḥadīth* examples, the date is not even mentioned, just the saliva. As reported by ʿĀʾisha, "[we] took ʿAbdallāh b. Zubayr to the prophet so that he [the prophet] would put saliva in his mouth" (Muslim, "Kitāb al-adab," no 5347). For other versions of the *taḥnīk* ceremony, see Aḥmad ibn Ḥanbal, *Musnad,* vol. II, 419; III, 315; Ṭayālisī, *Musnad,* no. 2056.

179. Bukhārī, *Ṣaḥīḥ,* "Kitāb al-ʿaqīqa," no. 378; Ibn Qayyim, *Tuḥfat,* 66; Ghazālī, *Etiquette,* 115.

180. On the association between the *taḥnīk* and the naming and blessing of the child, see Ibn Qayyim, who records the narration of Abū Mūsá, who reports that "a son was [first] born to me and I took him to the prophet, who named him Ibrāhīm, did *taḥnīk* with a date, invoked God to bless him, and returned him to me" (*Tuḥfat,* 65). See also Muslim, *Ṣaḥīḥ,* "Kitāb al-adab," no. 5340, where, after the prophet inserted the softened date into the child's mouth, he noted how the Anṣār have a liking for the dates, and then he gave the child the name ʿAbdallāh. On males being the primary target of the ceremony, see Avner Gilʿadi, *Taḥnīk,* 176.

181. Bukhārī, *Ṣaḥīḥ,* "Kitāb al-ʿaqīqa," no. 379; Muslim, *Ṣāḥīḥ,* "Kitāb al-adab," no. 5341; Ibn Qayyim, *Tuḥfat,* 65.

182. Ibn Kathīr, for example, relates that Umm Sulaym was with the prophet during the battle of Uḥud and Ḥunayn with a dagger at her waist.

She declared she would use it to stick it into the polytheists (*Al-sīra al-nabawīya,* 444). Ibn Hishām (as revised from Ibn Isḥāq) relates this story as well, and notes Umm Sulaym says she will take "this dagger so that if a polytheist came near me I could rip him up with it!" (vol. iv, 89, 2).

183. Al-Suyūṭī states, "Your womenfolk should eat dates, for whoever makes dates their food will produce children with ease." He then cites Sūra 19:25 (*Ṭibb,* 45).

184. See chapter 3, 92.

185. Kathryn Kueny, "Abraham's Test: Male Circumcision as Anti/Ante-Covenantal Practice," in *Bible and Qur'ān: Essays in Scriptural Intertextuality,* ed. John C. Reeves (Atlanta: Society of Biblical Literature, 2003), 161–82.

186. Abū Zakarīyā Muḥyī' al-Dīn al-Nawawī, *al-Majmū' sharḥ al-adhdhab,* 9 vols. (Cairo, 1925–29), vol. 1, 300–301, as cited by Jonathan Berkey in "Circumcision Circumscribed: Female Excision and Cultural Accommodation in the Medieval Near East," *International Journal of Middle Eastern Studies* 28, no. 1 (February 1996): 25.

187. Ibn Qayyim, *Tuḥfat,* 280.

188. Ibid., 260–61.

189. Ibid., 276. Ibn Qayyim suggests an uncircumcised (*aqlaf*) man must become circumcised in order to be a member of the Muslim community, even if he is eighty years old.

190. Qurṭubī, *Tafsīr,* vol. II, 100. Kister, 25. In medieval texts, there are few references to the prophet's circumcision, which raises the question whether he was at all.

191. Ibn Qayyim al-Jawzīya, *Tuḥfat,* 308. Another advocate for circumcision performed on the seventh day is Ghazālī (*Etiquette,* 114).

192. Ibn Qayyim, *Tuḥfat,* 305. Jews practice infant circumcision at eight days, which would coincide with the Muslims' seven days, given that Muslims do not factor in the actual day of birth in their equation. So both Jews and Muslims would perform the procedure at the same time. See also Ghazālī, who notes that circumcision is practiced by the Jews on the seventh day; therefore, "we must differentiate ourselves from them and wait until the child's hair begins to grow" (*Iḥyā' ulūm al-dīn* vol. 1 [Cairo: s.n., 1885], 132).

193. Ibn Qayyim, *Tuḥfat,* 307. Josephus, the first-century CE Jewish historian, also comments on how the Arabs "circumcise after the thirteenth year because Ishmael, the founder of their nation, who was born to Abraham of the concubine, was circumcised at that age" (Flavius Josephus quoted by Peters, *Hajj,* 41).

194. Ibn Qayyim, *Tuḥfat,* 308.

195. Ibid., 261. See also Qurṭubī, who notes uncircumcised males are not allowed to circumambulate the Kab'a (*Tafsīr,* vol. II, 39).

196. Ibn Qayyim adds one should not permit the *shahāda* of an uncircumcised male. *Shahāda* serves as the foundation of faith and an initial requirement for conversion *(Tuḥfat,* 276).

197. Ibid, 280.

198. C. D. Yonge, trans., "Questions and Answers on Genesis, III," *The Works of Philo: Complete and Unabridged* (Peabody, MA: Hendrickson Publishers, 1993), 841–63, quote on 857.

199. Otto Meinardus, "Mythological, Historical and Sociological Aspects of the Practice of Female Circumcision among the Egyptians," *Acta Ethnographica* 16 (1967): 388. Cited in Avner Giʿladi, "Normative Islam Versus Local Tradition: Some Observations on Female Circumcision with Special Reference to Eqypt," *Arabica*, T. 44, Fasc. 2 (April 1997): 258.

200. Carol Delaney, "Untangling the Meanings of Hair in Turkish Society," *Anthropological Quarterly* 67, no. 4 (1994): 164. She suggests that girls, by covering, veil the sight of their shame, while boys, who remain uncovered, display their glory.

201. Delaney, "Cutting," 449. Whether circumcision is imagined as a symbolic castration, a sacrifice, or a pruning in order to make the organ more fruitful (like haircutting, where it is believed cutting hairs make them stronger and fuller [see below]), the penis is the focus of the covenant as it is imagined as the organ of procreation. "Cutting," therefore, is connected with the idea that paternity is to a great extent imagined as *the* generative role (Delaney, "Cutting," 461).

202. Elizabeth Wyner Mark, *The Covenant of Circumcision: New Perspectives on an Ancient Jewish Rite* (Lebanon, NH.: University Press of New England, 2003), 61.

203. *The Arabian Nights Encyclopedia*, vol. 1, ed. Ulrich Marzolph, Richard Van Leeuwen, Hassan Wassouf (Santa Barbara: ABC-CLIO, 2004), 470.

204. Abū Ḥayyān, 439.

205. Ibn Qayyim suggests some scholars opt for the ritual to occur sometime between seven and ten years (*Tuḥfat*, 305).

206. Bilu, "Circumcision," 39.

207. Bilu, "Milah," 189.

208. Lawrence Hoffman, *Covenant of Blood: Circumcision and Gender in Rabbinic Judaism* (Chicago: University of Chicago Press, 1996), 147.

209. Delaney, "Cutting," 457. She notes how the power to procreate—imagined as divine power—transforms a merely patrilineal system into a patri archal one. In this way, the human father becomes a kind of naturalized divinity.

210. Ibid., 454.

211. Sūra 2:223.

212. Bilu, "Circumcision," 39.

213. Delaney argues in a patriarchal context, creative power *is* divinity ("Cutting," 454).

214. Bukhārī, *Ṣaḥīḥ*, "Kitāb al-anbiyāʾ" nos. 575, 576. Ibn Qayyim also views *khitān* as linked with the remembrance of Abraham, as he observes that "Abraham circumcised himself with a pick-axe [*qadūm*]. Or, with the tip [*ṭaraf*] of a pickaxe" (*Tuḥfat*, 76).

215. *Tuḥfat*, 276.

216. Abū Jaʿfar Muḥammad b. Jarīr al-Ṭabarī, *The History of al-Ṭabarī*, vol. 2, *Prophets and Patriarchs*, trans. William M. Brinner (Albany: State University of New York Press, 1991), 103.

217. Ibid., 104. Kueny, "Abraham's Test."

218. Abraham was known as a *ḥanīf*. In the Qurʾān, a *ḥanīf* is a monotheist who is neither a Jew nor Christian. One becomes a *ḥanīf* by means of logical reflection and empirical observation of nature. The monotheism of a *ḥanīf* is also

a part of one's natural constitution with which humans have been created by the one true God (Frank Griffel, "The Harmony of Natural Law and Shari'a in Islamist Theology," in *Shari'a: Islamic Law in the Contemporary Context,* ed. Abbas Amanat and Frank Griffel [Stanford: Stanford University Press, 2007], 43).

219. *Encyclopedia of the Qur'ān,* s.v. "covenant."

220. See, for example, Genesis 35:11–12.

221. *The Encyclopedia of the Qur'ān,* s.v. "covenant."

222. Mālik, *Muwaṭṭa',* 16.54. See also Bukhārī, *Ṣaḥīḥ,* "Kitāb al-janā'iẓ," no. 441.

223. Kueny, "Abraham's Test," 182.

224. Al-Bukhārī, *Ṣaḥīḥ,* "Kitāb al-libās," nos. 777, 779. See also Abū Dā'ūd, *Sunan,* "Kitāb al-tarajjul," no. 418; Ibn Ḥanbal, *Musnad,* vol. II, 229, 239, 283, 410, 489; vol. IV, 264; Mālik b. Anas, "Sāfat al-nabī," in *Al-Muwaṭṭa',* ed. Fārūq Sa'd (Beirut: Dār al-āfāq al-jadīda, 1981), 3.3; Muslim, "Kitāb al-ṭahāra," nos. 495, 496; Nasā'ī, "Kitāb al-zinā," *Sunan,* vol. 1, 75; Tirmidhī, *Ṣaḥīḥ,*"Abwāb al-adab," 14. Other scholars list ten *fiṭra* practices, but divide them into five in the head, and five in the body. The five in the head include cutting the mustache, rinsing, blowing out the nose, using the *siwāk* (tooth stick) and combing the hair; as for the body, the five include clipping the fingernails, shaving the pubes, circumcision, plucking out the armpit hairs, and washing after defecating and urinating with water (Ibn Qayyim, *Tuḥfat,* 268). Interestingly, Shī'ite traditions list five practices of the *fiṭra,* but eliminate circumcision from the list. For an examination of why this may be the case, see Kueny, "Abraham's test."

225. Ibn Qayyim, *Tuḥfat,* 267.

226. See Sūras 2:135–136; 3:95; 4:125; 6:161; 16:120; 16:123.

227. Bukhārī, *Ṣaḥīḥ,* "Kitāb al-buyū,'" nos. 299, 440; "Kitāb al-tafsīr," no. 408; "Kitāb al-ṭalāq," no. 259; "Kitāb al-ṭibb," no. 636; "Kitāb al-libās," nos. 815, 816, 820, 822, 823, 825, 826, 827, 829, 830, 831, 832, 845. See also Muslim, *Ṣaḥīḥ,* "Kitāb al-libās wa al-zīna," nos. 5300, 5301; Abū Dā'ūd, "Kitāb al-libās," 4038.

228. Bilu, "Circumcision," 38.

229. *Genesis Rabbah,* 11:6, cited in Bilu, "Circumcision," 38. He adds that cutting off, removing, and separating serve as key idioms for the transformation of nature into culture, that is, for the Judaizing of culture.

230. Some traditions assert twelve or more among the prophets were born circumcised (Majlisī, *Biḥār,* vol. 15, 296).

231. *Noah,* 5, quoted in Samuel A. Berman, *Midrash Tanhuma-Yelammedenu: An English Translation of Genesis and Exodus* (Jersey City: Ktav Publishing, 1996), 50–51. The *Avot D'Rabbi Nathan* notes thirteen individuals who were born without foreskins: Adam, Seth, Noah, Shem, Jacob, Joseph, Moses, Balaam, Samuel, David, Jeremiah, Zerubabel, and Job (2:5).

232. M. J. Kister, "Born Circumcised," 12–13, cites Ibn Jawzī, *al-Wafā bi-aḥwāli l-Muṣṭafa,* ed. Muṣṭafa 'Abd al-Wāḥid (Cairo: Dār al-Kutub al-Ḥadītha, 1966), 97.

233. Elliott Wolfson,"Circumcision, Vision of God, and Textual Interpretation: From Midrashic Trope to Mystical Symbol," *History of Religions* 27 (1987): 189–215.

234. *Genesis Rabbah,* 48:1; 48:9. See also Daniel Boyarin, "'This we know to be the Carnal Israel': Circumcision and the Erotic Life of God and Israel,"

Critical Inquiry 18, no. 3 (Spring 1992): 492. See also *Numbers Rabbah* 12:10 for examples of Abraham circumcising himself in order to invoke God to appear.

235. Boyarin, 495. See also Bilu, "Circumcision," 42.

236. Boyarin, 495.

237. In the context of medieval Christianity, Caroline Walker Bynum has pointed out that "men—powerful, clerical, authoritative, rational, 'divine' men—needed to become weak and human, yet spiritual, 'women' in order to proceed toward God" (*Holy Feast Holy Fast: The Religious Significance of Food to Medieval Women* [Berkeley: University of California Press, 1987], 287). The neutering of one's body in the Islamic context may be done for similar purposes. For a discussion of gender reversals in the Song of Songs, see Hildegard Elisabeth Keller, *My Secret is Mine: Studies on Religion and Eros in the German Middle Ages* (Leuven: Peeters Publishers, 2000), 248–60.

238. Sūra 84:1–3.

239. Ibn Qayyim, *Tuḥfat,* 291.

240. Ibid., 289. Ibn Qayyim notes that circumcision cannot serve as the sole distinguishing feature of a true believer. He states that some Christians are also circumcised (e.g., the Copts), so circumcision cannot always distinguish between Muslim and *kāfir.* There is tacit recognition in many sources that Jews are also marked by circumcision. However, there is no systematic effort to explain precisely what differentiates Jew from Muslim with regard to the practice, or, in fact, what unites them. For speculation on this issue, see Kueny, "Abraham's Test."

241. *Tuḥfat,* 211–13.

242. Ibid., 291.

243. *Midrash Tanḥuma,* Tazriʿa, 5, as cited in Elliot Wolfson, "Circumcision and the Divine Name: A Study in the Transmission of Esoteric Doctrine," *The Jewish Quarterly Review* LXXVII, nos. 1–2 (July-October 1987): 78, 85.

244. Ibn Qayyim, *Tuḥfat,* 257. See also Ibn Ḥanbal, *Musnad,* vol. 5, 75.

245. Abū Dāʾūd records a tradition that shows how the prophet advocated circumcision for women, as long as the cutting was not too severe as to inhibit pleasure for either the man or the woman (*Sunan,* "Kitāb al-adab," no. 5251). Ghazālī mentions a similar tradition regarding Umm ʿAṭīya: she should circumcise, but not exceed the appropriate bounds (*ʿIḥyā,* vol. 1, 90–92).

246. Ibn Qayyim, *Tuḥfat,* 258.

247. Ibn Qayyim noted in Avner Giʿladi, "Normative Islam Versus Local Tradition: Some Observations on Female Circumcision with Special Reference to Egypt," *Arabica* T. 44, fasc. 2 (April, 1997): 263–64.

248. Ghazālī, *Kīmiyāʾ al-saʿāda,* 47, notes music is lawful for celebratory occasions, such as weddings, feasts, returning from a journey, or circumcision.

249. Giʿladi, "Normative Islam," 263–64.

250. Berkey mentions one example in which the caliph ʿUthmān ordered excision performed upon female prisoners who converted to Islam (24). This practice, however, does not seem to be normative.

251. Kister notes that the intent of female circumcision is to diminish a woman's sexual desire; male circumcision is to secure the proper performance of his religious duties (23).

252. Ghazālī notes that the Sufis have adopted this view (*Etiquette,* 52).

253. A number of other traditions mention that circumcision provides a good means through which male sexual appetite, which often leads to distraction, can be curbed. On the curbing of pleasure through circumcision, Philo notes: "the flesh of the foreskin [symbolizes] those sense-pleasures and impulses which afterward overcome the body" (Boyarin, "'This we know to be the Carnal Israel,'" 486; Philo, *Questions and Answers on Genesis,* 3.52, supp. 1 of *Philo,* trans. Ralph Marcus [Cambridge: Harvard University Press, 1953], 253). In the Jewish context, Maimonides worked to limit indulgence of the body through food and sex (Michael S. Berger, "Judaism," in *Sex, Marriage, and Family in World Religions,* ed. Don Browning, M. Christian Green, and John Witte Jr. [New York: Columbia University Press, 2009], 10).

254. Tirmidhī, *Ṣaḥīḥ,* 41:63; Nasāʾī, *Sunan,* 40:5. See also Ibn Qayyim, where the prophet said, "every *ghulām* should be mortgaged with his *ʿaqīqa*: Slaughter for him on the seventh day, name him and shave his head" (*Tuḥfat,* 72, 159, 167). Also, Ibn Māja records the prophet as saying, "Every boy is mortgaged by his *ʿaqīqa,* so slaughter for him on the seventh day, shave his head, and name him" (*Sunan,* no. 3165). In this example, the man performs the ceremonies. Ibn Qayyim notes the rituals may also be performed on the fourteenth or twenty-first days, that is, in seven-day cycles (*Tuḥfat,* 108).

255. Ibn Qayyim, *Tuḥfat,* 59–87, deals with various discussions on the proper time for naming male children, and provides lists for recommended, ugly, and forbidden names, and underscores the exclusive right of the father to choose the name due to the fact that the father is genealogically related to the child. See also Annemarie Schimmel, *Islamic Names* (Edinburgh: Edinburgh University Press, 1995), 14–24. Only exemplary women in sacred history are allowed to name their children. For example, Zamakhsharī notes how Ḥanna, Mary's mother, named her own daughter (*Kashshāf,* vol. I, 355–57).

256. Ibn Qayyim, *Tuḥfat,* 233.

257. Sūra 2:31.

258. Ibn Qayyim, *Tuḥfat,* 233.

259. For a description of the process by which persons may be socialized into social systems that value linkage, bonding, and sociability at the same time it facilitates the exercise of patriarchal power by crafting selves subject to control, see the introduction to *Intimate Selving in Arab Families: Gender, Self, and Identity,* ed. Suad Joseph (Syracuse: Syracuse University Press, 1999), 9–13.

260. Ibn Qayyim, *Tuḥfat,* 233.

261. Ibid., 236. See also Muslim, *Ṣaḥīḥ,* nos. 5321; 5323. Ghazālī agrees that the prophet's *kunya* is prohibited (*Etiquette,* 114–15). The name Muḥammad, however, is perfectly acceptable. Ghazālī asserts further it is important for a name to have *ʿabd* (servant) associated with it, like ʿAbdallāh or ʿAbd al-Raḥmān.

262. See, for example, chapter 4, where Eve gives her sons inappropriate names.

263. Ibn Qayyim, *Tuḥfat,* 184–85.

264. Ghazālī, *Etiquette,* 114–15.

265. Ibn Qayyim, *Tuḥfat,* 189.

266. Ibid., 200.

267. Ibid., 225.

268. In Mālik's *Muwaṭṭa*ʾ, the *ʿaqīqa* is noted as being desirable, even if what is sacrificed is only a sparrow (26.2.5).

269. Ibn Rushd al-Qurṭubī provides a fairly extensive discussion about the *ʿaqīqa*. He points out two conflicting traditions on which scholars base their opinions about the practice. On tradition argues the necessity that very child be redeemed by his *ʿaqiqa,* which is to be sacrificed for him on the seventh day to remove evil from him. The other tradition indicates the prophet does not love the *ʿaqīqa,* but allows it to be performed anyway. This perspective is summarized by Ibn Qayyim, *Tuḥfat,* 70. See also Mālik, *Muwaṭṭa*ʾ, 26.1.1, 26.1.2.

270. Bukhārī suggests the *ʿaqīqa* ceremony resembles the *ʿatīra* and the *faraʾ*, both *jāhilīya* practices. *Faraʾ* refers to the first offspring sacrificed to idols; *ʿatīra* was in *rajab*. See Ibn Qayyim's summary of Bukhārī in *Tuḥfat,* 71.

271. Ibid.

272. Ibn Māja reports the prophet as saying, "Offer an *ʿaqīqa* for the boy, but do not smear his head with blood" (*Sunan,* 3166). See also Ibn Qayyim, *Tuḥfat,* 121. Here, the prophet decides that touching the child with the blood is unacceptable. Rather, he advocates shaving the head of the child, and declares it is *sunna* to put saffron of the head of the child (130). Mālik notes the *ʿaqīqa* is not obligatory but desirable. If someone makes an *ʿaqīqa* for his children, the same rules apply as with all sacrificial animals. One-eyed, emaciated, injured, or sick animals must not be used, and neither the meat nor the skin is to be sold. The bones must be broken and the family must eat the meat and give some of it away as charity. The child is not smeared with any of the blood (*Muwaṭṭa*ʾ, 26.2.7).

273. Ayoub, *Redemptive Suffering,* 74.

274. Ibn Qayyim, *Tuḥfat,* 86.

275. Bukhārī, "Kitāb al-ʿaqīqa," no. 388. See also Ibn Māja, who records "Salmān b. ʿĀmir heard the prophet say, 'for the boy there should be an *ʿaqīqa,* so shed blood for him and remove the harm from him'" (*Sunan,* no. 3164). Ghazālī argues for one sheep for a female, two for a male. He also adds that the prophet said for every male, there must be a sacrifice (*Etiquette,* 115). A father should shed blood on his child's behalf in order to remove harm from him (Ibn Qayyim, *Tuḥfat,* 71). Harm is also associated with hair, or even, perhaps, foreskin (ibid., 75).

276. Ibn Qayyim, *Tuḥfat,* 70, 112, 113.

277. Ibn Māja, *Sunan,* no. 3162: "Sibaʿ b. Thābit: his mother Kurz said, "I heard the prophet say, on behalf of a boy, two sheep of equal age and behalf of a girl one sheep." See also no. 3163. For similar traditions, note Ibn Qayyim, *Tuḥfat,* 73, 74, 76; Bukhārī, *Ṣaḥīḥ,* "Kitāb al-ʿaqīqa," no. 380; Ghazālī, *Etiquette,* 115.

278. Ibn Qayyim insists Mālik says one sheep for a boy and one for a girl; both sexes are equal. He also notes the prophet slaughtered a sheep apiece for Ḥasan and Ḥusayn. But, he suggests, Abū Dāʾūd, and Nisāʾī called for two sheep apiece (*Tuḥfat,* 74, 114). See Mālik, *Muwaṭṭa*ʾ, 26.2.7; 26.2.4, for confirmation of Ibn Qayyim's assessment.

279. For example, the Qurʾān condemns the burying of infant daughters alive (Sūras 16:57–58; 81:8–9).

280. Ibn Qayyim notes that the phrase "removing harm from him," which accompanies discussions of the *ʿaqīqa,* actually means removing "hair" from him (*Tuhfat,* 88).

281. The fact that in this case the mother cuts the hair as opposed to the father suggests bias against ʿAlī. The child is socialized into the family of the prophet, rather than that of ʿAlī. Perhaps the haircutting serves to replace the sacrifice, since women would not perform the sacrifice.

282. *Sadaqa* really refers to free will offerings. See Ibn Qayyim, *Tuḥfat,* 71; 160–63. See also Mālik, *Muwaṭṭa,* 26.1.2, 26.1.3., 26.2.64.

283. Ibn Qayyim, *Tuḥfat,* 126.

284. Other traditions assert the father is the one who performs the act of cutting the child's hair. For example, when Ḥusayn was born, the prophet took him in his arms, shaved the child's hair, gave its weight in silver alms and performed the *ʿaqīqa* (See Ayoub, *Redemptive Suffering,* 74).

285. Bilu, "Milah," 190, quoting Molly Myerowitz Levine, "The Gendered Grammar of Ancient Mediterranean Hair," in *Off With Her Head: the Denial of Women's Identity in Myth, Religion and Culture,* ed. H. Eilberg Schwartz and Wendy Doniger (Berkeley: University of California Press, 1995), 85.

286. Bilu, "Milah," 190, referencing Bartlett, 1994.

287. Bilu, "Milah," 190, citing Myerowitz Levine, 87.

288. Carol Delaney argues in the context of contemporary Turkey that haircutting indicates an entry into society, and a recognition of the replacement of one form of social control with another ("Untangling," 164).

289. Harm is often associated with hair, or even, perhaps, foreskin (Ibn Qayyim, *Tuḥfat,* 75).

290. Ibid., 152.

291. For those who support the practice of *adhān,* see Abu Dā'ūd, *Sunan,* "Kitāb al-adab," 106; Ibn Ḥanbal, vol. 6, 391, 392; Ṭayālisī, *Musnad,* no. 970. The practice also has prophetic precedence. Ibn Qayyim records that the prophet gave the call to prayer in the ear of Ḥasan after Fāṭima gave birth to him (*Tuḥfat,* 61).

292. Ghazālī also suggests it is desirable that the first words a child is taught to speak when he learns to talk be "there is no god but God" so that the words constitute his first utterance (*Encyclopedia of Religion and Ethics,* ed. James Hastings, Part 9 [Whitefish, MT: Kessinger Publishing, LLC, 2003], s.v. "Education [Muslim]").

293. Ibn Qayyim, *Tuḥfat,* 64.

294. Ibn Māja, *Sunan,* no. 2889, for example, states, "Whoever performs *ḥajj* to this house and does not have sexual relations nor commit any disobedience will go back *like the day his mother bore him*" (emphasis mine).

295. *Bodily Citations,* 7. Here, the editors discuss Butler's views on how social norms define the realm of viable subjectivity. However, just as such norms demarcate what is intelligible and acceptable, they also determine what lies outside those borders. These outlying areas are called the "abject" by Butler. Those who reside there are given no status in society, but at the same time they are necessary for the legitimation of viable subjectivities.

296. Jāḥiẓ, *"Chance or Creation,"* 72.

297. Ibid.

298. In the *Babylonian Talmud,* Hannah is presented as praying for a child in the following way: "Sovereign of the Universe, among all the things that Thou has created in a woman, thou has not created one without a purpose: eyes to see, ears to hear, a nose to smell, a mouth to speak, hands to do work, legs to walk with, breasts to give suck. These breasts that thou has put on my heart, are they not to give suck? Give me a son so that I may suckle with them" (*Berakhot,* 31b).

299. For example, according to Ibn Kathīr, after the prophet divorced al-ʿĀlīya, daughter of Ẓabyān, she went on to marry a cousin and was able to have children with him (Ibn Kathīr, *The Life of the Prophet Muḥammad [al-Sīra al-al-Nabawīya]*, trans. Trevor Le Gassick [Reading: Garnet Publishing, 2000] 426). Another of the prophet's wives, Umm Salama, also had children with her husband Abū Salama, before he was killed in the Battle of Uḥud (Fatima Mernissi, *The Veil and the Male Elite: A Feminist Interpretation of Women's Rights in Islam* [New York: Basic Books, 1991], 116). However, after she married Muḥammad, she remained barren.

300. Sūra 33:40.

301. In fact, it appears the prophet often passed on women who already had young children to take care of; in other words, he did not deem them to be suitable wives for him. Apparently once the prophet found out that Umm Hāniʾ, Fākhita, daughter of Abū Ṭālib, had small children, he left her, even though she had proposed marriage to him (Ibn Kathīr, *Life of the Prophet Muḥammad,* 427).

302. Sūras 33:6; 33:53.

303. Stowasser, 99, no. 90, notes Zamakhsharī, *Kashshāf,* vol. 3, 414. She also refers to Bayḍawī, *Anwār,* vol. 2, 123; Ibn Kathīr, *Tafsīr,* vol. 3, 468–69; Ṭabarī, *Tafsīr,* vol. 21, 77.

304. See Stowasser, 87–103, for an exhaustive list of the ways the wives are supposed to conduct themselves.

305. Mālik, *Muwaṭṭaʾ*, 8.8.26, 8.8.27; Abū Dāʾūd, *Sunan,* "Kitāb al-ṭahāra," nos. 33, 42, 50, 52, 55, 76.

306. See Ibn Saʿd, *Nisāʾ*, 44ff; Ibn Ḥanbal, *Musnad,* vol. VI, 151, 213, 260. Note also Ibn Māja, *Sunan,* no. 3739, where ʿĀʾisha said to the prophet, "All of your wives have a *kunya* except me." He said [to her], you are Umm ʿAbdallāh.

307. Ibn Māja, *Sunan,* no. 1607.

308. Ibid, no. 1512.

309. Ibid., no. 1511, notes Ibrāhīm had a wet nurse in paradise.

310. Bukhārī, *Ṣaḥīḥ,* "Kitāb al-janāʾiz," nos. 340, 413, 463.

Chapter 5. Mother as Monster

1. Marie-Hélène Huet, *Monstrous Imagination* (Cambridge: Cambridge University Press, 1993) 34. She notes that Michel de Montaigne asserts Aristotle stated "that in a certain nation where the women were in common they assigned children to their fathers by resemblance" (*Essays,* II:37, 578). According to Huet, resemblance imposes a temporary if superficial order while masking a fundamental, primordial disorder. And what the resemblance conceals, the

monster—that is, what stands outside the ordered features—unmasks. Not surprisingly, resemblance closes the distance between fathering and childbirth. In the Islamic context, the caliph ʿUmar assigned children of the *jāhilīya* to fathers via resemblance (see above and below).

2. Abū Ḥayyān, 454. Such observations reflect those of Aristotle, who notes the monstrous was a curiosity of nature. For the pseudo-Albertus Magnus (thirteenth and fourteenth centuries), monsters were created for the adornment of the universe. Ambroise Paré (1537) suggests the causes of monstrosity are as follows: the first whereof is the glory of God, that his immense power may be manifested to those which are ignorant of it . . .another cause in that God may punish men's wickedness, or show signs of punishment (Shildrick, *Embodying the Monster,* 12).

3. David Williams, *Deformed Discourse; The Function of the Monster in Medieval Thought and Literature* (Montreal: McGill Queen's University Press, 1996), 4–6.

4. Erika Elizabeth Hess, *Literary Hybrids: Crossdressing, Shapeshifting, and Indeterminacy in Medieval and Modern French Narrative* (New York: Routledge, 2004), 5 See also Williams, 5; Shildrick, 12.

5. Williams, 4.

6. Negative theology is native to the Muslim tradition, in particular, in the realm of mysticism. It is not as if a postmodern critique must be imposed on the tradition from the outside. For examples of negative theology in the Islamic tradition, see Michael Sells, *Mystical Languages of Unsaying* (Chicago: University of Chicago Press, 1994), in which he discusses the phenomenon of *apophasis* in the works of Ibn ʿArabī.

7. See chapter 2, 57.

8. Qazwīnī, *Nuzhatu al-qulūb,* 2. Here, Qazwīnī states zoological catalogues only reveal what human understanding can reach in its limited capacity. Only God knows the full extent of the variety of his creations. As God has said, "None knows the hosts of the Lord except Himself" (Sūra 74:34).

9. Examples include Damīrī.

10. Fedwa Malti-Douglas, *Structures of Avarice: The Bukhalāʾ in Medieval Arabic Literature* (Leiden: Brill, 1995), 34.

11. Shildrick, *Embodying the Monster,* 2.

12. Jāḥiẓ writes that physical deformities serve as calamities to discipline men (*"Chance or Creation,"* 113).

13. *Ḥiyāt al-ḥayawān,* 625. The Talmud notes the opposite of a giant is the *nannas* in Hebrew or *nannos* in Greek. Both terms mean dwarf. Such a figure cannot serve as a priest (*Sifra Emor,* 3.956). The Talmud further asserts an abnormally tall man should not marry an equally tall woman, lest their offspring be like a mast. Likewise, a male dwarf should not marry a female dwarf, lest their offspring be no larger than a thimble (*Bechnoth* 45b); (Preuss, *Biblical and Talmudic Medicine,* 201).

14. Jāḥiẓ, *"Chance or Creation,"* 113–20.

15. Jeffrey Jerome Cohen, *Monster Theory: Reading Culture* (Minneapolis: University of Minnesota Press, 1996), 12.

16. Ibid., 13.

17. Sūra 32:7–9.

18. Sūra 2:30. See chapter 1 for further discussion on how human creation differs from the creation of nonhumans.

19. *Mishkāt,* 763. The fact that the condemnation of such practices was based on a crossing of categories and not on a fear of what might be produced from such actions is evident in the fact that Ibn ʿAbbās is shown to believe the animal should be killed because of defilement. The prophet disapproved of its flesh being eaten or of any use being made of it when such a thing had been done to it. Like their Muslim neighbors, medieval rabbis also rule that sodomy with an animal cannot yield progeny, although they do note cases where women abort fetuses that *resemble* birds or beasts (Schochet, *Animal life,* 100). Here, again, resemblance becomes a tool through which to identify sexual deviance. In the Christian context, Alfonso the Wise (1252–1284) also notes that anyone who has intercourse with an animal will suffer death. He adds that the animal, too, shall be killed in order to obliterate the memory of the deed (noted in *La setena partida,* 21, *Los códigos espanoles* [Madrid: Imprenta de La Publicidad, 1848], quoted by John Boswell, *Christianity, Social Tolerance, and Homosexuality: Gay People in Western Europe from the Beginning of the Christian Era to the Fourteenth Century* [Chicago: University of Chicago Press, 1981], 289). It could be that Muslim scholars shared the same view. In the Talmudic texts, according to Rabbi Meir, if the woman aborts something that looks like a beast, or a wild animal or a bird, she is considered a parturient woman and must abide in uncleanness according to the sex of the fetus (*Niddah* 3:2). Sages make a general statement that an aborted fetus that does not have features of a human being should not to be considered a human child. Such is so in the case of a woman in Zidi who, three times, gave birth to the form of a raven (*Tosefta Niddah* 4:6). The Talmud never speaks of the birth of an animal to a human or vice versa, only resemblances.

20. Qazwīnī, *Nuzhatu,* 68. This particular zoological work contains sections that deal specifically with land animals, domestic animals, wild animals, beasts of prey, poisonous animals and creeping things, and animals of which certain members resemble man, sea animals, and air animals. Humans do not receive any consideration as a category among the *ḥayawānāt.*

21. Ibid., 48.

22. Ibid.

23. Ibid., 49.

24. For Greek and Roman references to "dog-headed peoples" that occupy Libya, Ethiopia, or the Indian mountains, see Hesiod (ca. 700 BCE), *Catalogues of Women Fragment 44;* Hesiod, *Catalogues of Women Fragment 40A,* trans. G. M. Most, in *Hesiod: The Shield, Catalogue of Women, Other Fragments,* Loeb Classical Library 503 (Cambridge: Harvard University Press, 2007); Claudius Aelianus (d. 230 CE), vol. 1, *On Animals,* 4.46; vol. 2, 10:25, 10:30, trans. A. F. Scholfield, Loeb Classical Library (Cambridge: Harvard University Press, 1958). Aelianus mentions they eat meat. However, in Aelianus's account, the dog-eared people are humans resembling animals, rather than vice versa. Pliny the Elder, also, mentions a tribe of human beings with dogs' heads in the Indian mountains. He takes the opposite view of Qazwīni by suggesting these creatures are men who look like dogs, and not the opposite (Pliny, *Natural History,* 7.23).

25. Qazwīnī, *Nuzhatu,* 48. Stephenson notes this animal resembles the *cynocephali* of Herodotus. See Herodotus, *Histories,* 4.191.3, ed. and trans. A. D. Godley (London: Heinemann, 1921).

26. Qazwīnī may be referring to Siamese twins here, but this theory is far from certain (*Nuzhatu,* 48). Qazwīnī describes this being as having one body but two heads, four arms and four legs, as if two men were to put their backs together. It crawls on all fours, with one form reclining on the back of the other. Other depictions of Siamese twins appear in the travel stories of the pseudo-Shāfiʿī. While in Yemen, Shāfiʿī saw two sisters who had two distinct trunks, four hands, two heads, and two faces. After one died, her body was tied with a rope until it rotted away. The remains were cut way and buried, and the living sister went about her business (Houari Touati, "Travel," in *Medieval Islamic Civilization,* ed. Josef W. Meri and Jere L. Bacharach [New York: Taylor and Francis, 2006]).

27. Qazwīnī, *Nuzhatu,* 48.

28. Ibid.

29. Ibid.

30. John Block Friedman, *The Monstrous Races in Medieval Art and Thought* (Syracuse: Syracuse University Press, 2000), 200.

31. Aristotle, for example, believed that hair was associated with heat and, therefore semen (Cobb, 175–76, notes 46, 47). Although apparently Aristotle argues that baldness is the result of excess semen (which apparently draws the heat away from the front of the head) (ibid.).

32. Ibn Māja, *Sunan,* no. 4071. The false Christ will emerge in a land in the east called Khurasān and will be followed by people with faces like hammered shields (ibid., 4072; 4075). Abū Ḥayyān notes that he who has protruding eyes does not see well what is far from him; but deep set eyes discern what is distant from them; for their movement is neither deviant nor scattered (420).

33. Qazwīnī, *Nuzhatu,* 48.

34. Communal identity and the significance of communal relations, as they are tied to essential elements of faith, are clearly illustrated, and underscored, by the five pillars of faith.

35. The *mālūf* is a form of *nasnās,* a kind of ape resembling a man. The Egyptian *nasnās* is hairy and has a tail (Qazwīnī, 50).

36. Ibid.

37. Damīrī, *Ḥayawān,* vol. II, 6.

38. Qazwīnī, *Nuzhatu,* 1.

39. Ibid., 59. See also Damīrī, *Ḥayawān,* vol. 1 606. This example illustrates the dehumanization of other groups of peoples. A Byzantine psalter, copied and illuminated by a monk named Theodore in 1066, depicts verses of the psalm by painting Christ surrounded by dog-headed men (*cynocephali*) with lolling tongues. The *cynocephali* are labeled as "Hebrews are dogs." Thus, Theodore characterizes the Jews as half-animal monsters (Alixe Bovey, *Monsters and Grotesques in Medieval Manuscripts* [Toronto: University of Toronto Press, 2002], 10–11).

40. On those who have intercourse with animals see Ibn Ḥanbal, *Musnad,* vol. I, 217, 269, 300, 317. Certainly, bestiality is also used to convey layers

of meaning in mystical works. Jalāl al-Dīn, for example, relays a story of a maidservant having improper relations with an ass. In this example, bawdy tales referring to acts of bestiality are presented within a broader poetic tapestry to demonstrate the presence of the divine in every aspect of the everyday world (Mahdi Tourage, *Rūmī and the Hermeneutics of Eroticism* [Leiden: Brill, 2007], 9–35). Clearly, bestiality is not a practice the mystics want to celebrate, but rather serves to reveal the inner workings of the divine just like any other.

41. Damīrī, *Ḥayawān*, 194–201.

42. Ibid. See also Saʿīd Ḥ. Manṣūr, *The Worldview of al-Jāḥiẓ* (Alexandria: Dar al-Maaref, 1977), 251. For Jāḥiẓ, hybrid animals have the worst nature among all the animals. As for humans, a child of a masculine female and an effeminate male has a worse nature than the mule (ibid.).

43. ʿArīb ibn Saʿd, *Khalq*, 34. Ibn Qutayba argues that frequent sexual intercourse causes one to become old. He notes that eunuchs attain old age because they do not engage in sexual intercourse. Mules also have long lives because they do not engage in sex. Sparrows have short lives because of the frequency with which they engage in coitus (*ʿUyūn al-akhbār*, 63).

44. Damīrī, *Ḥayawān*, 194–201. ʿArīb ibn Saʿd also mentions that mules do not bear offspring, although pregnant mules have been noted on rare occasion (*Kitāb khalq*, 34). For Abū Ḥayyān, mules are crossbreeds that do not propagate (443).

45. Abū Ḥayyān, 426.

46. Ibid., 415 The panther (*fahd*) seeks human excrement, eats it and is cured after eating "strangler of the panthers" (*khāniqat al-fuhūd*), a type of herb.

47. Ibid., 420. The wild ass may also couple with the bear, which produces a strange shape (*kawshāl*) that resembles both animals.

48. Ibid., 424.

49. Qazwīnī, *Nuzhatu*, 33.

50. For the negative properties of wine, see Kathryn Kueny, *The Rhetoric of Sobriety* (Albany: State University of New York Press, 2001).

51. In the human realm, there are a few exceptions where crossbreeding apparently does not result in deficient offspring. Damīrī discusses the waterman (*insān al-māʾ*), which resembles a man except for a tail. He is married and has a son (*Ḥayawān*, vol. 1, 63). Damīrī also refers to the mermaid (*bināt al-māʾ*), who is also capable of copulating with humans and can produce a child (ibid., 222).

52. Aristotle, for example, equated excess and deficiency with conditions of moral failing. Disordered bodies imply bodily imperfection but more starkly, immoral being (Shildrick, 32).

53. See above, note 42; Ibn Qutayba notes, "They also say, the son of a masculine woman or an effeminate man is as wicked as one can possibly be, for he inherits the worst of the qualities of his father and mother (*ʿUyūn al-akhbār*, 65.36.20).

54. Manṣūr, 251.

55. Damīrī vol. II, 35. See also Jacob Lassner, *Demonizing the Queen of Sheba: Boundaries of Gender and Culture in Postbiblical Judaism and Medieval Islam* (Chicago: University of Chicago Press, 1993), 208.

56. Damīrī, *Ḥayawān,* vol. 1, 558. Jāḥiẓ, too, supports the possibility of humans having sex with jinn (*Ḥayawān,* 114).

57. Ibid., 555–56.

58. Carol Bakhos, *Ishmael on the Border: Rabbinic Portrayals of the First Arab* (Albany: State University of New York Press, 2007), 117.

59. See, for example, Aḥmad ibn ʿAbd al-Ḥalīm ibn Taymīya (d. 1328 CE), *Idāḥ al-dalāla fī ʿumūm al-risāla,* translated as *Ibn Taymiyya's Essay on the Jinn,* by Abu Ameenah Bilal Philips (New Delhi: Islamic Book Service, 2002), 31.

60. Hishām ibn al-Kalbī, *Kitāb al-asnām,* trans. Nabih Amin Faris (Princeton: Princeton University Press), 170. Damīrī, *Ḥayawān,* vol. 1, 302, notes a party of Ḥanbalī *imāms* have ruled against marriage between a human being and a jinn. They said it is not allowable on account of the difference between the two classes. There seems to be much debate in antiquity over this issue. Aristotle, for example, did not entirely dismiss cross-species fertilization, but suggested that gestational periods as well as size of the animals involved would limit the extent to which this phenomenon could take place (*GA* II. 738b28, 746a30).

61. Damīrī, *Ḥayawān,* vol. 1, 302.

62. Robert Lebling, *Legends of the Fire Spirits: Jinn and Genies from Arabia to Zanzibar* (Berkeley: Counterpoint Press, 2010), 42.

63. According to legend, Solomon had a potion of slaked lime and ash made to remove the hair on her legs (Nicholas Clapp, *Sheba: Through the Desert in Search of the Legendary Queen* [Boston: Mariner Books, 2002], 41).

64. Damīrī, *Ḥayawān,* vol. 1, 288, 289.

65. Ibid., 297.

66. See chapter 2, 57. See also Qazwīnī, *ʿAjāʾib al-makhlūqāt,* 351, who notes if the strengths of the two sperm are equal a hermaphrodite will result.

67. Muḥammad ibn Aḥmad al-Sarakhsī, *Kitāb al-Mabsūṭ* (Cairo: Maṭbaʿat al-saʿada, 1906–1913), summarized in Paula Sanders, "Hermaphrodites in Medieval Muslim Law," in *Women and Middle Eastern History,* ed. Nikki Keddie and Beth Baron (New Haven: Yale University Press, 1993), 74–95. Sarakhsī suggests hermaphrodites must be treated in such a way that their presence does not violate the divinely sanctioned positioning of men above women. So, for example, a hermaphrodite would pray behind the men in the prayer line, and yet in front of the women's prayer line. That way, if the hermaphrodite is "really" a male he is not praying behind a female, and if she is a female she is not praying in front of the men (80–81).

68. *Nuzhatu,* 75.

69. Ibid., 51–52.

70. Ibid., 31. In addition to the hyena, other animals are also endowed with the organs of both sexes. The tortoise (*al-sulaḥfāh al-barrīya*), for example, has two penises and two vulvae (Damīrī, *Ḥayawān,* vol. 1, 560), as does the thorn tail lizard (*ḍabb*), which is described as being crafty (Ibn Qutayba, *ʿUyūn al-akhbār,* 74). It is forbidden to eat the tortoise (Patricia Curtis, *Guide to Food Laws and Regulations* [Hoboken: Wiley-Blackwell Publications, 2005], 187), and there is some debate over the permissibility of consuming the lizard (Qazwīnī, *Nuzhatu,* 19).

71. Abū Ḥayyān, 434; Aristotle, *HA* 579b 16–17. See also Damīrī 641, who attributes this observation to Jāḥiẓ (*Ḥayawān*), Zamakhsharī (*Rabīʿ al-abrār*), and Ibn al-Ṣalāḥ (*Riḥla*) who have mentioned it on authority of Aristotle and others (*Ḥayawān*, vol. 1, 641).

72. Damīrī, *Ḥayawān*, 641. See also Jāḥiẓ, *Al-Ḥayawān*, vol. 6 (Cairo: Muʾassasah al-Miṣrīya al-ʿĀmma li al-Taʾlīf wa al-tarjama wa al-ṭibāʿa wa al-nashr, 1964), 50–51, for a complete description of the hyena's sexual violation of male corpses.

73. See note 67 above.

74. *Ḥayawān*, vol. 1, 297. Damīrī notes another tradition that states the mother of these devils was actually Ṭurṭubba; however, al-Naqqāsh denies her motherhood by stating that she only hatched the eggs that were already fertilized (ibid., 298).

75. Sanders, 74–76. The Qurʾān's numerous verses on the subject of marriage support the point that this institution was considered normative (e.g., Sūras 2:221, 4:21, 4:22, 4:23, 4:24, 4:25, 5:5, 24:32, 25:74, 40:8, 30:21).

76. Qazwīnī, *Nuzhatu*, 44.

77. Ibid., 67. See also Ibn Qutayba, who notes that the author of "Agriculture" points out how the eagle and the kite become converted into each other with the eagle becoming a kite and the kite an eagle. Ibn Qutayba points out this transformation is equivalent to the hare's, where the hare becomes a female and then the female a male (*ʿUyūn al-akhbār*, 93.69.2).

78. Qazwīnī, *Nuzhatu*, 67–68.

79. Ibid., 11. See also Ibn Qutayba *ʿUyūn al-akhbār*, 93. Damīrī also categorizes the hare as a hermaphrodite in addition to a transsexual. He reports how Ibn al-Athīr relates that a friend of his once hunted a hare having two testicles and a male organ of generation but also a female one. When they cut open its abdomen they saw signs indicative of its hermaphroditism (*Ḥayawān*, vol. 1, 31–32). Such anomalous animals are also used to demonstrate God's glory in Christian texts. For example, Clement of Alexandria (d. 215 CE) suggests the creator, as "a proof and indication of his provenance, has ordained a few animals to preserve their stock on the earth in an exceptional way: for example, the crow conceives through the mouth, the weasel brings forth through the ear; and some birds, such as hens, sometimes produce eggs conceived of wind or dust; other animals convert the male into female, and change their sex every year, as hares and hyaena, which they call monsters" (*Recognitions*, Bk VIII, ch. 25 in *The Ante-Nicene Christian Library: Translations of the Writing of the Fathers down to A. D. 325*, vol. 3 *Tatian, Theophilus, and the Clementine Recognitions*, ed. Alexander Roberts and James Donaldson [Edinburgh: T. and T. Clark, 1867-]).

80. Qazwīnī, *Nuzhatu*, 11. A question arises, however, as to whether or not hares have fangs, and should be prohibited on that basis.

81. See note 75 above.

82. Damīrī, *Ḥayawān*, vol. 1, 31–32.

83. Rosenthal, 54.

84. See note 75 above.

85. *Khalq*, 34.

86. Ibn Sīnā, *Qānūn,* vol. 2, 603.
87. Bukhārī, *Ṣaḥīḥ,* "Kitāb al-libās," no. 773.
88. Pellat, 142.
89. Damīrī, *Ḥayawān,* vol. 1, 534.
90. 449.
91. Qazwīnī, *Nuzhatu,* 2. He suggests it has been said that every animal that goes on two legs takes only a single mate, and while mated is jealous, but that all those that go on four legs become enamored of numerous mates.
92. *ʿUyūn al-akhbār,* 81.
93. Damīrī, *Ḥayawān,* vol. 1, 534.
94. Jāḥiẓ vehemently disagrees with this position on the basis that few animals can actually fertilize another species (*"Chance or Creation,"* 55–56). He declares the giraffe is simply an amazing creation of God.
95. *Muwaṭṭa'*, 28.8.21.
96. 712.
97. Ibn Qutayba reports that Abū Ḥātim, on the authority of Aṣmaʿī, stated, "Two men once quarreled about a boy's mother. The mother said that one of the two men had intercourse with her, after which she menstruated; afterward the other one had sex with her. ʿUmar called in two *qā'if*s to ask their opinion. One of them said, 'shall I divulge my answer or inform you secretly?' ʿUmar replied, 'Inform me secretly.' And [the *qā'if*] said, 'Both of them shared in begetting him.' ʿUmar struck the *qā'if* until he fell to the ground. Then he asked the other, who gave the same answer, after which ʿUmar exclaimed, 'It never occurred to me that such a thing could happen, although I knew that if several dogs leg one bitch she brings forth young resembling the different males' " (*ʿUyūn al-akhbār,* 69).
98. The *Babylonian Talmud* denies possibility of superfetation; a woman cannot conceive and conceive again (*Niddah* 27a). This same passage claimed, however, that it once happened. A child was born and then three months later another was born. Abaye explains this anomaly by saying the sperm divided into two sections: the features of one section was completed at the beginning of the seventh month, and features of the other were completed at end of the ninth month (*Niddah* 27a; 45). In the *Jerusalem Talmud,* a woman can become pregnant a second time but only within first forty days *(Yerushalmi Yebamoth* 5c), so in this context superfetation can occur (Preuss, *Biblical and Talmudic Medicine,* 386–87).
99. See, for example, Ṭabarī, *Tafsīr,* vol. 1, 205ff. Strangely, Ṭabarī, for the most part, maintains the Qur'ān's insistence on the anonymity of the brothers, and employs such ambiguous statements as "The son of Adam killed his companion" (ibid., 222). However, given that he does relate traditions that do identify the animal sacrifice as being Abel's and the agricultural sacrifice as being Cain's, we can surmise it was Cain who killed Abel (ibid., 204).
100. For an in-depth discussion of "mother blame" in contemporary American society, see Molly Ladd-Taylor and Lauri Umansky, eds., *"Bad Mothers," The Politics of Blame in Twentieth Century America* (New York: New York University Press, 1998).
101. The Qur'ānic "Eve" is never singled out for punishment, nor is she prescribed any gender-specific punishments, as is the case in Genesis 3.

102. Ṭabarī, *Tārīkh,* vol. 1, 106. See also D. A. Spellberg, "Writing the Unwritten Life of the Islamic Eve: Menstruation and the Demonization of Motherhood," in *International Journal of Middle Eastern Studies* 28, no. 3 (August 1996): 314.

103. Kisā'ī, *Qiṣaṣ,* 72.

104. Rabbān al-Ṭabarī, *Firdaws,* 33–34.

105. Ibid., 39.

106. See chapter 2, 70.

107. See M. J. Kister, "Call Yourselves By Graceful Names...," in *Society and Religion fron Jāhiliyya to Islam* (Aldershot: Variorum, 1990), 7. Interestingly, Kister notes that the name of al-Ḥārith, the name of Iblīs and apparently the name of an idol (or son of Adam) during the *jāhilīya* period, survived into the period of the prophet, and was even recommended by the prophet.

108. Spellberg, "Writing," 315. She notes how Ibn Sa'd reports on an exchange between Eve and Satan, who comes to her in disguise, during which Satan asks her what is in her womb. He plants the notion in her mind that it may be a monster. As she draws near her time for delivery, he reappears, suggesting that he will pray to Allāh that he makes a boy resembling Eve and Adam. A perfect boy was born to them (ibid.).

109. See Ibn Kathīr, *Qiṣaṣ,* 311; Kisā'ī, *Qiṣaṣ,* 215–16; Bukhārī, *Ṣaḥīḥ,* "Kitāb al-'aqīqa," no. 379; Muslim, *Ṣaḥīḥ,* "Kitāb al-adab," no. 5341; Ibn Qayyim, *Tuḥfat,* 65.

110. Kisā'ī, *Qiṣaṣ,* 72–73. See also Ibn Kathīr, *Qiṣaṣ,* 60. Here, Ibn Kathīr notes Abū Ja'far bin Jarīr mentioned in his *tārīkh* that Eve gave birth to forty children in twenty pregnancies. In another tradition, he notes, it is suggested that she had 120 pregnancies, and with every birth there were one boy and one girl.

111. See Ṭabarī, *Tārīkh,* vol. 1, 322, where Adam refuses to listen to Satan (since he had misled him in the Garden), and names his son Ṣāliḥ. So, Satan killed the boy.

112. Sūra 22:2. Bukhārī, *Ṣaḥīḥ,* "Kitāb al-anbiyā'," no. 567; "Kitāb tafsīr al-nabī," no. 265.

113. Preuss, *Biblical and Talmudic Medicine,* 413; *BT Shabbath* 32b.

114. What exactly is meant by a "half-person"? In other contexts, Qazwīnī states it is one of the diabolical beings, a creature having the appearance of half a human being. For example, it is asserted that the *nasnās* is a cross (*murakkab*) between a *shiqq* (a half-human being that is hairy, with one foot and one eye) and a human being (Damīrī, *Ḥayawān,* vol. 1, 601).

115. Bukhārī, *Ṣaḥīḥ,* "Kitāb al-nikāḥ," no. 169; "Kitāb al-adab," nos. 634, 711.

116. Judith Z. Abrams, *Judaism and Disability: Portrayals in Ancient Texts from the Tanach through the Bavli* (Washington, DC: Gallaudet University Press, 1998), 116. The *Babylonian Talmud* discourages any sort of indecorous sexual intercourse by linking it to birth defects. The correlation between decorum during sexual intercourse and positive outcomes in terms of fetal development was a widely held notion in other cultures. For examples, see Peter Brown, *The Body and Society: Men, Women, and Sexual Renunciation in Early Christianity* (New York: Columbia University Press, 1988).

117. Bukhārī, *Ṣaḥīḥ,* "Kitāb al-nikāḥ," no. 94; Nīsābūrī, 127. Nīsābūrī also underscores the necessity of reciting 16:7–9; to make sure the child is born healthy. Nīsābūrī also reports that to remedy a lack of children, one ought to recite Sūra 71:10–12, then have sex with one's wife (171).

118. Ghazālī, *Etiquette,* 106.

119. Ibn ʿArabī, *Tafsīr,* 180 (commentary on Sūra 3:35).

120. Ghazālī, *Etiquette,* 114.

121. Ibid, 21.

122. Bukhārī, "Kitāb al-nikāḥ," no. 94; see also Bukhārī, *Ṣaḥīḥ,* "Kitāb al-aymān wa al-nudhūr," no. 78, no. 634; "Kitāb kaffārāt al-aymān," no. 711.

123. *Ṭibb,* 10.

124. Rahman, 122.

125. Ibn Qutayba records that Al-Aṣmaʿī related a certain man once said, "The daughters of paternal uncles are more patient, but strangers are better fit to give birth to virtuous sons." He adds, no one is more capable of cutting off the heads of heroes than the son of a Persian woman. He notes now the Arabs say that if you go abroad you will not beget weak offspring, meaning, believers should marry foreign women (*ʿUyūn al-akhbār,* 67).

126. Sūra 2:222.

127. Ghazālī, *Etiquette,* 185.

128. *Kitāb khalq,* 28.

129. Ibid.

130. *Mishkāt,* 659; Ibn Māja, *Sunan,* nos. 1923, 1923; Bukhārī, *Ṣaḥīḥ,* "Kitāb tafsīr al-Qurʾān," no. 51.

131. Ibn Māja, *Sunan,* nos. 1923, 1924. See also *Mishkāt,* where Ibn ʿAbbās reported the prophet as saying when a man calls another a Jew, give him twenty lashes. When he calls someone a *mukhannath* (hermaphrodite), give him twenty lashes, and kill anyone who has intercourse with a woman who is within the prohibited degrees (774).

132. *Mishkāt,* 659, records how the phrase, "so come to your tilth as you please" (Sūra 2:223) allows for vaginal intercourse from the front or behind; however, men are not free to enter the anus, and must avoid intercourse during menstruation.

133. Nīsābūrī, 175.

134. Ibid., 176.

135. Cited in Etan Kohlberg, "The Position of the '*walad zina*' in Imami Shiʿism," *Bulletin of the School of Oriental and African Studies* 48, no. 2 (1985): 259.

136. Ibid., 247.

137. Ibid., 244.

138. Nīsābūrī, 175.

139. Ibid., 173.

140. Ibid., 174. Ibn Qutayba also relies on such folklore when he relates what the Arabs say: "If a woman conceives at the beginning of the time after the menstruation period or at the beginning of a month at daybreak, and therefore gives birth to a son, this one will become an unbearable person" (*ʿUyūn al-Akhbār,* 65).

141. Nīsābūrī, 174.

142. Ibn Sa'd, *Nisā'*, 24–25.

143. Ghazālī, *Etiquette*, 107.

144. Ibid. Ibn Ḥanbal confirms this statement by claiming a child born out of an adulterous relationship should not be held responsible for its parents' actions (*Musnad*, vol. VI, 109).

145. Sūra 3:6 (*Huwa allathī yusawwirukum fī al-arḥāmi kayfa yashā'u lā ilāha illa huwa al-'azīzu al-ḥakīmu*).

146. *'Uyūn al-akhbār,* 65.

147. Kisā'ī, *Qiṣaṣ*, 72.

148. Rabbān al-Ṭabarī, *Firdaws*, 36. See also Hippocrates, 322–23.

149. Ibid.

150. 'Arīb ibn Sa'd, *Kitāb khalq*, 10.

151. Ibn Kathīr, *Qiṣaṣ*, 54; Ṭabarī, *Tārīkh*, 309–10.

152. Tha'labī, *Qiṣaṣ*, 74.

153. Tha'labī, 75, records a tradition to this effect whose authority is traced back to Imām Ja'far al-Ṣādiq (*Qiṣaṣ*, 75). Theoretically, the *ḥūrīya* (a paradisiacal woman whose sole purpose is to pleasure the righteous in the Garden) would have been more attractive than the *jinnīya* (a female spirit or demon), which suggests that already God rewarded the righteous, prior to Cain's slaying of Abel.

154. Ibid.

155. This claim against incest is confirmed also by Arab wisdom. According to Ibn Qutayba, the Arabs say that if you go abroad you will not beget weak offspring. Only kindred wives give birth to weak offspring (*'Uyun al-akhbār*, 67).

156. Ṭabarī, *Tārīkh*, 310.

157. Sūra 17:11.

158. Sūra 51:49.

159. Abū Dā'ūd, *Sunan*, "Kitāb al-ṭahāra," no. 236. This phrase, which is often used by Muslims to support the equal status of women and men, is embedded in a discussion of nocturnal wetness: 'Ā'isha said: The Prophet was asked about the man who found wetness, and he did not remember a wet dream. He said, "He must bathe." He was asked abut the man who had a wet dream, but did not find wetness. He said, "He does not need to bathe." Then Umm Sulaym said, "And if a woman found that, must she bathe?" He said, "Yes, for women are twins of men (*innima 'l-nisā'u shaqā'iqu al-rijāli*)."

160. Sūra 4:11.

161. In biblical tradition, the firstborn receives double the amount of his brothers. See Dt 21:17; I Chr 5:1–2.

162. *Tosefta Baba Bathra* 2:2.

163. In fact, many traditions posit that Abel was born before Cain, and not vice versa. See Ṭabarī, *Tafsīr*, 222.

164. See Ibn Qayyim, *Tibyān*, 305. Dean-Jones discusses how the Hippocratics describe the womb as having two horns. The womb can contain many pockets and those animals that produce a great many offspring at one birth do so because the semen is divided between several pockets and a separate fetus develops in each (66–67). Ḥunayn ibn Isḥāq reports that living creatures that produce few offspring, such as the lion or woman, do so because they have few "wombs"; hence, the number of young is thus in accordance with the number

of wombs (439). ʿArīb ibn Saʿd records that some prominent scholars said that if the sperm falls in two wombs and is very hot, a small piece gets cut off, and separates into two to three sections, then there will be two or three embryos (*Kitāb khalq*, 26). In the Jewish context, it is said twins occur as a result of the drop of sperm dividing into two parts (*Yebamoth*, 98B).

165. Ibn Qayyim, *Tibyān*, 305. He states that twinning occurs when the womb moves around and some of the sperm ends up on one side of the womb, and some of it ends up on the other side.

166. Ibid. The same story is repeated in ʿArīb ibn Saʿd, *Kitāb khalq*, 27.

167. Ibn Qayyim *Tibyān*, 305. Rabbān al-Ṭabarī records that once a woman bore twenty children during four pregnancies. In every womb there were five fetuses, and they all lived (*Firdaws*, 35). He reports further that he has heard from another woman (note the source of authority is a woman) that a black woman bore thirty children, and this was in the course of thirty-five pregnancies. Mostly, she put out twins, and miscarried a time or two (ibid.).

168. ʿArīb ibn Saʿd, *Kitāb khalq*, 27.

169. Ḥunayn ibn Isḥāq, 459.

170. Ibid. He notes the substance of human beings usually produces single children. If it produces twins, that is accidental and nonnatural. If they are twins, and one is a male and the other female, it is more obvious that this phenomenon is unnatural.

171. Rabbān al-Ṭabarī, 35. Hippocrates also notes how certain animals, such as the dog and the pig, produce two or more offspring from one act of intercourse, as they have multiple pouches which "hold" the mixed seed (345). Abū Dāʾūd links together clothes stained with menstrual blood with dead dogs and other stinking things (*Sunan*, "Kitāb al-ṭahāra," no. 66). Some scholars link multiples with unnatural, bodily forms. For example, Ḥunayn ibn Isḥāq asks "Why do some animals get many young, and others few? The living creatures which get many young are pigs, dogs and hares, while those which get few offspring are a woman and a lion. That is because the animals which get many young have many wombs; when the seed is divided among their wombs they bear very many young. But this is not present in the living creatures which get few offspring. That is because they have few wombs. Hence the number of young is in accordance with the number of wombs" (439).

172. Qazwīnī, *Nuzhatu*, 17.

173. Ibid.

174. Ibn Qutayba, *ʿUyūn al-akhbār*, 81.

175. See chapter 5, 174.

176. John Andrew Boyle, "The Hare in Myth and Reality: A Review Article," *Folklore* 84, no. 4 (Winter 1973): 313. See also *The Encyclopaedia of Islam, New Edition: Supplement*, vols. 3–4, s.v. "arnab," by Clifford Edmund Bosworth.

177. It is mentioned that angels will never enter homes where there are pictures and dogs (Bukhārī, *Ṣaḥīḥ*, "Kitāb al-taṣwīr," nos. 833, 834, 835, 839, 840, 846; Abū Dāʾūd, *Sunan*: "Kitāb al-ṭahāra," no. 227; "Kitāb al-libās," no. 4140.

178. Abū Ḥayyān, 431. He notes lions and cats practice the same disgusting habit.

179. *Encyclopaedia of Islam*, s.v. "arnab."

180. In general, the issue at stake seems to have to do with the presence of fangs, which would allow an animal to rend meat. However, given the hare's rather suspect sexual qualities, it may be there were deeper suspicions regarding its inherent impurity.

181. *ʿUyūn al-akhbār,* 74.

182. Ibid.

183. ʿArīb ibn Saʿd, *Kitāb khalq,* 33–34. For other examples of such lengthy periods of gestation, some going as long as five years, see Ibn Qutayba: ʿAbdallāh ibn Ṣāliḥ said, "I have been informed by al-Layth on the authority of Ibn ʿAjlān that the latter's wife became pregnant and remained in that state for five years after which she gave birth. Another time she was pregnant for three years before being delivered of a child. Al-Layth added that a freed female slave of ʿUmar ibn ʿAbd al-ʿAzīz had been pregnant for three years, so that she feared a disease might be in her belly; after that she gave birth to a boy" (*ʿUyūn al-akhbār,* 66). Ibn Qutayba relates further that he has been informed by Thābit ibn Jābān alʿIjli that al-Ḍaḥḥāk ibn Muzāhim was born as a child of sixteen months. Yet Yazīd ibn Hārūn via Juwaybīr said al-Ḍaḥḥāk was born after two years. Shuʿba was born after two years also (ibid.). See also Damīrī, who provides the names of the persons whom their mothers carried in their wombs beyond the point of pregnancy: Sufyān b. Ḥayyān, who was born after having spent four years in his mother's womb; Muḥammad b. ʿAbdallāh b. Ḥasan al-Ḍaḥḥāk ibn-Muzāhim, who was born having been sixteen months in his mother's womb; Yaḥyā b. ʿAlī b. Jabir al-Bagawi, who was born in the same manner, and Salmān al-Ḍaḥḥāk who was born a boy of two years during which period he remained in his mother's womb (*Ḥayawān,* vol. 1, 80).

184. Such mothers would not be called "bearers of elephants" for nothing (ʿArīb ibn Saʿd, *Kitāb khalq,* 34).

185. Shuʿba, after all, was a prolific transmitter of *ḥadīth.*

186. ʿArīb ibn Saʿd, *Kitāb khalq,* 12: If the sperm is great in the man and the woman, or in both of them together, then from that will be two or three children on one pregnancy. These chances increase in some of the offspring of animals, whose wombs are differentiated via cavities.

187. Sailesh Kumar, *Handbook of Fetal Medicine* (Cambridge: Cambridge University Press, 2010), 131.

188. Rabbinic discussions about monstrous births reveal medieval Jewish concerns over where to draw lines between human/nonhuman. For rabbinic scholars, human features refer solely to features of the face (*Niddah* 23a). Sages make a general statement that the aborted fetus that does not not have features of a human being is not to be considered a human child. Such is so in the case of a woman who three times gave birth to the form of a raven (*Tosefta Niddah* 4:6). However, according to Rabbi Meir, if a woman aborts something that looks like a beast, or a wild animal, or a bird, she is considered a parturient woman and must abide in uncleanness according the sex of the fetus (*Niddah* 4:6; Preuss, *Biblical and Talmudic Medicine,* 415). Other references explore infants with one eye, unrecognizable skulls, bodies with the lower portion of the torso missing, fingers not separated, fusion of lower limbs, wings, two backs and two spinal columns, or with two heads (*Menachoth,* 37a).

189. *Kitāb khalq,* 34. In rabbinic literature there is mention of a "sandal fetus" that often accompanies birth of a named child (Preuss, 417; *Niddah* 25b and 26a). In this case, one child lies on top of another and flattens it, which results in a contorted form.

190. ʿArīb ibn Saʿd, *Kitāb khalq,* 34.

191. Ibid.

192. According to medieval Muslim sources, people will be resurrected in the state in which they were created, a stance that differs from Augustine, for example, who asserted bodies would be resurrected without blemish (Beth Felker Jones, *Mark of His Wounds: Gender Politics and Bodily Resurrection* [Oxford: Oxford University Press, 2007], 28); Ṭayālisī, *Musnad,* 2638, Aḥmad ibn Ḥanbal, *Musnad,* vol. I, 220, 223, 229, 235, 253, 398. In these examples from the medieval Muslim tradition, there is no need for perfection of the body; by comparison with the Christian examples, Muslim tradition is much more open to deviance.

193. Despite such "open" perspectives, the tradition still treats physical anomalies as less than ideal. Ibn Māja, *Sunan,* nos. 3144, 3145, reports one cannot sacrifice animals with obvious defects; however, minor nicks are acceptable. Muslim reports on the authority of Abū Hurayra that the messenger of God used to dislike the *shikāl* horse (*Ṣaḥīḥ,* "Kitāb al-imāra," no. 623). "*Shikāl*" refers to a horse whose right back foot and left front or left back foot and right front foot are white (ibid., 4624).

194. Damīrī, *Ḥayawān,* vol. 1, 226.

195. Darrel W. Amundsen, *Medicine, Society, and Faith in the Ancient and Medieval Worlds* (Baltimore: Johns Hopkins University Press, 1997), 65; Augustine of Hippo, *Writings of St. Augustine* (New York: Cima, 1947), 87.

196. ʿArīb ibn Saʿd, *Kitāb khalq,* 26–27.

197. Ibn Qayyim, *Tibyān,* 304. See also al-Suyūṭī, *Ṭibb al-nabawī,* 193, who notes that after a drop of semen reaches the womb, a woman will no longer desire to have sexual intercourse.

198. The reason why Islamic law abhors adultery is to prevent a child whose descent is (literally) "mixed up." The *Jerusalem Talmud,* by way of contrast, suggests a woman may indeed become impregnated by two men. If a woman has intercourse with a second man within three days of having sex with the first man, the sperm could mix together and produce a child with two fathers (*Yerushalmi Yebamoth* 4; 5c). See below.

199. Rabbān al-Ṭabarī, *Firdaws,* 305.

200. Ḥunayn ibn Isḥāq, 517. Such views are based on Aristotelian science (Dean-Jones, 199). For Aristotle, monstrosities are often caused by an extraneous amount of matter.

201. Ibn Qayyim, *Tibyān,* 304. Rabbinic sources note how intercourse during the middle three months becomes important in generating a healthy fetus (Preuss, *Biblical and Talmudic Medicine,* 385).

202. Ibid., 386: Aristotle, *Des Generationes* 4:87–88.

203. *Firdaws,* 35. Rabbinic literature claims it happened once. A child was born and three months later another was born from the same womb. Abaye says the sperm divided into two sections, and the features of one form were completed at the beginning of the seventh month, and the features of the other

completed at end of nine months (*Niddah* 27a; 45). However, contradictory positions exist as well. The Talmud denies the possibility of superfetation: "A woman does not conceive and conceive again" (*Niddah* 27a) (Rosner, *Biblical and Talmudic Medicine,* 386–87).

204. Aristotle, *HA* VII, iv. 585a8–27, notes no female among males is receptive to coitus after impregnation except for the woman and the mare. Likewise, he records a narrative about a certain woman who miscarried twelve children in successive pregnancies. Another woman committed adultery after having become pregnant. She gave birth to two sons, of whom one resembled the husband and the other the adulterer. Certain women miscarry and become pregnant at the same time, so that one fetus leaves the womb and the other is conceived. In these instances, biological "fact" makes it easier for women to be accused of adultery. With Muslim theories on resemblance, heredity is used by the prophet either to refute or support Greco-Roman theories.

205. *ʿUyūn al-akhbār,* 69.

206. The "evil twin" figures prominently in a number of creation mythologies, in particular those of the Iroquoi, the Yuma tribe of Arizona, the Aztecs, and Melanesian Banks island people (David Adams Leeming, *Creation Myths of the World: An Encyclopedia,* vol. 1 [Santa Barbara: ABC-CLIO, 2009], 327); Zurvanism offers another example. In this tradition that may have existed prior to Zoroastrianism, Zurvan's wife bore him twins, Ahura Mazda and Ahriman. Zurvan decreed Ahura Mazda would rule the universe, but upon hearing this Ahriman ripped his way out of the womb in anger. He thus became the opponent of Ahura Mazda for the rest of time (Robert Ellwood, *Tales of Darkness: The Mythology of Evil* [London: Continuum, 2010], 45ff).

207. See Florentino Garcia Martinez, "Eve's Children in the Targumim," in *Eve's Children: The Biblical Stories Retold and Interpreted in Jewish and Christian Traditions,* ed. Gerard P. Luttikhuizen (Leiden: Koninklijke, Brill, 2003), 30–31.

208. Qazwīnī, *Nuzhatu,* 38.

209. Gordon Newby, *The Making of the Last Prophet: A Reconstruction of the Earliest Biography of Muḥammad* (Columbia: University of South Carolina Press, 1989), 48.

210. Qazwīnī, *Nuzhatu,* 36; Shildrick, *Embodying the Monster,* 31.

211. Abū Ḥayyān, 425. Abū Ḥayyān also notes that snakes are gluttonous, insatiable, and immoral creatures. They drink little water but cannot restrain themselves when smelling wine, since they have a great craving for it (410). See also Pliny, *Natural History* Book 10, ch. 72 for the same lore about snakes.

212. *Ḥayawān,* vol. I, 57.

213. Boswell, 137–38, notes the Epistle of Barnabas on this issue.

214. Damīrī, *Ḥayawān,* vol. 1, 405.

215. Pellat, 162.

216. A similar tale of twins (with cognate names for the sisters: Qlimta and Lbuda) appears in the VI century Syriac "Cave of Treasures." See Jurgen Tubach, "Seth in Early Syriac Literature," in *Eve's Children,* 187–208.

217. Ibn Kathīr, *Qiṣaṣ,* 54; Thaʿlabī, 74.

218. Thaʿlabī, 74.

219. Ibid., 55.

220. Ibid., 74.

221. Majūsī, *Kitāb kāmil*, vol. 2, 56.

222. Ibn Qutayba, *ʿUyūn al-akhbār*, 68.

223. Bukhārī, *Ṣaḥīḥ*, "Kitāb al-ḥayḍ," nos. 41, 43, 46; "Kitāb al-nikāḥ," nos. 39, 41, 46, 166.

224. Ibn Sīnā, *Qānūn*, vol. 1, 53.

225. See Mālik, *Muwaṭṭa'* (Cairo: Dar al-Nafa'is, 1977), 414. Note, however, that there are also statements to the contrary, which suggest the issue was far from resolved. Ibn Sa'd, for example, reports how the prophet once stated that he wanted to forbid the *ghīla* (a man having intercourse with his wife while she is breastfeeding) but then remembered that the Greeks and Persians used to practice it and it did not harm their children (*Nisā'*, 172).

226. Ṭabarī, *Tārīkh*, 310; Thaʿlabī, 74.

227. Ṭabarī, *Tārīkh*, 310–11.

228. Ibid., 311.

229. *ʿUyūn al-akhbār*, vol. 2, 67.

230. Thaʿlabī, 75. See also Ṭabarī, *Tafsīr*, vol. 10, 205.

231. Thaʿlabī, 75. Kisāʾī makes the exact opposite claim, and suggests Cain offered from the best of his grain (*Qiṣaṣ*, 77). In his commentary on Sūra 5:27, Ṭabarī records traditions that support both views, and also includes neutral reports that Cain simply offered grain that was not accepted by God (*Tafsīr*, vol. 10, 204–205).

232. Tha'labī, 77, reports how Ibn Jurayj said, "Cain did not know how to kill his brother, so Iblis appeared to him and took a bird, placed its head on a stone, and then crushed it with another stone" (77). For the same narrative, see also Ṭabarī, *Tafsīr*, vol. 10, 222.

233. Ṭabarī, *Tārīkh*, 314.

234. Ibid., 338.

235. Ibid., 338–39.

236. Ibid., 341.

Chapter 6. The Cure of Perfection

1. Stone, 49. See also Monique Wittig, *Straight Mind and Other Essays* (Boston: Beacon Press, 1992), who argues the categories of man and woman are political categories and not natural givens (14). In other words, such categories are social and ontological. Thus, the marking of those parts of the body tend to be those that are most useful to sexual reproduction. Therefore, binary categories of sex would be defended so vehemently precisely because they constitute the foundation upon which the *heterosexualization* of society and the imperative of sexual reproduction rest. Wittig argues the category of sex is detrimental to all women inasmuch as it "conceals the political fact of the subjugation of one sex by the other" while grounding heterosexual relations in the order of nature itself (5). Stone reiterates this view in his discussion of Genesis, when he suggests this text does much to promote, naturalize, and sanctify a particular obligatory social relationship between man and woman (50). He emphasizes

further notions of complementarity: what governs human/divine, male/female relationships becomes normative and ingrained in nature (53).

2. See Stone, who describes this phenomenon in the biblical context (54). See also Judith Butler, *Bodies that Matter,* 237.

3. See chapter 1, 21.

4. See chapter 1, 25.

5. See chapter 1, 23.

6. See chapter 1, 27

7. See chapter 1, 24.

8. See chapter 1, 25.

9. The "heterosexual dynamic" assumes the male/female binary to be both natural and normative, and privileges reproduction as the primary goal of human sexuality (Stone, 49–50).

10. Heterosexuality is a requirement for procreation. Other types of pairings would obviously not result in the mixing of the two sperms to create life. However, this assertion does not mean that there is no room for humans (and God) to enter into other types of intimate, sexual relationships or pairings, which are often observed among the *ḥayawānāt*. For example, Ibn Qutayba records a tradition on the authority of al-Muthanná ibn Zuhayr, who said: "I have never seen anything in the behavior of a man or woman that I have not seen in pigeons. I have seen a female pigeon, which desired but its own mate, and I have seen one which denied nothing to the other males. I have observed a female pigeon, which did not drag its tail ready to be trod, save after persistent endeavor on the part of the male, and another which yielded to the male at the first overtures. I have seen a female pigeon which allowed one specific male only to approach it, none other, and I have seen a female pigeon treading another female, a female treading a male, a male treading another male, a male treading whatever female it came across without regular pairing, and a male having two females and brooding on the eggs and feeding the young in company of neither" (*ʿUyūn al-akhbār,* 67).

11. Sūra 2:117.

12. Abū Ḥayyān, 406, in *Osiris.* For more on partridges, see *HA* 541 a 27; 560 b 13; *Ale.* xvii 15; *Antig.* 87. See also Eugene McCartney, "Spontaneous Generation and Kindred Notions in Antiquity," *Transactions and Proceedings of the American Philological Association* 51 (1920): 110.

13. Ibn Qutayba, *ʿUyūn al-akhbār,* 67. He also notes how eggs may be generated within females via dust or copulation, in addition to wind. See also Abū Ḥayyān, 448.

14. Aristotle refers to wind eggs in *GA,* Bk. III, ch. 1, 749b. He notes that some embryos are formed in birds spontaneously (without coitus and without a male presence). He refers specifically to the partridge in *HA* Book VI, ch. 2. Pliny also mentions wind eggs that occur in partridges, hens, and other fowl. For Pliny, wind eggs may be a product of mutual treading, a bird's lustful imagination, or (like Ibn Qutayba) dust (*Natural History,* X, 102). Qazwīnī also refers to wind eggs in his discussion of hens. At the time of sexual desire, if the hen does not meet with a cock, she rolls in the dust, and from that rolling small eggs are formed inside her, but their flavor is bad and they produce no

young. But if the cock treads her before she forms her eggs, the eggs are good (*Nuzhatu*, 70). See also Conway Zirkle, "Animals Impregnated by the Wind," *Isis* 25, no. 1 (May 1936): 111. In theory, pullets lay eggs without coition, but these are thought to be sterile, unfertilized eggs, or "virgin eggs."

15. Ibn Qutayba, *ʿUyūn al-akhbār*, 67.

16. A *hippomane* is described by Aristotle as a growth found on the forehead of a foal, which the mare consumes, along with the afterbirth. If confiscated by a human, the smell sends the mare into a rage (J. M. King, "The Origin and Development of the *Hippomanes* in the Horse and Zebra," *Journal of Anatomy* [1967]: 277).

17. *HA*, Book VI, 18.572a; Zirkle, 97. Virgil's *Georgics* describes how certain mares were impregnated by the west wind. Varro adds that the foals produced by such an encounter only live about three years; clearly, they are inferior products (*De re rustica*, II; i, as cited by Zirkle, 98).

18. ʿArīb ibn Saʿd, *Kitāb khalq*, 18.

19. Book VI, ch. 27, as cited by Zirkle, 98. Here, the Roman author views such conceptions as deviant, the result of inappropriate female sexual behavior.

20. *Natural History*, Pt. 1, Bk. 8, 222, as cited by Zirkle, 99. The story of the mares is also repeated in Christian works such as Augustine, *The City of God*, Bk. XXI, ch. 5.

21. Eusebios, *Praeparationes evangelicae*, Bk. III, ch. 12, as cited by Zirkle, 106.

22. Horapollon Nilous, as referenced by Zirkle, 106.

23. This observation was made by Remke Kruk, "A Frothy Bubble: Spontaneous Generation in the Medieval Islamic Tradition," *Journal of Semitic Studies* XXXV, no. 2 (Autumn 1990): 279.

24. Zirkle, 118.

25. The Qurʾān, of course, also suggests life may be generated from water (*māʾ*).

26. Sūras 21:30, 24:45, 25:54. Qazwīnī (revised geographical writings?) also refers to the isles of women, where women conceive by the wind and bring into the world females like themselves. "It is also said they conceive by eating the fruit of a tree which is on there itself. Qazwīnī goes on to describe a large city on one of the isles of the sea of Maghrib, where women kill male children" (as referenced by Zirkle, 120).

27. Zirkle, 119.

28. Jāḥiẓ, for example, notes how God created the Messiah in Mary's bosom, without the help of a man. That God would create a child out of a woman without the intervention of any man, but not a child out of a man without a woman, elevates the status of women, according to Jāḥiẓ (Pellat, 258).

29. Ibid., 275. Jāḥiẓ likewise underscores the miraculous nature of this event, and emphasizes the essential significance of the female in this event. After all, God created a child out of a woman without the intervention of any man, but never a child out of a man without a woman. Thus it is especially to woman and not to man that he vouchsafed this wonderful sign. This signal is a token, when he created the Messiah in Mary's bosom, without a man.

30. Sūras 23:12–14 and 22:5 discuss in detail the divinely created stages of fetal development that proceed via God's discrete creations.

31. Chapter 12 as referenced by Zirkle, 100. Origen, also, in the *Errors of Celsos* (I:37), defends the virgin birth by stating, "For it is ascertained that there is a certain female animal which has no intercourse with the male (as writers on animals say is the case with vultures), and that this animal, without sexual intercourse, preserves the succession of the race." Origen goes on to suggest that because God wished to send a divine teacher to humanity, why wouldn't he cause him to be born in some uncommon manner? "Nay, according to the Greeks themselves, all men were not born of man and woman" (Origen, cited by Zirkle, 106). Other defenders of the virgin birth who reference wind eggs include St. Basil (*The Hexaemeron,* Homily VIII, Sec. 6), and St. Ambrose (*Hexaemeron,* V:20), who states, "A bird bears without a mate and none confutes it, and because Mary bore when betrothed they question her chastity" (cited by Zirkle, 107).

32. Kruk, "A Frothy Bubble," 267.

33. Aristotle, *HA* 5.19.550b. This theory of spontaneous generation also appears in Pliny, *Natural History,* 11:37–39.

34. McCartney, "Spontaneous Generation," 105; Ovid, *Met.* xv 368.

35. McCartney, "Spontaneous Generation," 104; Aristotle, *HA* 551 a 1.

36. McCartney, "Spontaneous Generation,"107. *HA* 569a10–27. Ovid reflects on the fact that on hornets are generated in horses, or mules (*Met.* xv 368).

37. *Recognitions* of Clement, Bk VIII, ch. 25, as referenced by Zirkle, 112.

38. Damīrī, *Ḥayawān,* vol. 1, 646 on *al-ḍifdiʿ* (frog). Damīrī records how frogs are not the product of the male and female. There is a well-established notion in antiquity that frogs were generated from mud (McCartney, "Spontaneous Generation," 109; Ovid, *Met* xv 375; Kruk, "Spontaneous Generation," 266; al-Waṭwāt, *Mabāhij,* MS Leiden Or. 219 fols. 84b–85a; Ibn Abī al-Ḥawāfir, MS Chester Beatty 4352 fols. 94a–94b. See also Augustine, *City of God,* trans. Marcus Dods (New York: Modern Library, 1950), Book 16, ch. 7.

39. *Ikhwān al-Ṣafāʾ*, vol. 2, 231, 1928, as cited by Kruk, "Spontaneous Generation," 266.

40. Nuwayrī, 1923, vol. x, 152; Remke, 266.

41. Ibn Ḥayyān, 452; Muḥammad ibn ʿAbd al-Mālik Ibn Ṭufayl, *Ḥayy ibn Yaqẓān* (Cairo: Dār al-Maʿārif, 1966), 88; Kruk, "Spontaneous Generation," 266.

42. Abū Ḥayyān, 452.

43. Qazwīnī, *Nuzhatu,* 90; Abū Ḥayyān, 449.

44. Abū Ḥayyān, 452. Perhaps the reason why ants and bees are venerated in the Qurʾān with their own chapter headings has to to do with the fact that each are generated spontaneously, or, more specifically, in extraordinary ways by will of God. Abū Ḥayyān, 449, for example, notes bees bring forth young without impregnation by males. Ibn Abī al-Ashʾath, as quoted by Aḥmad ibn ʿAbd al-Wahhāb al-Nuwayrī, suggests ants drop something insignificant on the earth, and this grows until it becomes sperm and from that they come into being (parthenogenesis). Here, a combination of organic matter plus inorganic matter unites together to create a new animal (*Nihāyat al-arab fī funūn al-adab,* vol. X [Cairo, 1923], 174, as cited by Kruk, "Spontaneous Generation," 267).

45. Qazwīnī, *Nuzhatu,* 86. Of course, this generation only occurs because God allows it to be. To emphasize this point, Qazwīnī ends his tale with the proclamation, "And praise be to him. How great is his glory in the creation of the animals!" The peculiar reproduction of the phoenix is also mentioned in Theophylactos, who notes "The regeneration of the Phoenix, a virgin bird, must be conceded to spontaneous generation" (Bk VI, ch. 7, 956, as cited by Zirkle, 111).

46. Kruk, "Spontaneous Generation," 274.

47. Ḥayy, the hero of Ibn Ṭufayl's novel, grows up on an island with no contact with human society. Eventually, he gains uncorrupted knowledge of the world. His intellectual development allows him to move from grasping simple scientific truths to comprehending abstract philosophical truth, where Aristotelian and Neoplatonic philosophies are combined in a mystical view of the world. Later he meets a representative of traditional religion, and Ḥayy realizes he had intuited the same truths on his own (Hans Daiber, "The Reception of Islamic Philosophy at Oxford in the 17th Century: The Pecocks' (Father and Son) Contribution to the Understanding of Islamic Philosophy in Europe," in *The Introduction of Arabic Philosophy into Europe,* ed. Charles E. Butterworth and Blake Andrée Kessel, [Leiden: Brill, 1997], 76).

48. The other perfectly balanced and blended man was Adam, who contained the four natures: heat, cold, wetness, and dryness, that were prepared within four things: yellow bile, black bile, phlegm, and blood (*Ikhwān al-Ṣafā,* as cited by Murata, 42).

49. For examples of Qur'ānic portrayals of God creating man from clay and delivering a spirit or breath into him (that animates the clay), see Sūras 38:71–72 and 32:9.

50. Observation by Kruk, "Spontaneous Generation," 275, who quotes Ibn Ṭufayl (trans. Goodman, 1972), 106.

51. See chapter 1, 29.

52. Ibn Khaldūn, *Muqaddima,* vol. 2, 371.

53. Kruk, "Spontaneous Generation," 272. See also McCartney, "Spontaneous Generation," 103, who notes how Aristotle takes pains to express his own views about the process of spontaneous generation (*GA* 762 a 10). Aristotle maintains that animals do not originate from putrefied matter, but rather from an admixture of rainwater with matter undergoing putrefaction. The sweet elements in this combination produce the animals, and the putrefied matter is the residue in the process.

54. Ibn Qutayba *ʿUyūn al-akhbār,* 67; see also Ḥunayn ibn Isḥāq, 629, who states the limbs of the *zanj* are twisted because the seed that produces them is cooked.

55. Here, such heterodox theories about how life begins contrast sharply with, for example, the Muʿtazilite acceptance of creation *ex nihilo.* For Muʿtazilte views on creation *ex nihilo,* see Ibrahim Kalin's "Will, Necessity, and Creation as Monistic Theophany in the Islamic Philosophical Tradition," in *Creation and the God of Abraham,* ed. David B. Burrell, Carlo Cogliati, and Janet M. Soskice (Cambridge: Cambridge University Press, 2010), 116ff.

56. Kruk, "Spontaneous Generation," 270.

57. Ibn ʿArabī, *Futūḥāt,* vol. I, 138.17, as cited by Murata, 145.

58. Ibid., vol. I, 131.23, as cited by Murata, 143.

59. Ibid, vol. I, 131.23, cited by Murata, 143. Here, Ibn ʿArabī notes God "made the earth like the wife and the heaven like the husband. The heaven cast something off the command that God reveal to it into the earth, just as the man casts water into the woman through intercourse."

60. Ibid., vol. III, 440.25, cited by Murata, 152.

61. Stone (54) refers to Michel Foucault (*The History of Sexuality,* vol. 1), who notes that there may be no naturalized categories of sex; however, the alternative is not the transcendence of culture and power relations but rather the proliferation of power relations within them.

62. See chapter 2, 69.

63. The Qur'ān has no precise word for "metamorphosis"; rather, it refers more generally to the idea that one species can be created (*jaʿala*), and then essentially that form can be destroyed and another created in its place. The word also means "to appoint" or designate, a meaning that fleshes out further the idea that God's establishment of a thing, person, position, or identity prevails over any type of transformation that might take place in nature, or as a result of individual desire.

64. See also Sūra 5:60, which describes those whom God has cursed and on whom he has poured forth his wrath; he has "transformed them into monkeys and swine and worshipers of the devil." In similar fashion, Sūra 7:166 states that "then, when the disdained arrogantly do what they were forbidden, we said to them be miserable monkeys." Of course, in some instances God allows Jesus to perform such transformations. Qazwīnī, for example, notes that when the Banū Isrā'īl desired of Jesus the miracle of the production of an animal, he made a mouse of clay and blew upon it, and it became a bat (*khuffāsh*) and flew away (*Nuzhatu,* 69). This act, however, differs from the Qur'ānic reference to Jesus animating a clay bird. There, he does not transform that clay object into something else, but rather gives it life.

65. See, for example, Sūra 3:47, where God created Adam from dust and then said, "Be!" and he was.

66. *Ṣaḥīḥ,* "Kitāb al-zuhd wa al-raqā'iq," nos. 7135, 7136. See also Ibn Qutayba, *ʿUyūn al-akhbār,* 71, who refers to a Jewess as a mouse that would not drink camel's milk.

67. *The Arabian Nights Encyclopedia,* 53, which mentions such temporary or permanent metamorphoses of humans into animals, and vice versa, in the tales of *The Second Shaykh's Story; The Tale of the Ensorcelled Prince; The Second Qalandar's Tale; Jullanār the Sea-born and Her Son King Badr Bāsim of Persia;* and the *History of Sīdī Nuʿmān.*

68. *The Arabian Nights Encyclopedia,* vol. 1, 53.

69. See Ibn Sīnā, *De congelatione et conglutinatione,* referred to by Caroline Bynum, *Metamorphosis and Identity* (New York: Zone Books, 2001), 83. The idea of change is linked with identity. In the Christian context, Church lawyers continued to employ the famous *Canon episcopi* of ca. 900, that prohibited as blasphemy the belief in metamorphosis or body exchange. Theologians repeated Augustine's statement that humans do not become animals, although demons may utilize extremely complex strategies to make it appear that they do (Bynum, 82). See

also Joyce E. Salisbury, *The Beast Within: Animals in the Middle Ages* (New York and London: Routledge, 1994), 160.

70. Damīrī, *Ḥayawān*, vol. 1, 402.

71. *Sīrat rasūl Allāh*, 412. Likewise, the *Sīra* mentions how God transformed the people of Moses into apes for their sins (251).

72. Schochet, *Animal Life*, references *Genesis Rabbah* 23:6; *Sanhedrin*, 109ca. Louis Ginzberg, *The Legends of the Jews*, trans. Henrietta Szold (Philadelphia: The Jewish Publication Society of America, 1936–1942), 5:152, no. 55.

73. Schochet, references to *Genesis Rabbah* 23:6; *Sanhedrin*, 109ca.

74. Ibid.

75. *Sunan*, no. 4020.

76. Pellat, 158.

77. Muḥammad ibn ʿAlī bn Abī Jumhūr al-Aḥsāʾī, *Hādhā huwa al-kitāb al-ma'rūf bi-al-Mujallī al-mawsūm bi-Masālik al-afhām wa-al-Nūr al-munjī min al-ẓalām* (Tehran: s.n., 1911), 507.

78. Pellat, 153.

79. In similar fashion, Jāḥiẓ states, "Why should such things happen to people at all? We say, to stop them relying on the continuance of that security which encourages the wicked to trust in sinful things and slackens the efforts of the righteous to to good. Disastrous events make them humble and rouse them do to what is right" (*"Chance or Creation,"* 118). Such transformations of the self are also implied in discussions about resurrection. The resurrection on the last day is only possible through the suffering of afflictions. According to Jāḥiẓ, those who suffer afflictions have rewards in the hereafter, but only if they bear them patiently and thank their Lord and turn toward him. These rewards are so great as to make them regard the affliction as something small, so small that, if they were given the choice of the resurrection, they would choose to be returned to such suffering in order to have their rewards increased (ibid.). Here, without the opportunity to experience affliction, one presumably would not have the opportunity to transcend one's moral failures.

80. Muslim, *Ṣaḥīḥ*, "Kitāb al-qadar," nos. 6425, 6426, 427, 6428, 6429.

81. Ibid., no. 6423.

82. Each of these practices is mentioned as being characteristic of the *fiṭra* (Bukhārī, *Ṣaḥīḥ*, "Kitāb al-libās," nos. 777, 779). See also Abū Dāʾūd, *Sunan*, "Kitāb al-tarajjul," 418; Aḥmad b. Muḥammad ibn Ḥanbal, *al-Musnad*, vol. II, 229, 239, 283, 410, 489; vol. IV, 264; Mālik, "Sīfat al-nabī," in *Al-Muwaṭṭaʾ*, ed. Fārūq Saʿd (Beirut: Dār al-āfāq al-jadīda, 1981), 3.3; Muslim, "Kitāb al-ṭahāra," in *Ṣaḥīḥ*, nos. 495, 96; Nasāʾī, "Kitāb al-zinā," in *Sunan*, vol. 1, 75; Tirmidhī, "Abwāb al-adab," in *Ṣaḥīḥ*, 14. The list often expands to include letting the beard grow, washing the finger joints, and cleansing one's private parts with water (Abū Dāʾūd, *Ṣaḥīḥ*, "Kitāb al-ṭahāra," no. 52; Muslim, *Ṣaḥīḥ*, "Kitāb al-ṭahāra," nos. 502, 503).

83. Ibn Māja, *Sunan*, no. 1989.

84. Jāḥiẓ, *"Chance or Creation,"* 84.

85. See, for example, the *Gospel of Matthew* 18:9, for a similar sentiment. It states "If your eye causes you to sin, tear it out and throw it away. It is better

for you to enter into life with one eye than with two eyes than to be thrown into hell." See also the *Gospel of Mark* 9:47. A hand, too, may fall by the wayside if it "causes you to sin" (Mt. 5:30), as well as a foot (Mk 9:45).

86. *Kitāb khalq,* 10.

87. In addition, foreskin and excess hair impedes one's ability to cleanse oneself fully; in order to realize full, bodily purity it must be cut off. For example, the Shīʿite scholar Kulaynī records, "Do not grow your mustache long, for it is as if Satan took it as a hiding place, and concealed himself in it" (Kulaynī, *Furūʿ min al-kāfī,* "Kitāb al-ziyy wa ʿl-tajammul wa ʿl-murūʿa," [Tehrān: Maktabat al-Ṣadūq, 1957], 489, no. 11). See also no. 7.

88. Jāḥiẓ, *"Chance or Creation,"* 90.

89. Kister, 13, states Ibn Bābūya al-Qummī claimed every Shīʿite imam to be born circumcised and purified.

90. Ibid.

91. Ibn Khaldūn, *Muqaddima,* vol. 2, 370.

92. 430. See also Qazwīnī, *Nuzhatu,* 29; Ibn Qutayba, *ʿUyūn al-akhbār,* 84. Such a practice was also observed by Pliny, *Natural History,* vol. 3, books 8–9.

93. Ibn Māja, *Sunan,* nos. 2470, 2471.

94. Ibn Qutayba, *ʿUyūn al-akhbār,* 76.

95. The Qurʾān advocates this general ethical premise. "Let there be one community of you, calling to good, and commanding right and forbidding wrong" (Sūra 3:102, as quoted in Michael Cook, *Forbidding Wrong in Islam: An Introduction* [Cambridge: Cambridge University Press, 2001], 11). A *ḥadīth* supports this Qurʾānic maxim, but states the obligation more succinctly and explicitly: The prophet said, "Whoever sees a wrong, and is able to put it right with his hand, let him do so; if he can't, then with his tongue; if he can't, with his heart, and that is the bare minimum of faith" (ibid., 4). This study does not attempt to trace all the sources on this issue, but it simply asserts the more general principle of the need for humans to rectify what is wrong by doing what is right. Even women fall under this umbrella, according to most medieval scholars (Cook, 15–16).

96. *Kitāb khalq,* 44.

97. The *Materia Medica,* 51, also talks about *sausan,* in that it stops excessive flow of fluid of the prostate gland and excessive ejaculation.

98. Ibid., 131.

99. Ibid., 165, citing Yuḥanna Ibn Māsawayh's *Nawādir al-ṭibbīya.*

100. *Kitāb al-qarābādhīn ʿala tartīb al-ʿilal,* trans. Martin Levey and Noury al-Khaledy (Philadelphia: University of Pennsylvania Press, 1967), 68.

101. John Riddle, *Contraception and Abortion from the Ancient World to the Renaissance* (Cambridge: Harvard University Press, 1994), 70.

102. Qazwīnī, *Nuzhatu,* 11–12.

103. Robert E. Hall," Intellect, Soul, and Body in Ibn Sīnā: Systematic Synthesis and Development of the Aristotelian, Neoplatonic, and Galenic Theories," in *Interpreting Avicenna: Science and Philosophy in Medieval Islam,* ed. John McGinnis and David Reisman (Leiden: Brill, 2004), 76.

104. Schochet, *Animal Life,* 89; *Tosefta ʿatikata* 5:19; Ginzberg, *Legends,* 6:206, n. 111.

105. Rabbān al-Ṭabarī, *Firdaws,* quoted in Plinio Prioreschi, *History of Medicine,* vol. 1 (Omaha: Horatius Press, 1996), 355. See also Manfred Ullmann, *Islamic Medicine* (Edinburgh: Edinburgh University Press, 1978), 108.

106. The associations between frogs and fertility most likely go back to Sumerian times, as noted by P. B. Adamson, "Some Rituals Associated with Parturition in Ancient Antiquity," *Folklore* 96, no. 2 (1985): 176. The frog-headed *Heket* was also a lesser birth goddess of upper Egypt.

107. Damīrī, *Ḥayawān,* vol. 1, 496.

108. Interestingly, the life forces within the pregnant women can also be tapped into in order to cure illnesses. Rāzī, in his *Kitāb al-ḥāwī fī al-ṭibb,* states quartan fever can be cured if the patient wears the unwashed sweaty shirt of a woman in labor (Prioreschi, 355; Ullman, 109).

109. Qazwīnī, *Nuzhatu,* 30.

110. Namu Jia, "Myths and Traditional Beliefs about the Wolf and the Crow in Central Asia: Examples from the Turkic Wu-Sun and the Mongols," *Asian Folklore Studies* 65, no. 2 (2006): 170.

111. J. H. Hutton and J. P. van den Brand de Cleverskerk, "Wolf-Children," *Folklore* 51, no. 1 (March 1940): 10.

112. Rabbān al-Ṭabarī, *Firdaws,* quoted by Prioreschi, 354. See also E. Savage-Smith, "Medicine," in *Encyclopedia of the History of Arabic Science,* ed. Roshdi Rashed, vol. 3 (London: Routledge 1996), 903–62.

113. Jürgen W. Frembgen, "The Folklore of Geckos: Ethnographic Data from South and West Asia," *Asian Folklore Studies* 55 (1996): 140. See also James Frazer, *The Golden Bough: A Study in Magic and Religion,* vol. 9, part 6: *The Scapegoat* (New York: Macmillan, 1951), 302. Ibn Qutayba also notes how the thorn-tailed lizard (*ḍabb*) has two penises and two vulva, which would make it that much more fertile (*ʿUyūn al-akhbār,* 74).

114. Damīrī, *Ḥayawān,* vol. 2, 178. In ancient Indian traditions, the elephant was associated with water, and thus fertility. Buddhists believe elephants to be incarnations of the future Buddha. Queen Maya, after all, was approached by a young white elephant coming down from the heavens to enter into her womb to be born as Siddhartha (Hope B. Werness, *The Continuum Encyclopedia of Animal Symbolism in Art* [London, New York: Continuum, 2006], 161).

115. Suyūṭī, *Ṭibb,* 77.

116. Qazwīnī, *Nuzhatu,* 92.

117. Damīrī, *Ḥayawān,* vol. 1, 157.

118. Rabbān al-Ṭabarī, *Firdaws,* 39.

119. For Jewish references, see Preuss, *Biblical and Talmudic Medicine,* 385. Preserving stones may be appropriated by women who have already miscarried, those who are pregnant, and those who wish to become pregnant (*Shabbath* 66b).

120. Ibn Qutayba, *ʿUyūn al-akhbār,* 65.

121. *Mishkāt,* 659. On the authority of Abū Dāʾūd, Nisāʾī, and Tirmidhī, the *Mishkāt* states, "Marry women who are loving and very prolific; for I shall outnumber these peoples by you." See also Ghazālī, *Etiquette,* 53.

122. Ghazālī, *Etiquette,* 57.

123. Joseph and Najmabadi, *Encyclopedia,* 401.

124. Muḥammad ibn Aḥmad al-Bīrūnī, *Ṣaydana fī al-ṭibb*, trans. Hakim Mohammed Said as *Al-Biruni's Book on Pharmacy and Materia Medica* (Karachi: Hamdard Academy, 1973), 81.

125. Suyūṭī, *Ṭibb*, 49.

126. Ibid. 54; Ibn Jazzār, 243.

127. Suyūṭī notes how a man once went and complained to the prophet that he had very few children, and the prophet told him to eat eggs (*Ṭibb*, 19). Qazwīnī explains that three eggs steeped in vinegar will increase seminal fluid and give sexual power (*Nuzhatu*, 71). See also Ibn Jazzār, 243.

128. Ibn Jazzār, 243.

129. Suyūṭī, *Ṭibb*, 73.

130. Ibid., 93.

131. Ibid., 74.

132. Qazwīnī, *Nuzhatu*, 71. The *durrāj* will also increase brain power along with a quick intelligence.

133. Suyūṭī, *Ṭibb*, 81.

134. Ibid., 74.

135. See above. Also, Pliny the Elder, *Natural History*, 10.51.99–103.

136. Isodore of Seville, *The Etymologies of Isodore of Seville*, trans. Stephen A. Barney, W. J. Lewis, J. A. Beach, and Oliver Berghof (Cambridge: Cambridge University Press, 2006), 12.7.93.

137. Suyūṭī, *Ṭibb*, 46.

138. Ibid., 48.

139. Ibid., 66. Suyūṭī notes here that because saffron stimulates sexual intercourse, wearing garments dyed with saffron are forbidden during *muḥarram*. Such garments would instigate a desire for sex, which is prohibited during *muḥarram*.

140. Suyūṭī, *Ṭibb*, 66.

141. Ibid., 108.

142. Suyūṭī notes parsley increases sexual desire on the part of both men and women (89).

143. Ibid., 93.

144. ʿArīb ibn Saʿd, *Kitāb khalq*, 16.

145. Suyūṭī, *Ṭibb*, 67.

146. Qazwīnī, *Nuzhatu*, 87.

147. Ibid.

148. Qazwīnī, *Nuzhatu*, 78. He notes the flesh of the sparrow invokes sexual power and allays wind; consumption of its brain greatly increases sexual power.

149. Qazwīnī, *Nuzhatu*, 69.

150. Suyūṭī, *Ṭibb*, 64.

151. Qazwīnī, *Nuzhatu*, 84.

152. Ibid., 77.

153. Ibid., 70.

154. Ibid., 35.

155. Female vipers are notorious for being driven by lust, so much so they bite the males' heads off in fits of sexual ecstasy. See Pliny the Elder, *Natural History*, Book 10.82; Isodore of Seville, *Etymologies*, 12.4.10–11.

156. Qazwīnī, *Nuzhatu,* 16.
157. Ibid., 71.
158. Ibid., 52.
159. Ibid., 55.
160. Ibid., 56–57.
161. Suyūṭī, *Ṭibb,* 20.
162. Qazwīnī, *Nuzhatu,* 12.
163. Ibid. Hyenas, after all, have the ability to change their sex from male to female, and female to male. See also Pliny the Elder, *Natural History,* 8.30; Ovid, *Metamorphoses,* 15.391–417.
164. Qazwīnī, *Nuzhatu,* 16.
165. Ibid., 85–86.
166. Ibid., 18.
167. Ibid., 5.
168. Ibid., 72.
169. The oil of Spanish chamomile has the same function (inducing the facilitation of an erection) in Tamil medicine.
170. The *euphorbium* plant is worshipped by Hindus as Manusa, the serpent Goddess (Edward Balfour, *The Cyclopaedia of Eastern and Southern Asia,* vol. 1 [London: Bernard Quritch, 1885], 1061). Perhaps there are some associations here with fertility.
171. Qazwīnī, *Nuzahtu,* 40.
172. See above.
173. For example, Sūras 34:37; 58:17; 63:9; 71:21.
174. Valerie French estimates 5 percent of all infants born alive in Greco-Roman times would die before they reached the age of one month, and that among every twenty thousand women giving birth, five would die. Late fetal and in-childbirth deaths would raise the probability of infant mortality from 5–8 percent. She mentions how Caesar's daughter Julia died in childbirth, and the younger Pliny reports how both the daughters of his friend Helvidius died during the act of giving birth. An Athenian philanthropist (Herodes Atticus) was devastated when his first son died on the day after his birth ("Midwives and Maternity Care in the Roman World," in *Midwifery and the Medicalization of Childbirth: Comparative Perspectives,* ed. Edwin R. Van Teijlingen, Maureen Porter, George W. Lowis, and Peter McCaffery [Hauppauge, NY: Nova Science Publications, 2004], 53).
175. "Ancient Civilizations and Birth Control," in *Encyclopedia of Birth Control,* ed. Vern Bullough (Santa Barbara: ABC-CLIO, 2001), 18. The lactic anhydride that comes from acacia serves as a contraceptive; colocynth is known for its abortifacient properties and is still utilized by modern women in Arab countries.
176. J. Gwyn Griffiths, "Atlantis and Egypt," in *Historia: Zeitschrift für Alte Geschichte* 34, no. 1 (1st qtr. 1985): 7.
177. Arthur E. Robinson, "The Cult of the Crocodile," in *American Anthropologist,* New Series 34, no. 3 (July-September 1932): 550.
178. Riddle, *Contraception,* 18.
179. Musallam, 65. See the same Hippocratic tradition as quoted by Rabban al-Ṭabarī, in *Firdaws.*

180. *Laws*, as cited by Riddle, *Contraception*, 18.
181. Riddle, *Contraception*, 18–19.
182. Ibid., 18.
183. Ibid., 20.
184. Ibid., 20.
185. Musallam states Maimonides asserted it is forbidden to destroy seed (23). Therefore, a male may not practice *coitus interruptus* (24). In general, medieval Christianity forbids *coitus interruptus* and all other forms of birth control.
186. Musallam, in reference to Qurṭubī (52). Ghazālī argues a crime can be committed only after the sperm coagulates with a woman's fluid, for offspring are not produced by the sperm of the male alone but from the mixing of the mates, either from both his and her fluid or from his fluid and the blood of menses (*Etiquette*, 110).
187. Ibn Sīnā, *Ḥayawān*, Ix, 1 (Tehran ed. 428).
188. Musallam, 37–38. Jurists believed female contraceptive devices required a husband's consent. Clearly, this seems to be an issue in Jewish tradition as well. In an actual case, Judith, the wife of a rabbi, having suffered agonizing pains during childbirth, drank a sterilizing potion without her husband's knowledge (*Yebamoth* 65b; Preuss, *Biblical and Talmudic Medicine*, 412).
189. Joseph and Najmabadi, *Encyclopedia*, 406. Likewise, Musallam demonstrates most jurists argue withdrawal can only be practiced with a woman's permission, as children are a woman's right and she may suffer harm as a result of withdrawal practices (31–32). Ibn Māja 1928 concurs that *coitus interruptus* is only permissible with a free woman if she consents (*Sunan*, no. 1928). See also Delia Cortese and Simonetta Calderini, *Women and the Fatimids in the World of Islam* (Edinburgh: Edinburgh University Press, 2006), 217.
190. Joseph and Najmabadi, *Encyclopedia*, 406; Ghazālī, *Etiquette*, 111.
191. Ibn Sīnā, *Qānūn*, *Kitāb* 3, *Fann* 21, *Maqāla* 1 as cited by Joseph and Najmabadi, *Encyclopedia*, 405.
192. Ibn Sīnā (*Qānūn*, vol. 2, 579) as cited by Musallam, 69. The medical condition most likely referred to here is the "vesiculovaginal fistula," which results from a hole torn between the bladder and vagina, or the rectum and the vagina. This hole is the result of an extended and painful labor where a young girl is unable to deliver the child, because the child's head could not pass through her pelvic bones. As a result of the head pressing against the walls of the vagina and the bladder (along with inadequate medical care), a fistula would result (L. L. Wall, S. D. Arrowsmith, N. D. Briggs, A. Browning, Anyetei Lassey, "The Obstetric Vesicovaginal Fistula in the Developing World," in *Obstetrical and Gynecological Survey* 60, no. 7 [Suppl 1] [July 2005]: 1405–30). For a particularly grim account of a girl plagued with a fistula, see Abraham Verghese, *Cutting for Stone* (New York: Random House, 2010), 347.
193. Abū al-Ḥasan al-Ṭabīb, *Kitāb khalq al-insān*, f. 28, cited by Musallam, 70. He adds that "if the pregnant woman was a virgin, prematurely deflowered while still of tender age, she would surely die during childbirth."
194. ʿAlī ibn ʿAbbās al-Majūsī, *Kāmil*, vol. 2, 439–40.
195. Musallam, 25.
196. Musallam, 22. See also Ghazālī, *Etiquette*, 111.

197. *Genesis Rabbah,* 23.2; Preuss, *Biblical and Talmudic Medicine,* 412.

198. Ghazālī, *Etiquette,* 111. This statement appears to have something to do with the prohibition against sexual intercourse between a man and a woman who is experiencing postpartum bleeding.

199. Jāḥiẓ, *Ḥayawān,* vol. 4, 614.

200. Musallam argues withdrawal was the most significant and widely used form of birth control (76). Interestingly, it is Islamic jurisprudence, and not medicine, that contains detailed information on this technique.

201. Bukhārī, for example, records traditions in which the prophet claims it is better *not* to engage in withdrawal, since "God has written whom he is going to create [from now] until the day of resurrection" (*Ṣaḥīḥ,* "Kitāb al-tawḥīd," no. 506; "Kitāb al-nikāḥ," no. 137; "Kitāb al-maghāzī," no. 459).

202. *Sunan,* nos. 1926, 1927.

203. 659.

204. Ghazālī, *Etiquette,* 110, 113.

205. Ibn Taymīya, *Kitāb ʿilm al-sulūk,* in *Majmūʿ fatāwā Ibn Taymiyya,* ed. ʿAbd al-Raḥmān ibn Qāsim (Riyad: Matabiʾ al-Riyadh, 1961), 26.

206. Abdel Rahman Omran, *Family Planning and the Legacy of Islam* (London and New York: Routledge, 1992), 169.

207. Ibn Jazzār, 293. See also Rāzī's *Kitāb al-ṭibb al-Manṣūrī* (Musallam, 83), which recommends pepper after coitus.

208. Rāzī's *Kitāb al-ḥāwī* recommends that many of these ingredients should also be taken orally to produce the same contraceptive effect, including cyclamen, male fern, cinnamon with myrrh, leaves of weeping willow (Musallam, 77–78). Muḥammad b. ʿAlī b. ʿUmar al-Samarqandī suggests that some of these same ingredients—such as cinnamon—can also be used to cure diseases in the womb and reproductive organs (Levey, 135).

209. Musallam, 79. Ibn Sīnā makes this same references in his *Qānūn* (Musallam, 84).

210. Ibid., 78–79.

211. ʿAlī ibn ʿAbbās al-Majūsī, *Kitāb kāmil al-ṣināʿa,* as cited by Musallam, 83.

212. Many of these ingredients have been proven among contemporary scientists to contain contraceptive elements. Pomegranates for example, contain a high concentration of naturally occurring estrogens, which have a contraceptive effect, especially when applied directly to the uterus as a suppository (John Riddle, *Goddesses, Elixirs, and Witches: Plants and Sexuality throughout Human History* [New York: Palgrave Macmillan, 2010], 18). Greek physician Aetius of Amida (ca. sixth c. CE) likewise recommended rubbing an ointment made from pomegranate to prevent conception (Robert Jütte, *Contraception: A history* [Cambridge: Polity Press, 2008], 46).

213. Ibn Jazzār, 292.

214. Dill may have also had an adverse effect on the male penis. Bīrūnī, for example, referencing Dioscorides, suggests dill reduces the generation of seminal fluid (*Ṣaydana fī al-ṭibb,* 348).

215. Rāzī, *Kitāb al-ḥāwī,* as referenced by Musallam, 77.

216. 97. See also Rabbān al-Ṭabarī, *Firdaws,* 405.

217. *Kāmil al-ṣināʿa,* as cited by Musallam, 83; Ibn Jazzār, 292.
218. Rāzī, *Kitāb al-ḥāwī,* as cited by Musallam, 77.
219. Ibn Māsawayh, as cited by Musallam, 78.
220. Ibn Jazzār, 29.
221. Damīrī, *Ḥayawān,* vol. 1, 207, 208. See also Qazwīnī, *Nuzhatu,* 4. A more extreme form of contraception appears among asses. For example, Qazwīnī notes how the wild ass (*farā*) tears out the male testicles with her teeth so that he may not make her pregnant again (*Nuzhatu,* 22–23).
222. Musallam, 102.
223. Qazwīnī, *Nuzhatu,* 4.
224. Ibid., 7–8.
225. Damīrī, *Ḥayawān,* vol. 2, 189. See also Musallam, where it is mentioned that elephant dung is used as a contraceptive suppository (102).
226. Damīrī, *Ḥayawān,* vol. 1, 34. Qazwīnī reports if a woman takes hare (*arnab*) blood internally she will never become pregnant (*Nuzhatu,* 11–12).
227. Ibn Qutayba, *ʿUyūn al-akhbār,* 83. Dioscorides believed rennet to serve as a contraceptive (*De Materia Medica,* trans. Lily Y. Beck [Hildesheim; New York: Olms-Weidmann, 2005], 2.210.255). Rennet may have functioned as an effective contraceptive because of its coagulating tendencies (Soranus, 238).
228. Damīrī, *Ḥayawān,* vol. 1, 159.
229. Isodore of Seville, *Etymologies,* 12.7:55–56.
230. Sir Ernest Alfred Wallace Budge, *The Gods of the Egyptians, or Studies in Ancient Mythology,* vol. 1 (London: Methuen, 1904), 322.
231. Rabbān al-Ṭabarī, *Firdaws,* as noted by Prioreschi, 354.
232. Damīrī, *Ḥayawān,* vol. 1, 649. See note above, where the same remedy is proposed to increase fertility.
233. Damīrī, *Ḥayawān,* vol. 2, 178.
234. Qazwīnī, *Nuzhatu,* 11. According to Abū Ḥayyān, weasels conceive and give birth in unusual ways: they conceive through their mouths and bring forth through their ears (164). See also *Recognitions* of Clement, Bk VIII, ch. 25, who states that the creator, as a proof and indication of his provenance, has ordained a few animals to preserve their stock on the earth in an exceptional way: for example, the crow conceives through the mouth, the weasel brings forth through the ear. In the writings of Trotula of Salerno (ca. eleventh-twelfth c. CE), weasel testicles serve as a contraceptive. See *On the Diseases of Women,* trans. Elizabeth Mason-Hohl (Los Angeles: Ward-Ritchie Press, 1940), 18.
235. Qazwīnī, *Nuzhatu,* 22.
236. Ibid., 28.
237. Ibid., 30. It is believed the wolf (*dhiʾb*) breeds for only twelve days out of the year, which may have led people to believe that wolf blood would limit the amount of time a woman could actually be fertile (Pliny the Elder, *Natural History,* 8.34; Isodore of Seville, *Etymologies,* 12.2:23–24).
238. Qazwīnī, *Nuzhatu,* 19.
239. Ibid., 6.
240. Ibid, 10.
241. Qazwīnī mentions goat flesh is warm and dry, but does not explicitly detail how that might counter menstrual flow (*Nuzhatu,* 10).

242. For example, Herodotus mentions Egyptians do not sacrifice goats because Pan (who has the face and legs of a goat) is part of the pantheon of gods (*An Account of Egypt*, trans. G. C. MacCauley [Rockville, MD: Arc Manor Publishing, 2008], 30).

243. The tiger, for example, has associations with Shiva and Durga (*The Encyclopœdia Britannica: A Dictionary of Arts, Sciences, Literature, and General Information*, ed. Hugh Chisholm, vol. 2 [London: The Encyclopœdia Britannica Co., 1926], 52). However, Egypt, too, had its own tiger-gods (Gabriel de Tarde, *The Laws of Imitation*, trans. from the French by Elsie Clews Parson [New York: H. Holt, 1903], 277).

244. Damīrī, *Ḥayawān*, vol. 1, 61.

245. Ibn Qutayba *ʿUyūn al-akhbār*, 65.

246. Rabbān al-Ṭabarī, *Firdaws*, 39.

247. Ibn Qutayba, *ʿUyūn al-akhbār*, 83.

248. Qazwīnī, *Nuzhatu*, 10, on the goat (*maʿz*).

249. *"Chance or Creation,"* 90.

250. Stanley J. Tambiah, "The Magical Power of Words," *Man* 3 (1968): 175–208.

251. Qazwīnī, *Nuzhatu*, 92.

252. Ibid., 40, on the earthworm (*kharaṭīn*).

253. Damīrī, *Ḥayawān*, vol. 1, 649.

254. Qazwīnī, *Nuzhatu*, 30.

255. Ibid., 32.

256. David Frankfurter, "The Perils of Love: Magic and Countermagic in Coptic Egypt," *Journal of the History of Sexuality* 10, no. 3/4, Special Issue: *Sexuality in Late Antiquity* (July-October 2001): 486.

257. Qazwīnī, *Nuzhatu*, 32, on the hyena (*ḍabuʿ*). See also Damīrī, who notes, "If a woman be given to drink without her knowledge, the organ of generation of a male hyena ground fine, it will take away from her the desire for sexual intercourse. He who hangs on himself a piece of the vulva of a female hyena will be desirable to men (*maḥbūban li al-nās*) (*Ḥayawān*, vol. 1, 644). It is interesting that the subject of this discussion is a male.

258. Damīrī, *Ḥayawān*, vol. 1, 643.

259. Qazwīnī, *Nuzhatu*, 69, on the swallow (*khuṭṭāf*).

260. Muslim, *Ṣaḥīḥ*, "Kitāb al-salām," no. 5542. See also nos. 5544, 5550. No. 5545 adds the "short-tailed snake." Damīrī suggests the *al-abtar* is a variety of serpent (blue in color with its tail short or cut off) that causes women to miscarry if they so much as glance in its direction (*Ḥayawān*, vol. 1, 306).

261. Qazwīnī, *Nuzhatu*, 19.

262. Ibid., 37.

263. Suyūṭī, *Ṭibb*, 74.

264. *Ṣaydana*, 212.

265. Ibid., 78.

266. Suyūṭī, *Ṭibb*, 76.

267. Bīrūnī, *Ṣaydana*, 362.

268. *Ḥayawān*, vol. 1, 208.

269. Much rejoicing occurred over the birth of ʿAbdallāh, for the spell the Jews cast over the Muslims was believed to have been broken.

270. Bukhārī, *Ṣaḥīḥ,* "Kitāb al-aṭʿama," no. 659. See also his "Kitāb al-ṭibb," where ʿĀʾisha discusses how magic was worked on the prophet so that he used to think he had sexual relations with his wives while he—in reality—had not.

271. See Sūras 6:151; 60:12. Sūra 60:12 implies *jāhilīya* women were the ones who would kill their own children, which suggests female infanticide posed a direct threat to the patriarchal order. For further discussions on the banning of infant exposure, see Amundsen, 56, who suggests the Jews of Tacitus's time regarded the killing of infants as a reprehensible act, violating sacred law (as evident in the writings of Philo and Josephus). He notes further that Diodorus Siculus remarks how Moses required the Jews to rear their children, and says virtually the same thing about the Egyptians. Likewise, Oribasius maintains that Aristotle also attributed the same practice to the Egyptians; the geographer asserts that the Egyptians most zealously observe the custom of raising every child who was born (57). Exposure is thought to have included the condemnation of killing a defective newborn, along with the exposure of healthy infants. Aristotle supports this view, as he suggests that "as to exposing or rearing the children born, let there be a law that no deformed child shall be raised or reared" *(Politics,* II, 1335b).

272. Musallam, 57–58.

273. 290.

274. Bīrūnī, *Ṣaydana,* 149.

275. Ibn Jazzār, 291.

276. Bīrūnī, *Ṣaydana,* 367.

277. Ibn Jazzār, 291.

278. Bīrūnī, *Ṣaydana,* 347.

279. Ibn Jazzār, 291.

280. Bīrūnī, *Ṣaydana,* 43.

281. Damīrī, *Ḥayawān,* vol. 1, 35–36.

282. Ibid., 68.

283. Ibid., vol. 1, 214. Damīrī notes if the dung of a horse is used as a fumigatory, it will cause a fetus to come out of the womb (ibid., vol. 2, 167). See also Ibn al-Jawzī, *Kitāb iltiqāṭ al-manāfiʿ* as cited by Musallam, 103. In general, fumigations with the hooves of the horse, mule, or donkey prevent pregnancy.

284. Diane S. Aschenbrenner and Samantha J. Venable, *Drug Therapy in Nursing* (Philadelphia: Lippincott Williams and Wilkins, 2008), 1164.

285. See Zahrāwī on the necessity of extracting dead fetuses from the mother's womb (462–78).

286. See Ibn Taymīya, *Kitāb ʿilm al-sulūk,* 26, who discusses the stupidity of humans who assume God will simply grant them a child without any effort on their part. Jāḥiẓ, of course, claims humans are responsible for maintaining pure and clean bodies, as God did not create them as such (*"Chance or Creation,"* 90). Of course, in this context, God purposely did not create perfected bodies because his intention was to make humans willfully responsible for removing any sort of wickedness that might detract them from the faith. Finally, the Qurʾān advocates

human cultivation of righteous practices and habits. For example, humans are responsible for the consumption of good food (Sūra 5:88); eating what is lawful and wholesome (2:168); not hoarding their wealth (Sūras 3:180; 4:37); etc.

287. ʿArīb ibn Saʿd, *Kitāb khalq,* 49.

288. Ṭabarī, *Tafsīr,* vol. VI, 393–98.

289. *Kitāb khalq,* 41.

290. Ibid., 48–49.

291. Ibid., 40. Interestingly, Bīrūnī states that according to Ibn Māsawayh, *dār ṣīnī* should *not* be given to pregnant women (*Ṣaydana,* 156).

292. Suyūṭī, *Ṭibb,* 76.

293. Aḥmad ibn Muḥammad ibn Yaḥyá al-Baladī, *Tadbir kitāb al-ḥabālá wa al-aṭfāl wa al-ṣibyān,* quoted by Prioreschi, 356. See also Ullmann, 109.

294. *Ṣaydana,* 167.

295. ʿArīb ibn Saʿd, *Kitāb khalq,* 49. Interestingly, colocynth is used to ward off the hypersexed hyena (Abū Hayyān, 429).

296. Qazwīnī, *Nuzhatu,* 77, on the peacock (*ṭāʾūs*).

297. Ibid., 15.

298. Ibid., 62.

299. Damīrī, *Ḥayawān,* vol. 1, 591.

300. Ibid., 598.

301. Ibid., 57–58.

302. Ibid., 208.

303. Ibid., 210. See Sūra 99:5, for an example of how the earth receives God's revelation in order that she may declare her tidings.

304. Damīrī, *Ḥayawān,* vol. 1, 209.

305. See, for example, ʿArīb ibn Saʿd, *Kitāb khalq,* 10–20.

306. *ʿUyūn al-akhbār,* 67.

307. ʿArīb ibn Saʿd, *Kitāb khalq,* 49.

308. *Ṣaydana,* 146. Note the default mode of the fetus is male and not female.

309. Damīrī, *Ḥayawān,* vol. 1, 34.

310. Qazwīnī, *Nuzhatu,* 74. One may also "read" signs in nature to determine whether the child is going to be a boy or a girl. For example, Damīrī notes how every one of the birds of prey indicates a male child (*Ḥayawān,* vol. 1, 624). Notably, too, the vulture was worshipped by the ancient Arabs in the time of Noah, according to the Qurʾān, and also generally throughout semitic lands (Theodor Nöldeke, *Geschichte der Perser und Araber zur Zeit der Sasaniden* [Leiden: Brill, 1979], 27). The vulture was, as has been said, the goddess of maternity in Egypt (Florence Waterbury, "Bird Deities in China," *Artibus Asiae, Supplementum* 10 [1952]: 1–191).

Conclusion

1. Jāḥiẓ, *"Chance or Creation,"* 76.
2. Ibid., 72.
3. Sūra 39:6.

4. Sūra 50:6.

5. Sūra 50:7–8.

6. According to John Wansbrough, the pagan practices of the *jāhilīya* often serve as "foils" against which the articulation of the Muslim community can be measured (*The Sectarian Milieu: Content and Composition of Islamic Salvation History* [Oxford: Oxford University Press, 1978], 33).

7. Bukhārī, *Ṣaḥīḥ*, "Kitāb al-ṭalāq," nos. 230, 236.

8. See Mālik, *Muwaṭṭa'*, 36.21.22.

9. Ibid.

10. See Abū Dā'ūd, *Sunan*, "Kitāb al-ṭalāq," no. 31; Nasā'ī, *Sunan*, "Kitāb al-ṭibb," 50; Ṭayālisī, *Musnad*, no. 187.

11. Leor Halevi employs the term *Islamicization* in his study on *Muḥammad's Grave* (New York: Columbia University Press, 2007) 236–37. In general, he suggests the term refers to those activities and endeavors that somehow contribute to the making of an Islamic society.

12. Helen King, *Hippocrates' Women*, 1.

13. Jāḥiẓ, *"Chance or Creation,"* 76.

14. Such a perspective seems to contradict the view of sex put forth in prophetic medicine. For example, Ibn Qayyim emphasizes the importance of female pleasure during sex (*Ṭibb*, 188). However, it is unclear the extent to which more pleasure would produce too much sperm that may come to challenge or dominate male sperm.

15. Helen King notes that women portrayed in Greek literature appear to know nothing about what is happening inside of their bodies; rather, they trust that the doctor is the only one capable of reading the "signs" (*Hippocrates' Women*, 47).

16. Claude Levi-Strauss, *Totemism*, trans. Rodney Needham (Boston: Beacon Press, 1963), 89.

17. Nancy Tischler and Ellen Johnston McHenry, *All Things in the Bible: An Encyclopedia of the Biblical World*, vol. 1 (Santa Barbara: Greenwood, 2006), 298.

18. *Nedarim*, 65a.

19. Chapter 13, no. 14, as quoted in *A Talmudic Miscellany: A Thousand and One Extracts from the Talmud, the Midrashim, and the Kabbalah*, ed. Paul Isaac Hershon (London: Trübner and Co., Ludgate Hill, 1880), 326.

20. *Baba Kamma*, 16a.

21. Barbara Creed, "Lesbian Bodies: Tribades, Tomboys, and Tarts," in *Feminist Theory and the Body: A Reader*, ed. Janet Price and Margrit Shildrick (New York: Routledge), 119.

22. *Epistle of Barnabas*, in *Early Christian Writings: The Apostolic Fathers*, ed. Andrew Louth, trans. Maxwell Staniforth (New York: Penguin, 1987), 171. See also *Barnabas* 10:9: "Moses received three decrees about food and uttered them in the spirit, but they in their fleshly desire received them as having to do with eating" (Boswell, 1980, 137–38). Here, Barnabas makes it clear that the food laws have a spiritual dimension. This explains why the Jews have misunderstood them. And their misunderstanding is due to their fleshly desire. Their lack of understanding is thus connected with a moral defect (Reidar Hvalvik, *Struggle for Scripture and Covenant: The Purpose of the Epistle of Barn-*

abas and Jewish-Christian Competition in the Second Century, Wissenschaftliche untersuchungen zum Neuen Testament 2, Reihe, 82 [Tübingen: J. C. B. Mohr, Paul Siebeck, 1966], 188).

23. *Epistle of Barnabas,* 171; Boswell, 1980, 137–38. Robert McQueen Grant notes the *Physiologus,* which quotes the condemnation of eating the hyena in Leviticus, and then states the hyena is bisexual, sometimes male, sometimes female. It is a polluted animal because it changes sex (*Early Christians and Animals* [London, New York: Routledge, 1999], 63).

24. *Epistle of Barnabas,* 171; Boswell, 1980, 137–38; and Grant, *Early Christians and Animals,* 62, who again quotes the *Physiologus,* which states the mouth of the weasel "conceives from the male, and when pregnant gives birth through the ears."

25. Qazwīnī, *Nuzhatu,* 11. See also Ibn Qutayba, *ʿUyūn al-akhbār,* 93. Damīrī also categorizes the hare as a hermaphrodite in addition to its ability to transform its sex on a yearly basis. He reports how Ibn al-Athīr relates that a friend of his once hunted a hare that had two testicles and a male organ of generation but also a female one. They discovered this after they cut open its abdomen saw signs indicative of it (*Ḥayawān,* vol. 1, 31–32). Such animals are also used to demonstrate God's glory in Christian texts. In the *Recognitions* of Clement, Bk VIII, ch. 25, notes how the creator, as "a proof and indication of his provenance, has ordained a few animals to preserve their stock on the earth in an exceptional way: for example, the crow conceives through the mouth, the weasel brings forth through the ear; and some birds, such as hens, sometimes produce eggs conceived of wind or dust; other animals convert the male into female, and change their sex every year, as hares and hyaena, which they call monsters."

26. See chapter 5, 188.

27. See chapter 5, 189.

28. See chapter 5, 192.

29. Qazwīnī, *Nuzhatu,* 31. In addition to the hyena, other animals are also endowed with the organs of both sexes. The tortoise (*al-sulaḥfāh al-barrīya*), for example, has two penises and two vulvae (Damīrī, *Ḥayawān,* vol. 1, 50), as does the thorn tail lizard (*ḍabb*), which is described as being crafty (Ibn Qutayba, *ʿUyūn al-akhbār,* 74). It is forbidden to eat the tortoise, (Damīrī, *Ḥayawān,* 641), and there is some debate over the permissibility of consuming the lizard (Qazwīnī, *Nuzhatu,* 19).

30. These would include, for example, the bee, ant, camel, and sheep.

31. See above, notes 24 and 25, and chapter 5, note 234.

32. Muhammad Abdul-Rauf, *The Islamic View of Women and the Family* (Cairo: Al-Saadawi Publications, 1993), 99. See also Muhammad Aftab Khan's *Sex and Sexuality in Islam* (Karachi: Nasrhiat, 2006).

33. Stetkevych, 24. She notes that Aḥmad ibn Ḥanbal also renders the hyena as permissible to eat. Mālik suggests it is reprehensible (*makrūh*), but not *ḥarām*. Abū Ḥanīfa, on the other hand, prohibits it because of its fangs. The Ḥanafī juridical work, the *Hidāya,* however, declares weasels to be prohibited based on the fact that they are quadrupeds that seize their prey with their teeth (Thomas Patrick Hughes, *A Dictionary of Islam: Being a Cyclopœdia of the Doctrines,*

Rites, Ceremonies, and Customs, Together with the Technical and Theological Terms, of the Muhammadan Religion [London: W. H. Allen, 1896], s.v. "food").

34. See Damīrī, *Ḥayawān*, vol. 1, 34; Qazwīnī, *Nuzhatu*, 11–12.

35. Ibn Qayyim discusses the prohibitive nature of anal sex among heterosexual couples (*Ṭibb*, 186–89).

36. *The Code of Maimonides: Mishneh Torah*, trans. L. I. Rabinowitz and P. Grossman (New Haven: Yale University Press, 1995), s.v. "The Book of Holiness: Laws Concerning Illicit Intercourse," 21:18.

37. Men, for example, might be tempted to ensure their beautiful wives would not be compromised by pregnancy; likewise, in the context of a levirate marriage, the child conceived would not belong to the man, so there would be no reason to beget one. These reasons are put forth in the story of Tamar and Onan in Genesis 38:7, and elaborated by rabbis (*Yebamoth*, 34b).

38. Ruth Mazo Karras, *Sexuality in Medieval Europe: Doing unto Others* (New York: Routledge, 2012), 74.

39. Musallam, 77–79.

40. Baumgarten, 124. See also Lawrence H. Fuchs, *Beyond Patriarchy: Jewish Fathers and Families* (Waltham, MA: Brandeis University Press, 2000), 61.

41. Karras, 74.

42. See, for example, BT *Yebamoth* 34a-b; *Genesis Rabbah*, 23:2; *Yerushalmi Yebamoth* 6:5.

43. Schaus, s.v. "contraception."

44. BT *Kethubboth* 37a; *Yabamoth* 35a; see also Karras, 74.

45. Michele Klein. *A Time to Be Born: Customs and Folklore of Jewish Birth* (Philadelphia: The Jewish Publication Society, 1998), 46.

46. *Oholot* 7:6 cited by Klein, 46.

47. Klein, 46, who references *Sefer ha-toledet, op. cit.*, part 5, sign. 1, 112.

48. John Riddle, *A History of the Middle Ages, 300–1500* (Lanham, MD: Rowan and Littlefield, 2008), 54.

49. Karras, 32.

50. In *Apostolic Fathers: A New Translation and Commentary*, trans. Robert M. Grant and H. H. Graham (New York: T. Nelson, 1964–68), II, 2.

51. *The Instructor of Children* 2:10:91:2.

52. Ibid, 2:10:95:3.

53. *Homilies on Matthew* 28:5 (AD 391). As noted above, the Mālikites also hold this view.

54. *Encyclopedia of Birth Control*, ed. Vern L. Bullough (Santa Barbara: ABC-CLIO, 2001), s.v. "Augustine, Saint."

55. *Questionum in Heptateuchum* 2:80, as cited in Riddle, *A History of the Middle Ages*, 54.

56. *Augustine Through the Ages: An Encyclopedia*, ed. John C. Cavadini, Allan Fitzgerald, and Marianne Djuth (Grand Rapids: Eerdmans, 1999], s.v. "conception." Aquinas agrees but suggests abortion is the second to homicide (*Summa Contra Gentiles*, trans. Anton Pegis [South Bend: University of Notre Dame Press, 1975], 122).

57. Riddle, *A History of the Middle Ages*, 54.

58. Ghazālī, after all, also suggested that contraceptives in cases of poverty may not be used as a reason for practicing contraception. The Christian scholar Lactantius also states poverty does not present a legitimate reason for contraceptive use (*Divine Institutes,* trans. Anthony Bowen and Peter Garnsey: [Liverpool: Liverpool University Press, 2003], 6:20).

59. Sūra 3:6.

Bibliography

Abbott, Nabia. *Aishah, the Beloved of Mohammed*. Chicago: The University of Chicago Press, 1942.

ʿAbd al-Razzāq b. Hammām al-Ṣanʿānī. *Al-Muṣannaf*. Ed. Ḥabīb al-Raḥmān al-Aʿẓamī. 2d ed. 11 vols. Al-Majlis al-ʿilmī and Beirut: Al-Maktab al-islāmī, 1970–72.

Abdul-Rauf, Muhammad. *The Islamic View of Women and the Family*. Cairo: Al-Saadawi Publications, 1993.

Abrams, Judith Z. *Judaism and Disability: Portrayals in Ancient Texts from the Tanach through the Bavli*. Washington, DC: Gallaudet University Press, 1998.

Abū Dāʾūd Sulaymān ibn al-Ashʿath al-Sijistānī. *Sunan Abī Dāʾūd*. 3 vols. Beirut: Dār al-kutub al-ʿilmīya, 1996.

Abū al-Futūḥ Rāzī, Ḥusayn ibn ʿAlī. *Rawẓ al-jinān wa rūḥ al-janān fī tafsīr al-Qurʾān*. Tehran: Kitābfurūshī-yi Islāmīya, 1963.

Abū al-Ḥasan al-Ṭabīb. *Kitāb khalq al-insān*. Bodleian MS. Pococke 66.

Abū Ḥayyān al-Tawḥīdī. *Kitāb al-imtāʾ wa al-muʾānsa*. Trans. by L. Kopf as *The Zoological Chapter of the Kitab al-imtaʿ wa al-muʾānsa of Abū Ḥayyān al-Tawḥīdī (10th century). Osiris* 12 (1956): 390–466.

Adamson, P. B. "Some Rituals Associated with Parturition in Ancient Antiquity." *Folklore* 96, no. 2 (1985): 176–83.

Aelianus, Claudius (Aelian). *Aelian—On Animals: De Peculari Quadam Pisato insu Macedonia* (*On the Nature of Animals*). Vol. I, Books 1–5. Trans. A. F. Scholfield. *Loeb Classical Library*. Cambridge: Harvard University Press, 1958.

———. *De Natura Animalium* (*The Characteristics of Animals*). Vol. II, Books 6–11. Trans. A. F. Scholfield. *Loeb Classical Library*. Cambridge: Harvard University Press, 1959.

Agwan, A. R., and N. K Singh. *Encyclopedia of the Holy Qurʾān*. Vol. 1. New Delhi: Global Vision Publishing House, 2000.

Aḥsāʾī, Muḥammad ibn ʿAlī ibn Abī Jumhūr. *Hādhā huwa al-kitāb al-maʿrūf bi al-Mujallī al-mawsūm bi Masālik al-afhām wa-al-Nūr al-munjī min al-ẓalām*. Tehran: s.n., 1911.

Algra, Keimpe, Jonathan Barnes, Jaap Mansfeld, and Malcolm Schofield, eds. *The Cambridge History of Hellenistic Philosophy*. Cambridge: Cambridge University Press, 2000.

Ali, Kecia. *Marriage and Slavery in Early Islam.* Cambridge: Harvard University Press, 2010.

Althaus-Reid, Marcella. *Indecent Theology: Theological Perversions in Sex, Gender and Politics.* London, New York: Routledge, 2001.

Ambrose of Milan. *Hexameron, Paradise, and Cain and Abel.* Trans. John J. Savage. *Fathers of the Church A New Translation,* Vol. 42. Washington, DC: Catholic University of America Press, 1961.

Amundsen, Darrel W. "Medicine and the Birth of Defective Children: Approaches of the Ancient World." In *Euthanasia and the Newborn: Conflicts Regarding Saving Lives.* Ed. Richard C. McMillan, Hugo Tristram Englehardt and Stuart S. Spicker, 3–32. New York: Springer, 1987.

———. *Medicine, Society, and Faith in the Ancient and Medieval Worlds.* Baltimore: Johns Hopkins University Press, 1997.

Aptowitzer, Victor. *Kain und Abel in der Agada, den Apokryphen, der hellenistischen, christlichen und muhammedanischen Literatur.* Wien, Liepzig: R. Löwit, 1922.

Aquinas, Thomas. *Summa contra Gentiles.* Vol. 3. Trans. Anton Pegis. South Bend: University of Notre Dame Press, 1975.

The Arabian Nights Encyclopedia. Ed. Ulrich Marzolph, Richard van Leeuwen, and Hassan Wassouf. Vol. 1. Santa Barbara: ABC-CLIO, 2004.

ʿArīb ibn Saʿd. *Kitāb khalq al-janīn wa-tadbīr al-ḥabālā wa ʾl-mawlūdīn.* Al-Jazāʾir: Maktabat farrāris, 1956.

Aristotle. *Generation of Animals.* Trans. A. L. Peck. *Loeb Classical Library.* Cambridge MA: Harvard University Press, 1943.

———. *History of Animals.* 3 Vols. Trans. A. L. Peck. *Loeb Classical Library.* London: Heinemann; Cambridge: Harvard University Press, 1965-.

———. *Politics.* Trans. Stephen Everson. Cambridge: Cambridge University Press, 1996.

Armour, Ellen T., and Susan M. St. Ville, eds. *Bodily Citations: Religion and Judith Butler.* New York: Columbia University Press, 2006.

Aschenbrenner, Diane S., and Samantha J. Venable. *Drug Therapy in Nursing.* Philadelphia: Lippincott Williams and Wilkins, 2008.

Augustine of Hippo. *City of God.* Trans. Marcus Dods. New York: Modern Library, 1950.

———. *Writings of Saint Augustine.* New York: Cima, 1947.

Ayoub, Mahmoud. *The Qurʾan and Its Interpreters. Volume II, The House of ʿImrān.* Albany: State University of New York Press, 1992.

———. *Redemptive Suffering in Islām: A Study of the Devotional Aspects of ʿĀshūrāʾ in Twelver Shīʿism.* The Hague: Mouton, 1978.

ʿAyṭa, Durrīya. *Fiqh al-ʿibādāt ʿalá al-madhhab al-Shāfiʿī.* Damascus: Maktaba Dār Bayān, 1975.

Bakhos, Carol. *Ishmael on the Border: Rabbinic Portrayals of the First Arab.* Albany: State University of New York Press, 2007.

Baladī, Aḥmad ibn Muḥammad ibn Yaḥyā. *Tadbir al-ḥabālá wa-al-aṭfāl wa-al-ṣibyān.* Beirut: Dār al-kutub al-ʿilmīya, 2004.

Balme, D. M. "Development of Biology in Aristotle and Theophrastus: Theory of Spontaneous Generation." *Phronesis* 7, no. 1 (1962): 91–104.

Balsamo, Anne Marie. *Technologies of the Gendered Body: Reading Cyborg Women.* Durham: Duke University Press, 1995.

Baraitser, Lisa. *Maternal Encounters: The Ethics of Interruption.* London, New York: Routledge, 2009.

Barkai, Ron. *A History of Jewish Gynaecological Texts in the Middle Ages.* Leiden, Boston: Brill, 1998.

Bartlett, Robert. "Symbolic Meanings of Hair in the Middle Ages." *Transactions of the Royal Historical Society* 4 (1994): 43–60.

Basil of Caesarea. *Hexameron.* In *A Select Library of Nicene and Post-Nicene Fathers of the Christian Church.* Second Series. Vol. 8. Ed. Philip Schaff. New York: The Christian Literature Company, 1890–1900.

Baumgarten, Elisheva. *Mothers and Children: Jewish Family Life in Medieval Europe.* Princeton: Princeton University Press, 2004.

Bayḍawī, ʿAbdallāh ibn ʿUmar. *Anwār al-tanzīl wa asrār al-taʾwīl.* Istanbul: s.n., 1911.

Beattie, Tina. *God's Mother, Eve's Advocate: A Marian Narrative of Women's Salvation.* New York: Continuum, 2002.

Beckwith, John. *Early Christian and Byzantine Art.* New Haven: Yale University Press, 1986.

Berger, Michael S. "Judaism." In *Sex, Marriage, and Family in World Religions,* ed. Don Browning, M. Christian Green, and John Witte Jr. New York: Columbia University Press, 2009.

Berkey, Jonathan. "Circumcision Circumscribed: Female Excision and Cultural Accommodation in the Medieval Near East." *International Journal of Middle East Studies* 28, no. 1 (February 1996): 19–38.

Bertholet, Alfred. "*Das Wesen der Magie.*" In *Magie und Religion. Beitrdge zu einer Theorie der Magie,* ed. L. Petzoldt, 108–34. Darmstadt: Wissenschaftliche Buchgesellschaft, 1978.

Bilu, Yoram. "Circumcision, the First Haircut and the Torah: Ritual and Male Identity among the Ultraorthodox Community of Contemporary Israel." In *Imagined Masculinities: Male Identity and Culture in the Modern Middle East,* ed. Mai Ghoussoub and Emma Sinclair-Webb, 33–64. London: Saqi Books, 2000.

———. "From *Milah* (Circumcision) to *Milah* (Word]): Male Identity and Rituals of Childhood in the Jewish Orthodox Community." *Ethos* 31, no. 2 (2003): 172–203.

Bird, Phyllis. *Missing Persons and Mistaken Identities: Women and Gender in Ancient Israel.* Minneapolis: Fortress Press, 1997.

Birke, Lynda. "Bodies and Biology." In *Feminist Theory and the Body: A Reader,* ed. Janet Price and Margrit Shildrick, 42–49. Oxford: Oxford University Press, 1999.

———. *Feminism and the Biological Body.* Edinburgh: Edinburgh University Press, 1999.

Bīrūnī, Muḥammd ibn Aḥmad. *Ṣaydana fī al-ṭibb.* Trans. Hakim Mohammed Said as *Al-Biruni's Book on Pharmacy and Materia Medica.* Karachi: Hamdard Academy, 1973.

Blackledge, Catherine. *The Story of V: A Natural History of Female Sexuality.* New Brunswick: Rutgers University Press, 2003.

Bondeson, Jan. *A Cabinet of Medical Curiosities*. Ithaca: Cornell University Press, 1997.

Bos, Gerrit. "Ibn Jazzār on Sexuality and Sexual Dysfunction." *Jerusalem Studies in Arabia and Islam* 19 (Jubilee 1995): 250–66.

Boswell, John. *Christianity, Social Tolerance, and Homosexuality: Gay People in Western Europe from the Beginning of the Christian Era to the Fourteenth Century*. Chicago: University of Chicago Press, 1981.

Bosworth, Clifford Edmund. "Arnab." In *The Encyclopaedia of Islam*, new edition: Supplement.

Bourdieu, Pierre. *Masculine Domination*. Trans. Richard Nice. Cambridge: Polity Press, 2001.

———. *Outline of a Theory of Practice*. Trans. Richard Nice. Cambridge, New York: Cambridge University Press, 1977.

Bovey, Alixe. *Monsters and Grotesques in Medieval Manuscripts*. Toronto: University of Toronto Press, 2002.

Bowley, James E. *Living Traditions of the Bible: Scripture in Jewish, Christian, and Muslim practice*. Atlanta: Chalice Press, 1999.

Boyarin, Daniel. "'This we know to be the Carnal Israel': Circumcision and the Erotic Life of God and Israel." *Critical Inquiry* 18, no. 3 (Spring 1992): 474–505.

Boyle, John Andrew. "The Hare in Myth and Reality: A Review Article." *Folklore* 84, no. 4 (Winter 1973): 313–26.

Braswell, Bruce Karl. *A Commentary on the Fourth Pythian Ode of Pindar*. Berlin, New York: Walter de Gruyter, 1988.

Brenner, Athalya. *A Feminist Companion to Samuel and Kings*, Volume 5. London: Sheffield Academic Press, 1994.

———. *The Intercourse of Knowledge: On Gendering Desire and "Sexuality" in the Hebrew Bible*. Leiden, New York: Brill, 1997.

Brockopp, Jonathan E. *Early Mālikī Law: Ibn ʿAbd al-Ḥakam and his major compendium of jurisprudence*. Leiden: Brill, 2000.

Brown, Peter. *The Body and Society: Men, Women and Sexual Renunciation in Early Christianity*. New York: Columbia University Press, 1988.

Browne, Edward Granville. *Arabian Medicine*. Cambridge: Cambridge University Press, 1921.

Budge, Sir Ernest Alfred Wallace. *The Gods of the Egyptians, or Studies in Egyptian Mythology*. 2 vols. London: Methuen, 1904.

Bukhārī, Abū ʿAbdallāh Muḥammad b. Ismāʿīl b. Ibrāhīm. *Jāmiʿ al-ṣaḥīḥ*. Al-Riyāḍ: Bayt al-afkār al-dawlīya li al-nashr, 1998.

Bürgel, J. Christoph, "Secular and Religious Features of Medieval Arabic Medicine." In *Asian Medical Systems: A Comparative Study*, ed. Charles Leslie, 44–62. Delhi: Motilal Banarsidass, 1998.

Burnell, C. S. F. "The Planets and the Development of the Embryo." In *The Human Embryo: Aristotle and the Arabic and European Tradition*, ed. G. R. Dunstan. Exeter: University of Exeter Press, 1990.

Butler, Judith. *Bodies that Matter: On the Discursive Limits of Sex*. London, New York: Routledge, 1993.

———. *Gender Trouble: Feminism and the Subversion of Identity*. London, New York: Routledge, 2006.

———. *The Judith Butler Reader*. Ed. Sara Salih with Judith Butler. Hoboken: Blackwell Publishing, 2004.

———. "Performative Acts and Gender Constitution: An Essay in Phenomenology and Feminist Theory." In *Performing Feminisms: Feminist Critical Theory and Theatre*, ed. Sue-Ellen Case, 270–82. Baltimore: Johns Hopkins University Press, 1990.

Bynum, Caroline Walker. *Holy Feast Holy Fast: The Religious Significance of Food to Medieval Women*. Berkeley: University of California Press, 1987.

———. *Metamorphosis and Identity*. New York: Zone Books, 2001.

Cadden, Joan. *The Meanings of Sex Difference in the Middle Ages*. Cambridge: Harvard University Press, 1993.

Canaan, T. "Mohammedan Saints and Sanctuaries in Palestine." *Journal of the Palestine Oriental Society* IV, no. 1–2 (1924): 1–84.

Cavadini, John. C., Allan D. Fitzgerald, and Marianne Djuth, eds. *Augustine Through the Ages: An Encyclopedia*. Grand Rapids: Eerdmans, 1999.

Cherewatuk, Karen. *Marriage, Adultery and Inheritance in Malory's Morte Darthur*. Suffolk and Rochester, NY: Boydell and Brewer, 2006.

Chodorow, Nancy. *Feminism and Psychoanalytic Theory*. New Haven: Yale University Press, 1991.

———. *The Reproduction of Mothering: Psychoanalysis and the Sociology of Gender*. Berkeley: University of California Press, 1978.

Chrysostom, John. *Homilies on Matthew*. In *Select Library of the Nicene and Post-Nicene Fathers of the Christian Church*. Ed. Philip Schaff. New York: The Christian Literature Co., 1886–1890.

Clapp, Nicholas. *Sheba: Through the Desert in Search of the Legendary Queen*. Boston: Mariner Books, 2002.

Clement of Alexandria. *The Ante-Nicene Christian Library: Translations of the Writings of the Fathers down to A.D. 325*. Vol. 3. *Tatian, Theophilus, and the Clementine Recognitions*. Ed. Alexander Roberts and James Donaldson. Edinburgh: T. and T. Clark, 1867.

Cobb, L. Stephanie. *Dying to Be Men: Gender and Language in Early Christian Martyr Texts*. New York: Columbia University Press, 2008.

The Code of Maimonides (Mishneh Torah): Book 5, the Book of Holiness. Ed. and trans. Leon Nemoy, Louis I. Rabinowitz, and Philip Grossman. New Haven: Yale University Press, 1995.

Cohen, Jeffrey Jerome. *Monster Theory: Reading Culture*. Minneapolis: University of Minnesota Press, 1996.

The Continuum Encyclopedia of Animal Symbolism in Art. Ed. Hope B. Werness. London, New York: Continuum, 2006.

Cook, Michael. "Early Islamic Dietary Law." *Jerusalem Studies in Arabic and Islam* 7 (1986): 217–77.

———. *Forbidding Wrong in Islam: An Introduction*. Cambridge: Cambridge University Press, 2003.

———. "Ibn Qutayba and the Monkeys." *Studia Islamica* 89 (1999): 43–74.

Cortese, Delia and Simonetta Calderini. *Women and the Fatimids in the World of Islam*. Edinburgh: Edinburgh University Press, 2006.

Coulson, N. J. *Succession in the Muslim Family*. Cambridge: Cambridge University Press, 1971.

Covington, Sharon N., and Linda Hammer Burns. *Infertility Counseling: A Comprehensive Handbook for Clinicians*. Cambridge: Cambridge University Press, 2006.

Creed, Barbara. "Lesbian Bodies: Tribades, Tomboys, and Tarts." In *Feminist Theory and the Body: A Reader*, ed. Janet Price and Margrit Shildrick, 111–24. London, New York: Routledge, 1999.

Crone, Patricia. *Roman, Provincial, and Islamic Law: The Origins of the Islamic Patronate*. Cambridge: Cambridge University Press, 2002.

Curtis, Patricia. *Guide to Food Laws and Regulations*. Hoboken: Wiley-Blackwell, 2005.

The Cyclopœdia of Eastern and Southern Asia. Vol. 1. Ed. Edward Balfour. London: Bernard Quritch, 1885.

Daiber, Hans. "The Reception of Islamic Philosophy at Oxford in the 17th Century: The Pococks' (Father and Son) Contribution to the Understanding of Islamic Philosophy in Europe." In *The Introduction of Arabic Philosophy into Europe*, ed. Charles E. Butterworth and Blake Andrée Kessel, 65–82. Leiden: Brill, 1997.

Dalley, Stephanie, ed. and trans. *Myths from Mesopotamia*. London: Oxford University Press, 1989.

Dalton, Ormonde Maddock. *Byzantine Art and Archeology*. Ithaca: Cornell University Library, 2009.

Damīrī, Muḥammad ibn Mūsā. *Ḥiyāt al-ḥayawān al-kubrā*. 3 vols. Qum: Manshūrāt al-Raḍī, 1985.

Dārimī, ʿAbdallāh b. ʿAbd al-Raḥmān. *Al-Sunan*. Ed. Muḥammad Aḥmad Duhmān. Cairo: Dār al-iḥyāʾ, 1974.

Davis, Natalie Zemon. *Society and Culture in Early Modern France: Eight Essays*. Stanford: Stanford University Press, 1975.

Dean-Jones, Lesley. *Women's Bodies in Classical Greek Science*. London: Oxford University Press, 1996.

Delaney, Carol. "Cutting the Ties that Bind: The Sacrifice of Abraham and Patriarchal Kinship." In *Relative Values: Reconfiguring Kinship Studies*, ed. Sarah Franklin and Susan McKinnon, 445–67. Durham: Duke University Press, 2001.

———. *The Seed and the Soil: Gender and Cosmology in a Turkish Village*. Berkeley: The University of California Press, 1992.

———. "Untangling the Meanings of Hair in Turkish Society." *Anthropological Quarterly* 67, no. 4 (1994): 159–72.

Demand, Nancy. *Birth, Death, and Motherhood in Classical Greece*. Baltimore: Johns Hopkins University Press, 1994.

Dhahabī, Muḥammad ibn Aḥmad. *Siyar aʿlām al-nubalāʾ*. Cairo: Ma'had al-makhṭūṭāt al-ʿarabīya, 1956.

———. *Ṭibb al-nabawī*. Mecca, al-Riyāḍ: Maktabat nizār muṣṭafā al-bāz, 1976.

Didache. In *Apostolic Fathers: A New Translation and Commentary*, trans. Robert M. Grant and H. H. Graham. New York: T. Nelson, 1964–68.

Dioscorides Pedanius. *De Materia Medica.* Trans. Lily Y. Beck. Hildesheim, New York: Olms-Weidmann, 2005.

Doniger, Wendy, and Gregory Spinner. "Misconceptions: Female Imaginations and Male Fantasies in Parental Imprinting." *Daedalus* 127, no. 1c (Winter 1998): 97–129.

Dreger, Alice Domurat. *One of Us: Conjoined Twins and the Future of Normal.* Cambridge: Harvard University Press, 2004.

Ellingson, Stephen, and M. Christian Green, eds. *Religion and Sexuality in Cross-cultural Perspective.* New York; London: Routledge, 2002.

Ellwood, Robert. *Tales of Darkness: The Mythology of Evil*. New York: Continuum, 2010.

Encyclopedia of Birth Control. Edited by Vern Bullough. Santa Barbara: ABC-CLIO, 2001.

The Encyclopœdia Britannica: A Dictionary of Arts, Sciences, Literature, and General Information. Vol. 2. Ed. Hugh Chisholm. London: The Encyclopœdia Britannica Co., 1926.

The Encyclopedia of Islam. Ed. M. T. Houtsma et al. 9 vols. Leiden: E. J. Brill, 1913–34. Supplement, 1938.

The Encyclopedia of Islam. 2d. ed. Ed. H. A. R. Gibb et al. 12 vols. Leiden: E. J. Brill, 1986–2004.

The Encyclopedia of Islam. 3d. ed. Ed. Gudrun Krämer, Denis Matringe, John Nawas, and Everett Rowson. Leiden, E. J. Brill, 2007–.

The Encyclopedia of Religion and Ethics. Ed. James Hastings. Part 9. Whitefish, MT: Kessinger Publishing, 2003. S.v. "Education (Muslim)."

Endress, Gerhard. *An Introduction to Islam*. New York: Columbia University Press, 1988.

Epistle of Barnabas. In *Early Christian Writings: The Apostolic Fathers*, ed. and trans Maxwell Staniforth. Harmondsworth: Penguin, 1968.

Ernst, Carl. *Following Muḥammad: Rethinking Islam in the Contemporary World.* Chapel Hill: University of North Carolina Press, 2004.

Eusebios of Caesarea. *La Préparation évangélique.* 5 vols. Paris: Éditions du Cerf, 1974–.

Evetts, B. T. A. *Churches and Monasteries of Egypt and Some Neighboring Countries Attributed to Abu Salih the Armendian, Anecdota Oxoniensa,* Semitic Series 7. Oxford: Oxford University Press, 1895.

Fausto-Sterling, Anne. *Sexing the Body: Gender Politics and the Construction of Identity.* New York: Basic Books, 2000.

Featherstone, Brid, ed. *Mothering and Ambivalence*. London, New York: Routledge, 1997.

Feldman, Ruth, Aron Weller, Orna Zagoory-Sharon, and Ari Levine. "Evidence for a Neuroendocrinological Foundation for Human Affliliation: Plasma Oxytocin Levels across Pregnancy and Postpartum Period Predict Mother-Infant Bonding." *Psychological Science* 8, no. 11 (November 1995): 965–70.

Flemming, Rebecca. *Medicine and the Making of Roman Women: Gender, Nature, and Authority from Celsus to Galen*. Oxford, New York: Oxford University Press, 2000.

———. "The Pathology of Pregnancy in Galen's Commentaries on the *Epidemics*." In *The Unknown Galen*, ed. Vivian Nutton, 101–12. London: Institute of Classical Studies, 2002.

Foltz, Richard C. *Animals in Islamic Tradition and Muslim Cultures*. Oxford: Oneworld, 2006.

Foster, J. Andrew, and Kathryn Kueny. "From the Bodies of Bees: Classical and Christian Echoes in Surat al-Nahl." *Comparative Islamic Studies* 3, no. 2 (2007): 145–68.

Foucault, Michel. *Ethics: Subjectivity and Truth. The Essential Works of Michel Foucault, 1954–1984*. Vol. 1. Ed. Paul Rabinow. Trans. Robert Hurley. New York: New Press, 1997.

Frankfurter, David. "The Perils of Love: Magic and Countermagic in Coptic Egypt." *Journal of the History of Sexuality* 10, no. 3/4. Special Issue: *Sexuality in Late Antiquity* (July-October 2001): 480–500.

Frazer, James. *The Golden Bough: A Study in Magic and Religion*. Vol. 9, part 6: *The Scapegoat*. New York: Macmillan, 1951.

Frembgen, Jürgen W. "The Folklore of Geckos: Ethnographic Data from South and West Asia." *Asian Folklore Studies* 55 (1996): 135–43.

French, Valerie. "Midwives and Maternity Care in the Roman World." In *Midwifery and the Medicalization of Childbirth: Comparative Perspectives*, ed. Edwin R. Van Teijlingen, Maureen Porter, George W. Lowis, and Peter McCaffery, 53–62. Hauppauge, NY: Nova Science Publications, 2004.

Friedman, John Block. *The Monstrous Races in Medieval Art and Thought*. Syracuse: Syracuse University Press, 2000.

Fuchs, Lawrence H. *Beyond Patriarchy: Jewish Fathers and Families*. Waltham, MA: Brandeis University Press, 2000.

Galen. *On Semen*. Ed., trans., and commentary Phillip de Lacy. Berlin: Akademie Verlag, 1992.

Garcia, Guy. *The Decline of Men*. New York: Harper Perennial, 2009.

Ghazālī, Abū Ḥāmid Muḥammad ibn Muḥammd. *Iḥyā᾽ ulūm al-dīn*. 5 vols. Ḥalab: Dār al-waʿy, 1998.

———. *Iḥyā᾽ ʿulūm al-dīn*. Part 12. Trans. Madelain Farah as *Marriage and Sexuality in Islam*. Salt Lake City: University of Utah Press, 1984.

———. *Kasr al-shahwatayn*. Trans. Caesar D. Farah as *Abstinence in Islam: Curbing the Two Appetites, from the Iḥyā᾽ ʿulūm al-dīn*. Minneapolis: Bibliotheca Islamica, 1992.

———. *Kīmiyā᾽ al-saʿāda*. Trans. Claud Feld as *The Alchemy of Happiness*. Armonk, NY: M. E. Sharpe, 1991.

Gilʿadi, Avner. *Children of Islam: Concepts of Childhood in Medieval Muslim Society*. New York: Macmillan, 1992.

———. *Infants, Parents, and Wetnurses: Medieval Islamic Views on Breastfeeding and Their Social Implications*. Leiden: Brill, 1999.

———. "Liminal Craft, Exceptional Law: Some Notes on Midwives in Medieval Islamic Writings." *International Journal of Middle East Studies* 42 (2010): 185–202.

———. "Normative Islam Versus Local Tradition: Some Observations on Female Circumcision with Special Reference to Eqypt." *Arabica* T. 44, Fasc. 2 (April 1997): 254–67.

———. "Some Notes on Taḥnīk in Medieval Islam." *Journal of Near Eastern Studies* 47, no. 3 (July 1988): 175–79.

Gilmore, David D. *Manhood in the Making: Cultural Concepts of Masculinity*. New Haven: Yale University Press, 1990.

Ginzberg, Louis, *The Legends of the Jews*. 7 vols. Trans. Henrietta Szold. Philadelphia: The Jewish Publication Society of America, 1936–1942.

Goldziher, Ignaz. *Muhammedanische Studien*. Halle: Max Niemeyer, 1889. Trans. and ed. C. R. Barber, and S. M. Stern as *Muslim Studies*. 2 vols. Chicago: Aldine, 1968, 1971.

González-Crussi, F. *On Being Born and Other Difficulties*. Woodstock, NY: Overlook, 2004.

Grant, Robert McQueen. *Early Christians and Animals*. London, New York: Routledge, 1999.

Green, Monica. *Making Women's Medicine Masculine: The Rise of Male Authority in Pre-Modern Gynœcology*. Oxford: Oxford University Press, 2008.

———. "Women's Medical Practice and Health Care in Medieval Europe." *Signs* 14 (1989): 434–73.

Grensemann, H., ed. *Hippokratische Gynäkologie: die gynäkologischen Texte des Autors C nach den pseudohippokratischen Schriften* De Muliebribus I, II *und* De Sterilibus. Wiesbaden: Steiner, 1982.

Greppin, John A. C., Emilie Savage-Smith, and John L. Gueriguian, eds. *The Diffusion of Greco-Roman Medicine into the Middle East and the Caucasus*. Delmar, NY: Caravan Books, 1999.

Griffel, Frank. "The Harmony of Natural Law and Shariʾa in Islamist Theology." In *Shariʾa: Islamic Law in the Contemporary Context*, ed. Abbas Amanat and Frank Griffel, 38–61. Stanford: Stanford University Press, 2007.

Griffith, R. Marie. *Evangelical Women and the Power of Submission*. Berkeley: University of California Press, 2000.

Griffiths, J. Gwyn. "Atlantis and Egypt." *Historia: Zeitschrift für Alte Geschichte*. Bd. 34, H. 1 (1st Qtr. 1985): 3–38.

Guillaume, Alfred. *The Life of Muḥammad: A Translation of Ibn Isḥāq's* Sirat Rasūl Allāh. Karachi: Oxford University Press, 1995.

Halevi, Leor. *Muḥammad's Grave: Death Rites and the Making of Islamic Society*. New York: Columbia University Press, 2007.

Hall, Robert E. "Intellect, Soul, and Body in Ibn Sīnā: Systematic Synthesis and Development of the Aristotelian, Neoplatonic, and Galenic theories." In *Interpreting Avicenna: Science and Philosophy in Medieval Islam*, ed. John McGinnis and David Reisman, 62–86. Leiden: Brill, 2004.

Hallaq, Wael. *The Origins and Evolution of Islamic Law*. Cambridge: Cambridge University Press, 2005.

Hamarneh, Sami K. "Al-Ṭabarī." In *Encyclopedia of the History of Science, Technology, and Medicine in Non-Western Cultures*. Dordrecht: Kluwer, 1997.

Hameesh, A. H. Abdul Haq. "Rulings Concerning Tattooing in Islamic Jurisprudence." *Contemporary Jurisprudence Research Journal* 63 (2004): 14–16.

Hanson, Ann. "Hippocrates: Diseases of Women 1." *Signs* 1, no. 2 (Winter 1975): 567–84.

———. "The Medical Writers' Women." In *Before Sexuality: The Construction of Erotic Experience in the Ancient Greek World,* ed. Froma I. Zeitlin, John J. Winker, and David Halperin, 309–37. Princeton: Princeton University Press, 1990.

Harms, Roger. *Mayo Clinic Guide to a Healthy Pregnancy*. New York: Harper Paperbacks, 2004.

Herapollo Nilous. *Hieroglyphica*. Trans. by George Boas as *The Hieroglyphics of Horapollo*. New York: Pantheon Books, 1950.

Herodotus. *An Account of Egypt*. Trans. G. C. MacCauley. Rockville, MD: Arc Manor, 2008.

———. *Histories*. Ed. A. D. Godley. London: Heinemann, 1921.

Hershon, Paul Isaac, trans. *A Talmudic Miscellany: A Thousand and One Extracts from the Talmud, the Midrashim, and the Kabbalah*. London: Trübner, Ludgate Hill, 1880.

Hesiod. *Catalogues of Women*. In *Hesiod: The Shield, Catalogue of Women, Other Fragments,* ed. G. M. Most. Loeb Classical Library 503. Cambridge: Harvard University Press, 2007.

———. *Theogony*. Trans. Norman O. Brown. New York: Prentice-Hall, 1953.

———. *Works and Days*. Trans. M. L. West. Oxford: Oxford University Press, 1999.

Hess, Erika Elizabeth. *Literary Hybrids: Cross-dressing, Shapeshifting, and Indeterminancy in Medieval and Modern French Narrative*. New York: Routledge, 2003.

Heyneman, Stephen P. *Islam and Social Policy*. Nashville: Vanderbilt University Press, 2004.

Hillenbrand, Robert. "Mamlūk and Īlkhānid Bestiaries: Convention and Experiment." *Ars Orientalis* 20 (1990): 149–87.

Ḥimyārī al-Qummī, ʿAbdallāh ibn Jaʿfar. *Qurb al-isnād*. Al-Najaf: al-Maṭba'ah al-ḥaydarīya, 1950.

Hippocrates. *Hippocratic Writings*. Trans. J. Chadwick. Ed. G. E. R. Lloyd. New York: Penguin, 1978.

———. *Hippokratische Gynäkologie: Die gynäkologischen Texte des Autors C nach den pseudohippokratischen Schriften* De Muliebribus I, II *und* De Sterilibus. Ed. H. Grensemann. Wiesbaden: Steiner, 1982.

Hoffman, Lawrence. *Covenant of Blood: Circumcision and Gender in Rabbinic Judaism*. Chicago: University of Chicago Press, 1995.

Huet, Marie-Hélène. *Monstrous Imagination*. Cambridge: Harvard University Press, 1993.

Hughes, Thomas Patrick. *A Dictionary of Islam: Being a Cyclopædia of the Doctrines, Rites, Ceremonies, and Customs, Together with the Technical and Theological terms, of the Muhammadan Religion*. London: W. H. Allen, 1896.

Ḥunayn ibn Isḥāq al-ʿIbādī, Abū Zayd. *The Problemata Physica Attributed to Aristotle: The Arabic Version of Ḥunayn ibn Isḥāq and the Hebrew Version of Moses ibn Tibbon. Aristoteles Semitico-latinus,* vol. 11. Ed. L. S. Filius. Leiden, Boston: Brill, 1999.

Hutton, J. H., and J. P. van den Brand de Cleverskerk. "Wolf-Children." *Folklore* 51, no. 1 (March 1940): 9–31.

Hvalvik, Reidar. *Struggle for Scripture and Covenant: The Purpose of the Epistle of Barnabas and Jewish-Christian Competition in the Second Century. Wissenschaftliche untersuchungen zum Neuen Testament* 2. Reihe 82. Tübingen: J. C. B. Mohr (Paul Siebeck), 1996.

Hyginus. *The Myths of Hyginus.* Trans. and ed. Mary Grant. University of Kansas Publications in Humanistic Studies, no. 34. Lawrence: University of Kansas Press, 1960.

Ibn Abī Ḥawāfir. *Kitāb badā'ī al-akwān fī manāfi' al-ḥayawān.* MS Dublin, Chester Beatty 4352.

Ibn al-ʿArabī, Muḥyī al-Dīn. *Tafsīr al-Qur'ān al-karīm.* 2 vols. Bayrūt: Dār al-thaqāfa al-ʿarabiyya, 1968.

Ibn ʿAsākir, ʿAlī ibn al-Ḥasan. *Tārīkh al-kabīr.* Damascus: Maṭbaʿat rawḍat al-shām, 1911.

Ibn Bābawayh al-Qummī, Muḥammad ibn ʿAlī. *ʿUyunu akhbarī al-riḍā.* 2 Vols. Najaf: Haydariyyah Press, 1970.

Ibn Ḥajar al-ʿAsqalānī, Aḥmad ibn ʿAlī. *Kitāb al-iṣābah fī tamyīz al-ṣaḥābah.* 4vols. Beirut: Dār ṣādir, 1900.

Ibn Ḥajar al-Haythamī, Aḥmad ibn Muḥammad. *Ṣawāʿiq al-muḥriqa fī al-radd ʿalá ahl al-bidaʿ wa al-zandaqa.* 2 vols. Riyad: Dār al-waṭan; Beirut: Mu'assasat al-Risāla, 1997.

Ibn Ḥanbal, Aḥmad ibn Muḥammad. *Faḍā'il ahl al-bayt min Kitāb Faḍā'il al-Ṣaḥāba.* Tehran: al-Majmaʿ al-ʿālamī li al-taqrīb bayna al-madhāhib al-islāmīya, 2004.

———. *Musnad.* 6 Vols. Cairo: al-Maṭbaʿa al-maymanīya, 1895.

Ibn Hishām, ʿAbd al-Mālik. *Al-Sīra al-nabawīya.* See Ibn Isḥāq, Muḥammad.

Ibn Isḥāq, Muḥammad. *Sīrat rasūl Allāh,* in the recension of ʿAbd al-Mālik ibn Hishām's *al-Sira al-nabawīya.* 3 vols. Dār al-kutub al-misrīya, n.d. Trans. Alfred Guillaume as *The Life of Muḥammad: A Translation of Ibn Isḥāq's sīrat rasūl Allāh.* Oxford: Oxford University Press, 1955.

Ibn al-Jawzī, Abū al-Faraj ʿAbd al-Raḥmān ibn ʿAlī. *Kitāb aḥkām al-nisā'.* Beirut: Mu'assasat al-kutub al-thaqāfīya, 1988.

———. *Kitāb iltiqāt al-manāfīʿ.* Bodleian MS. Hun. Donat. 31, ff. 178–207.

———. *Al-Wafā bi aḥwāl al-muṣṭafá.* 2 vols. Ed. Muṣṭafa ʿAbd al-Wāḥid. Cairo: Dār al-kutub al-ḥadītha, 1966.

Ibn Jazzār, Abū Jaʿfar Aḥmad ibn Ibrāhīm ibn Abī Khālid. *Zad al-musāfir wa qūt al-ḥāḍir.* Book 6. Trans. Gerrit Bos. Sir Henry Wellcome Asian Series. London, New York: Kegan Paul International, 1997.

Ibn al-Kalbī, Hishām. *Kitāb al-aṣnām.* Trans. Nabih Amin Faris. Princeton: Princeton University Press, 1952.

Ibn Kathīr, Ismāʿīl ibn ʿUmar. *Al-Sīra al-nabawīya.* Trans. Trevor Le Gassick. Reading, UK: Garnet, 1999.

———. *Qiṣaṣ al-anbiyā'.* Dimashsq: Dār Ibn Kathīr, 1992.

———. *Tafsīr al-Qur'ān al-ʿazim.* 15 vols. Jīza: Mu'assasat qurṭuba; Maktabat awlād al-shaykh li al-Turāth, 2000.

Ibn Khaldūn. Abū Zayd ʿAbd al-Raḥmān ibn Muḥammad. *The Muqaddimah: An Introduction to History*. Ed. N. J. Dawood. Trans. Franz Rosenthal. 3 vols. Princeton: Princeton University Press, 1989.

Ibn Māja, Muḥammad ibn Yazīd. *Kitāb al-sunan*. Ed. Muḥammad Fūʾād ʿAbd al-Bāqī. 5 vols. Cairo: Dār iḥyā al-kutub al-ʿarabīya, 1953.

Ibn Māsawayh, Yuḥanna. *al-Nawādir al-ṭibbīya*. Trans. as *Les axiomes médicaux de Yohanna ben Massawaïh*. Annotated by Le R. P. Paul Sbath. Le Caire: N.G. Thamaz, 1934.

Ibn Qayyim al-Jawzīya, Muḥammad ibn Abī Bakr. *Ṭibb al-nabawī*. Trans. Penelope Johnstone as *Medicine of the Prophet*. Cambridge: The Islamic Texts Society, 1998.

———. *Al-Tibyān fī aqsām al-qurʾān*. Beirut: Muʾassasat al-risāla, 1994.

———. *Tuḥfat al-mawdūd bi-aḥkām al-mawlūd*. Dimashq: Maktabat dār al-bayān, 1971.

Ibn Qutayba, ʿAbdallāh ibn Muslim. *ʿUyūn al-akhbār*. 4 vols. Cairo: al-Muʿassasa al-miṣrīya al-ʿāmma li al-taʾlīf wa ʿl-tarjama wa al-nashr, 1964.

Ibn Saʿd, Muḥammad. *Ṭabaqāt al-kabīr, juzʾ 8*. Trans. Aisha Bewley as *The Women of Madina*. London: Ta-Ha, 1995.

Ibn Shahrāshūb, Muḥammad ibn ʿAlī. *Manāqib Āl Abī Ṭālib*. Najaf: al-Maṭbaʿa al-ḥaydarīya, 1956.

Ibn Sīnā, Abū ʿAlī al-Ḥusayn ibn ʿAbdallāh. *Āthār al-ʿulwīya. Avicennae de congelatione et conglutinatione lapidum: being sections of the Kitāb al-shifāʾ*. The Latin and Arabic texts with an English translation of the latter and with critical notes by E. J. Holmyard and D. C. Mandeville. Paris: Geuthner, 1927.

———. *Al-Qānūn fī al-ṭibb*. 3 vols. Beirut: Dar Sader Publishers, 1970.

———. *al-Shifāʾ*. Vol. 2, *Ṭabīʿīyāt*. Qum, Īrān: Maktabat āyat Allāh al-ʿuẓmá al-marʿashī al-najafī, 1983.

Ibn Taymīya, Aḥmad ibn ʿAbd al-Ḥalīm. *Fatāwā al-kubrá*. 5 vols. Cairo: Dār al-kutub al-ḥadītha, 1966.

———. *Idāḥ al-dalāla fī ʿumūm al-risāla*. Trans. Abu Ameenah Bilal Philips. New Delhi: Islamic Book Service, 2002.

———. *Kitāb ʿilm al-sulūk*. In *Majmūʿ fatāwā Ibn Taymiyya*, ed. ʿAbd al-Raḥmān ibn Qāsim. Riyad: Matabiʾ al-Riyadh, 1961.

Ibn Ṭufayl, Muḥammad ibn ʿAbd al-Mālik. *Ḥayy ibn Yaqẓān*. Misr: Dār al-maʿārif, 1966.

Inhorn, Marcia Claire. *Infertility and Patriarchy : The Cultural Politics of Gender and Family Life in Egypt*. Philadelphia: University of Pennsylvania Press, 1996.

———. "'The Worms are Weak': Male Infertility and Patriarchal Paradoxes in Egypt." In *Islamic Masculinities*, ed. Lahoucine Ouzgane, 217–37. New York: Zed Books, 2006.

———, ed. *Reconceiving the Second Sex: Men, Masculinity, and Reproduction*. New York, Berghahn Books, 2009.

Isodore of Seville. *The Etymologies of Isodore of Seville*. Trans. Stephen A. Barney, W. J. Lewis, J. A. Beach, and Oliver Berghof. Cambridge: Cambridge University Press, 2006.

Izbicki, Thomas. "Doctrine of the Immaculate Conception." In *Women and Gender in Medieval Europe: An Encyclopedia,* ed. Margaret Schaus. New York: Routledge, 2006.

Jāḥiẓ, Abū ʿUthmān ʿAmr ibn Baḥr. *"Chance or Creation"? God's Design in the Universe.* Trans. M. A. S. Abdel Haleem. Reading, Berks.: Garnet, 1995.

———. *Al-Ḥayawān.* Miṣr: Muṣṭafā al-bābī al-ḥalabī, 1966.

———. *Rasāʾil.* Cairo: Maktabat al-khānjī, 1964.

Jay, Nancy. *Throughout Your Generations Forever: Sacrifice, Religion, and Paternity.* Chicago: University of Chicago Press, 1992.

Jerome. *Saint Jerome's Hebrew Questions Genesis.* Oxford Early Christian Studies. Trans. C. T. R. Hayward. Oxford: Oxford University Press, 1995.

Jia, Namu. "Myths and Traditional Beliefs about the Wolf and the Crow in Central Asia: Examples from the Turkic Wu-Sun and the Mongols." *Asian Folklore Studies* 65, no. 2 (2006): 161–77.

Joseph, Suad. *Intimate Selving in Arab Families: Gender, Self, and Identity.* Syracuse: Syracuse University Press, 1999.

———, and Afsaneh Najmabadi, ed. *Encyclopedia of Women and Islamic Cultures: Family, Body, Sexuality, and Health.* Leiden: Brill, 2005.

Josephus, Flavius. *Jewish Antiquities.* 9 vols. Trans. Louis H. Feldman. *Loeb Classical Library.* Cambridge: Harvard University Press, 1998–.

Jütte, Robert. *Contraception: A History.* Cambridge: Polity Press, 2008.

Kalin, Ibrahim. "Will, Necessity and Creation as Monistic Theophany in the Islamic Philosophical Tradition." In *Creation and the God of Abraham,* ed. David B. Burrell, Carlo Cogliati, and Janet M. Soskice, 107–32. Cambridge: Cambridge University Press, 2010.

Karras, Ruth Mazo. *Sexuality in Medieval Europe: Doing unto Others.* London, New York: Routledge, 2005.

Kearns, Cleo McNelly. *The Virgin Mary, Monotheism, and Sacrifice.* Cambridge: Cambridge University Press, 2008.

Keller, Hildegard Elisabeth. *My Secret is Mine: Studies on Religion and Eros in the German Middle Ages.* Leuven: Peeters Publishers, 2000.

Kessler, Gwynn. *Conceiving Israel: The Fetus in Rabbinic Narratives.* Philadelphia: University of Pennsylvania Press, 2009.

Khalidi, Tarif. *Arab Historical Thought in the Classical Period.* Cambridge: Cambridge University Press, 1996.

Khan, Muhammad Aftab. *Sex and Sexuality in Islam.* Karachi: Nashryat, 2006.

Khaṭīb al-Tabrīzī, Muḥammad ibn ʿAbdallāh. *Mishkāt al-Maṣābīḥ.* 2 vols. Trans. James Robson. Lahore: Sh. Muhammad Ashraf, 1981.

Kisāʾī, Muhammad ibn ʿAbdallāh. *Qiṣaṣ al-anbiyāʾ.* Trans. W. M. Thackston Jr. as *Tales of the Prophets of al-Kisāʾī.* Boston: Twayne, 1978.

King, Helen. *Hippocrates' Women: Reading the Female Body in Ancient Greece.* London, New York: Routledge, 1998.

King, J. M. "The Origin and Development of the *Hippomanes* in the Horse and Zebra." *Journal of Anatomy* (1967): 277–84.

Kirkham, Mavis. *Exploring the Dirty Side of Women's Health.* New York: Routledge, 2006.

Kister, M. J. "Call Yourself By Graceful Names . . ." *Society and Religion from Jāhilīya to Islam* 12: 3–25. Aldershot: Variorum, 1990.

———. "'. . . And He Was Born Circumcised . . .': Some Notes on Circumcision in *ḥadīth*." *Oriens* 34 (1994): 10–30.

———. "Sons of Khadīja." In *The Life of Muḥammad,* ed. Uri Rubin, 57–93. Sydney: Ashgate Variorum, 1998.

———. "*Al-Taḥannath*: An Inquiry into the Meaning of a Term." *Bulletin of the School of Oriental and African Studies* 31, no. 2 (1968): 223–36.

Klein, Lilian R. "Hannah: Marginalized Victim and Social Redeemer." In *A Feminist Companion to Samuel and Kings, Volume 5,* ed. Athalya Brenner, 77–92. Sheffield: Sheffield Academic Press, 1994.

Klein, Michele. *A Time to Be Born: Customs and Folklore of Jewish Birth.* Philadelphia: The Jewish Publication Society, 1998.

Knight, Lisa I. *Contradictory Lives: Baul Women in India and Bangladesh.* Oxford: Oxford University Press, 2011.

Kohlberg, Etan. "The Position of the '*walid zina*' in Imami Shi'ism." *Bulletin of the School of Oriental and African Studies* 48 no. 2 (1985): 237–66.

Kriss, R., and H. Kriss-Heinrich. *Volksglaube im Bereich des Islam.* I., Wiesbaden: Wallfahrtswesen und Heiligenverehrun, 1960.

Kruk, Remke. "A Frothy Bubble: Spontaneous Generation in the Medieval Islamic Tradition." *Journal of Semitic Studies* XXXV, no. 2 (Autumn 1990): 265–82.

———. "Ibn Tufayl: A Medieval Scholar's Views on Nature." In *The World of Ibn Tufayl; Interdisciplinary Perspectives on Hayy ibn Yaqzân,* ed. Lawrence I. Conrad, 69–89. Leiden: Brill, 1996.

———. "Popular Arabic Literature as a Mirror of Social Attitudes and Preoccupations." In *Individu et Société dans le monde méditerranéen musulman; Questions et sources,* ed. Randi Deguilhem, 99–112. Aix-en-Provence: Université de Provence, 1998.

———. "Pregnancy and Its Social Implications in Mediaeval and Traditional Arab Society." In *Quaderni di studi arabi* 5–6. *Atti del XIII congresso dell' union européenne d'arabi-sants et d'islamisants,* 418–39. Venice: Università degli studi di Venezia, 1987–88.

———. "Traditional Islamic Views of Apes and Monkeys." In *Ape, Man, Apeman: Changing Views since 1600,* ed. Raymond Corbey and Bert Theunissen, 29–42. Leiden: Department of Prehistory of Leiden University, 1995.

Kueny, Kathryn M. "Abraham's Test: Male Circumcision as Anti/Ante-Covenantal Practice." In *Bible and Qur'ān: Essays in Scriptural Intertextuality,* ed. John C. Reeves, 161–82. Atlanta: Society of Biblical Literature, 2003.

———. *The Rhetoric of Sobriety: Wine in Early Islam.* Albany: State University of New York Press, 2001.

Kulaynī, Abū Jaʿfar Muḥammad ibn Yaʿqūb ibn Isḥāq. *Al-Kāfī.* 15 vols. Qum: Dār al-ḥadīth, 2008.

Kumar, Sailesh. *Handbook of Fetal Medicine.* Cambridge: Cambridge University Press, 2010.

Lactantius. *Divine Institutes.* Trans. Anthony Bowen and Peter Garnsey. Liverpool: Liverpool University Press, 2003.

Ladd-Taylor, Molly, and Lauri Umansky, eds. *"Bad Mothers," The Politics of Blame in Twentieth Century America*. New York: New York University Press, 1998.

Lammens, H. "Fāṭima." In *The Encyclopedia of Islam*.

Lassner, Jacob. *Demonizing the Queen of Sheba: Boundaries of Gender and Culture in Postbiblical Judaism and Medieval Islam*. Chicago: University of Chicago Press, 1993.

Lauwers, Judith, and Anna Swisher. *Counseling the Nursing Mother*. Sudbudy, MA: Jones and Bartlett, 2010.

Lane, Edward. *Arabic English Lexicon*. London: Williams and Norgate, 1863.

Lapidus, Ira. "Knowledge, Virtue, and Action: The Classical Muslim Conception of *adab* and the Nature of Religious Fulfillment in Islam." In *Moral Conduct and Authority*, ed. Barbara Metcalf, 38–61. Berkeley: University of California Press, 1984.

Laqueur, Thomas. *Making Sex: Body and Gender from the Greeks to Freud*. Cambridge: Harvard University Press, 1990.

de Lauretis, Teresa. "The Female Body and Heterosexual Presumption." *Semiotica* 67, no. 3–4 (1987): 259–79.

Lebling, Robert. *Legends of the Fire Spirits: Jinn and Genies from Arabia to Zanzibar*. Berkeley: Counterpoint Press, 2010.

Leeming, David Adams. *Creation Myths of the World: An Encyclopedia*. Vol 1. Santa Barbara: ABC-CLIO, 2009.

Leftkowitz, Mary R., and Maureen B. Fant. *Women's Life in Greece and Rome: A Source Book in Translation*. Baltimore: Johns Hopkins University Press, 2005.

Levey, Martin. *Early Arabic Pharmacology: An Introduction Based on Ancient and Medieval Sources*. Leiden: Brill, 1973.

———, and Safwat S. Souryal. "Galen's *On the Secrets of Women* and *On the Secrets of Men*: A Contribution to the History of Arabic Pharmacology." *Janus* 55, no. 2–3 (1968): 208–19.

Lévi-Strauss, Claude. *Totemism*. Trans. Rodney Needham. Boston: Beacon Press, 1963.

Lichtenstaedter, Ilse. "And Become Ye Accursed Apes." *Jerusalem Studies in Arabic and Islam* 14 (1991): 153–75.

Luttikhuizen, Gerard P., ed. *Eve's Children: The Biblical Stories Retold and Interpreted in Jewish and Christian Traditions*. Leiden: Koninklijke Brill, 2003.

Mabilia, Mara. *Breast Feeding and Sexuality: Behavior, Belief, and Taboo among the Gogo Mothers in Tanzania*. New York: Berghahn Books, 2005.

Mahler, Margaret, Fred Pine, and Anni Bergman. *The Psychological Birth of the Human Infant*. New York: Basic Books, 1975.

Mahmood, Saba. "Feminist Theory, Embodiment, and the Docile Agent: Some Reflections on the Egyptian Islamic Revival." *Cultural Anthropology* 16, no. 2 (May 2001): 202–36.

———. *The Politics of Piety: The Islamic Revival and the Feminist Subject*. Princeton: Princeton University Press, 2005.

Maimonides, Moses. *Fuṣūl Mūsā. The Medical Aphorisms of Moses Maimonides*. Trans. Fred Rosner. Haifa: Maimonides Research Institute, 1989.

Majlisī, Muḥammad Bāqir ibn Muḥammad Taqī. *Biḥār al-anwār*. Tehran: Dār al-kutub al-islāmīya, 1957–.
———. *Jalā' al-'uyūn*. Tehran: Kitābfurūshī-i al islamīya, 1974.
Majūsī, 'Alī ibn al-'Abbās. *Kitāb kāmil al-ṣinā'a al-ṭibbīya al-ma'rūf bi-al-malakī*. Ḥarrān, 1877.
Mālik ibn Anas. *Muwaṭṭa'*. Beirut: Dār al-gharb al-islāmī, 1994.
Malti-Douglas, Fedwa. *Structures of Avarice: The Bukhalā' in Medieval Arabic Literature*. Leiden: Brill, 1995.
Manṣūr, Sa'īd Ḥ. *The World View of al-Jāḥiẓ in Kitāb al-Ḥayawān*. Alexandria: Dar al Maaref, 1977.
Marcus, Ivan G. *Rituals of Childhood: Jewish Acculturation in Medieval Europe*. New Haven: Yale University Press, 1996.
Marghīnānī, 'Alī ibn Abī Bakr. *Hidāya*. Trans. Charles Hamilton. New Delhi, Kitab Bhavan, 1985.
Mark, Elizabeth Wyner. *The Covenant of Circumcision: New Perspectives on an Ancient Jewish rite*. Lebanon, NH.: University Press of New England, 2003.
Martinez, Florentino Garcia. "Eve's Children in the Targumim." In *Eve's Children*, 27–56.
Mas'ūdī, 'Alī ibn al-Ḥusayn al-Mas'ūdī. *Murūj al-dhahab wa ma'ādin al-jawhar*. Cairo: al-Maṭab'a al-azharīya, 1885–87.
Mauss, Marcel. *Manual of Ethnography*. Oxford, New York: Berghahn Books, 2009.
McAuliffe, Jane Dammen. "Mary and Fāṭima in Qur'ānic Exegesis." *Islamochristiana* 7 (1981): 19–28.
———, ed. *Encyclopedia of the Qur'ān*. 6 vols. Leiden: Brill, 2001–2006.
McCartney, Eugene Stock. "Sex Determination and Control in Antiquity." *American Journal of Philology* 43, no. 1 (1922): 62–70.
———. "Spontaneous Generation and Kindred Notions in Antiquity." *Transactions and Proceedings of the American Philological Association* 51 (1920): 101–15.
McConkey, Edwin H. *How the Human Genome Works*. Sudbury, MA: Jones and Bartlett, 2004.
Menachem ben Aron ibn Zeraḥ. *Tsedah al-derekh*. Warsaw: Bi-defus Ḥ. Ḳelṭer, 1880.
Meinardus, Otto. "Mythological, Historical, and Sociological Aspects of the Practice of Female Circumcision among the Egyptians." *Acta Ethnographica Academiae Scientiarum Hungaricae* 17 (1967): 387–97.
Mernissi, Fatima. *The Veil and the Male Elite: A Feminist Interpretation of Women's Rights in Islam*. New York: Basic Books, 1992.
Midrash Tanhuma-Yelammedenu: An English translation of Genesis and Exodus. Trans. Samuel A. Berman. Jersey City: Ktav Publishing, 1996.
Miller, Sarah Alison. *Medieval Monstrosity and the Female Body*. New York: Routledge, 2010.
Mishnah Berurah: The Classic Commentary to Shulchan aruch Orach. Trans. and commentary Israel Meir (ha-Kohen), Aharon Feldman, and Aviel Orenstein. Vol. 3. Feldheim Publishers, 1986.
Moore, Lisa Jean. "Killer Sperm: Masculinity and the Essence of Male Hierarchies." In *Reconceiving the Second Sex*, 45–71.

Motzki, H. "*Das Kind und seine Sozialisation in der islamischen Familie des Mittelalters.*" *Zur Welt des Islams* 27 (1987): 82–90.

Murata, Sachiko. *The Tao of Islam*. Albany: State University of New York Press, 1992.

Musallam, Basim. *Sex and Society in Islam*. Cambridge: Cambridge University Press, 1983.

Muslim ibn al-Ḥajjāj al-Qurshayrī. *Jāmiʿ al-ṣaḥīḥ* (*Ṣaḥīḥ Muslim*). 5 vols. Bayrūt: Dār Ibn Ḥazm, 1995.

Myerowitz Levine, Molly. "The Gendered Grammar of Ancient Mediterranean Hair." In *Off with Her Head: The Denial of Women's Identity in Myth, Religion, and Culture*, ed. H. Eilberg Schwartz and W. Doniger, 76–130. Berkeley: University of California Press, 1995.

Nabielek, Rainer. "*Sexualerziehung im Werk des Avicenna: Ein Beitrag zur arabisch-islarnischen sexualgeschichte.*" *Schriftenreihe für Geschichte der Naturwissenschaften, Technik und Medizin* 13, no. 2 (1976): 82–87.

Nafzāwī, ʿUmar Ibn Muḥammad. *Al-Rawḍ al-ʿāṭir fī nuzhat al-khāṭir*. Trans. Jim Colville as *The Perfumed Garden of Sensual Delight*. London: Kegan Paul, 1999.

Nasāʾī, Aḥmad b. Shuʿayb. *Sunan al-Nasāʾi*. Ed. Jalāl al-Dīn al-Suyūṭī. 8 vols. Cairo: Al-Maṭbaʿa al-misrīya, 1930.

Nawawī, Abū Zakarīyā Muḥyīʾ al-Dīn al-Sharaf. *Al-Majmūʿ Sharḥ al-Muhadhdhab*. 9 vols. Cairo: Zakarīyā ʿAlī Yūsuf, 1925–29.

Der Nersessian, Sirarpie. *Études byzantines et arméniennes: Byzantine and Armenian Studies*. Louvain: Impr. orientaliste, 1973.

Newby, Gordon D. *The Making of the Last Prophet: A Reconstruction of the Earliest Biography of Muḥammad*. Columbia: University of South Carolina Press, 1989.

Nīsābūrī, ʿAbdallāh ibn Busṭām. *Islamic Medical Wisdom: The ṭibb al-aʾimma*. Trans. Batool Ispahamy. London: The Muhammadi Trust, 1991.

Nöldeke, Theodor. *Geschichte der Perser und Araber zur Zeit der Sasaniden*. Leiden: Brill, 1879.

Nutton, Vivien. *Ancient Medicine*. London, New York: Routledge, 2004.

Nuwayrī, Aḥmad ibn ʿAbd al-Wahhāb. *Nihāyat al-arab fī funūn al-adab*. Cairo: National Government Publication, 1923.

Olsan, Lea T. "Charms and Prayers in Medieval Medical Theory and Practice." *Social History of Medicine* 16, no. 3 (2003): 343–66.

Origen. *Contra Celsum*. Trans. Henry Chadwick. Cambridge: Cambridge University Press, 1953.

Omran, Abdel Rahman. *Family Planning in the Legacy of Islam*. London, New York: Routledge, 1992.

Oswald, Dana. *Monsters, Gender, and Sexuality in Medieval English Literature*. Cambridge: D. S. Brewer; Rochester, NY: Boydell and Brewer, 2010.

Ovid. *Metamorphoses*. Trans. Z. Phillip Ambrose. Newburyport, MA: Focus Publishing, 2004.

Papaconstantinoue, Arietta, and Mary Alice Talbot. *Becoming Byzantine: Children and Childhood in Byzantium*. Cambridge: Harvard University Press, 2009.

Paulus, Aegineta. *The Seven Books of Paulus Ægineta.* Trans. Francis Adams. 3 vols. London: Printed for the Sydenham Society, 1844–47.

Pellat, Charles. *The Life and works of al-Jāḥiẓ: Translations of Selected Texts.* Trans. D. M. Hawke. London: Routledge and Kegan Paul, 1969.

Peters. F. E. *The Hajj: The Muslim Pilgrimage to Mecca and Holy Places.* Princeton: Princeton University Press, 1995.

Philo. *Questions and Answers on Genesis.* Trans. Ralph Marcus. *Loeb Classical Library.* Cambridge: Harvard University Press, 1953.

Pliny the Elder. *Natural History.* Book 7. Trans. Mary Beagon. Oxford: Clarendon Press; New York: Oxford University Press, 2005.

Pomeroy, Sarah. *Families in Classical and Hellenistic Greece: Representations and Realities.* Oxford: Clarendon Press, 1997.

Poor, Sara. *Mechthild of Magdeburg and Her Book: Gender and the Making of Textual Authority.* Philadelphia: University of Pennsylvania Press, 2004.

Pormann, Peter and Emilie Savage-Smith. *Medieval Islamic Medicine.* Edinburgh: Edinburgh University Press, 2007.

Powers, David. *Muḥammad Is Not the Father of Any of Your Men.* Philadelphia: University of Pennsylvania Press, 2009.

Preuss, Julius. *Biblisch-talmudische Medizin: Beiträge zur Geschichte der Heilkunde und der Kulture überhaupt.* Trans. Fred Rosner as *Biblical and Talmudic Medicine.* Lanham, MD: Jason Aronson, 2004.

Prioreschi, Plinio. *History of Medicine.* 2nd ed. 2 vols. Omaha: Horatius Press, 1996–.

Qazwīnī. Ḥamdallāh Mustawfī. *Nuzhatu al-qulūb.* Trans. Lieut-Col. J. Stephenson as *The Zoological Section of the Nuzhatu-l-qulūb.* London: Royal Asiatic Society, 1928.

Qazwīnī, Zakarīyā ibn Muḥammad. *ʿAjā'ib al-makhlūqāt wa gharā'ib al-mawjūdāt,* 1973.

Qummī, ʿAlī ibn Ibrāhīm. *Tafsīr al-Qummī.* Qum: Dhawā al-qurbā, 2007.

Qummī, Muḥammad ibn Muḥammad Riḍā. *Tafsīr kanz al-daqā'iq wa baḥr al-gharā'ib.* Qum: Dār al-ghadīr, 2003.

Qurṭubī, Muḥammad ibn Aḥmad. *Jāmiʿ li-aḥkām al-Qur'ān.* Al-Qāhira: Dār al-maṭābiʿ al-shaʿb, 1961.

Rabbān al-Ṭabarī, ʿAlī ibn Sahl. *Firdaws al-ḥikma fi al-ṭibb.* Beirut: s.n., 1970.

Rahman, Fazlur. *Health and Medicine in the Islamic Tradition.* New York: Crossroad, 1987.

Rasā'il Ikhwān al-Ṣafā' wa khillān al-wafā'. 4 vols. Beirut: Dār Bayrūt, 1957.

Rāzī, Abū Bakr Muḥammad ibn Zakarīyā. *Kitāb al-ḥāwī fī al-ṭibb.* 17 vols. Haydarabad: Osmania Oriental Publications Bureau, 1960.

———. *Kitāb ṭibb al-Manṣūrī.* Bodleian MS. Marsh 376.

Rāzī, Fakhr al-Dīn. *Al-Tafsīr al-kabīr.* Cairo: Al-Maṭbaʿa al-bahīya, n.d.

Reynolds, Gabriel Said. *The Qur'ān and its Biblical Subtext.* New York: Routledge, 2010.

Riddle, John. *Contraception and Abortion from the Ancient World to the Renaissance.* Cambridge: Harvard University Press, 1994.

———. *Eve's Herbs: A history of Contraception and Abortion in the West.* Cambridge: Harvard University Press, 1997.

———. *Goddesses, Elixirs, and Witches: Plants and Sexuality throughout Human History*. New York: Palgrave Macmillan, 2010.
———. *A History of the Middle Ages, 300–1500*. Lanham, MD: Rowman and Littlefield, 2008.
Rider, Catherine. *Magic and Impotence in the Middle Ages*. Oxford: Oxford University Press, 2006.
Robinson, Arthur E. "The Cult of the Crocodile." *American Anthropologist*. New Series 34, no. 3 (July–September 1932): 550.
Rosenthal, Franz. "Al-Rāzī on the Hidden Illness." In *Science and Medicine in Islam*, 45-60. Hampshire: Variorum, Gower, 1990.
Rosner, Fred. *Medicine in the Mishneh Torah of Maimonides*. Northvale, NJ: Jason Aronson, 1997.
Rubin, Uri. "Apes, Pigs, and the Islamic Identity." *Israel Oriental Studies* 17 (1997): 89–105.
———. *The Eye of the Beholder: The Life of Muḥammad as Viewed by the Early Muslims*. Princeton: The Darwin Press, 1995.
———, ed. *The Life of Muḥammad*. Brookfield, VT: Ashgate, 1998.
Sachedina, Abdulaziz. *Islamic Biomedical Ethics: Principles and Applications*. Oxford: Oxford University Press, 2010.
Sadtler, Samuel Philip, and Henry Trimble. *A Text Book of Chemistry: Intended for the Use of Pharmaceutical and Medical Students*. Philadelphia: J. B. Lippincott, 1895.
Salih, Sarah, and Denise N. Baker. *Julian of Norwich's Legacy: Medieval Mysticism and Post-Medieval Reception*. New York: Palgrave Macmillan, 2009.
Salisbury, Joyce E. *The Beast Within: Animals in the Middle Ages*. New York, London: Routledge, 1994.
———. *Perpetua's Passion: The Death and Memory of a Young Roman Woman*. New York, London: Routledge, 1997.
Samarqandī, Najīb al-Dīn Abū Ḥāmid Muḥammad ibn ʿAlī ibn ʿUmar. *Kitāb al-qarābādhīn ʿala tartīb al-ʿilal*. Trans. Martin Levey and Noury al-Khaledy. Philadelphia: University of Pennsylvania Press, 1967.
Sanders, Paula. "Gendering the Ungendered Body: Hermaphrodites in Medieval Islamic Law." In *Women in Middle Eastern History*, ed. Nikki R. Keddie and Beth Baron, 74–95. New Haven: Yale University Press, 1993.
Sarakhsī, Muḥammad ibn Aḥmad. *Kitāb al-Mabsūṭ*. 30 vols. Misr: Maṭbaʿat al-saʿada, 1906–1913.
Sasson, Vanessa R., and Jane Marie Law. *Imagining the Fetus: The Unborn in Myth, Religion, and Culture*. Oxford: Oxford University Press, 2009.
Savage-Smith, E. "Medicine." In *Encyclopedia of the History of Arabic Science*. 3 vols. Ed. Roshdi Rashed, 903–62. London: Routledge, 1996.
Schaus, Margaret. *Women and Gender in Medieval Europe: An Encyclopedia*. New York: Routledge, 2006.
Schimmel, Annemarie. *Islamic Names*. Edinburgh: Edinburgh University Press, 1990.
Schleifer, Alieh. *Mary: The Blessed Virgin of Islam*. Louisville: FonsVitae, 1998.
———. *Motherhood in Islam*. Cambridge: Cambridge University Press, 1986.
Schochet, Elijah Judah. *Animal Life in Jewish Tradition: Attitudes and Relationships*. Jersey City: Ktav Publishing, 1984.

Schwartz, Howard, and Caren Loebel-Fried. *Tree of Souls: The Mythology of Judaism*. Oxford: Oxford University Press, 2004.

Sells, Michael. *Approaching the Qur'an*. Ashland: White Cloud Press, 1999.

———. *Mystical Languages of Unsaying*. Chicago: University of Chicago Press, 1994.

Sered, Susan. "Rachel, Mary, and Fatima." *Cultural Anthropology* 6, no. 2 (May 1991): 131–46.

Sharīf al-Murtaḍá, ʿAlam al-Hudá ʿAli ibn al-Ḥusayn. *Kitāb al-intiṣār*. Islamic Manuscripts, Garrett No. 2751Y.

Shatzmiller, Maya. "Aspects of Women's Participation in the Economic Life of Later Medieval Islamic Occupations and Mentalities." *Arabica* 35, no. 1 (March 1998): 36–58.

———. "Women and Wage Labour in the Medieval Islamic West: Legal Issues in an Economic Context." *Journal of Economic and Social History of the Orient* 40 no. 2 (1997): 174–206.

Shaw, Theresa M. *The Burden of Flesh: Fasting and Sexuality in Early Christianity.* Philadelphia: Fortress Press, 1998.

Shildrick, Margrit. *Embodying the Monster: Encounters with the Vulnerable Self.* London, Thousand Oaks: Sage, 2002.

Singh, Yii-Jan. "Semen, Philosophy, and Paul." *Journal of Philosophy and Scripture* 4 no. 2 (Spring 2007): 32–45.

Smith, Jane Idleman and Yvonne Haddad. *The Islamic Understanding of Death and Resurrection.* Albany: State University of New York Press, 1981.

deSomogyi, Joseph. "Ad-Damiri's Ḥiyāt al-ḥayawān: An Arabic Zoological Lexicon." *Osiris* 9 (1950): 33–43.

Soranus. *Gynecology*. Trans. Owsei Temkin. Baltimore: Johns Hopkins University Press, 1956.

Spellberg, Denise. *Politics, Gender, and the Islamic Past: The Legacy of ʿĀʾisha bint Abī Bakr.* New York: Columbia University Press, 1996.

———. "Writing the Unwritten Life of the Islamic Eve: Menstruation and the Demonization of Motherhood." *International Journal of Middle Eastern Studies* 28 no. 3 (August 1996): 305–24.

Squire, Caroline. *The Social Context of Birth.* London: Radcliffe Publishing, 2009.

Stetkevych, Susan Pinckney. "Sarah and the Hyena: Laughter, Menstruation, and the Genesis of a Double Entendre." *History of Religions* 36 no. 1 (August 1996): 13–41.

Stone, Ken. "The Garden of Eden and the Heterosexual Contract." In *Bodily Citations: Religion and Judith Butler,* ed. Ellen T. Armour and Susan M. St. Ville, 48–70. New York: Columbia University Press, 2006.

Stowasser, Barbara Freyer. *Women in the Qur'an, Traditions, and Interpretation.* New York: Oxford University Press, 1996.

Sturtevant, A. H. *A History of Genetics*. Cold Spring Harbor, NY: Cold Spring Harbor Laboratory Press, 2001.

Stoller, Robert. *Presentations of Gender.* New Haven: Yale University Press, 1985.

Sujimon, M. S. "Istilḥāq and Its Role in Islamic Law." *Arab Law Quarterly* 18, no. 2 (2003): 117–43.

Suyūṭī, Jalāl al-Dīn. *Bushrá al-ka'ib bi liqā' al-ḥabīb*. Al-Zarqā', al-Urdun: Maktabat al-manār, 1988.

———. *Ṭibb al-nabawī*. Trans. as *As-Suyuti's Medicine of the Prophet*. London: Ta-Ha, 1994.

Ṭabarī, Abū Ja'far Muḥammad ibn Jarīr. *Jām' al-bayān 'an ta'wīl āy al-qur'ān* (*Tafsīr al-Ṭabarī*). 7 Vols. Bayrūt: Mu'assasat al-Risāla, 1994.

———. *Tārīkh al-rasūl wa'l-mulūk*. Trans. Franz Rosenthal. Vol. 1, *General Introduction and From the Creation to the Flood*. Albany: State University of New York Press, 1989.

———. *Tārīkh al-rasūl wa'l-mulūk*. Trans. William M. Brinner. Vol. 2, *Prophets and Patriarchs*. Albany: State University of New York Press, 1991.

Talmud Bavli. Ed. I. Epstein. 34 vols. London: Soncino Press, 1935–1952.

Talmud Yerushalmi. Ed. Chaim Malinowitz, Yisroel Simcha Schorr, and Mordecai Marcus. 10 vols. Brooklyn: Mesorah Publications, 2005–.

Tambiah, Stanley J. "The Magical Power of Words." *Man* 3 (1968): 175–208.

Ṭayālisī, Sulaymān ibn Dāwūd. *Musnad*. Ḥaydar Ābād al-Dakn: Maṭba'at majlis dā'irat al-ma'ārif al-niẓāmīya, 1903.

Tesseron, Ella Landau. "Adoption, Acknowledgment of Paternity and False Genealogical Claims in Arabian and Islamic Societies." *Bulletin of the School of Oriental and African Studies* 66, no. 2 (2003): 169–92.

Tha'labī, Abū Isḥāq Aḥmad ibn Muḥammad ibn Ibrāhīm. *'Arā'is al-majālis fī qiṣaṣ al-anbiyā'*. Trans. William Brinner as *Stories of the Prophets*. Leiden: Brill, 2002.

Thurkill, Mary F. *Chosen Among Women: Mary and Fatima in Medieval Christianity and Shi'ite Islam*. South Bend: University of Notre Dame Press, 2007.

Tinsman, Heidi. *Partners in Conflict: The Politics of Gender, Sexuality, and Labor in the Chilean Agrarian Reform, 1950–1973*. Durham: Duke University Press, 2002.

Tirmidhī, Abū 'Īsā Muḥammad b. 'Īsā. *Ṣaḥīḥ al-Tirmidhī*. Ed. Aḥmad Muḥammad Shākir. 5 vols. Cairo: Al-Maṭba'a al-misrīya, 1931–34.

Tischler, Nancy, and Ellen Johnston McHenry. *All Things in the Bible: An Encyclopedia of the Biblical World*. 2 vols. Santa Barbara: Greenwood, 2006.

Touati, Houari. "Travel." In *Medieval Islamic Civilization*, ed. Josef W. Meri and Jere L. Bacharach. New York: Taylor and Francis, 2006.

Tourage, Mahdi. *Rūmī and the Hermeneutics of Eroticism*. Leiden: Brill, 2007.

Trotula of Salerno. *Passionibus Mulerium Curandorum*. Trans. Elizabeth Mason-Hohl as *On the Diseases of Women*. Los Angeles: The Ward-Ritchie Press, 1940.

Tuana, Nancy. "Aristotle and the Politics of Reproduction." In *Engendering Origins: Critical Feminist Readings of Plato and Aristotle*, ed. Bat-Ami Bar On, 189–206. Albany: State University of New York Press, 1994.

Tubach, Jurgen. "Seth in Early Syriac Literature." In *Eve's Children*, 187–208.

Ṭūsī, Muḥammad ibn al-Ḥasan. *Tibyān fī tafsīr al-Qur'ān*. 10 vols. Al-Najaf: al-Maṭba'a al-ilmīya, 1957–1963.

Ullman, Manfred. *Islamic Medicine*. Trans. Jean Watt. Edinburgh: Edinburgh University Press, 1978.

Varro. *De re rustica*. Trans. William Davis Hooper. *Loeb Classical Library*. Cambridge: Harvard University Press, 1934.

Verghese, Abraham. *Cutting for Stone*. New York: Knopf, 2009.

Wadud, Amina. *Quran and Woman*. Kuala Lumpur: Penerbit Fajar Bakti Sdn. Bhd., 1992.

Wall, L. L., S. D. Arrowsmith, N. D. Briggs, A. Browning, Anyetei Lassey. "The Obstetric Vesicovaginal Fistula in the Developing World." *Obstetrical and Gynecological Survey* 60 (7 Suppl. 1) S3-S51 (July 2005): 1405–30.

Wansbrough, John. *The Sectarian Milieu: Content and Composition of Islamic Salvation History*. New York: Oxford University Press, 1978.

Warner, Marina. *Monsters of Our Own Making: The Peculiar Pleasures of Fear*. Lexington: University Press of Kentucky, 2007.

Waterbury, Florance. "Bird Deities in China." In *Artibus Asiae Supplementum* 10 (1952): 1–191.

Watt, W. Montgomery. "Khadīja." In *Encyclopedia of Islam*. 2d. ed.

———. *Muḥammad at Medina*. Oxford: Clarendon Press, 1956.

Waṭwāṭ, Muḥammad ibn Ibrāhīm ibn Yaḥyá. *Mabāhij al-fikar wa manāhij al-ʿibar*. Beirut: al-Dār al-ʿarabīya li al-mawsūʿāt, 2000.

Weiss-Amer, Melitta. "Medieval Women's Guides to Food During Pregnancy: Origins, Texts, and Traditions." *Canadian Bulletin of Medical History/Bulletin canadien d'histoire de la médecine* 10 (1993): 5–23.

Weisser, Ursula. *Zeugung, Vererbung und pränatale Entwicklung in der Medizin des arabisch-islamischen Mittelalters*. Erlangen, H. Lüling, 1983.

Wensinck, A. J. *Concordance et indices de la tradition musulmane*. 7 vols. Leiden: Brill, 1936–1969.

———, and Penelope Johnstone. "Maryam." In *Encyclopedia of Islam*. 2d ed.

Wheeler, Brannon. *Mecca and Eden: Ritual, Relics, and Territory in Islam*. Chicago: University of Chicago Press, 2006.

White, L. Michael. *Scripting Jesus: The Gospels in Rewrite*. New York: HarperOne, 2010.

Wilensky, Mordechai L. "Health Conduct in Intercourse Taken from Rabbi Moshe Maimon." *Proceedings of the American Academy for Jewish Research* LVI (1990): 101–13.

Williams, David. *Deformed Discourse: The Function of the Monster in Medieval Thought and Literature*. Montreal: McGill Queen's University Press, 1996.

Wilson, Adrian. "Ceremonies of Childbirth and Its Interpretation." In *Women as Mothers in Pre-Industrial England, Essays in Memory of Dorothy McLaren*, ed. Valerie Fildes, 68–107. London, New York: Routledge, 1990.

Wilson, Deborah S. "Technologies of Misogyny: The Transparent Maternal Body and Alternate Reproductions in *Frankenstein, Dracula*, and Some Selected Media Discourses." In *Bodily Discursions: Genders, Representations, Technologies*, ed. Deborah S. Wilson and Christine Moneera Laennec, 105–34. Albany: State University of New York Press, 1997.

Wittig, Monique. *Straight Mind and Other Essays*. Boston: Beacon Press, 1992.

Wittkower, Rudolph. "Marvels of the East: A Study in the History of Monsters." *Journal of the Warburg and Courtauld Institutes* 5 (1942): 159–97.

Wolfson, Elliott. "Circumcision and the Divine Name: A Study in the Transmission of Esoteric Doctrine." *The Jewish Quarterly Review* LXXVII, no. 1–2 (July-October 1987): 77–112.

Wolfson, Elliott. "Circumcision, Vision of God, and Textual Interpretation: From Midrashic Trope to Mystical Symbol." *History of Religions* 27 (1987): 189–215.

Yonge, C. D., trans. "Questions and Answers on Genesis, III." In *The Works of Philo: Complete and Unabridged,* 841–63. Peabody, MA: Hendrickson Publishers, 1993.

Zahrāwī, Abū al-Qāsim Khalaf ibn ʿAbbās. *Kitāb al taṣrīf li man ʿajiza ʿan al-taʾlīf.* Trans. Martin S. Spink and Geoffrey L. Lewis as *Abulcasis on Surgery and Instruments*. Berkeley: University of California Press, 1973.

Zamakhsharī, Maḥmūd ibn ʿUmar. *Khashshāf ʿan ḥaqāʾiq al-tanzīl wa-ʿuyūn al-aqāwīl fī wujūh al-taʾwīl*. 4 vols. Miṣr: al-Bābī al-ḥalabī, 1966.

Zirkle, Conway. "Animals Impregnated by the Wind." *Isis* 25 no. 1 (May 1936): 95–130.

Index